Leaving Certificate

BREAKING GROUND

AGRICULTURAL SCIENCE

CAROL CRONIN • SANDRA TIERNAN

3rd Edition

The Educational Company of Ireland

The Educational Company of Ireland
Ballymount Road
Walkinstown
Dublin 12

www.edco.ie

A member of the Smurfit Kappa Group plc

ISBN: 978-1-84536-842-5

The paper used in this book comes from Managed Forests in Northern Europe For every tree felled, at least one new tree is planted

Editor: Life Lines Editorial Services
Design and layout: Global Blended Learning, Daghda, QBS Learning
Artwork: Global Blended Learning
Proofreaders: Sally Vince, Geraldine Begley
Indexer: Geraldine Begley

Author acknowledgements
We would like to thank everyone at Edco for their support, help and advice from the beginning to the end: Martina Harford, Ruth Smyth, Declan Dempsey, Martina Garvey, Victoria Lemaire, Diarmuid O'Hegarty, Julie Glennon, Rochelle Lazario and all the Edco sales representatives. Sincere thanks to Amanda Harman and Mike Harman at Life Lines Editorial and to Global Blended Learning.

We would also like to thank everyone who gave their time and expert knowledge to us in writing this book:

John Griffin, Department of Agriculture, Food and the Marine; Gabrielle Kelly, Tracy Clegg, Ian O'Boyle at UCD; Anthony Duignan at Roscommon District Veterinary Office; Stanley Hunter, Joanne Harmon and Brenda Guihen and the Health and Safety Authority (HSA); Anthony Walsh, Russell Waldron and Robert Hosey at Aurivo Dairy Ingredients, Ballaghadereen, Co. Roscommon; Christopher Daly and the ICBF, Bandon, Co. Cork; John Fagan at Independent Newspapers; John Bell; Donagh Berry, Padraig French, Bernadette O'Brien and Sinéad McParland at Teagasc Animal and Grassland Research and Innovation Centre, Moorepark, Fermoy, Co. Cork; Ewen Mullins at Teagasc Crops Research Centre, Oakpark, Carlow; Ciarán Carroll at Teagasc Pig Development Department, Animal and Grassland Research and Innovation Centre, Moorepark, Fermoy, Co. Cork; Aidan Murray, Beef Specialist at Teagasc, Ballybofey, Co. Donegal; Catherine Carty at UCD, School of Medicine; Gareth Carroll and Kiernan Milling, Granard, Co. Longford; Padraig and Rita Shannon; Karl McDermottroe; Clare Noone; Fidelma Lipsett, Fiona Kilroy and Bryan Henry; Martin Minchin and Kverneland Group Ireland Ltd; Justina and Liam Gavin and Drumanilra Farm Kitchen; Gerald and Julian Burns and Lullaby Milk; Jerry Kennedy and Donncha Ó Céileachair and Blasket Islands Lamb; Marion Roeleveld and Killeen Farmhouse Cheese; Donal Sheehan and the BRIDE Project; Tom Keane and Droimeann Cattle; Ken McGrath and Ashleigh Environmental; Dr Kenneth Lipsett; Lilian O'Sullivan, Teagasc; Abbey Community College, Boyle, Co. Roscommon; Sligo Grammar School, Sligo.

We would also like to acknowledge Teagasc and their research centres at Grange, Moorepark and Athenry; Coilte; Department of Agriculture, Food and the Marine; Central Statistics Office; Health and Safety Authority; without whose research and information this book would not be possible. We would like to thank the Cronin and Tiernan families for their ongoing support while writing this book.

Contents

Guide to features in the book   iv

List of Specified Practical Activities   v

Introduction   vi

STRAND 1

Scientific Practices

1   Hypothesising and experimenting   2
2   Evaluating evidence and communicating   21
3   Working safely   39

STRAND 2

Soils

4   Soil formation and classification   58
5   Physical characteristics of soil   72
6   Chemical characteristics of soil   92
7   Biological characteristics of soil   100
8   Soil management   114

STRAND 3

Crops

9   Plant physiology   134
10   Applied plant genetics   144
11   Plant classification   165
12   Principles of crop production and management   184
13   Barley   206
14   Potatoes   219
15   Catch crop: Kale 🅗 (Higher Level Only)   231
16   Energy crop: Miscanthus 🅗 (Higher Level Only)   240
17   Grassland characteristics and growth   252
18   Grazing and grassland management   265
19   Sowing and reseeding grassland   279
20   Conservation of grass   287

STRAND 4

Animals

21   Animal nutrition   300
22   Animal physiology   313
23   Animal reproduction   323
24   Applied animal genetics   335
25   Dairy breeds, nutrition and management of a dairy herd   349
26   Milk composition, milk production and the dairy industry   371
27   Beef breeds and beef production: dairy calf to beef and suckler beef production   394
28   Sheep breeds and production   413
29   Lamb production and husbandry   425
30   Pig breeds, management, nutrition and production   443
31   Animal health and disease   466
32   Environmental impact of agriculture and markets for Irish produce   491

Synoptic Questions   511

Glossary   514

Index   524

Guide to features in the book

Learning objectives box	Key concepts dealt with in the chapter
DEFINITION ⬡ **Definition box**	Key terms associated with agriculture
Literacy box	Words that may be new or unfamiliar to students
🧪 Activity	Activity
🧪 SPA SPECIFIED PRACTICAL ACTIVITY	Specified practical activity
H (Higher Level only)	Higher Level only material

Digital Resources

The *Breaking Ground* digital resources will enhance classroom learning by encouraging student participation and engagement.

To provide guidance for the integration of digital resources in the classroom and to aid lesson planning, they are **referenced throughout the textbook** using the following icons:

Engaging **videos** allow students to observe agricultural science in action.

Animations bring diagrams to life and reinforce the topic at hand.

Weblink documents provide links to additional material.

PowerPoint presentations provide chapter summaries that highlight key themes and topics.

Solutions to textbook questions.

Teachers can access the *Breaking Ground* digital resources via the interactive e-book, which is available online at **www.edcolearning.ie**.

SPA

LIST OF SPECIFIED PRACTICAL ACTIVITIES

5.1a	To determine the soil texture of a soil sample by hand testing	74
5.1b	To determine the soil texture of a soil sample by sedimentation	75
5.1c	To determine the soil texture of a soil sample using a soil sieve	76
5.2	To calculate the percentage water content of a soil sample	83
5.3a	To demonstrate capillarity in a compacted soil and an uncompacted soil	84
5.3b	To compare the infiltration rate of a compacted soil and an uncompacted soil	86
6.1	To show flocculation in a soil sample	93
6.2	To demonstrate cation exchange capacity in a soil **H** (Higher Level only)	95
6.3	To determine the pH of a soil	96
7.1	To determine the percentage organic matter in a soil sample and convert that to organic carbon	103
7.2	To isolate and grow bacteria from clover root nodules	108
7.3	To show the activity of earthworms in a soil and estimate the number of earthworms in a pasture	110
10.1	To investigate the complexity associated with the genetic inheritance of traits by hybridising two varieties to determine the rate of transfer of the required trait to the next progeny	160
12.1	To compare plant uniformity from certified and uncertified seed **H** (Higher Level only)	185
12.2	To investigate the effect of weather and soil conditions on the percentage germination of an agricultural seed	189
12.3	To investigate the effect of nutrients on the growth of a sample of plants and measure the biomass of these plants above and below ground	192
14.1	To determine the dry matter (DM) content of different potato varieties	228
17.1	To investigate the botanical composition of an old permanent pasture or a new ley	253
17.2	To investigate the dry matter (DM) content of grass	257
19.1	To compare the establishment of grass with that of one other crop **H** (Higher Level only)	283
26.1	To investigate the quality of a sample of milk over time	378
32.1	To plan the layout of a farm	506

Introduction

This comprehensive third edition of *Breaking Ground* has been written for the new Agricultural Science Specification for both the Higher and Ordinary level courses. Material applicable specifically to the Higher-Level course has been identified in the book.

The book is subdivided into the four strands in line with the specification – Scientific Practices, Soils, Crops, Animals. Learning objectives are identified at the start of each chapter, highlighting the key concepts of each of the strands. There is a summary at the end of every chapter, followed by multiple-choice questions, short-answer questions and structured questions. Synoptic type questions are also included at the end of the textbook.

Every effort has been made to ensure all the material is up to date with current agricultural practices and that the material is accurate. While writing this textbook, many experts were consulted. Strand 1, Scientific Practices, is a key focus of the new specification. We aimed to reinforce the concepts from Strand 1 in the other three strands where appropriate. Students must complete the range of Specified Practical Activities outlined in the specification. All Specified Practical Activities are included, and these are indicated in the textbook. Students must maintain a record of all activities carried out. This record can be in a variety of formats, including written, video, audio and graphical.

Farm Safety is another key component in the new specification and there is a dedicated chapter to Farm Safety in Strand 1. Farm Safety is also integrated into the other three strands.

Students are often asked to analyse and interpret secondary data as part of the new specification. Secondary data has been provided in the book with worked examples included to aid students in their analysis and interpretation of this data. A range of scientific information related to agriculture, including sources from the media, websites, scientific articles and people involved in the agri-food industry have been included to provide a comprehensive resource for both teachers and students.

The book has a range of labelled diagrams, colour photos and definitions throughout to aid learning and understanding. Literacy is an important component of all science subjects. Words that students may not be familiar with, especially those related to agriculture, are highlighted and explained in literacy boxes throughout this book.

Additional resources – including videos, animations, PowerPoint presentations and solutions to questions in the book – can be accessed via the interactive *Breaking Ground* e-book, which is available online at **www.edcolearning.ie**. These materials can be used in class to aid student learning and for revision purposes.

The textbook has been structured to begin with Strand 1: Scientific Practices followed by Strand 2: Soils, Strand 3: Crops and Strand 4: Animals. Although the textbook follows the layout of the specification, teachers may choose to teach the strands and their content in whichever order they prefer. In Strand 3, both Ordinary and Higher-level students must study grassland and one other food crop. A choice of barley or potatoes has been provided as examples of food crops. Higher-level students must also study an energy crop or a catch crop. Miscanthus has been included as an example of an energy crop and kale has been included as an example of a catch crop. In Strand 4, students are required to study cattle and sheep enterprises and one other animal enterprise. Pigs has been included as the additional animal enterprise.

Carol Cronin and Sandra Tiernan

Scientific Practices — STRAND 1

Soils — STRAND 2

Crops — STRAND 3

Animals — STRAND 4

Scientific Practices

1	Hypothesising and experimenting	2
2	Evaluating evidence and communicating	21
3	Working safely	39

STRAND
1

CHAPTER 1 Hypothesising and experimenting

When you have completed this chapter you should be able to:

- Write a hypothesis based on an observation
- Make a prediction based on the hypothesis
- Identify independent and dependent variables in an experiment
- Identify controlled variables in an experiment
- Distinguish between primary and secondary data
- Identify ways to collect, organise and present data
- Analyse and interpret primary and secondary data with and without the use of technology
- Describe relationships between sets of data (qualitative and/or quantitative)
- Distinguish between causation and correlation
- Distinguish between statistical and systematic uncertainty
- Identify methods used to reduce statistical and systematic uncertainty
- Recognise uncertainty as a limitation of the process of measurement
- Appreciate the difference between accuracy and precision.

Scientific method

Scientific practices are also known as the scientific method. The scientific method is a step-by-step approach to answering a question or solving a problem. It is used worldwide in all areas of science and engineering. This chapter aims to remind you of those practices and expand on them further.

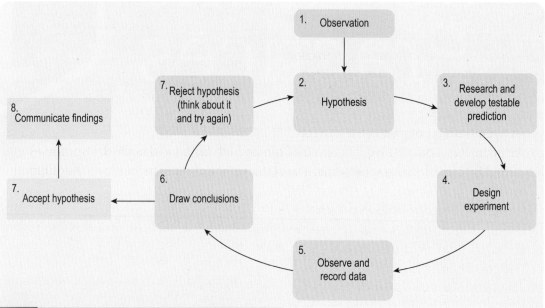

| 1.1 | *Flow chart showing the scientific method* |

The scientific method is made up of the following steps:

1. Observing (identifying a problem or a question)
2. Formulating a hypothesis
3. Making a prediction
4. Designing an experiment

5. Recording data

6. Drawing conclusions

7. Accepting or rejecting the hypothesis

8. Communicating the results.

Even though the main steps are listed above, it is better to think of these steps in a cycle, as the data and conclusions obtained from an experiment can lead to further investigation or a new hypothesis (see Fig. 1.1).

Hypothesising

Observation

Any scientific investigation usually starts with an observation, such as 'A fertiliser high in nitrate gives good crop growth'.

Observations form the basis on which to formulate a hypothesis.

Hypothesis and predictions

> **DEFINITION**
>
> **Hypothesis:** a proposed explanation for an observation. A hypothesis must be both testable and falsifiable.
> **Prediction:** the outcome you would expect to observe if the hypothesis is correct. A prediction is often written as an 'If … then …' statement.

Falsifiable: something that can be proven to be false.

A hypothesis is often referred to as an 'educated guess', and it is an attempt to answer an observation or a problem. For example, a farmer observes that there is poor plant growth and the leaves of the crop are yellow. The farmer forms the hypothesis that the crop must be suffering from a nitrogen deficiency. From this they make a prediction: **if** a nitrogen fertiliser is added to the crop **then** there will be improved plant growth and dark green foliage.

1.2   *The farmer hypothesises that this plant is suffering from nitrogen deficiency*

Foliage: the leaves of a plant or a tree.

A hypothesis is not always the correct explanation; it is a possible explanation that can be both tested and falsified. Hypotheses are tested by carrying out experiments. The outcome of the experiment may either support or reject the hypothesis. If the results of the experiment support the hypothesis, then this means that the hypothesis is likely to be correct. In the example above, the farmer notices an improvement in the crop's growth and foliage after the addition of a nitrate fertiliser. The farmer can **accept** their hypothesis that the crop was **most likely** suffering from a deficiency in nitrogen. In science we cannot prove anything with 100% certainty, hence the term 'most likely'. However, if after a period of time the farmer sees no improvement in the plant growth or the colour of the foliage, and the results of

Table 1.1 Summary of the scientific process as used by the farmer	
Observation	Farmer observes their crop and notices poor growth and yellow leaves
Hypothesis	Crop is suffering from a nitrogen deficiency
Prediction	If a nitrogen fertiliser is added **then** there will be improved plant growth
Experiment	Apply nitrogen to crop
Result	Crop growth improves: **accept hypothesis** No improvement in crop: **reject hypothesis**

the experiment go against the hypothesis, then it is likely that the hypothesis is incorrect and the crop is not suffering from a nitrogen deficiency. In this case the farmer would **reject** their hypothesis and review the situation and formulate a new hypothesis.

If a hypothesis stands up to testing over a long period of time, it becomes a theory. Hypotheses are used to form the basis of a prediction.

Writing a hypothesis and a prediction

Sinéad and Rory keep hens at home to supply the family with eggs. Both Rory and Sinéad noticed that during the summer months the hens laid an egg every day or two, but as autumn arrived the hens did not produce eggs as frequently and stopped laying eggs over the winter months altogether.

Sinéad formed the hypothesis that the hens stopped laying eggs as the daylight hours were too short during the winter.

Rory formed the hypothesis that the hens stopped laying eggs as the temperatures over the winter months were too cold for the hens.

From their hypotheses, both Sinéad and Rory formulated predictions. Sinéad predicted that **if** she artificially provided the hens with extended hours of light during the winter days **then** the hens would continue to lay eggs in the winter months. Rory predicted that **if** he raised the temperature in the hens' shed **then** they would continue to lay eggs over the winter.

Both Sinéad and Rory's hypotheses are testable. Their predictions indicate the outcome they would observe if their hypothesis were correct. A prediction typically focuses on the relationship between two different variables.

> **Theory:** an explanation for some aspect of the natural world that is based on facts that have stood up to repeated testing by the scientific method over a period of time.

1.3   *Sinéad and Rory have different testable hypotheses as to why their hens stop laying eggs over the winter months.*

Experimenting
Designing the experiment
Variables

Hypotheses are tested using a **controlled experiment**. In a controlled experiment there are three types of variable:

- **Independent variable:** the factor that is changed in the experiment, e.g. the length of daylight or the temperature.
- **Dependent variable:** the factor that depends on the independent variable. This is the variable you observe during the experiment. You often record some measurement of this variable, e.g. the number of eggs laid by the hens.
- **Controlled variables:** all other variables that must be kept constant in order to ensure that the experiment is a fair test.

> **Variable:** any factor or condition that can be changed in an experiment.

1.4   *Dependent variable: the number of eggs laid by the hens*

When writing a prediction for an experiment the independent and the dependent variables can be identified. For example, Sinéad's prediction stated that if she artificially provided the hens with **extended hours of light** during the winter days then the hens would continue to **lay eggs in the winter months**.

In Sinéad's prediction the **independent variable** is the number of hours the hens would receive artificial light and the **dependent variable** is the number of eggs the hens lay in the winter months.

Rory's prediction stated that if he raised the **temperature** in the hens' shed then the hens would continue to **lay eggs over the winter months**.

In Rory's prediction the **independent variable** is the temperature of the hens' shed and the **dependent variable** is the number of eggs the hens produce over the winter months.

Table 1.2 A summary of the scientific process as used by Sinéad and Rory		
	Sinéad	**Rory**
Observation	Hens stop laying eggs during the winter months	Hens stop laying eggs during the winter months
Hypothesis	Hens stop laying as daylight hours in winter are too short	Hens stop laying as temperatures during winter are too cold
Predictions	**If** hens are provided with extended hours of light **then** the hens will continue to lay egg during winter months	**If** the temperature is raised in the hens' shed **then** the hens will continue to lay eggs over the winter months
Independent variable	Hours of light	Temperature
Dependent variable	Number of eggs laid over the winter months	Number of eggs laid over the winter months

Exercise 1.1

1. Using the internet or other sources, investigate both Sinéad and Rory's predictions.
2. What evidence can you find to support either of their predictions?
3. In groups, devise an experiment you would carry out to test both hypotheses.
4. What variables would need to be controlled when carrying out the experiments?

Conducting a controlled experiment

All experiments should have only one independent variable. Experimental results are easier to interpret and analyse when there is just one independent variable. All other variables should be kept **constant**; otherwise they could affect the outcome of the experiment.

Example of a controlled experiment

Hypothesis
That mammalian enzyme amylase will break down starch faster at higher temperatures

Prediction
If the temperature is increased **then** the time taken by amylase to break down starch will decrease.

Independent variable
Temperature

Dependent variable
Time taken for the enzyme amylase to break down the starch

Controlled variables
- Volume and concentration of the starch solution
- Volume and concentration of the amylase solution
- Volume and concentration of the iodine solution
- Size of the test tubes

Apparatus and chemicals
Test tubes, water baths, thermometers, spotting tiles, Pasteur pipettes, iodine solution, 0.3% amylase solution (freshly prepared), 0.2% starch solution

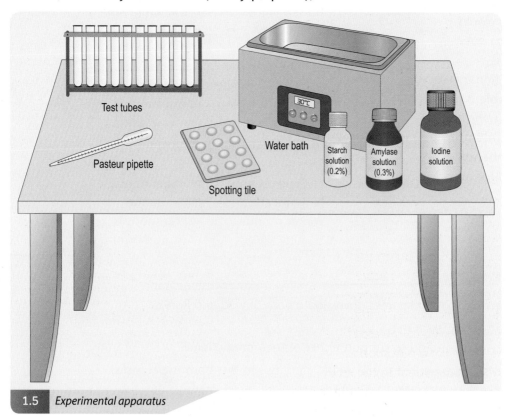

1.5 *Experimental apparatus*

Procedure
1. Label five test tubes A to E.
2. Set up five water baths at the following temperatures: 20°C, 30°C, 40°C, 50°C, 60°C.
3. Fill the compartments of a spotting tile with iodine.
4. Add 5 cm³ of starch solution to each test tube.
5. Place each test tube into a separate water bath for 5 minutes to allow it to adjust to the relevant temperature:
   - Test tube A at 20°C
   - Test tube B at 30°C
   - Test tube C at 40°C
   - Test tube D at 50°C
   - Test tube E at 60°C.
6. Add a second test tube containing 5 cm³ of starch to each water bath and label it as a control. Do not add amylase to this test tube.
7. After 5 minutes add 5 cm³ of amylase solution to each test tube labelled A to E.
8. Using a pipette, remove one drop of the starch amylase solution from each test tube every minute and add it to the iodine in the spotting tile.
9. Measure the amount of time it takes for the amylase to completely digest the starch. Once the starch is digested, the iodine solution will no longer turn blue-black.

10. Repeat steps 3 to 8 twice, and calculate the average time taken for the amylase to break down the starch at each temperature.

Results

Table 1.3 The time taken for amylase to digest starch at 20°C, 30°C, 40°C, 50°C and 60°C					
Temperature (°C)	1st time	2nd time	3rd time	Average (min)	Observation
20	7	8	9	8	
30	5	4	6	5	
40	3	3	3	3	
50	8	10	12	10	
60	No digestion	No digestion	No digestion		Iodine stayed blue-black throughout the experiment

Discussion

The results of this experiment show that as the temperature is increased the time taken for amylase to break down starch decreases up to a point. Amylase breaks down starch fastest at 40°C. As this is mammalian amylase, it is obvious from the graph that this enzyme works best at a temperature close to body temperature. However, once the temperature is increased to 50°C, the time taken for amylase to digest the starch increases. At 60°C, there is no digestion of starch by amylase – this is evident in the fact that the iodine remained blue-black and did not change colour. Amylase is composed of protein, and the shape of this protein can be altered by high temperatures. The enzyme is damaged at high temperatures and is unable to digest the starch.

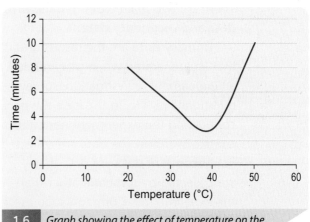

1.6   *Graph showing the effect of temperature on the time taken for amylase to digest starch*

Conclusion

An increase in temperature from 20°C to 40°C does decrease the time taken for amylase to break down starch; however, temperatures above 40°C increase the time, and at 60°C there is no digestion as the enzyme amylase is denatured.

Do the results of this experiment support the hypothesis?

The original hypothesis was that mammalian amylase will break down starch faster at higher temperatures. The results of this experiment do not fully support this hypothesis. Up to 40°C, an increase in temperature does decrease the time that amylase takes to break down starch. However, at temperatures greater than 40°C the results do not support the hypothesis. In this case the students should re-evaluate their hypothesis and try to refine it and then retest their new hypothesis.

In the above experiment, both **qualitative** and **quantitative** data are recorded. Qualitative data are data that cannot be measured accurately and that we observe with our senses, such as colour changes, smells and tastes. The iodine turning blue-black, therefore indicating the presence of starch, is an example of qualitative data. Quantitative data involve measurement and are always numerical values, such as the time taken for amylase to digest the starch in the experiment.

SCIENTIFIC PRACTICES

Qualitative data: data that we observe with our senses, e.g. colour changes, smells, tastes.

Quantitative data: data that involve measurement and will always be numerical values.

When conducting an experiment it is important to have an adequate **sample size**. This is achieved by carrying out an experiment in replicates. In the above experiment, the time taken for amylase to digest starch was tested three times at each temperature and an average was calculated. **Increasing the sample size and repeating an experiment a number of times makes it more likely that your results are reliable and minimises error. In addition, it is important to include all data from an experiment, whether or not they support the hypothesis.**

Collection, organisation and presentation of data (results)

There are two main types of data: **primary data** and **secondary data**.

Primary data are the results or data that are generated when carrying out an experiment, investigation, survey, questionnaire, etc. In this case the person conducting the experiment has direct control over how the data are collected.

Secondary data are data that are collected by someone other than the experimenter. Common sources of secondary data include censuses,

1.7 *Collecting water samples for testing*

information from government departments (such as the Department of Agriculture, Food and the Marine) and experimental data originally collected for other research purposes (such as research data from Teagasc).

The data collected during an investigation or from a secondary source are normally recorded in a table. One of the most common types of table used to present and organise data is a **frequency distribution table** (Table 1.4).

A **frequency distribution table** summarises values and their frequency (how often that value occurs).

Table 1.4 Frequency distribution table of the number of ewes giving birth to a single lamb, twins, triplets and quads	
Number of lambs	**Frequency**
Single lamb	25
Twins	40
Triplets	27
Quads	8

1.8 *A ewe with twin lambs*

Using the table above, work out the total number of lambs born on this farm. What percentage of ewes gave birth to twins?

There are certain conventions for recording data in a table, to make them clear for readers.
- Always give the table a title so that the reader knows what it is about
- Provide column and row headings as appropriate
- Include units of measurement in column/row headings, e.g. 'Weight (kg)', 'Distance (m)' (see Table 1.5 below as an example)
- Record the independent variable in the first column and the dependent variable in subsequent columns
- Present numerical data in its simplest form; round up/down numbers where appropriate.

Table 1.5 is an example of a table used to record the number of bubbles of oxygen gas produced by *Elodea* when the light intensity was changed. The set-up of the apparatus is shown in Fig. 1.9.

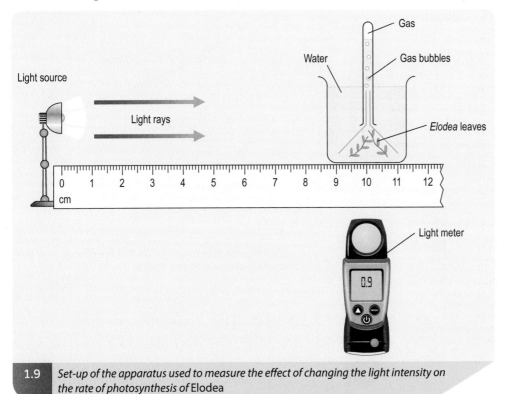

1.9 *Set-up of the apparatus used to measure the effect of changing the light intensity on the rate of photosynthesis of* Elodea

Table 1.5 The effect of light intensity on the rate of photosynthesis of *Elodea*				
Distance from the lamp (cm)	Light intensity (lux)	No. bubbles per min 1st trial	No. bubbles per min 2nd trial	Average (bubbles/min)
100	0.02	7	5	6
75	0.03	15	17	16
50	0.05	21	22	21.5
25	0.2	39	35	37
10	0.9	80	76	78

Tables can contain very detailed information, making it difficult to see any patterns or trends that might be present. For this reason data are often presented in the form of a chart or a graph.

The chart or graph used to present data depends on the type of data involved. The most common ways of presenting data include:
- Bar charts – used to show frequency or the mean for different categories
- Line graphs – used to show how one or more variables changes over time; for this reason time is recorded on the horizontal axis (*x*-axis)
- Pie charts – used to show percentages of different categories

SCIENTIFIC PRACTICES

- Scatter graphs – used to show the relationship between two variables (the **independent variable** and the **dependent variable**). The independent variable is placed on the horizontal axis (*x*-axis) and the dependent variable is placed on the vertical axis (*y*-axis).

Some examples of the different types of graphs are shown below. Graphs like these can be drawn by hand or using a software package such as Microsoft Excel.

It is important that when you draw a graph or chart that you include the following:

- A title summarising what the graph or chart is showing
- An appropriate scale
- A label on both the *x*-axis and the *y*-axis; the labels should also include the units of measurement
- A legend to explain different colours/fill patterns
- An acknowledgement of the source if the graph contains secondary data.

ppm: parts per million (mg/l); 1 ppm = 1 mg per litre.

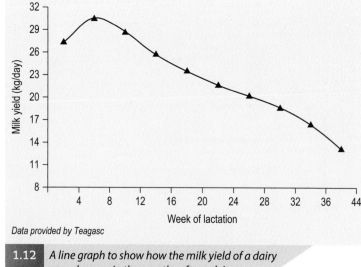

Data provided by Teagasc

1.12 *A line graph to show how the milk yield of a dairy cow changes in the months after calving*

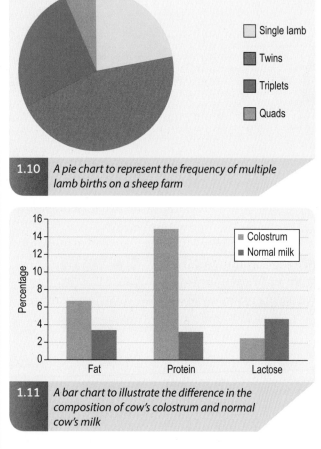

1.10 *A pie chart to represent the frequency of multiple lamb births on a sheep farm*

Legend:
- Single lamb
- Twins
- Triplets
- Quads

1.11 *A bar chart to illustrate the difference in the composition of cow's colostrum and normal cow's milk*

Legend:
- Colostrum
- Normal milk

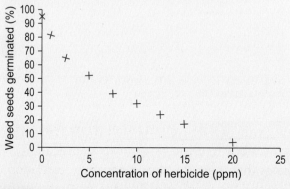

1.13 *A scatter graph showing the relationship between the concentration of herbicide and the percentage germination of broadleaf weeds. This graph shows an obvious trend between the concentration of the herbicide (independent variable) and the percentage of weed seeds that germinated (dependent variable). The correlation coefficient, r = −0.96404.*

Analysis: an identification of trends and patterns in data. Examining or scrutinising results.

Analysis and interpretation of data with and without the use of technology

The analysis and interpretation of data or results of an experiment is an integral part of the scientific method. Analysis of results involves identifying **trends** and **patterns** in quantitative data. Quantitative data can be analysed statistically. Statistical calculations are used to analyse results and investigate whether there is a relationship between the independent and dependent variables.

The mean (or average) is one of the simplest statistical calculations that can be carried out when an experiment is done in duplicate or triplicate. Calculating the mean of a set of results is more **reliable** than an individual, one-off result. This will help to reduce the effect of **random errors** and give a value close to the true value (see page 14). The **correlation coefficient** is a common statistical calculation carried out on the data collected from experiments. A correlation indicates that there is a connection or a **relationship** between two variables (or **two sets of data**).

DEFINITION

Mean: the sum of all the values in a set of data divided by the total number of values.

Correlation coefficient: a statistical measure (expressed as a value between -1 and $+1$) that describes the size and direction of a relationship between two or more variables. The correlation coefficient is denoted by the letter *r*.

A correlation coefficient of -1 indicates a negative correlation, i.e. as one variable increases the other variable decreases. A correlation coefficient of $+1$ indicates a positive correlation, i.e. as one variable increases the other variable also increases. A correlation coefficient of zero indicates that there is no relationship between the two variables. Correlation coefficients can be calculated using the CORREL function in a spreadsheet such as Excel or on a scientific calculator.

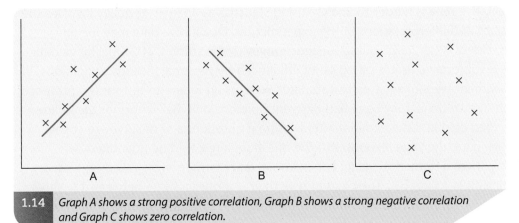

A   B   C

1.14   *Graph A shows a strong positive correlation, Graph B shows a strong negative correlation and Graph C shows zero correlation.*

Fig. 1.13 on page 10 shows the relationship between the concentration of a herbicide and the germination of weed seeds, with a correlation coefficient $r = -0.96404$. This *r* value indicates that there is a strong negative correlation between the concentration of the herbicide and the number of weed seeds that germinate.

 Activity 1.1   **To test the effect of nitrogen fertiliser on the growth of barley seedlings**

A student investigated whether there is any relationship between the height that barley seedlings grow in 2 weeks and the amount of nitrogen fertiliser they receive. Table 1.6 shows the average heights the plants grew in a 2-week period in relation to the amount of nitrogen fertiliser they received. The student plotted this information in a graph in a spreadsheet and calculated the correlation coefficient.

Results

Table 1.6 Results of an experiment to test the effect of nitrogen fertiliser on the growth of barley seedlings over 2 weeks	
Concentration of nitrogen fertiliser (ppm)	Height of plants (cm)
0	2
5	5
12	11
15	17
20	21
25	26

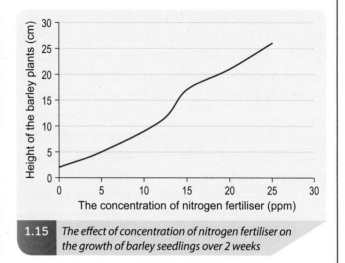

1.15 *The effect of concentration of nitrogen fertiliser on the growth of barley seedlings over 2 weeks*

In the graph in Fig. 1.15 there is a strong positive correlation between the concentration of nitrogen fertiliser and the height of the barley plants. The correlation coefficient was calculated as $r = +0.9921$.

Objective: a way of looking at something that is not influenced by personal feelings or opinions.

Subjective: a way of looking at something that is based on personal feelings, tastes or opinions.

Interpretation: the process of explaining the meaning of your data and drawing conclusions or findings.

Quantitative data analysis is often viewed as being reliable and sound, as it uses numerical data and can be viewed **objectively**.

Qualitative data is harder to analyse using statistics as analysis normally involves the impressions and interpretations of the experimenter. Qualitative data may include pictures, videos, interviews, questionnaires, surveys, case studies, etc. Qualitative data analysis is **subjective**, as it is based on or influenced by personal feelings or opinions. In the experiment we looked at earlier, students were using iodine to test for the presence of starch; the students may have had different opinions on whether or not the iodine has changed colour. If the experimenter is using a questionnaire or survey to collect qualitative data, then the responses to the questionnaire could be quantified by allocating them a numerical value. For example, dairy farmers were asked on a survey 'How difficult is your job?'. They had to give their response a value between 1 = Very easy and 10 = Very difficult. This would allow for some statistical analysis of the data. When analysing qualitative data the experimenter would look for behaviours or interactions between the variables.

Interpretation of results

Interpretation of data (results) is the process of explaining or demonstrating an understanding of your results or findings. Interpretation of results would be the basis for writing a conclusion. Interpretation of results could also involve discussing the implications or significance of your findings. Do your findings agree or disagree with investigations carried out previously, or are your findings novel and add additional knowledge or understanding to an area of science or agriculture?

Causation and correlation

Determining the correlation coefficient when analysing data is a useful technique. However, it has its limitations because it is normally associated with graphs that show linear relationships (variables that show proportionality to produce a straight line). In addition, even if two variables show a correlation, this does not imply that there is causation. Causation means that a change in one variable will cause a change in another.

Causation: indicates that a change in one variable is the direct result of a change in another variable (i.e. that there is a cause-and-effect relationship).

During the 1980s, one American academic investigating crime rates in New York City found that there was a strong correlation between the sales of ice cream and the amount of crime committed in the summer. Therefore it would appear that the two were linked and that an increase in crime rates was **causing** the increase in ice cream sales. However, in this case is there a third variable that is the cause of both? Crime rates normally increase during the summer months when the weather is warmer. The warm summer weather is also responsible for an increase in ice cream sales.

In order to determine causation, a cause-and-effect relationship between two variables, a **randomised controlled experiment** must be carried out. When carrying out this type of experiment there must be two groups; an **experimental group** and a **control group**. For example, if a drugs company wanted to investigate the effects of a new dose to remove liver fluke from dairy cattle, two groups of dairy cattle would be selected: an experimental group and a control group. To avoid **bias**, the two groups would be composed of randomly selected dairy cattle of similar age, breed, feed requirements, etc. The new dose would be administered to the experimental group and the control group would receive no treatment or the normal treatment (normal dose for liver fluke). Both groups would be treated the same in terms of feed, grazing, housing, etc. and they would be monitored for signs of infestation using faecal egg counts, bulk milk antibody levels and reports from the abattoir on post-mortem liver examination. If at the end of the trial the experimental group had lower levels of fluke infestation or were free of liver fluke altogether, then it may be the case that the new dose is a better treatment for removing liver fluke from dairy cattle. Having a control group in an experiment increases the **reliability** of the results.

1.16 *Causation versus correlation*

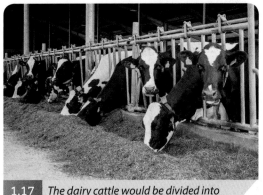

1.17 *The dairy cattle would be divided into an experimental group and a control group in this fictitious randomised controlled experiment.*

Randomised controlled experiment: an experiment in which the subjects are randomly divided into two groups: an experimental group and a control group. The experimental group receives the treatment under investigation while the control group receives no treatment or the standard treatment. Using a randomised control experiment reduces bias.
Control: The control is commonly the normal or usual state; the only difference between the control and the experimental group is the independent variable. The results of the control can be compared to the results of the experimental group.

Uncertainty is a limitation of the process of measurement

There is a saying among trade and craft people, 'Measure twice, cut once'.

Uncertainty in the process of measurement is the doubt that exists about the results of any measurement (hence those wise words above indicate that a measurement should be taken at least two times before anything is cut). For every measurement, regardless of how carefully it is taken, there is always a **margin of error**. Sometimes this margin will be known – for example, an electronic balance is known to have a margin of error of ±0.2 g. This margin of error of ±0.2 g is the difference between the measured value and the 'true value' of the item being measured. Manufacturers often provide a margin of error in the manual that accompanies a measuring device.

More often than not this uncertainty is not known. Uncertainty can be estimated by carrying out statistical analysis of a set of measurements. Calculating **standard deviations** can give an indication of the spread of the results. The spread indicates the uncertainty of a measurement.

Measuring uncertainties can be caused by a number of factors:

- The measuring device – errors in measurement due to wear and tear of the device, drift, poor readability
- The item being measured – difficulties in trying to measure the mass of an animal on a scales if the animal keeps moving
- Environmental influences – temperature, humidity, etc. might interfere with the measuring device
- The person taking the measurements – they may not have the required skill and precision in taking the measurement, or they might be careless.

1.18 *Always be aware of potential sources of uncertainty when taking measurements and take precautions to reduce them.*

Taking the following precautions when taking measurements can help to reduce measurement uncertainties:

- Check that the measuring device is working properly
- Calibrate the measuring instrument prior to use
- Make careful calculations, especially when using formulas, and ask a competent person to check your results
- Read the measurement carefully
- Make good data records
- Check results.

Statistical and systematic uncertainty

Statistical and systematic uncertainties arise from errors associated with the taking of measurements.

Statistical uncertainties are usually the result of **the experimenter's inability to take the same measurement in exactly the same way each time**. Systematic errors are more difficult to detect and

1.19 *An anemometer*

can often persist throughout the entire experiment. They are usually associated with **faulty measuring equipment** or **consistently taking a measurement incorrectly**, e.g. measuring the volume of water in a measuring cylinder from the top of the meniscus rather than the bottom of the meniscus. Systematic uncertainty can also be caused by interference from the environment with the measuring process, e.g. trying to measure wind speed using an anemometer.

DEFINITION

Statistical uncertainty: random fluctuations in measurements (also known as random errors). Random errors can occur in either direction, above and below the true value.

Systematic uncertainty: consistent, repeatable error usually caused by measuring instruments that are incorrectly calibrated, a defect in the measuring equipment or the measuring equipment being used incorrectly. Systematic errors are always of the same value in the same direction, e.g. +0.05 g.

Table 1.7 provides examples of both statistical and systematic uncertainty and ways to reduce these errors.

Table 1.7 How to reduce statistical uncertainty and systematic uncertainty		
Type of uncertainty	**Example**	**How to minimise this error**
Statistical uncertainty (random error)	• You measure a sample of soil in a crucible three times and you get the following masses: 15.35 g, 15.28 g and 15.32 g. You have not been consistent in how the measurement is taken.	• Random errors can be reduced by increasing the sample size and taking more measurements. The error can then be reduced by averaging your results. The average or mean value will be closest to the true value.
Systematic uncertainty	• The electronic balance that is used to measure the mass of the soil sample has been incorrectly tared and reads 0.03 g too high for all the measurements taken. • Zero error: an electronic balance giving a false reading when you know its true value is zero.	• In this situation all the data are off in the same direction, all masses are 0.03 g more than their true value. Systematic errors can be difficult to spot. • Reducing systematic error in this case involves the experimenter learning to tare the electronic balance correctly.

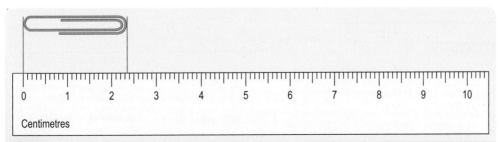

1.20 *The measurements on this ruler do not start at the start of the ruler. Therefore it is important to remember when using this ruler to measure the length of the paper clip that you place the start of the clip at zero and not at the start of the ruler. If the clip is measured from the start of the ruler then the experimenter is introducing zero error.*

Other ways of reducing systematic uncertainty include:
- Always reading measurements at eye level thus avoiding parallax error
- Avoiding zero error
- Identifying the causes of systematic error and eliminating them, e.g. calibrating a pH probe correctly before using it to measure pH or correctly taring an electronic balance.

Precision and accuracy

Measurements should always be taken as accurately and precisely as possible. **Accuracy refers to how close a measurement is to its 'true value', whereas precision refers to how close the measurements are to each other.** If measurements are taken with precision, then there will be little variation seen when taking the same measurement repeatedly using the same measuring instrument.

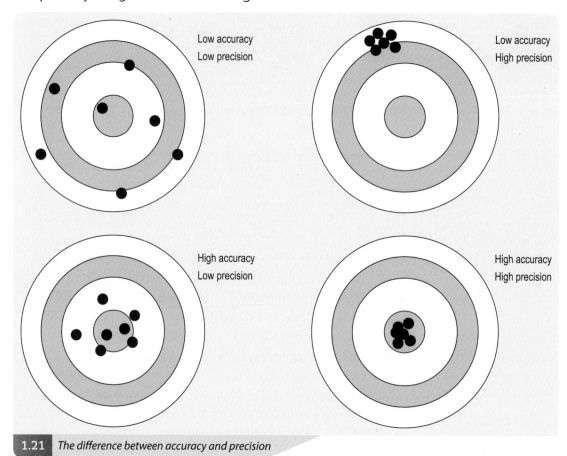

1.21 *The difference between accuracy and precision*

How to improve accuracy and precision when taking measurements:
- Ensure all measuring instruments are calibrated and functioning correctly
- Ensure that measuring cylinders, burettes and pipettes are clean prior to use; debris remaining in these pieces of equipment will influence measurements of volume
- Take measurements multiple times.

> An **accurate** measurement is close to the true value; precise measurements repeatedly give a similar value, but this might not be the true value.

Summary

- The scientific method is made up of the following steps: observing, formulating a hypothesis, making a prediction, designing an experiment, recording data, drawing conclusions, accepting or rejecting the hypothesis and communicating the results.
- Observations form the basis of a hypothesis.
- A hypothesis is a proposed explanation for an observation. A hypothesis must be testable and falsifiable.

- A variable is any factor or condition that can be changed in an experiment.
- Qualitative data are data that we observe with our senses, e.g. colour changes, smells, tastes.
- Quantitative data are data that involve measurement and are always numerical values.
- Primary data are the results or data that are generated when carrying out an experiment, investigation, survey, etc.
- Secondary data are the data collected by someone other than the experimenter.
- Data collected during an investigation are normally recorded in a table.
- Data are often presented in the form of a chart or a graph.
- The most common ways of presenting data include: bar charts, line graphs, pie charts and scatter graphs.
- Analysis of results involves the identification of trends and patterns in the quantitative data and drawing conclusions from the data.
- Quantitative data can be analysed statistically. Statistical calculations can be used to investigate whether there is a relationship between the independent and dependent variables.
- The correlation coefficient is a statistical measure that describes the size and the direction of a relationship between two or more variables.
- Qualitative data analysis normally involves the impressions and interpretations of the person conducting the investigation.
- Causation indicates that a change in one variable is the direct result of a change in the other variable, i.e. that there is a cause-and-effect relationship.
- In order to determine causation, a randomised controlled experiment must be carried out.
- Statistical uncertainties are the result of an experimenter's inability to take the same measurement in exactly the same way each time.
- Statistical uncertainty, also known as random errors, is random fluctuations in measurements. Random errors can occur in either direction, above and below the true value.
- Systematic uncertainty is a consistent, repeatable error usually caused by measuring instruments that are incorrectly calibrated or a defect in the measuring equipment.
- Systematic errors are always the same value in the same direction.
- Reducing systematic errors involves learning how to use the measuring device correctly, calibrating the device correctly and avoiding zero error.
- Uncertainties of measurement can be caused by a number of factors: the measuring device, the item being measured, environmental influences and the person taking the measurements.
- Statistical uncertainty can be reduced by increasing the sample size and taking more measurements. The error can then be reduced by averaging the results.
- Accuracy refers to how close a measurement is to its 'true value'.
- Precision refers to how close the measurements are to each other.

PowerPoint Summary

QUESTIONS

1. Which of the following is a step-by-step approach used to help answer a question or solve a problem?

   (a) Experiment

   (b) Hypothesis

   (c) Scientific method

   (d) Prediction

2. A hypothesis is:

   (a) An educated guess

   (b) A proposed explanation for an observation

   (c) Both testable and falsifiable

   (d) All of the above.

3. The independent variable in an experiment is:

   (a) The factor that is changed

   (b) The factor that is measured

   (c) The factor that is controlled

   (d) None of the above.

4. An experiment that tests only one variable at a time using an experimental group and a control group as a comparison is called:

   (a) An investigation

   (b) A theory

   (c) A prediction

   (d) A controlled experiment.

5. Which of the following are examples of quantitative data?

   (a) The iodine turned blue-black.

   (b) There was a 2 cm increase in the growth of the barley seedlings.

   (c) After drying, the mass of the grass dropped by 2 g.

   (d) There was a rancid smell given off by the fermented grass.

6. Rearrange the following to give the correct order of steps in the scientific method.

   (a) Form a hypothesis.

   (b) Analyse the results.

   (c) Draw conclusions.

   (d) Test the hypothesis.

   (e) Observe and record data.

   (f) Communicate the findings.

7. A student wanted to investigate the optimum depth at which to plant runner bean seeds that would still allow the bean seedlings to emerge from the ground.

   (a) What is the independent variable in this experiment?

   (b) What is the dependent variable?

   (c) Identify two conditions that would need to be controlled in this experiment.

8. Which type of graph or chart would be used to show the relationship between two variables?

   (a) A pie chart

   (b) A line graph

   (c) A scatter graph

   (d) A bar chart

9. Explain how a hypothesis differs from a theory.

10. Lucy decides to investigate the effect of a nitrogen fertiliser on the yield of tomatoes from tomato plants. She divides 50 tomato plants into two equal groups.

    (a) Why did Lucy divide the tomato plants into two equal groups?

    (b) What are the independent variable and the dependent variable in this experiment?

    (c) During the experiment Lucy kept the two groups of tomato plants under the same conditions. Why was this?

1.22 *The effect of nitrogen fertiliser on the yield of tomatoes*

(d) Identify two conditions that Lucy would have to keep constant during the experiment.

(e) The results of Lucy's experiment were as follows:

The effects of nitrogen feed on the yield of tomatoes	
Group	**Average number of tomatoes**
Experimental group	21.5
Control	15

What conclusion can be drawn from Lucy's results?

(f) Lucy repeated her experiment several times. Give a reason why she did this.

(g) Explain the purpose of a control in an experiment.

11. A scientist was investigating the number of lactobacillus bacteria growing in a milk sample over a number of hours.

(a) What are the independent and dependent variables for this experiment?

(b) What type of graph would you use to present these data?

(c) Plot these data on a graph. Label both the horizontal and vertical axes.

(d) Write a title for this graph.

(e) Analyse the data. What trend, or pattern, is emerging about the growth of the bacteria?

The number of lactobacillus bacteria growing in a milk sample	
Time (hours)	**Number of bacteria**
0	21
1	42
2	84
3	168
4	336
5	672

12. A soil scientist was investigating the amount of lime required to raise the pH of a sample of acidic soil (pH 5.2). The table shows the mass of lime added to 100 g of soil and the resulting pH after the samples were left for a month.

(a) What is the independent variable and its units?

(b) What type of graph would be used to present these data?

(c) Plot these data on a graph and draw a trend line.

(d) What type of correlation exists between the independent and the dependent variables?

The mass of lime required to raise the pH of a soil sample	
Mass of lime added to the soil (g)	**pH of the soil**
0	5.2
0.5	5.4
1	5.55
2	5.76
4	6.1
5	6.26
10	7

13. Using the internet, research and investigate whether there is a cause-and-effect relationship for each of the following:

    (a) As the number of trees cut down increases, the probability of soil erosion increases.

    (b) As temperature decreases, the speed at which molecules move decreases.

    (c) As the amount of moisture increases in an environment, the growth of mould spores increases.

14. Describe how systematic uncertainties arise during an experiment.

15. Outline ways in which both statistical and systematic uncertainties could be reduced during an experiment.

16. Distinguish clearly between the members of each of the following pairs of terms:

    (a) Qualitative and quantitative data

    (b) Primary and secondary data

    (c) Causation and correlation

    (d) Statistical and systematic uncertainty

    (e) Precision and accuracy.

17. A farmer has 40 lambs that he wants to raise and finish for the market. All the lambs were born within 2 weeks of each other and all are of a similar weight. The co-op advises that the lambs should be switched to a diet that is high in energy and protein. The adviser tells the farmer that the ratio of energy to protein in the lambs' diet must be balanced as lambs on a high-energy diet that have inadequate levels of protein will not put on the necessary weight gain. The co-op recommends that the lambs are fed a creep crunch with 16% protein. However, this feed is very expensive. The farmer is not convinced and decides to buy enough of the 16% protein crunch to feed half of the lambs and another cheaper feed with only 8% protein to feed the remainder of the lambs. Design a feed trial that the farmer could use to test the different lamb feeds. In your design you must state each of the following:

    - Hypothesis
    - Prediction
    - Independent variable
    - Dependent variable.

    (a) What control variables are needed?

    (b) What other factors would the farmer need to consider before starting the feed trial?

    (c) How would you track the weight gain of the animals?

    (d) In the first week of the feed trial the lambs on 16% protein put on an average of 2.38 kg of live weight while the lambs on the 8% protein put on an average of 2.03 kg of live weight. In the second week the lambs on 16% protein put on 2.4 kg of live weight and the lambs on 8% put on 2.05 kg of live weight. In the third week the lambs on 16% protein put on 2.39 kg of live weight while the lambs on 8% protein put on 2.04 kg. In the fourth week of the trial the lambs on 16% protein put on 2.4 kg of live weight and the lambs on 8% put on 2.035 kg of live weight.

        (i) Represent the above data in a table.

        (ii) Use a graph of your choice to represent the above data.

    (e) If all the lambs roughly weighed the same at the start of the feed trial (20 kg) and they continued to put on live weight at the same rate as shown in the data above, calculate the total weight of both the lambs on the 16% protein and the lambs on 8% protein at the end of the sixth week.

    (f) What conclusion can be drawn from the results of this feed trial?

 Solutions Weblinks

CHAPTER 2 Evaluating evidence and communicating

When you have completed this chapter you should be able to:

- Critically examine the scientific process that was used to present a scientific claim
- Use your knowledge and understanding of science and nature to develop arguments or draw conclusions related to agriculture
- Make judgements and draw informed conclusions arising from the result of the investigation of others
- Appreciate the limitations of scientific evidence
- Distinguish between the reliability and validity of data
- Identify ways in which you can increase the reliability and validity of data
- Make predictions on the behaviours of systems based upon interpretation of numeric, graphic and symbolic representations
- Evaluate any ethical issues
- Read and evaluate scientific information related to agriculture.

Evaluating evidence

Critically examining the scientific process that was used to present a scientific claim

How many of you have heard the following claims?

- Eating carrots gives you night vision
- Eating food within five seconds of dropping it on the floor is safe
- Eating chocolate gives you acne.

All of the above are common everyday claims but all in fact are false. There is no scientific evidence to back up any of those claims, and although the examples given above don't have any serious implications it is important when we read about scientific claims that we don't just accept them without looking at them carefully and evaluating them critically.

So, how do you critically examine the scientific process used to present a scientific claim? There are a number of things you can look for when evaluating a scientific claim.

2.1 *When evaluating a scientific claim, you should look for accuracy, validity, reliability and peer review*

1. **Accuracy:** How accurate is the research? Accuracy depends on the design of the experiment and the instruments used to record the results. Accuracy is critical in making the results of an experiment or study reliable and valid. Other questions that you can ask about the accuracy of the study include:
   - Did the experiment last long enough? Was the experiment conducted over a sufficient time period?
   - Was the sample size large enough for statistical analysis?
   - Have the findings been checked by experts?

2. **Validity:** Does the experiment test the hypothesis stated (is it a fair test)? Reliability and validity are discussed in more detail in the next section.

3. **Reliability:** Is the experiment replicable? If the experiment was repeated under the same conditions would the results be the same? Are the results of this study consistent with the findings of other scientists? If the experiment were repeated and it produced a different set of results, then this would question the reliability and the validity of the original results. Some experiments are performed numerous times, especially when there are uncontrolled variables. Other scientists will also try to replicate the results.

4. **Peer review:** Peer review involves the evaluation of the experiment and its findings by expert scientists. Before scientists publish their research in a scientific journal, their work has to be externally reviewed. When Gregor Mendel's research data on the inheritance of traits in garden peas was analysed by Ronald A Fisher, he found discrepancies in the data which led him to question the accuracy and reliability of Mendel's research.

> **Validity:** how well a scientific test measures what it set out to measure. Can the results of the study be trusted or believed?

Mendel's perfect experimental ratios

Gregor Mendel is known as the Father of Modern Genetics as a result of the experimental work he completed on the inheritance of traits in garden peas in the mid nineteenth century. Mendel performed hundreds of crosses and collected large amounts of data, which allowed him to come up with simple ratios for the inheritance of traits. In the early 1900s, British statistician and geneticist Ronald A Fisher analysed Mendel's experimental data and found that they were too good a fit to Mendel's theoretical expectations. Ronald Fisher found that the probability of obtaining such a good fit was only 7 in 100,000. Further analysis of Mendel's data identified other discrepancies. Ronald Fisher concluded that most if not all of Mendel's experimental data had been falsified so as to agree closely with Mendel's expectations (confirmation bias). Ronald Fisher attributed this falsification of data to Mendel's assistants. It is probable that they were aware of the results Mendel was expecting and either ignored results that did not agree with this or misinterpreted or misidentified some of the experimental results.

2.2 *Gregor Mendel, the Father of Modern Genetics*

2.3 *Ronald A Fisher, a renowned statistician and geneticist who reviewed and analysed Gregor Mendel's research*

> **Bias:** prejudice or a preconceived opinion about something.

DEFINITION

Confirmation bias: the tendency to search for, interpret or favour information that confirms our existing beliefs or ideas.

Exercise 2.1

Read the following article published in the *Communicable Disease Update* Volume 17 Issue 1 by Health Service Executive (HSE) South (South East), Department of Public Health, and then answer the questions.

The risk of spread of infection from animals to humans: farmers' knowledge, and their transmission prevention practices

Of all human pathogens, 60% are zoonotic, i.e. infections that are naturally transmissible from vertebrate animals to humans. The One Health approach recognises that the health of people is connected to the health of animals, and the health of the environment.

> **One Health** is an international collaboration of doctors, veterinarians and other health professionals to attain optimal health, for people, animals and the environment.

> DEFINITION
>
> **Zoonoses** or **zoonotic diseases**: diseases that can be passed from animals to humans.

Zoonoses are transmitted by ingestion, bite, scratch, inhalation or skin contact. Indirect transmission of zoonotic gastrointestinal pathogens has been documented in outbreak settings, with illness being associated with contact with contaminated clothing or shoes, animal bedding, flooring, barriers, and other environmental surfaces. Farmers, because of their work with livestock, in an environment often contaminated with animal faeces or by-products, may be at higher risk for zoonotic disease. Other members of farming households, even if not working on the farm, may also be at higher risk through direct and indirect contact with animals.

> **Gastrointestinal** refers to the stomach and small intestine.

> DEFINITION
>
> **Pathogen**: a disease-causing organism such as a bacterium, virus or fungus.

This is a summary of the findings from a study published in the Journal of Epidemiology and Infection last year [1]. It was a pen and paper survey to ascertain farmers' knowledge of the risk of spread of infection from animals to humans, and their transmission prevention practices. It was a survey of 1,044 farmers who submitted material to Ireland's Regional Veterinary Laboratories in 2015, with an 84% response rate.

> **Epidemiology** is the study of how often diseases occur in different populations or groups of people, and why.

The age of the respondents ranged from 12 to 91 years, with a mean age of 46 years. More than 90% were male. A variety of farming types were reported.

Ninety percent of farmers did not know that healthy animals may be a source of infection for themselves or family members. Over half did not realise that disease can be contracted from sick poultry or pets. On the other hand, farmers' knowledge of the risk to pregnant women of infection from birthing animals was high (88%). Younger farmers (<45 years) were more likely than older farmers (45+ years) to know what a zoonosis is, that one can catch an infection from healthy animals, from sick poultry, and from pets. Older farmers were more likely than younger farmers to identify aborting animals as a source of infection.

> **Response rate:** the number of people who answered the survey divided by the number of people who were asked to fill in the survey. It is expressed in the form of a percentage.

Ninety three percent of respondents reported washing their hands before eating or smoking while on the farm. Younger farmers were less likely than older farmers to wash their hands before eating or smoking on the farm, after handling sick animals and, in the morning and evening. One-third of respondents reported that they did not wear a boiler-suit/wet-gear while working. Of those who did, almost one-quarter did not remove it on entering the home.

The Environmental Protection Agency recommends annual testing of private well water for bacterial contamination. In our survey, almost three-quarters of farmers reported sourcing their drinking water from a private well. Of these farmers, 62% tested their water less frequently than once a year.

Approximately 40% of dairy farmers surveyed drank unpasteurised milk once a week or more frequently, indicating that dairy farmers continue to potentially expose themselves, and their families, unnecessarily, to pathogenic organisms in their milk.

Most respondents accessed information on diseases on the farm from multiple sources. The most common information sources were the veterinary practitioner, newspapers, Teagasc (the Agriculture and Food Development Authority) and the Department of Agriculture, Food and the Marine. Consistent, thorough hand hygiene is the single most important measure that can be taken to reduce the risk of disease transmission, most particularly gastrointestinal infections but also respiratory tract and skin infections. The Food Safety Authority of Ireland recommends that farm work clothes or footwear are not worn in the home because they can spread *E. coli*.

Consumption of unpasteurised milk or untreated water may also put farmers and their families at risk of contracting zoonotic infection. Unpasteurised (raw) milk can carry harmful bacteria such as *Campylobacter*, *Listeria*, *Brucella*, *Mycobacterium bovis*, *Salmonella*, *Verotoxigenic E. coli* (*VTEC*). The significant infection risks associated with the consumption of raw milk or raw milk derived products are well documented internationally.

Half of Irish agricultural households get water from a private source. This contrasts with private well ownership in Ireland generally, which is about 10%. Well water can be vulnerable to contamination, particularly if the well is not properly constructed or protected. The Environmental Protection Agency (EPA) has reported that 25% of groundwater supplies in Ireland are contaminated with faecal coliforms.

The results illustrate the need for further education, in plain language, to increase the awareness of potential biohazards on farms, and practical measures that can be taken to mitigate the risk of zoonotic infection. The fact that most farmers accessed information on diseases on the farm from multiple sources, suggests that a multi-faceted, One Health approach to infectious disease prevention in the farming community is merited. Evidence shows that building partnerships with agencies providing services in rural communities and trusted sources of information for the target population (e.g. farmer and country women's organisations, government departments, financial organisations, etc.), to provide information and training are effective ways of engaging with health promotion activities in farming and rural communities.

The Health Service Executive (HSE), with Department of Agriculture and Local Authority Veterinarians undertake health education and promotion activities directed at farmers throughout the year. The results of the survey have been published in Epidemiology and Infection [1] and presented at international public health and veterinary conferences. Posters and leaflets with advice about handwashing, protective clothing, pasteurising milk and private well water have been developed and will be distributed to Teagasc, the Regional Vetinary Laboratories (RVLs) and farming organisations.

[1] MAHON, M., SHEEHAN, M., KELLEHER, P., JOHNSON, A., & DOYLE, S. (2017). An assessment of Irish farmers' knowledge of the risk of spread of infection from animals to humans and their transmission prevention practices. *Epidemiology and Infection*, **145**(12), 2424-2435, © Cambridge University Press 2017

By Dr. Sarah Doyle, Consultant in Public Health Medicine & Dr. Marrita Mahon, Surveillance Scientist

---

The Environmental Protection Agency is an independent public body that is responsible for protecting and improving the environment for the people of Ireland.

E. coli are a large group of bacteria commonly found in the environment and the intestines of humans and animals. Many types of *E. coli* are harmless; however, some forms (e.g. VTEC) can cause severe illness.

Water contamination with faecal coliforms: coliforms are a group of bacteria that are normally found in the intestines of warm-blooded animals. Water polluted with animal or human faeces has the potential to spread diseases.

An example of a **biohazard** is a microorganism that is a risk to human health.

Multi-faceted: using several approaches.

Questions

1. Is this article from a reliable source? Justify your answer.

2. According to the article, what percentage of human pathogens are zoonotic?

3. Why are farmers and members of their families at a higher risk of becoming infected with a zoonotic disease?

4. Where were the findings of this study published?

5. What was the aim of this study?

6. (a) In this study 1044 farmers completed the survey. There was an 84% response rate. How many farmers were asked to complete the survey?

   (b) What was the average age of the farmers that were surveyed?

   (c) In your opinion, was the sample size used in the study adequate? Justify your answer.

7. What were some of the main findings of this study?

8. Outline some of the measures identified in the study that a farmer should take to prevent the transmission of a pathogen to a farmer or their family.

9. The study lists a number of bacteria that are found in unpasteurised milk. What diseases in cattle can you link to any of the bacteria found in the milk?

10. What recommendations does the study make in order to raise awareness among the farming community about the risks of zoonotic diseases?

11. Is there scope for further research/studies based on the findings of this study? Explain your answer.

Limitations of scientific evidence

Scientific method, the basis of investigation

The scientific method is based on the testing of hypotheses. Some investigations are beyond the scope of the scientific method – for example, we cannot set up an experiment to test for the existence or absence of God. The scientific method highlights challenging ethical issues, such as stem cell research. The scientific method cannot make moral decisions; it cannot decide whether something is right or wrong.

Our ability to interpret results

The results and conclusions drawn from the testing of hypotheses can be easily misinterpreted. Scientists can make mistakes or demonstrate bias when interpreting data. Both cultural and personal beliefs can influence our interpretation of data and the conclusions drawn. Many scientific theories have changed or evolved over time, mainly due to improvements or advances in technologies used in scientific research.

Stem cell research: in particular, embryonic stem cell research involves the use of human embryos.

The application of the scientific method to the natural world is always subject to change

The scientific method uncovers new knowledge about the living world on a continuous basis, which leads to new hypotheses, so the scientific method must be applied again and again. For example, the discovery of penicillin allowed doctors to treat bacterial diseases. However, today many bacteria have developed a resistance to antibiotics, which means that scientists are now trying to find ways to treat and cure diseases caused by antibiotic-resistant bacteria.

Scientific investigations are carried out in an environment where variables are controlled and measurements are accurately taken. However, translating what happens in the laboratory to the real world can be difficult. In science we cannot prove anything with a 100% certainty in the natural world. When a hypothesis stands up to testing we can only refer to it as being mostly true, because if we were to say it were 100% true then it would not be falsifiable.

The extent of our own knowledge

Observations that scientists make are based on the extent of their own scientific knowledge. A lack of knowledge often means that we are not asking the right questions or coming up with the right hypothesis or designing the appropriate experiment to test a hypothesis.

Accidental discoveries

Louis Pasteur once said that, 'In the fields of observation chance favours only the prepared mind'. What he implied by this is that occasionally advances in our scientific knowledge are made quite by accident, but opportunities that occur by chance can be seized only by a mind that is ready to recognise and accept them. Many accidental scientific discoveries were preceded by years of dedicated work and failure. The discovery of penicillin by Alexander Fleming and the discovery of radioactivity by Henri Becquerel are probably the most notable ones. Accidental discoveries have allowed for huge advancements in scientific knowledge.

Drawing conclusions from scientific investigations

After the analysis of the results of an experiment is completed, conclusions are made based on the findings. When drawing conclusions from data, it is important that the experimenter considers the reliability and validity of the data.

Reliability refers to the repeatability of the results. If the experiment/investigation were to be repeated a second or third time under the same conditions, would the results be the same? In addition, repetition of an experiment minimises the effects of random errors. Many experiments are carried out in replicates for this reason. Carrying out a **blind** or **double-blind** experiment can help to eliminate bias of the experimenter and the subject being tested. This increases the reliability of the results. Blind and double-blind experiments are often carried out in clinical trials, for example when testing a new drug. In a blind test on the new drug, the participants do not know whether they are in the experimental group (receiving the new drug) or in the control group (receiving a placebo). In a double-blind test, neither the participant nor the experimenter know which participants are receiving the new drug or the placebo. This is to prevent bias.

Placebo: a substance that resembles a drug but contains inactive ingredients such as sugar or starch.

DEFINITION

Blind and double-blind experiments: a blind experiment is an experiment in which information is withheld from the participant. A double-blind experiment is when information is withheld from both the participant and the experimenter. Blind and double-blind experiments eliminate or prevent bias.

For the results of an experiment to be reliable they also need to be valid. Are the instruments being used accurately, measuring what they are supposed to? For example, an electronic balance that is 1 g (gram) off will give you the same result each time but the results will not be valid as the readings are not accurate.

Validity of an experiment means that the experiment or investigation is accurately measuring what it is supposed to be measuring. A valid experiment should have the following criteria:

- Accurately test the hypothesis
- Have a large sample size
- Be conducted over a sufficient time period
- Control all other variables except for the independent and dependent variables
- Have appropriate measuring procedures
- Have a control experiment
- Follow the steps of the scientific method.

Measuring procedures will depend on the dependent variable. Are you measuring time, for example? Will you use a stopwatch?

A researcher would also assess whether the results and conclusions of the experiment can be applied in the real world outside the controlled environment of the laboratory.

The conclusions from a study or investigation are then compared to the original hypothesis. If the conclusions agree with the original hypothesis then the hypothesis is accepted. If not, then the hypothesis is rejected and from that a new hypothesis can be formed and tested. In this case, information gathered from the initial experiment may prove useful in forming the new hypothesis. If the hypothesis is accepted, then further research and experimenting are required to ensure the results are reproducible, which would add reliability to the experiment.

The experimenter may also make suggestions for further research based on their findings. The experimenter then communicates their scientific process and its findings to the scientific community, either through a scientific journal or by presenting a paper at a scientific conference. It is important that scientists communicate their findings, as it allows other researchers to repeat the experiment and build on it. These researchers can then confirm and validate the findings.

2.4   *Communicating findings of research allows collaboration between scientists to find solutions to world problems such as climate change.*

Making predictions based on analysis and interpretation of tables, graphs and symbolic representations

Earlier in this chapter we discussed how we can make predictions based on hypotheses. However, we can also make predictions based on our analysis of tables, graphs and diagrams. Look at the following example.

A student observed the growth of two species of coniferous tree (Norway spruce and Serbian spruce) for 8 years. Twenty of each type of tree were grown in a clay soil. The height of each tree was measured each year and the average was calculated. Heights were recorded in metres. The results are shown in Fig. 2.5 overleaf.

SCIENTIFIC PRACTICES

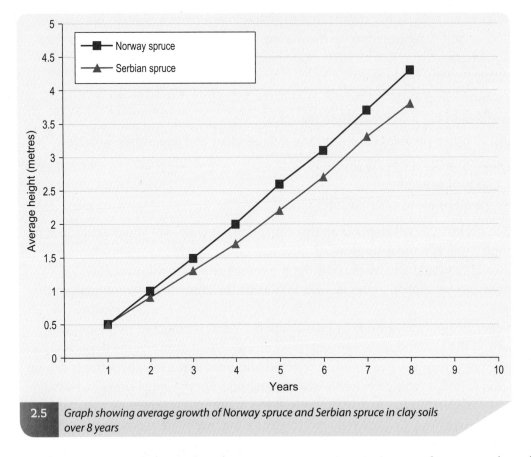

| 2.5 | *Graph showing average growth of Norway spruce and Serbian spruce in clay soils over 8 years* |

The graph in Fig. 2.5 shows that the Norway spruce is growing at a faster rate than the Serbian spruce in the clay soil. By extrapolating the graph, it will allow you to predict the average height of both the Norway spruce and Serbian spruce in years 9 and 10. By looking at the data in the table we can see that the Norway spruce is growing an average of 0.54 m per year while the Serbian spruce is growing an average of 0.47 m per year. Using this information we could predict what height the trees would be in 5 or 10 years if the trees continue to grow at the same rate.

Table 2.1 The average growth of Norway spruce and Serbian spruce over 8 years				
Year	Norway spruce (height in metres)	Growth per year (metres)	Serbian spruce (height in metres)	Growth per year (metres)
1	0.5	–	0.5	–
2	1.0	0.5	0.9	0.4
3	1.49	0.49	1.3	0.4
4	2	0.51	1.7	0.4
5	2.6	0.6	2.2	0.5
6	3.1	0.5	2.7	0.5
7	3.7	0.6	3.3	0.6
8	4.3	0.6	3.8	0.5
Average growth per year (metres)		0.54		0.47

DEFINITION

Extrapolating: the extension of a graph/data to estimate something by assuming that an existing trend will continue.

Symbolic representations

According to the National Council for Curriculum and Assessment (NCCA), symbolic representation involves the analysis of information presented verbally and the translation of that information into a mathematical form. One example of where this technique could be used is in genetics to predict the outcome of a cross between two parents. In genetic crosses the **genotypes** of both parents are represented using symbols. In cattle the polled (hornless) condition is represented with a capital P, as it is **dominant**, and the horned condition is represented with a lowercase p, as it is **recessive**. Cattle can have three possible genotypes for this trait (Table 2.2).

Table 2.2 The genotypes and phenotypes of the polled condition in cattle		
Genotype	Symbol	Phenotype
Homozygous dominant	PP	Polled (hornless)
Heterozygous	Pp	Polled (hornless)
Homozygous recessive	pp	Horned

Both the homozygous dominant and the heterozygous genotype for this trait will produce the same **phenotype**. Only the homozygous recessive genotype will give the horned condition.

In the example below, the genotypes of the cattle are given verbally. This information must be changed into the genotypes of the cattle using symbols. The gametes produced in this cross will carry only one of the pair of alleles present in the genotype. A Punnett square is then used to determine or predict the probability of the offspring being polled or having horns.

Verbally: by means of words.

> DEFINITION
>
> **Gametes:** sex cells, e.g. egg and sperm.
> **Alleles:** alternative forms of the same gene.
> **Dominant:** expressed in the phenotype when present in the genotype; normally represented by a capital letter, e.g. T.
> **Recessive:** expressed only when an individual has no dominant allele present; usually represented with a lower-case letter, e.g. t.
> **Genotype:** the genes present in the organism, whether they are expressed or not, e.g. Tt.
> **Phenotype:** the outward appearance of the organism.
> **Homozygous:** when the alleles present in the genotype are the same, e.g. PP or pp.
> **Heterozygous:** when the alleles present in the genotype are not the same, e.g. Pp.

Example

In cattle the polled condition (P) is dominant over the horned condition (p).
A **heterozygous polled cow** is crossed with a **heterozygous polled bull**.

Parents:	Heterozygous polled cow	×	Heterozygous polled bull
Parents' genotypes:	Pp	×	Pp
Gametes:	(P) (p)		(P) (p)

Punnett square:

	P	p
P	PP	Pp
p	Pp	pp

Table 2.3 The probability of the three genotypes for the polled condition in cattle		
Genotype of offspring	Phenotype	Probability
PP	Polled	25% or 1 in 4
Pp	Polled	50% or 1 in 2
pp	Horned	25% or 1 in 4

From this cross, the probability of the offspring having the polled condition is 75% and the probability of the offspring having the horned condition is 25%. Further information on genetic crosses is provided in Chapter 10.

Exercise 2.2

Data can be presented in a variety of formats. The following example was taken from the National Farm Survey, 2017. This is an annual report produced by Teagasc. Data is presented graphically, in graphs and pie charts, as well as numerically. Examine the information given in Fig. 2.6 and answer the following questions.

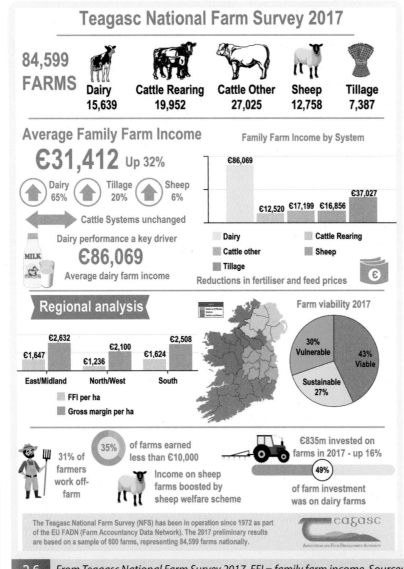

2.6 *From Teagasc National Farm Survey 2017. FFI = family farm income. Source: Teagasc*

Questions

1. In Ireland there are 84,599 farms in total. The breakdown of that number into the different farm systems is provided for all sectors except for mixed livestock farms. Using the information provided, calculate the number of mixed livestock systems in Ireland.

2. What percentage of Irish farms are dairy production systems?

3. What farming system was the most profitable in 2017? Justify your answer.

4. Did the average income of a dairy farmer increase or decrease compared with their income in 2016?

5. Using the information on incomes provided calculate the average income of a dairy farmer in 2016.

6. What costs decreased for farmers in 2017?

7. How many geographical regions is Ireland subdivided into? Identify those regions.

8. In the regional analysis, dairy farmers in the East Midlands had an average gross margin of €2632 per hectare. Their average family farm income was €1647 per hectare. What were the average costs for farmers in the East Midlands?

9. In which region of Ireland did dairy farmers have the lowest gross margin per hectare? Suggest reasons why this region of Ireland has a smaller gross margin per hectare. How did the costs of these farmers compare to those of the East Midlands?

10. Using the information provided, calculate the amount of money invested in Irish dairy farms in 2016.

11. How much money did Irish farmers invest in their farms in 2017? Was this an increase or decrease in the amount of money invested in Irish farms in 2016?

Gross margin per hectare: the amount of money available to pay for costs, e.g. hired labour, insurance, veterinary costs, loans, repairs and maintenance, and electricity. When these costs are deducted from the gross margin what remains is the net margin (farm family income).

Ethical issues when evaluating evidence

Ethics deals with decision-making and whether something is right or wrong. Scientific ethics requires honesty and integrity in all areas of the scientific method. Many scientific research areas, such as stem cell research, have many difficult ethical considerations. Over the last few decades scientists have developed a code of ethics when conducting, evaluating and publishing their findings. This has mainly been as a result of the mistreatment of both animals and human beings that have taken part in scientific experiments in the past.

2.7 *Scientists have a code of ethics to follow when conducting experiments and communicating their results*

1. All findings from research should be published or communicated to the wider scientific community and the public in a transparent way. The results of experiments should never be altered or exaggerated.

2. Scientists should always be open and willing to share their findings. The open publication of findings provides the opportunity for other scientists to build upon or extend this research further.

3. A lot of scientific research is publicly funded and people are more likely to fund research if the findings are communicated to them in a transparent and truthful way.

4. The researcher should avoid bias in all aspects of the experiment from the set-up of the experiment through to data analysis and the reporting of the findings.

5. Very often scientific research requires the collaboration and co-operation of many researchers. All contributors to a piece of work should be acknowledged. A scientist should never plagiarise another person's work.

6. The use of animals in research is an area with huge ethical issues. Animals used in research should always be treated respectfully and be properly cared for.

7. People often take part in clinical trials, especially in the area of medicine. If people are involved in research then they should be fully informed on what is being conducted, and written consent from them is required. No harm should come to any person involved in scientific research.

A national policy statement was developed in 2013 by a group that included universities, institutes of technology, the Royal Irish Academy and other funders of research to ensure research integrity in Ireland. The principles of this policy are:

- Honesty in presenting research goals and intentions, in the precise reporting of research methods and procedures, and in conveying valid interpretations and justifiable claims with respect to possible applications of research results.

- Reliability in performing research and in communicating the results.

- Interpretations and conclusions must be founded on facts and data capable of proof and secondary review, there should be transparency in the collection, analysis and interpretation of data and verifiability of the scientific reasoning.

Commissioning: authorising the production of a study, etc. A scientific study should never be funded by a particular organisation, as that might lead to the organisation applying pressure on the researchers to draw a favourable conclusion for the commissioning body.

- Impartiality and independence from commissioning or interested parties, from ideological or political pressure groups, and from economic or financial interests. For example, a multinational company could not commission or pay for research to prove that a chemical they produced did not contribute to pollution. Doing so might put undue pressure on the researchers to provide favourable evidence in support of the multinational company.

- Open communication, in discussing the work with other scientists, in contributing to public knowledge through publication of findings, in honest communication to the general public.

- Duty of care for participants in and the subject of research, be they human beings, animals, the environment or cultural objects.

- Fairness, in providing proper references and giving due credits to the work of others, in treating colleagues with integrity and honesty.

- Responsibility for future science generations. The education of young scientists and scholars requires binding standards for mentorship and supervision. In addition, we recognise that research should always be designed and conducted in accordance with ethical principles, and with appropriate review processes in place to ensure this.

Sourced from: National policy statement on Ensuring Research Integrity in Ireland, published by Irish Universities Association in June 2014

All third level institutes in Ireland have an ethics board or committee that view research proposals and highlight any ethical issues arising.

Communicating

Reading and evaluating scientific information related to agriculture

As part of the syllabus you must be able to evaluate scientific information related to agriculture from a variety of sources: media, websites, agri-food events and other agricultural resources. Learning to critically read scientific information and evaluate it will develop and improve your research skills. When reading any article, whether it be in a newspaper or on the internet, it is important that you keep an open mind, and try to look at the information in an objective manner. Do not disregard new ideas just because they contradict or confirm your thinking (avoid bias).

There are a number of things you can look for to check the reliability of the information.

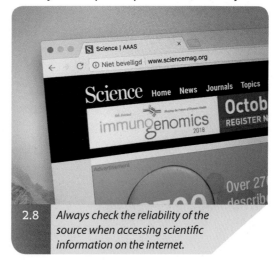

2.8　*Always check the reliability of the source when accessing scientific information on the internet.*

- Check the source of the information: whether it is an educational site, a government site, a commercial site, etc. Look at the last portion of a website's URL. Websites that end in '.com' (commercial), '.net' (network) and '.org' (organisation) are public domain names. Some URL addresses are more restrictive and are available only to state or government institutions. URLs ending in '.edu' (education) are American universities and other educational institutes. UK university URLs end in '.ac.uk'. Governments and government agencies have '.gov' at the end of their URL (e.g. www.nasa.gov). In some cases the .gov can be combined with a country domain; for example, the Department of Agriculture, Food and the Marine (DAFM) in Ireland is www.agriculture.gov.ie. The '.ie' stands for Ireland.

- Who wrote the information in the article or website? What level of expertise does this person have? Has the content of the article been peer reviewed? Are there contact details for the author or the publication?

- Cross-check the information with numerous sources. Do other sources confirm or refute the information in question?

- Consider the quality of the content. Are there spelling or grammatical errors? Does the site or article look like a professional publication? Are the sources of information cited reliable? When examining articles check when the information was published. This will give you an idea of the relevance of the information. Material published online should also indicate when it was published and when it was updated. If there are links embedded in the article, check that the links come from a credible source (e.g. established publications, research institutions, universities).

- Does the article or website present only one side of the issue or does it have a balanced approach? Is the author demonstrating bias? Is the material factual or is the author just expressing their opinion? Are the author's claims supported by evidence?

> **URL (uniform resource locator):** also known as a web address, a URL is a reference to a web source.

SCIENTIFIC PRACTICES

Exercise 2.3

Read the following article, which was published in *New Scientist* magazine, issue 3185 on 7 July 2018 and amended on 16 July 2018.
The author of the article is Michael Le Page, a UK news reporter at *New Scientist*.

The second great battle for the future of our food is underway

First it was GM food. Now battle lines are being drawn over whether crops and animals modified with CRISPR gene-editing can make it on to supermarket shelves

By **Michael Le Page**

YOU have probably heard of CRISPR, the gene-editing technique set to cure diseases and modify our DNA. The real revolution, however, may be in its ability to transform our food. "The biggest impact is going to be in agriculture," Jennifer Doudna, who helped develop the method, told *New Scientist* earlier this year.

This is because older, cruder techniques make it expensive to develop genetically modified (GM) foods, so they are mostly the domain of big multinationals. In contrast, CRISPR has made genetic tinkering cheap and easy.

"It takes a firm on average 13 years and costs $130 million to launch a GM crop"

"Rather than just four or five large multinationals dominating the market, you're going to have an explosion of companies all over the world innovating and coming up with improved crop varieties," says Tony Moran of US biotech company Cibus.

But just how far this revolution goes depends on how countries regulate CRISPR foods. The US and some others have decided that simple gene tweaks don't require special regulation. But the world's biggest market – the European Union – has yet to decide. A court decision due later this month could determine the technique's fate in the EU, which is historically anti-GM, and perhaps the world.

So why are people keen to CRISPR our food? For starters, genome-edited plants and animals could make what we eat safer by removing allergens and cancer-causing substances such as acrylamides. CRISPR could also make crops resistant to diseases and more nutritious.

Amend: to make minor changes in order to make it fairer or to reflect a changing situation.

CRISPR: a gene editing technology that allows scientists to change an organism's DNA. Using this technology, genetic material can be altered at particular locations in the DNA (see page 153).

Genome: the genetic material present in a cell.

Genome-edited refers to plants that have had a change made to their DNA sequence using gene editing. The change usually involves the changing of only one base in the DNA sequence.

Acrylamide: a chemical substance that can cause mutations in DNA. A mutation is any change that occurs to the DNA sequence of a cell.

Meta-analysis: a statistical procedure for combining data from multiple studies.

We need the next generation of food to tackle challenges such as a growing population and climate change, says Nigel Halford of plant research centre Rothamsted Research in Harpenden, UK. "The idea that we don't need new technologies is utterly ridiculous," he says.

We have been here before, though. Critics of GM crops say they were supposed to have all kinds of benefits, from boosting food production to helping the environment, but haven't delivered. That is probably wrong. For instance, a 2018 meta-analysis found that GM maize yields are up to 25 per cent higher. Several reports, including one in 2016 from the US National Academies of Sciences, also suggest that GM crops are no worse for the environment, and are sometimes better.

What is true is that most GM crops are designed to enrich big companies. That is because it takes on average 13 years and costs $130 million to launch one. "When you have an intensely demanding regulatory system, only big multinationals can afford to do it," says Joyce Tait at the University of Edinburgh in the UK, who studies the governance of new technologies.

Genome editing means you no longer need to be Monsanto to launch a new crop. "We are a small company," says Federico Tripodi of Calyxt, a US firm that has just begun growing soybeans edited using another gene-editing tool that can produce small and permanent changes to the DNA sequence of organisms on a commercial scale.

By opening biotech up to small companies and non-profit groups, CRISPR offers us a chance to avoid the mistakes made with genetically modified organisms (GMOs) and ensure more people benefit, says Tait. "Whether it happens or not depends entirely on how we regulate this technology," she says.

The deciding factor is whether regulators see CRISPR as a smarter form of conventional breeding or treat it as a new form of GM. The science is clear. All breeding involves genetic modification of some kind. Farmers who select a prize cow to mate are choosing to propagate its genes. Older genetic modification techniques add extra DNA to a plant or animal – often taken from a different organism. It is an old and clumsy technology, says Peter Beetham, CEO of Cibus. "We see GMOs as Windows 95."

By contrast, the most common use for CRISPR is to change just one or two DNA letters. Such mutations occur with no human intervention all the time, so CRISPR proponents argue that there is no logical reason to treat them differently.

"Conventional breeding can result in hundreds of unpredictable changes to an animal's DNA," says Kris Huson of Recombinetics, a Minnesota firm that has made hornless dairy cattle by inducing a mutation already present in some beef cattle. "Gene editing results in an intentional, predictable one."

In fact, plant breeders in the 1950s gave up waiting for natural mutations and started inducing them with radiation or toxic chemicals, called mutagenesis. Much of our food was created in this way, such as some wheat varieties and red grapefruit. "From a scientific point of view, regulating genome editing and mutagenesis differently makes absolutely no sense," says Halford.

Natural mutations

Anti-GM activists disagree. They want all edited crops to be treated as GM. "It is not whether or not something similar already exists, or whether the modification could occur naturally," says Franziska Achterberg of Greenpeace's European unit.

Only a few countries have made their position clear so far. In the US, crops created by minor gene-editing tweaks are being treated as normal, but animals created in the same way are subject to additional regulation.

Monsanto is a US company specialising in agrochemicals and agricultural biotechnology. Monsanto developed a herbicide called Roundup and is a major producer of genetically engineered crops. It was acquired by Bayer (German multinational pharmaceuticals company) in 2018.

Proponents of CRISPR: people who are in favour of or supporters of this new technology.

Mutagenesis: the process of changing the genetic information of an organism by exposing the DNA to mutagens (substances that cause a mutation).

Activist: a person who campaigns to bring about political or social change.

Greenpeace is an international non-governmental environmental organisation that campaigns on worldwide issues such as climate change, deforestation, overfishing and genetic engineering.

Matters could be complicated by a new law requiring GM foods to be labelled as "bioengineered" in the US. The biotech industry fears this label will deter both consumers and investors.

That might not be true: firms that labelled food as "genetically engineered" because of a short-lived law in Vermont say they saw no fall in sales. There was also a slight fall in opposition to GM in the state, according to research published last week.

However, it seems likely that CRISPR-edited foods will not require labelling. The details were meant to be finalised this month, but the process is running late.

As for the rest of the world, Canada, Argentina, Brazil and Chile will regulate on a case-by-case basis, with most edited varieties being treated as normal ones. Colombia could soon follow suit – it has already said it will treat gene-edited cacao (chocolate) as a normal crop.

The big question is what will happen in the largest market of all: the EU. It was supposed to make a final ruling several years ago, but still has not done so.

"Conventional breeding can result in hundreds of unpredictable changes to an animal's DNA"

All eyes are on the European Court of Justice, which is hearing a case challenging the definition of GMOs. A legal opinion published early this year hints that the ruling will be that gene-edited organisms do not count as GM under EU law. If so, it could spark a massive CRISPR boom globally. The decision is expected on 25 July, so watch this space – your food may never be the same.

Note: In July 2018, the European Court of Justice ruled that all gene-edited crops must be labelled as genetically modified organisms (GMOs).

This article appeared in print under the headline "The second great food war"

Article amended on 16 July 2018

> **European Court of Justice:** the supreme court of European Union in all matters of European Union law. It interprets EU law and ensures that all members states adhere to these laws.

Questions

1. (a) Who is making the claim that the second great battle for the future of our food is underway?

   (b) What evidence can you find in the article to support this claim?

   (c) Checking other sources of information, what evidence can you find to support or refute this claim?

2. Is this article published by a reliable source? Give a reason for your answer.

   (a) Do some research into *New Scientist* to find out how long they have been producing this publication.

   (b) What type of publication is it?

   (c) Are readers able to contact *New Scientist* and, in particular, the author of this article? Where can you find information on contacting the author or the publication itself?

3. What makes CRISPR different to normal methods of genetically modifying organisms?

4. What evidence does the author include to show that genetically modified (GM) maize produces higher yields and that 'GM crops are no worse for the environment'? What type of evidence is it?

5. In your opinion, does the author try to present a balanced argument for and against GM crops or is he slanting the article for GM crops? What evidence can you find in this article to support your opinion?

6. Has the author consulted experts in the area of CRISPR and GM? Give a reason for your answer. What level of expertise do these people have?

7. Have a class discussion on this article and the answers to the questions.

Summary

- There are a number of points to look out for when critically evaluating the process used to present a scientific claim. These include evaluating:
  - The accuracy of the research: Was the experiment conducted over a sufficient time period? Was the sample size large enough? Have the findings been checked by experts?
  - Validity: Does the experiment test the hypothesis stated?
  - Reliability: Is the experiment replicable? If the experiment were repeated again under the same conditions would the results be the same?
  - Peer review: This involves the evaluation of the experiment and its results by expert scientists.
- The scientific method does have limitations, including:
  - Some things are beyond the scope of the scientific method (e.g. we cannot set up an experiment to test for the existence or absence of God)
  - Our ability to interpret our results
  - Its application to the natural world, which is always subject to change
  - The extent of our knowledge
  - Accidental discoveries.
- Reliability refers to the repeatability of the results. Repetition of an experiment minimises the effect of random errors.
- Validity of an experiment means that the experiment or investigation is accurately measuring what it is supposed to be measuring.
- Extrapolating is the extension of a graph/data to estimate a value by assuming that an existing trend will continue.
- Ethics deals with decision-making and whether something is right or wrong.
- Scientists have developed a code of ethics when conducting, evaluating and publishing their findings.
- Some ethical considerations in science include:
  - Research should always be published or communicated to the wider scientific community and public in a transparent way
  - Scientists should always be open and willing to share their findings
  - Bias should be avoided in all aspects of the experiment
  - Animals used in research should always be treated respectfully and be properly cared for
  - People participating in scientific research should be fully informed on what is being conducted. No harm should come to any person involved in scientific research.
- When evaluating scientific articles written online or in magazines, there are a number of things you can look for to check the reliability of the source of information.
  - Check the website URL – is it a trusted source, e.g. a university, government department or agency?
  - What level of expertise does the person who wrote the article have?
  - Cross-check the information with numerous sources.
  - Consider the quality of the content – are there errors in spelling and grammar? When was the article published?
  - Is there a balanced approach to the issue involved? Is the author demonstrating bias? Is there evidence to support the claim?

PowerPoint Summary

QUESTIONS

1. When evaluating the scientific process involved in presenting a scientific claim you would look at the:

    (a) Accuracy of the research

    (b) Reliability of the experiment

    (c) Validity of the experiment

    (d) All of the above

2. Which of the following is a limitation of the scientific process?

    (a) Graphing results

    (b) Recording results

    (c) Interpreting results

    (d) None of the above

3. Which of the following is the correct definition for a double-blind experiment?

    (a) Information is withheld from the experimenter only.

    (b) Information is withheld from the experimenter and the participant.

    (c) Information is withheld from the participant only.

    (d) Information is made available to both the experimenter and the participant.

4. Why is repeatability of results important in scientific experiments?

5. When examining scientific research it is important to check the **accuracy**, **validity** and **reliability** of the experiment and data. Write a brief note on each of the bold words.

6. Identify any **two** limitations of the scientific method. Explain each one.

7. How can bias be avoided in scientific experiments?

8. How can scientists ensure the validity of the experiments that they conduct?

9. Why is it important that scientists publish the findings of their research?

2.9   *Peer-reviewed scientific journals*

10. Discuss the benefits of scientists adhering to an ethical code when carrying out scientific research.

11. Identify criteria you would use to check the reliability of an agricultural article online.

 Solutions — Weblinks

CHAPTER 3 Working safely

When you have completed this chapter you should be able to:

- Identify health and safety hazards associated with agricultural practices
- Discuss controls and precautions necessary to prevent accidents, injury and ill-health
- Discuss the health and safety considerations of using agricultural machinery and equipment
- Recognise the need for safe work practices in all agricultural activities.

According to the Health and Safety Authority, farming is one of the most dangerous occupations in Ireland. Over one-third of all workplace fatalities in Ireland occur in farming. **Vehicles** and **machinery** are the **main causes** of farm accidents. In the past 10 years they account for approximately 50% of all farm deaths, with elderly farmers and children most at risk. Being crushed, struck, pinned under or falling from vehicles are the main causes of deaths with farm vehicles. Being entangled in power take-off (PTO), crushed under a machine part, caught in a machine mechanism, crushed between vehicles and struck by a machine object are the main causes of deaths with farm machinery. Between 2010 and 2017 a total of 172 agricultural fatalities was reported. The keys to prevention are training, good maintenance and safe work practices.

Table 3.1 Agriculture – number of reported fatalities (worker and non-worker) 2010–2017								
2010	2011	2012	2013	2014	2015	2016	2017	Total
22	22	20	16	30	18	20	24	172

Source of information: Health and Safety Authority

In Ireland the 2005 Safety, Health and Welfare at Work Act requires all farmers to prepare and implement a safety statement. A safety statement contains a health and safety policy and risk assessments. It is a legal requirement for all farmers to carry out a risk assessment of their farm. If a farmer has three or fewer people working on their farm then they can use the Health and Safety Authority Farm Safety Code of Practice, Risk Assessment Document to comply with this legal requirement.

Risk assessment is central to all work activities. It involves the following four steps:

1. Identification of hazards
2. Assessment of the risk
3. Identification and implementation of controls
4. Regular review and update of the hazards and risk assessment.

It is only through raising awareness of the need for safe working practices in agriculture that we can decrease the number of agriculture-related injuries and deaths that occur each year.

Health and safety hazards associated with agricultural practices

Identifying hazards and associated controls to prevent accidents and injury

Farms are a unique working environment as they normally contain the family home. Many farms have children and young people (under the age of 18) who grow up on the farm. As a result, all family members and adults working on the farm have a legal obligation to do everything reasonably possible to ensure the safety and health of children and young people on the farm.

Some of the most common hazards for children on a farm include tractors and agricultural machinery or equipment, livestock (e.g. cattle, especially bulls), drowning and falls (see Fig. 3.1).

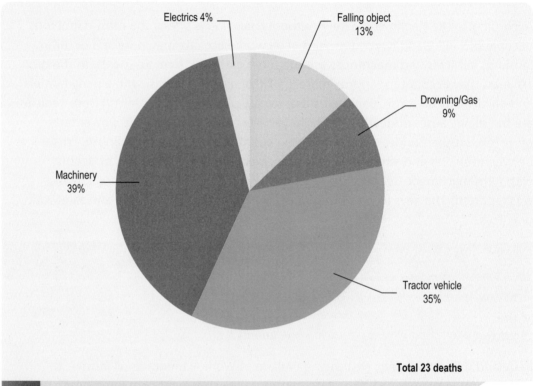

Total 23 deaths

3.1　*Deaths of children on farms, which represent 11% of all fatalities between 2008 and 2017 (courtesy of the Health and Safety Authority)*

The following pages contain a summary of safety hazards (hazards and risks) associated with farming practices and control measures that should be implemented as set out by the Health and Safety Authority in their Code of Practice for Preventing Injury and Occupational Ill Health in Agriculture. This document is available in full on their website.

3.2　*A warning sign on farmland*

3.3　*Children are at risk of injury if the farm is used as a playground.*

Table 3.2 Safety hazards and the controls necessary to prevent accidents and injury to children

Hazard	Risk	Controls and precautions
• Moving tractors and machinery around the farm	• Struck or crushed by tractors and agricultural machinery.	• Children must not be allowed unsupervised access to tractors and farm machinery. • No child under the age of 7 should be carried inside the cab of a tractor, harvester or other farm vehicle. • Children under 14 should not be allowed to drive or operate tractors or machinery. • Children over 14 should receive formal training before they are allowed to operate tractors. • No persons under the age of 18 should operate a harvester, power driven machine, sprayer, slurry spreader or chainsaw. These machines are particularly high risk and require specialist knowledge to operate them safely.
• Stacks of silage and hay bales, pallets or timber. Large tractor wheel, gates and pillars	• Falls from a height • Child crushed by bales or tractor wheels falling on them	• Children might be tempted to climb stacks of bales, pallets or timber. All stacks should be built carefully so that they do not collapse. • Tractor wheels should be stored on the flat so that there is no risk of them falling over and crushing a child. • Gates and pillars should be properly erected and secure.
• Livestock	• Child struck and crushed by an animal	• Children should never be allowed near female animals with newborn young. • Children should not be allowed near bulls, stallions and rams. • Avoid having children present when animals are let out of winter housing or when animals are being loaded onto a trailer, as these animals may be agitated or excited.
• Slurry pits, slurry storage areas, water tanks, etc.	• Drowning	• Provide a safe play area for children that has childproof fencing and is in sight of the home. • Slurry pits and water sources should be surrounded by secure fencing at least 1.8 metres high. • Access manholes to slatted slurry tanks should be secure and not easily opened by a child. A safety grid should be fitted below the manhole cover.

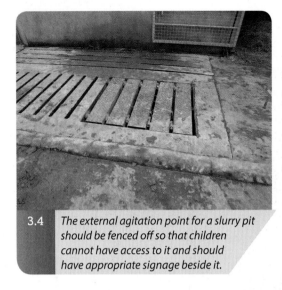

3.4 | *The external agitation point for a slurry pit should be fenced off so that children cannot have access to it and should have appropriate signage beside it.*

3.5 | *This sign is displayed on the entrance to every farm, indicating some of the hazards to be found on farms.*

Famers over the age of 65 have a greater risk of accidents and injury due to lack of mobility and agility, hearing loss, poor vision or medication they may be on. It is important that older farmers consider their limitations as they get older and avoid some types of work, such as working at heights and herding animals.

According to the Health and Safety Authority by far the greatest cause of farm deaths and accidents is caused by farm vehicles and machinery. People at risk include the operator of the vehicle, passengers and anyone in the vicinity of the vehicle or machine while it is being operated.

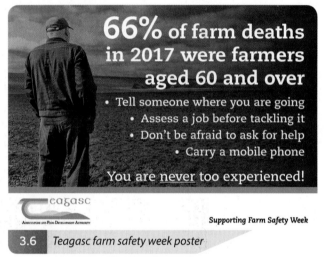

3.6 | *Teagasc farm safety week poster*

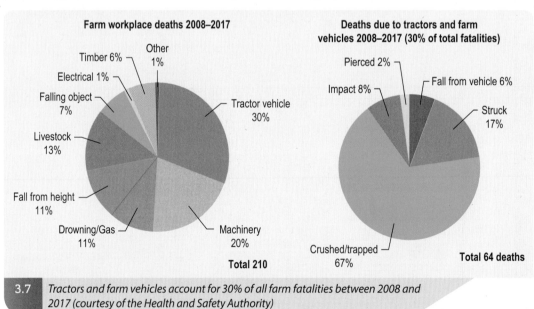

3.7 | *Tractors and farm vehicles account for 30% of all farm fatalities between 2008 and 2017 (courtesy of the Health and Safety Authority)*

An overview of the general safety hazards and appropriate controls for farmers is contained in Table 3.3.

Table 3.3 Overview of the general safety hazards and appropriate controls and precautions for farmers

Hazard	Risk	Controls and precautions
Tractors	• Crushed • Pinned or thrown from the tractor • Being struck by a tractor • Falling from the tractor	• Any person operating a tractor should receive training on how to use and operate the vehicle safely. • Keep the vehicle in good working order and well maintained. • Do not drive at speed. • Do not carry passengers on the tractor/machinery or inside a cab unless it is fitted with a passenger seat. • Ensure that the engine stop control is working effectively. • Ensure that the cab floor is kept clear to allow the brakes and clutch to be used. • Ensure that the brakes are in good working order. • Ensure that the power take-off (PTO) U-guard is kept in place at all times and that the PTO can be turned on and off correctly. • Do not leave the tractor while the engine is running. • Ensure that you have insurance and the appropriate licence for driving a tractor on a public road. • Use a four-wheel-drive tractor when driving on a slope. Assess the risk of overturning if working on a slope and avoid severe slopes. • When attaching any machine to a tractor, take precautions to prevent getting crushed. Never stand in the crush zone between the back of the tractor and the piece of machinery. • When finished using a tractor always use the safe stop procedure.

3.8 *The safe stop procedure*

Hazard	Risk	Controls and precautions
Quad bikes or all-terrain vehicles (ATVs)	• Driver's lack of experience • Overturning • Crashing	• Appropriate training on how to drive or use the quad bike or ATV. • Do not allow children under the age of 14 to drive a quad or ATV. • Wear personal protective equipment (PPE) and a helmet. • Keep the quad or ATV well maintained. • Check that tyre pressure is correct to ensure stability and control of ATV. • Vehicle speed and body weight placement is crucial for the operating and cornering of the quad or ATV.
Livestock	• Crushed or struck	• This is dealt with in greater detail in Chapter 25.
Falls or collapse of buildings	• Falling from roofs and from ladders • Falling from bales • Collapse of walls and gates • Falling objects	• Avoid working at heights with the use of ladders if at all possible. If not, work with someone to foot the ladder and tie the top of the ladder to a secure part of the building. Place the base of the ladder on firm, level and secure ground. The ladder must be in good condition. • Extensive work at height may require scaffolding. Scaffolds should be erected by appropriately trained personnel. • Use a mobile elevated platform with an operator with the appropriate training and experience. • Check for overhead electrical wires.
Drowning	• Drowning involving slurry	• Fence off water hazards and take precautions when working near water. • Slatted tank access manholes should not be easily opened and should have a safety grid below the manhole cover.
Poisoning	• Slurry gas	• This is dealt with in greater detail in Chapter 8.
Silage pit	• Tractor overturning when filling or rolling the pit • Excessive filling of a silage pit can overload walls and increase risk of a tractor overturning • Suffocation from fermenting gases	• Silage pits should never be overfilled. • Machine operators should be competent. • Never go underneath a silage cover once in place. Fermenting grass uses up oxygen under the cover quickly. • An open silage pit, with earth embankments, should have the sides and ends of the silage sloped off at a safe angle (less than 45 degrees). • Silage pits should be designed in accordance with the specifications set out by the Department of Agriculture, Food and the Marine (DAFM).

SCIENTIFIC PRACTICES

Hazard	Risk	Controls and precautions
Bales	• Crushed by falling bales • Rolled over by bale on sloped ground • Crushed or spiked by bale-handling equipment • Falling from trailers while tying down loads	• Choose a location which allows for the safe stacking and removal of the bales. • Store bales on a level, smooth and hard or well-draining surface. • Ensure stacks are stored away from overhead power lines. • When possible, round bales should be stored on their flat ends, one bale high. • If round bales have to be stacked, they should be placed on their curved side in a pyramid shape with supports to stop them moving. The maximum height of the stack should be three bales high. • Square bales should be stacked using an interlocking pattern to tie in the bales with the row underneath. The maximum height should be one and a half times the width of the base. Avoid getting on top of the bales. • Use suitable bale-handling equipment operated by a competent person to remove bales. Remove bales from the upper rows first.

Controls and precautions necessary to prevent ill-health

3.9 *Silage bales stored correctly*

3.10 *Silage bales stored incorrectly*

DEFINITION

Agrochemical: a chemical used in agriculture, e.g. pesticide, herbicide or fertiliser.

Agrochemicals are often used on a daily basis in farming. Agrochemicals cover a wide variety of substances, including detergents, fertilisers, pesticides and herbicides. It is vital that these chemicals are stored, handled and disposed of correctly. There is a high number of incidents involving agrochemicals reported to the National Poisons Information Centre every year, and many of these incidents involve children under the age of 10. All chemicals must be stored in a secure location. The storage area must be dry and well ventilated and constructed of material that is not combustible. A warning sign should be displayed at the entrance to the chemical store. Important information regarding the potential hazards of agrochemicals is shown on the products label.

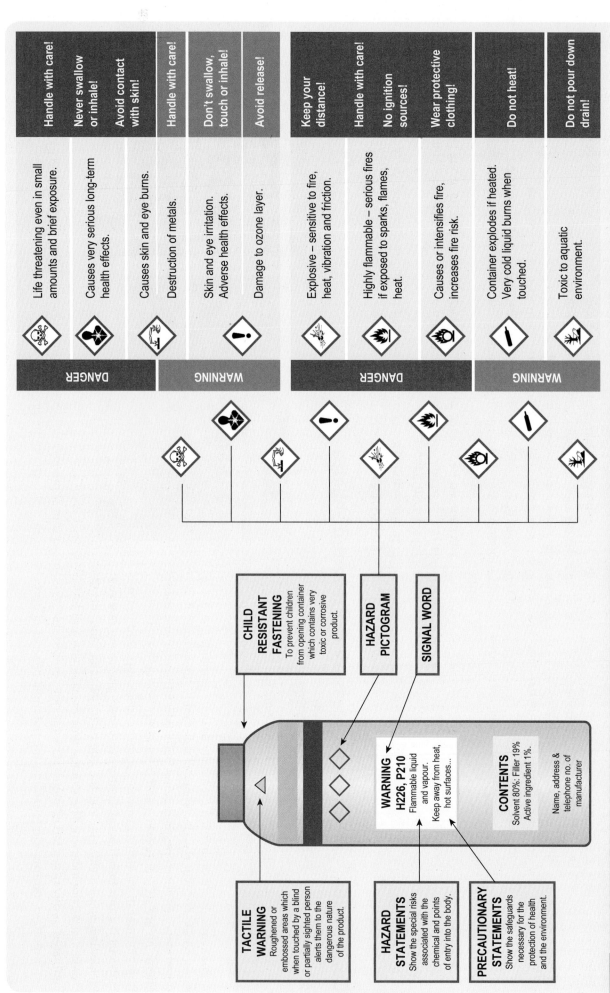

DANGER

Pictogram	Hazard	Warning
	Life threatening even in small amounts and brief exposure.	Handle with care!
	Causes very serious long-term health effects.	Never swallow or inhale!
	Causes skin and eye burns.	Avoid contact with skin!

WARNING

	Destruction of metals.	Handle with care!
	Skin and eye irritation. Adverse health effects.	Don't swallow, touch or inhale!
	Damage to ozone layer.	Avoid release!

DANGER

	Explosive – sensitive to fire, heat, vibration and friction.	Keep your distance!
	Highly flammable – serious fires if exposed to sparks, flames, heat.	Handle with care! No ignition sources!
	Causes or intensifies fire, increases fire risk.	Wear protective clothing!

WARNING

	Container explodes if heated. Very cold liquid burns when touched.	Do not heat!
	Toxic to aquatic environment.	Do not pour down drain!

CHILD RESISTANT FASTENING
To prevent children from opening container which contains very toxic or corrosive product.

HAZARD PICTOGRAM

SIGNAL WORD

WARNING
H226, P210
Flammable liquid and vapour.
Keep away from heat, hot surfaces....

CONTENTS
Solvent 80%: Filler 19%
Active ingredient 1%.

Name, address & telephone no. of manufacturer

TACTILE WARNING
Roughened or embossed areas which when touched by a blind or partially sighted person alerts them to the dangerous nature of the product.

HAZARD STATEMENTS
Show the special risks associated with the chemical and points of entry into the body.

PRECAUTIONARY STATEMENTS
Show the safeguards necessary for the protection of health and the environment.

3.11   *The label on a chemical container provides detailed information on the hazardous properties of that chemical. (Based on Health and Safety Authority material)*

Table 3.4 Safety hazards and controls for the use of agrochemicals

Type of agrochemical hazard	Risk	Controls and precautions
Fertilisers – calcium ammonium nitrate and urea	• Oxidising – they can cause or contribute to the combustion of other materials.	• This is dealt with in Chapter 8.
Pesticides	• Potential to cause serious harm including cancer; can cause damage to the brain and spinal cord, immune system and reproductive system.	• The sale and use of pesticides is regulated by the DAFM. • Handling and application of the pesticide should be carried out by a competent person. • Read the label and safety data sheet (SDS). The SDS contains more detailed information than that found on the label. • Use the pesticide in such a way as to minimise drift, run-off and volatilisation.
Fuels, oils, paints, etc.	• Respiratory problems • Skin irritation	• Wear appropriate PPE, e.g. gloves. • Avoid spraying. • Ensure there is good ventilation.
Acids and bases	• Acids and bases are generally corrosive to skin, eyes and the respiratory system.	• Wear PPE, e.g. gloves, goggles as directed.
Veterinary medicines (antibiotics, vaccines, wormers and drenches and dips)	• Puncture wounds from needles • Accidental injection • Inhalation • Poisoning	• Use proper handling facilities for the administration of injections. • Use needle guards. • Wear gloves, aprons, face shields and respiratory protective equipment when necessary.

Acids are commonly used in agriculture as cleaning agents or as an additive for the preservation of silage. Bases are also used in cleaning. Lime (calcium carbonate) is a base that is commonly used to raise the pH of soil.

DEFINITION

Safety data sheet (SDS): a sheet that provides information on chemicals describing hazards, handling, storage and disposal of the chemical, as well as emergency measures in case of an accident.

Drift: the unintentional movement of a pesticide from an area of application to any unintended site. Drift can cause the accidental exposure of the pesticide to people, animals and plants.

Volatilisation: the evaporation or sublimation of a substance into a gas.

Pesticide run-off: caused by rain washing the pesticide off plants and carrying it into drains, streams and rivers or washing the pesticide through the soil and into the groundwater. Pesticide run-off contributes to water pollution.

3.12 *Safety signage related to the use of medicines*

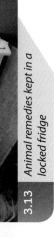

3.13 *Animal remedies kept in a locked fridge*

3.14 *Warning sign indicating a storage press for herbicide*

As farming involves a considerable amount of manual handling, farmers are at risk of suffering an injury due to this. The most common type of injury is a back injury. Other causes of ill-health in farmers include lung problems, infections and noise.

Table 3.5 Safety hazards and controls associated with ill-health in farmers

Hazard	Risk	Control
Lifting loads or weights	Back injury caused by: • Incorrect posture when lifting heavy weights • Repetitive bending and twisting postures • Lifting objects in confined spaces with unstable footing	• If the load is excessively heavy (50 kg or more) and has to be manually lifted, then have two people lift the load. • Use a front loader to lift heavy loads. • If possible, break the load down into a smaller size. • Use handling aids to reduce the need for lifting. • Use a calving jack when pulling a calf. • Improve the layout of the farm yard so that heavy loads can be stored in mobile storage units and reduce the need for manual handling. • Have clear access routes and space to allow for the use of handling aids or for the movement of loads. • Use a meal bin rather than handling large meal bags. • Always plan jobs ahead and consider ways of reducing the risk of an injury being caused by lifting heavy loads. • When lifting a heavy load, slightly bend your back, hips and knees, keep the load close to your waist and adopt a stable posture. Avoid twisting or leaning sideways. Do not lift more than you can manage.

Hazard	Risk	Control

Inhalation of dust or spores	• Farmer's lung:
	  • Mouldy feed or grain contains minute spores that cause an inflammation of the alveoli within the lungs.
	  • These spores trigger an allergic reaction which causes headaches, coughing and a shortness of breath upon physical exertion.
	  • Long-term exposure can lead to permanent damage to the lung tissue.
	• Exposure to mould can also lead to asthma.
		• Ensure buildings are well ventilated.
		• Do not disturb mouldy bales by opening out, as this releases spores into the air.
		• Damp down any sources of dust or spores.
		• Wear a suitable mask that is a respiratory protective device (Type FFP2 or P3).

Infections (zoonoses)	• There is a range of diseases that can be transmitted from animals and contaminated materials.	• This is dealt with in Chapter 31.
Noise	• Exposure to high levels of noise over an extended period of time or intense noise over a short period of time can cause permanent damage to a person's hearing.	• Purchase equipment with low noise level ratings. • Keep tractor doors shut. • Have a silencer on equipment such as a chainsaw. • Use mechanical or automatic feeding systems in pig and poultry houses. • If the noise level exceeds 80 decibels, ear defenders must be worn.
Stress	• Stress can be caused by numerous factors, including: fluctuations in market and farm prices, financial worry, long working hours, poor working conditions, poor health, poor weather, etc. • Isolation and lone working are contributing factors that cause stress. • Stress is associated with an increased risk of accidents and diseases of the circulatory system. • Stress can also lead to increased alcohol consumption, unhealthy eating habits, poor decision making and self isolation.	• Get sufficient sleep. • Good diet and exercise. • Seek professional help from medical, community or representative bodies. • Talk to family, friends, etc. • Get help with the workload.

Health and safety considerations when using agricultural machinery and equipment

Each year incidents involving tractors, machinery and equipment cause serious injury and even death. Agricultural machinery should be operated only by competent and fully trained people. The operator should be totally familiar with all the controls and operating procedures of the machinery.

One of the most commonly used pieces of machinery is a power take-off (PTO) drive shaft. PTO shafts are the source of power for many machines that are attached to a tractor and powered by the tractor's engine. PTOs can rotate at speeds up to 1000 rpm (revolutions per minute). Unguarded PTOs can cause serious injuries including death.

3.15   *Correctly guarded PTO*

3.16   *PTO partially guarded*

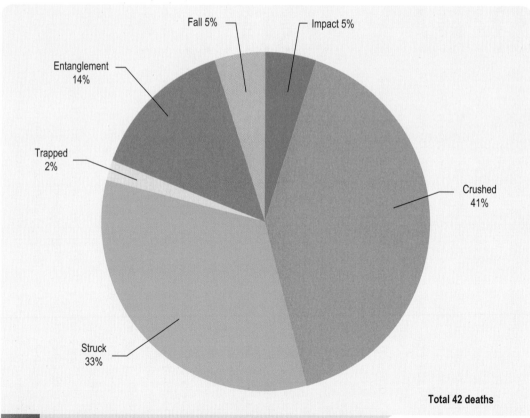

3.17   *Machinery accounted for 20% of all fatalities between 2008 and 2017 (courtesy of the Health and Safety Authority)*

Table 3.6 Safety hazards and controls for the use of farm machinery

Hazards	Risks	Controls and precautions
Power take-off (PTO)	• Entanglement in the PTO	• Rotating PTO shafts must be totally enclosed by the guard. The guard should be undamaged and match the shaft in both length and size (see Fig. 3.13). • The machine end O-guard and the tractor end U-guard must be in place. • The PTO guard should be greased regularly and should rotate on its bearings. • Avoid wearing loose clothing and jewellery and tie long hair up when using the PTO to reduce the risk of entanglement.
Tractor loader and telehandler	• Collapse	• It is a legal requirement to have equipment used to lift loads examined regularly by a competent person. • All lifting equipment must be checked after any substantial alteration or repair affecting its strength and stability. • Hydraulically operated machines used to lift more than 1000 kg must be fitted with a suitable device to prevent collapse if there is a hydraulic failure.
Harvest machinery	• Pressure to get harvesting work completed leads to time pressure and long working days • Driver fatigue from excessive hours • Increased risk of road collisions due to large number of agricultural machines using public roads	• Inspect and prepare all machinery before starting. • Ensure all safety guards are in place. • Check for any hydraulic leaks. • Be aware of any exposed moving parts and crop intake points. • Ensure the engine is off and the handbrake is on before removing any blockages from the machine. • Ensure operators have work breaks and plenty of food and water, and change operators regularly to prevent driver fatigue. • Ensure farm machinery is roadworthy and has proper working brakes and lights. • Beware of overhead electrical lines. • Watch out for other road users when using public roads at harvest time.
Silage machinery	• Pressure to get silage cut, collected and saved • Long working hours lead to driver fatigue • Increased risk of collision due to large number of agricultural machines using public roads	• All tractors, harvesters, balers, etc. should be properly prepared, maintained and in good working condition. • Only competent operators should be allowed to operate machinery. • Do not carry passengers. • All machinery should be roadworthy with working brakes and lights. • Beware of overhead electrical lines. • Watch out for other road users. • All guards should be in place on all equipment, especially the PTO shafts. • Keep individuals well away from mowers when they are in use, as there is an increased risk of being hit by projectile stones. • Ensure good communication between all operators of silage harvesters, loaders and tractors. • Beware of driver fatigue; ensure all operators have regular breaks, food and water and change operators regularly.

Safe work practices in all agricultural activities

As stated earlier, the farm is a unique working environment as it is the home of many farming families. To keep it a safe environment for everyone, all members of the family must be aware of potential hazards on the farm and take the necessary precautions and controls to prevent accidents and injuries. One way of alerting persons on the farms to hazards is using safety signs, although such signs should not be a substitute for trying to reduce the risk. Safety signs should be easily seen and kept clean. Any contractors or other personnel visiting the farm should be instructed on safety measures that need to be taken on the farm and the meaning of any safety signs. Examples include:

- Emergency routes and exits
- Working at height danger area
- Risk of falling objects
- Area of excessive noise (>85 dBA)
- Bull present in field.

3.18 *Warning sign for an electric fence*

Decibel (dbA): most noise levels are measured in dbA, which are decibels adjusted to reflect the ear's response to sound levels.

3.19 *Warning sign for a bull in a field*

3.20 *Warning sign for farm machinery*

The Health and Safety Authority recommends that all farmers and farm personnel have a safe system of work in place. Some basic rules that farmers must consider and follow include:

- Plan ahead and prioritise work
- Carry out essential safety checks
- Use proper equipment
- Ensure signs are in place
- Communicate with other workers and family and provide instructions where necessary
- Put measures in place to protect children and the elderly.

There are a number of steps that you can take when working on a farm or even visiting a farm in order to stay safe.

- Keep well away from tractors and machines that are in operation, as these machines can be very noisy and the person operating them may not be able to hear you or know that you are there.
- Stay clear of any stacked bales as they could fall and crush you.
- Give animals lots of space, especially those that have young.
- If you are carrying out work on the farm, always ask for help if you need it. Ensure that you fully understand the job that you are doing and that you understand and follow any instruction given to you. You should be supervised by a responsible adult while carrying out these activities.

- You must be 14 years or older to operate a tractor and you should have received formal training in the safe operation of the tractor. Never carry a passenger in the tractor with you unless there is a seat provided. You must be 16 years of age and have a licence to drive a tractor on a public road.
- Always wear proper protective equipment (including a helmet) if operating a quad. You must be 16 years or older to drive a quad.
- Keep away from slurry tanks and never enter a building where slurry is being agitated.
- Wash your hands regularly, especially after coming in contact with animals, their housing or feedstuffs. This can reduce the risk of picking up some infectious zoonotic diseases.
- Pay attention to all warning signs; these signs are there for your protection as they identify hazards.
- If you see something unsafe or some damaged equipment, always report this to a responsible adult.

There are a number of online health and safety courses on farm safety for farmers, parents and children (primary school), to outline the dangers on a farm and how to prevent accidents and injuries, at the Health and Safety Authority (HSA) website.

Summary

- Some of the most common hazards for children on a farm include tractors and agricultural machinery, livestock, drowning and falls.
- Children under the age of 7 should not be carried inside the cab of a tractor, harvester or other farm vehicle.
- Children under 14 should not be allowed to drive or operate a tractor.
- All stacks of silage and hay bales, pallets or timber should be built carefully so that they do not collapse.
- Children should never be allowed near livestock, especially bulls and livestock with young, or when livestock are being moved or let out of housing.
- Slurry pits and water sources should be surrounded by secure fencing. Slurry access manholes should be secure and not easily opened.
- Farmers over the age of 65 should avoid some types of work including working at heights and herding animals.
- There are many risks associated with the operation of a tractor. Any person driving a tractor must know how to operate the tractor safely. Quad bikes are especially hazardous, as speed and body weight placement is crucial in maintaining balance and avoidance of overturning the quad. Protective equipment and a helmet should be worn at all times.
- To reduce the risk of injury caused by falls, always ask someone to foot a ladder, and secure the top of the ladder to part of the building. If extensive work has to be done at height, e.g. repairing a roof, use scaffolding.
- Never overfill a silage pit. Any person using machinery to roll the silage should be competent to do this. Silage pits should be designed in accordance with the specifications as set out by the Department of Agriculture, Food and the Marine (DAFM).
- Agrochemicals are chemicals used in agriculture, e.g. pesticides, herbicides and fertilisers.
- The handling and application of pesticides should be carried out by a competent person. Pesticides should be applied in such a way as to avoid drift, run-off and volatilisation.
- Wear gloves, goggles and personal protective equipment (PPE) when handling and using acids and bases.

- Avoid a back injury by not lifting excess loads (50 kg), by using lifting aids where possible, or have two people lift the load.
- Farmer's lung is a serious health condition caused by exposure to dust and spores, which trigger an immune response that can lead to permanent damage to the lungs.
- Exposure to high levels of noise can result in permanent hearing damage. Always wear ear defenders when the noise level exceeds 80 decibels.
- Try to reduce stress by getting adequate sleep, watch your diet and get some exercise. Seek professional help if required and talk to family and friends.
- The power take-off (PTO) shaft must be completely enclosed by the guard. Avoid loose clothing, jewellery and tie back long hair to reduce the risk of entanglement.
- At harvest time ensure that all operators are competent in operating the machinery.
- Avoid driver fatigue by ensuring all operators have regular breaks and plenty of food and drinks, and change operators regularly.
- Ensure all machinery is roadworthy to drive on public roads. Watch for other road users and be aware of overhead electrical lines.
- Be familiar with any safety signs used on farms you are working on or farms that you visit.
- All farmers are legally required to prepare and implement a Safety Statement for their farm.

PowerPoint Summary

QUESTIONS

1. Complete an online course on farm safety using the Health and Safety Authority website. There are two courses available, one on an introduction to tractor safety (40 minutes to complete) and another on farm safety with slurry (30 minutes to complete). At the end of both courses you will receive a certificate if you pass the assessment.

2. At what age are children legally allowed to drive a tractor once they have had formal training?

   (a) 13   (c) 15
   (b) 14   (d) 16

3. Which of the following are hazards regarding a quad or ATV?

   (a) Driving too fast for cornering

   (b) Head injuries from being thrown off and not wearing a helmet

   (c) Incorrect tyre pressure

   (d) All of the above

4. Round bales should be stored where possible:

   (a) On their curved side, one on top of the other

   (b) On their flat side, maximum height two bales high

   (c) On their flat side in a pyramid shape with a maximum height of three bales high

   (d) On their flat ends, one bale high.

5. What does 'SDS' stand for?

   (a) Same day sheet

   (b) Specific data sheet

   (c) Safety data sheet

   (d) Safety date sticker

6. What is the main cause of the respiratory disease farmer's lung?

   (a) Inhalation of slurry gases

   (b) Smoking

   (c) Poor diet

   (d) Inhalation of dust or spores

7. Which of the following are recommended ways to deal with stress?

   (a) Ignore the problems

   (b) Get enough sleep and eat a healthy diet

   (c) Talk to friends and family

   (d) Get help with the workload

8. Ear defenders should be worn when the noise level exceeds:

   (a) 50 decibels

   (b) 60 decibels

   (c) 70 decibels

   (d) 80 decibels.

9. 'PTO' stands for:

   (a) Please turn off

   (b) Past the office

   (c) Power take-off

   (d) Power take-on.

10. To avoid entanglement in the PTO, persons should:

    (a) Ensure their shoe laces are tied

    (b) Avoid wearing a scarf

    (c) Close up all jackets and high-vis vests

    (d) All of the above.

11. What does the safety sign in Fig. 3.21 tell you?

    (a) Goggles should be worn

    (b) Gloves should be worn

    (c) High-vis vest should be worn

    (d) Ear defenders should be worn

3.21   *Safety sign*

12. Discuss why farm safety is an important issue in Irish agriculture and why it is necessary to identify hazards and put in place controls and precautions to reduce these.

13. Farm safety week is an annual event led by the Irish Farmers' Association and supported by a number of agencies. Its aim is to reduce the number of accidents on farms. Fig. 3.22 shows a poster that was used during farm safety week to highlight some of the dangers posed to children.

3.22   *Safety poster*

    (a) Whose responsibility is it to ensure the health and safety of children and young people on a farm?

    (b) What hazard or risk is posed to the child in Fig. 3.22?

    (c) Identify and explain other key hazards or risks to children growing up on a farm.

14. Outline measures that can be taken to reduce the risk of children being struck or crushed by tractors.

15. Discuss measures that can be taken to reduce the risk of children accidently drowning in a slurry pit or water source.

16. Why are farmers over the age of 65 at a greater risk of accidents or injury?

17. Explain the safe stop procedure for tractors and other self-propelled agricultural machinery.

18. Fig. 3.23 shows symbols from a label of a fungicide used to prevent blight in potatoes. Analyse the information carefully and answer the questions below.

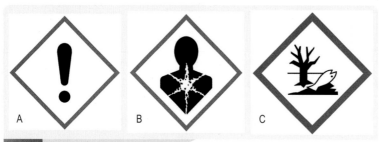

3.23 *Hazard pictograms*

(a) What hazards are identified by the labels A, B and C?

(b) What pieces of personal protective equipment (PPE) should be worn when preparing and handling this chemical?

(c) How should this chemical be stored?

(d) How would a farmer dispose of this chemical?

(e) What precautions should a farmer take to prevent contamination of water sources with this chemical?

19. Identify any hazards or risks in (a) to (d) below. Describe any controls or precautions you would put in place to eliminate these hazards.

(a)

(b)

(c)

(d)

 Solutions   Weblinks

Soils

STRAND 2

4	Soil formation and classification	58
5	Physical characteristics of soil	72
6	Chemical characteristics of soil	92
7	Biological characteristics of soil	100
8	Soil management	114

Soil formation and classification

When you have completed this chapter you should be able to:

- Describe the factors involved in soil formation
- Describe and classify the different soil types and groups
- Describe the different soil profiles and their distribution in Ireland
- Compare soils with respect to their varied properties and land use potentials.

The functions of soil

Soil is the top layer of the earth's surface. It consists of mineral and rock particles, organic matter, water and air. Soil is developed over thousands and millions of years through weathering. The soils of Ireland are considered to be young, since they were formed only after the last Ice Age. Much of the parent material from which the soils developed was transported, deposited and broken down by glaciers. This is known as parent rock material. Plant residues, known as organic parent material, also contribute to soil formation.

Residue: remains of a substance.

Agriculture could not exist without soil. Soil provides a medium in which crops can be grown and provides physical support for plant roots. It also provides a medium in which plant and animal remains can be decomposed, allowing for the recycling of nutrients. Soil also allows for the retention and provision of water and air, which are necessary for plant growth. Farmers choose to grow different crops depending on the type of soil they have on their land. Poor yields of crops can result from growing a crop in an unsuitable soil. Farmers also have to consider sustainable methods of farming to ensure the ability to grow crops on an ongoing basis. This chapter focuses on the materials and the factors that contribute to soil formation.

Parent material

Physical and chemical weathering of rocks is an important step in soil formation.

Rocks are divided into groups based on how they are formed. There are three groups of rocks, all of which are found in Ireland: igneous, sedimentary and metamorphic rocks. All three groups provide parent material from which the mineral matter in our soils originates.

Igneous rock

A liquid called magma is found underneath the earth's crust. Magma is molten (melted) rock. When magma cools it solidifies and forms rock. When magma appears above the earth's surface it is called lava. This also cools to form rock. The type of rock that is formed when magma or lava solidifies is called igneous rock.

As magma cools it forms crystals that consist of minerals. If magma cools quickly, the crystals will be small; if it cools rapidly, the crystals will be large. The three most common crystals formed are quartz, feldspar and mica. Their properties determine the characteristics of the rock in which they are found and, in turn, the soil that is formed when that rock is weathered. Quartz is acidic in nature, while feldspar is alkaline.

Granite and basalt are the two most common igneous rocks found in Ireland. Granite contains a lot of quartz and, therefore, is an acidic rock. The soils formed from granite are also acidic. Basalt is less acidic, since it contains only a small amount of quartz. Basalt also contains feldspar, which makes it smoother and more fine-grained. The soils formed from basalt are smooth and fine.

4.1 Granite

4.2 Basalt

Sedimentary rock

Millions of years ago, layers of sediment were deposited at the bottom of seas and lakes. These layers built up over millions of years and slowly compacted in the process. As they compacted, they solidified to form what is known as sedimentary rock.

Mineral sediments are of different sizes. The largest particles (quartz) were washed up on shores and are commonly known as sand. Smaller particles known as clay were brought further out to sea for deposition. Clay particles are a result of the weathering of igneous rock. The shells of fossils that contain lime were deposited in deep water. Each of the three types of sediment was compacted over time to form a different type of rock: sandstone, shale and limestone, respectively.

Sediment: small particles that settle to the bottom of a liquid.

Table 4.1 Characteristics of sedimentary rock		
Particle type	**Rock formed**	**pH**
Sand (quartz)	Sandstone	Acidic
Clay	Shale	Less acidic
Fossils and shells	Limestone	Alkaline

4.3 Sandstone

4.4 Shale

4.5 Limestone

Metamorphic rock

Metamorphic rocks are formed from igneous or sedimentary rocks (see Fig. 4.9). Heat or pressure brings about a change in the rock and its mineral content. Metamorphic rocks have an influence on the acidity or alkalinity of the soils formed from them. If the metamorphic rock is acidic, the soil formed when it is weathered will also be acidic.

Table 4.2 Metamorphic rock formation	
Rock type	**Metamorphic rock formed**
Limestone	Marble
Shale	Slate
Granite	Gneiss
Sandstone	Quartzite

4.6 *Gneiss rock formed by heat and pressure on granite rock*

4.7 *Marble is formed by intense heat on limestone*

4.8 *Slate is formed by intense pressure on shale*

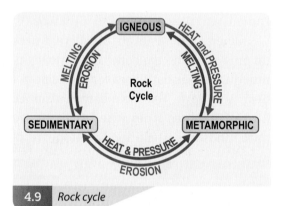

4.9 *Rock cycle*

Weathering and decomposition of rock

Weathering of rock takes place when rock is broken down by physical (mechanical), chemical or biological means. Physical weathering involves the breakdown of rocks into sediments. Chemical weathering brings about a chemical change during the decomposition process. Biological weathering involves the breakdown of rock by the actions of living organisms. The main methods of physical, chemical and biological weathering are outlined below.

> **Weathering:** decomposition of rock without changing its location.

Physical weathering

There are many types of physical weathering, each of which breaks down rock into smaller particles.

- **Heating and cooling:** increased temperatures can cause minerals in rock to expand. Minerals will expand at different rates, causing rock to shatter and disintegrate. Minerals will also contract as they cool, contributing to the weathering process.
- **Freezing (frost action):** water fills cracks in the rock. As it freezes and turns to ice, it expands, causing the rock to shatter and break. This leads to more cracks in the rock, which will subsequently fill with water and undergo the same process.
- **Activity of roots:** roots of trees penetrate cracks in rock. As the roots grow, they put pressure on rock and cause it to break.

- **Activity of animals:** animals digging and burrowing contribute to rock breakdown.
- **Grinding action:** glaciers levelled hills and moved boulders and rock over long distances by grinding action. Rocks and rock particles are also moved by water (rainfall and rivers), wind (sand) and gravity.

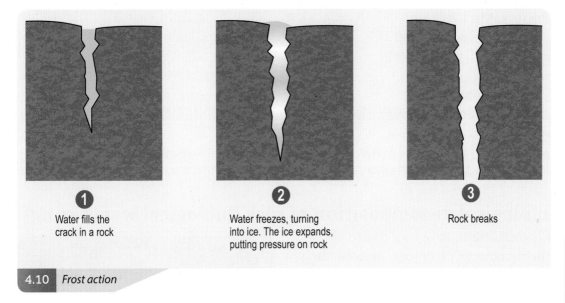

① Water fills the crack in a rock

② Water freezes, turning into ice. The ice expands, putting pressure on rock

③ Rock breaks

4.10 *Frost action*

Erosion: the breakdown of rock particles by wind, water or ice.

Chemical weathering

Chemical reactions with rock bring about a change in rock minerals. There are a number of ways in which rock is weathered chemically.

Hydrolysis

Hydrogen ions in water react with rock minerals. The result is that hydroxide compounds are formed which, in turn, release minerals into the soil (e.g. potassium).

Hydrolysis: chemical breakdown of a substance when it reacts with water.

Oxidation and reduction

Oxidation is the loss of electrons; reduction is the gain of elections (OIL RIG). Oxidation is also the addition of oxygen to a substance; reduction is the removal of oxygen from a substance. Oxidation of iron in rock is a common occurrence and it takes place in dry conditions. Haematite is a mineral formed by oxidation.

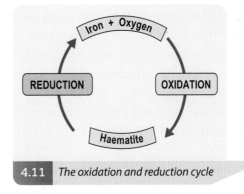

4.11 *The oxidation and reduction cycle*

Haematite: a reddish-black mineral that contains iron.

Hydration

Hydration is the addition of water to a rock mineral. It frequently takes place after oxidation where iron oxide is produced. When the water molecule combines with the iron oxide, it causes the rock to expand and decompose.

Solution and carbonation

Water is a natural solvent and it dissolves minerals in rock as it percolates through the rock. Metal ions such as potassium, sodium and calcium are highly soluble in water.

Carbon dioxide	+	Water	$\longrightarrow$	Carbonic acid
CO_2	+	H_2O	$\longrightarrow$	H_2CO_3

Carbonic acid	+	Limestone	$\longrightarrow$	Calcium hydrogen carbonate*
H_2CO_3	+	$CaCO_3$	$\longrightarrow$	$Ca(HCO_3)_2$

*Calcium hydrogen carbonate is also known as calcium bicarbonate and it is soluble, hence limestone is readily dissolved by carbonic acid.

4.12 *Formation of carbonic acid and its reaction with limestone*

If water reacts with carbon dioxide gas it forms carbonic acid. The carbonic acid dissolves the alkaline minerals in rock faster than water. Limestone in particular is weathered quickly by carbonic acid.

Biological decomposition of rock (biological weathering)

Microorganisms have their role to play in the decomposition of rock. Bacteria, fungi and lichens colonise bare rocks. Some of these microorganisms are able to utilise nitrogen and carbon dioxide from the atmosphere. The microorganisms secrete acids that dissolve mineral nutrients such as calcium and phosphorus in rock. This leads to the decomposition of rock and contributes to soil formation.

4.13 *Lichen*

Carbonation: dissolving carbon dioxide in a liquid (water).

Lichen consists of an alga and a fungus.

Organic parent material

Organic parent materials consist of the remains of plants which have partially decomposed. These remains accumulate in wet, waterlogged conditions and often in lakes. Oxygen is necessary for the decomposition of the plant material and the wet, waterlogged conditions in which these plant remains are found lack the oxygen necessary for this process to occur. Peat is the main material that is produced from these plant remains. An area where peat accumulates is known as a bog. There are three types of bogs in Ireland: basin peats (also called fens), raised bogs and blanket bogs (see Table 4.3).

Table 4.3 Summary of basin peat, raised bog and blanket bog characteristics			
Characteristic	**Basin peat**	**Raised bog**	**Blanket bog**
Depth (m)	2	8–12	2.6
Shape	Flat	Dome shaped	Sloped or flat, depending on the landscape
pH	6.0	4.0–6.0	5.0
Location	Valleys, lakes	Lakes	Mountains and lowlands on the west coast

Basin peats or fens are flat bogs that have developed in hollows in the landscape (e.g. lakes and waterlogged areas) where there is a mineral-rich water supply. When the water supply no longer exists, and more material accumulates on top of the basin peat, a raised bog forms. The basin peats or fens are only slightly acidic, but as they form raised bogs they become more acidic and their pH lowers.

Blanket bogs develop in areas of high rainfall and low evaporation in anaerobic conditions. They are found in mountainous areas all along the west coast of Ireland from Co. Donegal to Co. Clare and Co. Kerry. They are not as deep as basin peats. They are very acidic with low fertility and have limited agricultural use.

Factors of soil formation

Five factors affect the formation of soil:

1. Parent material
2. Climate
3. Living organisms
4. Topography
5. Time.

> **Topography:** mapping/shape of the surface of the land.

Parent material

Soils are hugely influenced by parent material. Forty-five per cent of soil consists of mineral matter (see Chapter 5). Therefore, the characteristics of parent material, particularly its acidity and texture, will influence the acidity and texture of the soil formed from it. Soil formed from granite contains quartz, which is weathered into sand particles and is acidic in nature. The mica particles in the rock are weathered into clay particles.

Limestone is alkaline in nature and the calcium and magnesium present in limestone raise the pH of the soil formed from it. Broadleaf tree species are best suited to growing on soils which are derived from limestone. They continue to contribute to the alkalinity of these soils through the organic matter they produce.

Climate

The climatic conditions that have the most effect on soil formation are temperature and precipitation. Water contributes to the physical and chemical weathering of rock through freezing, solution, hydrolysis and hydration. Temperature plays a role in the heating and cooling of rock. Low temperatures lead to low evaporation levels. This means that more water is available for chemical weathering.

Living organisms

Plant and animal species contribute to soil formation. Both contribute humus when they die and microorganisms help to decompose the organic matter in soil. If soils are lacking in vegetation they will also lack in organic matter. Organic matter contributes to the structure and fertility of a soil. Soils that develop under grassland benefit from the fibrous root system of grass. The grass roots bind the soil together, preventing erosion but also contributing large amounts of humus as they die and decompose. Grasses also contain higher levels of alkaline compounds, which reduce acidity levels in soil and make them more suitable for cultivation.

> **Humus:** the dark-coloured, decomposed plant and animal material found in soil. It is rich in nutrients and contributes to soil structure.

Soils that develop under forests can suffer from acidification, particularly if the trees are conifers. The needles from conifers are acidic and as these accumulate in the soil they have an acidifying effect on the soil. Deciduous, broadleaf species do not have as severe an effect on soil acidity. Also, the roots of trees are large and they do not contribute the same levels of humus to the soil as the fibrous roots of grass.

Topography

Topography refers to the slope of the landscape: whether it is level or hilly. On steep slopes, erosion will carry soil from the top of the hillsides to the valleys below. This leads to thin soils on the hillsides and deep fertile soils in valleys. Water also contributes to soil erosion on hillsides. Water is evaporated rapidly from the hillsides in comparison to the fertile soils in the valleys. The moisture content that remains in these lowland soils makes them particularly suitable for cultivation.

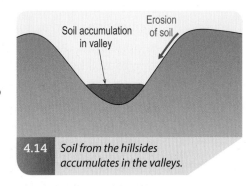

4.14 *Soil from the hillsides accumulates in the valleys.*

Time

The length of time that the other four factors have had to influence soil formation is important. In soils that are considered to be old, much of the material available for soil formation through weathering has already been eroded or decomposed. Fertility often comes from organic materials in old soils. In young soils, such as those found in Ireland, there is a high level of parent rock material available for weathering and soil formation, contributing to the overall fertility of the soil.

Soil classification

It is important for farmers to know what types of soils exist on their land. Soil fertility can be improved through fertilisation and liming. Soil structure can be maintained and improved by the addition of organic manures and by crop rotation. However, the overall soil type that exists on a farm remains largely the same, and this must be taken into account when deciding how to use the land. Knowing the type of soil that exists on a farm will also determine what steps can be taken to improve the land.

Soil profiles

The materials provided by parent rock and organic matter for soil formation form layers in the soil, known as horizons. Soils have a number of horizons, each with their own characteristics. Excavation of a soil will show these horizons in a vertical section from the uppermost layer at ground level to the bedrock. This vertical section showing all of the soil horizons is known as a soil profile. A typical soil profile is shown in Fig. 4.15.

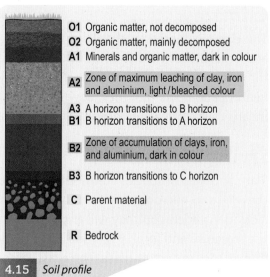

O1 Organic matter, not decomposed
O2 Organic matter, mainly decomposed
A1 Minerals and organic matter, dark in colour
A2 Zone of maximum leaching of clay, iron and aluminium, light / bleached colour
A3 A horizon transitions to B horizon
B1 B horizon transitions to A horizon
B2 Zone of accumulation of clays, iron, and aluminium, dark in colour
B3 B horizon transitions to C horizon
C Parent material
R Bedrock

4.15   *Soil profile*

- **O horizon:** this is not always present, due to the absence of vegetation. It consists of organic material.
- **A horizon:** this is commonly known as topsoil. It contains minerals and may have organic matter mixed through it. However, it can experience the effects of leaching and so it may be lacking in minerals in certain conditions.
- **B horizon:** this is known as subsoil. It is normally a lighter colour than topsoil, except where minerals have been leached and have accumulated in this horizon.
- **C horizon:** this contains parent material and is rocky in nature.
- **R horizon:** this is bedrock and is solid.

Each of the horizons O, A and B may be split into smaller horizons. These sub-horizons are not present in all soil types. Two sub-horizons of importance are A2 and B2.
- Horizon A2 is known as the zone of maximum leaching. Many minerals are present in topsoil because of the decomposition of organic matter and the application of fertilisers and manures. Heavy rainfall may lead to the leaching of these minerals from the A2 layer, leaving it pale and bleached in colour.
- Horizon B2 is known as the zone of accumulation. The minerals leached from the A2 horizon are washed down into the subsoil and accumulate in the B2 horizon. The presence of these minerals gives the soil a dark colour but it can also lead to the formation of an iron-pan, which may lead to waterlogging in this horizon.

> **Leaching:** the process in which soluble matter, such as minerals, dissolves in water filtering through soil and is carried downwards. The leached minerals may accumulate at a lower horizon.

Soils of Ireland – the system of soil classification

Under the most recent classification of soils in Ireland, soils are categorised into 11 distinct 'great soil groups'. The soils are grouped by distinguishing criteria and have their own characteristic profiles and uses. The soil profiles of a number of these soils will be studied in greater detail.

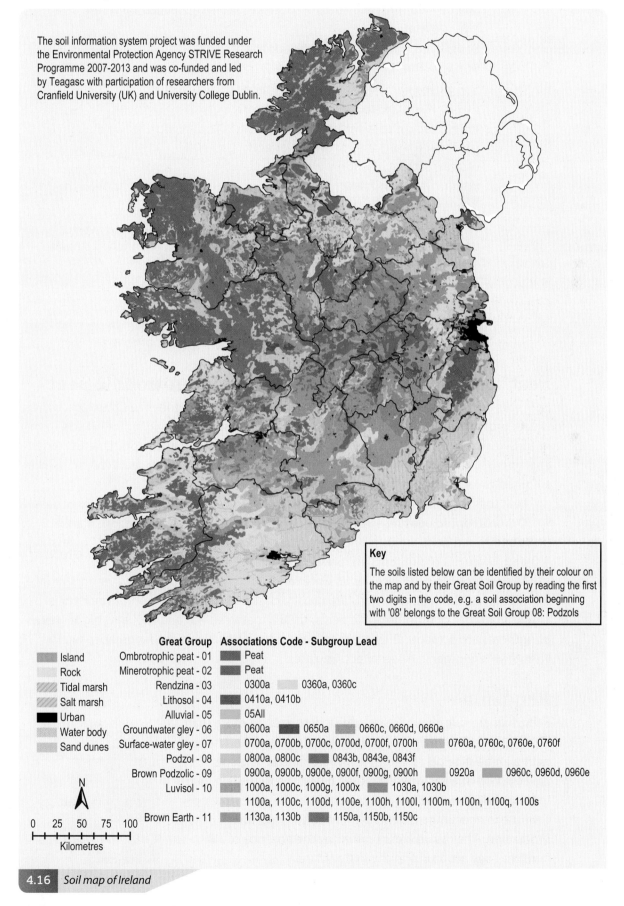

The soil information system project was funded under the Environmental Protection Agency STRIVE Research Programme 2007-2013 and was co-funded and led by Teagasc with participation of researchers from Cranfield University (UK) and University College Dublin.

Key

The soils listed below can be identified by their colour on the map and by their Great Soil Group by reading the first two digits in the code, e.g. a soil association beginning with '08' belongs to the Great Soil Group 08: Podzols

	Great Group	**Associations Code - Subgroup Lead**
Island	Ombrotrophic peat - 01	Peat
Rock	Minerotrophic peat - 02	Peat
Tidal marsh	Rendzina - 03	0300a 0360a, 0360c
Salt marsh	Lithosol - 04	0410a, 0410b
Urban	Alluvial - 05	05All
Water body	Groundwater gley - 06	0600a 0650a 0660c, 0660d, 0660e
Sand dunes	Surface-water gley - 07	0700a, 0700b, 0700c, 0700d, 0700f, 0700h 0760a, 0760c, 0760e, 0760f
	Podzol - 08	0800a, 0800c 0843b, 0843e, 0843f
	Brown Podzolic - 09	0900a, 0900b, 0900e, 0900f, 0900g, 0900h 0920a 0960c, 0960d, 0960e
	Luvisol - 10	1000a, 1000c, 1000g, 1000x 1030a, 1030b
		1100a, 1100c, 1100d, 1100e, 1100h, 1100l, 1100m, 1100n, 1100q, 1100s
	Brown Earth - 11	1130a, 1130b 1150a, 1150b, 1150c

N

0 25 50 75 100
Kilometres

4.16 *Soil map of Ireland*

Great Soil Group	Description	Distinguishing criteria
Table 4.4 The Irish soil classification system		
1 Ombrotrophic peat	Rain-fed peat	Soils with thick organic layers
2 Minerotrophic peat	Groundwater-fed peat	
3 Rendzina	Shallow calcareous soil (<40 cm deep)	Shallow or extremely gravelly soils
4 Lithosol	Shallow non-calcareous soil (<40 cm deep)	
5 Alluvial	Soil derived from alluvium; no distinct layer development	Soils influenced by water
6 Groundwater gley	Soil gleyed within 40 cm of the surface due to water table	
7 Surface-water gley	Soil gleyed within 40 cm of the surface due to slowly permeable horizon	
8 Podzol	Infertile acidic soils with an ash-like subsurface layer; they show the effects of acid leaching; typically formed under coniferous forest	Soils affected by Fe/Al
9 Brown podzolic	Some leaching has taken place but not as severe as in podzols	
10 Luvisol	Loss of clay minerals from the surface horizon to lower horizons (clay illuviation); generally found in limestone areas	Soils with clay-enriched subsoil
11 Brown earth	Uniform throughout	Relatively young, or soils with little profile development

> **Illuviation:** the accumulation or deposition of soil particles or minerals from one soil horizon to another by percolating water or leaching.

Peat soils: ombrotrophic peat and minerotrophic peat

Peat soils are characterised by their absence of horizons except for the O horizon, which is dark brown/black in appearance. Peats are widely used for providing fuel in the form of turf. Peat soils are characterised by their poor drainage and acidic pH. Due to these characteristics, basin peats are mainly restricted to forestry. Blanket peats can be used in a limited capacity for grazing.

Peat soils are classified as ombrotrophic or minerotrophic based on their water supply.

Ombrotrophic peat receives its water and nutrients from precipitation. Blanket peats and raised bogs are usually classified as ombrotrophic. They have a pH of less than 4.0 and low levels of nutrients are present.

Minerotrophic peat receives its water and nutrients from groundwater and surface-water sources. Basin peats or fens are usually classified as minerotrophic. Their pH is higher than that of ombrotrophic peats, usually between 4.0 and 6.0, and higher levels of nutrients are present. They are most common in hollows in the landscape, such as valleys, where organic material accumulates.

> **Ombrotrophic:** describes a bog or its vegetation which depends on atmospheric moisture for its nutrients.

> **Minerotrophic:** describes a fen or peatland supplied with dissolved minerals from groundwater or surface water.

> **Calcareous:** describes a material which is chalky or contains calcium carbonate.

Rendzina

Rendzinas are calcareous (chalky) shallow soils of no more than 30 cm depth. They are derived from limestone rock and have a neutral or alkaline pH (5.0–8.0) and high mineral content. They are common in areas where exposed limestone is present. Due to their shallow nature and the presence of limestone outcrops, their use in agriculture is generally limited to grassland production. Their structure is typified by the absence of a B horizon. They are found chiefly in Co. Clare.

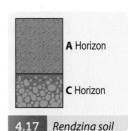

4.17 *Rendzina soil profile*

Lithosol

Lithosols are shallow, stony soils of less than 30 cm depth. They are non-calcareous and contain partially weathered rock fragments. They are found over solid or fragmented bedrock and the soil is stony in nature. Lithosols are frequently associated with rocky outcrops at higher elevations. As a result, they have limited agricultural use and are usually confined to rough grazing.

Alluvial soils

Alluvial soils are formed from the deposition of materials (alluvium) by rivers and lakes. Their characteristics can differ depending on location, but they are rich in minerals due to their clay content, and have a high water table.

> **Alluvium:** particles of sand, silt and clay deposited by rivers or lakes or marine deposition.

Gley soils: groundwater gley and surface-water gley

Gleys are poorly drained soils that form in waterlogged, anaerobic conditions. The formation of a gley soil is called **gleisation**. Water movement in the soil is restricted and can occur in areas of high rainfall or in soils that have poor drainage. A high water table may also be present. Reduction of minerals such as iron, results in a mottled effect, with blue and grey colouring in the B horizon. Gleys have poor structure. They can be improved through drainage, but due to their high water content their use is limited.

> **Water table:** the level below which the ground (soil) is completely saturated with water.

Gley soils are typically confined to light grazing and planting of some broadleaf tree species. There are two types of gley soils categorised by their method of formation: groundwater gleys and surface-water gleys.

Groundwater gleys are formed in areas where there is a depression in the landscape, such as a valley, and where there is high rainfall. Water runs off the surrounding hillsides and accumulates in the depression in the landscape. These soils typically have a high water table. This means there is little space for soil water to drain off, leading to waterlogging.

> **Mottling:** spots, blotches or speckles of colour.

> **Groundwater:** water that seeps down through the soil and is found in underground soil pores and cracks in rock above the water table.

A — Presence of vegetation provides a limited structure

B — Mottled appearance due to oxidation and reduction of minerals

C

4.18 *Gley soil profile*

Surface-water gleys are formed in areas where water does not drain freely through the soil as it has low permeability.

- **A horizon:** there is no definition in the A horizon and A1 and A2 horizons are not identified. The presence of vegetation gives it a limited structure.
- **B horizon:** there is also no definition within the B horizon. Oxidation and reduction of minerals give it a mottled appearance.

> **Surface water:** water found on the upper layer of soil which has not penetrated soil pores.

Podzol

Podzols are found overlying acid parent material such as sandstone. They are found in mountainous and hillside areas. They are mainly used for forestry or rough grazing because of their acidic nature. They are prone to leaching of minerals. Acid leaching of minerals causes the leaching of iron and aluminium from the A horizon. This causes the bleaching of the A horizon. The minerals accumulate in the B horizon and form an iron-pan. The iron-pan is impermeable to water. This can cause waterlogging above the iron-pan and also prevent roots from penetrating deeper into the soil. The iron-pan can be broken up with a subsoiler. Liming may also be carried out to raise the pH of the soil.

> **Podzolisation:** occurs in acidic pH conditions where minerals such as iron and aluminium are leached from the A horizon, leaving it bleached in colour. They accumulate in the B horizon, forming an iron-pan that is impermeable to water.

- **O horizon:** organic matter has not decomposed due to acidic conditions
- **A horizon:** thin A1 horizon and thick A2 horizon, bleached in colour due to leaching of minerals
- **B horizon:** red-brown colour due to accumulation of minerals. Iron-pan is formed at B2 horizon.

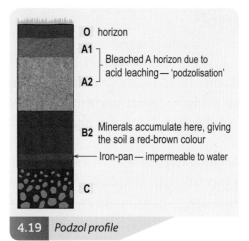

4.19 *Podzol profile*

Brown podzolic soils

Brown podzolic soils are found in lowland areas. They are suitable for forestry but can also be used for crops and grazing. Liming and fertilisation contribute to the improvement of these soils. They are like podzols in that they are found overlying acid parent materials such as shale, sandstone and granite. However, they are not as severely leached.

- **A horizon:** large quantity of organic matter in A1 horizon, A2 horizon is thin and shows little development.
- **B horizon:** red-brown in colour due to the accumulation of minerals, particularly iron.

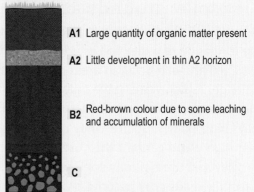

4.20 *Brown podzolic soil profile*

Luvisols

Eluviation: the transport of soil particles or minerals from the upper layers of a soil to the lower layers by precipitation of water.

Luvisols are soils with high levels of clay content. Clay particles are eluviated from horizon A to horizon B, where they accumulate as illuvial deposits. Luvisols are found overlying lowland areas with limestone parent material and have a high pH. They can be used for tillage farming for cereal and root crops.

Brown earths

Brown earths are found in lowland areas. They are very suitable for crop production. They are found mainly overlying limestone or lime-rich parent materials and have a high pH. They require little lime or fertiliser and have good drainage. Very little leaching takes place in these soils. They are dark brown in colour with no distinct horizons:

- High levels of organic matter give the soil a darker appearance at the surface (topsoil)
- Uniform brown colour throughout, showing little leaching of minerals
- Very fertile soils.

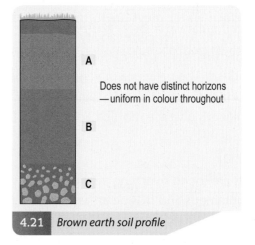

4.21 *Brown earth soil profile*

Summary

- There are three groups of rocks: igneous (e.g. basalt, granite), sedimentary (e.g. limestone, sandstone, shale) and metamorphic (e.g. marble, quartzite).

- Rocks undergo a number of types of physical weathering processes, including: heating and cooling, freezing, activity of animals, activity of roots and grinding action.

- Rocks undergo chemical weathering processes such as: hydrolysis, oxidation and reduction, hydration, solution and carbonation.

- Organic parent materials consist of the remains of plants that have partially decomposed.

- There are three types of bogs in Ireland: basin peats (fens), raised bogs and blanket bogs.

- Basin peats (fens) are flat bogs that have developed in hollows in the landscape, e.g. lakes and waterlogged areas where there is a mineral-rich water supply.

- A raised bog is formed when material accumulates on top of basin peat.

- Blanket bogs develop in areas of high rainfall and low evaporation in anaerobic conditions. They are found in mountainous areas all along the west coast of Ireland.

- Five factors affect the formation of soil: parent material, climate, living organisms, topography and time.

- A soil profile is a vertical section from the uppermost layer of soil at ground level to the bedrock. Each layer is known as a horizon.

- The O horizon consists of organic material; the A horizon is commonly known as topsoil; the B horizon is called subsoil; the C horizon is parent rock material; and the R horizon is bedrock.

- The soils of most importance in Ireland include: podzols, brown podzolics, brown earths and gleys.

- Podzols are found overlying acid parent material such as sandstone. They are prone to leaching of minerals such as iron and aluminium from the A horizon to the B horizon. This causes bleaching of the A horizon and the formation of an impermeable iron-pan in the B horizon.

- Leaching is a process in which soluble matter such as minerals dissolves in water filtering through soil and is carried downwards. The leached minerals may accumulate at a lower horizon.

- Brown podzolic soils are found in lowland areas overlying acid parent materials. They are suitable for forestry but can also be used for crops and grazing.

- Brown earths are found in lowland areas overlying limestone parent materials. They are very suitable for crop production as they require little lime or fertiliser and have good drainage.

- Gleys are poorly drained soils that form in waterlogged conditions. There are two types of gleys: groundwater gleys formed in depressions in the landscape and surface-water gleys found overlying land impermeable to water. They can be improved by drainage but their use is limited.

PowerPoint Summary

QUESTIONS

1. Name the three different rock types.
2. Explain how igneous rock is formed.
3. Which of the following is a crystal found in igneous rock?
   (a) Magma　　　　(b) Shale　　　　(c) Quartz　　　　(d) Marble
4. Explain how sedimentary rocks are formed.
5. Which of the following are not sedimentary rocks?
   (a) Shale　　　　(b) Marble　　　　(c) Granite　　　　(d) Limestone
6. Name the metamorphic rocks formed from (a) granite and (b) limestone.
7. How are metamorphic rocks formed?
8. Which of the following pairs are types of physical weathering?
   (a) Activity of roots and grinding action
   (b) Carbonation and freezing
   (c) Hydrolysis and activity of animals
   (d) Oxidation and reduction and activity of roots
9. Which of the following are types of chemical weathering?
   (a) Solution and carbonation
   (b) Heating and cooling
   (c) Frost action
   (d) Hydration
10. What role do microorganisms play in the decomposition of rocks?
11. What are organic parent materials and where are they found?
12. Name two types of peats.
13. Where are blanket peats found and how are they formed?
14. Where are basin peats found and how are they formed?
15. Complete the following table:

Characteristic	Raised bog	Blanket bog
Depth (m)	8–12	
pH		5.0
Shape		

16. How does parent material influence soil formation?
17. What two climatic factors have the most influence on soil formation?
18. How does topography influence soil formation?
19. What is a soil profile?
20. What is found in the O horizon?
    (a) Rocks　　　　(b) Subsoil　　　　(c) Humus　　　　(d) Topsoil
21. What is the A horizon more commonly known as?
    (a) Humus　　　　(b) Topsoil　　　　(c) Subsoil　　　　(d) Bedrock
22. What process is commonly seen in the A2 horizon?
    (a) Accumulation　(b) Decomposition　(c) Leaching　(d) Carbonation
23. What is the B horizon commonly known as?
    (a) Bedrock　　(b) Parent material　　(c) Iron-pan　　(d) Subsoil
24. What process is commonly seen in the B2 horizon?
    (a) Eluviation　(b) Illuviation　(c) Decomposition　(d) Humification
25. Indicate whether each of the following statements is true or false:
    (a) Granite is an igneous rock.

(b) Quartz is alkaline in nature.

(c) Basalt rock is mainly found in Co. Cork.

(d) Shale is formed from sand particles.

(e) Repeated heating and cooling will cause rocks to shatter and disintegrate.

(f) Hydrolysis is a reaction of the hydrogen in water with the minerals in rock.

(g) Carbonic acid does not dissolve limestone.

(h) Oxygen is not necessary for the decomposition of plant material.

(i) Horizon B2 in soil is where most soil leaching takes place.

26. What parent material is typically associated with podzols?

   (a) Shale   (b) Marble   (c) Sandstone   (d) Limestone

27. What is acid leaching?

28. What causes the light colour of the leached horizons in a soil?

29. Which minerals are leached from the podzol?

   (a) Nitrogen and carbon   (c) Iron and aluminium

   (b) Chlorine and helium   (d) Sodium and phosphorus

30. Where do minerals accumulate?

   (a) O horizon   (b) A horizon   (c) B horizon   (d) C horizon

31. What is podzolisation?

32. Explain how an iron-pan is formed.

33. What negative effects does an iron-pan have on a soil?

34. How can an iron-pan be removed?

   (a) Harrow   (b) Crop rotation   (c) Subsoiler   (d) Liming

35. What parent materials are associated with brown podzolics?

36. Suggest an agricultural use for a brown podzolic.

37. Why are brown earths considered to be good agricultural soils?

38. Distinguish between ombrotrophic and minerotrophic peats.

39. Which description best describes a rendzina?

   (a) Deep soil, sandstone parent material, no B horizon

   (b) Shallow soil, no C horizon, sandstone parent material

   (c) Deep soil, limestone parent material, no B horizon

   (d) Shallow soil, limestone parent material, no B horizon

40. Name the two types of gley soils found in Ireland.

41. Why are gleys limited in their suitability for agriculture?

42. What form of chemical weathering gives gleys a mottled appearance?

43. Which soils are formed from the deposition of material from rivers and lakes?

   (a) Alluvial   (b) Lithosol   (c) Rendzina   (d) Podzol

44. Give one common use for blanket and basin peats.

45. Compare granite and limestone as parent materials in soil formation.

46. Describe four methods of physical weathering.

47. Explain the following soil-related terms:

   (a) Topography   (b) Topsoil.

48. Give a scientific explanation for the presence of an iron-pan in a soil profile.

49. Using a labelled diagram, describe any named soil profile.

 Solutions   Weblinks

Physical characteristics of soil

CHAPTER 5

When you have completed this chapter you should be able to:

- Examine the physical features of soil including structure, particle size, texture and drainage
- Examine the impact of compaction and organic matter loss
- Determine and compare the total pore space in a compacted soil and an uncompacted soil
- Examine the impact of erosion, sedimentation and weathering
- Carry out an investigation to determine the texture of a soil sample by feel and sedimentation and soil sieve (SPA)
- Carry out an investigation to calculate the percentage water content of a soil sample (SPA)
- Carry out an investigation to compare the capillarity and infiltration rate of a compacted and an uncompacted soil (SPA).

Soil composition

Soil consists of solid, liquid and gas components. Each is necessary for the growth and development of plants.

The solid components of soil include mineral matter, which is derived from parent rock material, and organic matter, which is derived from the remains of plant and animal material. Together, mineral and organic matter occupy 50% of soil volume. They are responsible for providing nutrients for plants and providing the medium to anchor plants in the ground. The other half of the soil consists of soil pores, which are spaces in the soil. These pores are filled with air and water. Typically, half the soil pores in a soil will be filled with air and the other half with water. However, these proportions can change under different conditions. During a period of heavy rainfall, the level of water in the soil rises and subsequently the level of air drops. This is common in winter, when rainfall levels are high. In periods of drought and low rainfall, the water level in the soil falls and the amount of air increases. This is more common in the summer.

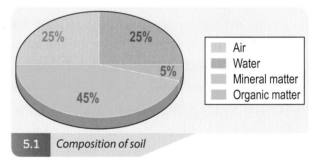

5.1 Composition of soil

Mineral matter

Parent rock material is broken down into mineral particles. The mineral particles are classified by size. The Irish Soil Survey categorises the particles into five different sizes. The five types of particle are: gravel, coarse sand, fine sand, silt and clay (see Fig. 5.2). The particles also have a number of properties associated with them that contribute to the overall characteristics of a soil.

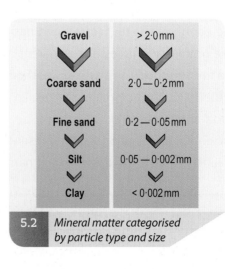

5.2 Mineral matter categorised by particle type and size

Table 5.1 Soil mineral particles and their properties		
	Gravel and sand (coarse and fine)	**Silt and clay**
Particle size	Large soil particles	Small soil particles
Pore space between particles	Large pore space between particles	Small pore spaces between particles
Drainage	Free-draining due to large pore spaces	Poor drainage due to small pore spaces
Aeration	Well aerated due to large pore spaces	Poor aeration due to small pore spaces
Waterlogging/drought	Can be prone to drought in prolonged periods of dry weather	Do not suffer from drought, retain water in dry weather but can become waterlogged after prolonged rainfall
Fertility/ion exchange	No contribution to fertility or ion exchange	Clay is a source of K, P, Ca, Mg ions; its large surface area allows for ion exchange to take place

Ion exchange: this process takes place in soil where ions are attracted to soil particles (clay) and are held on the surface of these particles. This is known as **adsorption**. The clay particles also contain ions of their own and they release these particles in the exchange. The smaller the particle, the greater the ion exchange that takes place. Colloidal clay particles are the smallest type of clay particles: they are less than 0.001 mm in size, but they have the greatest capacity for ion exchange. (Ion exchange is discussed in greater detail in Chapter 6.)

Physical properties of soil

The physical properties of soil play a large role in determining its suitability for crop growth. The physical properties of soil are:

- Texture
- Structure
- Porosity and density
- Colour
- Temperature.

Porosity describes materials that contain tiny holes or pores that allow gases and liquids to pass through the material.

Soil texture

Soil texture has a huge influence on a soil's characteristics. It is a permanent property of the soil that cannot be changed. Sand, silt and clay particles all have different properties (e.g. effect on drainage, aeration and fertility). Therefore, the proportions of these mineral particles present in a soil will largely influence the water and nutrients available to crops, the aeration of the soil, drainage of the soil, and how easy it is to cultivate.

The proportions of sand, silt and clay in a soil determine the soil texture. An ideal soil for cultivation contains 40% sand, 40% silt and 20% clay. A loam soil contains equal amounts of all three soil particles.

There are a number of ways of determining the texture of a soil. Three of these methods are outlined in the following experiments.

DEFINITION

Soil texture: a measure of the proportion of different-sized mineral particles (sand, silt, clay) that are found in a sample of soil.
Loam soil: soil that contains equal amounts of sand, silt and clay.

SPA 5.1a To determine the soil texture of a soil sample by hand testing

SPECIFIED PRACTICAL ACTIVITY

State your hypothesis and prediction.

Materials
Soil samples, water

Method

1. Take a dry sample of soil and rub it between your thumb and fingers. Take note of its grittiness or smoothness.

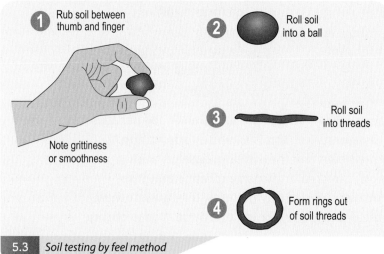

5.3 *Soil testing by feel method*

2. Wet the soil sample with some water and rub it between your finger and thumb, again noting its grittiness or smoothness. Also note the plasticity (ability to be moulded) of the sample; check if the wet sample is sticky or not. Use the flow chart (see Fig. 5.4) to identify the texture of the soil sample. Roll the sample into a ball. Record if this is possible or not.

3. Roll the sample into threads on a flat surface. Record if this is possible or not.

4. If the soil can be rolled into threads, attempt to make a ring out of the thread. Record your observations.

5. Compare your results with the flow chart.

Validation

1. Do the results of this experiment support the hypothesis?

2. What types of data are collected?

3. Comment on the validity and reliability of your results.

4. Are the results of this investigation objective or subjective? Justify your answer (refer to Chapter 1 page 12).

5. If the same soil sample is used for all three investigations, compare your results and identify and justify which method is the most accurate and reliable in determining soil texture.

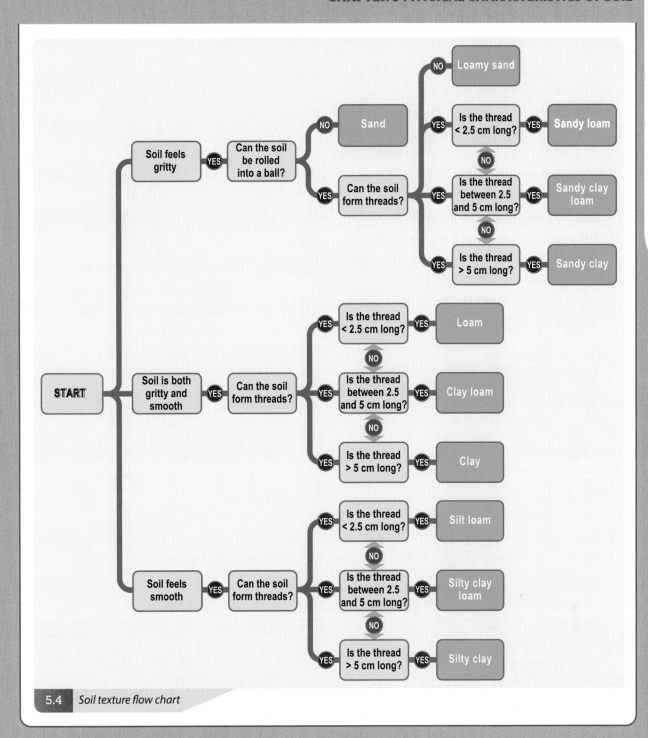

5.4 *Soil texture flow chart*

 SPA 5.1b To determine the soil texture of a soil sample by sedimentation

SPECIFIED PRACTICAL ACTIVITY

Note: Sedimentation is the process that occurs when particles of a material (in this case soil) settle at the bottom of a container of liquid. The largest particles settle at the bottom with the smaller particles forming layers above them.

State your hypothesis, prediction, independent variable, dependent variable and controlled variable.

Materials

Different soil samples, beaker, stirring rod, graduated cylinders, water, stopper, 2 mm sieve

Method

1. Add a sample of sieved soil to a beaker of water and stir it with the stirring rod.

2. Pour the mixture of soil and water into the graduated cylinder, rinsing all soil from the beaker into the cylinder. Add enough water to cover the soil completely.

3. Place a stopper on the cylinder and shake it to mix the soil and water thoroughly.

4. Leave to settle for a few hours or overnight.

5. Observe the layers that have settled in the graduated cylinder. Sand settles at the bottom, silt above the sand layer and clay on top of the silt.

6. Using the graduation marks on the cylinder, record the amount of sand, silt and clay in the soil sample as a percentage of the total soil solids.

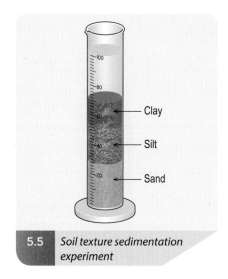

Clay
Silt
Sand

5.5 *Soil texture sedimentation experiment*

Table 5.2 Percentages of sand, silt and clay in a soil sample		
Sand %	Silt %	Clay %

Use the soil triangle (Fig. 5.7, page 77) to help you to classify your soil sample.

Validation

1. Do the results of this experiment support the hypothesis? Explain your answer.

2. What types of data are collected?

3. Identify any sources of error in the recording of your results (see Chapter 1 page 15).

4. What measures were taken to reduce errors when taking measurements?

 SPA 5.1c To determine the soil texture of a soil sample using a soil sieve

SPECIFIED PRACTICAL ACTIVITY

State your hypothesis, prediction, independent variable, dependent variable and controlled variable.

Materials

Different soil samples, oven, pestle and mortar, electronic balance, weighing boats, soil sieves

Method

1. Place soil sample in an oven to dry it out completely.

2. When soil is dry, crush it with a pestle and mortar.

5.6 *Soil sieves*

3. Weigh an empty weighing boat; place the crushed sample into the boat and reweigh. Subtract the mass of the empty boat to calculate mass of the soil.

4. Place crushed soil sample in the largest soil sieve. Place cover on sieve and shake.

5. Remove the cover from the sieve and separate out each sieve.

6. Weigh the empty weighing boats.

7. Pour the contents of each sieve into separate pre-weighed boats.

8. Weigh each sample in turn.

9. Calculate each separate sample of sand, silt and clay as a percentage of the total soil mass.

10. Use the soil triangle (Fig. 5.7) to help you to classify your soil sample.

Validation

1. Do the results of this experiment support the hypothesis? Explain your answer.

2. What type of data is collected?

3. Identify any sources of error in the recording of your results (see Chapter 1 page 15).

4. What measures were taken to reduce systematic uncertainty when recording measurements?

5. Comment on the validity and reliability of your results.

6. Are the results of this investigation objective or subjective? Justify your answer.

Determination of soil textural class

The soil textural triangle in Fig. 5.7 is used to classify a soil sample by the proportions of sand, silt and clay it contains. The percentages of sand, silt and clay are marked out on each side of the triangle.

Coarse sand and fine sand are grouped together under sand for classification purposes.

How to use the soil triangle

- Taking the three percentage values of sand, silt and clay determined by sedimentation or by using a soil sieve, mark the percentage of clay on the left-hand side of the triangle along the scale for clay.

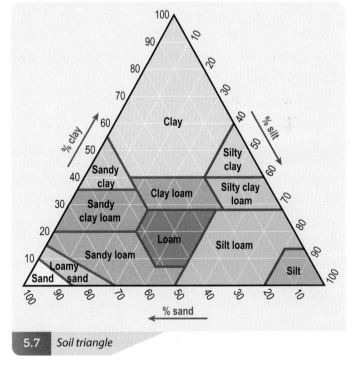

5.7   *Soil triangle*

- Draw a line from this mark across the triangle, parallel to the side marked '% sand'.
- Mark the percentage of silt on the scale for silt on the right-hand side of the triangle.
- Draw a line from this mark, parallel to the '% clay' side.
- The two lines drawn should intersect in the triangle. The area in which they intersect gives the name of the soil texture of the sample.
- To confirm the soil texture of the sample, mark the percentage of sand on the bottom of the soil triangle and draw a line parallel to the '% silt' side of the triangle.
- The three lines should meet, confirming the soil texture of the sample.

Activity 5.1

A soil sieve was used to determine the percentage of sand, silt and clay in a soil sample. The percentages were determined to be: sand 50%, silt 20% and clay 30%. Use the soil texture triangle to determine the soil texture of the sample.

1. Place a mark at 30 on the clay scale and draw a line across the triangle parallel to the % sand scale.

2. Place a mark at 20 on the silt scale and draw a line across the triangle parallel to the % clay scale.

3. The two lines intersect in the sandy clay loam section of the triangle. This shows that the sample is a sandy clay loam.

4. To confirm this classification, place a mark at 50 on the sand scale and draw a line parallel to the % silt scale. This line will intersect with the other two lines in the sandy clay loam section of the triangle.

 Activity 5.2

Use the soil textural triangle to determine the soil textures for each of the following soil samples.

Table 5.3 Soil samples for classification			
Soil sample	**% Sand**	**% Silt**	**% Clay**
A	22	24	54
B	41	43	16
C	31	57	12
D	27	43	30
E	48	10	42

Table 5.4 Soil textural properties			
	Sandy soils[1]	**Loam soils[2]**	**Clay soils[3]**
Drainage	Well drained, free-draining	Good drainage	Poor drainage
Aeration	Well aerated	Good aeration	Poor aeration
Fertility	Low fertility	Good fertility	Fertile, retains nutrients
Tillage capabilities	Easily tilled	Easily tilled	Not suited to tillage due to plasticity
Temperature	Warm up quickly in spring	Will warm up in spring	Do not warm up due to lack of aeration; cold soils
Drought/ waterlogging	Prone to drought, do not get waterlogged	Will retain water but will not become waterlogged or be prone to drought	Retain water during drought but are prone to waterlogging

[1] **Sandy soils:** *sand, loamy sand*
[2] **Loam soils:** *loam, sandy loam, silt loam, clay loam*
[3] **Clay soils:** *clay, silty clay, silty clay loam*

Plasticity: easily shaped or moulded.

Soil structure

Soil structure describes the arrangement of soil particles within a soil. Sand, silt and clay particles are the primary particles from which soil is composed. They form clusters in the soil known as aggregates or peds. It is the coming together of these aggregates that determines the soil pore space. Since pore space determines how much water and air is in the soil, this is an important characteristic of soil. A good soil structure has a large volume of pores: 50% of the total soil volume and approximately half the pores are filled with air and the other half with water.

Good soil structure is necessary for:

- Drainage of excess water
- Retention of water for plant growth
- Emergence of seedlings
- Air movement within the soil
- Root penetration.

As the primary soil particles aggregate, pores are formed between the particles within the aggregates. These are called **micropores**. As the aggregates cluster together, more pores are formed between the aggregate units. These are called **macropores**. Both micropores and macropores are necessary for good soil structure. A well-structured soil containing approximately 50% pore space contains both micropores and macropores.

A poorly structured soil typically does not form aggregates. As a result, the only pore space within this soil is between the primary soil particles and may be as low as 20%.

> **Aggregate:** a substance formed by combining several separate elements.

Aggregate formation

An aggregate is formed when sand, silt and clay particles cluster together.

They are held together by the clay particles and other polymers. These particles are colloidal clay and colloidal organic matter particles. The process by which the particles join together is known as flocculation.

Flocculation is the clustering together of soil particles to create larger structures called floccules (see Chapter 6 for how flocculation occurs).

Structural development of a soil

All soils are structureless to begin with. Soil particles join to form aggregates and over time a soil develops and becomes structured. Other activities can also influence the development of soil structure. Some of these activities are climatic, some are biological or chemical and some are human-influenced. All the activities that influence soil structure can be classified as either cementation or separation processes.

> **DEFINITION**
>
> **Cementation:** the binding together of soil particles, e.g. when silt and sand particles are cemented together in aggregates during flocculation by clay particles.
>
> **Separation:** soil aggregates are broken up within the soil. Large cracks may develop in the soil, which damages its overall structure.

Factors affecting structural development

- **Freezing and thawing:** water in the soil expands and contracts, causing a change in the soil volume. This leads to aggregation of soil.
- **Wetting and drying:** this causes the soil volume to change as it expands and shrinks. As the soil dries out, the particles are cemented together. When the soil is wet again, the soil breaks up and cracks may form.

- **Soil organic matter:** this provides a substrate for building aggregates. The presence of organic matter in the soil will lead to aggregation of the soil, particularly in the upper horizons.
- **Plant root activity:** small roots compact the soil and bind it together. The roots of larger plants and trees can break up the soil, forming cracks in the structure.
- **Animal activity:** small burrowing animals, in particular earthworms, contribute to soil cementation, forming aggregates. Earthworms also contribute to the organic matter in the soil through the ingestion and egestion of soil.
- **Cultivation and tillage:** agricultural activities such as ploughing and harrowing break up soil and encourage aggregation.

Soil porosity

Porosity refers to the total volume of the soil occupied by soil pores. A soil with good structure should have 50% of its volume occupied by soil pores. These pores are filled with air and water. Approximately half of the pores are air-filled, and the other half occupied by water. The levels of water and air in the soil can fluctuate with heavy rainfall or drought conditions. The number of pores present in a soil and the size of the pores are also important factors in determining the characteristics of a soil.

Soil air

Air is necessary in the soil for plant root respiration.

Soil air has almost the same composition as atmospheric air; the main difference is the higher level of carbon dioxide in soil air than in atmospheric air and there is a lower level of oxygen in soil air than in the atmosphere. The main reason for this is that the plant roots take in oxygen when they are respiring and release carbon dioxide. This leads to a depletion of oxygen in the soil and a build-up of carbon dioxide.

A continual depletion of oxygen and subsequent build-up of carbon dioxide

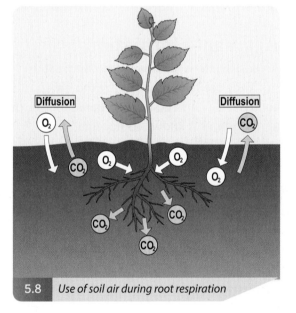

| 5.8 | *Use of soil air during root respiration* |

would negatively affect crop growth and development. The plant would be starved due to a lack of oxygen but also affected by carbon dioxide toxicity. It is important for crop growth that the carbon dioxide can be continually removed from the soil to the atmosphere and that oxygen will be replaced. This process is known as diffusion.

> **DEFINITION**
>
> **Diffusion** is the movement of a substance from an area of high concentration to an area of low concentration, along a concentration gradient. It is a passive process and so does not require energy.

Carbon dioxide will diffuse from the soil into the atmosphere and oxygen will diffuse from the atmosphere into the soil. Diffusion of carbon dioxide and oxygen is dependent on there being sufficiently large pores in the soil for this process to take place. Soils with a good soil structure will have sufficient pore spaces for diffusion to take place. A soil with poor structure will have fewer air-filled pores. Crops can fail if the level of air-filled pores drops drastically.

Soil aeration can be improved by mechanical means. Compacted soil can be broken up using a subsoiler. A subsoiler is also used to break up compacted soil that has been repeatedly ploughed at the same depth. This layer of compaction is known as the **plough pan**.

Soil compaction

Soil compaction occurs when soil particles are pressed together, and aggregates are destroyed. This reduces the total pore space in the soil. Heavily compacted soils have few large pores which are essential for drainage of water and diffusion of gases. As the overall proportion of the soil which consists of pore space has been reduced this increases the density of the soil.

The impact of compaction

- A compacted soil has a reduced rate of water infiltration and drainage. Large pores are necessary to drain water efficiently. This cannot happen in a compacted soil.
- Gaseous exchange is reduced in compacted soils as there are insufficient large pore spaces for diffusion of carbon dioxide back to the atmosphere and oxygen into the soil for plant root respiration. This will stunt plant growth.
- Plant roots cannot remove water from small capillary pores. This reduces water availability to growing plants even if the soil contains large amounts of water.
- Plant roots have difficulty in penetrating dense compacted soils so root development, mineral uptake and water intake are limited, which leads to reduced plant growth. Roots will also have limited ability to anchor the plant.
- Repeated tillage operations can cause a plough pan. This can also cause the soil to form a crust after rainfall, which further affects drainage and infiltration rates.
- Compaction reduces optimum conditions for living organisms in the soil habitat. While this may lead to a reduction in nematodes that feed on root crops, it will also lead to a reduction in earthworms, which are beneficial to the soil.

> **Nematodes** are a diverse group of worms, including roundworms and eelworms.

 Activity 5.3 | To determine and compare the total pore space in a compacted soil and an uncompacted soil

State your hypothesis, prediction, independent variable, dependent variable and controlled variable.

Materials
Soil samples: a compacted soil and an uncompacted soil sample, two graduated cylinders, mortar and pestle, water

Method
1. Take a dry sample of an uncompacted soil and add 50 cm³ of the sample to a graduated cylinder.
2. Tap the cylinder to remove any large air pockets in the soil.
3. Take another 50 cm³ sample of a compacted soil. Add this soil to a second graduated cylinder.

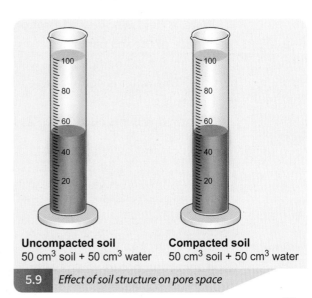

Uncompacted soil
50 cm³ soil + 50 cm³ water

Compacted soil
50 cm³ soil + 50 cm³ water

5.9   *Effect of soil structure on pore space*

4. Add 50 cm³ of water to the first cylinder. Repeat for the second cylinder.

5. Allow the cylinders to stand for 1 hour. Record the total volume of soil and water in each cylinder on the table below.

Table 5.5 Results		
	Compacted soil	**Uncompacted soil**
Initial volume of soil (A)	_____ cm³	_____ cm³
Total volume of soil and water (B)	_____ cm³	_____ cm³
Total volume when soil and water are combined after 1 hour (C)	_____ cm³	_____ cm³
Volume of water occupying pore spaces (B–C)	_____ cm³	_____ cm³
Percentage of soil that is pore space:	Pore space (B–C) × 100/Volume of soil (A)	

Compare the percentage pore space for the compacted soil and uncompacted soil.

Validation

1. Do the results of this experiment support the hypothesis? Explain your answer.

2. What types of data are collected?

3. Comment on the validity and the reliability of your results.

4. Identify any sources of error in the recording of your results.

5. What measures were taken to reduce both statistical and systematic uncertainty?

Soil water

The size of pores is important in determining water levels in the soil. Large soil pores are needed for adequate drainage, while small soil pores are needed for water retention for plant uptake. Sandy soils, because of their larger particles, tend to have large pores that lead to good drainage in the soil but can also contribute to drought in a prolonged period of dry weather, since the soil is unable to retain water.

Clay soils contain the smallest particles and contain the smallest pores. These pores are better at retaining water but a soil with high clay content may also become waterlogged. An ideal soil, such as a loam soil, will contain sand, silt and clay in equal amounts. As a result, it will also contain an equal proportion of large and small pores that allow for good drainage, while still retaining enough water for plant uptake.

Water is held in soil by adsorption and capillary action. Adsorbed water is held on the surface of the soil particles because it is **polarised** and is attracted to negative charges on the soil particles. The water forms a thin film around the surface of the soil particles. This water is not available to plants and cannot be removed from the soil by their roots.

Adsorbed water is also known as **hygroscopic water**.

Polarised: having a positive (+) charge at one end and a negative (–) charge at the opposite end of a particle.

DEFINITION

Hygroscopic water (adsorbed water): water that forms a thin film around a soil particle and is held on the surface of the particle by force of attraction. It cannot be removed from the soil and is unavailable to plants.

Capillary action occurs when water is drawn into pores in the soil and is drawn upwards through the soil against the force of gravity. The water molecules are attracted to the soil particles and held in the soil by adsorption. The water molecules are also attracted to other water molecules in the soil. The smaller the pores in the soil, the more water will be held in the pores and the further it will travel upwards through the soil. Therefore, water is drained from large cracks in the soil but is retained in the smaller pores.

SPA 5.2 To calculate the percentage water content of a soil sample

SPECIFIED PRACTICAL ACTIVITY

State your hypothesis, prediction, independent variable, dependent variable and controlled variable.

Materials
Soil samples (sandy soil, clay soil, loam), beaker, weighing scales, oven or microwave

Method
1. Find the mass of a clean, dry beaker.
2. Add moist soil sample to beaker.
3. Find the mass of the beaker and soil.
4. Place beaker and soil in an oven at 105°C and dry to a constant mass.
5. Calculate loss in mass of soil.
6. Repeat for all other soil samples.

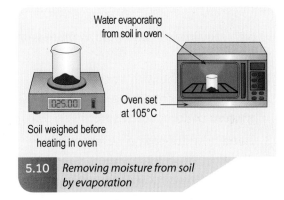

5.10 *Removing moisture from soil by evaporation*

Results

Table 5.6 Results	
Mass of beaker (A)	_____ g
Mass of beaker and soil (B)	_____ g
Mass of moist soil (B–A)	_____ g
Mass of beaker and soil dried to constant mass (C)	_____ g
Mass of dry soil (C–A)	_____ g
Mass of water lost = Moist soil – Dry soil	_____ g
Percentage water content of soil: Mass of water lost/Mass of moist soil × 100/1	_____ %

Validation
1. Identify any sources of error.
2. How would you improve the reliability of this experiment?
3. If more than one soil sample was used, present your results in a chart or graph.
4. Investigate if there is a relationship between soil type and the percentage moisture.

SPA 5.3a To demonstrate capillarity in a compacted soil and an uncompacted soil

SPECIFIED PRACTICAL ACTIVITY

State your hypothesis, prediction, independent variable, dependent variable and controlled variable.

Materials

Two open-ended glass tubes of equal size, cotton wool or muslin cloth, rubber bands, sample of dry compacted soil, sample of dry uncompacted soil, water, water trough, ruler, cress seeds (optional)

Method

1. Plug the ends of both tubes with cotton wool or cover the ends of each tube with muslin cloth and hold in place with rubber bands.

2. Fill the first tube with uncompacted soil. Fill the second tube with an equal amount of compacted soil.

3. Stand both tubes in a water trough as shown in Fig. 5.11.

4. Leave the tubes in the water trough for a few hours.

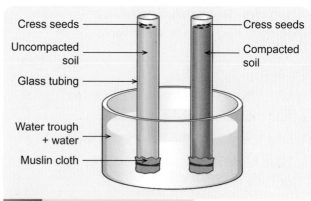

5.11 *Soil capillary action*

5. Observe the tubes and note any rise in water level in each tube. Use a ruler to measure the level to which the water has risen. Compare the level in the compacted soil with the uncompacted soil to determine which soil has the greatest capillary action.

Option: Add an equal number of cress seeds to the surface of the soil in each tube. The cress seeds will germinate if the water rises to a sufficient level so that it is available to the seeds for germination.

Validation

1. Do the results of this experiment support the hypothesis? Explain your answer.

2. Identify any sources of error.

3. Comment on the validity of this experiment (see Chapter 2 page 22).

Capillary water

Capillary water is held in the pores within the soil aggregates and in the pores between the soil aggregates. Capillary water that is held in small pores within the soil aggregates is unavailable to plants. Capillary water that is held in large pores between the soil aggregates is available for plant uptake.

Gravitational water

Gravitational water is moved through the soil by gravity. It is found in cracks in the soil and large soil pores. It is normally only available on a temporary basis to plants (e.g. after heavy rainfall) as it is drained away quickly. Air fills the pores when the gravitational water has drained away.

Water availability in the soil

Saturation

When the large pores are full of gravitational water, the soil is described as saturated. This may occur after heavy rainfall.

Field capacity

This is the water present in the soil after the gravitational water has been drained away. The large capillary pores contain air and the small capillary pores contain water. Plant uptake reduces the level of water in the soil. This water is replaced regularly from rainfall and Irish soils are normally at field capacity due to consistent rainfall. However, if there is a prolonged period of dry weather and water is constantly removed from the soil by plants and is not replaced, eventually all the capillary water will be used up. When no more water can be removed from the soil, the soil is said to be at its permanent wilting point.

Available water capacity

Soils that retain a high volume of water, such as clay soils, do not necessarily have a high available water capacity. This is because much of the water in clay soils is retained in small capillary pores and also as hygroscopic water, which is unavailable to plants.

Figure 5.12 shows that clay soils have a high field capacity. However, they also have a high permanent wilting point, which means that the available water capacity of these soils is quite small. This is due to the high number of small capillary pores found in clay soils. The water in these pores is unavailable to plants. The water in these pores is also hygroscopic in nature and cannot be removed from the soil.

In contrast, loam and clay loam soils have a much lower permanent wilting point, giving a higher available water capacity. This means that there is a greater volume of water available for plant uptake in these soils.

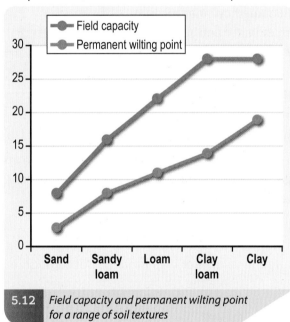

5.12 *Field capacity and permanent wilting point for a range of soil textures*

> ### DEFINITION
>
> **Field capacity:** the amount of water in a soil after the gravitational water has drained away.
> **Permanent wilting point:** the point at which no more capillary water can be removed from a soil (by plant roots). Plants will die from drought if the soil in which they are growing reaches its permanent wilting point.
> **Available water capacity:** the amount of water between the field capacity and permanent wilting point that is available for absorption by plant roots.
> Available water capacity = field capacity – permanent wilting point.

SPA 5.3b To compare the infiltration rate of a compacted soil and an uncompacted soil

SPECIFIED PRACTICAL ACTIVITY

State your hypothesis, prediction, independent variable, dependent variable and controlled variable.

Materials

Filter funnels, retort stands, beakers, filter paper, sample of dry compacted soil, sample of dry uncompacted soil, graduated cylinders, water, stopwatch

Method

1. Set up apparatus as shown in Fig. 5.13. Line a filter funnel with filter paper and fill it with compacted soil. Repeat with the second funnel but fill it with an equal amount of uncompacted soil.

2. Using a graduated cylinder measure out 20 cm³ of water and pour it into a beaker. Repeat with a second beaker.

3. Pour one beaker of water into each of the soil samples at the same time.

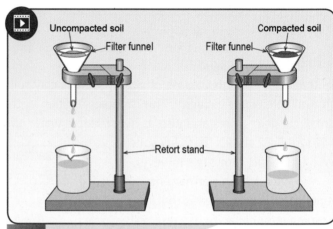

5.13 *Soil capillary action*

4. Infiltration rate can be measured in two ways:

   (a) Use a stopwatch to time how long it takes for the first drop of water to pass through the soil and be collected in the beaker below the funnel for each sample.

   or

   (b) Use a stopwatch for a set period of time (e.g. 5 minutes, 10 minutes) to measure the volume of water that passes through each soil sample in the time allowed. Compare the results of both samples.

> **Infiltration:** the rate at which water will pass or filter through soil.

Result

Table 5.7 Results		
	Compacted soil	**Uncompacted soil**
Time for first drop of water to be collected	_____ s	_____ s
Volume of water collected after _____ minutes	_____ cm³	_____ cm³

Validation

1. Do the results of this experiment support the hypothesis? Explain your answer.

2. Account for differences between the volumes of water added to both soil samples and the volumes of water collected.

3. Suggest ways that farmers could improve the infiltration rate of their soil.

Soil colour

In terms of physical properties, the colour of a soil can indicate its humus and mineral content. A soil that is dark brown/black in colour is usually rich in humus. These types of soil have high fertility and nutrient content, and a high humus content leads to good soil structure. Dark-coloured soils also absorb more sunlight and so they are warm soils.

Since humus tends to be found in the top layer of soil, it may be necessary to examine the subsoil and lower horizons to assess the soil colour. Soils that are light-coloured or grey tend to be low in fertility and nutrients and lacking in humus. This is particularly true of the soil horizons nearest the surface. These soils can suffer from leaching, where the minerals are washed out of the soil or accumulate in a lower horizon in the subsoil.

Red colouring in soil indicates the presence of iron. Often iron is leached from the upper layers of the soil and accumulates in the lower horizons, and there it forms an iron-pan that may be impermeable to water and roots. This will be characterised by a thin red layer in the subsoil.

Soil temperature

Air that is found in pores in the soil is more easily heated than water. Therefore, it is more advantageous to have a well-drained sandy soil or a loam soil for crop growth, since this soil will warm up quicker in springtime. Soil temperature is an important factor in crop growth, since cold temperatures will slow or stunt the growth of a crop.

The rate of chemical reactions doubles with every 10°C rise in temperature (Van't Hoff's Law) so the warmer the soil, the faster the growth rate.

Effects of soil temperature

- Soil temperatures affect the germination and growth of crops. This is particularly important for spring-sown cereal crops. If soils warm up quickly in spring, crops will germinate faster.
- Soil temperatures affect water and mineral uptake by a plant as well as root growth. At lower temperatures water and mineral uptake is decreased, which reduces crop growth.
- Temperature therefore is an important factor in crop development and can determine the length of the growing season. A cold spring will delay germination and growth, leaving a shorter growing season, which may result in a reduced yield, particularly for cereal crops.

The impact of erosion, sedimentation and weathering on soil

Soil erosion can have a detrimental effect on agricultural land. Topsoil, which is rich in nutrients and is vital for crop growth, is worn away by three main methods of erosion: wind, water and tillage.

Water erosion

Precipitation on soil surfaces, particularly on soils with poor drainage, can break down soil aggregates leading to further deterioration of the soil structure. Lighter soil particles can then be removed by rain and run-off from the surface of the soil. Soil compaction and soil capping also lead to reduced infiltration and an increase in erosion of topsoil. Land that has been left fallow with no vegetative cover can also be susceptible to soil erosion by water. Steeply sloped land can also contribute to soil erosion, as there is a greater chance of run-off.

Soil capping: a hard crust on the soil surface that limits permeability.

Wind erosion

Fine soil particles can be carried away by wind. Hillsides are susceptible to wind erosion due to the lack of shelter. Shelterbelts on farms can provide a windbreak and reduce soil erosion. Vegetative cover on land helps to bind soil together and reduce the effects of erosion.

Tillage erosion

Erosion of soil can be caused by tillage operations. The more passes over the soil, the more soil is moved. Conservation measures such as min-till or no-till operations can reduce soil erosion on tillage farms.

> DEFINITION
>
> **Minimum tillage (conservation tillage):** a method of cultivation in which ploughing is not carried out at any stage during the seedbed preparation.

Sedimentation

Sedimentation is the result of erosion. Eroded soil particles (or sediments) are transported from their place of origin (e.g. tillage land) and deposited in a different location (e.g. a river).

Effects of erosion and sedimentation

Soil erosion can result in the loss of topsoil from agricultural land. Topsoil can take in excess of 100 years to form, so if eroded, the rate of removal will exceed the rate of replacement. As this leads to a loss of a layer of soil rich in nutrients and organic matter, this leads to soils with a poorer structure and fewer nutrients, which in turn may result in poorer crop yields. Sediments that deposited elsewhere as a result of erosion may in turn reduce the water quality in aquatic habitats such as rivers, lakes and streams.

Methods of reducing the effects of erosion and sedimentation

- Use catch crops (Chapter 15) to provide vegetative cover on land that would otherwise lie bare
- Return land to pasture
- Install drainage to reduce the effects of heavy water run-off, which can erode topsoil
- Reduce effects of compaction as compacted soils have poor infiltration rates so soil can be eroded by run-off water
- Reduce tillage by employing a min-till or no-till system, as tillage can create a loose layer of topsoil easily eroded by wind.

Organic matter loss

Cation: a positively charged ion (e.g. H^+, Ca^{2+}, Al^{3+}).

If topsoil is eroded from a soil, this can lead to loss of organic matter as the majority of organic matter and humus is found in the upper layer of the soil. This can lead to poorer soil structure, less nutrient availability, less carbon sequestration, lower water retention and lower cation exchange capacity in the soil.

> DEFINITION
>
> **Carbon sequestration:** the removal of carbon dioxide from the atmosphere by plant photosynthesis and storing as plant biomass or organic soil matter.

Summary

- Soil consists of mineral matter (45%), air (25%), water (25%) and organic matter (5%).
- The five types of mineral particle found in soil are: gravel, coarse sand, fine sand, silt and clay.
- Gravel and sand lead to good drainage and aeration. Silt and clay are good for water retention and clay has high fertility levels.
- Ion exchange takes place in soil where ions are attracted to soil particles (clay) and are held on the surface of these particles.
- Organic matter consists of the remains of plants and animals.
- Humus is the dark-coloured, decomposed plant and animal matter found in soil. It is rich in nutrients and contributes to soil structure.
- The physical properties of soil are: texture, structure, porosity, colour and temperature.
- Soil texture is a measure of the proportion of different-sized mineral particles (sand, silt, clay) that are found in a sample of soil.
- Loam soil contains equal amounts of sand, silt and clay.
- Soil structure describes the arrangement of soil particles within a soil. A good soil structure has a large volume of pores – 50% of the total soil volume – and approximately half the pores are filled with air and the other half with water.
- Flocculation is the clustering together of soil particles to create larger structures called floccules.
- Cementation is the binding together of soil particles.
- Separation occurs when soil aggregates are separated within the soil.
- Structural development is affected by: freezing and thawing, wetting and drying, soil organic matter, plant root activity, animal activity, and cultivation and tillage.
- Porosity refers to the total volume of the soil occupied by soil pores.
- Soil compaction occurs when soil particles are pressed together and aggregates are destroyed. This reduces total pore space.
- Hygroscopic water (adsorbed water) forms a thin film around a soil particle and is held on the surface of the particle by force of attraction. It cannot be removed from the soil and is not available to plants.
- Capillary water is held in the pores within the soil aggregates and in the pores between the soil aggregates.
- Gravitational water is moved through the soil by gravity.
- Field capacity is the amount of water in a soil after the gravitational water has drained away.
- Permanent wilting point: the point at which no more capillary water can be removed from a soil (by plant roots).
- Available water capacity: the amount of water between the field capacity and permanent wilting point that is available for absorption by plant roots.
- The colour of a soil can indicate its humus and mineral content.
- The rate of chemical reactions doubles with every 10°C rise in temperature (Van't Hoff's Law), so the warmer the soil, the faster the growth rate.
- Soil erosion removes topsoil from the surface of the land. This can happen by wind, water or tillage erosion.
- Soil erosion can be reduced by employing min-till operations, installing drainage and by the use of catch crops.

PowerPoint Summary

QUESTIONS

1. What is the ideal composition of soil?

    (a) Mineral matter 50%, water 20%, air 20%, organic matter 10%

    (b) Mineral matter 25%, water 25%, air 25%, organic matter 25%

    (c) Mineral matter 55%, water 20%, air 20%, organic matter 5%

    (d) Mineral matter 45%, water 25%, air 25%, organic matter 5%

2. Arrange the mineral particles in soil from largest to smallest.

    (a) Silt   (c) Gravel

    (b) Clay   (d) Sand

3. Which of the following is not a property of clay particles?

    (a) Small soil particles   (c) Good drainage

    (b) Poor aeration   (d) High fertility

4. A loam soil is best described as:

    (a) A soil with equal proportions of sand, silt and clay

    (b) A soil that is mainly sand

    (c) A soil that is mainly silt

    (d) A soil that is mainly clay.

5. Which of the following are described as cementation processes?

    (a) Wetting and drying   (c) Burrowing of earthworms

    (b) Freezing and thawing   (d) All of the above

6. Compacted soil can be broken up using:

    (a) A harrow   (c) A subsoiler

    (b) A rake   (d) None of the above.

7. Water which is adsorbed on to the surface of soil particles is best described as:

    (a) Hygroscopic water   (c) Gravitational water

    (b) Capillary water   (d) Pore water.

8. Which of the following causes erosion of topsoil?

    (a) Wind   (c) Tillage

    (b) Water   (d) All of the above

9. Why is the air and water content of soil so variable?

10. Describe the properties of soils that contain sand and gravel under the following headings: Pore space, Drainage, Aeration, Fertility.

11. What is ion exchange?

12. What are colloidal clay particles?

13. Identify the soil textures for each of the following soils.

    (a) Sand 40%, silt 15%, clay 45%

    (b) Sand 24%, silt 34%, clay 42%

    (c) Sand 35%, silt 27%, clay 38%

    (d) Sand 56%, silt 36%, clay 8%

14. Compare sandy soils and clay soils under the following headings:

    (a) Drainage

    (b) Aeration

    (c) Fertility

    (d) Tillage capabilities.

15. List five physical properties of soil.

16. What is a loam soil?

17. A student tested a soil by the feel method to determine its texture. She found on testing that the soil was smooth and could form threads between 2.5 cm and 5 cm long. Use the flow chart of soil textures to determine the soil texture of the soil sample.

18. A student tested a soil using a soil sieve. He found that in a 100 g soil sample 30 g was sand, 60 g was silt and 10 g was clay. Identify the soil texture of the soil using the soil triangle.

19. List two advantages and two disadvantages of (a) sandy soils and (b) clay soils.

20. Why are loam soils considered to have the best soil texture?

21. What is meant by the term 'soil structure'?

22. List three reasons why a good soil structure is necessary.

23. What is meant by the term 'flocculation'?

24. List three factors that affect the structural development of a field.

25. Atmospheric air and soil air are almost identical in their composition. How do they differ?

26. What factor contributes to the difference between atmospheric air and soil air? Explain how this factor contributes to the difference.

27. Which type of water is best described by each statement below?

    (a) Water held in pores in soil aggregates and between soil aggregates

    (b) Water moved through the soil by gravity

    (c) Water held as a thin film on the surface of soil particles

28. Explain the terms:

    (a) Field capacity

    (b) Permanent wilting point

    (c) Available water capacity.

29. Explain how a named soil texture influences:

    (a) Water movement

    (b) Fertility

    (c) Pore spaces.

30. Outline four ways in which soil compaction affects soil.

Solutions   Weblinks

CHAPTER 6

Chemical characteristics of soil

When you have completed this chapter you should be able to:

- Explain the process of flocculation in soil
- Understand how cation exchange occurs in soil
- Understand the effect of pH in a soil
- Understand the relationship between pH and liming in soil
- Examine the importance of plant-available nutrients
- Carry out an investigation to determine the pH of a soil sample (SPA)
- Carry out an investigation to demonstrate cation exchange capacity (SPA – Higher Level only)
- Carry out an investigation to show flocculation in a soil sample (SPA).

Chemical properties of soil

The chemically active particles in soil are the clay and humus particles. These are also the smallest particles found in a soil. Clay and humus both have positive and negative charges on their surfaces. Their charges attract ions of the opposite charge. These ions are necessary for plant nutrition and also influence the acidity or alkalinity of the soil.

There are several chemical properties that are important in determining the characteristics of a soil:

- Flocculation
- Cation exchange
- pH
- Plant-available nutrients.

Flocculation

Flocculation is the clustering together of soil particles to create larger structures called floccules. These structures may also be called peds or aggregates. Floccule formation is an important process in maintaining good soil structure, and can be promoted by the presence of cations in the soil.

How flocculation occurs

1. Chemical reactions in the soil cause the formation of negative charges on the soil colloids.

2. Cations (ions with positive charges) are attracted to these charges and are adsorbed onto the surface of the soil colloids. Water between the soil colloids is polarised and acts as a link between the colloids. The colloids are linked together by the polarised water, and this is known as a floccule.

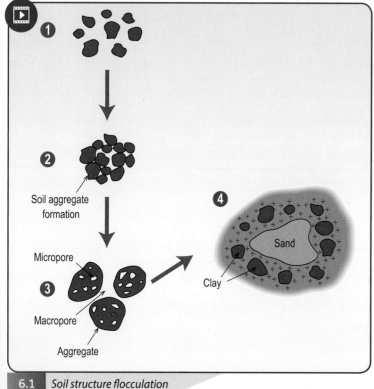

6.1   *Soil structure flocculation*

3. The floccule is essentially a chain of colloidal particles held together by water and the force of attraction between the water and the cations.

4. The floccules then trap larger particles such as sand and silt, forming aggregates.

> Cations that promote flocculation:
> Al^{3+}, Fe^{3+}, Ca^{2+}, Mg^{2+}, H^+, K^+, Na^+

 **SPA 6.1** | **To show flocculation in a soil sample**

SPECIFIED PRACTICAL ACTIVITY

State your hypothesis, prediction, independent variable, dependent variable and controlled variable.

Materials

Clay soil, deionised water, test tubes, test tube rack, stoppers, droppers, 0.1M hydrochloric acid (HCl), 0.1M sodium chloride (NaCl), 0.05M calcium chloride ($CaCl_2$), 0.02M aluminium chloride ($AlCl_3$)

Method

1. Add 1 g clay to 100 cm³ of deionised water and mix thoroughly.

2. Pour 10 cm³ of the clay-water suspension into each of four test tubes.

3. Add 1 cm³ hydrochloric acid to the first test tube.

4. Add 1 cm³ sodium chloride to the second test tube.

5. Add 1 cm³ calcium chloride to the third test tube.

6. Add 1 cm³ aluminium chloride to the fourth test tube.

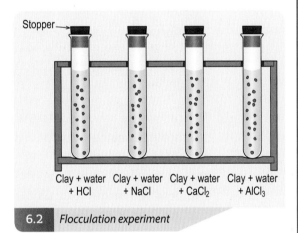

Stopper

Clay + water + HCl | Clay + water + NaCl | Clay + water + $CaCl_2$ | Clay + water + $AlCl_3$

6.2 *Flocculation experiment*

7. Place a stopper on each test tube and shake to mix.

8. Observe the test tubes and record the level of flocculation in each one at 5-minute intervals.

9. Determine which reagent (chemical) was the most effective flocculant.

10. Record your results in a table.

Validation

1. Based on the results of your investigation, list the cations in order of most effective to least effective as flocculating agents.

2. Do the results of this experiment support the hypothesis? Explain your answer.

3. Is the data recorded in this investigation subjective or objective? Explain your answer.

4. Identify any sources of error.

Cation exchange

Cations are positively charged ions such as H^+, K^+, Ca^{2+}. Positively charged cations are attracted to negatively charged humus and clay particles. They are held on the surface (adsorbed) as the opposite charges of the particles attract each other. Clay and humus particles can release cations that are adsorbed onto their surfaces and replace them with other cations. The ability of soil particles to attract, retain and release cations is called cation exchange.

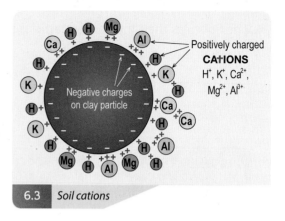

6.3   *Soil cations*

> **DEFINITION**
>
> **Cation exchange:** the ability of soil particles (clay and humus) to attract, retain and release cations.

Soil colloids are the smallest particles that exist in the soil. They are also the most chemically active. Colloidal clay and colloidal humus have the highest rates of cation exchange in the soil. The amount or volume of cation exchange that can take place on a soil particle is known as its cation exchange capacity (CEC).

> **DEFINITION**
>
> **Cation exchange capacity (CEC):** the quantity of cations that a soil adsorbs. It can also be described as the capacity of a soil to exchange cations between the soil surfaces and the soil solution (water).

The cations are released into the soil through weathering. Cations are present in the water in the soil, known as soil solution. A cation with two positive charges (e.g. Ca^{2+}) can displace (take the place of) two separate cations each with one positive charge (e.g. K^+).

6.4   *Cation exchange soil colloid*

Cation exchange is constantly taking place. Cations are removed from the soil solution by plant roots and replaced through cation exchange between the soil solution and the soil particles.

Factors affecting cation exchange capacity

There are a number of factors affecting CEC in a soil:

- **Humus content:** humus has the highest CEC value as colloidal humus has high quantities of negative charges which make it suitable for cation exchange. It can be up to 30 times more effective at cation exchange than clay
- **Clay content:** soils with a high clay content will have a higher CEC than those with a low clay content (see Table 6.1)
- **Soil texture:** soils with a fine texture have a higher CEC
- **pH:** fewer cations are available at lower pH levels, particularly when pH is lower than 5.0. Cation exchange levels can be maintained or raised by liming, which increases the amount of Ca^{2+} cations available for exchange. Also, as pH increases the number of negative charges on soil colloids increase, leading to greater CEC.

Table 6.1 CEC values for different soil textures	
Soil texture	**CEC range (mEq/100 g soil)**
Sand	1–5
Sandy loam	5–10
Loam	5–15
Silt loam	15–25
Clay loam	15–30
Clay	30–50
Organic soils/materials	50+

Milliequivalent (mEq): amount of a substance that will react with a certain number of hydrogen ions (H^+).

SPA 6.2 (H)   To demonstrate cation exchange capacity in a soil

SPECIFIED PRACTICAL ACTIVITY   (Higher Level only)

State your hypothesis and prediction and identify one safety precaution.

Materials

Dry soil sample with high pH, filter funnel, dropper, potassium chloride, beaker, 10% solution of ammonium oxalate, 2 mm sieve

Method

1. Add 5 g of dry, sieved soil to the filter funnel.

2. Use a dropper to add potassium chloride solution to the soil (drop by drop). Collect the water that filters from the soil in a clean dry beaker. This is known as leachate.

3. Test the leachate for calcium by adding 10 drops of ammonium oxalate to the leachate. If a white precipitate forms, calcium is present.

4. Discard the leachate and repeat the experiment by adding more KCl to the soil and testing the leachate for calcium.

5. Repeat until the leachate does not test positive for calcium.

KCl

Ammonium oxalate

Ammonium oxalate + leachate

Leachate

6.5   *Potassium–calcium ion exchange*

> **Leachate:** water that has percolated through soil, removing minerals and suspended solids from the soil.

Validation

1. Do the results of this experiment support the hypothesis? Explain your answer.

2. Is the data recorded qualitative or quantitative? Explain your answer.

3. Suggest reasons why the soil sample used in this experiment has a high pH.

4. Account for the presence of calcium ions in the leachate.

5. What result would you expect if you used a soil sample with a low pH?

pH

The term pH refers to the concentration of hydrogen ions in a solution. The solution in this case is the soil solution.

> **pH:** a measure of the concentration of the hydrogen ions in a solution. It can also be expressed as the negative log of the hydrogen ion concentration: $pH = -\log_{10}[H^+]$.

The pH scale extends from 0 to 14, where 7 is neutral. Values below 7 are described as acidic and values above 7 are described as alkaline (basic).

For each unit decrease on the pH scale, the H^+ ion concentration increases by a factor of 10. This means that a pH of 5 is ten times more concentrated than a pH of 6. The acidity of the soil is determined by the concentration of acidic ions adsorbed on the surface of the soil colloids. Hydrogen and aluminium ions (H^+ and Al^{3+}) are acidic ions and the soils in which they dominate will also be acidic. Calcium and magnesium (Ca^{2+} and Mg^{2+}) are alkaline ions and the soils in which they dominate will be alkaline. Hydrogen ions are derived from carbonic acids and aluminium ions from granite or sandstone. Calcium and magnesium are derived from limestone or from the application of lime to the land.

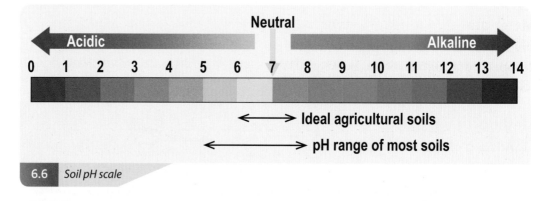

6.6 *Soil pH scale*

 SPA 6.3 To determine the pH of a soil

SPECIFIED PRACTICAL ACTIVITY

State your hypothesis, prediction, independent variable, dependent variable and controlled variable.

Materials
Different dry soil samples, beaker, distilled water, stirring rod, pH meter, pH paper/universal indicator, funnel, filter paper

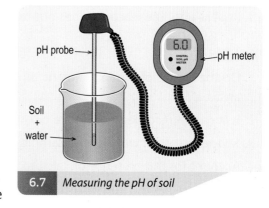

6.7 *Measuring the pH of soil*

Method

1. Add 20 g of a soil sample to a beaker. Add approximately 25 ml distilled water to the soil and stir for 5 minutes.

2. Turn on the pH meter and insert the electrode in a beaker of distilled water (pH 7) to ensure the probe is clean and reading the pH accurately.

3. Insert the electrode into the soil and water mixture. Note the pH reading on the meter. Clean the electrode with distilled water after use.

Alternative methods for determining pH

1. If a pH meter is not available, dip a strip of pH paper into the soil and water mixture. Observe the colour change (if any) of the pH paper. Compare the colour of the pH paper with the colour chart supplied to determine the pH of the soil.

2. If using universal indicator, set up a funnel and place filter paper in the funnel. Pour the soil and water mixture into the funnel and collect the water that is filtered from the soil in a clean, dry beaker. Add a couple of drops of universal indicator to the water and note the colour. Compare the colour of the indicator with the colour chart supplied to determine the pH of the soil.

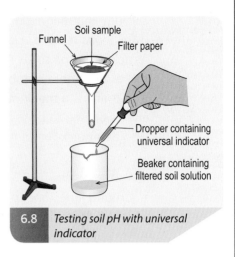

6.8 *Testing soil pH with universal indicator*

Validation

1. Do the results of this experiment support the hypothesis? Explain your answer.

2. Is the data recorded subjective or objective? Explain your answer.

3. If you used a pH probe to measure the pH of your soil sample, briefly describe how you calibrated and used the probe in order to reduce error.

4. Which of the methods is the most accurate method of determining pH? Justify your choice.

Importance of pH on soil activity

Most crops will grow in a pH range from 5.5 to 8.5. Some crops will grow at pH levels slightly above or below this range. The optimum pH level for crop growth is between 6.5 and 7.5. Outside these ranges, a very low or very high pH can reduce the availability of nutrients to plants. When essential nutrients are unavailable to plants, growth rates are limited and yields are reduced. Certain ions may become abundant in the soil, to the point where they are at toxic levels, and the activity of some microorganisms may decrease because of unsuitable environmental conditions.

Availability of soil nutrients

The availability of soil nutrients is shown in Fig. 6.9. As soils become increasingly acidic or alkaline, the availability of particular nutrients is reduced and in some instances, nutrients are unavailable. Most nutrients are available between pH 6 and 7. This is the optimum range for crop growth in a wide range of crops.

In soils that are acidic, availability of nutrients can be increased by raising the pH of the soil. This is normally achieved by liming.

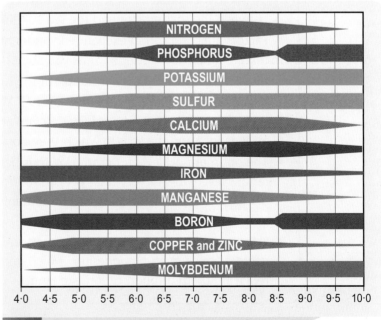

6.9 *Nutrient availability over a range of pH values*

Liming

Liming involves spreading ground limestone on the soil. Ground limestone contains calcium and magnesium, both of which are alkaline. The calcium (Ca^{2+}) and magnesium (Mg^{2+}) ions replace acidic hydrogen and aluminium ions through cation exchange. As acidity in the soil is reduced, the pH level increases. This reduces acid leaching and makes soils more suitable for crop growth.

Liming is a medium-term activity, since it takes approximately 2 years for the full effects of lime to be seen on the land. It is not suitable, therefore, to spread lime on the land as a quick-fix solution to a low pH soil.

Ground limestone

- Ground limestone for agricultural use should consist of crushed natural limestone containing calcium carbonate or magnesium carbonate.
- Moisture content should be no greater than 2.5%.
- Total neutralising value should be no less than 90%.
- All ground limestone should pass through a 3.35 mm sieve and not less than 35% of it should pass through a 0.15 mm sieve.

Summary

- The smallest and most chemically active particles in soil are clay and humus particles. They attract ions due to the charges on their surfaces, which affect plant nutrition and soil pH.
- The chemical properties of soil are: flocculation, cation exchange capacity, pH, plant available nutrients.
- Flocculation is the clustering together of soil particles to create larger structures called floccules.
- Cations are positively charged ions that are attracted and adsorbed onto the surface of soil particles.
- Cation exchange: the ability of soil particles (clay and humus) to attract, retain and release cations.
- Cation exchange capacity (CEC): the quantity of cations that can be adsorbed by a soil. It can also be described as the capacity of a soil to exchange cations between the soil surfaces and the soil solution (water).
- Factors affecting cation exchange include: humus content, clay content, soil texture and pH.
- pH: a measure of the concentration of the hydrogen ions in a solution.
- Hydrogen and aluminium ions (H^+ and Al^{3+}) are acidic ions and the soils in which they dominate will also be acidic. Calcium and magnesium (Ca^{2+} and Mg^{2+}) are alkaline ions and the soils in which they dominate will be alkaline.
- The optimum pH level for crop growth is between 6.5 and 7.5. Outside these ranges a very low or very high pH can reduce the availability of nutrients to plants, and the activity of some microorganisms may decrease because of unsuitable environmental conditions.
- Liming involves spreading ground limestone on the soil. Ground limestone contains calcium and magnesium which neutralise acidic ions in the soil by replacing them through cation exchange.

PowerPoint Summary

QUESTIONS

1. Which of the following are cations?

    (a) Ca^{2+}

    (b) Al

    (c) Cl^-

    (d) H^+

2. Rearrange these steps to show how floccule formation occurs.

    (a) Floccules trap larger particles such as sand to form aggregates.

    (b) Chemical reactions form negative charges on soil colloids.

    (c) The colloids are linked together by polarised water to form a floccule.

    (d) Cations are adsorbed onto the surface of soil colloids.

3. Cation exchange is best described as:

    (a) The ability of a soil to attract, retain and release cations

    (b) The ability of a soil to attract, retain and release clay particles

    (c) The removal of positively charged ions from the soil

    (d) The exchange of negative ions between the soil and soil water.

4. Which of the following soil textures has the lowest cation exchange capacity?

    (a) Clay

    (b) Loam

    (c) Sandy loam

    (d) Organic soils

5. pH measures the concentration of which ions in a solution?

    (a) Aluminium

    (b) Calcium

    (c) Potassium

    (d) Hydrogen

6. What is the normal pH range for agricultural land?

    (a) 5.0–8.0

    (b) 6.0–7.0

    (c) 4.0–7.5

    (d) 5.5–8.5

7. List four factors that affect cation exchange capacity.

8. Describe the effects that a pH outside the range of 5.5–8.5 can have on a crop.

9. Outline the chemical exchanges that would occur in the soil between lime, soil colloids and soil solution following the application of lime.

10. What are the properties of ground limestone?

 Solutions —  Weblinks

CHAPTER 7
Biological characteristics of soil

When you have completed this chapter you should be able to:

- Examine the microbiome of a soil
- Appreciate the importance of the rhizosphere
- Appreciate the relationship between soil fungi and roots and the impact of that relationship on productivity
- Explain the roles of the carbon cycle and nitrogen cycle
- Examine the importance of organic matter in soil
- Relate organic matter content to soil structure and other physical and chemical properties for soils of differing management
- Examine the role of earthworm activity in soil
- Carry out an investigation to determine the percentage organic matter in a soil sample and convert that to organic carbon (SPA)
- Carry out an investigation to isolate and grow bacteria from clover root nodules (SPA)
- Carry out an investigation to show the activity of earthworms in a soil (SPA)
- Carry out an investigation to estimate the number of earthworms in a pasture (SPA).

Biological properties of soil

Soil provides a habitat for a variety of living organisms. The list of organisms is extensive and includes insects, worms, small mammals, fungi and bacteria. These living organisms help to improve the soil through physical activity. Their activities improve the growing conditions available to crops.

A variety of plants need soil as a medium for growth. They extract water and nutrients from the soil and use it to anchor themselves. Plants also contribute large amounts of organic matter to the soil when they lose their leaves and when they die, and their remains decompose. All of these plants and animals are collectively known as soil biomass.

The plant and animal material which has decomposed is known as humus. Humification is the name given to the process of converting organic matter to humus.

> **DEFINITION**
>
> **Soil biomass:** the total mass of living organisms in the soil.
> **Humification:** the process by which soil organic matter is converted to humus.

Microbiome: a community of microorganisms (e.g. bacteria and fungi) that inhabit a particular environment.

Soil microbiome: soil bacteria and fungi

The soil microbiome consists of a wide range of bacteria and fungi. Soil microorganisms carry out several important processes. These include the recycling of plant nutrients such as carbon and nitrogen, supporting plant growth, and production of humus (known as humification) by feeding on plant and animal remains. These processes release nutrients into the soil, which are then available for plant uptake.

Types of microorganisms

- **Bacteria:** single-celled organisms that are responsible for converting soil organic matter into humus. They are also responsible for converting nitrogen into usable forms for plants (nitrogen fixation and nitrification) and converting usable nitrogen into atmospheric nitrogen, which is unavailable for plant use (denitrification) (see page 107, nitrogen cycle).
- **Actinomycetes:** mycelial bacteria that have thread-like extensions radiating from their single-cell structure. They are responsible for humification of soil organic matter.
- **Fungi:** fungi range from microscopic in size to large mushrooms. They are responsible for humification of soil organic matter, and some species form **symbiotic relationships** with other living organisms in the habitat. Some fungi are parasitic and can have a detrimental effect on a crop when they attack it.

> **DEFINITION**
>
> **Symbiotic relationship:** where different organisms live in a close relationship. In a **mutualistic relationship** both organisms benefit from the relationship.

The rhizosphere

The rhizosphere is the zone of soil surrounding a plant root where the biology and chemistry of the soil are influenced by the plant root. Typically, this area is a couple of millimetres wide, and is a region where many microorganisms feed on biological and chemical compounds released by the root.

As plant roots develop they release many water-soluble compounds into the soil including amino acids and sugars. These compounds provide a nutrient supply for the soil microorganisms. This results in a high concentration of microbial activity in the rhizosphere in comparison to the soil outside the rhizosphere. The bacteria and fungi in the rhizosphere create a nutrient-rich zone around the roots creating a symbiotic relationship.

One specific example of this symbiosis is the mycorrhizal relationship between fungi and the root system of a plant. The fungus benefits from the energy produced by the plant through photosynthesis and in turn the plant benefits from mineral nutrients and water supplied by the fungus, which are taken from the soil.

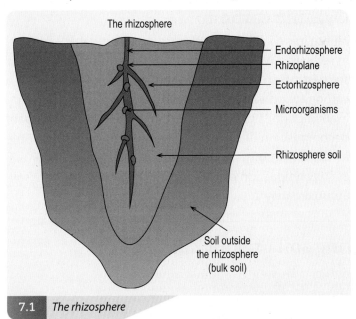

7.1 *The rhizosphere*

The rhizosphere — Endorhizosphere — Rhizoplane — Ectorhizosphere — Microorganisms — Rhizosphere soil — Soil outside the rhizosphere (bulk soil)

> **DEFINITION**
>
> **Rhizosphere:** the zone of soil surrounding a plant root where the biology and chemistry of the soil are influenced by the plant root. It is the most biologically active part of the soil with microorganisms benefitting from the chemical compounds released by the plant roots.

Nitrification: conversion of ammonia or ammonium compounds into nitrite or nitrate.

Parasite: an organism that lives on another host organism. The parasite usually benefits at the expense of the host and may cause damage to the host.

Endorhizosphere: area of the cortex and endodermis of root where microorganisms can occupy spaces between cells and make use of nutrients released by roots.

Rhizoplane: the external surface of the roots and adhering soil particles.

Ectorhizosphere: the area of the rhizosphere which extends from the rhizoplane to the bulk soil.

Advantages of mycorrhizal fungi

- The mycorrhizal fungi threads enhance the water-holding capacity of the soil, promoting drought resistance in the plant.
- The mycorrhizal filaments help bind soil particles together, improving soil structure and reducing erosion.
- The uptake of mineral elements by the fungi is selective, excluding toxic heavy metals such as lead.
- Disease resistance is increased as mycorrhizal fungi offer protection from plant pests such as soil-borne nematodes.

Organic matter

Organic matter consists of the dead remains of plants and animals. The type of organic matter found in soil can vary in terms of its source and the size of the particles. Some of it is clearly visible (e.g. twigs, leaves, dead insects) and it is not decomposed. The organic matter that has decomposed is called humus. Humus particles are very small.

Like mineral matter, the size of the particles of organic matter has an effect on their contribution to the soil's properties.

Table 7.1 Effect of organic matter particle size on soil properties	
Large particles of organic matter	**Small particles of organic matter**
Large pore spaces between particles: • Improve drainage • Do not contribute to ion exchange.	Small pore spaces between particles: • Provide a source of nutrients for plant growth • Are important in ion exchange. Colloidal humus has a higher rate of ion exchange than colloidal clay.

Organic carbon

Sequester: the act of forming a stable compound from an ion, atom or molecule so that it is unavailable for other chemical reactions.

All organic matter contains carbon. Soil organic carbon plays an important role in removing carbon dioxide from the atmosphere, in a process known as **carbon sequestration. Soil organic carbon accounts for 58% of soil organic matter.** Organic carbon found in the soil provides an energy source for the soil microbiome, which is an important part of the carbon cycle. Soil microorganisms are necessary for the decomposition of soil organic matter and recycling nutrients in the soil.

Soils with organic matter levels of 3.4% or higher are not considered to be at risk of soil compaction or capping. This is equivalent to a soil organic carbon content of approximately 2%.

Calculating soil organic carbon

Formula

Soil organic carbon (SOC) = Mass of soil organic matter (SOM) × 0.58

% SOC = % SOM × 0.58

Questions

A student conducted an investigation to determine the mass of soil organic matter in a 50 g sample of soil. The mass of soil organic matter was 2.5 g.

1. Calculate how many grams of soil organic carbon were present in the soil sample.

2. What percentage of the soil sample was organic carbon?

Answers

1. Mass (g) of SOC = Mass (g) of SOM × 0.58
   $$= 2.5 \text{ (g)} \times 0.58$$
   $$\text{SOC (g)} = 1.45 \text{ g}$$

2. % SOC = % SOM × 0.58
   $$\% \text{ SOM} = \frac{2.5}{50} \times \frac{100}{1} = 5\%$$
   $$\% \text{ SOC} = 5\% \times 0.58$$
   $$\% \text{ SOC} = 2.9\%$$

 SPA 7.1 To determine the percentage organic matter in a soil sample and convert that to organic carbon

SPECIFIED PRACTICAL ACTIVITY

Note: All organic matter contains carbon, which is combustible (it can be burned). In this experiment the organic matter will be removed from the soil by burning it off.

State your hypothesis and prediction.

Materials

Electronic balance/weighing scales, soil sample, crucible, pipe clay triangle, tripod stand, Bunsen burner, tongs, dry soil sample

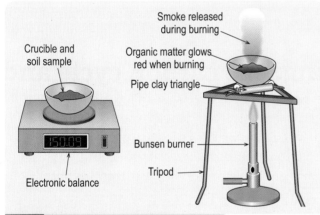

7.2 *Organic matter apparatus*

Method

1. Weigh an empty crucible and record its mass in the table below. (A)
2. Add a sample of dry soil to the crucible and record its mass. (B)
3. Subtract the mass of the crucible from the combined mass of the crucible and soil sample to calculate the mass of the soil. (C)
4. Put the crucible on the pipe clay triangle on the tripod stand.
5. Heat the soil in the crucible with the Bunsen burner. The humus (organic matter) should glow red as it burns, and smoke will be produced. Continue to burn off the humus until there is no more smoke and the soil does not glow.
6. Remove the crucible from the tripod with tongs and reweigh, noting the mass. (D)
7. Calculate the loss of mass in the soil by subtracting the mass of the crucible and burned soil (D) from the mass of the crucible and soil before burning. (B)
8. Calculate the mass of organic matter by subtracting the soil mass after burning from the soil mass before burning (C – E).

Table 7.2 Results		
Mass of crucible (A)	=	g
Mass of crucible + soil sample (B)	=	g
Mass of soil = B – A (C)	=	g
Mass of crucible + burned soil sample (D)	=	g
Soil mass after burning = B – D (E)	=	g
Mass of organic matter = C – E		

9. Calculate the percentage of organic matter in your soil sample, using the formula:

$$\frac{\text{Mass of organic matter}}{\text{Mass of original soil sample}} \times \frac{100}{1} = \text{percentage soil organic matter (SOM)}$$

10. Calculate the percentage soil organic carbon using the formula:
    % SOM × 0.58 = % SOC.

Validation

1. Describe **two** safety precautions taken when carrying out this investigation.

2. Do the results of this experiment support the hypothesis?

3. Is the data recorded quantitative or qualitative? Explain your answer.

4. Identify any sources of error.

5. Based on your results, comment on whether there is enough organic matter present in your soil sample to minimise soil compaction. Justify your response. If organic matter is low, identify ways that it can be increased.

Nutrient recycling: the carbon cycle and the nitrogen cycle

The carbon cycle

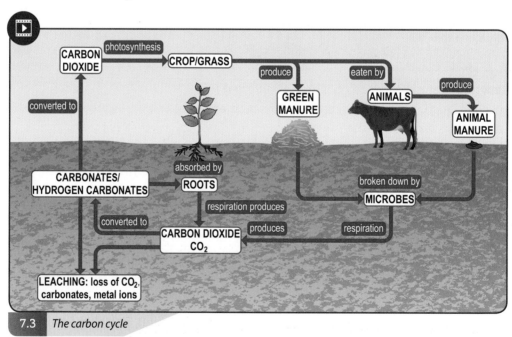

7.3   *The carbon cycle*

All organic matter contains carbon. Most living organisms derive their energy from material which contains carbon. Plants take carbon dioxide from the atmosphere during **photosynthesis**. Other living organisms produce carbon dioxide when they **respire**.

Many of the microscopic organisms in the soil convert carbon from one form to another in what is known as the carbon cycle:

- Plants take in carbon dioxide from the atmosphere during photosynthesis and convert it to carbohydrate. Plant roots respire, producing carbon dioxide.
- Animals eat plants. Animals respire to produce carbon dioxide and animal manure.
- Plants also produce manure, known as green manure, when they die.
- Microorganisms in the soil break down plant and animal manures. They respire, producing carbon dioxide.
- The carbon dioxide produced by plant roots and soil microorganisms is converted to carbonate ions in the soil. These can be taken up by plant roots but can also be lost due to leaching.
- Some of the carbon dioxide produced in the soil diffuses back into the atmosphere where it can be used by plants during photosynthesis.

Importance of organic matter

The presence of organic matter in soil is crucially important due to its role in several vital processes within the soil.

Biological

- **Nutrient reservoir:** carbon is sequestered in humus for long-term storage; other mineral nutrients are available for plant and animal uptake.
- **Biodiversity:** both micro- and macro-organisms are sustained in the soil ecosystem by the presence of organic matter, which provides a source of nutrients and energy.

Chemical

- **Soil pH buffering:** organic matter in the soil acts as a buffer on the pH of the soil, which encourages availability of plant nutrients and a suitable pH for organisms such as earthworms.
- **Cation exchange:** colloidal humus can increase cation exchange in soil.
- **Nutrient supply:** macronutrients such as nitrogen and phosphorus can be released into the soil from organic matter through mineralisation. This ensures an ongoing supply of essential nutrients to crops.

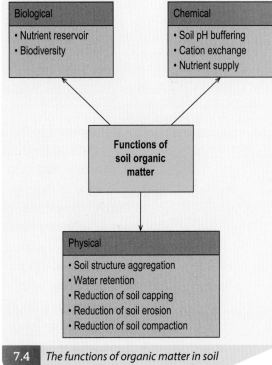

7.4 *The functions of organic matter in soil*

Physical

- **Soil structure aggregation:** organic matter encourages aggregates or peds to form in soil. This contributes to an improved soil structure. This in turn leads to improved drainage and aeration within the soil.
- **Water retention:** organic matter has a higher capacity to absorb and retain water than mineral matter. It also has the advantage that it will release the water to plant roots.
- **Reduction of soil capping:** organic matter improves soil structure, which leads to a reduction in soil capping, particularly in soils with a high sand and silt content.
- **Reduction/prevention of soil erosion:** erosion of soil is reduced by improved soil structure. This can be helped by the presence of organic matter in the soil, which aids water retention and infiltration and reduces surface erosion by wind or water.
- **Reduction of soil compaction:** increased levels of soil organic matter lead to lower levels of soil compaction.

Soil capping: when a crust forms on a soil surface and reduces the permeability of a soil. Capping can reduce aeration in a soil and increase run-off from the surface of the soil, and the surface crust can prevent the emergence of seedlings.

Levels of organic matter/organic carbon present in soil

The amount of organic matter present in soil is influenced by a number of factors. These include soil type, climate, topography, vegetation and land management practices. A combination of factors can lead to a decline in soil organic matter, which in turn leads to a decline in carbon sequestration in the soil ecosystem. Two of the main agricultural uses of land in Ireland are for grassland production and production of tillage crops. As both farming practices involve differing uses of land, they also have different effects on the amount of organic matter present in the soil.

Table 7.3 Effects of continuous tillage vs permanent grassland on soil organic matter		
	Continuous tillage	**Permanent grassland**
Presence of crop	Fallow period during winter when soil is bare	Under grass all year round
Cultivation	Cultivated regularly with the sowing of a new crop annually	Cultivation is minimal as permanent grassland is never ploughed
Level of organic matter	Lower levels of plant manures returned to the soil due to fallow period, leading to lower organic matter levels	Higher manure levels due to constant crop presence; plant material provides humus
Level of soil organic carbon	Lower in tillage enterprises	Higher in soils under permanent grassland

Methods of improving soil organic matter

There are many methods farmers can use to improve soil organic matter and in turn carbon sequestration in the soil, particularly on soils that are primarily used for tillage crops.

- **Catch crops/cover crops:** crops can provide cover in autumn/winter on soils that would otherwise lie fallow. This can maintain or improve soil organic matter. While catch crops may be used for winter fodder or sold for market, some cover crops may be ploughed into the soil as green manures, increasing the soil organic matter and increasing soil organic carbon.
- **Crop rotation:** implementing a crop rotation that includes grassland may improve organic matter levels in the soil and reduce soil erosion.
- **Farmyard manure/mushroom composts/organic fertilisers:** addition of manures or composts to the soil will improve soil organic matter levels and provide nutrients to the soil.
- **Straw:** organic matter levels and soil structure can be improved by ploughing straw back into the soil.
- **Reduced tillage/minimum tillage (min-till):** as cultivation of soil breaks up aggregates and leads to a decline in soil organic matter and organic carbon, reduction of tillage or implementing a min-till system slows the loss of organic matter and soil erosion.
- **Return to permanent pasture:** soils that have been under continuous tillage (tillage for 6 years or more) can benefit from being planted with grass, allowing organic matter levels to improve while the land is under permanent pasture.

The nitrogen cycle

Nitrogen, unlike other nutrients, is derived mainly from the atmosphere. It can also be added to the soil through the application of manures and artificial fertilisers. Like carbon, it is converted into usable forms in the soil, which can then be absorbed by plant roots. Nitrogen is converted into several different forms in the nitrogen cycle. Bacteria have a fundamental role in the conversion of nitrogen to usable forms.

- Nitrogen is applied to the land in the form of artificial fertiliser, e.g. in the form of calcium ammonium nitrate (CAN). N-fertiliser contains compounds such as nitrates, urea and ammonia. The nitrates (NO_3^-) are available immediately for plant uptake. Urea and ammonia must be converted to nitrates by the process of nitrification.
- Atmospheric nitrogen diffuses into the soil, where it undergoes nitrogen fixation.
- Nitrogen fixation is the process by which nitrogen gas is converted into nitrates, which can be used by plants. *Rhizobium* bacteria are an important part of this process.
- Rhizobia are found in nodules on the roots of leguminous plants, such as clover and beans. They form a symbiotic relationship with clover: they fix nitrogen, while at the same time receiving nutrition from the plant tissues. Planting clover in a pasture reduces the need to apply artificial nitrogen fertiliser to the land.
- Animals eat plants. Plant and animal manures are added to the soil. This organic matter undergoes mineralisation in the soil, producing ammonium ions (NH_4^+).
- The ammonium ions produced from organic matter and application of fertilisers undergoes nitrification.
- *Nitrosomonas* bacteria convert ammonium ions to nitrite ions and *Nitrobacter* bacteria convert nitrite ions to usable nitrate ions.
- Nitrate ions are then available for plant uptake.
- Some nitrates are used to provide proteins to soil microorganisms. They are not available again until the microorganism dies. This is known as immobilisation.
- Some of the nitrates are leached from the soil, while some nitrates undergo denitrification. This is where nitrates are converted to nitrogen gas and nitrogen oxide. These gases are not available to plants and diffuse back into the atmosphere.
- Nitrogen fixation also occurs in the atmosphere by lightning. Lightning splits nitrogen molecules (N_2) and the nitrogen atoms combine with oxygen in the atmosphere to form nitrogen oxides (NO and NO_2). These nitrogen oxides combine with water in the atmosphere and form nitrates, which are returned to earth by precipitation.

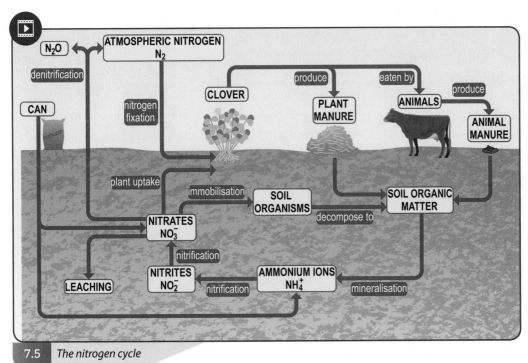

7.5   *The nitrogen cycle*

Rhizobium and clover

Some bacteria are extremely beneficial in agriculture. *Rhizobium* is a rod-shaped bacterium that has a symbiotic relationship with clover. These bacteria live in nodules attached to the roots of clover. Here, the *Rhizobium* bacteria fix atmospheric nitrogen (N_2) into nitrates. The clover plant uses nitrates produced by the *Rhizobium* to produce protein and, in return, the clover provides the bacteria with sugars.

 SPA 7.2 To isolate and grow bacteria from clover root nodules

SPECIFIED PRACTICAL ACTIVITY

Note: Alcohol is flammable, and containers of alcohol must be kept away from naked flames.

State your hypothesis and prediction.

Materials

Clover plant, sterile scalpel, disinfectant (Milton fluid), 70% alcohol solution, sterile water, sterile glass rod, sterile petri dish, inoculating loop, nutrient agar, incubator

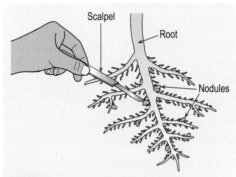

| 7.6 | *Removing the nodules from a clover root* |

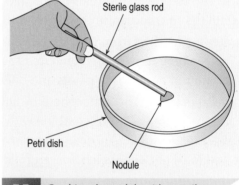

| 7.7 | *Crushing the nodule with a sterile glass rod* |

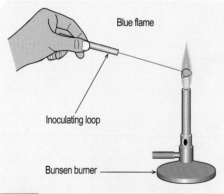

| 7.8 | *Sterilising the inoculation loop in a Bunsen burner flame* |

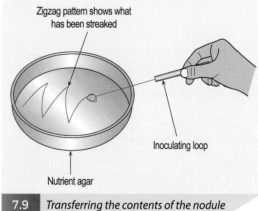

| 7.9 | *Transferring the contents of the nodule onto an agar plate* |

Method

1. Wash the roots of a clover plant under running water.
2. Use a scalpel to remove a portion of root with a large pinkish nodule.
3. Sterilise the surface of the nodule and the root with some Milton and then wash them with alcohol.

4. Rinse the root with sterile water to remove the alcohol and the disinfectant.

5. Crush the root nodule with the sterile glass rod in a sterile petri dish.

Note: The glass rod can be sterilised by dipping the end of the rod in a small amount of alcohol and then passing the end of the rod through the flame of a Bunsen burner. The alcohol will burn off the rod and sterilise it.

6. Sterilise the inoculating loop in a Bunsen burner flame until it glows red hot. Allow the loop to cool for 20 seconds.

7. Transfer some of the contents of the root nodule onto the nutrient agar.

8. Incubate upside down at a temperature of 25°C for one week.

Validation

1. Identify **two** safety precautions taken in this experiment.

2. Do the results of this experiment support the hypothesis? Explain your answer.

3. Is the data recorded quantitative or qualitative? Explain your answer.

4. What precautions were taken to ensure that there was no contamination of your agar plate?

Macroorganisms: the earthworm

Organisms that can be seen by the naked eye are described as macroorganisms. The macroorganism that is of most importance in soil and to the farmer is the earthworm.

The optimum environmental conditions for earthworm populations are in moist soils rich in organic matter, with a pH close to neutral. Earthworms prefer soils with a pH range of 6 to 8. Earthworm populations are also affected by temperature and prefer warm soil conditions above 12°C.

7.10 *The earthworm* (Lumbricus terrestris)

Benefits of earthworms

The benefits of earthworms are numerous:

- They convert organic matter (e.g. leaf litter) into humus, which improves soil fertility
- They improve soil structure through burrowing, creating channels that improve and aid aeration and drainage
- They mix layers of soil by bringing organic matter to deeper levels through burrowing
- Worm casts created by excretion are high in nitrogen, phosphates and potash due to the breakdown of organic and mineral matter by the earthworm's digestive system. This leads to higher nutrient levels in the soil. Worm casts also provide many beneficial bacteria to the soil.

SPA 7.3   To show the activity of earthworms in a soil and estimate the number of earthworms in a pasture

SPECIFIED PRACTICAL ACTIVITY

Part A: To show the activity of earthworms in a soil

State your hypothesis, prediction, independent variable, dependent variable and controlled variable.

Materials

Wormery x 2, earthworms, soil, sand, chalk and clay, leaf litter, water

Method

1. Obtain two wormeries. Fill each wormery with layers of soil, sand, clay and chalk. Alternate the layers so they can clearly be seen.

2. Add some organic matter (e.g. leaf litter) on the top layer of each wormery.

3. Add earthworms to one wormery. Leave the other wormery without worms; this will act as a control.

4. Add water to moisten the soil.

5. Cover both wormeries with a black plastic bag or cloth to block out light.

6. Leave in a cool place for at least one week ensuring that the soil is kept moist.

7. After a week, remove the cover and note any changes in the wormeries.

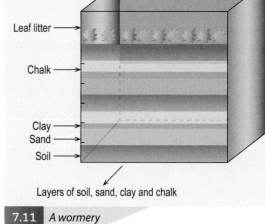

7.11   *A wormery*

Part B: To determine the population of earthworms in a pasture

State your hypothesis, prediction, independent variable, dependent variable and controlled variable.

Materials

Quadrat, shears, washing-up liquid and water solution, watering can, bucket, trundle wheel

Method

1. Mark out an area of a field or pasture with a quadrat (1 m², 0.25 m², etc.).

2. Use shears or scissors to remove all vegetation and ground cover within the quadrat.

3. Make up a solution of warm water and washing-up liquid.

4. Use a watering can to apply the solution to the area inside the quadrat.

5. Wait for a few minutes for the earthworms to come to the surface.

6. Count each worm that comes to the surface and place the worm in a bucket or suitable container so that it will not be counted a second time. Do not count worms that surface outside the quadrat.

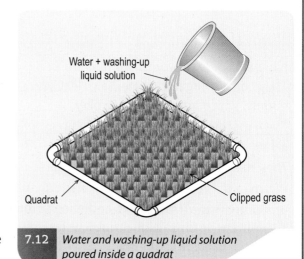

7.12   *Water and washing-up liquid solution poured inside a quadrat*

7. Record the number of worms that were collected and return the earthworms to the ground.

8. Repeat the experiment in other areas of the field.

9. Calculate an average number of earthworms per quadrat.

Results

Calculate the area of a field by measuring its length and width with a trundle wheel.

- If the quadrat was 1 m², multiply the average number of earthworms by the area of the field in metres squared to calculate the average population for the field.
- If the quadrat was 0.25 m², multiply the earthworm number by four to calculate the number of worms per metres squared and then multiply by the area of the field.

Validation

1. Do the results of these experiments support the hypothesis? Explain your answer.

2. Is the data recorded quantitative or qualitative? Explain your answer.

3. Identify ways of increasing the earthworm population in a pasture.

Worked example

A group of students carried out the above experiment to determine the earthworm population of their school football pitch. The pitch was measured with a trundle wheel and was found to be 80 m wide and 130 m long. The students sampled the earthworm population in five areas of the pitch using a 0.25 m² quadrat. The number of earthworms found in each quadrat is shown in Table 7.4.

Table 7.4				
Site 1	Site 2	Site 3	Site 4	Site 5
18	23	20	22	17

Use the above figures to calculate the earthworm population of the pitch.

Area of pitch = 130 m × 80 m = 10,400 m²

Average number of earthworms per 0.25 m² quadrat = (18 + 23 + 20 + 22 + 17) / 5 = 20

Average number of earthworms per 1 m² = 20 × 4 = 80

Area of pitch × Number of earthworms/m² = 10,400 × 80 = 832,000 earthworms in the pitch

Summary

- Soil biomass is the total mass of living material in a habitat.
- Humus is the dead and decomposing remains of plants and animals.
- Humification is the process by which soil organic matter is converted to humus.
- A microbiome is a community of microorganisms (bacteria and fungi) that inhabit a particular environment.
- Microorganisms that live in the soil include bacteria, fungi and actinomycetes.
- A parasite is an organism that lives on another host organism. The parasite usually benefits at the expense of the host and may cause damage to the host.
- The rhizosphere is the zone of soil surrounding a plant root where the biology and chemistry of the soil are influenced by the plant root.

- Mycorrhizal fungi enhance the water-holding capacity of the soil, help bind soil particles together and have a selective intake of minerals, preventing toxicity from heavy metals.
- Organic matter consists of the dead remains of plants and animals.
- The carbon cycle is the way carbon is used, reused and recycled in nature by living organisms converting it from carbon dioxide (photosynthesis) to carbohydrate and in the soil to carbonate ions.
- Soil organic matter plays an important role in the soil, including acting as a nutrient reservoir, pH buffering, cation exchange, soil structure aggregation, reduction of soil compaction.
- Organic matter levels can be improved through the use of catch crops, crop rotation, farmyard manure, min-till and return to permanent pasture.
- The nitrogen cycle is the way nitrogen is recycled in nature, being converted from atmospheric nitrogen to ammonia and then to nitrates and nitrites before being converted back into nitrogen gas.
- A symbiotic relationship is a mutually beneficial relationship between two unrelated species.
- Nitrification is the conversion of urea and ammonia into nitrates.
- Denitrification is the conversion of nitrates to nitrogen gas.
- *Rhizobium* bacteria found in the nodules on clover roots can convert nitrogen gas into nitrates in a process known as nitrogen fixation.
- Earthworms provide many benefits to soil, including converting organic matter to humus, improving soil structure, mixing layers of soil and releasing nutrients in worm casts.

PowerPoint Summary

QUESTIONS

1. What is soil biomass?
   (a) Microorganisms that live in a habitat
   (b) Decayed material found in soil
   (c) Plants and animals that live in the soil habitat
   (d) Dead plant and animal remains

2. Mycelial bacteria that have thread-like extensions are best described as:
   (a) Viruses
   (b) Parasites
   (c) Fungi
   (d) Actinomycetes

3. Carbon sequestration is the removal and storage of which gas from the atmosphere?
   (a) Oxygen
   (b) Nitrogen
   (c) Carbon dioxide
   (d) Hydrogen

4. Which percentage best represents the amount of organic matter found in soil?
   (a) 2%
   (b) 5%
   (c) 7%
   (d) 12%

5. Which of the following is a benefit of soil organic matter?
   (a) Nutrient reservoir
   (b) Reduction of soil capping
   (c) Soil pH buffering
   (d) All of the above

6. Which of the following is not a method of improving soil organic matter?

    (a) Crop rotation

    (b) Addition of fertiliser

    (c) Minimum tillage

    (d) Return to permanent pasture

7. Which of the following bacteria is involved in nitrogen fixation?

    (a) *Rhizobium*

    (b) *Nitrosomonas*

    (c) *Nitrobacter*

    (d) *E. coli*

8. *Rhizobium* bacteria are found in the root nodules of:

    (a) Perennial ryegrass

    (b) Barley

    (c) Clover

    (d) Oats.

9. Distinguish between humus and soil biomass.

10. List and describe an example of a symbiotic relationship that exists in the rhizosphere of a plant root.

11. State two benefits that mycorrhizal fungi offer to a plant.

12. (a) For the following soil samples, calculate the mass of soil organic carbon and percentage of organic carbon in the soil sample:

    (i) 50 g of soil containing 2 g of soil organic matter

    (ii) 40 g of soil containing 2.4 g of soil organic matter

    (iii) 75 g of soil containing 2.25 g of soil organic matter.

    (b) Which of the three soils would be at risk of low organic matter?

13. With the aid of a labelled diagram, outline the main steps of the carbon cycle.

14. Give two examples each for the biological, chemical and physical functions of organic matter in soil.

15. Compare the effects of continuous tillage and permanent grassland on soil organic matter under the following headings:

    (a) Cultivation

    (b) Level of soil organic carbon.

16. List and describe three methods of improving soil organic matter.

17. With the aid of a labelled diagram outline the main features of the nitrogen cycle.

18. Distinguish between nitrification and denitrification.

19. Describe four benefits of earthworms in soils.

20. A group of students carried out a survey of the earthworm population on 1 hectare of land. They sampled the population in five parts of the land using a 1 m² quadrat. The population of earthworms in each of the five areas was found to be 77, 79, 81, 70 and 73. Calculate the earthworm population per hectare (1 hectare = 10,000 m²).

 Solutions   Weblinks

8 Soil management

When you have completed this chapter you should be able to:

- Discuss the importance of drainage and soil health and fertility for good soil management
- Describe the importance of soil sampling, testing and analysis of results in relation to good soil management
- Discuss the importance of fertiliser or slurry/manure application in relation to soil management
- Identify health and safety hazards associated with soil management
- Discuss controls and precautions necessary to prevent accidents, injury and ill-health
- Appreciate the need for safe work practices, including the safe handling, use and storage of chemicals, slurry/farmyard manure and machinery
- Appreciate the impact of animals on the chemical, physical and biological properties of soil
- Describe the causes and effects of soil compaction and pollution
- Outline methods of soil conservation
- Discuss the importance of good soil management on the impact on water quality, air quality and greenhouse gas emissions
- Describe methods of maintenance of soil organic matter and soil carbon sequestration
- Consider sustainable land use and management of soil.

Management principles

Arable: land that is ploughed and used to grow crops.

The main processes that take place on farms are crop and livestock production. Good management principles are key to successful production in both arable and livestock farming. One key component of successful production is good soil management. Soil provides a medium in which crops grow, delivering nutrients and water to the crop and a medium to anchor the crop. In livestock production, grassland and other forage crops are grown on land for livestock consumption and winter fodder production. It is important that sufficient quantities of good quality fodder are produced for livestock. It is also important that livestock (in particular cattle and sheep) receive sufficient quantities of nutrients from grazing and fodder intake. While deficiency diseases can be treated and prevented with dietary supplements, this measure can be contained by ensuring there are adequate nutrients available in the soil, through the addition of fertilisers or the prevention of run-off. Soils can also harbour pests and diseases of crops and livestock and good management of soils can reduce the threat of disease on the farm.

Soil health and fertility

Essential elements, macronutrients and micronutrients

Plants would not be able to grow or complete their life cycles without 17 **essential elements**.

Three of the elements are carbon, hydrogen and oxygen. Together they form the carbohydrate glucose ($C_6H_{12}O_6$), which is produced during photosynthesis. Carbon and oxygen come from carbon dioxide, which comes from the atmosphere, and hydrogen comes from water, which plants extract from the soil.

The remaining 14 elements are classified as macronutrients or micronutrients. Macronutrients are used in large quantities by plants and micronutrients are used in small quantities. Plants extract these elements from the soil.

They are:
- **Macronutrients**: nitrogen, phosphorus, potassium, calcium, magnesium, sulfur.
- **Micronutrients**: iron, zinc, manganese, copper, boron, molybdenum, chlorine, nickel.

The macronutrient and micronutrient elements are normally found in ionic form and are derived from rock or organic parent materials. A deficiency of essential minerals might be caused by:
- The soil's low fertility, e.g. a sandy soil
- Unsuitable pH (reduced availability of nutrients).

Of most importance are the macronutrients nitrogen, phosphorus and potassium.

Nitrogen

Nitrogen (N) is the most important of the macronutrients. Without it, plant and animal life would not exist. The many ways in which nitrogen is used and recycled have already been outlined in Chapter 7, the nitrogen cycle (page 107). Nitrogen has many essential functions in both plants and animals:
- Component of chlorophyll, which is needed for photosynthesis
- Component of amino acids, which are needed to create protein
- Component of DNA, which is responsible for growth and reproduction in plants
- Component of ATP, a compound responsible for the control of metabolic energy in the plant.

Table 8.1 Nitrogen	
Sufficient nitrogen	**Nitrogen deficiency**
Rapid plant growth	Slow growth, small plants
Dark green vegetation	Pale green or yellow due to a lack of chlorophyll
High protein content in seeds	Necrosis (death) in older leaves as nitrogen is used in younger leaves

Phosphorus

Phosphorus (P) is the second most important macronutrient. Phosphorus, like many mineral elements, is found in ionic compounds in the soil. It is soluble in water and it is taken up by plants in this soluble form. However, phosphorus uptake is largely dependent on the pH of the soil. At pH levels below 5 and above 7.5, phosphorus forms compounds that are insoluble in water and unavailable to plants. This is known as the immobilisation of phosphorus. Like nitrogen, phosphorus has many essential roles in the plant:
- Required for optimum growth and reproduction
- Involved in energy transfer in the plant
- Production and development of new cells
- Transfer of DNA to new cells
- Seed formation and development.

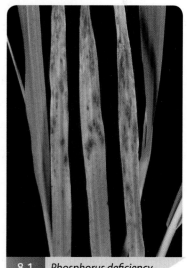

8.1 *Phosphorus deficiency in barley leaves*

Table 8.2 Phosphorus	
Sufficient phosphorus	**Phosphorus deficiency**
Vigorous growth	Stunted growth
Early maturing	Lack of fruit or flowers
Increased resistance to plant disease	Wilting
Improved flower formation	Discoloured blue-purple leaves
Increased stalk/stem strength	Delayed maturity

Potassium

Potassium (K) carries out a number of important functions in the plant:
- Protein synthesis
- Translocation of carbohydrates
- Regulation of plant stomata and water use
- Promotion of disease resistance
- Activation of plant enzymes.

Table 8.3 Potassium	
Sufficient potassium	**Potassium deficiency**
Increased crop yields	Reduced crop yields
Increased root growth	Scorching of leaves (browning) along leaf margins
	Slow growth
	Poorly developed root system
	Weak stalks leading to lodging in cereals
	Low sugar content in fruit
	Chlorosis (yellowing of leaves)

8.2   *Scorching of leaves on a potato plant*

> **DEFINITION**
>
> **Lodging:** the tendency of cereal crops to bend over so that they lie almost flat on the ground. This makes it difficult to harvest the crop and reduces the yield.

Calcium, magnesium, sulfur

Soils do not suffer from the same level of depletion of calcium, magnesium and sulfur as they do other nutrients. Of the three, sulfur is the mineral most likely to be deficient in a soil. Sulfur is now added to many of the compound fertilisers available to farmers to rectify this problem. Calcium and magnesium deficiencies are less common as both elements are present in lime, which is spread on the land to raise pH levels. These three macronutrients play an important role in plant development and without them deficiencies would occur.

Table 8.4 Role of calcium, magnesium and sulfur in plant growth		
Macronutrient	**Role in plant**	**Deficiency symptom**
Calcium (Ca)	Needed for cell wall formation	No development of terminal buds
Magnesium (Mg)	Part of the chlorophyll molecule	Chlorosis of lower plant leaves
Sulfur (S)	Contained in amino acids for protein	Chlorosis of upper plant leaves

Micronutrients

Although plants need only small amounts of the micronutrient elements, they are still important and a deficiency of one or more can cause problems, as shown in Table 8.5. A deficiency in the plant can cause a deficiency in the livestock that eats it.

Table 8.5 Deficiencies caused by lack of micronutrients	
Micronutrient	**Deficiency disease**
Iron (Fe)	Chlorosis leading to reduced yield/poor-quality fruit in pears and raspberries Anaemia in pigs
Zinc (Zn)	Yield reduction in cereals, stunted growth and reduced flowering in legumes
Manganese (Mn)	Grey speck in oats, marsh spot in peas, speckled yellows in sugar beet
Copper (Cu)	Swayback in sheep, and curled, distorted ears in wheat
Boron (B)	Heart rot/crown rot in sugar beet and carrots
Molybdenum (Mo)	Whiptail (narrow distorted leaves) in cauliflower

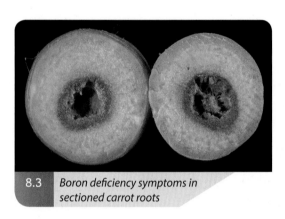

8.3   *Boron deficiency symptoms in sectioned carrot roots*

8.4   *Copper deficiency in wheat*

Availability of soil nutrients

The availability of the macronutrients and micronutrients in the soil was briefly discussed in Chapter 6 (see pages 97–98). As soils become increasing acidic or alkaline, the availability of particular nutrients is reduced and in some instances is unavailable. Most nutrients are available between pH 6 and 7. This is the optimum pH range for crop growth for a wide range of crops. In soils that are acidic, availability of nutrients can be increased by raising the pH of the soil; this is normally achieved by liming.

Soil testing

Soil testing allows farmers to determine the nutrients available on their land and to determine how suitable an area is for crop growth. Soils can be tested for a variety of nutrients, lime requirement and for pH. Once carried out, a soil test is valid for 5 years. However, farmers engaged in intense crop production may test their soils more often to optimise crop production.

Guidelines for taking a soil sample
- Divide the area to be sampled into regions 2–4 ha in size.
- Take samples from a wide range of areas, accounting for differences including different soil types, previous cropping history and slopes.
- Avoid taking samples from areas that are not typical of the area, e.g. entrances and exits to fields, around drinking troughs, beside ditches and on marshland.

- Do not sample for P and K for at least 3 months after the last P and K application.
- Do not sample for lime for at least 2 years after the last application.
- Samples should be taken using a soil auger. At least 20 samples should be taken in a W shape across the field. The samples should be 10 cm in depth.
- Samples from the same field should be stored together and sent to Teagasc for analysis.

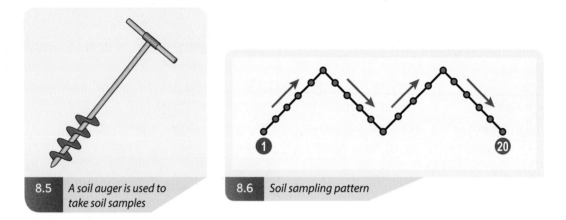

| 8.5 | A soil auger is used to take soil samples |
| 8.6 | Soil sampling pattern |

The soil index system

A soil test is best carried out every 2 to 3 years to determine the nutrient requirements of an area of land. This is particularly important if the land is farmed intensively. When a soil test has been completed, it is possible to determine which fertiliser should be applied to the land and what quantity of the fertiliser should be used. Teagasc categorises soils in a soil index system. This ranks a soil by its fertility level and its likely response to fertiliser application. The level of nutrients required to grow a particular crop and the pH of the soil are also taken into account. If the pH is too low, liming may be recommended.

When a soil test is completed, the soil sample will be given an index value. The levels of mineral nutrients in the soil are included in the results of the analysis and a recommendation is made with regard to fertiliser application.

Soils tested are ranked on the soil index from 1 to 4, where 1 is the poorest soil and 4 is the best. A soil given a rank of 1 for the availability of a particular nutrient will need a high level of fertiliser applied, whereas a soil ranked 4 will not need any. Soil tests are essential in order to be able to apply the correct fertiliser to the soil and in the correct quantities. It will also help to determine the suitability of a soil for the production of a particular crop.

Tenuous: something that is very unlikely, or has only a weak or slight effect.

Table 8.6 Teagasc soil index		
Teagasc soil index	Index description*	Response to fertiliser
1	Very low	Definite
2	Low	Likely
3	Medium	Unlikely/tenuous
4	Sufficient/excess	None

* The index description refers to the fertility levels in the soil

Fertilisers and manures

Fertilisers and manures are any naturally or artificially produced materials that can be added to soil to provide one or more of the elements that are essential for plant growth. They exist in solid, liquid and gaseous forms. The quantity of an essential element present in a fertiliser can vary enormously and it is important for a farmer to know how much of a particular element is present when spreading the fertiliser or manure on their crop. This is to ensure that the crop is receiving the correct level of nutrients. It is also important not to waste fertiliser, since this will increase the famer's costs and can also contribute to pollution.

> DEFINITION
>
> **Fertiliser:** an inorganic, manufactured material that may contain one or more of the essential elements required for crop growth.
> **Manure:** an organic material that consists of the wastes of plants and animals.

Fertilisers and essential elements

The most important elements needed for crop growth are nitrogen (N), phosphorus (P) and potassium (K). The vast majority of fertilisers sold in Ireland contain at least one of these essential elements. There are a number of commercially produced fertilisers available to farmers. The most common N, P and K straight fertilisers are listed in Table 8.7.

Table 8.7 Fertilisers		
Fertiliser	**Nutrient**	**% nutrient present**
Urea	N	46
Calcium ammonium nitrate (CAN)	N	27.5
Sulfate of ammonia	N	21
Ground rock phosphate	P	12
Superphosphate	P	7
Triple super phosphate	P	16
Muriate of potash	K	50
Sulfate of potash	K	42

Inorganic: made from material that has not come from living matter (plants or animals).

Organic: made from material that was once living matter and contains carbon.

Straight nitrogen fertilisers

The most commonly used straight nitrogen fertilisers in Ireland are urea and calcium ammonium nitrate (CAN). Ground rock phosphate is used as a straight fertiliser in forestry. The other straight fertilisers listed in Table 8.7 are not widely used as straight fertilisers but are used to produce compound fertilisers.

> DEFINITION
>
> **Straight (simple) fertiliser:** contains only one of the essential elements.
> **Compound fertiliser:** any fertiliser that contains two or more elements. Compound fertilisers are often produced by the combination of two or more straight fertilisers.

Important fertilisers

Calcium ammonium nitrate (CAN)

CAN contains nitrogen in two forms: nitrate and ammonium ions. The ammonium ions are acidic and can lower the pH of the soil. A lower soil pH would normally have a negative effect on crop growth, since some elements become unavailable to plants. However, since CAN contains calcium, which is alkaline, this acts as a buffer against the acidic ammonium ions and prevents pH levels from becoming too acidic.

One of the main advantages of CAN is that it is a fast-acting fertiliser. The nitrate in CAN is immediately available for uptake by crops. The ammonium ions are slower-acting as they must first be converted to the nitrate form. The combination of fast-acting and slow-acting fertilisers means that nitrogen is available on a long-term basis when CAN is spread on the land.

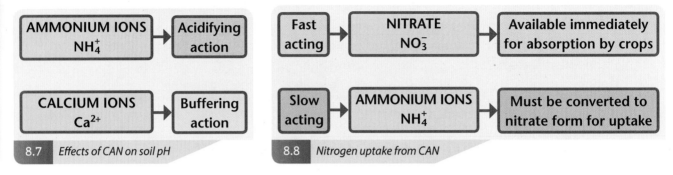

| AMMONIUM IONS NH_4^+ | → | Acidifying action |
| CALCIUM IONS Ca^{2+} | → | Buffering action |

8.7 *Effects of CAN on soil pH*

| Fast acting | → | NITRATE NO_3^- | → | Available immediately for absorption by crops |
| Slow acting | → | AMMONIUM IONS NH_4^+ | → | Must be converted to nitrate form for uptake |

8.8 *Nitrogen uptake from CAN*

8.9 *Granulated fertiliser*

8.10 *Urea and CAN are the most common straight nitrogen fertilisers used in Irish agriculture*

Granulated: describes the texture of a substance that is made up of grains or particles.

A substance is described as **hygroscopic** if it can absorb moisture from the atmosphere.

CAN is sold in granulated form, which allows for uniform spreading. CAN must be stored carefully, since it is hygroscopic. Containers should remain sealed until they are needed and should be used immediately when they are opened. If CAN is not kept in airtight conditions, the granules will cake together and cannot be spread on the land.

Urea

Urea is not as popular as CAN in terms of fertiliser usage; however, it does contain a higher concentration of nitrogen, which means less fertiliser is needed for spreading on the land. This can reduce costs and labour. Urea is a slower-acting fertiliser than CAN. It must be converted from urea to ammonium form and then into nitrate before it is available to crops. This results in a slower crop response. One of the other disadvantages of urea as a nitrogen fertiliser is that it undergoes volatilisation.

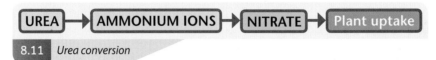

| UREA | → | AMMONIUM IONS | → | NITRATE | → | Plant uptake |

8.11 *Urea conversion*

DEFINITION

Volatilisation: a process in which the ammonium ions produced are converted to ammonia gas, which is then lost to the atmosphere.

Volatilisation is wasteful, since the ammonia lost to the atmosphere cannot be used by the growing crop. A high level of ammonia gas in the atmosphere, particularly at ground level, will cause toxicity in germinating seedlings. Volatilisation most commonly occurs when the weather is warm and dry. It can be avoided by spreading urea when rain is due, and the soil is moist. Crop losses due to volatilisation may also be reduced by spreading urea on established crops. Applying a fertiliser to an established crop is known as top-dressing. Urea is hygroscopic and needs to be stored in a similar manner to CAN.

Controls and precautions when using CAN and urea

Table 8.8 Hazards and controls when using CAN and urea		
Hazards	**Risks**	**Control**
• Calcium ammonium nitrate • Urea	• Oxidising – can cause or contribute to the combustion of other materials • Volatilisation of the fertiliser to produce toxic gases such as ammonia • Cause irritation or burning to the eyes, skin and respiratory system	• Use an automated sprayer to spread the fertiliser • Wear goggles to protect eyes, gloves and overalls to protect skin and respiratory protection to protect the lungs from exposure to the fertiliser

Toxicity: the extent to which a (poisonous) substance can damage a living organism.

Compound fertilisers

Compound fertilisers can be produced by combining straight fertilisers and by mixing N, P and K compounds in their raw state. The main advantage of compound fertilisers is that only one fertiliser may be needed for application to a crop or grassland, since it provides all the nutrients required by the crop. Compound fertilisers may contain all three main minerals or just two of the minerals. There are many compound fertilisers available, which allows a farmer to choose the most suitable fertiliser for the land. A fertiliser may be applied after a soil test has been completed to determine which mineral nutrients are required.

Naming compound fertilisers

All compound fertilisers are labelled with three numbers. These numbers represent the percentages of N, P and K (in that order) present in the fertiliser mix. Fig. 8.12 shows a fertiliser called 10-10-20. This is a commonly used fertiliser in Ireland. This fertiliser contains 10% N, 10% P and 20% K. Table 8.9 shows a list of common compound fertilisers and their uses.

8.12 *10-10-20 is one of the most commonly used compound fertilisers in Ireland*

Table 8.9 Uses of N-P-K fertiliser	
N-P-K fertiliser	**Common use**
10-10-20	Grassland, potatoes, cereals
18-6-12	Grassland, cereals
27-2.5-5	Cereal crops, intense grazing
24-2.5-10	Grassland
7-6-17	Root crops

Handling, use and storage of fertilisers

It is important to store fertiliser carefully to prevent it from getting into waterways and causing pollution but also to reduce risks to health and safety on the farm. There are a number of considerations when storing and handling fertiliser:

- Store bagged fertiliser at least 10 m away from a waterway or drain and where there is no risk of flooding
- For indoor storage, do not store fertilisers beside other combustible materials (e.g. hay or straw) or other chemicals such as pesticides or oil
- Store fertilisers of the same type together
- Do not store bagged fertiliser near sources of heat or heating systems
- Handle bags carefully to avoid damage
- Clean up any fertiliser spills to prevent it entering a drain or watercourse
- When cleaning fertiliser spreaders do not allow washings to enter a watercourse
- Always wear gloves when handling fertiliser to prevent it getting into open cuts or wounds
- Wear a mask if opening and filling spreaders in an enclosed area
- When emptying a large bag of fertiliser into a spreader do not stand under the bag when it is suspended or cut it open from the bottom; instead, cut the bag on the side in a cross shape
- Ensure all machinery used to spread fertiliser (tractor and spreader) are in good working order.

Fertiliser application

A fertiliser spreader is used to spread fertiliser on a recently sown crop or an established crop. Fertiliser is spread uniformly (usually in granulated form) on the soil surface or the growing crop.

Fertiliser may be applied in one of three ways:

8.13 *Fertiliser spreader*

1. **Placed in soil:** fertiliser is applied to the land when the seeds are sown. The seed drill sows the seed and applies the fertiliser in a band close to the seed so that nutrients are available to the crop.

2. **Broadcast:** fertiliser is spread (broadcast) on the soil using a fertiliser spreader and then harrowed into the soil. This may take place prior to sowing.

3. **Top-dressing:** fertiliser is spread on an established crop.

Manures

There are a number of different manures used in agriculture. Manure is a cheap, alternative source of nutrients. It is a cost-effective way of recycling waste on a farm, particularly animal waste. It can also reduce the need to purchase artificial fertilisers. It adds organic matter/humus to the soil, which improves soil fertility and structure. Organic farmers can also use manures on their farms. The main source of manure on a farm is animal waste.

Farmyard manure

Farmyard manure (FYM) consists of animal dung, animal urine and straw from winter bedding. The manure rots over time and can be applied to the land. As it decomposes it releases nutrients. It also contributes to the organic matter content of the soil and helps to maintain soil structure. FYM is particularly useful on organic farms as a source of nutrients where artificial fertilisers are not used. FYM is a bulky fertiliser, since the nutrient level is quite low (see Table 8.10). FYM can be applied to the land with a muck spreader.

8.14 *Spreading manure with a muck spreader*

Table 8.10 Nutrient levels and nutrient availability in manures				
Type of manure	N content (%)	P content (%)	N availability (%)	P availability (%)
Cattle manure	0.35	0.09	40	100
FYM	0.45	0.12	30	100
Mushroom compost	0.80	0.25	45	100

Slurry

Slurry is a liquid manure that contains animal dung and urine. It is collected in a tank underneath the floor in slatted housing. The level of nutrients in animal slurry is similar to that in farmyard manure, but it contains less organic matter due to the absence of straw from winter bedding. Therefore, it does not have as great a benefit to soil structure. It can be spread on the land using a slurry spreader and it is absorbed quickly because of its liquid composition. As a result, it gives a faster growth response than farmyard manure.

8.15 *Slurry spreader*

The spread of pests and diseases is a factor to be considered when spreading slurry and as such it should be confined to grassland applications. It may be used for slurry seeding when re-seeding grassland. It can also contribute to weed dispersal, particularly dock leaves.

Table 8.11 Nutrient content of animal slurry		
Animal	N content (%)	P content (%)
Cattle slurry	0.50	0.08
Sheep slurry	1.00	0.15
Pig slurry	0.42	0.08

Slurry agitation: risks and precautions

There are two major health and safety risks associated with slurry: drowning and gas poisoning. Slurry is digested anaerobically by bacteria while it is stored in an underground tank. This anaerobic digestion produces a number of toxic gases: hydrogen sulfide (H_2S), ammonia (NH_3), methane (CH_4) and carbon dioxide (CO_2). Before slurry can be pumped into the slurry tank for spreading, it is agitated to give it a uniform consistency and to liquefy the slurry which has settled in the tank over several months. This agitation also breaks the crust on the surface of the slurry, which releases the toxic gases.

Anaerobic: describes respiration in the absence of oxygen.

Agitation: Rapid stirring of liquid.

ONE LUNGFUL OF SLURRY GAS CAN KILL

ALWAYS OBEY SAFE AGITATION GUIDELINES
- ✔ Agitate on Windy Days
- ✔ Remove all Livestock & Control Pets
- ✔ Open all Doors & Control Access
- ✔ Agitate/Ventilate & Stay Away for 30 minutes
- ✔ Work Upwind at all times
- ✔ Do not enter Tanks, even when empty
- ✔ Keep Tank Openings secure at all times
- ✔ If possible, avoid agitating alone

8.16 *Slurry hazard warning signs (source: HSA)*

Risks of slurry agitation

Toxic gases are released during the first 30 minutes of slurry agitation. They can also be released if silage effluent is added to the slurry tank. Hydrogen sulfide is the most dangerous of these gases to humans and livestock. It is a dense gas (heavier than air) that settles at ground level when there is no air movement. It can suffocate humans and livestock in a matter of minutes; therefore, farmers must take precautions when agitating slurry.

Precautions when agitating slurry

- Remove livestock from slatted sheds.
- Ensure nobody enters the building.
- Keep the shed well ventilated, with all doors open to provide a draught.
- It is recommended to agitate the slurry tank on a windy day to maximise ventilation in the shed and allow the gases to be dispersed by air currents.
- Agitate the slurry from outside the shed.
- Ensure that at least two persons are present; do not stand near the slats as toxic gases are emitted.
- Persons and livestock should not re-enter the shed for 30–60 minutes after agitation or until they are certain that gases have dispersed.
- Persons entering the shed should wear breathing apparatus.

Open slurry tanks should have barriers or fencing to prevent humans or livestock falling in. Openings or hatches to slurry tanks should not be left unprotected. Covered or slatted tanks require access manholes that children cannot open easily. Fit a safety grid below the manhole to give secondary protection.

Table 8.12 Comparison of farmyard manure and slurry		
	Farmyard manure	**Slurry**
Composition	Solid	Liquid
Application to land	Muck spreader	Slurry tanker with splash plate
Storage	Manure pit	Tank underground/ underneath slatted shed
Effect on soil	Improves soil structure	Little effect on soil structure
Toxicity	No toxic gases	Produces toxic gases such as H_2S and NH_3
Organic matter content	Greater than slurry	Less than FYM due to absence of straw
Release of nutrients	Slower than slurry as solid	Faster than FYM due to liquid composition

Straw/stubble

Straw is a green manure, as it is a by-product of crop production.

The straw or stubble that remains in a field after harvest of a cereal crop can be ploughed back into the field, providing organic matter that improves soil. As it decomposes, it also releases a small amount of nutrients.

Soil drainage

Soil fertility is not the only factor to be considered when implementing good soil management practices. Soil drainage is a major factor to be considered on Irish farms in the maintenance and improvement of land for grazing and tillage. One third of agricultural land in Ireland is classified as heavy or poorly drained soil. This creates a problem for the farmer who needs to graze heavy livestock on the land, for dairy or beef production, or for the growth of tillage crops. As most livestock enterprises in Ireland are grass-based, it is important for farmers to optimise land use, through longer growing seasons, increased growth rates in grass and forage crops, and reduction in damage to land through poaching. Some improvements in the land can be made through drainage.

Soil drainage can be affected by several different factors.
- **Soil type:** a heavy clay soil which has smaller pores will lead to less infiltration than a soil with a high sand content.
- **Precipitation:** some parts of the country are subject to high levels of precipitation. Coupled with a soil with a poor infiltration rate, this can lead to waterlogging very quickly, particularly in winter months.
- **Percolation:** the amount of water that drains through the soil. This is dependent on the soil type and its capacity to drain water.
- **Groundwater:** this is where the water table is located below the soil surface, and it is at this point that the soil is saturated with water. Soils with a high water table do not have much capacity for growth.

Poaching: damage caused to wet or waterlogged land where land is cut up by livestock movement on wet soils. It causes surface vegetation to be removed and soil to be washed away. Soil may also be compacted.

Drainage systems

There are two main drainage systems used on Irish farms: a groundwater drainage system and a shallow drainage system.

- **Groundwater drainage system:** this system makes use of a series of underground pipes which collect water from the permeable layer of soil and transport it to an outfall.
- **Shallow water drainage system:** used where there is little permeability of the soil at any level, so the objective is to improve drainage capacity by using a subsoiler, or through mole drainage using a mole plough.

Benefits of soil drainage

- Improved accessibility to land for machinery.
- Less poaching of land by livestock.
- Extended grazing season.
- Less reliance on winter fodder and concentrates as livestock can graze land for longer.
- Removal of favourable conditions for some pests (e.g. snails, which breaks the liver fluke life cycle).
- Increased yields of crops (tillage and grassland) as there is increased nutrient availability and uptake and drainage increases aerobic conditions for crop roots.
- Greater window of opportunity available for tillage operations on land that is drained.

Outfall: the point where a drain empties into a river, lake or sea.

Mole plough: creates cylindrical channels in the soil which increase the drainage ability of a soil with low permeability. This type of drainage is called mole drainage.

Impact of animals on the soil

Animals have a great impact on the physical, chemical and biological characteristics of the soil.

- Livestock such as cattle can contribute to compaction and poaching of heavy soils with poor drainage.
- Manure produced by livestock can contribute nutrients and organic matter to the soil, where it is broken down by invertebrates and bacteria.
- Earthworms can improve soil structure, drainage and aeration by breaking down ingested soil, and creating channels as they move through the soil.
- Organic matter is broken down by many invertebrates, which improves soil structure and increases nutrient availability.

Management practices to reduce soil compaction and poaching

Agricultural soils can be subjected to compaction by heavy machinery or poaching by livestock. Since many agricultural soils are heavy clay soils and in areas of high precipitation, this increases the chances of soil compaction when combined with machinery use or poaching. Compacted soils can reduce yields of crops through lower availability of oxygen, water and nutrients and poor root penetration. Run-off from surface water can lead to fertilisers and other nutrients entering waterways, which can lead to eutrophication (see next page). Good soil management practices can reduce compaction and its negative effects on Irish farms.

Methods of reducing compaction and poaching:

- Reduce the number of tillage operations by using min-till to reduce compaction by tillage machinery
- Use tramlines in tillage crops to confine effects of compaction to a smaller area of a field

- Reduce stocking densities of livestock on land and employ rotational grazing systems so livestock are not left on land for a lengthy period of time; this can reduce poaching of land
- Do not carry out operations involving machinery when soil is at field capacity to prevent compaction
- Do not put animals out on saturated land to prevent poaching.

Pollution

Eutrophication

Aquatic habitats can suffer as a result of eutrophication. Rivers, streams, lakes and ponds are all examples of aquatic habitats that are at risk. Run-off from fertilisers, slurry, silage effluent and milk can all cause eutrophication. The nutrients in these substances promote excessive growth of algae, known as algal bloom. Algae die off quickly, producing a high volume of dead organic matter. This organic matter is decomposed by bacteria aerobically. As the bacteria

8.17 *Algal bloom caused by eutrophication*

respire, they deplete the oxygen levels in the water. Other aquatic creatures such as fish are not able to survive due to the lack of oxygen, and they die. When this happens on a large scale it is known as a fish kill.

DEFINITION

Eutrophication: the artificial enrichment of a habitat or environment with nutrients.

Biochemical oxygen demand

Some organic materials are more polluting than others in terms of their biochemical oxygen demand (BOD) value. Clean water has a BOD value of 1–2. Polluted water has a BOD value of 100. Table 8.13 shows the values for some common organic pollutants. The higher the value, the more polluting the material.

Biochemical: relates to chemical processes or substances that occur in living organisms.

DEFINITION

Biochemical oxygen demand (BOD): the amount of dissolved oxygen needed to break down organic material in a water sample.

Milligrams (mg): 1000 milligrams = 1 gram.

Milligrams per litre (mg/l): the number of milligrams of a substance that are dissolved in 1 litre of water.

Table 8.13 BOD values of agricultural waste	
Organic materials	**mg/l**
Raw domestic sewage	300
Dilute dairy and parlour washings	1000–2000
Dirty yard water	1500
Cattle slurry	17 000
Pig slurry	25 000
Silage effluent	65 000
Whole milk	100 000

Conservation

Pollution can be prevented and minimised in an agricultural environment in several ways. Good farm practice (e.g. adhering to guidelines regarding the spreading of effluents and fertilisers) can prevent run-off from fields into waterways, springs and groundwater sources. Much of the water used for human consumption is from groundwater sourced through wells. Schemes created by the Department of Agriculture can help and encourage farmers to adhere to regulations regarding the disposal of organic wastes and spreading of fertilisers. Penalties and fines can be imposed on those who do not comply.

Spreading fertilisers and the Nitrates Regulations

There are restrictions on the spreading of fertilisers enforced by the Nitrates Regulations (also known as the Nitrates Directive). To minimise run-off, waste and water pollution, fertilisers should not be spread in the following conditions:

Effluent: discharge of liquid waste from a substance or run-off from land.

- If the land is waterlogged
- If the land is flooded or is likely to flood
- If the land is snow-covered or frozen
- If heavy rain is forecast within 48 hours
- If the ground is steeply sloped and, combined with other factors, poses a risk of water pollution.

Run-off from fertilisers can also be minimised by following the guidelines below.

- Do not apply fertiliser within 1.5 m of a watercourse.
- Do not spread fertilisers or effluents near watercourses, bore holes, springs or wells.
- Do not apply chemical fertiliser between 15 September and 15 January.*
- Do not apply organic fertilisers between 15 October and 15 January.*
- Do not apply farmyard manure between 1 November and 31 January.*

*Dates vary slightly with region.

Storage of organic waste and effluents

Farmyard manure, slurry, silage effluent, soiled water and fertilisers should be collected and stored on a farm until they can be spread on the land or disposed of appropriately. The storage facilities (e.g. dung stead, silage pit) should be maintained so that they are free from structural damage that would allow seepage of these materials into groundwater.

Impact on water quality and greenhouse gases

Water quality

There are a number of ways that water quality can be affected detrimentally in agriculture. Water pollution mainly results from run-off of fertilisers, effluent and slurry from land. If these pollutants enter a watercourse or contaminate groundwater, aquatic life can be adversely affected. Water sources used for domestic consumption may also be affected and may cause groundwater pollution.

- Eutrophication: excess nitrates and phosphates washed from soil into water can lead to algal bloom, depleted oxygen levels in waterways and in turn lead to fish kills.
- Sedimentation from soil erosion can be washed into streams and lakes which can reduce water clarity and quality.

Farmers are required to adhere to several practices to ensure good water quality and protection of water quality against pollution by nitrates. These practices include:

- Divert all clean water to a clean water outfall
- Prevent clean water from becoming soiled

- Minimise the amount of soiled water that is produced on the holding
- Collect and manage all organic fertilisers, effluents and soiled waters in a way that will prevent run-off or seepage, directly or indirectly, into ground waters or surface waters
- Have sufficient storage for all of the above and silage effluent, or effluent from other crops when required
- Do not stockpile or store farmyard manure on land during the prohibited spreading period
- The total amount of livestock manure applied to land in a calendar year must not contain more than 170 kg of nitrogen per hectare
- Apply fertilisers in a uniform manner
- Adhere to buffer zones when applying fertilisers
- Keep records of the quantity of fertiliser spread on the land and where it was spread.

Greenhouse gases and air quality

Methane (CH_4), nitrous oxide (N_2O) and carbon dioxide (CO_2) are all greenhouse gases that contribute to climate change. In an agricultural context, methane is produced by livestock, nitrous oxide from fertilisers and manures. Soils play an important role in the production and use of these gases. Any practice that increases the amount of organic matter in the soil decreases the amount of carbon dioxide that is released into the atmosphere. Microorganisms that live in wet, poorly aerated soils release methane gas as they decompose organic matter. Nitrous oxide is a product of denitrification in soil.

Ammonia emissions from animal manures have a negative impact on air quality. Ammonia particles in the atmosphere can cause respiratory problems in humans.

Buffer zone: land beside a waterway that controls and prevents pollution of the waterway. It helps to maintain water quality.

Maintenance of soil organic matter and soil carbon sequestration

To ensure sustainable land use and to maximise carbon sequestration through maintenance of soil organic matter, farmers need to prevent soil erosion. This can be achieved through minimum soil cover, particularly at times in the year when the land would otherwise lay bare. Minimum land management is also an important factor in the maintenance of soil. Min-till operations should be implemented where possible. Soil organic matter levels can be maintained by the addition of manures and by not burning stubble such as straw as it adds valuable organic matter to soil and maintains soil structure. Maintaining levels of organic matter in the soil in turn allows for carbon sequestration levels to be maintained.

Good management practices for sustainable land use

Farmers can implement a number of practices to ensure good soil management on the farm and to ensure a long-term plan of sustainable land use. These practices include:

- Crop rotation
- Nutrient management programmes
- Soil testing (nutrients, organic matter, pH)
- Min-till or no-till
- Protection of beneficial organisms
- Irrigation of land when necessary
- Drainage of land
- Encouraging biodiversity on farm land (see Chapter 32).

Summary

- Macronutrients are used in large quantities by plants and micronutrients are used in small quantities.
- Macronutrients: nitrogen, phosphorus, potassium, calcium, magnesium, sulfur.
- Micronutrients: iron, zinc, manganese, copper, boron, molybdenum, chlorine, nickel.
- Nitrogen is needed for photosynthesis, protein production, growth and reproduction in plants. Plants deficient in nitrogen show slow growth, appear pale green from a lack of chlorophyll and are necrotic.
- Phosphorus is needed for growth and reproduction, production of new cells and seed formation. Plants deficient in phosphorus have stunted growth, do not produce fruit and show signs of wilting and leaf discolouration.
- Potassium is needed for protein synthesis and translocation of carbohydrates. A lack of potassium leads to scorching of leaves, reduced crop growth, poor root development and slow growth.
- Most nutrients are available between pH 6 and 7. As soils become increasingly acidic or alkaline the availability of particular nutrients is reduced. In some instances these nutrients are unavailable.
- Soil testing allows a farmer to determine the nutrients available in their land and to determine how suitable an area is for crop growth.
- When sampling a soil, a soil auger should be used to take at least 20 samples from a variety of areas in a field.
- Teagasc categorises soils in a soil index system. This ranks a soil by its fertility level and its likely response to fertiliser application
- Fertiliser may be applied by placing it in the soil, broadcasting it or top dressing.
- Farmyard manure (FYM) consists of animal dung, animal urine and straw from winter bedding.
- Slurry is liquid manure that contains animal dung and urine.
- Slurry releases toxic gases such as hydrogen sulfide and methane when agitated. Proper ventilation is necessary when agitating slurry. Slurry tanks should have barriers or fencing to prevent humans or livestock falling in and drowning.
- Soil drainage can be affected by several factors: soil type, percolation, precipitation and groundwater.
- Animals have a range of influences on the soil, including damage by poaching, contribution of organic matter and nutrients from dung and improvement of soil structure by earthworms.
- Eutrophication is the artificial enrichment of a habitat with nutrients.
- Water quality on farms can be maintained by ensuring fertilisers, effluents and washings are collected and prevented from entering watercourses.

 PowerPoint Summary

QUESTIONS

1. Which of the following is not a macronutrient?

   (a) Nitrogen
   (b) Calcium
   (c) Sulfur
   (d) Zinc

2. Which of the following is not a micronutrient?

   (a) Iron
   (b) Copper
   (c) Selenium
   (d) Magnesium

3. Which of the following statements best describes the role of nitrogen in plants?

   (a) Component of chlorophyll
   (b) Sufficient nitrogen leads to high protein content in seeds
   (c) Component of DNA, which is responsible for growth and reproduction
   (d) All of the above

4. Swayback is a deficiency disease due to a lack of which element?

   (a) Iron
   (b) Zinc
   (c) Copper
   (d) Cobalt

5. Which of the following steps is recommended when soil sampling?

   (a) Take one soil sample from the centre of the field.
   (b) Take a sample immediately after applying fertiliser.
   (c) Take at least 20 samples in a W shape.
   (d) Include ditches, entrances and exits to fields when sampling.

6. What is the name given to the piece of equipment used to take soil samples?

   (a) Augur
   (b) Trowel
   (c) Hoe
   (d) Rake

7. Urea and sulfate of ammonia are examples of fertilisers that contain large amounts of:

   (a) Potassium
   (b) Phosphorus
   (c) Carbon
   (d) Nitrogen.

8. Which of the following are considered safety hazards when spreading CAN or urea?

   (a) They are oxidising substances.
   (b) They cause irritation to eyes and skin.
   (c) They can volatilise, producing ammonia.
   (d) All of the above.

9. Which of the following are toxic gases released when agitating slurry?

   (a) Oxygen and carbon dioxide
   (b) Carbon dioxide and nitrogen
   (c) Hydrogen sulfide and ammonia
   (d) Hydrogen sulfide and oxygen

10. State two functions of nitrogen in plants.

11. State two signs of nitrogen deficiency in plants.

12. What are the signs of phosphorus deficiency in plants?

13. Why is the pH of the soil important for the availability of phosphorus to plants?

14. Name the micronutrients with the following chemical symbols: Fe, Zn, Mn.

15. Name the deficiency disease associated with:

   (a) Molybdenum
   (c) Iron

   (b) Boron
   (d) Manganese.

16. At what pH range are most nutrients available for plant uptake?

17. Why is soil sampling carried out?

8.18   *Soil sampling*

18. List two areas that should not be sampled for soil testing.

19. How often should a soil be sampled?

20. If the results of a soil test record 1 for nitrogen, 4 for potassium and 3 for phosphorus, what does this mean in the context of soil fertility on the farm? Suggest a suitable fertiliser that may be applied to the land, if necessary.

21. Describe two precautions you would take to ensure the safe storage of fertiliser.

22. List three precautions you would take when handling and using fertiliser.

23. Compare and contrast slurry and FYM. Suggest two disadvantages of spreading slurry.

24. Describe four precautions that should be taken when agitating slurry.

25. Suggest two ways that drainage of land may optimise land use.

26. Describe two factors which may affect soil drainage.

27. Describe two positive effects animals may have on soil.

28. Outline how a farmer might reduce compaction of soil on a farm.

29. What is eutrophication? Name three pollutants which may contribute to eutrophication.

8.19   *Algal bloom resulting from eutrophication*

30. Identify four ways in which farmers can minimise the run-off of fertilisers into watercourses.

31. Describe four ways in which farmers can maintain water quality on a farm.

Solutions   Weblinks

Crops

STRAND

3

9	Plant physiology	134
10	Applied plant genetics	144
11	Plant classification	165
12	Principles of crop production and management	184
13	Barley	206
14	Potatoes	219
15	Catch crop: Kale (H)	231
16	Energy crop: Miscanthus (H)	240
17	Grassland characteristics and growth	252
18	Grazing and grassland management	265
19	Sowing and reseeding grassland	279
20	Conservation of grass	287

Plant physiology

When you have completed this chapter you should be able to:

- Identify the main structures of the leaf and outline their role in photosynthesis
- Explain the term 'aerobic respiration'
- Identify the role of mitochondria and the cytosol in aerobic respiration
- Identify the functions of xylem, root hairs and stomata in transpiration
- Explain osmosis
- Explain how transpiration occurs in plants
- Explain the role that root hairs, endoderm and xylem vessels have in nutrient absorption
- Outline the role that active transport plays in the absorption of nutrients by the root hairs.

Vascular tissue

Vascular tissue is transport tissue and is composed of xylem and phloem.

Xylem tissue transports water and minerals from the roots up to the leaves. Phloem transports sugars produced by photosynthesis from the leaves to other parts of the plant for storage or for use.

Xylem

Xylem tissue is composed of two types of cells: xylem vessels and xylem tracheids. All xylem tissue is dead tissue. There is no nucleus or cytoplasm in these cells. The cell walls of xylem cells are reinforced with lignin, a very strong, water-resistant and durable organic compound, which provides strength and support to the cell walls of the xylem vessels and tracheids. If the xylem walls were not reinforced with lignin, then the cell walls of the xylem vessels would collapse as a result of the constant tension created by the water moving through them.

Xylem vessels are much wider and shorter than xylem tracheids. Xylem vessels have no end walls, while tracheids have tapered perforated end walls. Pits in both the xylem vessels and tracheids allow for the lateral movement of water. Both xylem vessels and tracheids are arranged in plants so that there is a continuous route for water to travel from the roots up to the leaves.

Tapered: comes to a point.

Perforated: has small holes.

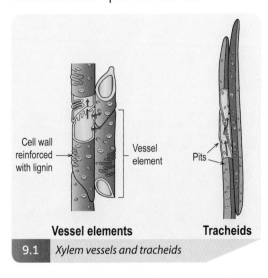

9.1 *Xylem vessels and tracheids*

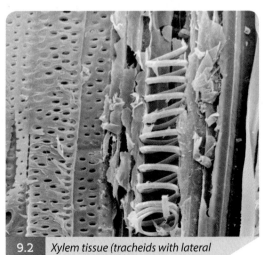

9.2 *Xylem tissue (tracheids with lateral pits and a spiral of lignin)*

Phloem

Phloem tissue is composed of sieve tubes and companion cells. Phloem tissue is living tissue; however, the sieve tubes do not have nuclei and require companion cells to control and maintain the sieve tube.

Sieve tubes are long cells with perforated walls known as sieve plates. The cell walls of phloem tissues are not lignified.

The main function of the phloem tissue is the transport of sugars. Sugars can move up and down the phloem tissue depending on where the food is needed. In the stems and the leaves of plants, xylem and phloem tissue are found together in vascular bundles.

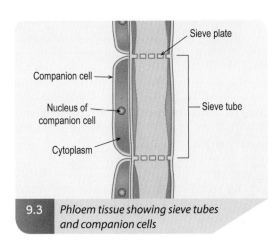

9.3 *Phloem tissue showing sieve tubes and companion cells*

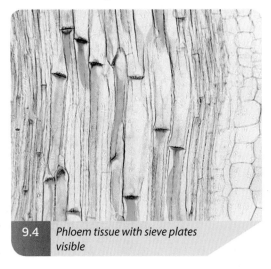

9.4 *Phloem tissue with sieve plates visible*

Vascular bundles: are found in the stems and leaves of plants. They are composed of xylem and phloem.

Photosynthesis

Photosynthesis and the structure of the leaf

Plants are autotrophic, meaning that they can make their own food. The leaves of plants are highly specialised organs and their main function is to produce food by photosynthesis. The cells in the leaves of plants are packed with chloroplasts. Chloroplasts contain the green pigment chlorophyll which is located within the thylakoid membrane. When a plant is photosynthesising, the chlorophyll molecule absorbs light energy from the sun and uses this energy to combine hydrogen from water and carbon dioxide from the atmosphere to produce glucose and oxygen.

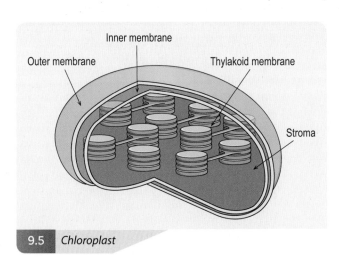

9.5 *Chloroplast*

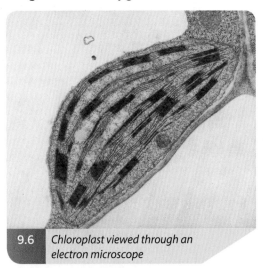

9.6 *Chloroplast viewed through an electron microscope*

Glucose produced by photosynthesis can have a number of different uses in the plant.

$$\text{Carbon dioxide} + \text{Water} \xrightarrow[\text{Sunlight}]{\text{Chlorophyll}} \text{Glucose} + \text{Oxygen}$$

$$6CO_2 + 6H_2O \xrightarrow[\text{Sunlight}]{\text{Chlorophyll}} C_6H_{12}O_6 + 6O_2$$

The glucose can be:
- Converted into starch and stored by the plant
- Converted into cellulose, which is used to provide strength and support to the plant cell wall
- Broken down in aerobic respiration in order to provide energy for the plant.

Likewise, oxygen (which is often seen as a waste product of photosynthesis) is not completely excreted by the plant. Some of the oxygen produced by photosynthesis is used for aerobic respiration. The excess oxygen is excreted through the stomata.

The leaf has many adaptations for photosynthesis (see Table 9.1).

9.7 *Elodea producing oxygen*

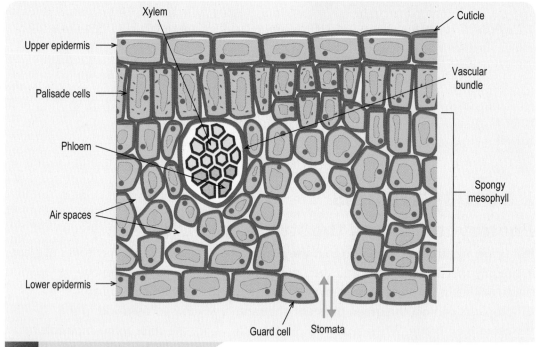

9.8 *A transverse section of a leaf*

Table 9.1 Adaptations of a leaf for photosynthesis	
Structure	**Adaptation**
Leaf	Flat shape gives a large surface area to maximise light absorption for photosynthesis; leaf is extremely thin and this facilitates the diffusion of gases
Waxy cuticle	Prevents water loss
Palisade layer	The cells are tightly packed together and contain a large number of chloroplasts to maximise the absorption of light for photosynthesis
Spongy mesophyll	Many air spaces allow for the rapid diffusion of gases
Vascular tissue (xylem and phloem)	Transport of water for photosynthesis and the removal of sugars for storage
Stomata	Gaseous exchange
Guard cells	Open and close stomata

Respiration

Both plant and animal cells obtain their energy in the form of adenosine triphosphate (ATP) by aerobic respiration. Aerobic respiration occurs in every living plant cell.

Aerobic respiration: the controlled release of energy from glucose in the presence of oxygen.

The overall balanced chemical equation for the reaction is:

Glucose + Oxygen $\longrightarrow$ Carbon dioxide + Water + Energy

$$C_6H_{12}O_6 + 6O_2 \longrightarrow 6CO_2 + 6H_2O + Energy$$

Respiration occurs in two parts. The first stage, glycolysis, takes place in the cytosol. This stage does not require oxygen and releases only a small amount of energy. During this stage, glucose is broken down into two molecules of pyruvic acid. The pyruvic acid passes into the mitochondria in the cells. Mitochondria are a type of cell organelle that is found in the cytoplasm and it is commonly referred to as the power house of the cell. In the presence of oxygen, the pyruvic acid is broken down further by a series of chemical reactions known as the Krebs cycle and the electron transport system. Pyruvic acid is completely broken down into carbon dioxide and water. The combination of the Krebs cycle and the electron transport system produces a large amount of ATP.

Cytosol: the liquid component of the cytoplasm.

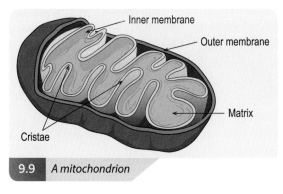

9.9 A mitochondrion

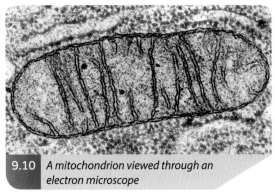

9.10 A mitochondrion viewed through an electron microscope

The Krebs cycle occurs in the matrix of the mitochondria and the electron transport system is located on the inner foldings of the mitochondria. The folding of the inner membrane creates a large surface area for the electron transport system.

Organelle: 'little organs'; specialised structures within a cell that carry out specific functions. Mitochondria and chloroplasts are types of organelles.

Water transport

In plants, xylem tissue is responsible for the transport of water and minerals from the roots to the leaves. Water is an essential ingredient for photosynthesis and it is vital that photosynthesising cells have a plentiful supply. The movement of water from the roots up to the leaves of plants can be explained by root pressure, cohesion–tension and transpiration. As a result, water moves as a continuous column up the xylem tissue from the roots to the leaves. This movement of water in the xylem vessels is known as the transpiration stream.

Transpiration stream: the uninterrupted passage of water in the xylem tissue from the roots up to the leaves in plants.

Root pressure

Root pressure is caused by the continuous movement of water by osmosis, from the soil into the root hairs. This causes a build-up of pressure, which forces water into the xylem vessels and tracheids. Root hairs increase the surface area for the absorption of water. Root pressure on its own is not sufficient to push water up to the leaves of large plants. Root pressure can be illustrated by cutting a herbaceous plant close to the bottom of the stem. A little bubble of water will form on the top of the cut stem. Root pressure can be responsible for forcing water out of the leaves of grasses and strawberry plants in a process known as guttation.

Guttation is the oozing of water from the leaves of plants as a result of root pressure.

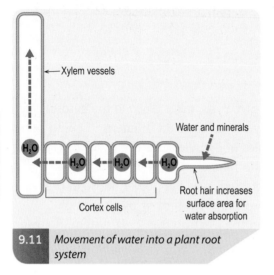

9.11 *Movement of water into a plant root system*

9.12 *Root pressure forces water out of the leaves of grass*

DEFINITION

Osmosis: the movement of water from an area of high concentration to an area of low concentration across a semi-permeable membrane. Osmosis does not require energy.

Transpiration

Many plant species have a waxy cuticle on the surface of the leaf. This prevents the loss of water from the leaf's surface. However, water is constantly lost through the stomata by evaporation on the underside of the leaf. As a result, water is drawn out of the xylem vessels in the leaf to replace that lost through evaporation. This pulls water up the xylem vessels. Transpiration is a passive process as it requires no energy; however, the rate of transpiration can be controlled by the opening and closing of the stomata. Specialised cells known as guard cells regulate the opening and closing of the stomata. Stomata are normally open during the day in order to facilitate photosynthesis. However, if water is in short supply the guard cells will close the stomata to prevent water loss.

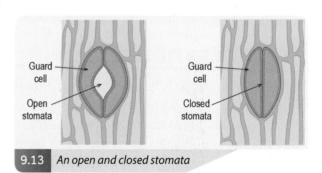

9.13 *An open and closed stomata*

DEFINITION

Transpiration: the loss of water by evaporation from the leaves.

Cohesion–tension model

Water molecules tend to stick together, causing a force known as cohesion. In addition, the loss of water from the leaves by transpiration creates a tension and the combination of these forces together pulls water as a continuous column up the xylem vessels and tracheids. As we have seen, the xylem vessels and tracheids are structurally adapted to cope with the constant changes of pressure caused by the movement of water up through them. The small perforations between the xylem tracheids reduce the number and size of air bubbles that can sometimes form. Xylem tissue is dead tissue, so the xylem tissue itself does not require water. This means that all of the water absorbed by the root can travel up through the xylem tissue without being used up along the way.

Factors that affect the rate of transpiration

The rate of transpiration is not constant and is influenced by a number of factors. The factors that affect transpiration are summarised in Table 9.2.

Table 9.2 Factors that affect the rate of transpiration	
Factor	**Effect**
Temperature	Evaporation of water from the leaves of plants helps to keep them cool. On hot days the rate of transpiration increases. The rate of transpiration decreases on cold days.
Wind	On calm days a layer of water vapour builds up around the stomata, increasing the humidity and decreasing the rate of transpiration. On windy days the rate of transpiration increases as air movement across the stomata prevents the build-up of humid air.
Soil water	If plants experience a water shortage, as in the case of droughts, the stomata of the leaves close in an effort to reduce transpiration and conserve water. When soil water is plentiful, plants respire at a higher rate.
Light	Light stimulates the opening of the stomata, increasing the rate of transpiration. Stomata are normally closed at night, reducing the rate of transpiration.
Humidity	If the air is dry and low in water vapour, the rate of transpiration increases. If there is rain or the air is high in water vapour, the rate of transpiration decreases as the air becomes saturated with water vapour and can hold no more water.

Cohesion: the sticking together of particles of the same substance.

Humidity: the amount of water vapour in the atmosphere.

Nutrient absorption

Nutrients are found either dissolved in the soil solution or attached to the soil colloids. Plant roots have millions of tiny outgrowths called root hairs. Root hairs are extensions of the epidermis and have very thin walls. They greatly increase the surface area for the uptake of water and the absorption of nutrients from the soil. The nutrients are absorbed into the root hairs from the soil solution by active transport.

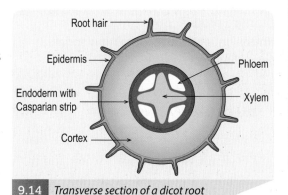

9.14 *Transverse section of a dicot root*

Dicotyledon (dicot): a flowering plant with two cotyledons (seed leaves), which are often the first leaves to emerge from the germinating seed.

The movement of the nutrient ions (calcium, magnesium, etc.) is from a region of low concentration (soil solution) to a region of high concentration (inside the root) against a concentration gradient. In order for this to occur, energy is required. Root cells have many mitochondria present in order to supply the energy required for the absorption of nutrients. The nutrients are then passed from the cortex towards the centre of the root to the xylem vessels.

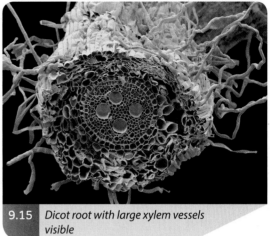

9.15 *Dicot root with large xylem vessels visible*

In order to reach the xylem vessels the nutrients must pass through the endoderm layer. The endodermis cells are embedded in the Casparian strip. The Casparian strip is a ring-like band of corky tissue that surrounds the cells of the endoderm but does not cover the front or the back of the cells. It prevents water moving between the cells of the endoderm, therefore forcing all the nutrients and water to pass through the cells of the endoderm. Special carrier molecules in the cell walls of the endoderm cells allow the cells to recognise and select specific nutrient ions. The nutrients then move through the endoderm cells and into the xylem vessels, where they are transported upwards from the roots to the stems and leaves.

Casparian strip: an important barrier in plants that protects the plant against microorganisms and regulates the uptake of water and minerals. The Casparian strip also prevents the leakage of nutrients from the plant root back into the soil.

> DEFINITION
>
> **Active transport:** the movement of a substance from an area of low concentration to an area of high concentration against a concentration gradient. Active transport requires energy.

Leguminous: describes members of the Fabaceae family (formerly known as Leguminosae). They have a symbiotic relationship with bacteria that allows them to fix nitrogen.

Some symbiotic relationships between plant roots and microorganisms also improve the uptake of nutrients from the soil. Mycorrhiza is a fungus that helps to create a larger root surface area, thus enhancing nutrient uptake. *Rhizobium* is a bacterium that lives in the nodules of leguminous plants (e.g. clover). The *Rhizobium* bacteria have the ability to fix atmospheric nitrogen into soluble nitrates, which can then be used by the plants to produce protein. Both mycorrhiza and *Rhizobium* benefit by obtaining sugars from the plants.

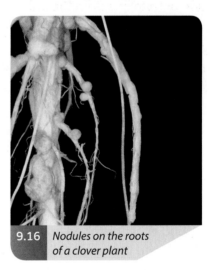

9.16 *Nodules on the roots of a clover plant*

Summary

- Vascular tissue is transport tissue that is composed of phloem and xylem.
- Xylem tissue transports water and minerals from the roots up to the leaves. Phloem transports sugars produced by photosynthesis from the leaves to other parts of the plant for storage.
- Plants are autotrophic, which means they can produce their own food.
- The chlorophyll molecule absorbs light energy from the sun and uses this energy to combine hydrogen from water and carbon dioxide from the atmosphere to produce glucose and oxygen.

- Excess oxygen is excreted by the stomata.
- The palisade layer of cells are packed with chloroplasts and it is these cells that carry out the majority of photosynthesis.
- Stomata allow for gaseous exchange to occur, with carbon dioxide diffusing into the leaf for photosynthesis and oxygen and water vapour diffusing out.
- The opening and closing of the stomata are controlled by the guard cells.
- Both plant and animal cells obtain their energy in the form of ATP by aerobic respiration.
- Aerobic respiration is the controlled release of energy from glucose in the presence of oxygen.
- Glycolysis is the first stage of respiration. It occurs in the cytosol of the cell and produces two molecules of pyruvic acid and a small amount of energy. Oxygen is not required for this stage.
- Inside the mitochondria, in the presence of oxygen, the pyruvic acid is completely broken down into carbon dioxide and water. This produces a large of amount of ATP.
- The movement of water from the roots to the leaves of plants is caused by a combination of root pressure, cohesion–tension and transpiration.
- The movement of water in the xylem vessels from the roots to the leaves is called the transpiration stream.
- Root pressure is caused by the continuous movement of water by osmosis from the soil into the root hairs.
- Water is constantly lost through the stomata in the leaves by evaporation, which draws the water out of the xylem vessels to replace water lost.
- Root hairs greatly increase the surface area for the uptake of water and the absorption of nutrients from the soil.
- The nutrients are absorbed into the root hairs from the soil solution by active transport.
- The endodermis cells are embedded in the Casparian strip. The Casparian strip is an important barrier that regulates the uptake of water and nutrients and also protects the plant.
- Some symbiotic relationships between plants and microorganisms help to improve the uptake of nutrients from the soil.

PowerPoint Summary

QUESTIONS

1. Xylem tissue is composed of which two types of cells?
   (a) Xylem vessels and companion cells
   (b) Xylem vessels and sieve tubes
   (c) Tracheids and sieve tubes
   (d) Xylem vessels and tracheids
2. The walls of xylem tissue are reinforced with:
   (a) Cellulose
   (b) Lignin
   (c) Starch
   (d) Glucose.

3. The function of the companion cells in phloem tissue is to:

    (a) Control the movement of water in the tracheids

    (b) Produce lignin

    (c) Control and maintain the sieve tube

    (d) Control the movement of minerals in the sieve tube.

4. The purpose of the palisade layer in the leaf is to carry out:

    (a) Gaseous exchange   (c) Transpiration

    (b) Photosynthesis   (d) Active transport.

5. Which of the following facilitates the diffusion of gases in the leaf?

    (a) The thinness of the leaf   (c) Open stomata

    (b) The spongy mesophyll layer   (d) All of the above

6. The rate of transpiration from a leaf is regulated by:

    (a) The presence of a waxy cuticle

    (b) The evaporation of water from the stomata

    (c) The opening and closing of the stomata by the guard cells

    (d) The loss of water from the xylem vessels.

7. How are the xylem vessels and tracheids adapted to facilitate the movement of water through them?

    (a) They have pits to allow lateral movement of water   (c) Xylem tissue is dead tissue

                                           (d) All of the above

    (b) The cell walls are reinforced with lignin

8. Nutrients are absorbed into the root hairs from the soil solution by:

    (a) Osmosis   (c) Active transport

    (b) Diffusion   (d) None of the above.

9. The function of the Casparian strip is to:

    (a) Regulate the movement of water and minerals towards the xylem tissue

    (b) Regulate the movement of sugar and water towards the xylem tissue

    (c) Regulate the movement of minerals and sugar towards the xylem tissue

    (d) Regulate the movement of sugars and water towards the phloem tissue.

10. The correct sequence for the movement of nutrients from the soil solution into the xylem vessels is as follows:

    (a) Root hairs, endoderm, cortex and xylem vessels

    (b) Endoderm, root hair, cortex and xylem vessels

    (c) Root hairs, Casparian strip, endoderm and xylem vessels

    (d) Root hairs, cortex, endoderm and xylem vessels.

11. Fig. 9.17 represents two forms of vascular plant tissue.

    (a) Name this type of vascular tissue.

    (b) Identify the two forms of this tissue.

    (c) What plant process are these tissues necessary for?

    (d) Explain two features of this tissue that are necessary for its function in part (c) above.

12. Name another vascular tissue.

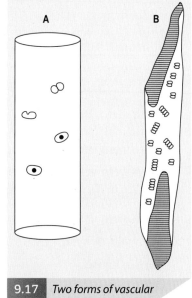

9.17   *Two forms of vascular plant tissue*

13. Identify each of the cell organelles in Fig. 9.18.

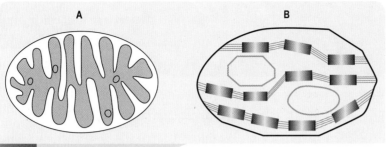

A   B

| 9.18 | *Two cell organelles* |

(a) What process is cell organelle A essential for?

(b) Give a reason for the many inner foldings in organelle A.

(c) Give one location in plants where you would find a high concentration of organelle A and give a reason why.

(d) What pigment is normally found in cell organelle B? What is the function of this pigment?

(e) What plant process is cell organelle B required for?

(f) In what precise location in the plant would you find a high concentration of organelle B?

14. (a) Name the openings in leaves that allow the entry of carbon dioxide for photosynthesis. State a factor that regulates the diameter of these openings.

(b) Draw a clearly labelled diagram of the internal structure of the leaf.

(c) Identify four features of the leaf that are fundamental in enabling it to carry out photosynthesis.

(d) Explain briefly how these features adapt the leaf to its function in photosynthesis.

15. Fig. 9.19 represents a transverse section through a root.

(a) Name the parts labelled A to D.

(b) Nutrients are absorbed from the soil solution into the root cells by the root hairs.

(i) Identify two features of root hairs that facilitate the absorption of plant nutrients.

(ii) Explain how plant nutrients enter root hairs and then pass to the vascular tissue.

(iii) Discuss the importance of the Casparian strip in protecting the plant and regulating the uptake of nutrients.

(iv) In which vascular tissue will the nutrients now rise up through the plant?

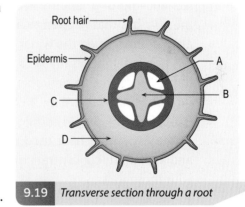

Root hair

Epidermis   A

C   B

D

| 9.19 | *Transverse section through a root* |

16. Distinguish between osmosis and active transport.

Solutions — Weblinks

When you have completed this chapter you should be able to:

- Describe the principles of genetic improvement and selection: natural selection, progeny testing, performance testing, physical traits, genotyping and genomic selection
- Appreciate the role of innovation and biotechnological applications in crop development and management
- Understand the principles of genetic engineering, identifying genes in characterised crop genomes and understanding how they produce proteins to tackle specific crop diseases
- Evaluate the ethical and economic considerations and arguments arising from biotechnological applications as applied to crop management; for example, the genetic enhancement of crop varieties against pests and diseases using traditional biotechnology and more recent technologies such as genome editing
- Investigate the complexity associated with the genetic inheritance of traits by hybridising two varieties to determine the rate of transfer of the required trait (e.g. petal colour) to the next progeny (SPA).

The principles of genetic improvement and selection

Genetic improvement involves change in a plant or animal. In an agricultural context the changes that happen to a plant or animal must provide a benefit to the plant or animal, the farmer, the wider community or the environment.

Applied genetics involves the manipulation of hereditary characteristics in order to improve or produce desirable characteristics in offspring. Desirable characteristics might include improved fertility, increased milk production or better growth rates in breeds of cattle (see Chapter 24) or higher yields and better disease resistance in plants. For centuries, farmers have used controlled breeding, known as selective breeding, in plants and animals to concentrate desirable traits in offspring by careful selection of parents with those traits.

In addition, genetic engineering allows the production of new plant species that contain genes from unrelated organisms, providing a new generation of plants known as genetically modified organisms.

Natural selection

The theory of biological evolution by natural selection was proposed by British naturalist Charles Darwin.

Darwin proposed that because resources are limited in nature, organisms with traits that favour their survival and ability to reproduce tend to produce more offspring than those lacking in these heritable traits.

As more offspring survive with the favourable trait, the incidence of this trait in the population gradually increases. As a result of natural selection, populations adapt to an environment over time. Natural selection is dependent on the environment of a species and also on variations of a trait within the population.

Heritable: describes characteristics that are genetically transferred from parent to offspring.

10.1 *Charles Darwin proposed the theory of natural selection.*

Key observations by Darwin:

1. Traits are heritable: many characteristics are passed from offspring to parent.

2. More offspring are produced than survive: organisms produce more offspring than their environment can support. They compete for limited resources such as food, habitat space and mating opportunities.

Conclusions based on Darwin's observations:

1. Not all individuals will survive or reproduce; they must compete for resources as the environment cannot support all of them.

2. The individuals that have traits that allow them to adapt to the conditions of their environment will survive and reproduce and leave more offspring than those without the favourable traits, and this will increase the presence of the trait in the next generation of the species.

Natural selection favours traits that are beneficial. It acts on existing variations within heritable traits. A trait that is beneficial in one environment may not be in another. Heritable variations arise from random mutations in DNA. Over several generations a species becomes adapted to its environment. Brightly coloured petals and a strong scent are examples of how flowers are adapted to attract insects for pollination. Wind-pollinated plants have evolved to have reproductive parts that hang outside the flower, where feathery stigmas can catch pollen. Resistance to disease and attack from pests are also traits that will enable a plant to survive and reproduce.

Progeny testing

In crop production, trials are carried out to assess the progeny of a variety of plants of a particular species. Progeny with the most desirable traits are chosen and allowed to pollinate, and further selections are made from the resulting progeny. This process is repeated until a desirable species is developed. One such method of progeny testing is called the ear to row method. It is extensively used in selection of maize plants for seed production.

DEFINITION

Progeny testing: the comparison of an animal or plant's offspring with another animal or plant's offspring kept under the same conditions. The plants grown from the seeds of one plant can be compared with the plants grown from the seeds of another plant of that species when grown in trials under the same conditions.

Ear to row method

1. Fifty to one hundred plants are selected based on their phenotype. They are allowed to open pollinate.

2. The seeds from each plant are harvested separately.

3. A single row of plants is grown from each selected plant. Each row is called a progeny row.

4. The rows are evaluated for desirable characteristics and superior plants are identified based on their phenotypes.

5. The selected plants are allowed to open pollinate.

6. Small progeny rows are grown again from the seeds of the selected plants.

In the ear to row method, selection is based on progeny and not on individual plants, which allows superior genotypes to be identified. Large numbers of progeny can be grown to prevent inbreeding.

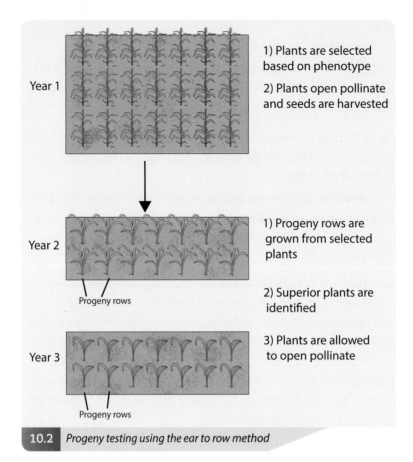

Year 1

1) Plants are selected based on phenotype

2) Plants open pollinate and seeds are harvested

Year 2

Progeny rows

1) Progeny rows are grown from selected plants

2) Superior plants are identified

Year 3

Progeny rows

3) Plants are allowed to open pollinate

10.2 *Progeny testing using the ear to row method*

DEFINITION

Open pollination: pollination that takes place between two plants of the same species, or by self-pollination. It also means pollination that takes place naturally by wind, insect, or water, i.e. without interference.

Performance testing

DEFINITION

Performance testing: comparing two animals or plants kept under the same conditions, such as housing and feeding for animals or crops grown in trials in fields under the same conditions.

Many crops are grown in trials annually by Teagasc. The crops are evaluated in a number of different categories and are chosen for traits that are important to crop growers. A variety is evaluated for several different reasons:

- As a legal requirement
- To be sold as a named variety, it must be certified to be included on a national list or EU common catalogue of listed varieties
- It must have value for cultivation or use (VCU), which relates to its agronomic performance as a crop
- It must also have distinctiveness, uniformity and stability (DUS)
- If the species is a grass species it must be able to adapt to conditions all over Ireland
- It must perform over an extended period of time
- It must be tested in a range of locations over a number of years.

If a variety has been performance tested based on the criteria above, it may be added to a recommended list of varieties published by the Department of Agriculture, Food and the Marine (DAFM) on an annual basis. Varieties on the list will be given values, usually on a scale of 1–10 for a number of different traits relating to yield, disease resistance and grain quality (for cereals).

Varieties that do not reach the standard set by control varieties in crop trials are discontinued from the trials and will not be put on the recommended list. Varieties are also tested for different markets. An example of this is barley, which may be suitable for malting or feeding.

Performance tests help farmers to choose a variety for their location and conditions, and also for the traits that they favour and that are most suitable for the end product. A grass variety may be chosen on early or late heading dates to suit local weather conditions, or for yield for silage production, for example. A farmer who grows malting barley on contract for a distiller might choose a barley for high grain quality or yield.

Physical traits

The DAFM produces annually a Recommended List for seed varieties for crops in five different areas (Table 10.1). The five areas are:

1. Cereals (wheat, oats, barley)
2. Herbage (grasses and clover)
3. Forage maize
4. Spring beans
5. Winter oilseed rape.

Table 10.1 Physical traits assessed on the DAFM Recommended Lists of crop varieties	
Crop	**Physical trait assessed**
Cereals	Straw height Resistance to lodging Straw breakdown Earliness of ripening Disease resistance Grain quality: • Hagberg falling number • Hectolitre weight • Grain protein content % • Thousand grain weight (TGW) • Hardness index
Herbage	Grass: • Heading date • Total yield • Ground cover • Spring growth • Silage yield • Dry matter digestibility Clover: • Total yield • Leaf size • Clover %
Forage maize	Dry matter yield Dry matter content Starch content

Dry matter is the matter remaining in a food or crop after the water has been removed.

Crop	Physical trait assessed
Spring beans	Yield
	% Crude protein
	Disease resistance
	Plant height
Winter oilseed rape	Relative seed yield
	Oil content
	Glucosilonate content
	Early vigour
	Full plant height
	Lodging resistance
	Full stem stiffness
	Earliness of flowering
	Earliness of maturity
	Shedding resistance
	Light leaf spot resistance

Glucosilonate: a bitter-tasting chemical compound found in cruciferous vegetables.

Genotyping and genomic selection

DEFINITION

Genotyping: the process of determining differences in the genetic make-up (genotype) of an individual organism by examining the individual's DNA and comparing it to a reference sequence or another organism's sequence.

Genotyping allows the identification of alleles an organism has inherited from its parents. In crop production it is important in identifying disease variants. It is also beneficial in controlling the spread of pathogens. Genotyping detects small genetic differences that may lead to major differences in the genotype of an organism. To identify specific genes, the genome of an organism must be examined.

DEFINITION

Genome: an organism's complete set of DNA, including all of its genes. Each genome contains all of the information needed to build and maintain that organism. It is a complete list of nucleotides (A, T, C, G) that make up the individual or species.

Nucleotide: a structural component or building block of DNA or RNA.

Polymorphism: a condition occurring in several forms. In genetics this is a form of variation where there are at least two forms of a gene called alleles.

The genome of an organism is a complete set of genetic instructions made up of DNA. DNA consists of biological compounds called nucleic acids. They are the building blocks of DNA. There are four types of base found in DNA: adenine (A), thymine (T), cytosine (C) and guanine (G). Adenine is always paired with thymine and cytosine with guanine. A handy way of remembering which bases are paired together is **A**ll **T**illage **C**rops **G**row. The pairs join together, binding two strands of DNA in a double helix shape, as shown in Fig. 10.3.

Trait selection in agriculture

Trait selection in plants and livestock is used to increase yield and quality. A process called single nucleotide polymorphism (SNP) genotyping is used.

SNP genotyping

SNP genotyping is a measurement of genetic variations (SNPs, pronounced 'snips') between members of a species. SNPs are one of the most common forms of genetic variation. A SNP is a **single base pair mutation at a single locus**, usually consisting of two alleles (Fig. 10.3b).

Locus: location of an allele.

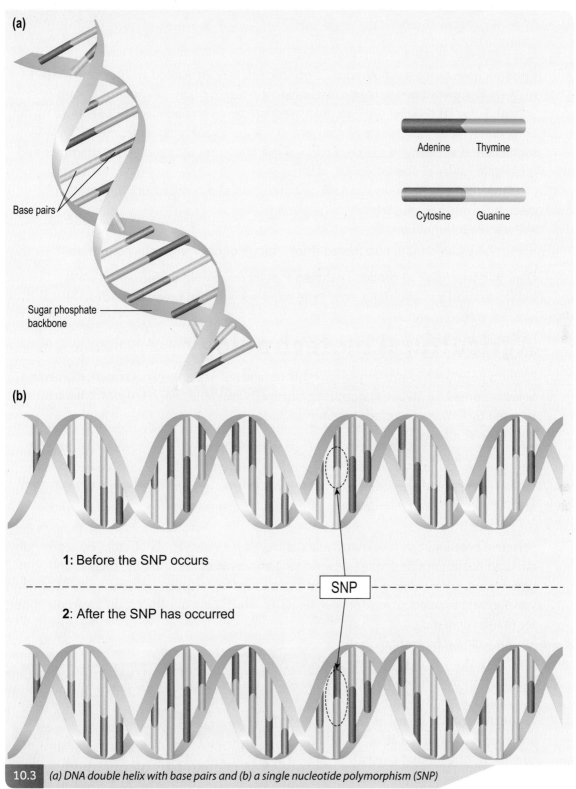

(a)

Base pairs

Sugar phosphate
backbone

Adenine   Thymine

Cytosine   Guanine

(b)

1: Before the SNP occurs

SNP

2: After the SNP has occurred

| 10.3 | *(a) DNA double helix with base pairs and (b) a single nucleotide polymorphism (SNP)* |

Selective breeding generates new breeds and varieties with more desirable phenotypes and changes to specific genomic regions associated with these phenotypes. Detecting these genetic changes allows a plant breeder to understand which specific genes and sequences are associated with particular phenotypic traits. This information can be used for designing new breeding programmes. SNP detection can be used to study a range of infectious diseases in plants.

DEFINITION

Allele: an alternative form of a gene, e.g. a gene for petal colour in flowers may have alleles red or white.
Genotype: the genetic make-up of an organism.
Phenotype: the physical representation of the genotype.

Genomic selection

Genomic selection uses thousands of genetic markers associated with genes. These markers along with performance tests help to assess the genetic merit of a plant or animal. For crop production, genomic selection allows a tillage farmer to choose a crop variety with an accurate assessment of the crop variety's genetic merit. It allows for increased accuracy in the prediction of the outcomes of breeding programmes and genotypic values of species.

Genomic selection uses a reference population as a comparison. Information is gathered from sources such as:

- Pedigree information
- Phenotypic information gathered from a range of environmental conditions.

Genomic selection can produce varieties that increase yield performance when hybridised and can also reduce the time required between breeding cycles.

Agricultural biotechnology

Farmers have been improving crops for thousands of years through selective breeding. Selective breeding involves choosing plants with desirable characteristics. Characteristics selected by farmers and plant breeders include:

- Disease resistance
- Pest resistance
- Yield
- Drought resistance
- Flavour.

Selective breeding can take many years to develop a new variety of crop, by repeatedly crossing plants with desirable traits. Advancements in biotechnology, such as SNP genotyping, have allowed farmers and plant breeders to speed up development of new varieties and to select plants for specific traits, which best suit the crop's environment or for market demands.

Agricultural biotechnology describes a variety of processes used to improve and enhance plants and animals. Being able to identify specific genes in an organism and to be able to remove or alter that gene provides a benefit to the farmer if it results in an improved crop. Some of the techniques used to identify and alter DNA lead to faster developments of new varieties and improvements that would not be possible by selective breeding alone.

10.4 *Potato crop damaged by potato cyst nematode (on the left) and nematode-resistant crop (on the right)*

Genetic improvement through biotechnology

There are several methods of improving or developing new varieties of crop through the use of biotechnology, including:

- Genetic engineering/genetic modification
- Gene editing
- Molecular markers
- Plant tissue culture (micropropagation).

The principles of genetic engineering

> DEFINITION
>
> **Genetic modification (GM):** the alteration of an organism's DNA for the purpose of improvement or to correct a defect in the organism.

Genetic engineering allows scientists to insert beneficial genes into the chromosomes of plants and animals. Plants and animals that are produced by genetic engineering are described as **genetically modified (GM) organisms**. In some cases, a gene from one organism (e.g. a bacterium) can be placed into a completely unrelated organism (e.g. a plant). The resulting organisms are known as **transgenic species**.

> DEFINITION
>
> **Transgenic species:** any organism that has had part of the DNA of another species (animal, plant, microorganism, etc.) inserted into its own DNA by genetic engineering.

GM maize contains a gene from a bacterium called *Bacillus thuringiensis* that codes for a toxin. This toxin is poisonous to insect pests, and in particular to the corn borer caterpillar. As a result, the plant can produce its own pesticide so that the caterpillars die when they eat the plant. This reduces the need to spray the crop with pesticides. Some varieties of maize can be genetically modified so that they can tolerate herbicides such as glyphosate. This allows farmers to spray crops with herbicides to kill competing weeds without killing the maize crop.

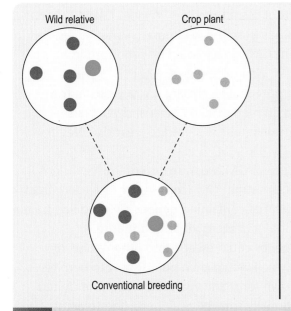
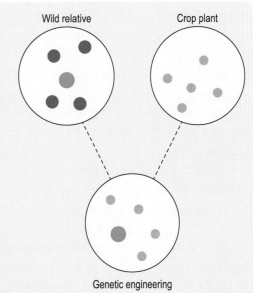

10.5 *Creating a transgenic species through genetic engineering*

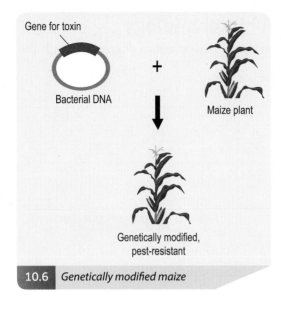

10.6 *Genetically modified maize*

10.7 *Tomato purée made from genetically modified tomatoes*

However, not all GM organisms have to be transgenic. Genetic information can be transferred between two varieties of the same crop or genus. This is called **cisgenesis**. Over the last number of years, Teagasc has seen the emergence of more aggressive strains of blight, some of which have been resistant to fungicides. As a result, Teagasc has completed a crop study designed to assess the impact of GM blight-resistant potatoes (variety Désirée) on soil biodiversity and also on the strains of blight themselves.

> DEFINITION
>
>
>
> **Cisgenic:** describes an organism that has been modified with a gene from an organism of the same species or a closely related species.

This GM variety of potato contains blight-resistant genes from species of wild potatoes that originated in South America. In this case, the gene has been transferred from a wild potato into a commercial variety by genetic engineering.

The results of the initial trial showed that the GM variety of potato had increased resistance to late blight in comparison with the non-GM variety.

One of the benefits of genetic engineering is that it can accelerate the breeding process of a crop. Using traditional methods of plant breeding, it could take 40 years to breed the blight-resistant variety of potatoes from the wild potato varieties. Using genetic engineering, the new blight-resistant GM variety could be produced in a laboratory within 18 weeks and could achieve varietal approval within 3–5 years.

Other benefits of GM crops include the potential to preserve crop yields in the presence of a disease or drought conditions. In medicine, bacteria and yeast are genetically modified so that they produce insulin, which is used to treat diabetes in humans.

Some of the concerns surrounding the use of GM organisms stem from a lack of understanding of the technology. One concern is that GM crops may cause allergies in the people consuming them. Any plant or animal containing genetically modified traits would have to be assessed to identify any potential allergy that might arise.

Another fear is that herbicide-resistant genes could escape into other plants by cross fertilisation to produce super weeds, which would then be resistant to herbicides. Herbicide-resistant GM crops have been grown for many years in parts of the United States and Canada. There, the farmers continually sprayed their herbicide-tolerant soya bean crop with the same herbicide to control weeds. As a result, weeds started to demonstrate resistance to the herbicide being used. The use of herbicide-resistant soya bean made many farmers complacent in their crop management. Instead of practising crop rotation and other methods of weed control, they had encouraged the development of herbicide resistance in weeds associated with the GM soya bean by continually using the same herbicide. Growing of GM crops has to be managed sensibly.

Many risk assessment studies have been carried out on GM organisms and these studies are ongoing. To date, no health issue has been identified. As part of the crop study being conducted by Teagasc and its partners, there is an aim to determine whether GM potatoes have a positive or a negative impact on insects, pollinators and soil microbes.

Table 10.2 Genetic modifications of agricultural crops

Crop	Genetic modification	Use
Soya bean	Herbicide tolerant	Food and food additives
Oilseed rape	Herbicide tolerant	Food and food additives
Maize	Herbicide tolerant and pest resistant	Food and food additives
Starch potato	Enhanced starch	Food
Sugar beet	Herbicide tolerant	Food

Genome editing

> **DEFINITION**
>
> **Genome editing:** the use of any technology that allows a change to an organism's DNA. Genetic material can be added, removed or altered at specific locations in the genome.

Genome editing increases the possibility of creating new varieties in crops that are difficult to breed. This would be a particular advantage in crops that are sterile or reproduce by vegetative propagation.

Genome editing is a precise way of altering a genome. A specific piece of DNA can be added or removed. Breeding through mutations induced by radiation or chemical mutagens can result in many thousands of new variations, some of which will be beneficial and some of which will not. Genome editing targets a specific gene leading to a specific outcome. One of the most recent developments in genome editing is a technique called CRISPR/Cas9.

CRISPR/Cas9

CRISPR/Cas 9 is a relatively recent innovation in gene editing technology. It was first developed in 2012. It is a **subgenic** form of genetic engineering. It has been adapted from a naturally occurring genome editing system in bacteria. The bacteria capture snippets of DNA from invading viruses and create DNA segments called CRISPR arrays. The arrays allow the bacteria to 'remember' the virus. If the virus attacks the bacteria again, the bacteria produce RNA segments from the CRISPR array to attack the virus' DNA. Bacteria use Cas9 or another enzyme to disable the virus.

How CRISPR technology can work in crops:

1. CRISPR technology can be used to make changes to the genome of a crop's DNA. The gene responsible for a specific trait is identified. A piece of RNA is created in a laboratory, along with the enzyme Cas9 to edit the gene.
2. The RNA and the Cas9 enzyme are introduced into the cell. The RNA mimics the DNA sequence.
3. The RNA contains a guide sequence which allows it to locate and bind to the correct DNA sequence. The DNA sequence consists of two strands wound around each

Risk assessment: a process of evaluating the potential risks involved in an activity.

CRISPR: Clustered regularly interspaced short palindromic repeats.

Cas9: an enzyme that targets specific strands of genetic information.

Subgenic engineering: the alteration of the genetic make-up of a plant by the removal of a gene or addition of DNA without inserting genes from other species.

Array: an ordered series or arrangement.

RNA: abbreviation for ribonucleic acid. RNA is a single strand of nucleotides.

other in a double helix shape. The RNA also binds to the Cas9 enzyme. Cas9 is like genetic scissors and cuts the DNA at the target location using the RNA as a cutting template.

4. Once the Cas9 enzyme has cut across the two strands of DNA, the change can take place. The gene can be removed or other DNA can be added.

5. Once the change has taken place, the DNA repairs itself.

6. The RNA and Cas9 enzyme are removed from the cell. The plant can now be crossed with another plant and the change in its DNA will be passed on in its genes.

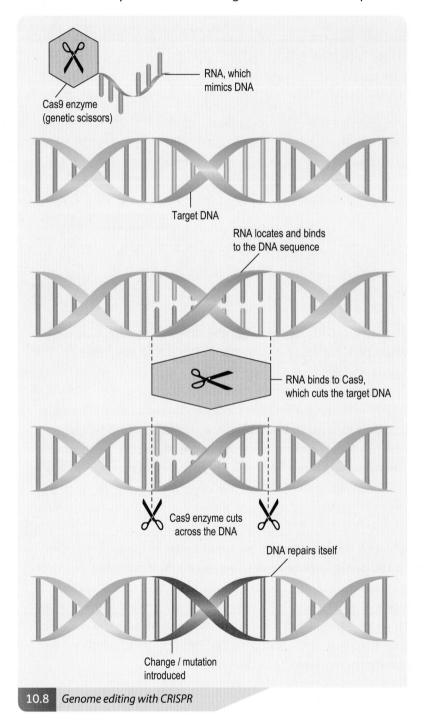

RNA, which mimics DNA

Cas9 enzyme (genetic scissors)

Target DNA

RNA locates and binds to the DNA sequence

RNA binds to Cas9, which cuts the target DNA

Cas9 enzyme cuts across the DNA

DNA repairs itself

Change / mutation introduced

10.8 *Genome editing with CRISPR*

Crops created using gene editing techniques such as CRISPR/Cas9 are subject to the same regulations as genetically modified crops under EU legislation.

Table 10.3 Comparison of transgenic engineering and gene editing		
Type of genetic modification	**Transgenic engineering**	**Gene editing**
DNA origin	Genes come from another species	DNA, if inserted, is from the same species
DNA technique used	Change is made at a random location in the genome	Change is made at a specific location in the genome
Breeding	The inserted gene cannot be generated by breeding so the GM plant is different to the original plant	Practically identical to traditional selective breeding
Regulation	Banned in Ireland; approved in USA for some crops after rigorous testing by US Dept of Agriculture	Currently treated the same as GM organisms under EU law; legal in USA
Timeline for development	5–10 years	3–5 years

Molecular markers

A molecular marker is used to select a plant for a specific trait if it has a desirable gene in its DNA. The marker is a fragment of DNA that is found at a particular location in the genome. The marker is used to identify a specific sequence of DNA in a longer sequence. The molecular markers can also be used to identify plants with undesirable genes to ensure they are not used for breeding. Examples of molecular markers include identification of *Fusarium* head blight in wheat. The marker is used to identify a blight-resistant gene in the cereal crop, so varieties that have the resistant gene can be selected for breeding. The advantage for farmers is the ability to sow a crop that does not need to be treated with fungicide.

Tissue culture

Tissue culture is a method of genetic engineering in which disease-free plants are produced in a laboratory in sterile conditions from pieces of plant tissue on a nutrient culture medium. The plant tissue cultures are used to produce clones of a plant species.

There are several advantages to micropropagation of plant tissues, including:
- To be able to produce exact genotypic copies (clones) of plants with desirable traits, e.g. petal colour, fruit, starch content
- To produce large numbers of plants in a short period of time
- To produce disease- and pest-free plants that can be sold on to farmers
- To produce plants quickly without the need for pollination.

A common example of plant production through tissue culture is the micropropagation of potatoes.

Micropropagation of potatoes

1. Sprouts are removed from a disease-free parent plant.
2. Sprouts are grown in a sterile medium that contains plant hormones and sucrose.
3. Tissue cultures are incubated under low light conditions at 25°C.

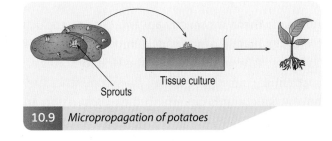

Sprouts   Tissue culture

10.9 *Micropropagation of potatoes*

Callus: a mass of unorganised plant cells.

4. The shoots form a callus, which is removed from the nutrient culture.

5. The callus is divided into sections and re-inoculated on fresh nutrient medium.

6. The process can be repeated many times to produce thousands of genetically identical plants.

Protein production for disease prevention

Genetic resistance to disease in plants results from a plant's ability to produce a gene that is resistant to a specific disease. The resistant gene is known as an R-gene. The R-gene present in the plant targets the specific disease-causing gene in the pathogen.

The inheritance of resistance in the host plant to a specific disease and the pathogen's ability to cause that disease is controlled by a pair of matching genes in a gene-for-gene relationship (Table 10.4). A disease-causing gene is known as an avirulent gene (Avr-gene).

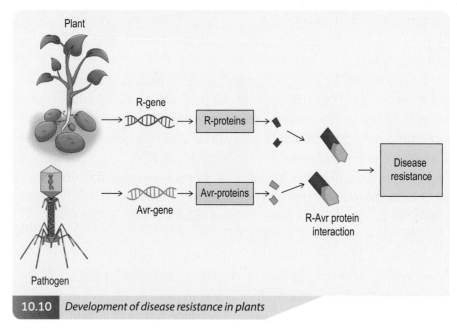

| 10.10 | *Development of disease resistance in plants* |

Table 10.4 R-genes and Avr genes in host plants and plant pathogens			
Host plant	**R-gene in host plant**	**Plant pathogen**	**Avr-gene in plant pathogen**
Barley (*Hordeum vulgare*)	Mla	Powdery mildew (*Blumeria graminis*)	AvrMla
Maize (*Zea mays*)	Rp1	Common rust (*Puccinia sorghi*)	Avr-RP-1-D
Potato (*Solanum tuberosum*)	R1	Potato blight (*Phytophthora infestans*)	Avr1

Ethical and economic considerations for biotechnological innovations in crop development

Although there are several advantages to producing GM crops, there are also other factors to be taken into consideration. GM crops have only existed for approximately 25 years. While countries like the United States and Canada have introduced these crops successfully into tillage farms, many countries are opposed to the use of GM crops or have strict controls governing their production and use.

The ethical and economic considerations could include:
- **Access to technology:** there are a large number of plant breeders located throughout Europe. The biotechnology available to edit genomes should be regulated for safety, but also with consideration to cost so that expense does not exclude all but the largest multinational plant breeders. Wider availability of genome editing technology would lead to a larger range of developments and would prevent the market for genome edited crops being dominated by a few companies.
- **Crop testing:** crops that are developed with the use of mutagens should undergo rigorous evaluation and testing before new varieties can be approved for sale. Consideration should be given to the evaluation and testing procedures for genome edited crops and whether the current procedures are fit for purpose.
- **Increased production:** gene editing technologies allow for the development of crops with increased yields to meet the demands for food production for an increasing global population.
- **Benefits to biodiversity:** as crop varieties are developed to be pest resistant, this leads to a reduction of pesticide application on these crops. This is of benefit to the environment, as there is less risk of pollution from pesticides, but also a benefit to biodiversity, as other living organisms do not get killed by pesticides that are intended for one particular pest.
- **Effect on food chain:** GM crops are tested and compared with non-GM crops to ensure they provide the same nutrients if the crop is to be used as a food source. GM crops should also be tested to ensure that alteration of their genetic make-up does not lead to the production of allergens or toxins entering the food chain or having a negative effect on biodiversity.
- **Environmental impact:** environmental impact should be considered when deciding to plant a crop that has been genetically modified. As the phenotype of a plant or animal can be controlled by several genes interacting with each other and the environment, the introduction of a gene may influence the other characteristics of the plant. The impact on biodiversity is another consideration. If a plant is developed to be pest resistant, the presence of the pest in the habitat may decline. This may impact other living organisms in a positive or negative way.

Genetic enhancement of crop varieties

There are many advantages to genetically modifying crop varieties.
- **Disease resistance:** if they are able to grow crops that are disease resistant, farmers can be assured that their crop will not be destroyed from a particular bacterial, viral or fungal attack.
- **Pest resistance:** the cost of pesticide application and labour costs are reduced as farmers are not required to apply pesticides to crops to prevent attack by insects. This also has positive implications for other insects that are negatively affected by insecticide application.
- **Virus resistance:** plants can be genetically modified to resist viruses that cause damage to the crop. As many viruses are transmitted by aphids, this also reduces the need to apply aphicides to the crop.
- **Herbicide tolerance:** farmers can apply herbicides to crops to control weeds without affecting the growth of the crop.
- **Drought tolerance:** while it is not a major problem in Ireland, crops that have been genetically enhanced to retain moisture are better able to tolerate drought conditions, without the need for irrigation of the crop.

- **Reduction of food waste/improved shelf life of crops:** some crops turn brown if they are bruised or have been stored for a long period of time. While these crops are edible, they are often not appealing to the consumer. Gene editing techniques can prevent bruising and browning of crops – apples, potatoes and mushrooms in particular.
- **Delayed fruit ripening:** fruit that takes longer to mature will have a longer shelf life from the time it is harvested to the time it appears on a supermarket shelf. This reduces waste and also gives the produce a longer shelf life from the time it is purchased by the consumer.
- **Enhanced nutrient content:** crops can be genetically modified to increase the nutrient content of the crop. An example of this is GM soya beans, which have been developed to be trans-fat free and have increased oil content. Rice called 'golden rice' has also been developed that is enriched with Vitamin A.

Inheritance of traits

Chromosomes carry all the genetic information of a living organism in the form of genes. Chromosomes occur in pairs, and the chromosomes in a pair have similar genes. As we have already seen, genes that exist in two different forms (e.g. for petal colour in plants) are called alleles. When different alleles exist for a gene, usually one will be **dominant** and one will be **recessive**.

When an organism has a copy of each of the different alleles, the one that is expressed physically is the dominant one. Dominant alleles mask or hide recessive alleles. For example, in pea plants, flowers may be purple or white, and purple petal colour is dominant over white petal colour. When a purple pea plant that carries only purple genes is crossed with a white pea plant, all of the offspring will be purple.

Purple pea plant

White pea plant

Purple offspring

10.11 *Inheritance of petal colour in peas*

Each parent plant has two alleles for the gene for petal colour, one on each of a pair of chromosomes. However, when it produces gametes only one of the alleles is found in the gamete, as gametes contain only single chromosomes. During fertilisation when the male and female gametes fuse together, the chromosomes containing these genes form pairs and the offspring receive two copies of the gene, one from each parent. Both genes may be the dominant allele, both may be recessive or there may be one of each.

Therefore, for pea plants there are three different combinations of genes possible. The genotypes are PP, Pp and pp. When both genes are the same, e.g. PP or pp, they are described as homozygous. The genotype PP is described as homozygous dominant and the genotype pp is described as homozygous recessive. When the two genes in a pair are different, e.g. Pp, they are described as heterozygous. A summary of the combination of genotypes and phenotypes is shown in Table 10.5.

Table 10.5 Genotypes and phenotypes		
	Genotype	**Phenotype**
Homozygous dominant	PP	Purple
Heterozygous	Pp	Purple
Homozygous recessive	pp	White

Predicting the outcome of a cross

What will happen if two purple pea plants that are both heterozygous are crossed? As they are both heterozygous, they both carry a purple gene and a white gene.

Step 1: Identify the genotypes of the parents (Fig. 10.12).

Step 2: Each parent produces gametes with only one gene in each gamete. Identify all possible gametes that each parent can produce (Fig. 10.13).

Step 3: Draw a Punnett square. This is a grid that allows you to identify all possible combinations of gametes from each parent. List all of the gametes from Parent 1 on one side of the Punnett square and list all possible gametes from Parent 2 on the other side.

The Punnett square is completed by combining one allele from the left-hand side with one allele from the top of the square. The two letters are written together as a pair and are called the genotype. If a dominant allele (e.g. P) and a recessive allele (e.g. p) form a pair, the dominant gene is usually written first.

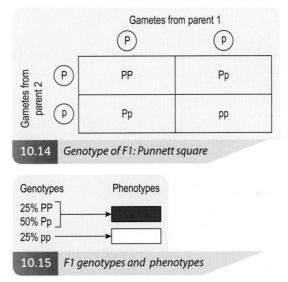

Genetic cross

	Parent 1	Parent 2
Parents:	Pp	Pp

10.12 *Parent's genotype*

Gametes: (P) (p)   (P) (p)

10.13 *Gametes*

Gametes from parent 1

	P	p
P	PP	Pp
p	Pp	pp

Gametes from parent 2

10.14 *Genotype of F1: Punnett square*

Genotypes   Phenotypes

25% PP ⎤
50% Pp ⎦ → ▇
25% pp → □

10.15 *F1 genotypes and phenotypes*

Step 4: Identify the phenotypes of each of the genotypes listed in a grid.

Genotypes	Phenotypes
1 × PP	Purple
2 × Pp	Purple
1 × pp	White

In this example, three of the genotypes produced were purple and one was white. This can be expressed as a ratio, a fraction, a decimal or a percentage (Table 10.6).

Table 10.6 Methods of expressing phenotype	
Method	**Result**
Ratio	3 purple : 1 white
Percentage	75% purple, 25% white
Fraction	¾ purple, ¼ white
Decimal	0.75 purple, 0.25 white

Incomplete dominance

In the previous cross, purple petal colour was dominant over white petal colour and the offspring produced had either purple or white petals. However, this is not always the case. When red snapdragon flowers are crossed with white snapdragon flowers, all the offspring are Rr and have pink petals. This is an example of **incomplete dominance**. In this case, neither the allele for red nor for white is dominant. Therefore, when both alleles occur together (Rr), the phenotype is a combination of both alleles.

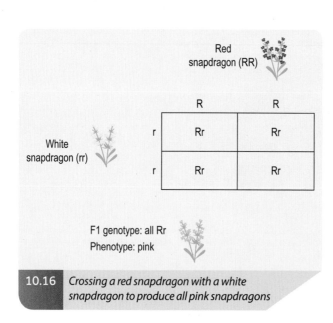

Red snapdragon (RR)

White snapdragon (rr)

	R	R
r	Rr	Rr
r	Rr	Rr

F1 genotype: all Rr
Phenotype: pink

10.16 *Crossing a red snapdragon with a white snapdragon to produce all pink snapdragons*

10.17 *Pink snapdragon flower*

Incomplete dominance occurs when two alleles are equally dominant. When both occur together in the genotype, the resulting phenotype is a blend of the two.

SPA 10.1 To investigate the complexity associated with the genetic inheritance of traits by hybridising two varieties to determine the rate of transfer of the required trait to the next progeny

SPECIFIED PRACTICAL ACTIVITY

Note: This experiment can be carried out with a wide variety of plants. Different plants produce different numbers of seeds and grow in a variety of conditions at different times of the year. Check what time of year and conditions your chosen plant variety is best suited to before setting up your experiment.

State your hypothesis, prediction, independent variable, dependent variable and controlled variable.

Materials

Seeds of two different varieties of the same plant, seed trays, water, fertiliser, soil or vermiculite, light source, cotton buds, scissors, plant pot

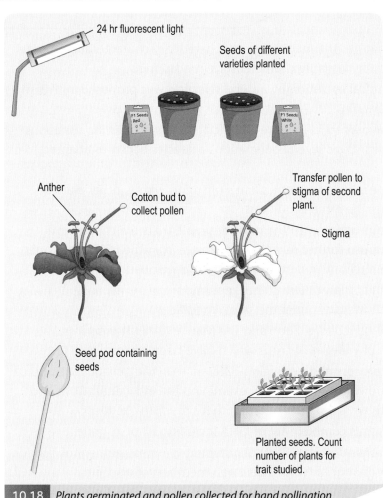

24 hr fluorescent light

Seeds of different varieties planted

F1 Seeds Red

F1 Seeds White

Anther

Cotton bud to collect pollen

Transfer pollen to stigma of second plant.

Stigma

Seed pod containing seeds

Planted seeds. Count number of plants for trait studied.

10.18 *Plants germinated and pollen collected for hand pollination*

Method

1. Plant seeds of one plant variety (e.g. a plant with red petals) in a seed tray or plant pot. Plant the seeds of the second variety (e.g. a plant with white petals) of the plant in another seed tray, petri dish or plant pot.

2. Seeds should be supplied with water and fertiliser and have a source of light – ideally, a fluorescent light that can be left on 24 hours a day to maximise photosynthesis.

3. Once the seeds have germinated in the two containers, thin the poorer seedlings to allow the remaining seedling enough space to grow.

4. When the plants have flowered, rub a cotton bud on the anther of one plant and transfer the pollen to the stigma of the second plant. If the plants are a species that can self-fertilise, the anthers may be removed with scissors before pollen is produced in one of the plants.

5. Monitor the plants after pollination to ensure they have enough water and nutrients.

6. When the seed pod has swelled and the petals have died off, remove any remaining petals and the seed pod from the plant.

7. Open the seed pod and remove the seeds.

8. Depending on the type of plant, the seeds may need to be stored in a cool, dry place until they can be planted, as some plants are annuals which will grow only at a certain time of year.

9. Plant the seeds in a new seed tray, supplying them with water and nutrients and wait for them to germinate.

10. Once the plants have flowered, count the number of plants produced with either petal colour (or other trait). Compare the ratio of the phenotypes observed with the expected ratio.

Summary

- Applied genetics involves the manipulation of hereditary characteristics in order to improve or produce desirable characteristics in offspring.
- The theory of biological evolution by natural selection was proposed by British naturalist Charles Darwin.
- Natural selection favours traits that are beneficial. It acts on existing variations within heritable traits. Over several generations a species becomes adapted to its environment.
- Progeny testing: the comparison of a plant's offspring with another plant's offspring kept under the same conditions.
- In crop production, progeny with the most desirable traits are chosen and allowed to pollinate and further selections are made from the resulting progeny. This process is repeated until a desirable species is developed.
- Performance testing compares two plants kept under the same conditions, e.g. crops grown in trials in fields under the same conditions.
- The Department of Agriculture, Food and the Marine (DAFM) produces recommended lists of varieties of crops which have been performance tested.
- Genotyping is the process of determining differences in the genetic make-up (genotype) of an individual organism by examining the individual's DNA and comparing it to a reference sequence or another organism's sequence.
- Genome: an organism's complete set of DNA including all of its genes.
- Single nucleotide polymorphism (SNP) genotyping is a measurement of genetic variations (SNPs, pronounced 'snips') between members of a species.
- Genomic selection uses thousands of genetic markers associated with genes. These markers, along with performance tests, help to assess the genetic merit of a plant or animal.
- Selective breeding involves choosing plants with desirable characteristics. In crop production this includes disease resistance, pest resistance, yield, drought resistance and flavour.
- Developments in biotechnology such as SNP genotyping have allowed farmers and plant breeders to speed up development of new varieties and to select plants for specific traits.
- Genetic modification (GM) is the alteration of an organism's DNA for the purpose of improvement or to correct a defect in the organism.
- Transgenic species: any organism that has had part of the DNA of another species (animal, plant, microorganism, etc.) inserted into its own DNA by genetic engineering.
- Cisgenic refers to the genetic modification of a recipient organism with a gene from an organism of the same species or a closely related species.
- Genome editing is the use of any technology that allows a change to an organism's DNA. Genetic material can be added, removed or altered at specific locations in the genome.
- A molecular marker is used to select a plant for a specific trait if it has a desirable gene in its DNA. The marker is a fragment of DNA that is found at a particular location in the genome. The marker is used to identify a specific sequence of DNA in a longer sequence.
- Tissue culture is a method of genetic engineering in which disease-free plants are produced in a laboratory in sterile conditions from pieces of plant tissue on a nutrient culture medium. The plant tissue cultures are used to produce clones of a plant species.

- Genetic resistance to disease in plants results from a plant's ability to produce a gene that is resistant to a specific disease. The resistant gene is known as an R-gene. The R-gene present in the plant targets the specific disease-causing Avirulent gene (Avr gene) in the pathogen.

- There are a number of ethical and economic considerations with regard to GM crops. Crops have to be tested to prove they are as safe as non-GM crops for human consumption. There is the ability to increase yields to meet demands for food globally. Biodiversity can be enhanced with the reduction in the use of pesticides on GM crops.

- Advantages of genetically modifying crops include: disease resistance, pest resistance, virus resistance, increased yields, drought tolerance, herbicide tolerance, delayed maturity, reduced food waste and enhanced nutrient content.

- Alleles are alternative forms of the same gene.

- In genetic crosses, the parents' genotype has two alleles present for a gene, while the gametes have only one allele present.

- The inheritance of pink petal colour in snapdragon flowers demonstrates incomplete dominance.

 PowerPoint Summary

QUESTIONS

1. Which naturalist proposed the theory of natural selection?
   (a) Isaac Newton
   (b) Gregor Mendel
   (c) Charles Darwin
   (d) Marie Curie

2. Which of the following statements is not true of the theory of natural selection?
   (a) Many characteristics are passed from parent to offspring.
   (b) Organisms must compete for resources as there are not enough resources for all living organisms.
   (c) All offspring survive and reproduce at the same rate.
   (d) Organisms that best adapt to their environment will survive and reproduce more.

3. (a) Define progeny testing.
   (b) Outline how the ear to row method can be used in progeny testing of crops.

4. (a) Define performance testing.
   (b) Outline four reasons that performance tests are carried out by Teagasc before recommending a crop variety.

5. Crops that meet the required standards are placed on recommended lists by Teagasc. Identify two physical traits that are assessed for each of the following crops:
   (a) Cereals   (b) Forage crops   (c) Maize.

6. The DAFM releases a Recommended List for a variety of crops each year. Using the DAFM website, identify two recommended varieties for each of the following crops for the current year:
   (a) Spring barley
   (b) Wheat
   (c) Maize
   (d) Oats
   (e) Spring beans.

7. Differentiate between the following terms:

   (a) Genotyping   (b) Genome   (c) Genomic selection   (d) Genome editing.

8. List four characteristics of crops favoured by farmers through selective breeding.

9. What are the benefits of using genetically modified organisms?

10. Define the following terms in relation to genetic engineering:

   (a) Transgenic   (b) Cisgenic   (c) Subgenic.

11. Outline how CRISPR/Cas9 technology is used in gene editing of crops.

12. Compare transgenic engineering and gene editing under the following headings:

   (a) DNA origin   (b) DNA technique used   (c) Timeline for development.

13. Explain how molecular markers are used in gene editing.

14. Micropropagation is a form of plant tissue culture.

   (a) State three advantages of micropropagation.

   (b) Outline how potato plants can be produced through micropropagation.

15. Explain how disease resistance in a plant is developed genetically.

16. Discuss some of the ethical and economic issues surrounding the use of genetically modified organisms. Identify four advantages to genetically enhanced crops.

17. Explain the meaning of each of the following terms:

   (a) Gene   (b) Homozygous   (c) Dominant   (d) Recessive

   (e) Allele   (f) Genotype   (g) Phenotype.

18. In pea plants, round seeds (R) are dominant over wrinkled seeds (r). Answer the questions below using the genotypes, RR, Rr, rr.

   (a) What genotype is homozygous dominant?

   (b) What genotype will produce wrinkled seeds?

   (c) What two genotypes will produce round seeds?

   (d) What genotype is homozygous recessive?

   (e) What genotype is heterozygous?

19. In pea plants, purple flowers (P) are dominant over white flowers (p). A pea plant with purple flowers was crossed with a pea plant with white flowers. Fifty per cent of the F1 offspring had purple flowers and 50% had white flowers.

   (a) What were the genotypes of the parents?

   (b) Using a Punnett square, show how the purple and white flowers were obtained in the F1 generation.

20. Red flower colour in snapdragon plants is a homozygous dominant condition (RR). Pink-flowered snapdragons were crossed with pink-flowered snapdragons. The seeds from these plants were collected and sown, and the new plants produced flowers as shown:

   • Number of plants with red flowers   29
   • Number of plants with pink flowers   56
   • Number of plants with white flowers   27

   (a) State the genotype of the original pink snapdragons.

   (b) Explain how the three flower types above resulted from a cross between two pink-flowered plants.

   (c) What offspring would result if a pink-flowered snapdragon were crossed with a white-flowered snapdragon? Outline the cross and state the genotype and phenotype of the offspring produced.

Solutions   Weblinks

CHAPTER 11 Plant classification

When you have completed this chapter you should be able to:

- Apply knowledge of structure and function to identify a variety of grasses, cultivated crops and weeds
- Distinguish between annual, biennial and perennial life cycles
- Explain the importance of plant breeding and seed variety.

Identifying plant families

Plants are classified into many different families. There are many plants which are of importance in agriculture, including tillage crops such as cereals and potatoes, grass species, catch crops and weeds. Plants are classified by their physical characteristics. A key is shown in Fig. 11.1 to identify the physical features of each plant family. Each floral diagram in this chapter shows the arrangement of the sepals, petals, stamens and carpels in each flowering plant.

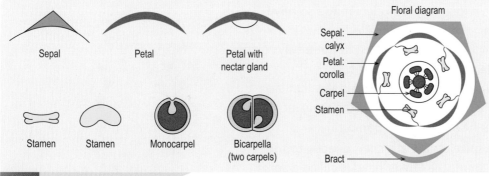

11.1 *Key to floral diagram*

- **Sepals:** leaf-like structures at the base of the flower, which protect the young flower bud before it opens and are usually green. This outer ring of sepals is called the calyx.
- **Petals:** inside the sepals is a ring of modified leaves called petals. They are often brightly coloured to attract insects. Collectively the ring of petals is called a corolla.
- **Stamen:** this is the male part of the flower consisting of the anther and filament. It produces pollen and there may be multiple stamens in a flower.
- **Carpel:** at the centre of the flower is the carpel. This is the female part of the flower consisting of the stigma, style and ovary. The ovary contains the ovule.
- **Bract:** a modified or specialised leaf, often associated with reproductive structures such as flowers.

Family Poaceae

Poaceae is the most important plant family in agriculture and is a very large one, with an estimated 10,000 species. This family contains productive perennial ryegrass varieties *Lolium perenne* (used for grazing, hay and silage), and cereals such as wheat (*Triticum aestivum*), barley (*Hordeum vulgare*) and maize (*Zea mays*), which are mainly used as animal feeds. All the members of this family are monocots, having one cotyledon in the seed. The part of the grass plant commonly referred to as the flower is composed of many florets (small flowers) contained in a structure called the spikelet.

> **Cotyledon:** part of the embryo within the seed of a plant. When the seed germinates, or begins to grow, the cotyledon may become the first leaves of the seedling. The cotyledon is often called the seed leaf and can provide energy to the germinating seed until the true leaves have formed and can photosynthesise.

Grass species are specialised for wind pollination. Their petals are reduced or absent, and lack scent and colour. Their stamens hang outside the plant and produce large amounts of pollen. They have feathery stigma to trap the pollen.

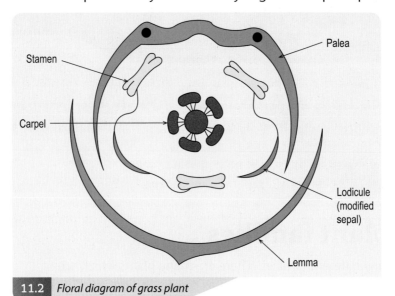

11.2　*Floral diagram of grass plant*

Palea: an internal bract that surrounds a floret.

Lemma: an external bract that surrounds a floret.

Lodicule: scale found at the base of an ovary that forces bracts to open to expose the reproductive parts of a flower.

Inflorescence in grass plants

A grass flower contains both male and female reproductive parts. A spikelet is the name given to the structure that contains a number of florets protected by glumes or bracts (leaf-like structures). Spikelets may also have small hair-like extensions called awns.

Awn: a long hair or needle-like structure extending from the lemma of the grass floret.

Spikelets can be arranged in three ways on a grass plant as shown in Fig. 11.3.

- If the spikelets are borne on stalks that are attached to branches from the main stem, the flower head is called a panicle.
- If the spikelets are attached directly to the main stem, the flower head is called a spike.
- If the spikelets are attached to the main stem by individual stalks, the flower head is called a raceme.

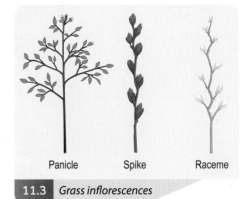

11.3　*Grass inflorescences*

Structure of a grass plant

- **Stem (culm):** the stem, also known as a culm, is hollow and cylindrical. It supports the plant.
- **Node:** nodes are points found along the stem, which give rise to a new leaf.
- **Internode:** the space along the stem between each node.
- **Flag leaf:** the uppermost leaf on the plant, it encloses the seed head before the plant flowers or heads out.

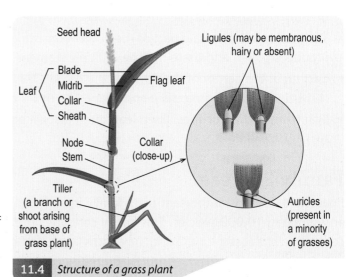

11.4　*Structure of a grass plant*

- **Petiole:** the stalk that connects the leaf to the stem.
- **Leaf sheath:** the lower section of the leaf that covers the petiole and surrounds the stem of the plant.
- **Leaf blade (lamina):** the part of the leaf above the sheath.
- **Midrib:** the main or central rib or vein running down the centre of the leaf.
- **Collar:** the junction between the leaf blade and leaf sheath.
- **Ligule:** a membrane-like tissue or row of hairs found at the junction of the leaf blade and leaf sheath. It is absent in some grasses.
- **Auricle:** extensions at the base of the leaf blade, which wrap around the stem. Auricles can be claw-like, short or absent.
- **Tiller:** a side shoot capable of producing a new plant.
- **Seed head:** the flowering part of the plant, also called an inflorescence.

Table 11.1 Characteristics of grasses found in Ireland				
Grass species	**Inflorescence**	**Awns**	**Leaf blades**	**Growth habit**
Perennial ryegrass	Spike	Absent	Glabrous	Tussock
Italian ryegrass	Spike	Present	Glabrous	Tussock
Timothy	Panicle	Present	Glabrous	Tussock
Meadow foxtail	Panicle	Present	Glabrous	Tussock
Cocksfoot	Panicle	Present	Glabrous	Tussock
Annual meadowgrass	Panicle	Absent	Glabrous	Rhizome
Scutch grass	Spike	Absent	Hair present	Rhizome

Glabrous: hairless or smooth.

Tussock: compact clump of grass that is thicker or longer than the grass growing around it.

The inflorescence of perennial ryegrass and Italian ryegrass is a spike. Italian ryegrass can be distinguished from perennial ryegrass by the presence of awns.

Meadow foxtail and timothy have similar inflorescence and are often confused with each other. Both have a compacted panicle that looks like a spike. Meadow foxtail has soft awns along the side of the seed head, making it appear fuzzy like a fox's tail. When comparing the two species side by side, the inflorescence of timothy is roughly twice the length of the inflorescence of meadow foxtail.

Rhizome: an underground stem that can send out both shoots and roots. If a rhizome is broken into pieces, each piece can produce a new plant.

Cocksfoot is a common perennial grass found in permanent grassland. Its inflorescence is a triangular-shaped panicle with green- or purple-tinged spikelets.

Annual meadow grass is an annual or short-lived perennial. It is often in flower even at short heights and tends to form small tussocks. Its inflorescence is a branched and spreading panicle with small spikelets. This grass is commonly found on acid soils.

Scutch grass is a perennial grass that is an invasive weed. It spreads rapidly by rhizomes (Fig. 11.5). It is best controlled using a systemic herbicide containing glyphosate.

Cereals are also part of the Poaceae family. The most common cereal plants grown in Ireland are barley, wheat, oats and maize. All of these cereals are used for production of animal feeds or for human consumption.

11.5 *Rhizomes on a scutch grass plant*

Noxious weeds are unwanted plants that grow aggressively, multiply quickly and are difficult to control. Some noxious weeds are poisonous to livestock, e.g. ragwort.

Wild oats is a noxious weed in tillage crops. It is highly competitive, multiplies rapidly to produce large numbers of seeds, acts as a host for a number of cereal diseases (e.g. barley yellow dwarf virus) and is difficult to control in cereal crops. It has an open-branched panicle inflorescence with spikelets held out on the branches.

Table 11.2 Grass species in Irish agriculture

11.11 *Timothy*

11.17 *Scutch grass*

11.10 *Meadow foxtail*

11.16 *Maize*

11.9 *Cocksfoot*

11.15 *Oats*

11.8 *Wild oats*

11.14 *Wheat*

11.7 *Italian ryegrass*

11.13 *Barley*

11.6 *Perennial ryegrass*

11.12 *Annual meadow grass*

Family Fabaceae

Family Fabaceae is also known as the pea family. White clover (*Trifolium repens*) and red clover (*Trifolium pratense*) are two important agricultural plants. The family also contains beans and peas. Both contain the bacterium *Rhizobium*, which lives in root nodules of these plants. *Rhizobium* can fix nitrogen into nitrates for plant use. The leaves of clover are trifoliate, and the flowers are normally white or red. Clover is commonly found in grassland, since it increases the protein content of the herbage and it provides good ground cover to help prevent weeds.

Flowers in plants in the Fabaceae family have five sepals, five petals, ten stamens and one carpel.

> **Trifoliate:** each leaf is composed of three leaflets.

> **Herbage:** vegetation or grass.

11.19 *White clover*

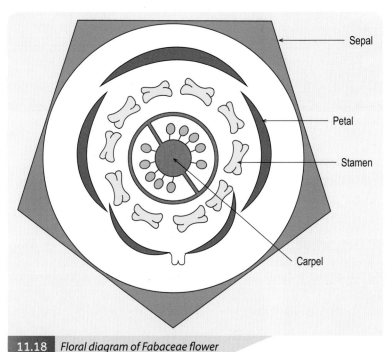

11.18 *Floral diagram of Fabaceae flower*

Sepal

Petal

Stamen

Carpel

11.20 *Red clover*

Family Asteraceae

This is the largest plant family, containing many grassland weeds (e.g. daisy, dandelion and ragwort) and commercial crops (e.g. sunflower). The flower heads of these plants are composed of many individual flowers all sharing the same receptacle. The individual flowers are so densely arranged that they resemble a single flower. There are two types of floret: ray florets and disc florets. Ray florets lack stamens, while disc florets contain both stamens and carpels. Members of the Asteraceae family use wind dispersal to disperse their seeds.

> **Receptacle:** the main stem of a flower.

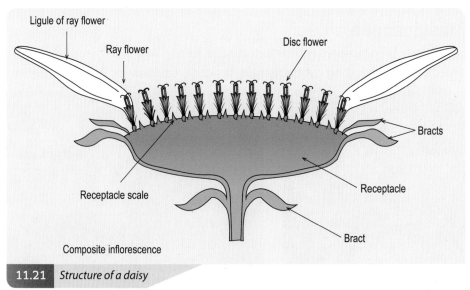

Ligule of ray flower

Ray flower

Disc flower

Bracts

Receptacle scale

Receptacle

Bract

Composite inflorescence

11.21 *Structure of a daisy*

Ragwort is a noxious weed and is poisonous to cattle and horses. Sheep can tolerate some ragwort. It is not usually grazed by livestock; however, care must be taken to ensure that this weed is not incorporated into silage as livestock selectivity is reduced and animals will eat it. Ragwort is a biennial plant. In its first year it can be identified as a rosette: a cluster of leaves in a circular form. In its second year it produces yellow flowers in late spring, which can produce thousands of seeds that are mainly dispersed by wind.

11.22 *Ragwort flowers*

11.23 *Dandelion flowers*

Selectivity: carefully choosing something.

Regenerate: the ability of the plant to regrow after loss of part of the plant or damage to the plant.

Dandelion is a common perennial weed of permanent grassland. It produces yellow flowers from early summer until October and a single flower head produces an average of 180 seeds. Dandelions can be difficult to remove, since they have a long tap root which can regenerate if broken. The dandelion plant overwinters as a rosette.

11.24 *Dandelion rosette*

11.25 *Spear thistle*

Spear thistle is a member of this family and is also listed as a noxious weed. Spear thistle is a biennial and can be a serious problem in grassland and in tillage crops. It can produce large numbers of seeds that are dispersed by wind.

Family Brassicaceae

The Brassicaceae family is commonly called the cabbage family. Many of the members of this family are vegetables, including cabbage, kale, broccoli, cauliflower, Brussels sprouts.

11.26 *Broccoli*

11.27 *Forage rape*

Catch crops such as forage rape, mustard, leafy turnip and tillage radish are also members of this family. They are described as cruciferous vegetables because of the similarity of its four-petal flowers to the shape of a cross. The flowers contain four sepals, four petals, four stamens and two carpels.

Charlock is a common annual weed found in arable land. It flowers between May and July with a bright yellow flower. Its seeds can remain dormant for many years and can appear on land that has been permanent grassland after it has been ploughed for the first time.

Shepherd's purse is also a member of the Brassicaceae family and a very common weed. It produces small white flowers and it can flower and produce seeds throughout the year. It can be recognised by its triangular-shaped seed heads.

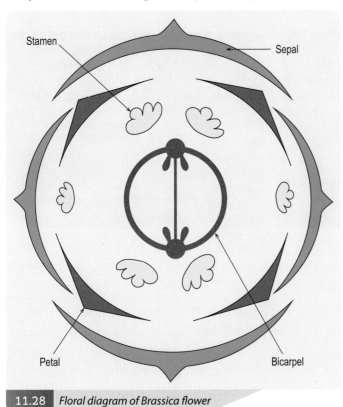

11.28   *Floral diagram of Brassica flower*

11.29   *Charlock*

11.30   *Shepherd's purse*

Family Polygonaceae

Common plants of agricultural importance in this family include the dock plant and buckwheat. There are two main species of dock: the curled dock (*Rumex crispus*) and the broadleaf dock (*Rumex obtusifolius*). Both species can affect the productivity of a grassland sward. Docks thrive in an open sward (presence of bare patches of soil) and as a result are a problem in pasture used for silage and in grassland that has been overgrazed or poached. Docks are a noxious weed. They are a perennial with a large tap root and leaves. They produce large clusters of green flowers which turn red when mature.

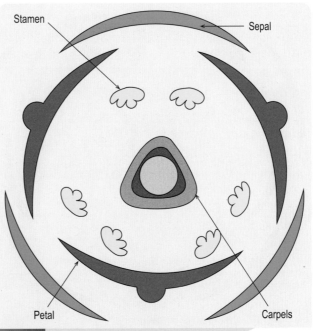

11.31   *Floral diagram of broadleaf dock*

Sward: land covered with grass.

Despite the name, buckwheat is not related to wheat and is not a member of the grass family. It is suitable as a short season crop and is sometimes described as a pseudocereal as its grain can be used in a similar way to the grains of the cereal family. Buckwheat can be used as a gluten-free alternative to cereal products and is a crop that is recommended as a catch crop for the GLAS scheme.

11.32   *Curled dock*

GLAS stands for Green, Low-Carbon, Agri-Environmental Scheme. It is an agri-environmental scheme.

11.33   *Broadleaf dock*

11.34   *Buckwheat*

Family Ranunculaceae

Creeping buttercup, meadow buttercup and lesser celandine are all members of this family, commonly called the buttercup family. Both creeping buttercup and meadow buttercup can reduce the productivity of a grassland sward, since they are unpalatable to livestock. Creeping buttercup can be identified by its bright yellow flower with five petals (flowers between May and July), hairy leaves and stem. It can reproduce both by seed and asexually by producing **stolons** which can rapidly colonise an area of land.

Unpalatable: something that does not taste nice.

Stolon: a horizontal stem that grows above the ground from the base of a plant and produces a new plant from its tip.

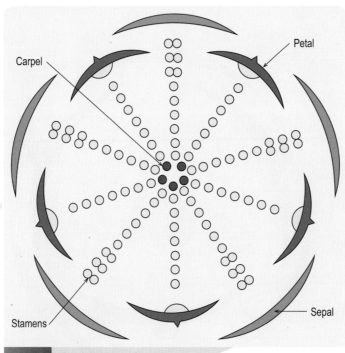

Carpel

Petal

Stamens

Sepal

11.35   *Floral diagram of buttercup*

11.36   *Creeping buttercup*

11.37   *Meadow buttercup*

Meadow buttercup is a strong weed of older permanent grassland. It has a more upright growth habit than creeping buttercup and it too can reproduce both by seed and asexually from an underground **rhizome**. Meadow buttercup flowers from May to July. Buttercups have five sepals, five petals and numerous stamens and carpels

Family Urticaceae

The common nettle is a member of this family and it is frequently found in hedgerows. The nettle is a plant that bears either male or female flowers and they are wind-pollinated. Livestock normally avoid eating the growing weed but will eat it in hay.

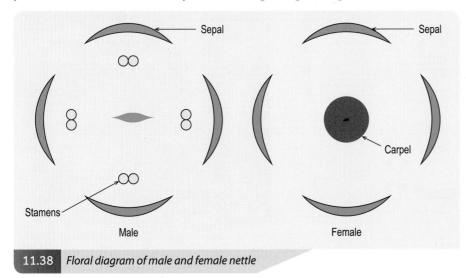

11.38 *Floral diagram of male and female nettle*

11.39 *Common nettle*

Family Solanaceae

This large group of plants contains one of the most important tillage crops in Ireland: the potato. Other members of the family include tomatoes, tobacco and chili peppers. Common varieties of potato grown commercially in Ireland include Kerr's Pink, Rooster, Maris Piper and Queens. The flower consists of five sepals, five petals, five stamens and two carpels.

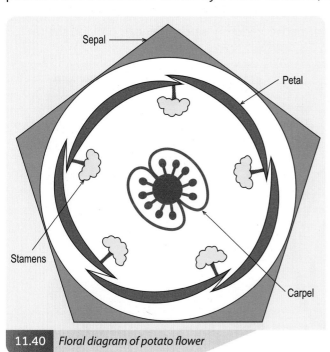

11.40 *Floral diagram of potato flower*

11.41 *Potato plant*

Family Rubiaceae

Goose grass is known by several names, including cleavers and robin-run-the-hedge. It is an annual plant that is a common weed in tillage crops and hedgerows. It can grow to form extensive masses which can drag down a cereal crop. The seeds of this plant contain little hooks which can attach to clothing or animals' coats. The flower has four sepals and four petals.

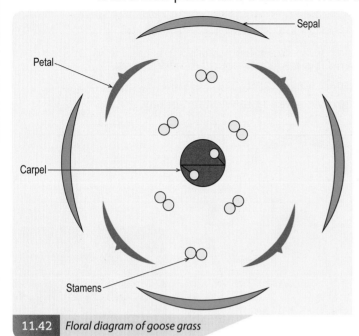

11.42 *Floral diagram of goose grass*

11.43 *Goose grass*

Family Rosaceae

This family produces large flowers with five petals and sepals and numerous stamens and carpels. There are a wide range of plants in this family including shrubs such as roses, raspberries, hawthorn and blackthorn; fruit trees such as apples, peaches and cherries, and plants such as silverweed. Silverweed is a perennial plant that produces small yellow flowers and can creep along the surface of the soil by producing stolons. Hawthorn and blackthorn are used for native hedging, since they can provide shelter for livestock and habitats for wildlife.

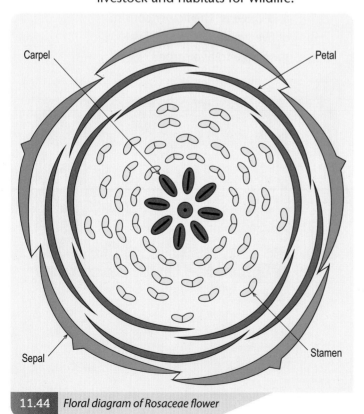

11.44 *Floral diagram of Rosaceae flower*

11.45 *Silverweed*

11.46 *Hawthorn*

Family Apiaceae

The Apiaceae family contains many important food crops including carrots, parsley and parsnip. Another member is cow parsley, which is is a common weed found in hedgerows and at the edges of fields. Its inflorescence is called an umbel, which consists of a number of short stalks with small white flowers all originating from the same point. The flower consists of five sepals, five petals, five stamens and two carpels (see Fig. 11.47).

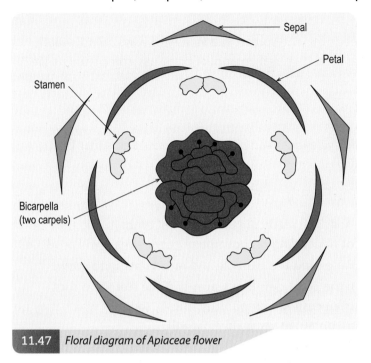

11.47   *Floral diagram of Apiaceae flower*

11.48   *Cow parsley*

11.49   *Carrot*

Plant life cycles

Plants can be categorised by the type of life cycle they have.

Annual plants

Annual plants complete their life cycle in one year. Examples of annual plants include maize, peas and annual meadow grass. Annual plants germinate, produce flowers or fruit and die in one season.

An annual plant goes through the following stages.

- **Seed:** the seed is sown in the soil. The seed contains the plant embryo and may be classified as a monocot or dicot depending on how many cotyledons it will produce.
- **Germination:** the seed germinates and the plumule and radicle begin to grow.

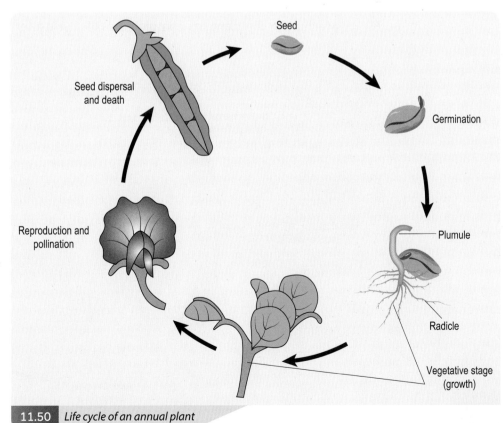

11.50   *Life cycle of an annual plant*

- **Vegetative stage (growth):** the plant develops leaves and the stem and root continue to grow. The plant produces food through photosynthesis, some of which may be stored in a tap root or used for continued vegetative growth. The plant then develops flowers.
- **Reproduction and pollination:** pollen from the anthers is carried by insects or wind and trapped on the stigma. The male gamete travels down the pollen tube to the ovary where it fuses with the ovule to become the seed. In flowering plants the fruit then develops.
- **Seed dispersal and death:** seeds may be spread in a variety of ways: wind, water, animal and self-dispersal. After seed dispersal an annual plant has completed its life cycle and dies.

Biennial plants

Biennial plants complete their life cycle in 2 years. Ragwort, carrots and sugar beet are biennial plants.

Year 1

- **Seed:** the seed is sown in the soil. The seed contains the plant embryo and may be classified as a monocot or dicot depending on how many cotyledons it will produce.
- **Germination:** the seed germinates and the plumule and radicle begin to grow.
- **Vegetative stage 1 (growth):** the plant develops leaves and the stem and root continue to grow. The plant produces food by photosynthesis, some of which may be stored in a tap root or used for continued vegetative growth.
- **Dormancy:** the plant undergoes a period of dormancy, usually during the winter. Growth and development cease during this time.

Year 2

- **Vegetative stage 2:** the plant undergoes further growth in year two and flowers develop during this growth period.
- Pollination, reproduction and seed dispersal take place as in the annual cycle, at which point the plant has completed its life cycle after 2 years and dies.

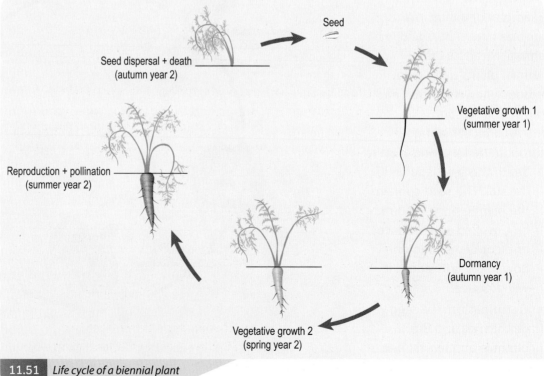

11.51 *Life cycle of a biennial plant*

Perennial plants

Perennial plants grow every year from the root, producing flowers and seeds. Perennial ryegrass and clover are important perennials in grassland production.

A perennial plant will germinate from a seed in its first year and go through a vegetative stage of growth, producing flowers and seeds and then undergo a period of dormancy, usually in winter. The following spring the plant will begin to grow again, flowering and producing new seeds before returning to dormancy. It can continue this life cycle for many years until the plant dies.

Plant breeding

Plant breeding is an important aspect of crop production. It involves deliberately choosing plants with specific traits which are beneficial to crop production. This process is called selective breeding. It allows a farmer to choose parent plants with specific desirable traits in order to produce offspring with those traits. Over time those traits can become concentrated within a species. Genetic engineering allows the production of new plant species which contain genes from unrelated organisms, giving rise to plants known as genetically modified (GM) organisms.

Selective breeding

Selective breeding is also known as artificial selection and it can be used to eliminate undesirable traits. Selective breeding of plants produces varieties or cultivars. Selective breeding can be of two types: inbreeding and crossbreeding.

Cultivars and varieties

A cultivar is a 'cultivated variety' that is propagated vegetatively (e.g. cutting, grafting, runners). It is genetically identical to its parent plant, but the seeds produced from the cultivar may not be true to type. A variety results from crossing two parent plants, occurs in nature and is often true to type.

> **True to type:** a plant whose seed will produce the same type of plant as the original plant.

Inbreeding

> DEFINITION
>
> **Inbreeding:** the mating of closely related organisms, which increase the chances of offspring being affected by undesirable recessive traits.

Inbreeding also has the advantage of fixing desirable genetic traits and creating uniformity among offspring. In plant breeding, inbred lines are used to create plant hybrids with desirable traits from the two highly homozygous parent plants. Inbreeding can also naturally occur in plants where self-pollination takes place. Peas are an example of a crop which can self-pollinate.

Crossbreeding

> DEFINITION
>
> **Crossbreeding:** the mating or crossing of animals or plants from two different breeds, varieties or species.

Crossbreeding or outbreeding involves the mating of animals or plants from two different breeds, varieties or species. The offspring in many instances inherit favourable genes from both parents, leading to improved health traits over either parent. This is known as hybrid vigour or heterosis.

> **Heterosis (hybrid vigour):** the increased productivity displayed by offspring from genetically different parents.

Crossbreeding is the opposite of inbreeding: it reduces the risk of harmful recessive genes being displayed in the phenotype by increasing the number of heterozygous pairs of genes. Crossbreeding also comes with disadvantages. There is a loss of hybrid vigour with subsequent crossing of the hybrids. This results in a reduction of the uniformity of the phenotype in the offspring. Crossbreeding also requires maintenance of two purebreds to produce the crossbreeds.

Crossbreeding in F1 hybrid seed varieties

Crossbreeding is extensively used to produce F1 hybrid seed varieties. These hybrid crosses are often stronger, have greater disease resistance and higher yields than their purebred parents. These F1 hybrid seeds are derived from the crossing of two genetically different parent cultivars.

> **F1:** the first (filial) generation of offspring produced by two parents.

F1 hybrid seed production

- Two parent plants are chosen, e.g. cultivar A and cultivar B. The parents have been inbred by repeated self-pollination over several generations, so they are highly homozygous for their traits. These parent plants are known as breeding stock.
- Cultivar A and cultivar B are then cross-pollinated by hand. This involves the removal of immature anthers that produce the pollen from cultivar A, and dusting the pollen from the anthers of cultivar B onto the stigma of cultivar A.

The seeds which are produced as a result of pollination are a hybrid of cultivars A and B and contain genes from both plants. These seeds are called F1 hybrid cultivars. They benefit from hybrid vigour and they have a uniform phenotype.

The production of F1 hybrid seeds is an expensive process, as the parent cultivars must be crossed every year. If the F1 hybrids are crossed for an F2 generation, the offspring have greater variability compared to the F1 generation and lose some of the hybrid vigour of the F1. Also, if a grower wants to ensure uniformity, they will need to purchase F1 hybrid seeds each year.

11.52   *F1 seed variety packets*

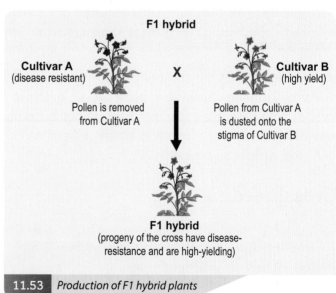

11.53   *Production of F1 hybrid plants*

Reproductive technologies

Reproductive technologies have led to an increase in the number of offspring that can be produced from genetically superior plants and animals that would not otherwise be possible naturally. Micropropagation, grafting, cuttings and layering are used extensively in horticulture to produce large numbers of plant offspring asexually.

Importance of seed variety

There are a wide variety of seeds for different crops available to Irish farmers. Choosing a seed variety is important as the decision should be made based on several factors, including soil type, climate and system of farming. Choosing a variety that provides optimum growth for the conditions on an individual farm will give the best return to the farmer.

Seed varieties are recommended based on different traits. The traits that are tested by growing the crop repeatedly in trials in different parts of the country vary for different types of crops and the requirements from farmers. The Department of Agriculture, Food and the Marine (DAFM) produces a list of recommended seed varieties annually recommending varieties of grass and clover, winter and spring cereals, legumes and catch crops. All the recommended seed varieties have been tested extensively in numerous locations around the country and have been deemed best suited for growing on Irish farms. Seed varieties sold also comply with the requirements of the Seed Certification Scheme which ensures standards of quality are maintained in seed production and sale.

Grass seed varieties

Grass species are assessed on several different characteristics when they are grown in trials. Their scores in each category are provided so farmers can make an informed choice about which grass variety to choose based on the needs of their farm.

Grass characteristics assessed for recommended varieties:
- Heading date
- Total yield (DM/ha)
- Ground cover score
- Spring, summer and autumn growth
- First and second cut silage
- Grass quality (DMD value).

Grass species recommended to farmers include perennial ryegrass, Italian ryegrass and hybrid ryegrasses. Perennial ryegrass is the most popular grass seed variety sown in Ireland and is categorised by maturing date.

Maturity: early, intermediate or late heading grasses. This indicates when the grass 'heads out', i.e. when the ear emerges on the plant. A farmer may choose an early, intermediate or late heading grass based on what the pasture is used for. This may be early spring grazing or first cut silage, long-term grazing usage or a variety of pasture and silage production. Some farmers choose to create a seed mixture with a range of heading dates to ensure a constant supply of grass.

Italian ryegrass is used mainly for silage production but persists only for 2–3 years before it has to be reseeded.

Hybrid ryegrasses are achieved by crossing perennial ryegrass and Italian ryegrass. The hybrid is chosen for the persistence inherited from perennial ryegrass and high yield of Italian ryegrass, but it does not quite achieve the yield of a purebred Italian ryegrass species.

Diploids versus tetraploid grasses

Tetraploid grass varieties are more palatable to livestock and are more resistant to drought than diploids. Diploid grasses have a higher tillering ability and higher dry matter content than tetraploids.

Cereals

The DAFM also releases an annual list of recommended cereal varieties which have been trialled and given scores on several characteristics including:

* Relative yield
* Straw height
* Resistance to lodging
* Straw breakdown
* Earliness of ripening
* Disease resistance (diseases are specific to each individual cereal).

Information is also provided on grain quality for cereals by giving specific values for each variety for the following tests:

* Hagberg falling number (wheat)
* Hectolitre weight (barley, wheat, oats)
* Kernel content (oats)
* Protein content (wheat)
* Screenings (barley)
* 1000 grain weight (barley, wheat, oats).

Exercise 11.1

Research what each of the grain tests assesses when analysing cereal quality.

Summary

* Poaceae is the most important plant family in agriculture.
* Members of this family include perennial ryegrass, wheat, barley, oats and maize.
* The members of this family can be distinguished from one another based on their inflorescence.
* Noxious weeds are unwanted plants that grow aggressively, multiply quickly and are difficult to control.
* Some noxious weeds are poisonous to livestock.
* Wild oats is a noxious weed. It can produce large numbers of seeds, act as a host to several cereal diseases and become difficult to control in cereal crops.
* Family Asteraceae is the largest plant family, containing many grassland weeds (e.g. dandelion, ragwort and thistles). Spear thistles and ragwort are noxious weeds.
* The Brassicaceae family gets its name from the similarity of its four-petal flowers to the shape of a cross. Many important agricultural crops belong to this family, e.g. turnips, oilseed rape, kale and cabbage.
* Red and white clovers belong to the Fabaceae family. Both contain the bacterium *Rhizobium*, which fixes nitrogen in the root nodules of these plants.
* Plants undergo one of three life cycles: annual, biennial or perennial. A plant with an annual life cycle completes its entire life cycle in 1 year. A biennial plant

completes its life cycle in 2 years. A perennial plant lives and produces seed for many years.

- Selective breeding is the process of breeding animals or plants with desirable traits and concentrating those desirable traits in their offspring.
- Selective breeding is also known as artificial selection and can be divided into inbreeding and crossbreeding.
- Inbreeding involves crossing closely related plants, which increases the chance of offspring being affected by undesirable recessive traits.
- Crossbreeding involves the crossing of animals from two different species or varieties.
- Hybrid vigour (heterosis) is the increased productivity displayed by offspring from genetically different parents.
- F1 seed varieties are produced by crossbreeding two genetically different cultivars. The F1 hybrids benefit from hybrid vigour and are all uniform in phenotype.
- Seed varieties sold in Ireland must comply with the standards set out by the Seed Certification Scheme. Seeds are tested in crop trials and several traits are assessed and scored. The DAFM recommends a variety of grass, cereal and catch crop seed varieties annually for growth on Irish farms.

 PowerPoint Summary

QUESTIONS

1. A ring of sepals is called a:
   - (a) Corolla
   - (b) Carpel
   - (c) Calyx
   - (d) Stamen.

2. Which of the following is not a member of the Poaceae family?
   - (a) Perennial ryegrass
   - (b) Buckwheat
   - (c) Barley
   - (d) Maize

3. Clover is known for its ability to fix which chemical element?
   - (a) Oxygen
   - (b) Nitrogen
   - (c) Carbon
   - (d) Hydrogen

4. Which of the following statements is true for ragwort?
   - (a) It is a noxious weed.
   - (b) Its leaves form a rosette.
   - (c) It is a member of Family Asteraceae.
   - (d) All of the above.

5. Which of the following describes the structure of a flower in the Brassicaceae family?
   - (a) Four sepals, four petals, four stamens, one carpel
   - (b) Four sepals, four petals, two stamens, one carpel
   - (c) Four sepals, four petals, four stamens, two carpels
   - (d) Four sepals, four petals, two stamens, two carpels

6. Dock leaves belong to which family?

   (a) Polygonaceae

   (c) Apiaceae

   (b) Ranunculaceae

   (d) Urticaceae

7. Place the stages of the life cycle of an annual plant in the correct order.

   (a) Seed dispersal and death

   (c) Germination

   (b) Vegetative growth

   (d) Reproduction and pollination

8. Identify each of the following plants and name its plant family:

   (a)

   (c)

   (b)

   (d)

9. Grasses are identified by their inflorescence. Explain the term 'inflorescence'.

10. Wild oats are described as a noxious weed. Explain the term 'noxious weed'.

11. Identify the plant family to which each of the following belongs.

    (a) Scutch grass

    (e) Dandelion

    (b) Raspberry

    (f) Parsnip

    (c) Kale

    (g) Potato

    (d) Meadow buttercup

    (h) Robin-run-the-hedge

12. Outline the advantages and disadvantages of inbreeding.

13. Explain the term 'hybrid vigour'.

14. Describe the production of F1 seed varieties. What are the advantages and the disadvantages of the production of F1 hybrid seed varieties?

15. Wild oats are described as a noxious weed. Give three reasons why this weed is described as noxious.

16. Search online for the DAFM webpage on the Control of Noxious Weeds and use the information to answer the following questions.

    (a) State which four weeds are considered noxious under Irish law.

    (b) What responsibility does a landowner/land occupier have in relation to noxious weeds?

17. Draw a floral diagram for a member of the family Fabaceae labelling the sepals, petals, stamens and carpels.

18. Compare the structure of the flowers from the Rosaceae and Brassicaceae families. In Fig. 11.54, identify the plants from each family in (a) and (b).

11.54   *(a) Rosaceae plant;*   *(b) Brassicaceae plant*

19. How can crossbreeding be used to improve the productivity of a crop production system?

20. State three characteristics tested in cereal crops which are listed on the DAFM's Recommended Cereals List.

21. Explain, giving an example, why a plant/crop breeding programme would be beneficial in Irish agriculture.

22. State two factors which you consider to be important when choosing a grass seed variety and give a reason why those factors are important.

 Solutions   Weblinks

Principles of crop production and management

When you have completed this chapter you should be able to:

- Evaluate the impact of different crop management practices on food-producing and other animals
- Understand how a variety of soil factors influence crop productivity
- Recognise the purpose of crop rotation and the benefits of, and alternatives to, crop rotation as a means of indirect disease control
- Discuss strategies for crop protection against diseases (fungal, bacterial or viral)
- Appreciate the importance of recognising and controlling disease in crops and evaluate the benefits and disadvantages of using chemicals for this purpose
- Appreciate the need for compliance in relation to notifiable diseases
- Discuss the implications of sustainable development for crop production
- Compare conventional and organic food production
- Recognise the need for safe work practices, including the safe handling, harvesting and storage of crops
- Identify farm health and safety hazards associated with the management of crops
- Discuss the controls and precautions necessary to prevent accidents, injury and ill-health on the farm
- Carry out an investigation to compare plant uniformity from certified seed and uncertified seed (SPA – Higher Level only)
- Investigate the effect of weather and soil conditions on the percentage germination of an agricultural seed (SPA)
- Investigate the effect of nutrients on the growth of a sample of plants and measure the biomass of these plants above and below ground (SPA).

Seed certification in Ireland

The Department of Agriculture, Food and the Marine (DAFM) is responsible for seed certification in Ireland. Potatoes, cereals, vegetables and fodder crops are just some of the crops included in the scheme.

Seeds included in the seed certification scheme must pass identity and purity tests. The main advantages of using certified seed are that a higher germination rate, and therefore a high yield, can be guaranteed. Seeds that are intended for sale are listed on the National Catalogue or EU Common Catalogue of Agricultural Plant Varieties. This means that the variety has passed certain identity and purity tests relating to **distinctness**, **uniformity** and **stability**.

Distinctness: whether a new variety differs from existing varieties within the same species.
Uniformity: whether the characteristics used to establish distinctness are expressed uniformly.
Stability: whether characteristics do not change over subsequent generations.

For agricultural crops, trials are also carried out to establish a variety's Value for Cultivation or Use (VCU).

Certified seed

- Must have a minimum germination rate of 85%
- Must have a minimum analytical purity rate of 98%
- Must be treated with fungicide/pesticide
- Must be completely free from wild oat seed.

These standards apply to barley, wheat and oats, grass and maize seed. However, the percentage germination for maize is 90% and for perennial ryegrass and white clover it is 80%. The purity rate for perennial ryegrass is 96%.

12.1 *Wild oats growing in wheat*

 **SPA 12.1** (H) | To compare plant uniformity from certified and uncertified seed

SPECIFIED PRACTICAL ACTIVITY (Higher Level only)

Note: This experiment can be performed with any crop where a sample of certified seed and uncertified or home-produced seed is used.

State your hypothesis, prediction, independent variable, dependent variable and controlled variable.

Materials

Sample of certified seed of choice, sample of uncertified seed of choice, beaker, water, petri dishes or seed trays, filter paper, area for planting

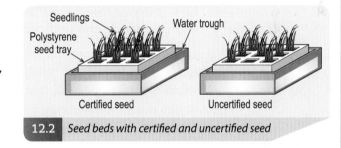

12.2 *Seed beds with certified and uncertified seed*

Method

1. Count out 100 certified seeds and 100 uncertified seeds. Do not mix the two samples.
2. Identify the characteristics of the certified seed that classify it as uniform.
3. In the case of cereal grains or similar, place each sample in a separate labelled beaker, add water and leave to soak for 24 hours.
4. Plant the seeds from each sample in separate trays. Larger seeds may be planted in separate labelled beds in a polytunnel or outdoors.
5. Both sets of seeds should be provided with the same amount of light, water and nutrients.
6. Monitor the seeds until both sets have reached establishment.
7. Examine both sets of seeds. Identify how many of the certified seeds have the characteristics that define its uniformity. Repeat for the uncertified seeds.

Result

Place the number of uniform seeds in each sample over 100, and multiply by $\frac{100}{1}$ to calculate the percentage uniformity. Compare the two results.

Validation

1. Construct a table to record your results.
2. Present your data in a suitable graph of your choice (bar chart, scatter graph or pie chart).
3. Do the results of this experiment support the hypothesis? Explain your answer.
4. Discuss how you established if your certified seed/uncertified seed demonstrated uniformity.
5. Based on your results, would you recommend the use of certified seed in crop production? Justify your answer.

Factors affecting crop management

There are several factors that affect crop management. While a farmer can maximise the germination rate of a crop by sowing certified seed, several other factors need to be considered to ensure establishment, to minimise competition from weeds, attack from pests and diseases, and to ensure optimal growth and yield at harvest.

1. **Seed variety selection:** the seed variety chosen has a major effect on the management of the crop. Seed varieties are developed for many reasons: yield, disease resistance, strength of stem, length of stem, resistance to lodging, earliness of harvesting and winter hardiness, as well as dry matter content, palatability, grain quality and productivity. The approach to crop management will depend on which factors are prioritised by the farmer: a variety that is disease resistant may need less pesticide and fungicide to be applied throughout the growing season; a variety chosen for winter hardiness may allow a farmer to spread out their workload on a mixed farm by sowing at a different time of year. Market factors will also have an influence on a chosen seed variety, as some varieties of root and vegetable crop are more popular than others.

2. **Soil and water:** soil type largely determines which crops can be grown, but also whether there is sufficient drainage and aeration for roots, mineral availability, suitable soil temperature for germination and whether the land needs to be irrigated during the growing season. Lighter sandy soils make crop planting, fertiliser application, herbicide and pesticide application and harvesting much easier than heavier clay soils.

3. **Previous crop history:** if the same crop is planted year after year, nutrients may be depleted in the soil or pests of that crop may build up. This has to be taken into account when planning for crop production during the following season. A good crop rotation can help to alleviate the problems with weed and pest build-up, and those associated with nutrient depletion from growing the same crop continuously. If crop rotation is not practised, management of the crop must take into account the application of fertiliser, herbicide and pesticide where necessary.

4. **Weed, disease and pest control:** competition from weeds is most prevalent during germination and establishment. This is particularly important in slow-growing crops such as kale. If weed control is not part of the crop management programme, then the crop will struggle to establish itself and compete with weeds and will fail to reach its optimal yield. An application of a pre-emergent herbicide at sowing following a post-emergent herbicide at establishment of the crop can keep weed infestations to a minimum (see pages 196, 235). Use of certified seed treated with pesticides and fungicides can also help to control pests and diseases in the growing crop.

Video
Spraying pesticides on crops

5. **Plant nutrition:** nitrogen, phosphorus and potassium are the three main nutrients required by the growing crop. Soil tests (see Chapter 8, pages 117–118) should be carried out prior to planting to determine the correct rate of fertiliser application at sowing, or broadcast on the growing crop. The correct type and rate of fertiliser is a crucial part of crop management for optimal plant growth and yield.

6. **Seeding rate:** the number of seeds sown to optimise yield of the crop. A low seeding rate leads to a lower overall yield, but also provides space for weeds to compete with the growing crop. A good crop management programme will optimise seeding rate, taking into account the size of seed and spacing required by the seed.

7. **Weather and timing:** weather has a direct effect on the sowing date, fertiliser application and harvesting of a crop. Farmers planting winter crops need to plant early enough that seedlings will establish and reach the grass corn stage (for cereals)

before cold winter temperatures stall growth until spring. Prolonged adverse weather conditions can reduce access to fields with heavy machinery, reducing the ability to apply fertiliser, pesticides or herbicides or to harvest the crop. Some farmers have to consider the advantages and disadvantages of planting winter and spring crops, as a prolonged winter season may delay the planting of a spring crop, which can lead to a reduced yield at harvest.

Impact of crop management practices on animals

Crop management practices have an impact on a wide variety of animals in farming environments.

- Grass and catch crops such as kale and stubble turnip provide a food source for grazing livestock, which can allow livestock to outwinter or to be zero grazed. They provide an alternative source of winter fodder to livestock.
- Weed control can improve the quality of pasture available to animals, as they graze on grasses such as perennial ryegrass and high-protein plant material such as clover. Weed control also reduces the presence of noxious weeds such as ragwort, which is poisonous to cattle.
- Drainage of soil in grassland crops leads to a reduction in pests such as liver fluke in cattle and sheep.
- Rotation of crops reduces the number of pests of plants and animals present in fields. This includes pests such as wireworms and leatherjackets.
- Application of pesticides reduces the number of aphids present in crops, particularly in cereal and potato crops, where they spread viral diseases.
- Energy crops such as miscanthus can provide shelter for nesting birds, and habitats for other small and medium-sized mammals such as mice, shrews, rabbits and foxes.
- The cover that energy crops and catch crops provide during a time period where land might lie fallow provides wildlife corridors, improving biodiversity.

Winter sowing versus spring sowing

As well as choosing a seed for its certified qualities, a farmer may choose to sow a crop (particularly cereals) either in winter or in spring. As a result, they will have to choose a seed type suitable to the seasonal conditions. Both winter and spring varieties of cereal seeds are available, each with their own properties.

Table 12.1 Characteristics of winter and spring seed varieties	
Winter variety seeds	**Spring variety seeds**
Frost resistant	Not frost resistant
Sown September to November	Sown February to April
Harvested mid-July onwards	Harvested August onwards
Longer growing season	Shorter growing season
Higher yield due to longer growing season	Lower yield due to shorter growing season

Ideally, farmers should sow as much as possible of their land with winter varieties, since this produces a higher yield with earlier harvesting. It may not always be possible to plant all winter varieties, however. If there is a crop rotation in place, one crop may be harvested in late autumn; sowing a spring variety may be more suitable in these circumstances. However, winter varieties have several advantages.

Advantages of sowing winter variety cereals:

- In a mixed farming system (tillage and livestock), labour may be spread out over the year by sowing winter varieties, since the farmer will be busy with calving and lambing in spring.
- Winter varieties have a longer growing season than spring varieties and, as a result, a higher yield by up to 20%.
- Harvesting dates for winter varieties are earlier, so they can be harvested in good weather conditions. Harvesting may prove to be difficult for spring varieties in poor autumn conditions and losses may occur as a result.
- Poor weather conditions in spring (late frost and snow, cold temperatures) may delay sowing, germination and establishment of a crop. This can lead to a delay in harvesting and lower yields than winter varieties.
- The suitability of the land to be used for growing crops must also be taken into account when planning for tillage. Soils that are lacking in nutrients, have a poor structure or are infested with pests will not lead to high crop yields. These problems can be overcome by crop rotation.

12.3　*Unripe winter wheat*

Germination of seeds: the influence of soil on crop productivity

While water, oxygen and temperature are all essential factors for seed germination, the environmental conditions in which seeds are sown can also influence the germination rate of a seed. As these factors influence the germination of a crop, this can have a knock-on effect on the establishment rate of a crop and ultimately the yield at the end of a growing season. As seeds are sown in the soil, the characteristics of soil have a major influence on crop productivity. Weather also has an influence as it determines temperatures of air and soil and the amount of sunlight available to a germinating crop.

Factors that can affect the germination of a seed include:

- Depth of sowing
- Soil compaction
- pH of soil
- Drainage/saturation of soil
- Soil type
- Photoperiod
- Temperature (weather or climatic conditions).

Photoperiod: the length of time each day that a living organism (plant or animal) receives exposure to light.

 **SPA 12.2** To investigate the effect of weather and soil conditions on the percentage germination of an agricultural seed

SPECIFIED PRACTICAL ACTIVITY

For each test, state your hypothesis, prediction, independent variable, dependent variable and controlled variable.

Materials

Seeds of an agricultural variety (e.g. barley, wheat, maize, perennial ryegrass), seed trays, water, different soil samples, buffer solutions for various pH values (e.g. pH 4, pH 10), desk lamps, heat mats or seed incubators

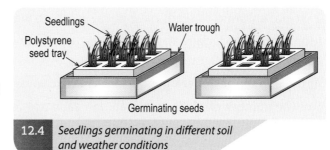

12.4 *Seedlings germinating in different soil and weather conditions*

Method

Test 1: Effect of temperature on percentage germination

1. Count out 100 seeds and split into two groups of 50.

2. Plant the two sets of seeds in separate seed trays.

3. Place one seed tray indoors in the laboratory or in a polytunnel and place one in a fridge. The trays kept indoors could also be kept in seed incubators or on heat mats to keep their temperature constant.

4. Monitor the temperature of both seed trays on a daily basis for 2 weeks. Count the number of germinated seeds in each tray each day for 2 weeks.

5. At the end of the 2-week period, count the number of seeds that germinated in the tray kept indoors/in a polytunnel, and count the number of seeds that germinated in the tray that was kept in the fridge.

6. Plot a graph of the cumulative total of seeds germinated each day for the 2-week period for the seeds kept indoors and the seeds kept in the fridge. Note the average temperature for each of the indoor and fridge trays.

7. Calculate the percentage germination for each tray by placing the number of germinated seeds over 50 (or other number used) and multiply by 100/1 to calculate the percentage germination. Compare the number of seeds germinated in each tray. Identify which tray (and temperature) showed the earliest seed germination.

Test 2: Effect of depth of sowing on percentage germination

1. As in the previous test, plant two equal size groups of seeds in two large plant pots. Plant the first set at a depth of 1 cm and plant the second set at a depth of 5 cm. More than two plant pots can be used for this experiment with an equal number of seeds, spaced at the same distance, but at different depths.

2. Keep all plant pots at the same temperature (i.e. in the laboratory or polytunnel) for 2 weeks, ensuring all seeds have equal access to water and light.

3. Monitor the seeds on a daily basis and record the cumulative total number of seeds germinated in each pot.

4. At the end of the 2-week period record the total number of seeds germinated in each pot.

5. Plot a graph of the number of seeds germinated in each pot for the 2-week period.

6. Calculate the percentage germination for each pot as in the previous experiment. Compare the results of each pot. Identify from your graphs and table of results if there is a correlation between depth of sowing and percentage germination.

Test 3: Effect of soil compaction on percentage germination

1. Count out two equal size samples of seeds and plant at the same depth in two equal size seed trays. The first seed tray should contain a compacted soil and the second tray should contain an uncompacted soil. A compacted soil sample can be obtained by taking a sample of the uncompacted soil and crushing it with a pestle and mortar to compact it before placing in the tray.

2. Keep both seed trays at the same temperature (i.e. in the laboratory or polytunnel) for 2 weeks, ensuring all seeds have equal access to water and light.

3. Monitor the seeds daily and record the cumulative total number of seeds germinated in each tray.

4. At the end of the 2-week period record the total number of seeds germinated in each tray.

5. Plot the number of seeds germinated in each tray for the 2-week period.

6. Calculate the percentage germination for each tray as in the previous experiment. Compare the results of each tray. Identify from your graphs and table of results if there is a relationship between soil compaction and percentage germination.

Test 4: Effect of soil type on percentage germination

1. As in the previous test, plant two equal size groups of seeds at equal depth in two seed trays. Plant the first set in a sandy soil and the second set in a clay soil. More than two seed trays can be used for this experiment with an equal number of seeds, spaced at the same distance, but with different soil types.

2. Keep all seed trays at the same temperature (i.e. in the laboratory or polytunnel) for 2 weeks, ensuring all seeds have equal access to water and light.

3. Monitor the seeds on a daily basis and record the cumulative total number of seeds germinated in each tray.

4. At the end of the 2-week period record the total number of seeds germinated in each tray.

5. Plot the number of seeds germinated in each tray for the 2-week period.

6. Calculate the percentage germination for each tray as in the previous experiment. Identify from your graphs and table of results if there is a relationship between soil type and percentage germination.

Test 5: Effect of pH on percentage germination

1. Count out multiple sets of 50 seeds. Place each set of seeds in a separate petri dish or seed tray with damp tissue or filter paper. Add a different buffer solution to each dish, e.g. pH 4, pH 6, pH 10. Ideally set up a petri dish for each pH from 4 to 10.

2. Keep all petri dishes at the same temperature (i.e. in the laboratory or polytunnel) for 2 weeks, ensuring all seeds have equal access to light. Keep the filter paper or tissue moist with its appropriate buffer solution.

3. Monitor the seeds on a daily basis and record the cumulative total number of seeds germinated in each tray.

4. At the end of the 2-week period record the total number of seeds germinated in each tray.

5. Plot the number of seeds germinated in each dish for the 2-week period for each pH value.

6. Calculate the percentage germination for each tray as in the previous experiment. Compare the results of each tray. Draw a graph showing the number of seeds germinated for each pH value tested. Identify from your graphs and table of results if there is a relationship between pH and percentage germination.

Test 6: Effect of soil saturation on percentage germination

1. Count out three equal size sets of seeds. Plant each set in a different seed tray with the same soil at equal spacings and depth.

2. Do not add any water to the first tray. Add enough water to the second tray to keep the soil moist. Add water to the third seed tray until the soil is saturated.

3. Keep all seed trays at the same temperature (i.e. in the laboratory or polytunnel) for 2 weeks, ensuring all seeds have equal access to light. Continue to add water to the second and third seed trays to keep them moist and saturated, respectively. The first tray should remain dry.

4. Monitor the seeds daily and record the cumulative total number of seeds germinated in each tray.

5. At the end of the 2-week period record the total number of seeds germinated in each tray.

6. Plot a graph of the number of seeds germinated in each tray for the 2-week period.

7. Calculate the percentage germination for each tray as in the previous experiment. Compare the results of each tray. Identify from your graphs and table of results if there is a relationship between soil water availability and percentage germination.

Test 7: Effect of photoperiod on percentage germination

1. Count out multiple sets of seeds of equal numbers. Place each set of seeds in a separate petri dish with damp tissue or filter paper.

2. Wrap one petri dish in two layers of aluminium foil to block out light. These seeds will receive no light for the duration of the experiment.

3. Place each of the remaining dishes under a lamp. Each set of seeds should get a varying amount of light (e.g. one dish could be exposed to light for 12 hours per day, a second dish could be exposed to light for 8 hours per day).

4. When not exposed to light, dishes of seeds should be wrapped in aluminium foil or placed in a dark cupboard. All dishes should be carefully labelled to identify how many hours of light they are exposed to each day.

5. At the end of the 2-week period count how many seeds have germinated in each dish.

6. Calculate the percentage germination for each dish as in the previous tests.

7. Plot a graph showing how many seeds have germinated compared to the number of hours of light the seeds were exposed to daily (the photoperiod).

8. Compare the results of each tray. Identify if there is a correlation between the photoperiod of the seeds and the percentage germination.

Validation

1. Do the results of these experiments support the individual hypotheses? Explain your answer.

2. Identify any problems or difficulties you encountered while conducting these investigations. Outline how you overcame them.

3. Identify any sources of error.

4. For each of your results identify if the data was qualitative or quantitative.

5. Based on your results, make recommendations for the most suitable weather and soil conditions for seed germination.

Crop rotation

Crop rotation is a system of tillage cultivation in which crops are grown in a defined sequence. Each subsequent crop is different from the previous crop: it has different nutritional needs, but also has different pests associated with it.

Crop rotation prevents a build-up of pests in a crop over time. It also prevents the soil being depleted of nutrients and maintains the soil structure.

Advantages of crop rotation

Prevention of the build-up of pests and diseases

If the same crop is grown in the same field year after year, the pests and diseases that affect that crop will accumulate. This will damage the crop and reduce yields. Some of these pests can live in the soil for many years. In order to reduce the risk of attack by pests and diseases, crop rotation using several unrelated crops is advised because the pests that attack each crop will be different, e.g. a root crop followed by a cereal or grassland. This can also help to prevent a build-up of weeds specific to a crop.

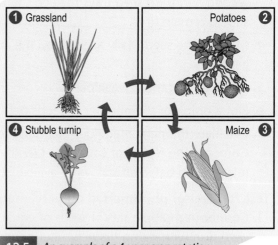

12.5 *An example of a 4-year crop rotation*

Nutrient management

Different crops make use of different nutrients at different rates. If the same crop is continuously grown, it will strip the soil of certain nutrients, making it infertile. Crop rotation prevents this and has the added benefit that some plants add nutrients to the soil. Examples of this include leguminous plants (e.g. peas, beans, clover), which can fix nitrogen.

Deep-rooted crops can be alternated with fibrous-root crops. This allows the use of nutrients that are deep in the soil but unavailable to some crops. For example, the roots of a maize plant can extend up to 1.5 m underground in good soil conditions. The fibrous roots of grass help to maintain the organic matter levels in soil. Therefore, grass is often included in crop rotation.

Soil structure

Fibrous plants such as grasses can help to bind soil together and improve soil structure. They also help to prevent soil erosion. When the grass is ploughed into the soil to prepare for sowing a new crop, the grass contributes to the fertility of the soil in the form of organic matter.

 SPA 12.3 To investigate the effect of nutrients on the growth of a sample of plants and measure the biomass of these plants above and below ground

SPECIFIED PRACTICAL ACTIVITY

State your hypothesis, prediction, independent variable, dependent variable and controlled variable.

Materials

Cereal seedlings, polystyrene seed trays, water troughs, water culture solution, air pump, shears, plastic bags, hook scales, tissue paper, weighing scales

Method

1. Set up four seed trays or flasks as shown in Fig. 12.6. Each polystyrene tray has holes in it to hold the seedlings.

2. Each tray should have an equal number of seedlings placed in it.

3. Place each seed tray into a separate water trough. Ensure that there is a supply of oxygen in each water trough.

4. Make up the mineral solutions using distilled water.

5. Add a different mineral solution (Sach's solution) to each trough as follows:
   - Trough 1: Solution contains all mineral nutrients
   - Trough 2: Contains all mineral nutrients except nitrogen
   - Trough 3: Contains all mineral nutrients except phosphorus
   - Trough 4: Contains all mineral nutrients except potassium.

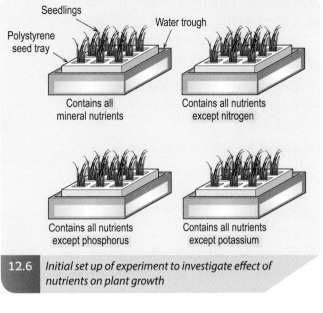

12.6 *Initial set up of experiment to investigate effect of nutrients on plant growth*

6. Leave all trays in sunshine for a week.

7. Observe any change in the seedlings.

8. Continue observations for 1 month.

9. After 1 month record the height of the plants in each tray. Calculate the average height of the plants in each tray.

10. Plot a graph showing the height of each plant and the nutrient absent compared to the control.

11. Record any observations about the physical appearance of the plants in each tray (e.g. wilted, stunted growth, withered or scorched leaves).

12. Compare the appearance of each crop sample (nutrient absent) and its height to the control.

Note: This experiment may be carried out in seed trays with moss peat low in nutrients.

Biomass measurement above ground:

1. In each seed tray harvest all the crop by cutting the stem of the plant at the base where it emerges from the polystyrene.

2. Put all the harvested crop from one tray in a labelled bag.

3. Repeat harvesting in each subsequent trays.

4. Record the mass of each bag by hanging it off the hook scales. This is measurement of the fresh biomass of each plant sample.

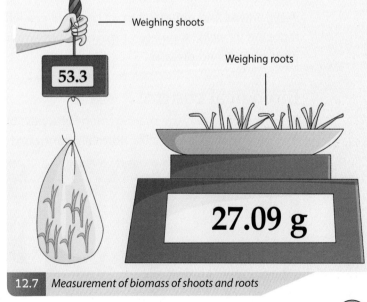

12.7 *Measurement of biomass of shoots and roots*

Biomass measurement below ground:

1. Collect all the roots from each seed tray and place in a labelled bag.

2. Repeat for each of the seed trays.

3. Dry off the roots with tissue paper and record the mass of roots with weighing scales.

4. Repeat for each sample of roots.

5. Plot a graph of mass of biomass above ground versus mass of biomass below ground for each of the samples. Discuss your results.

6. Draw a bar chart of biomass above ground, biomass below ground and total biomass for each tray, identifying each sample by the nutrient that was absent.

Validation

1. Do the results of this experiment support the hypothesis? Explain your answer.

2. Identify any sources of error.

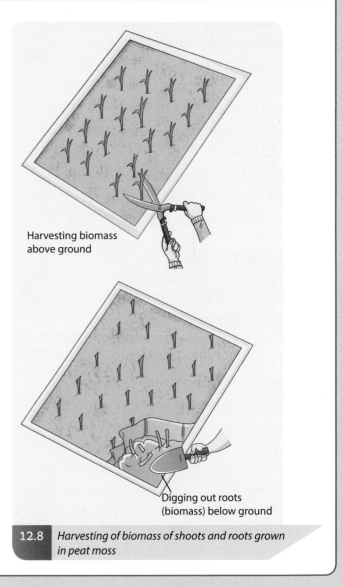

Harvesting biomass above ground

Digging out roots (biomass) below ground

12.8 *Harvesting of biomass of shoots and roots grown in peat moss*

Control of pests, weeds and diseases

Pests, weeds and diseases can all have adverse effects on a crop, damaging the crop and reducing its yield. A variety of methods are employed on farms to reduce the effect of pests, weeds and diseases.

Biological control

Biological control is the management of a pest by introducing a predator or parasite of that organism. The predator normally controls the pest organism by consuming the pest

12.9 *Leaf roll is a viral disease of potatoes that is transmitted by aphids.*

12.10 *A ladybird eating an aphid*

or killing or damaging it. A common example of a biological control is the ladybird and aphid. The ladybird is the natural predator of the aphid and will keep aphid populations under control. Controlling aphids is important in crop production, as they are a carrier of several viral diseases of cereal crops and potatoes in particular.

Indirect control

Indirect control is the implementation of agricultural practices that do not eradicate pests and diseases directly; instead, they discourage the establishment of those pests and diseases.

> DEFINITION
>
> **Indirect control of pests and diseases:** the implementation of agricultural practices that discourage the establishment of pests and diseases.

There are five methods of controlling pests, weeds and diseases indirectly: crop rotation, sowing resistant crop varieties, growth encouragement, timely harvesting and stubble cleaning.

1. **Crop rotation** prevents the build-up of pests, weeds and diseases of a specific crop by sowing dissimilar crops in the same place in subsequent years.

2. **Sowing resistant crop varieties** helps to prevent attack from pests and diseases, since these varieties are not affected by the disease. In some cases, the variety has been developed to resist the disease, particularly when there is no other way of preventing it. Examples of this include some varieties of sugar beet seed that are resistant to the *Rhizomania* virus, which has an adverse effect on the crop. The potato variety Sarpo Mira is blight resistant.

3. **Growth encouragement** promotes the growth of healthy crops, which prevents growth of weeds and attack by pests and diseases. A crop that has the optimum growing conditions to begin with will grow more efficiently and not be as susceptible to pest attack. Growth in plants is favoured by availability of nutrients (fertilisers), proper seedbed preparation and correct procedures when the seed is sown.

4. **Timely harvesting** ensures that the crop is less susceptible to attack. If a crop is not harvested on time and becomes over-ripe, there is an increased risk of damage to the crop by pests and diseases.

5. **Stubble cleaning** is very important in controlling weeds, pests and diseases. The term refers to the cultivation of the land with ploughs and harrows after harvest. Harrowing the land encourages weeds to germinate. When the weeds have germinated, the land is again harrowed, and the weeds are killed.

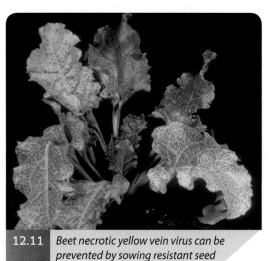

12.11 *Beet necrotic yellow vein virus can be prevented by sowing resistant seed varieties.*

Direct control (chemical control)

Direct control is the use of chemicals to control or eradicate weeds, pests and diseases. There are three types of chemical control: herbicides, fungicides and pesticides.

CHAPTER 12 PRINCIPLES OF CROP PRODUCTION AND MANAGEMENT

Herbicides

Selective herbicides and non-selective herbicides

There are two types of herbicide available to farmers: selective herbicides and non-selective (total) herbicides. Most herbicides are applied as a liquid spray.

1. **Selective herbicides** control or kill certain species of plant life without harming other plant species. Many of the herbicides used on crops are selective herbicides. Many are designed to kill off broadleaf weeds, particularly in grass and cereal crops. They are effective because a broadleaf plant (weed) will absorb more of the herbicide than a grass or cereal because of its foliage. A selective herbicide can become non-selective and kill off all plant life if too much of it is applied to the crop.

2. **Non-selective herbicides** are also known as total herbicides. They kill all plant life and do not distinguish between weeds and crops. They may be used to clear an area completely of vegetation. An example of a total herbicide is Roundup.

Pre-emergent and post-emergent herbicides

Herbicides work at one of two main times: before germination and after germination of weeds.

1. **Pre-emergent herbicides** prevent germinating weeds from establishing themselves in a crop. They should be applied before weeds have germinated. The chemical inhibits cell division within the weed plant and the seedling subsequently dies off.

2. **Post-emergent herbicides** kill weeds after they have germinated. They should be applied after the weed has germinated and can be seen in the crop.

Modes of herbicide action

Herbicides have three modes of action: contact, translocation and soil-acting.

1. **Contact herbicides** are chemicals that kill only the foliage with which they come into contact, so complete coverage of the plant is important. They are not translocated around the plant and do not affect underground root or rhizome systems. This means that while on the surface the weed has been killed off, underground the root system has not and the weed may grow back. Several applications of a contact herbicide may be necessary as a result. Contact herbicides are most effective on annual weeds, since perennial weeds have the ability to grow back.

2. **Translocated herbicides** are chemicals that are absorbed by the plant and are translocated to the stem, leaves and roots. The herbicide kills off each part of the plant with which it comes into contact. This type of herbicide is particularly suitable for perennial weeds that are not killed off by contact herbicides and weeds that have well-developed rhizomes or root systems.

3. **Soil-acting herbicides** are also known as residual herbicides. They are applied to the soil and absorbed by the germinating weed seedlings, killing them off as they grow. Since they are applied to the soil surface, they do not affect crops with deep root systems.

Fungicides

Fungicides work in a similar manner to herbicides except that they are designed to kill or control fungi rather than plant life. Fungicides are normally applied as a liquid spray.

Modes of fungicide action

There are many different types of fungicide. The main types of fungicides are contact, translocated (systemic or translaminar) or protective in their modes of action.

1. **Contact fungicides** work in a similar way to contact herbicides: they kill fungi on application to the crop. They will kill only the fungi with which they have come into contact. Therefore, it is important to apply the fungicide to the entire plant.

Herbicide: a chemical that kills plants or inhibits their growth.

Fungicide: a chemical that kills or inhibits the growth of fungi.

Pre-emergent: before a seed has germinated and appeared above the soil surface.

Post-emergent: after a seed has germinated and shoots can be seen above the soil surface.

2. **Systemic fungicides** are absorbed by the plant and translocated to the stem, leaves and roots. They kill any fungal infection with which they come into contact. They will also provide protection from further attack by fungi.

3. **Translaminar fungicides** are sprayed onto the crop and absorbed by the upper leaf surface and translocated to the lower leaf surface, giving it protection from fungal attack. It is not translocated to the stem and root system.

4. **Protective fungicides** work by preventing attack by fungi at the site of application. It is important to apply the fungicide before the crop is attacked by fungi, since it will not be effective on an infected crop. It is also advisable to ensure that the entire crop is protected, since this fungicide is not translocated by the plant. Do not apply in wet weather because the fungicide will be washed away.

Pesticides

The main pests of crops include insects, rodents, slugs and snails. A variety of chemicals are used to kill and control these pests. Pesticides can be found in solid, liquid or gaseous form, depending on their usage.

Insecticides are used to kill insects that are pests of plant crops and animals. Crops may be sprayed with a solution of the pesticide. The pesticide may work in contact or translocated form: it may remain on the surface of the plant or be absorbed by the plant's foliage. When an insect pest eats the plant foliage, it ingests the insecticide and dies. The insect may also be killed by contact with the insecticide. Some pesticides are designed to kill specific pests. For example, an aphicide is used to kill and control aphids, as the aphid will ingest the chemical when it sucks the sap from the treated plant.

Other pesticides are applied in the form of bait. The pest eats the bait, which is poisonous to the pest, and dies from ingesting toxic levels of the poison. Slug pellets are a common example of baits that are used to kill off the slugs that eat the foliage of plants. Slug pellets are spread on the ground around the plant and are eaten by the slugs.

Poisonous gases called fumigants may also be used in pest control. They are released in an enclosed space to kill off the pests. Fumigants may be used in greenhouses and mushroom tunnels.

> **Pesticide:** a chemical used to kill pests (particularly insects and rodents).

Advantages and disadvantages of using chemicals for weed, pest and disease control

Chemicals are considered a necessity in modern agriculture. They are applied to crops on a regular basis throughout the growing season to keep control of weeds, pests and diseases. Certified seed is treated with a pesticide and a fungicide before it is sold. Fertilisers are applied to crops to increase growth. Chemicals bring several benefits to agriculture but also have disadvantages.

Advantages of chemicals in agriculture:

- **Increased food production:** the use of chemical pesticides and fertilisers has meant that food production levels have increased on farms worldwide. Farmers can increase crop growth and harvest yields by using artificial fertilisers, which enhance the amount of nutrients available to the crop, far in excess of what would be available in the soil. The application of pesticides means that crops can grow with fewer attacks by pests and diseases, which means a higher percentage of the crop has the potential to reach maturity, leading to higher yields.

- **Increased profit for farmers:** as farmers are paid for their crop by the amount produced, the higher the yield at harvest time the more a farmer can potentially earn.

- **Decreased damage by weeds, pests and diseases:** crops can be attacked by a wide variety of pests and diseases. As these can be controlled or eliminated by chemicals, they are less susceptible to attack, improving yields but also the quality of the crop that can be sold.

- **Less labour required:** chemicals can be applied by machinery. This saves labour costs as weeds and pests do not have to be manually removed, which would be time-consuming on a large farm.

Disadvantages of chemicals in agriculture:
- **Build-up of toxins in the food chain:** chemicals applied to crops can be washed into waterways. This can result in the death of plants and animal species due to the build-up of chemicals in their environment. Some of these toxins build up and are stored in an animal's adipose tissue. The level of toxins becomes more concentrated at the top of a food chain because these organisms feed on organisms that have built up a concentration of the pesticide.
- **Harm to human health:** humans may consume animal or plant material that has built up a concentration of pesticides. This may adversely affect human health. Humans may also be at risk of exposure to various chemicals through application of chemicals to land or crops. Chemicals may be absorbed through skin or inhaled.
- **Killing living organisms that are not pests:** pesticides that are applied to crops may kill living organisms that are not the target of the pesticide. For example, bees and butterflies, which are vital for insect pollination of flowers and crops, may be killed by application of some pesticides on crops.
- **Pollution of air, water and soil:** run-off from various chemicals into waterways may lead to contamination of aquatic environments or groundwater sources. Residues may remain in soil and be taken up by the roots of other plants or by living organisms. Chemicals can be transported by volatilisation of fertilisers or in the application of liquid or gaseous sprays. They can be carried by air to areas for which they are not intended.
- **Pest resistance:** some weeds, pests and diseases have built up a resistance to some common herbicides and pesticides. This means they are no longer effective at controlling those weeds and pests. This may have a detrimental effect on crop production in the future if an effective chemical does not exist to control a particular weed, pest or disease.

Bacterial diseases of crops

Bacteria cause far fewer diseases of crops than viruses or fungi. However, they can cause many different types of symptoms, including leaf spots, blights, soft rot, scabs, wilt and cankers. Some plant pathogenic bacteria produce toxins or produce enzymes that break down components of plant cells. Soft rot bacteria break down the pectin layer that holds plant cells together. Some colonise the xylem vessels, which prevents the transport of water, causing wilting and death.

Bacteria can be carried by water, wind, birds or insects. Infected tools, particularly those used in greenhouse and fruit production, can carry disease from one plant to another.

The main methods of controlling bacterial disease in plants include:
- Choosing resistant varieties or hybrids
- Using bacteria-free seed or propagation materials
- Cleaning all tools used in crop production
- Crop rotation
- Application of compounds that contain copper or Bordeaux mixture
- Antibiotic sprays
- Control of insect pests, as they create points of entry to the plant when they feed on them.

Bordeaux mixture: a mixture of copper sulfate and slaked lime, which is used as a fungicide.

Quarantine diseases of crops

There are several bacterial diseases of crops that are classed as quarantine diseases in Ireland. They are infectious and cause considerable damage to crops. Two examples of these are brown rot and ring rot in potatoes (see Chapter 14). A full list of quarantine diseases is available from the DAFM. If a person wishes to import plant material that is an identified host of the quarantine diseases, a plant passport must be obtained for that plant material to certify that it is valid for entry to Ireland.

Implications of sustainable development for crop production

Crop production in Ireland requires the farmer to grow crops on an ongoing basis. Use of chemicals in crop production is widespread. Crops are planted year after year, either within a rotation or on a continuous basis. To meet demand, farmers must achieve high yields of crops while minimising damage to those crops during the growing season. This must also be achieved in a sustainable manner to avoid putting ecosystems at risk.

High yields can be achieved by using **integrated pest management** to protect crops and livestock from disease and minimising the use of pesticides that can harm the environment. It also requires a crop rotation to be implemented to protect against weeds and other invasive species. This also encourages soil retention and on mixed farms reduces compaction of soils by livestock. Farmers can implement sustainable crop production by carrying out several practices on the farm (see Table 12.2).

12.12 *Potato with ring rot, a quarantine disease*

Quarantine: a state, period or place of isolation for a plant or animal that has arrived from another location, where it may have been exposed to an infectious or contagious disease.

Table 12.2 Sustainable development practices in crop production	
Aim	**Practice**
The prevention or suppression of harmful organisms	Crop rotation
	Sterile seedbed technique
	Clean machinery
	Nutrient management programme
	Soil testing
	Certified seed
	Resistant varieties
	Minimum cultivation
	Optimal sowing dates
Monitoring of harmful organisms	Forecast systems (Met Éireann: Blight warnings)
	Identification of pests
	Traps or lures
Sustainable biological, physical or non-chemical methods of weed, pest and disease control	Natural predators
	Crop fleeces or nets
	Mechanical weeders or toppers for weed control
Target of specific pests and pesticide use at necessary levels	Avoid broad spectrum products
	Avoid insecticide use where bees forage
	Use seed dressings
	Consider spot dressing rather than blanket coverage
	Reduce frequency and rate of application

Graminicide: a herbicide that controls grass weeds, e.g. scutch grass.

Exercise 12.1

Read the following article published on the Farm Ireland pages of Independent.ie and then answer the questions.

Weedkiller ban will be 'disaster' for Irish farming
EU refuses to extend glyphosate licensing amid cancer scares

Sarah Collins
June 7 2016 2:30 AM

EU governments have refused to re-authorise agriculture's number one weedkiller glyphosate for use in Europe, over concerns that the product may be linked to cancer.

The licence for glyphosate – a key ingredient in Roundup – is due to expire at the end of this month.

In a tense vote yesterday, national representatives in the EU's plants, animals, food and feed committee threw out a European Commission proposal to extend the current authorisation for 12–18 months, pending new scientific advice.

If no solution is found before July 1, farmers will be forced to stop using products containing glyphosate, the world's most-used herbicide, by December 2018.

Farmers say there are no viable chemical alternatives for weed control, and that costs and carbon emissions will go up if they have to switch from glyphosate to ploughing.

"This would be a total disaster for Irish farming," said Carlow agronomist Pat Minnock.

"Glyphosate revolutionised cereal production here since it became available in the 1970s. It has increased cereal yields and reduced costs by controlling scutch.

"There is no other herbicide out there that will control scutch roots.

"A graminicide will control it temporarily, but there would be very limited options for its use in cereal crops," he said.

The issue has heralded an era of more politicised environmental lawmaking, with growing concerns that other commonly used pesticides will be subjected to a similar process.

Unusual
"It's unusual for the re-licensing of a product to receive such political attention," Fine Gael MEP Mairead McGuinness said. "I think this will extend to the re-licensing of other products."

The Glyphosate Task Force, representing manufacturers, has contacted the commission seeking a full licence renewal.

The issue will now be heard by an appeal committee made up of ambassadors from the EU's 28 countries, and will be discussed by commissioners at their weekly meeting today.

Although 20 EU countries, including Ireland, were in favour of reauthorising glyphosate, EU voting rules require a "qualified" majority of 55pc of EU countries that make up 65pc of the EU's population.

The fact that the EU's most populous states, Germany, France and Italy, abstained from Monday's vote, made re-approval impossible. Malta was the only country to vote against.

The vote follows several compromise proposals by the Commission, which says EU countries can ban the use of specific products containing glyphosate.

EU health chief Vytenis Andriukaitis has warned governments not to "hide behind" the Commission's decision.

Glyphosate came up for a 15-year renewal last year but a decision was put off after a World Health Organisation (WHO) body classified it as "probably carcinogenic to humans".

The advice conflicts with the European Food and Safety Agency, which found it was "unlikely" to be carcinogenic, a position echoed by a joint United Nations/WHO committee last month.

The European chemicals agency is now reviewing its toxicity but is not expected to rule before mid-2017.

One of the biggest issues surrounding glyphosate's use in Europe is the practice of 'burning off' cereal crops with the pesticide 10 days before harvest. "It is probably the issue that concerns people most," admitted Mr Minnock.

However, the crop advisor said that the technique was the only way for continuous cereal rotations to work in Ireland.

"You could increase the integrated pest management (IPM) techniques, but by waiting until the crop is harvested to deal with scutch, you will not get back in to sow until maybe November.

"That doesn't work in modern rotations where farmers are trying to spread the autumn workload and get crops planted in good conditions in September and October," he said.

Pesticide and herbicide application on crops

Spot treatment with glyphosate to control weeds in wheat crop

Indo Farming

Questions

1. The World Health Organization and the European Food and Safety Agency have differing views on the effects of glyphosate on human health. Why, do you think, are there such opposing views on the chemical? Does the article provide any evidence to support either recommendation? Give a reason for your answer.

2. Based on the information in the article, do you think glyphosate has more benefits or disadvantages?

3. What implications does this potential ban on glyphosate have for crop production in Ireland?

4. Suggest ways in which sustainability practices could be implemented to replace the effect of applying glyphosate to crops.

5. Since this article was published, the licence for glyphosate in Europe was renewed in 2018 for another 5 years. Why, do you think, did countries vote to retain glyphosate as a herbicide when there are concerns about its effect on human health and the environment?

Organic farming

Organic farming is an agricultural activity that does not rely on chemical fertilisers, pesticides, genetically modified crops and livestock antibiotics. While it doesn't mean that farmers have to return to traditional methods, it does mean farming in harmony with the natural environment. This can involve the use of biological pest controls, green manures, crop rotations, composting and mechanical methods of cultivating the land and controlling weeds and pests. The number of farmers engaged in organic methods of food production is increasing each year. As of 2018, there were approximately 1800 organic producers in Ireland.

Many people today, farmers and consumers alike, are increasingly concerned about where their food comes from. Consumers want to eat good-quality produce that is free from chemicals, pesticides and antibiotics. They are concerned about the conditions in which animals are raised. More and more people are looking for the organic option when they go to the supermarket and are willing to pay higher prices for organic produce.

Organic production principles

There are several requirements that farmers must follow for their farms to be certified organic by the Organic Certification Bodies (e.g. Organic Trust, Irish Organic Association). These requirements include:

- Products are produced without the use of genetically modified organisms or their derivatives
- Organophosphate-based compounds, e.g. pesticides, are not used
- Organic plant production uses tillage and cultivation practices that maintain or increase soil organic matter, enhance soil stability and soil biodiversity, and prevent soil compaction and soil erosion
- Where the nutritional needs of plants cannot be met by organic standard measures, only approved fertilisers and soil conditioners may be used, including fish meal, fur and feathers, calcium carbonate from natural sources, soft ground rock phosphate, plant by-products and seaweed
- Appropriate preparations of microorganisms may be used to improve the overall condition of the soil or the availability of nutrients in the soil or in the crops
- The soil management must ensure the regular input of organic residues in the form of organic manures/compost and plant remains to maintain the level of humus, biological activity and plant nutrients (except in the case of permanent pasture); it must also ensure a level of microbial activity sufficient for the decay of organic materials and breakdown of minerals into simple nutrients capable of being absorbed by the plant roots
- Farmers must make every effort to use organically certified seed
- Only organically produced seed and propagating material should be used for production
- Farmyard manures and slurries can be used as organic fertiliser if their origin is also certified organic.

Advantages to organic farming

There are many advantages to organic farming:

- Animals are reared on land free from chemicals (fertilisers, pesticides and herbicides)
- Animals are free-range and have suitable living conditions on the farm
- Crops have not been genetically modified
- Soil structure has been protected by means of rotations and the additions of green manures, farmyard manures and mulches
- Since there are no organic or chemical pollutants produced, waterways are not at risk of pollution
- Habitats are maintained, and this promotes and encourages biodiversity.

Safe work practices

There are a wide variety of risks to health and safety associated with crop production. These hazards range from accidents and injuries caused by tractors or machinery to health issues associated with the use of chemicals. Many of the health and safety risks and steps which may be taken to minimise risk are outlined in Table 12.3.

Table 12.3 Health and safety hazards of crop management		
Hazard	**Safety risk**	**Control**
Tractors	• Being crushed • Being pinned or thrown from the tractor • Being struck by a tractor	• Only trained operator to drive the tractor • Keep the tractor well maintained • Ensure PTO guard is in place • Do not carry passengers on the tractor/machinery or inside a cab unless it is fitted with a passenger seat • Use a four-wheel-drive tractor when driving on a slope; assess the risk of overturning if working on a slope and avoid severe slopes • When attaching any machine to a tractor, take precautions to prevent getting crushed; never stand in the crush zone between the back of the tractor and the piece of machinery
Harvest machinery	• Injury from moving parts of machinery	• Ensure all guards are in place • Beware of any moving parts • Avoid wearing loose clothes, jewellery • Turn off machine to clear blockages (e.g. combine harvester, baler) • Ensure all machinery is in good working order • Do not put hands or other body part into machinery while it is operating
Chemicals	• Poisoning • Fire • Respiratory problems • Skin and eye irritations	• Wear gloves, goggles and protective clothing when handling chemicals • Read all material safety data labels relating to chemicals • Keep all chemicals in a locked area, particularly to prevent children accessing them and ingesting them • Use automatic sprayers for fertilisers • Keep chemicals away from sources of heat or light, which could cause fire

Summary

- Certified seed is guaranteed to have 98% purity and 85% germination rate, to be free from wild oats and to have been treated with a fungicide and pesticide.
- Winter variety cereals are sown because they are frost resistant, have a longer growing season, have a higher yield, can be harvested in July in good weather and will lessen the labour load in spring on a mixed farm enterprise.
- Factors affecting crop management include seed variety selection, soil and water, previous crop history, weed, disease and pest control, plant nutrition, seeding rate and weather.
- Crop management practices can alleviate pests of crops such as aphids, wireworms and leatherjackets but also kill off beneficial insects such as bees and butterflies with pesticides.
- Seed germination can be influenced by depth of sowing, soil compaction, pH of soil, saturation of soil, soil type, photoperiod and temperature.
- Crop rotation occurs when different crops are grown in a defined sequence. It prevents a build-up of pests and diseases, is better for nutrient management (since nutrients are not continually depleted) and improves soil structure.
- Biological control is the control of a pest by introduction of a predator or parasite of the pest.

- Indirect controls of pests and diseases discourage the establishment of those pests and diseases. Methods of indirect control include crop rotation, growth encouragement, timely harvesting, sowing resistant crop varieties and stubble cleaning.
- Direct/chemical control is the use of chemicals (herbicides, pesticides, fungicides) to control weeds, pests and diseases.
- Herbicide is a chemical that kills plants or inhibits their growth. A total herbicide kills all plant life.
- A selective herbicide kills certain species of plant life without harming other plant species. Selective herbicides are mainly used to control broadleaf weeds.
- Herbicides can work on contact, by being translocated or by action in the soil.
- Fungicide is a chemical that kills or inhibits the growth of fungi. The main types of fungicides are contact, translocated or protective in their modes of action.
- Pesticide is a chemical used to kill pests (particularly insects and rodents).
- Insecticides are used to kill insects, which are pests of plant crops and animals.
- Bait is spread around a crop and is poisonous when eaten by a pest. Fumigants are poisonous gases that are used in an enclosed space to kill pests.
- Benefits of using chemicals in agriculture include increased food production, increased profit for farmers, and decreased damage caused by pests and diseases.
- Disadvantages of using chemicals include build-up of toxins in the food chain, harm to human health, killing of other living organisms, pollution of air, water and soil, and pest resistance.
- Bacterial diseases can be controlled by using resistant crop varieties, dressed seeds and crop rotations.
- Quarantine diseases are infectious bacterial diseases that cause considerable damage to crops. Plant material that may carry these diseases must have a plant passport when entering Ireland.
- Sustainable development involves practices that prevent harmful organisms, use of biological, physical or non-chemical controls of weeds, pests and diseases, and targeted application of pesticides.
- Organic farming does not allow the use of genetically modified crops, or use of organophosphates.
- Organic farming encourages tillage practices that increase soil organic matter and soil biodiversity.
- Farmers should put controls in place when operating tractors or other machinery to prevent accidents or injury through crushing, falls or injury to limbs by moving parts.
- Chemicals should be kept in a locked storage area away from light and heat. Goggles, gloves and protective clothing should be used when handling any hazardous chemicals.

PowerPoint Summary

QUESTIONS

1. Give three advantages of sowing winter variety seeds over spring variety seeds.

2. What are the four properties of certified seed?

3. In an experiment to compare uniformity of certified and uncertified seed, a student sowed two batches of 100 seeds: one batch certified and one batch uncertified. The trait the student was examining was height of plants.

   When the crop was established, the student counted how many had germinated. In the certified batch 88 were tall plants and in the other batch 71 were tall plants.

   Account for the difference in the uniformity of the two batches.

4. Identify four factors that affect crop management. Fully explain the effect of each of these factors.

5. Give two reasons for the importance of crop rotation.

6. How can pests and diseases of any crop build up in the soil?

7. Name three methods of weed, disease and pest control.

8. Explain how crop rotation can control weeds and pests.

9. What is stubble cleaning?

10. Explain how pests can be controlled biologically.

11. Direct (chemical) control is an effective way of controlling weeds. What is the difference between a selective and a nonselective herbicide?

12. What is (a) a contact herbicide, (b) a translocated herbicide and (c) a residual herbicide?

13. What is a fungicide? Describe two types of fungicides.

14. Outline three reasons that a farmer might choose not to use chemicals on a farm.

15. On the Plant Health and Trade section of the DAFM website, identify four diseases that are on the quarantine disease list. Identify the name of the disease, the crop it attacks and the damage it causes.

16. Outline four practices that a farmer may implement into an integrated pest management programme on a farm, to increase sustainable practices regarding pest control.

17. Outline the strategies, other than crop rotation, employed by organic farmers and environmentally conscious growers in dealing with:

    (a) Weeds   (b) Invertebrate pests   (c) Fungal diseases.

18. Identify three methods of reducing accidents with machinery in crop production and three methods of reducing accidents with chemicals.

Solutions   Weblinks

CHAPTER 13 Barley

When you have completed this chapter you should be able to:

● Describe the growth cycle of barley
● Discuss the effect of soil quality, seedbed preparation, seed selection and sowing on the production of the crop
● Understand how a variety of soil factors influence productivity
● Discuss strategies for crop protection against diseases (fungal, viral or bacterial)
● Discuss the implications of sustainable development for crop production
● Discuss the various factors involved in crop management including application of nutrients to match crop requirements
● Discuss harvesting techniques and storage methods for barley
● Recognise the need for safe work practices, including the safe handling, harvesting and storage of crops
● Discuss the controls and precautions necessary to prevent accidents, injury and ill-health on the farm
● Identify farm health and safety hazards associated with the management of crops.

13.1 Barley is easily distinguished from other cereal crops by the awns present on the grain

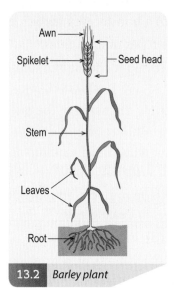

13.2 Barley plant

Barley

Barley (*Hordeum vulgare*) is a cereal and a member of the Poaceae family. It is by far the most widely grown cereal crop in Ireland with more than 200,000 hectares planted annually. Ninety per cent of the barley grown in Ireland is spring barley. Barley may be two-row barley or six-row barley. As the name suggests, two-row barley has two rows of seeds on each spike, while there are six rows of seeds on the spike of the six-row variety. Both two-row and six-row varieties are used for winter barley, but only two-row barley is used for spring planting. Barley is well suited to Irish soils and can be grown on a continuous basis if necessary, which is advantageous to farmers who are growing tillage crops on a continuous basis.

Uses of barley

There are two types of barley grown in Ireland: malting barley and feeding barley. Malting barley is grown on contract by farmers to produce alcohol in the brewing and distilling industry. It must be of a very high quality. Feeding barley is grown to produce animal ration and also for feeding livestock on farms. Barley straw is used for animal bedding and occasionally as an animal feed.

The growth cycle of barley

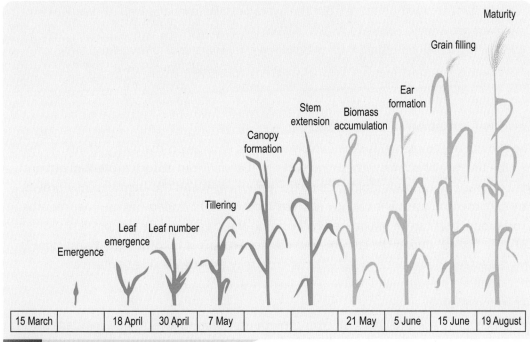

Maturity

Grain filling

Ear
formation

Stem
extension

Biomass
accumulation

Canopy
formation

Tillering

Leaf
emergence

Leaf number

Emergence

| 15 March | | 18 April | 30 April | 7 May | | | 21 May | 5 June | 15 June | 19 August |

13.3 *The growth cycle of spring barley*

The growth of barley or any cereal crop is dependent on several factors. Temperature is a major factor in the growth of the crop. The warmer the temperatures are, the faster the crop will grow. The higher the rate of photosynthesis that can take place also determines growth rates and yield. This is controlled by how much sunlight the plant can capture. The greater the canopy area of the crop, the greater the rate of photosynthesis. Optimum barley growth is favoured by bright, sunny conditions with warm temperatures.

Canopy: green area covered by the crop.

Growth stages

- **Leaf emergence:** after germination the first leaf emerges soon after the crop initially emerges. The crop continues to produce leaves at a continuous thermal rate. This thermal rate is a set number of degree days between the emergence of successive leaves. The length of time that elapses between the emergence of two successive leaves on the plant is called the phyllochron. Late-sown crops have a shorter phyllochron, as leaves emerge faster and have fewer leaves overall.
- **Leaf number:** spring-sown barley produces fewer leaves than autumn-sown barley as the crop has less time to grow. On average the plant will produce eight leaves.
- **Tillering:** the production of tillers is key in the production of grain and ultimately grain yield. Tillers emerge after the third leaf has emerged on the barley plant. Shoots are produced from the tillers, so the more tillers that are produced, the more shoots are produced. The number of ears produced on the barley plant is dependent on the number of shoots produced. The higher the number of ears the greater the potential for a high grain yield. Barley growers aim to have 750–1000 ears per m², with intensive growers aiming for over 900 ears per m². Ear production can be affected by competition from weeds in the crop such as wild oats, nutrient deficiencies and attack by pests and diseases. Optimum tiller and ear production can be enhanced by sowing certified seed, and application of fungicides and pesticides to the growing crop. Application of fertilisers also helps to maximise crop production.

Degree day: a unit of measurement of heat calculated by subtracting the plant's threshold temperature from the average daily temperature. It is used by plant growers to calculate heat available for crop growth.

Phyllochron: the time that elapses between the emergence of two successive leaves. It is influenced by the sowing date and the seed variety sown.

Canopy formation

The growth of the canopy is slow initially as leaves emerge on the barley plants. As leaves emerge the rate of photosynthesis increases as the plant can absorb more sunlight and the crop canopy expands rapidly. Once the ear emerges and the stem has fully grown, canopy growth ceases. The canopy absorbs most sunlight during the summer months. Crop production can be maximised by ensuring the crop has sufficient nutrients to optimise growth during the summer period. Application of fungicides and pesticides is also necessary to prevent any setback the crop may experience due to disease.

Stem extension

Until the stem begins to grow, all crop growth is at ground level. Once the stem starts to grow, the crop is more susceptible to frost damage at the growth point. Four of the leaves on the barley plant will grow at ground level and four will be on the stem. The crop will be at its maximum height after the ear emerges and biomass accumulation begins in the grains. At harvest the ear bends over and lies parallel to the stem. It is of benefit to farmers to choose a seed variety that is resistant to lodging to prevent stems breaking and reducing crop yield.

Biomass accumulation

Senescence is the process in which a plant starts to die back.

As the crop develops more leaves and has a bigger canopy, it increases the amount of sunlight it absorbs. In turn, the biomass it produces accumulates at a greater rate. Once the ear emerges on the plant, the leaf senescence begins. Barley produces on average 13 t/ha dry matter (DM) at the time of harvest. Grain yield accounts for approximately 7 t/ha of this biomass.

The production of biomass goes through several different stages of production. Initially biomass production centres on leaf emergence. This is followed by stem production and ear production. Once the stem has reached its maximum height, biomass production is focused on grain production, as starch accumulates in the developing grains.

Ear formation

The greater the number of shoots produced, the greater the number of ears formed on the barley plant. Grain yield is determined by the number of ears per m². The crop ceases vegetative growth when ears start developing. It takes approximately 35 days for an ear to fully form on the barley plant.

Grain filling

Grains begin to fill once the ear has emerged. It takes approximately 40 days for the completion of grain filling in the barley ear. The products of photosynthesis, which were stored in the stem, are now transferred to the grains. Crop production can be maximised through adequate fertiliser application to ensure the maximum number of tillers on each plant, which in turn maximises ear production and grain filling. The crop should be ripe before harvesting.

Cereal crop varieties and seed selection

The Department of Agriculture, Food and the Marine (DAFM) releases a list of recommended cereal varieties annually. Winter and spring varieties of barley that appear on the list have been grown over several years and are chosen based on a number of characteristics:

- Relative yield
- Shortness of straw
- Resistance to lodging
- Straw breakdown
- Earliness of ripening
- Resistance to disease.

Relative yield scores are based on the average yield of a crop being assigned a score of 100. Scores above this value indicate a higher than average yield. Other characteristics are scored on a scale from 1 to 9, where 9 is the best and 1 is worst. For example, a seed variety scoring 8 on resistance to disease is highly resistant, whereas a seed variety scoring 2 is highly susceptible to that disease. When choosing a seed variety to maximise productivity of the crop, a farmer can assess each seed variety on the scores attained in each category. A high resistance to disease and earlier ripening may compensate for a slightly lower yield. Varieties scoring high values in each category would contribute to a higher overall productivity of the crop.

Table 13.1 Recommended barley varieties				
Variety	Thousand grain weight (g)	Relative yield (average yield = 100)	Resistance to lodging (scale = 1–9)	Resistance to mildew (scale = 1–9)
Winter				
KWS Kosmos	49.3	105	6	8
Quadra	45.8	105	7	7
KWS Cassia	54.7	97	7	5
Spring				
KWS Irina	51.5	103	7	8
Mickle	51.2	100	7	5
RGT Planet	52.9	105	5	8

> **Thousand grain weight (TGW)** is the mass of 1000 grains of a cereal variety in grams. It is used to calculate the seeding rate.

Cultivation of barley

Soil suitability

Soil requirements differ for malting barley and feeding barley. Malting barley requires a well-drained soil and is best suited to brown podzolics and light sandy loam soils. Feeding barley can be grown on soils that retain more moisture, such as brown earths and deep sandy loam soils. The pH of the soil is an important consideration. A soil pH of 6.5 is ideal for barley but a crop will grow on soils of pH 6.0 or greater. Barley is highly sensitive to acidity, so soils used for regular barley production should be tested for pH and limed where appropriate to ensure a suitable pH is maintained. A pH below 6.0 will result in less availability of nutrients to the crop and reduced productivity.

Climate

Moisture is important for barley growth, since drought leads to a lower yield and a poorer quality grain. However, dry conditions are necessary for harvesting and a wet summer can have a detrimental effect on the barley crop. Drier grain is preferable at harvesting. The south-east region of Ireland, where temperatures are warmer and there is less precipitation, is best suited to barley growing.

Preparation of seedbed

Winter barley: when preparing the land for winter barley, soil should be ploughed in autumn and then harrowed with a one-run harrow.

Spring barley: autumn ploughing is not possible for spring barley. Under the Nitrates Regulations it is only permitted if the crop is emerged 6 weeks after sowing. This is to prevent nitrogen leaching. Therefore, cultivations for spring barley may not take place until seed is being sown. When preparing a seedbed for spring barley, the land may also be rolled after sowing seed to ensure good seed–soil contact. For rapid establishment of spring barley, to achieve higher productivity, ploughing should take place to a depth of 175–250 mm. This is most effective on clay loam soils and ensures a high establishment rate which is best suited to intensive crop production.

Minimum tillage: this is mainly confined to winter cereals. Minimum tillage involves the least amount of cultivation possible when preparing a seedbed for a crop. This means that the soil is not ploughed during seedbed preparation. The seed can be sown by direct drilling. Minimum tillage (also known as conservation tillage) reduces labour costs and energy consumption (fuel) on the farm. It also retains moisture in the soil and retains plant cover (e.g. stubble), which reduces soil erosion.

Ploughing and harrowing of soil provides a good seedbed for the barley crop and ensures that the crop has a high rate of establishment. Min-till provides a less intensive system of seedbed preparation for sustainable establishment of the crop but can prove difficult in a short growing season, and farmers need to consider the effect of grass weeds in the barley crop in this system, particularly where high productivity is important. While min-till promotes sustainable tillage production, establishment rates for barley are lower using this system. As there are lower establishment rates, herbicides need to be applied to offset the increased rates of weed growth. Min-till is best suited to lighter sandy soils.

> **DEFINITION**
>
> **Minimum tillage (conservation tillage):** a method of cultivation in which ploughing is not carried out at any stage during the seedbed preparation.

Grass corn stage is when the plant reaches a height of 8–10 cm.

Video
Sowing barley

Time, rate and method of sowing

Winter barley is usually sown in September; the optimum sowing date is 1 October. If sown at this time, it reaches the grass corn stage by winter and will survive the winter frost and cold temperatures. If sown any earlier, it grows past the grass corn stage and will grow too tall. When growth recommences in spring, the crop can be prone to lodging, which leads to a reduced yield.

Spring barley is sown between February and April, as soon as weather conditions will allow. The later spring barley is sown, the lower the yield will be. The seeding rate is determined by the time the seed is sown and the variety chosen. Establishment rates of 90% can be achieved in late September/early October, with a decline in the establishment rate to 75% by late October, resulting in 260–320 plants per m². As a result, seeding rate increases the later the crop is sown: this ensures optimum establishment rates.

Seeding rates are determined by several factors:
- Seedbed/soil conditions   • Seed quality   • Time of planting.

The use of certified seed will guarantee a minimum of 85% germination, and also ensure the seed is free of weeds and disease.

Seeding rate

The seeding rate is calculated by the following formula:

$$\text{Seed rate (kg/ha)} = \frac{\text{target population} \times \text{TGW}}{\text{expected establishment (\%)}}$$

For example, if the desired plant population is 250 plants per m² and the barley seed has a thousand grain weight (TGW) of 50 g with an expected establishment rate of 90%, then the seeding rate is:

$$250 \times \frac{50}{90} = 138.9 \text{ kg/ha}$$

Earlier sown crops such as winter barley will produce more leaves than later sown crops such as spring barley.

Seeding rates can range from 100 kg/ha in late September to 244 kg/ha in late October for winter barley, depending on the variety chosen and the time of sowing. Barley is sown with a combine drill. The drill sows seed and fertiliser at the same time.

Some farmers leave tramlines in the field at the time of drilling.

Tramlines are parallel lines in the crop that allow farmers to access the crop by tractor to fertilise the crop and spray pesticides and herbicides without damaging the crop with the machinery.

Tramlines can be created at the time of sowing by switching off the drill, which leaves rows through the crop without seed. These bare rows are then used for access throughout the growing season. They also ensure that no area of the crop is missed or is sprayed or fertilised more than once.

13.4 *Tramlines in a barley crop*

Application of fertilisers

The application of N, P and K can vary depending on the fertility of the soil, region of the country and previous use of the field. Nitrogen is mainly supplied by application of fertilisers such as calcium ammonium nitrate (CAN), and phosphorus and potassium are mainly supplied by the application of 18-6-12 and 10-10-20. Some farmers are beginning to use more specialised fertiliser compounds based on the results of soil tests. Farmers must also carry out regular soil tests on their land to meet the requirements of cross-compliance and are subject to maximum fertiliser application rates under the Nitrates Regulations. The maximum application rates for cereals are determined by the soil index results for the area to be sown.

For spring barley about 30% of the total nitrogen requirement can be applied at the time of sowing. The remaining nitrogen can be applied at the mid tillering stage. This is called split dressing and can maximise uptake of nitrogen for the crop, particularly during the rapid growth phase during late spring and early summer.

For malting barley, only P and K should be applied at sowing. Malting barley has a low N requirement so N should not be applied and split dressings should not be used. The application of nitrogen fertiliser at sowing or soon after emergence will encourage development of tillers. Further application of nitrogen will encourage the continued growth of tillers and development of canopy. CAN is the most popular straight N fertiliser that is applied to spring barley.

> **Cross-compliance** is a set of legal requirements a farmer must adhere to under the Common Agricultural Policy (CAP).

Table 13.2 Fertiliser applications for winter barley					
Variety	Nutrients	Soil index			
		1	2	3	4
Winter barley	Nitrogen (kg/ha)*	160	135	100	60
	Phosphorus (kg/ha)*	45	35	25	0
	Potassium (kg/ha)*	70	50	35	0

* Maximum rate that can be applied. Farmers are not obliged to apply this level of fertiliser

Table 13.3 Fertiliser application for spring barley					
Variety	Nutrients	Soil index			
		1	2	3	4
Spring barley 6.5 t/ha	Nitrogen (kg/ha)*	135	100	75	40
Barley 7.5 t/ha	Nitrogen (kg/ha)*	155	120	95	60
Barley 8.5 t/ha	Nitrogen (kg/ha)*	175	140	115	80
	Phosphorus (kg/ha)*	45	35	25	0
	Potassium (kg/ha)*	65	50	35	0

* Maximum rate that can be applied. Farmers are not obliged to apply this level of fertiliser

It is also essential that phosphorus and potassium are applied during sowing to ensure proper crop development. Phosphorus is necessary for root and tiller development. Optimum availability of crop nutrients is at a soil pH of 6.5. Trace elements such as copper, zinc and manganese should be applied at sowing if soil tests have indicated low levels.

Organic manures

Farmyard manure and slurry may be applied to the soil to provide N, P and K. Levels of artificial fertiliser may be reduced based on the rate of application of organic manures.

Diseases, pests and weed control

Several common diseases that affect barley are fungal diseases. The first step to preventing fungal disease attacks on a growing crop is to choose a disease-resistant seed variety from the DAFM's Recommended Cereals List. The seed should be certified, which ensures it has been treated with fungicide and pesticide. Fungal diseases may attack a growing crop early in the season, damaging tillers, and it is important to spray the crop when it is tillering. A second application of fungicide is also recommended when the flag leaf emerges on the crop. Planting disease-free certified seed also reduces the chances of a crop being attacked by fungal diseases such as loose smut and leaf stripe.

Rhynchosporium

Rhynchosporium (leaf blotch or scald) is a fungal disease that causes large yield losses and a decrease in grain quality. Leaves affected by the disease have diamond-shaped, chlorotic, blue-grey patches. The fungal spores are spread by rain splash, and the disease is prevalent in wet weather conditions. It can be treated or controlled using a fungicide, which should be sprayed twice during the growing season or by sowing a resistant variety.

Powdery mildew

Powdery mildew is a fungal disease that affects the leaves of the plant. It can overwinter on volunteer barley or stubble. It forms grey-white patches of fungus on the leaves, and the underside of the leaves turns yellow. It should be treated by spraying a fungicide or by sowing resistant varieties. It causes a loss of yield in the crop as grains are not filled.

Leaf rust

Leaf rust is also known as brown rust. It can be identified by the orange-brown circular spores that are found on leaf surfaces. It causes premature death of leaves and a reduction in yield. It can be controlled using a fungicide spray.

Net blotch

Net blotch is a fungal disease caused by *Pyrenophora teres*. It is characterised by brown marks in the leaves in a net pattern. The fungus affects the developing tillers and reduces the green leaf area on the plant. Application of fungicides and using resistant varieties can help to control the disease.

Fusarium head blight

Fusarium head blight is caused by the fungus *Fusarium*. The fungus affects the head of the crop, which introduces mycotoxins into the grain. The grain is then contaminated and is not suitable for human or animal consumption. The fungus favours wet conditions. It can be controlled by spraying fungicide.

Barley yellow dwarf virus

Barley yellow dwarf virus (BYDV) is a viral disease transmitted by aphids. It is transmitted to the plant when the aphid feeds on it. The leaves turn bright yellow and yield is reduced as a result. Disease can be controlled using an aphicide during the growing season. The aphicide should be applied when the crop is at the three to five leaf stage.

Wireworms

Wireworms are the larvae of the click beetle. They are yellow-orange in colour. The female click beetle lays her eggs near the roots of the plant. When the eggs hatch, the wireworms feed on the seeds, roots and stem. This can reduce the yield of the plant and cause lodging in cereals. To reduce the threat of wireworm infestation, barley should not be grown after grass in rotation.

Leatherjackets

Leatherjackets are the larvae of the crane fly. They cause damage by eating the roots and underground stems of the plant. Crops at early emergence are most at risk. They can be controlled by spraying the crop with a pesticide.

Weed control

Selective herbicides can be used to control weeds in a barley crop. Herbicides should be chosen on identification of the weeds present in the crop. Wild oats and charlock are common weeds that compete with barley. The crop should be sprayed with a post-emergent herbicide at the three to five leaf stage for successful control of weeds. This is particularly important for spring crops. For greatest effect, herbicides should be sprayed during good growing conditions and a mix of herbicides should be used to prevent resistance from weeds. Field history should be taken into account when choosing a herbicide. Other herbicides can be sprayed up to the flag leaf stage. Crop rotation and stubble cleaning can also help in the control of weeds.

Volunteer: a plant that has not been planted deliberately. It may have remained after harvest or overwintered after a rotation.

Rotation

Feeding barley: soil-borne pests and diseases do not seriously affect barley. Barley will give higher yields when grown in rotation, particularly in intensive tillage enterprises. The crop can also be affected by pests if grown after grassland. Rotation is considered advantageous as it helps to maintain the soil structure. However, feeding barley can be grown continuously.

Malting barley: since it has a lower nitrogen requirement than feeding barley, malting barley should not be sown after grass or legumes in a rotation.

Harvest, yield and storage

Barley is harvested with a combine harvester. When the crop is ripe, the ear bends over and lies parallel to the stem. The grains are hard and dry and the golden colour of the crop fades. It is important for the grain to have low moisture levels; otherwise it will have to be dried out. Farmers are also paid based on the moisture content of the grain. Winter barley is higher yielding than spring barley and can be harvested earlier in the summer.

> ▶ **Video**
> Harvesting barley

Table 13.4 Barley yield and harvest date			
Crop	**Grain yield (tonnes/ha)**	**Straw yield (tonnes/ha)**	**Harvest date**
Winter barley	8–9	4.2	July
Spring barley	6–8	3.6	August

Grain is stored in large ventilated sheds. Grain that is kept in storage is treated with propionic acid, which prevents the grain from being attacked by pests, fungi and bacteria. Low temperatures and low moisture content are important for grain storage to prevent germination and spoilage. Ventilation systems can keep temperatures low and also dry out grain to a low moisture level.

Barley straw can be used for animal feed and bedding or ploughed into the soil for winter crops. Straw can be made into round or square bales and used on the farm or sold. Barley straw can be burned in a biomass boiler to provide energy. One tonne of barley straw provides the same amount of energy as 406 litres of kerosene (*source: Teagasc*).

13.5 *A combine harvester*

13.6 *Barley grain storage*

Safety considerations for barley production and harvesting

There are several health and safety hazards to consider as a tillage farmer. These hazards involve the use of machinery for cultivation of soil, harvesting and storage of barley, and application of fertilisers, pesticides, herbicides and fungicides. Farmers must also consider the health implications when spreading fertilisers and chemicals on the crop.

Some general precautions tillage farmers should take include:

- Ensure all machinery is in good working order (tractor, plough, combine harvester)
- Ensure all machinery is operated by persons over 18 years of age
- Wear goggles, gloves and protective clothing to prevent skin and respiratory problems associated with fertilisers, herbicides, pesticides and fungicides
- Apply all chemicals to avoid or minimise run-off, leaching and volatilisation.

Precautions to consider when operating a combine harvester

There are a number of safety risks to consider when operating a combine harvester. These include:

- Being pulled into the cutting mechanism
- Coming into contact with the knife, reel or stripper rotor or straw chopper or spreader
- Being injured by the drive mechanisms or trapped when automatic sensors operate
- Becoming entangled with the levelling or discharge augers in the grain tank
- Coming into contact with overhead power lines
- Falling from machinery or being run over.

Farmers can minimise risk to themselves when operating a combine harvester by putting the following safety precautions in place:

- Apply the handbrake, place the harvester in neutral and turn off the engine when checking the harvester for blockages
- Do not carry passengers, especially children, in the cab
- Do not reach into the harvester to clear blockages when the harvester is switched on
- Plan a safe travel route and know the height of the harvester to avoid coming into contact with overhead power lines.

Machinery used in barley production

Harrow

A harrow is a tool that is towed behind a tractor and is used to break up the surface of the soil. Any clods of soil left on the surface after ploughing are broken up and the surface is levelled. The harrow is an important tool in the formation of a seedbed. It breaks up only the surface soil – unlike the plough, which breaks up and turns soil at a greater depth.

There are many different types of harrows available to farmers, including disc harrows and chain harrows. A harrow that is driven by the power take-off (PTO) shaft of a tractor is called a power harrow.

| 13.7 | *Power harrow* |

| 13.8 | *Disc harrow* |

Roller

A roller is used to break up clods of soil on the soil surface. It is also used to create a firm seedbed. Rollers are of particular importance when sowing cereal crops. Rolling can take place before or after sowing seed. When the soil is rolled after sowing, this promotes better contact between the newly sown seed and the soil, improving germination and establishment. It can also help to prevent water loss from the soil. Rollers may be smooth or ribbed.

13.9 *Actiroll roller*

Seed drill

A seed drill is a machine that automates the sowing of a crop. Seeds are placed in a storage bin called a hopper and fed to tubes that are evenly spaced. The seed drill allows the farmer to sow seeds in drills that are equally spaced in a field and also at a specific depth.

When the seed is placed in the soil by the seed drill, it is covered over with soil to complete the process. The use of a seed drill to plant seeds can greatly increase the germination and establishment rates of a crop.

There are many different types of seed drill available. A seed drill that also places fertiliser in the soil along with the seed is known as a combine drill or one pass machine. The sowing rate and depth can be adjusted on a seed drill to suit different crops of a similar type (e.g. cereals such as barley and wheat). Other crops require a specialised seed drill due to size and shape of the seed.

13.10 *Seed drill specialised for sowing maize seed*

The use of a seed drill may be described as precision seeding, because it regulates the number of seeds that are sown and the depths at which they are sown. It reduces wastage when sowing, as the required sowing rate can be used to calculate the volume of seed required by the drill. It also ensures that seeds are sown uniformly, and this leads to better rates of germination and establishment. Use of a seed drill ensures that crop seeds are provided with optimum space for growth and development, which leads to better yields.

Combine harvester

A combine harvester is used to harvest cereal crops such as barley, wheat and oats. It combines three separate functions:

* **Reaping:** cutting the stalks of grain
* **Threshing:** loosening the grain seeds from the straw and the chaff
* **Winnowing:** separating the seeds from the straw and the chaff.

The three processes are carried out by the combine harvester in one continuous operation.

Chaff: the inedible husks or seed casings on cereal grains.

Summary

- Barley grown in Ireland is either malting barley or feeding barley. Malting barley is used for the production of alcohol and feeding barley is used for the production of animal feed. Barley straw is used as animal bedding.
- Barley can be identified by the awns present on its grains.
- Soils such as brown earths with good drainage and a pH of 6.5 are best suited for growing barley.
- Warm temperatures are needed for optimum barley growth and yield and dry weather is necessary for harvesting.
- When sowing barley, land should be ploughed, harrowed and rolled in the case of spring barley. Winter barley is sown with a corn drill in September with the optimum sowing date being 1 October, so that the plant will reach the grass corn stage by winter. This also prevents lodging. Spring barley is sown from February to April.
- Lodging is the tendency of cereal crops to bend over, so that they lie more or less flat on the ground. This makes it impossible to harvest the crop and reduces the yield.
- Barley varieties are chosen for their yield, strength of straw, shortness of straw, earliness of ripening, disease resistance and, in the case of winter varieties, winter hardiness.
- CAN, 18-6-12 and 10-10-20 are the main fertilisers used to supply N, P and K nutrients.
- Fungal diseases that affect barley include *Rhynchosporium*, powdery mildew and leaf rust, all of which can be treated and controlled by spraying fungicides.
- Barley yellow dwarf virus is spread by aphids. Aphids, wireworms and leatherjackets can all be controlled by spraying suitable pesticides.
- Pests and diseases do not seriously affect barley, so rotation is not essential; however, it does lead to higher yields.
- Barley is ripe when the grains are dry and hard and their colour has faded. The ear lies parallel to the stem. It is harvested in July (winter barley) or August (spring barley) with a combine harvester.
- Average yields are 8–9 tonnes/ha (winter) and 6–8 tonnes/ha (spring).
- Grain is treated with acid to prevent attack from pests and disease and stored in a ventilated shed.

PowerPoint Summary

QUESTIONS

1. To which family does barley belong?
   - (a) Fabaceae
   - (b) Apiaceae
   - (c) Poaceae
   - (d) Rosaceae

2. State one way of identifying barley.
   - (a) The seeds are on a panicle
   - (b) The presence of awns on the ear
   - (c) The presence of multiple florets
   - (d) Broad leaves

3. When are the winter varieties of barley sown?
   - (a) 1 September
   - (b) 15 September
   - (c) 1 October
   - (d) 15 October

4. The length of time that elapses between the emergence of two successive leaves on a barley plant is called a:

   (a) Degree day
   (c) Phyllochron
   (b) Senescence
   (d) Biomass.

5. Identify four factors that should be considered when calculating seeding rate.

6. Calculate the seeding rates for the following seed varieties:

   (a) 300 plants, TGW = 45 g, expected establishment rate 85%
   (b) 275 plants, TGW = 48 g, expected establishment rate 90%
   (c) 250 plants, TGW = 50 g, expected establishment rate 95%

7. Give two reasons for planting winter barley instead of spring barley.

8. What are tramlines and what is their purpose?

9. Outline the differences in soil requirements and climate that are needed for growing feeding barley and malting barley.

10. Account for the differences in nitrogen application rates for soil Index 1 and soil Index 3.

11. Why are split dressings used in nitrogen applications for barley?

12. What characteristics of barley (seed) are important when choosing a variety for sowing?

13. Name one winter variety and one spring variety of barley.

14. From Table 13.1 identify a suitable seed variety that could be sown to maximise yield and also provide a high resistance to powdery mildew and lodging.

15. What is meant by min-till? List one advantage and one disadvantage of min-till cultivation.

16. Name two common fungal diseases of barley, describe their symptoms and state two methods of prevention or treatment.

17. What are the signs that barley is ready for harvesting?

18. Identify two factors that affect the storage of barley and how spoilage may be prevented.

19. Give two uses for barley straw.

20. State the straw yield for high-yielding winter barley and spring barley.

21. What is the average yield in tonnes per hectare of (a) winter barley and (b) spring barley?

22. State three hazards that may be a risk when using a combine harvester and state three controls to prevent these risks.

23. Describe the production of a cereal crop under each of the following headings:

   (a) Soil suitability
   (d) Use of fertiliser on spring barley
   (b) Preparation of seedbed
   (e) Harvesting time and storage.
   (c) Sowing rate and method

24. List four factors that are considered by the DAFM when recommending varieties of cereals to be grown by farmers.

Solutions   Weblinks

Potatoes

When you have completed this chapter you should be able to:

- Describe the growth cycle of potatoes
- Discuss the effect of soil quality, seedbed preparation, seed selection and sowing on the production of potatoes
- Understand how a variety of soil factors influence productivity
- Discuss strategies for crop protection against diseases (fungal, viral or bacterial)
- Discuss the various factors involved in crop management including application of nutrients to match crop requirements
- Appreciate the need for compliance in relation to notifiable diseases
- Appreciate the role of innovation and biotechnological applications in crop development and management
- Discuss harvesting techniques and storage methods for potatoes
- Identify farm health and safety hazards associated with the management of crops
- Discuss the controls and precautions necessary to prevent accidents, injury and ill-health on the farm
- Recognise the need for safe work practices, including the safe handling, harvesting and storage of crops
- Carry out an investigation to measure the dry matter (DM) content of potatoes (SPA).

It is believed that potatoes were first cultivated in Ireland around the 1600s. By the 1700s, they were part of the staple Irish diet, especially of the poor. This had devastating consequences when blight destroyed the potato crops between 1845 and 1852; this period of history is now remembered as the Great Famine. Despite this, the potato remains one of the most popular vegetables in Ireland, with 95% of households buying potatoes regularly. Approximately 9000 hectares of land is planted with potatoes each year.

Table 14.1 Potato production in Ireland			
Year	Area grown (000 ha)	Yield (tonnes/ha)	Crop production (000 t)
2017	9.2	44.9	412.4
2016	9.0	38.9	352.0
2015	8.5	42.3	360.1
2014	9.5	40.5	383.0

Potatoes belong to the family Solanaceae. Other members of this family include tomatoes and tobacco. A potato tuber is a modified stem used for food storage by the plant.

The growth cycle of potatoes

Potatoes are a biennial plant. However, potatoes that are grown and harvested for human consumption are usually harvested 3–6 months after they were initially sown. The potato plant goes through five stages of growth prior to harvest.

14.1 *Potato plant with flowers*

Growth cycle of a potato

1. **Sprout development:** sprouts develop from the eyes on the seed tubers and grow upwards, emerging from the soil. Roots begin to develop from the base of the emerging sprouts.

2. **Vegetative growth:** leaves and stems develop from nodes on the emerged sprouts. Roots and stolons begin to develop from nodes below the ground. Once the leaves have emerged the plant begins to photosynthesise.

3. **Tuber initiation:** tubers begin to form at the tips of the stolons but do not develop further at this stage. Flowers begin to emerge on the plant.

4. **Tuber bulking:** water, nutrients and carbohydrates begin to accumulate in the tubers. The tubers begin to grow. Most of the carbohydrate storage in the potato plant at this stage of development is in the tubers.

5. **Maturation:** the plant begins to turn yellow and lose its leaves. Photosynthesis decreases, and tuber growth also decreases. The dry matter (DM) content of the tubers reaches its optimum level and the potato skins begin to harden.

Categories of potato and seed selection

Potatoes are classified as:

- First earlies
- Second earlies
- Maincrop.

First and second earlies are planted as early as February. However, potatoes are not frost-resistant, and for this reason they are grown in coastal areas of counties Cork and Wexford. The soils in these regions are sandy soils and warm up early in spring. Earlies are harvested immaturely from May onwards. As a result, there is a lower yield, but they obtain a higher price. Home Guard and British Queen are the most popular early varieties grown in Ireland.

Maincrop potatoes are harvested fully mature in September and October and give higher yields than early varieties. Maincrop potatoes are used to supply the consumer market until May of the following year.

Rooster, Kerr's Pink, Record and Golden Wonder are the most popular maincrop varieties in Ireland, since these varieties have high DM content and produce floury tubers. Over half of all land planted with potatoes in Ireland is planted with Roosters. In contrast, Cara, a variety that is popular on the Continent, has low DM content but is very high yielding. Production of maincrop potatoes is mainly confined to counties Meath, Dublin, Louth, Cork and Wexford.

Potato seed selection

Potatoes are assessed under several characteristics. Growers may choose different characteristics based on their needs.

1. **Disease resistance:** the ability to resist certain diseases is important in potato production. Loss in yield can be minimised by choosing a variety that is resistant to certain diseases and being aware of the measures necessary to control other diseases.

2. **Yield:** most potato growers are involved in maincrop production. The higher the yield the more profitable the crop will be. Some varieties are higher yielding than others.

3. **Maturity:** when a potato matures will determine when it can be harvested. As most potatoes are harvested as maincrop potatoes, growers want varieties that will be mature by October.

4. **Keeping quality:** maincrop potatoes supply the Irish market for most of the year. This means that they must be kept in storage for many months. Some varieties such as Roosters are better suited to prolonged storage.

5. **Eating quality:** Irish consumers prefer potatoes with a high DM content (floury potatoes). Red skinned varieties such as Rooster and Kerr's Pink are popular in Ireland.

6. **Seed availability:** while the Irish market is dominated by a few popular varieties, the availability of other varieties can be determined by seed availability.

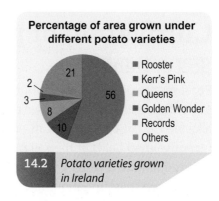

Percentage of area grown under different potato varieties

- Rooster
- Kerr's Pink
- Queens
- Golden Wonder
- Records
- Others

56, 21, 2, 3, 8, 10

14.2 *Potato varieties grown in Ireland*

Table 14.2 Potato varieties and characteristics		
Category	**Variety**	**Characteristics**
First earlies	• Home Guard • Epicure	• Good eating quality, good yield
Second earlies	• British Queen • Maris Piper	• Excellent eating quality • Good yield
Maincrop	• Rooster • Kerr's Pink • Golden Wonder • Cara	• Moderately high yield, good disease resistance • Good eating quality, high yield • Excellent eating quality, low yield • Low DM, poorer eating quality, very high yield

14.3 *Home Guard potatoes*

14.4 *Kerr's Pink potatoes*

Seed production

Commercial potato production can be divided into two categories:

1. Certified seed potatoes

2. Ware production (potatoes for human consumption).

Seed potato production is centred in Donegal. The windy conditions keep the aphid population low and Donegal is isolated from other potato-growing counties, preventing the spread of diseases. Certified seed potatoes that are distributed to commercial ware growers are grown under strict regulations. Seed potatoes can be produced only from fields free from potato cyst nematode and they must be free from plant viruses, e.g. leaf mosaic virus, leaf roll and virus Y. Certified seed is also produced using micropropagation. Some growers reduce the cost of producing their ware potatoes by using their own potatoes for seed, which can produce a good yield. However, it is advisable to purchase certified seed every 3 years, since viruses can build up in a producer's stock.

14.5 *Aphids are carriers of a number of viral diseases that affect potatoes*

Cultivation of potatoes

Soil suitability

Potatoes are grown in a wide variety of soils. However, deep, well-drained loams and sandy loams are ideal. Potatoes prefer a pH of 5.5 to 6.0. If the pH of the soil is very alkaline (>7), it can cause scab on potatoes. For this reason, potatoes are not grown in recently limed fields. If the soil pH is less than 5.5, the availability of trace elements is affected, and as a result crop growth is affected. When potatoes are grown in sandy or sandy loam soils, irrigation may be required if drought occurs in late summer. Drought affects tuber development and reduces crop yield. Adding manure to the soil helps it to retain more water, especially in sandy soils, and this helps prevent drought damage to the potato crop.

Rotation

Rotation is vital in the production of potatoes, since it prevents the build-up of potato cyst nematode and other soil-borne pests and diseases. Ware potatoes should not be grown in the same area for more than one year in four, and in seed production that is increased to one year in five.

14.6 *Potato cyst nematode on the roots of a potato plant*

Preparation of seedbed

Potatoes need deep and well-cultivated soil. Since potatoes are sown in spring, soil should be ploughed to a depth of 22 cm. It should be rotavated and beds should be formed at this time. Each seedbed contains two drills and is 172–182 cm wide. If potatoes are grown in a rotation after grass, grass should be burned off with glyphosate prior to cultivation.

Commercial growers also practise stone and clod removal. This prevents bruising and contamination of the potatoes at harvesting. The stones and large clods are removed, using a machine similar to a potato harvester, and are placed in a line at the side of the machine. The following year the land is ploughed at a right angle to distribute the stones again. Clods in seedbeds can cause slow crop growth, irregular emergence and lower rates of stem emergence. To ensure a good yield of potatoes, rapid emergence and subsequent crop growth is necessary. Wet soils are also susceptible to compaction, which impacts on root development and yield of potatoes. Soils should be well drained to maximise crop production. Drill formation is the final stage of cultivation and is done either before sowing or when the potatoes are sown.

14.7 *Grimme de-stoner*

14.8 *Drill formation*

Table 14.3 Recommended potato seed spacing and seeding rate		
Seed size (mm)	Spacing (cm)	Seeding rate (seeds/ha)
35–45	20–25	60,000
45–55	30–35	40,000

Sowing the seed potatoes

Potatoes are sown 10 cm below the ridge. The spacing between the seed potatoes is determined by the size of the seed. Seeds are divided into two categories in a process called split grading. This produces a more uniform crop. The recommended spacing and seeding rate for seed potatoes is shown in Table 14.3. Seeds can be planted by hand, but commercial farmers use an automated planter. Seed spacing and seeding rate is determined by the type of tubers required. Factors such as cost of seed, variety and growing conditions are also a consideration when determining seeding rate.

▶ **Video**
Sowing potatoes

Time of planting

Potatoes are usually sown in March or April in frost-free conditions. While farmers in coastal areas can plant potatoes without the risk of frost damage, in other areas of the country planting usually takes place from late March onwards when soil temperatures are 7°C or higher to minimise risk of frost.

Sprouting (chitting)

Seed potatoes can be sprouted before planting. This process is also known as chitting, and it involves exposing the potato seeds to light so that they develop shoots. Sprouting potatoes gives the potato seeds a head start and is an essential practice if growing early varieties, to allow for an earlier harvesting date and an increased yield. In order to sprout potatoes, the seeds are placed in shallow trays that are kept in a greenhouse or in a building using artificial light at a temperature of 5.5°C. Sprouting

14.9 *Sprouted potatoes*

seeds speeds up growth, plant emergence and yield. Sprouts should be 1 cm in length. Seed potatoes need to be stored in refrigerated conditions at 4°C to prevent excessive sprouting.

Fertiliser application

As with any crop, it is important to establish first the inherent fertility of a soil. A soil test is used to establish the N, P and K content of the soil. Most growers apply a compound fertiliser such as 10-10-20 or 7-6-17 to their potato crop before planting the seed. This is done by broadcasting the fertiliser and then incorporating it into the soil in one of the final cultivations.

Commercial growers place the fertiliser in two bands, one either side of the potato drill. Placing the fertiliser in bands ensures an even distribution between the potato plants which promotes uniform growth. This method is a more beneficial and cost-effective mechanism of fertiliser application, with less wastage than broadcasting the fertiliser. The amount of fertiliser added to potatoes must be judged carefully, since excess fertiliser can have a negative effect on tuber development.

Nitrogen: Tuber yield may be increased through the application of nitrogen, but excess nitrogen depresses the dry matter content of the tuber and produces a more watery tuber. The plant may also be more susceptible to blight.

Phosphorus: application of phosphorus can increase dry matter and encourage early rooting.

Potassium: like nitrogen, application of a potassium source such as sulfate of potash can increase tuber yields. Excessive application of potassium can lead to a reduction in dry matter in the potato.

Adding farmyard manure improves the soil structure and helps to prevent drought damage.

Weed control and earthing up

Once 15–20% of the potato plants have emerged after sowing, the potato crop is sprayed, usually with a contact and a residual herbicide. The contact herbicide kills all plants including the potatoes; however, the potato crops will quickly recover. The residual herbicide prevents any weed seeds from germinating. Weeds are controlled by shading once the potato crop has become established. At this point, the haulms (shoots and leaves) of the potatoes meet across the ridges and prevent sunlight reaching the soil, which prevents any weed seeds present in the soil from germinating.

Weeds can also be controlled by earthing up. This means covering the growing haulms with more soil, which prevents light getting to the tubers and turning them green. Green tubers cannot be sold, as they contain the toxin solanine, which is harmful if consumed. Earthing up also supports the growing haulms and helps to prevent blight spores being washed from the leaves down onto the tubers. However, earthing up is no longer practised by commercial farmers, since the potatoes are sown deep enough in the drills to prevent the tubers being exposed to sunlight.

> **Toxin:** a poisonous substance that is produced by a living organism.

Diseases

Potato blight

Potato crops can be attacked by several pests and diseases, but by far the most common is potato blight. Blight is caused by an airborne fungus called *Phytophthora infestans*. Its spores can travel from fields up to 1.6 km away. The spores germinate in humid weather when the temperature is greater than 10°C. The first signs of blight are yellow spots that turn black on the leaves. If the underside of the leaf is inspected, a white furry growth should be visible: these are the sporangia. The fungus produces more spores on the infected leaves of the plant and these spores can be washed down into the soil by rain, where they will then infect and rot the tubers. The most reliable way to prevent fungal infection is to spray the potato crop with a fungicide.

Met Éireann issues blight warnings when weather conditions are right for the spread of blight. When blight warnings are issued, commercial growers spray their crop and continue to spray it every 10 days until the crop is harvested. In severe cases of blight, farmers are advised to spray every 7 days. Since blight is not a risk until the summer months, farmers who grow earlies do not usually have a problem: their crop is harvested before blight becomes a threat. Blight is a problem for organic farmers, who cannot spray their crop with any chemicals. If blight strikes, the infected haulms should be removed and burned to prevent further spread of the fungus. Blight-resistant potato varieties such as Sarpo Mira are available. Since the leaves die due to the blight attack, no photosynthesis occurs and potatoes have a reduced yield.

14.10 *Leaf showing potato blight*

Blackleg

Blackleg is an increasingly worrying disease for commercial potato growers. It is caused by the bacterium *Pectobacterium carotovorum*, which is also responsible for causing the soft rot of tubers. The bacterium can affect the potato seed and prevent the emergence of the plant, but more commonly it affects the established crop, causing the leaves to turn yellow and the stems to turn black just above or below ground level. The disease itself is spread through contaminated seed potatoes.

The multiplication of blackleg bacteria is totally weather dependent. Cool, wet weather favours the multiplication of the bacteria, which spread to developing tubers. Therefore, blackleg outbreaks are more common in windy, wet springs than in drier springs. Poor-draining soils that retain water also facilitate the spread of the disease.

Seed potatoes need careful inspection for blackleg, since the bacteria spread from the infected tubers to others during storage. Damaged or bruised seeds or sprouts allow entry of the bacteria more easily, and for this reason damaged seeds should not be sown.

In order to prevent blackleg, growers should plant only clean, disease-free certified seed. If an outbreak of blackleg occurs, the infected stems and tubers, including the original seed potato, should be removed. The original seed potato was probably the source of the infection. Removal of all tubers at harvest will prevent any diseased potatoes harbouring the disease for the following year. The bacterium itself does not survive very long in the soil, so crop rotation will help in controlling the disease.

14.11 *A potato plant with blackleg*

Common scab

Common scab is a potato disease caused by the bacterium *Streptomyces scabies*. Potatoes are most susceptible to this disease in dry conditions and free-draining soils and during the first 6 weeks of growth. The quality of the potatoes is reduced. Scab can be reduced by maintaining a crop rotation and planting scab-free seed potatoes. Irrigation in dry conditions can help to control scab.

14.12 *Potato with common scab*

Quarantine diseases

Brown rot and ring rot are two serious diseases of potatoes found in crops in continental Europe. Neither of these diseases are present in Ireland. Under the EU Plant Health Directive both of these diseases are categorised as quarantine diseases and notifiable diseases.

Brown rot (*Ralstonia solanacearum*)

Brown rot is a bacterial disease of potatoes that causes rotting of tubers, which leads to large yield losses. It causes wilting in the potato plant and rotting of the tubers. The bacterium is found in a host plant called woody nightshade, which is found in Ireland.

Should this disease establish in Irish potato crops it would cause widespread losses in the seed potato and ware potato sectors. Importation of potatoes carrying this disease is prohibited. Annual inspections of potato stocks are carried out by the DAFM to check for signs of the disease.

Ring rot

Ring rot is a highly infectious bacterial potato disease. It is identified by wilting in the lower leaves, leaf margins rolling inwards, and loss of shiny appearance of leaves. Leaves turn from light green to yellow and eventually become necrotic. Soft rot of the vascular ring in tubers is also a symptom. The disease favours hot, dry weather conditions. Like brown rot, ring rot is a quarantine disease, and surveys are carried out annually to ensure it is not present in Irish potato stocks.

Threat from quarantine diseases can be minimised by planting only certified seed, maintaining a crop rotation and ensuring there are no groundkeepers. Groundkeepers are potatoes left in the ground after harvest.

Pests

Wireworms, the insect larvae of the click beetle, can sometimes be a problem if potatoes are planted after grassland. In order to reduce risk of attack, soil may be treated with an insecticide before planting. Wireworms attack tubers, eating them and lowering tuber yield and tuber quality. They can be treated using an insecticide. Some varieties are more prone to slug damage than others. Slugs eat tubers and can be a problem in wet summers, when the slug population rises. These pests are killed using slug pellets. Aphids not only cause damage to the crop but are also vectors of viral diseases. Control of aphids is vital in seed potato production. The potato crop should be sprayed with a suitable insecticide.

A **vector**, usually an insect, is a carrier of a parasitic agent: bacteria, fungi, protozoans or viruses.

Table 14.4 Aphid transmitted potato viruses	
Name	**Effect**
Leaf roll	Leaves roll up, chlorosis and stunted growth
Virus Y	Mosaic/mottled leaves, necrotic spots on tubers

Harvest and storage

Early potatoes are harvested from late May onwards, and maincrops are harvested in late September or October. The haulms are first killed off using a contact herbicide. The potatoes are left in the ground for up to 3 weeks to allow the skins of the tubers to harden; this prevents them from being bruised when harvesting. The potato crop is then harvested with a potato harvester, usually an elevator digger.

The machine separates the potatoes from the soil and either leaves the potatoes on the top of the soil to be gathered by hand or carries them to a storage bin. Care is taken to remove all potatoes, so that none are left behind.

14.13 *A potato harvester*

Storage

Losses during storage can reduce a farmer's profit and should be minimised as much as possible. Common reasons for loss of potatoes during storage include frost damage, sprouted potatoes, overheating, damage by pests (rodents), poor ventilation, and tubers harvested when wet or damaged during harvesting.

In order to minimise these potential losses, potatoes must be stored in purpose-built buildings that are well ventilated, leak-proof, insulated and frost-proof. They must allow access to a tractor and trailer. Potatoes are stored in stacks. If the stack is 1.8 m high, natural ventilation is adequate to dry out the potatoes. However, if potatoes are stored in stacks higher than this, a forced draught ventilation system is required. Any heat generated by the stacks must be allowed to escape, otherwise the potatoes will start to sprout. To further reduce the risk of sprouting, potatoes are often sprayed with a sprout inhibitor. Sprouted potatoes are unsellable. Since the demand for potatoes is all year round, many commercial growers store their potatoes in refrigerated units, and this further extends the availability of the potatoes.

Yield

First and second earlies yield around 7–10 tonnes per hectare. Maincrop potatoes have a much higher yield of 30–40 tonnes per hectare, since they are harvested when they are fully mature.

Genomics research

To improve varieties of potato available for crop production, the main potato research focuses on selecting varieties which have genes that control the characteristics for disease resistance and quality. Research at Teagasc and other similar institutions focuses on sequencing the potato genome to identify genes that provide resistance to diseases. Diseases of importance include blight and potato cyst nematode, both of which have a detrimental effect on the crop, reducing yields. Being able to produce resistant varieties of the crop means that crop yields can be improved with less reliance on chemicals such as fungicides and pesticides to control disease. This is an important factor for both sustainability of potato crops and also because several pesticides once used to control potato cyst nematode are now banned.

Sustainability in potato production

To ensure sustainability in potato production a number of factors should be considered:
- Breed varieties with high yield, high nutritional value, resistance to main diseases and high adaptability to less favourable conditions
- Promote varieties adapted to the range of existing climatic conditions to ensure wide adaptability and stable production
- Focus breeding programmes on achieving long-term benefits, including not only resistance to insect pests and diseases but also high, stable yield, greater resource efficiency, better nutritional quality and better storage capabilities
- Store only seed tubers taken from healthy plants and ensure they are devoid of storage diseases such as late blight, bacterial rot and silver scurf
- Plant seed potatoes that are uniform in size to improve uniform crop emergence and an overall better yield
- Use only certified disease-free seed
- Produce certified seed only in disease-free areas
- Practise crop rotation and remove groundkeepers.

Health and safety considerations in potato production

Potato production is highly mechanised, which increases risk of injury to the farmer. Several precautions should be taken in potato crop production:

- Ensure all machinery (potato planter, fertiliser spreader, elevator digger) are operating correctly and all guards are in place where relevant
- Ensure all machinery is switched off and disengaged before cleaning, servicing or removing blockages
- Do not walk behind the harvester when it is moving
- Ensure only people who have been trained operate specialised machinery
- Wear protective clothing, goggles and gloves when handling and spreading fertilisers, pesticides, fungicides or herbicides.

 **SPA 14.1** To determine the dry matter (DM) content of different potato varieties

SPECIFIED PRACTICAL ACTIVITY

Note: This investigation can be carried out with any crop.

State your hypothesis, prediction, independent variable, dependent variable and controlled variable.

Materials
Different varieties of potatoes, weighing scales, beakers, knife, oven

Method

1. Choose two or more varieties of potatoes.

2. Wash any soil from the potatoes and dry the tubers.

3. Weigh each group of potatoes separately.

4. Weigh an empty beaker or suitable container.

5. Cut the potatoes into equal-sized pieces and place the pieces into beakers, using a different beaker for each variety.

6. Place each beaker into an oven at 100°C. After 15 minutes remove the beakers from the oven and reweigh.

7. Put the beaker back in the oven. Continue to weigh the beaker of potatoes until there is no change in mass.

8. Calculate the mass of the dry matter in the potatoes for each variety by subtracting the mass of the beaker from the final mass of potatoes and beaker.

9. Calculate the percentage dry matter content of each potato variety from the following formula:

$$\frac{\text{Final mass of potatoes}}{\text{Initial mass of potatoes}} \times \frac{100}{1}$$

Validation

1. Present your data in a suitable table and a graph of your choice.

2. Do the results of this experiment support the hypothesis? Explain your answer.

3. Identify any sources of error.

4. Based on your results, identify a variety that gives a floury potato. Justify your choice.

Summary

- Potatoes belong to the family Solanaceae.
- Potatoes go through five stages of growth: sprout development, vegetative growth, tuber initiation, tuber bulking, maturation.
- Potatoes are classified as first earlies, second earlies and maincrop.
- Earlies are harvested immaturely from May onwards.
- Maincrop potatoes are harvested fully mature in September to October and give higher yields than early varieties.
- Potatoes are assessed under several characteristics: disease resistance, yield, maturity, keeping quality, eating quality and seed availability.
- Certified seed potatoes are produced in Donegal. The windy conditions keep the aphid population low and prevent the spread of diseases.
- Potatoes grow well in deep, well-drained loam soils and sandy loam soils with a pH between 5.5 and 6.0.
- Rotation is vital, since it prevents the build-up of potato cyst nematode and other soil-borne pests and diseases.
- Potatoes need deep and well-cultivated soils.
- Soil cultivation for potatoes involves ploughing to a depth of 22 cm, rotavation to produce a fine seedbed 172–182 cm wide, and each seedbed containing two drills.
- Commercial growers remove stones and clods; this prevents bruising and contamination of the potatoes at harvesting.
- Potatoes are sown 10 cm below the ridge. The seed size determines the spacing between the seed potatoes.
- In the sowing of early varieties the seed potatoes are sprouted before planting. Sprouting seed potatoes speeds up growth, plant emergence and yield.
- Fertiliser requirements are determined by soil tests.
- Excess nitrogen depresses the dry matter content of the tuber and produces a watery tuber.
- Weeds are controlled initially by using a contact and residual herbicide. Once the crop becomes established, shading prevents the growth of weeds.
- An airborne fungus causes blight.
- In order to prevent fungal infection, farmers spray the potato crop with a fungicide.
- Blackleg is caused by a bacterium, which is also responsible for causing soft rot of tubers and affects the established crop, causing the leaves to turn yellow and the stems to turn black.
- Brown rot and ring rot are quarantine diseases that are notifiable under the EU Plant Health Directive.
- The potato crop is harvested with a potato harvester.
- Potatoes in storage should be protected from frost damage, overheating, sprouting and pests to prevent yield losses.

PowerPoint Summary

QUESTIONS

1. Identify the family to which the potato belongs.

   (a) Apiaceae   (b) Fabaceae   (c) Rosaceae   (d) Solanaceae

2. Which of the following is not a type of potato grown in Ireland to harvest for human consumption?

   (a) First earlies   (b) Seed potatoes   (c) Second earlies   (d) Maincrop

3. Which of the following is not a maincrop potato variety?

   (a) Maris Piper   (b) Rooster   (c) Golden Wonder   (d) Cara

4. Which of the following statements is true with regard to seed potato production?

   (a) Seed potatoes are produced in Co. Donegal.

   (b) Cool temperatures keep aphid populations low.

   (c) Seed potatoes must be grown in fields free of potato cyst nematode.

   (d) All of the above.

5. Production of early potatoes is mainly confined to coastal regions of counties Cork and Wexford. Give a reason for this.

6. Why are potato growers recommended to use certified seed?

7. State three characteristics that a potato grower might consider when choosing a seed potato variety for potato production.

8. Why is crop rotation important in the production of potatoes?

9. Why is it important for potato growers to remove clods from the soil prior to planting?

10. Outline the cultivation of potatoes under the following headings:

    (a) Seedbed preparation   (c) Use of fertiliser   (e) Pest control

    (b) Sowing seed   (d) Weed control   (f) Harvesting the crop.

11. What is chitting? Under what conditions should chitting take place? What are the advantages of chitting?

12. What are the effects of applying excess fertiliser to a potato crop?

13. What is earthing up and why is it carried out?

14. Describe the conditions necessary for potato blight to develop in a growing crop.

15. Quarantine diseases are of concern to potato growers and the DAFM.

    (a) What is meant by a quarantine disease?

    (b) Name two quarantine diseases of concern to potato growers.

    (c) Why are quarantine diseases of such concern to potato production?

    (d) Outline three ways in which the risk of infection by a quarantine disease can be reduced.

16. Blackleg is a problem in potato crops due to our favourable climate in Ireland.

    (a) What type of organism causes blackleg?

    (b) What effect does blackleg have on the established crop?

    (c) What precautions should a farmer take to prevent blackleg occurring in their crop?

17. Identify four ways in which sustainable potato production can be implemented in Ireland.

18. Give a reason for each of the following processes:

    (a) Sprouting   (b) Earthing up   (c) Burning off the haulms.

19. Outline four reasons for losses occurring in potato crops during storage.

20. Outline three safety precautions a farmer should take in the production of a potato crop.

 Solutions   Weblinks

CHAPTER 15

Catch crop: Kale Ⓗ

When you have completed this chapter you should be able to:

- Describe the growth cycle of kale
- Discuss the effect of soil quality, seedbed preparation, seed selection and sowing on the production of the crop
- Understand how a variety of soil factors influence productivity
- Discuss the various factors involved in crop management including application of nutrients to match crop requirements
- Appreciate the importance of recognising and controlling disease in crops
- Discuss strategies for crop protection against diseases (fungal, viral or bacterial)
- Discuss harvesting techniques (grazing) for kale
- Identify farm health and safety hazards associated with the management of crops
- Discuss the controls and precautions necessary to prevent accidents, injury and ill-health on the farm
- Recognise the need for safe work practices, including the safe handling, harvesting and storage of crops.

Catch crops: facts

DEFINITION

Catch crops: fast-growing crops grown between two main crops when land would otherwise lie idle. Also known as fodder crops.

Catch crops are cultivated primarily for animal feed. They are usually incorporated into a crop rotation, where they can provide some quickly grown livestock feed. For example, a gap between the harvest of winter-sown barley and sowing a spring ley provides farmers with the opportunity of growing a catch crop, thus providing additional winter fodder. Ploughing a catch crop back into the soil can also help to improve soil structure.

Ley: a field or pasture sown by the farmer which is temporary in nature.

Advantages of catch crops

- Fast growing
- High yielding
- Provide farmers with additional winter feeds with a high dry matter (DM) content: less risk of fodder shortage in winter months
- Reduce winter feed costs: fewer concentrated feeds purchased
- Feed is fully traceable: grown on the farmer's own land
- Break crop between grass and cereals
- Help to prevent nitrogen leaching
- Early bite for dairy cows and early lambs when grazed in February
- Some crops, e.g. kale, have high crude protein content.

Disadvantages of catch crops

- Labour intensive, if strip grazed or zero grazed
- Many are low in fibre so hay or silage must be fed with the catch crop
- Vulnerable to attack from pests and diseases; crop rotation must be employed
- Uneconomical to plough a productive perennial ryegrass pasture for sowing a catch crop unless reseeding is planned
- Risk of poaching land if a catch crop is grazed in situ during wet winter months on heavy soils
- Iodine deficiency can occur when livestock are fed on brassica crops; brassicas are low in iodine, and chemicals produced by the plants can inhibit the uptake of iodine in animals.

Kale

Kale is a popular catch crop grown in Ireland. It has a longer growing season than stubble turnip, and if a farmer is planning to use it as winter fodder (for cattle or sheep) it must be sown between April and early July. Kale gives its maximum yield after a growing period of 5 to 6 months. It is a traditional winter feed but can also be used as a summer feed. It has a deep root system and good tolerance to drought. While it can be susceptible to club root (see page 236), and attack by insect pests, it is not as badly affected as other brassica crops. It responds well to moist, fertile soils which can affect yield, as does the variety sown.

The growth cycle of kale

Kale, like other members of the Brassicaceae family is a biennial plant. However, it is generally sown as a catch crop for autumn/winter and is grazed as a fodder crop when it is approximately 6 months old.

Seed   Seedling   6–8 true leaves   9–12 true leaves   Mature plant

15.1 *Growth cycle of kale*

Table 15.1 Growth stages of kale	
Growth stage	**Description**
Cotyledon (emergence)	Cotyledons emerge from the soil
Seedling	Up to five true leaves may be produced
True leaves present	Beginning of uptake of nitrogen and period of vegetative growth
First harvest	Leaves have grown to the stage where they may be harvested or grazed in situ
Stem elongation	7–12 cm of visible stalk from centre of rosette to the top of the growing plant
Plant decline	Leaf quality declines and is no longer suitable for grazing/harvesting
Bolting	Main shoot begins to elongate

Cultivation practices and feeding

Soil suitability

Kale grows best on a free-draining loam or sandy soil with a pH of 6–7, ideally a pH of 6.5. Land must be suitable for grazing if a farmer plans to graze the kale in situ (for cattle or sheep); otherwise, kale can be zero grazed or harvested in August to September and baled like silage to produce kaleage.

Planning to include kale or any other brassica crop in a rotation should take into consideration the crop sequence planned for the rotation, and maintenance of soil structure and fertility. Soil should be suitable to create a firm seedbed. As the land that will be under kale may be used for grassland once the catch crop is harvested, soil fertility needs to be managed for future reseeding. Depending on what the land has been used for prior to sowing kale, provision must be made for access to water for livestock grazing on kale, ease of dividing land (e.g. for strip grazing) or access to land with machinery (e.g. zero grazing, ensiling), and provision of a run-back for livestock.

The ideal site for kale production would be:
- Land with a free-draining soil that dries out quickly
- Relatively flat land (avoid steep slopes)
- Land that has not been sown with brassica crop in the last 4 years, to avoid club root
- Land that is not close to a watercourse
- Land where grassland productivity has decreased.

> **Run-back:** an area at the end of a field where livestock can graze.

Seedbed preparation and sowing

A soil test should be carried out approximately 8 weeks prior to sowing. If the land was previously used for pasture, the sward should be killed off by spraying glyphosate.

Usually the land is ploughed and then power harrowed to produce the seedbed. Kale can be broadcast, or it can be sown with a precision drill or by direct drilling. Seeding rates are adjusted depending on the seeding method used. Sow seeds in a firm seedbed, at a depth of 10 mm to ensure uniform germination. Roll after sowing to ensure good soil–seed contact. Kale is sown between April and July. Early sown crops that establish well are more likely to give the highest yields. The target population is 70 plants/m² whichever sowing method is used.

15.2 *Direct drilling of kale*

Jan	Feb	Mar	Apr	May	Jun	Jul	Aug	Sep	Oct	Nov	Dec
					Sow						
Graze								Graze			

15.3 *Sowing and harvesting year for kale*

Table 15.2 Seeding methods and rates for kale	
Method	**Seeding rate (kg/ha)**
Precision drilling	3
Direct drilling	4
Broadcasting	5–6

Seed selection

Maris Kestrel, Caledonian, Grampian and Keeper are common varieties of kale. Maris Kestrel is the most popular variety of kale in Ireland.

Table 15.3 Kale varieties and characteristics	
Variety	**Characteristics**
Caledonian	Good yield from a short winter hardy variety High leaf to stem ratio Suitable for dairy and beef cattle
Keeper	High yielding Winter hardy High leaf to stem ratio Good nutritional value for finishing lambs Good lodging resistance
Maris Kestrel	Good yield from a short winter hardy variety High leaf to stem ratio
Grampian	Excellent autumn or winter feed for both sheep and dairy cows Very high dry matter yields Some club root resistance

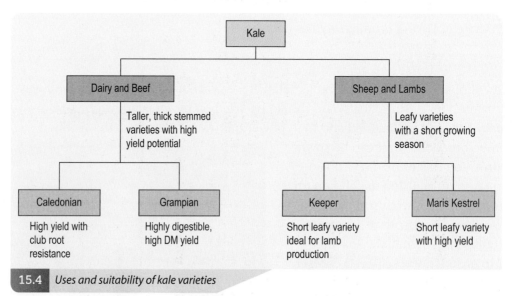

15.4 *Uses and suitability of kale varieties*

15.5 *Kale variety Maris Kestrel*

Table 15.4 Features of Maris Kestrel	
Variety	Maris Kestrel
Crop sowing time	May–June
Seed rate/ha	4 kg
Time of utilisation	November–February
Expected DM yield (t DM/ha)	10–12
DM%	14–16
Crude protein %	16–18
Metabolisable energy (MJ/kg DM)	12.5–13.5

Maris Kestrel is suitable for sheep and cattle grazing. It has high digestibility and a long utilisation period. Animals can utilise the entire plant by grazing on leaves and stems. It is a suitable autumn feed for cattle or sheep, when grazing is limited. It allows a farmer to outwinter livestock. It has good winter hardiness and is resistant to lodging.

Rotation

Like all members of the Brassicaceae family, kale is prone to club root. For this reason, it should not be grown continuously in the same field. Ideally, it should be incorporated in a 5-year rotation. Varieties with club root resistance are available.

Fertiliser requirements

Soil tests should be carried out to determine the fertiliser application. All fertiliser can be applied before sowing. Alternatively, half of the N fertiliser required can be applied at sowing, and the remaining fertiliser applied 2–3 weeks after crop emergence. Crops in the Brassica family have a sulfur requirement, so sulfur should be applied at a rate of 15–20 kg/ha. This is important for light sandy soils, or soils with low organic matter, where sulfur deficiencies are more common. Boron can also be applied to crops growing in these soils. Soil test results may also highlight deficiencies in other trace elements, which should be applied where necessary.

Table 15.5 Nutrient requirements for kale*			
Soil index	N	P	K
1	150	60	220
2	130	50	210
3	100	30	170
4	70	0	0
* For late sown crops (i.e. sown after April), reduced N requirement by 20%			

Weed control

An excellent seed bed and vigorous early growth leads to a well-established kale crop. This helps to control weeds within the crop. Weeds can be controlled in several ways, but the main method is by application of herbicide.

If a kale crop is sown after pasture, there may be weed seeds of broadleaf weeds such as dock and thistle present in the field. Spraying a pre-emergent herbicide prior to cultivation can reduce the incidence of broadleaf weeds in the crop. Post-emergent herbicides may also be used to control broadleaf weeds. Early sown crops may be more prone to weed infestation due to slow germination and competition with broadleaf weeds.

Pests

Flea beetles

Flea beetles can cause considerable damage to young kale seedlings. Holes are eaten in the stems, leaves and cotyledons at emergence. This is more problematic in warm, dry conditions, when damage can kill the seedlings. Most crops are not severely affected where rapid establishment takes place. In a slow-growing crop where incidence of flea beetle attack is prevalent, crops can be sprayed with a contact insecticide.

15.6 *Flea beetle*

15.7 *Flea beetle larva*

Diamondback moth

The caterpillar of the diamondback moth causes damage to the crop. The moth lays its eggs on the underside of kale leaves. When they hatch, the caterpillars feed on the leaves of the crop. Application of a contact insecticide will control caterpillar numbers.

Diseases
Club root

Club root represents the main disease threat in kale. It also affects other members of the Brassicaceae family. It is a soil-borne fungus, so control is by using good rotations. Avoid growing kale on any fields which have a history of club root; however, planting resistant varieties such as Caledonian can reduce the risk to the crop.

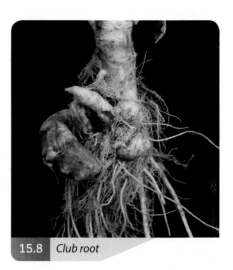

15.8   *Club root*

Club root causes the roots to swell and reduces their ability to absorb water and nutrients. This causes the plant to wilt. Eventually affected roots will rot, which reduces yield of the crop. Club root spores can remain in soil for up to 20 years. While some varieties of kale are resistant to the disease, a different variety may be affected in a subsequent rotation.

Feeding livestock

Kale can be zero grazed, strip grazed or ensiled. Strip grazing kale is the most popular use of the crop. An electric fence is used, allowing a space of 3 m per cow. The crop should be grazed in long, narrow strips to ensure all animals can graze at the same time and to minimise trampling of the crop at feeding. Strip grazing will maximise utilisation of the crop and minimise wastage.

Livestock should be introduced to the crop slowly – allow 1–2 hours access per day and build up to full-time access after 7–10 days. Kale or other brassicas should form no more than 70% of the diet, with 30% coming from fibre sources such as silage, hay or straw. There should be access to roughage, e.g. silage bales – place bales in the field during the summer or at sowing as this will avoid machinery traversing the field in winter (reducing soil damage such as compaction) and reduce workload. A run-back area will also contribute to the fibre in the diet in the form of grazing.

Excessive intake of kale can lead to anaemia. It can also cause nutritional red water in livestock as it contains a non-protein amino acid that is converted into a compound in the rumen, which damages red blood cells. The damaged cells release haemoglobin and the haemoglobin appears in the urine of the animal. In order to prevent this happening, livestock should be gradually introduced to kale and the crop should not be grazed if it is in flower, since red water is more common then. Kale is high in calcium but low in phosphorus, manganese and iodine, so mineral supplements must be provided to livestock.

15.9   *Dairy cows strip grazing kale*

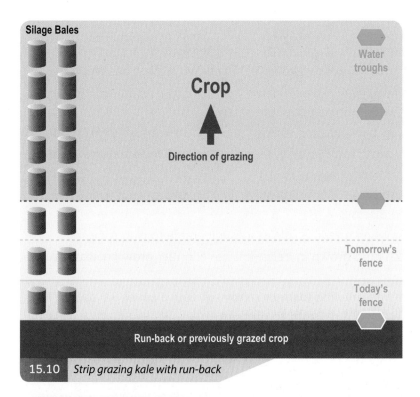

15.10 *Strip grazing kale with run-back*

Table 15.6 Yield	
Average DM yield	8–10 tonnes/ha
Average fresh yield	60–65 tonnes/ha

Benefits of grazing kale and other brassicas

There are several other benefits to the farmer in growing kale as a catch crop for winter grazing:

- It reduces winter housing costs
- It reduces labour and machinery requirements for feeding and silage production
- It allows livestock to overwinter outdoors
- It has a high crude protein content
- It is economical to grow
- It contributes to sustainability through acting as a cover crop when land would otherwise lie fallow. Cover crops prevent soil erosion, reduce nitrogen leaching, reduce nitrate levels in ground water, increase soil organic matter and contribute to biodiversity.

Health and safety risks and precautions in kale production

- Ensure all machinery (tractor, plough, fertiliser spreader, sprayers) are in good working order and guards are in place where applicable.
- Wear protective clothing, goggles and gloves when spraying fertiliser, insecticides or herbicides.
- Ensure all machinery is switched off if a blockage needs to be cleared. Do not put hands into machinery while operating.
- Take care when moving livestock when strip grazing. Ensure all boundary fencing in the strip grazed field is adequate.

Summary

- Catch crops are fast-growing crops, grown between two main crops when the land would otherwise lie idle.

- Catch crops are cultivated primarily for animal feed.

- Ploughing a catch crop back into the soil can also help to improve soil structure.

- Advantages of catch crops: fast growing, high yielding and reduce winter feed costs.

- Disadvantages of catch crops: labour intensive, low in fibre and vulnerable to attack from pests and diseases.

- Rotation is important when growing kale as it is vulnerable to club root.

- Kale is a popular catch crop grown in Ireland. It has a longer growing season than stubble turnip.

- Kale grows best on a free-draining loam or sandy soil with a pH of 6.0 to 7.0. It has a deep root system and is resistant to drought.

- Kale is a biennial plant and a member of the Brassicaceae family.

- Land for growing kale should be sprayed with herbicide to kill off old pasture prior to ploughing and harrowing.

- Kale can be sown by broadcasting, direct drilling or precision seeding at a depth of 10 mm.

- Seed should be sown between April and July with a density of 70 plants per m^2.

- Maris Kestrel, Caledonian, Grampian and Keeper are common varieties of kale. Maris Kestrel is the most popular variety of kale in Ireland.

- Kale is susceptible to attack by flea beetles and diamondback moths. The crop should be sprayed with a suitable insecticide.

- Club root is a soil-borne fungal disease which causes the roots to swell and rot, reducing yield.

- Kale can be strip grazed by livestock, using an electric fence, or harvested and baled like silage. Kale should be grazed in long, narrow strips to maximise grazing.

- Livestock should be provided with hay or silage at all times when grazing kale.

- Kale is high in calcium but low in phosphorus, manganese and iodine, so mineral supplements should also be given to livestock grazing it.

- Excess kale intake can lead to nutritional red water in livestock.

- Grazing kale can reduce winter feed costs, allow livestock to overwinter outdoors, produce a high DM fodder crop in a short period of time, and provide a cover crop to land where it would otherwise lie fallow.

PowerPoint Summary

QUESTIONS

1. (a) Define the term 'catch crop'. (b) Give two examples of catch crops.

2. Give four advantages and two disadvantages of growing catch crops.

3. To which family does kale belong?
   (a) Apiaceae
   (b) Fabaceae
   (c) Poaceae
   (d) Brassicaceae

4. Which soil conditions best describe those suited to kale production?
   (a) Clay soil, pH 6.5
   (b) Sandy soil, pH 5.0
   (c) Sandy soil, pH 6.5
   (d) Loam soil, pH 7.5

5. Identify three factors that would make a site suitable for kale production.

6. Describe the cultivation of kale under the following headings:
   (a) Seedbed preparation
   (b) Sowing rate
   (c) Variety
   (d) Fertiliser requirement.

7. Identify a suitable variety of kale for:
   (a) Dairy production
   (b) Lamb production.

8. Account for the popularity of Maris Kestrel as the most common variety of kale sown in Ireland.

9. How often should kale be sown in rotation?

10. Why are pre- and post-emergent herbicides necessary?

11. Describe the damage caused and control measures taken against:
    (a) Flea beetles
    (b) Diamondback moths.

12. Why is club root considered to be a serious disease of brassica crops?

13. Outline how a farmer might maximise access to and intake of kale by livestock and identify any precautions that should be taken when introducing it as a winter feed.

14. Hay and silage must be fed to livestock when on kale or other brassicas. Explain why this is important.

15. State four benefits of grazing kale.

16. Outline two precautions a farmer should take when sowing/harvesting kale.

17. Give two reasons why the intake of fodder crops in the diet of a farm animal should be limited.

18. Identify the type of organism that causes club root in kale and explain how this disease could be controlled or prevented.

Solutions — Weblinks

Energy crop: Miscanthus Ⓗ

When you have completed this chapter you should be able to:

- Describe the growth cycle of miscanthus
- Understand how a variety of soil factors influence productivity
- Discuss the effect of soil quality, seedbed preparation, seed selection and sowing on the production of the crop
- Discuss the various factors involved in crop management including application of nutrients to match crop requirements
- Discuss strategies for crop protection against diseases (fungal, viral or bacterial)
- Discuss harvesting techniques and storage methods for miscanthus
- Discuss the implications of sustainable development for crop production
- Evaluate the impact of different crop management practices on food-producing and other animals
- Recognise the need for safe work practices, including the safe handling, harvesting and storage of miscanthus
- Identify farm health and safety hazards associated with the management of crops
- Discuss the controls and precautions necessary to prevent accidents, injury and ill-health on the farm.

Miscanthus is a member of the Family Poaceae. Also known as elephant grass, it is a perennial species, originating in Asia. It is a high-yield energy crop that resembles bamboo. One of the major benefits of miscanthus is that it produces a crop every year without the need for replanting, and it can grow to over 3 m in a single growing season. *Miscanthus giganteus* is the species that is used for biomass production in Ireland. Miscanthus spreads by means of rhizomes. Farmers can use pieces of rhizome to produce new plants. Once the crop is planted it will produce an annual crop for at least 15 years.

The main products associated with miscanthus are for combustion. Bales are used in power stations to produce heat and electricity. Chips, pellets and briquettes can be used in boilers and stoves to produce heat. Miscanthus can also be used for animal bedding.

16.1 *Miscanthus*

The growth cycle of miscanthus

Miscanthus rhizomes are planted in early spring and the first shoots are produced from the underground rhizomes in March. In the first year of planting these shoots develop into stems 0.5–1.0 m in height by August. The canes resemble bamboo and contain a solid pith. From late July the lower leaves of the plant undergo senescence. Once the temperatures start getting colder in autumn, senescence increases and nutrients are translocated back to the rhizomes. Leaves fall from the plant, producing a deep leaf litter that is valuable to the soil in terms of organic matter. The stems dry during the winter months to a low moisture content of 30–50%. The canes are harvested in winter or early spring, when they are almost bare.

As the crop does not reach its full height in the first 3 years, it is not worth harvesting during this time period. From the third year onwards, the crop reaches a height of over 3 m.

The plant follows a simple growth pattern each year after harvest.

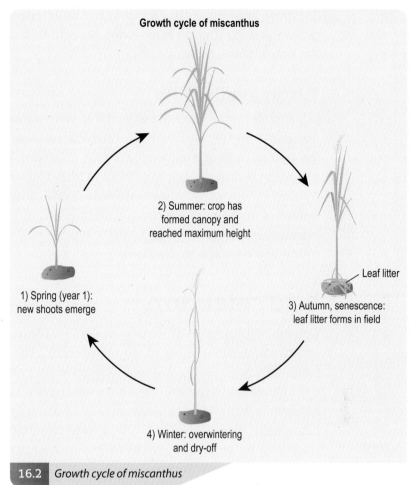

Growth cycle of miscanthus

1) Spring (year 1): new shoots emerge

2) Summer: crop has formed canopy and reached maximum height

Leaf litter

3) Autumn, senescence: leaf litter forms in field

4) Winter: overwintering and dry-off

16.2 *Growth cycle of miscanthus*

Spring: emergence

After establishment, shoots emerge from underground rhizomes in March/April.

Summer: growth

In summer miscanthus undergoes a period of vegetative growth, reaching a height of greater than 3 m in July/August.

Autumn: senescence

Senescence is triggered by colder autumn temperatures. Nutrients are translocated to the underground rhizomes. The deep leaf litter that results forms a mulch and controls weeds, while also providing nutrients and organic matter to the soil.

Winter/early spring: harvest

The crop overwinters in the field. This aids drying by reducing moisture content. Miscanthus is ready to harvest in winter or early spring (January–March).

Factors for growth

Soil suitability and quality

Miscanthus grows on a wide variety of soils and is tolerant of a large pH range. The optimum pH for growing miscanthus is between 5.5 and 7.5. As miscanthus is harvested in winter or early spring, it is important that the soil does not get waterlogged, which could cause access issues for heavy machinery and damage soil structure (although the leaf litter and rhizome mat do provide some structure for the soil). For this reason, heavy clay soils may not be the most suitable for miscanthus production.

Climate and temperature

Sunshine, water availability and temperature are the three key factors that affect the yield of miscanthus. The plant has a threshold temperature of 6°C, below which it will not grow. However, as this temperature is quite low, it allows the crop to have a long growing season. During early spring growth, frosts can destroy early foliage and reduce the length of the growing season.

Water availability

Miscanthus makes good use of available water as its roots can penetrate soil up to a depth of 2 m. The availability of water from annual rainfall and soil water retention to the crop has a strong influence on yield at harvest. Limited soil water availability during a growing season will prevent the crop from reaching its optimum yield for that year. A dense canopy of leaves can intercept rainfall, and this water will evaporate off the surface of the plant rather than infiltrating through the soil. Water intercepted in this manner can reduce all water available from rainfall by a third. Drought will lead to leaf rolling and die-back on the plant.

Site selection

As a miscanthus crop will remain on site for at least 15 years after initial planting, careful consideration should be given to site selection. The crop can also reach a maximum height of 3.5 m, so this may also have an impact on the local landscape. Consideration has to be given to the effect the crop may have on local wildlife or conservation areas: miscanthus has the potential to provide a habitat for wildlife and encourage greater biodiversity. Also, as the roots have a deep penetrating ability, their impacts on any neighbouring archaeological sites and public areas need to be considered.

Planting and establishment

Soil preparation

As the crop will grow on the same site for at least 15 years, careful soil preparation is essential to ensure good establishment and high yields. Proper site preparation will also mean crop management is easier. The site should be sprayed with a broad-spectrum herbicide for controlling perennial weeds prior to cultivation. This is of particular importance if the site was previously under grass. After spraying, the soil should be ploughed from 15 January onwards. This also reduces attack of the newly established plants by the larvae of two moths: the ghost moth (*Hepialus humuli*) and the common rustic moth (*Mesapamea secalis*).

In March or April, the site should be rotavated or power harrowed immediately before planting. This aids good root development and improved soil aeration. Rolling leads to better root soil contact and also improves the effectiveness of any residual herbicides that have been applied. This leads to better establishment and overall better crop productivity.

Rhizome selection

Miscanthus is a sterile crop and does not produce seed. The crop is produced from rhizomes. There is no current rhizome certification scheme available in Ireland or Europe. Miscanthus rhizomes should be sourced from nurseries in European countries and rhizome cuttings should come from young plants.

Miscanthus propagation

Rhizome division is one of the most common ways of producing plant rhizomes. Two- to three-year-old plants are split while dormant using a rotary cultivator and the rhizome pieces are collected for planting. Rhizome pieces must have at least two to three buds and be kept moist before replanting. Germination tests carried out by Teagasc have shown germination rates of greater than 90% for rhizomes with two to three buds. For best results, rhizomes should be planted within 4 hours of harvesting. If rhizomes are to be stored, they should be kept in cold conditions at a temperature of 3–5°C. Rhizomes can be stored in these conditions for several weeks. Rhizomes that are kept in cold storage should be planted within 4 hours of being removed from storage. To ensure crop establishment, soils should have a moisture content above 40%.

16.3 *Miscanthus rhizomes*

Plant density

Rhizomes are planted at a depth of 5–10 cm and at a rate of approximately 16,000 rhizomes per hectare. This gives an establishment rate of 10,000–15,000 plants per hectare after the third year. This planting density also suppresses weed growth through competition. Rhizomes are usually planted in March or April, which allows for a longer growing season and spring soil moisture. However, planting can take place as late as May to June. The longer growing season allows for the growth of large rhizomes, which makes them more tolerant to adverse weather conditions, such as drought, in subsequent years.

Planting and planting machinery

Miscanthus can be planted using a specialised miscanthus planter or a potato planter. Specialist miscanthus planters can plant rhizomes in rows, and typical planters are two- or four-row planters. Rhizomes are planted in rows 1 m apart and with 0.7–0.8 m spacings. If a potato planter is used, rhizomes must be graded to ensure they fit the potato planter. Soil should be rolled immediately after planting to ensure good soil–rhizome contact. Any gaps that emerge when the crop has established can be filled by stitching-in rhizomes.

16.4 *Autumn senescence in miscanthus*

Fertiliser requirement

Miscanthus is very efficient at nutrient uptake and use. The crop is deep rooted and can extract nutrients from a large area of soil that other crops cannot access. Fewer nutrients are needed per kilogram of crop in comparison with traditional tillage crops such as barley, or grassland. As senescence occurs in early autumn, nutrients are translocated from the leaves to the rhizomes, where they are stored during the winter. These nutrients are available for shoot growth and development the following spring.

The dense leaf litter that is produced by miscanthus in autumn decomposes over time and nutrients are recycled in the soil and can be absorbed again by the plant's root system. The movement of nutrients goes through an annual cycle of translocation from the rhizomes to the shoots in spring and summer and back to the rhizomes from the leaves in autumn. Nutrient levels in rhizomes have a direct effect on the growth and yield of the crop, which in turn affects the crop's productivity. Nutrient off-take is low in miscanthus, as most nutrients are translocated to the rhizomes prior to harvest and

Nutrient off-take: nutrient removal from soil through the harvest of crops.

nutrients in leaf litter are returned to the soil. Crop productivity is also heavily reliant on suitable temperatures and available water.

Miscanthus does not have a heavy reliance on artificial fertilisers. Crops show a better response to nitrogen fertilisers on less fertile soils. Soil tests allow miscanthus growers to determine if there are sufficient nutrients in the soil for their crop.

Teagasc recommends that artificial fertiliser application is not necessary for the first 2 years as there are usually sufficient nutrients in the soil. Fertiliser recommendations are based on growth from year three onwards and are also dependent on soil index value results from soil tests. Organic manures including slurry, manure and sewage sludge may also be applied to miscanthus.

Table 16.1 Miscanthus nutrient requirements			
Soil index	Nitrogen (kg/ha)	Phosphorus (kg/ha)	Potassium (kg/ha)
1	100	23	120
2	80	13	75
3	50	0	40
4	30	0	0
Source: Teagasc			

Weed, disease and pest control

Weed control

Control of weeds is important in miscanthus, particularly in the establishment of the crop. Slow growth during establishment means that it is hard to compete with weeds for light, water and nutrients. Weeds can also establish quite easily if planting densities of the crop are low and leave bare patches of soil. Once miscanthus becomes established, weeds can be controlled by application of selective herbicides. The germination and establishment of weed seedlings is reduced once the full canopy develops in the summer.

At this point the main weeds of miscanthus are shade-tolerant weeds such as chickweed and black bindweed. Annual meadow grass can also provide competition in autumn after crop senescence. Weeds can be kept under control in the first year of growth by ensuring a broad-spectrum translocated herbicide such as glyphosate is applied prior to planting. This is important if old pasture was present before planting, as this can harbour many broadleaf weeds such as dock.

16.5 *Chickweed*

Herbicide should be applied in January to kill off vegetation. Ten days should be allowed for the translocated herbicide to take effect before ploughing. Fourteen days after planting a pre-emergent herbicide should be sprayed along with an insecticide if miscanthus follows a grass ley. This removes the risk of crop attack by leatherjackets. Selective herbicides may be used post emergence to reduce competition from weeds such as thistles.

At the end of the first growing season glyphosate can be applied to control weeds. If any green leaves remain on the crop, the crop should be topped within 48 hours of glyphosate application to prevent translocation of the herbicide to the rhizomes.

Once the crop is mature, the canopy reduces light availability to weeds, controlling their growth. The leaf litter produced on an annual basis also suppresses weed growth. In a fully established crop, the need for weed control is low.

Pests and diseases

The growth and production of miscanthus is not seriously affected by pests. The larvae of two moths, the common rustic moth and the ghost moth, can cause problems to a newly established crop as the moth larvae feed on the leaves. This problem is most prevalent where the crop has been sown after a ley. Crops are most at risk in the 2 years following permanent pasture. Control of grass weeds is also effective in control of pests found in pasture. Rabbits may cause problems by feeding on the leaves of the crop, but fencing can reduce this damage. Miscanthus is not adversely affected by bacterial, fungal or viral diseases.

Table 16.2 Pests of miscanthus	
Pest	**Damage caused**
Common rustic moth larvae	The larvae of the common rustic moth overwinter before becoming adults and feed on the roots of the crop from autumn until May.
Ghost moth larvae	The ghost moth larvae overwinter twice before becoming adults and live in the soil, feeding on the roots of the miscanthus crop.
Wireworms	The wireworms bite holes in the stem/shoots at the soil surface.

16.6 *Common rustic moth and its larva*

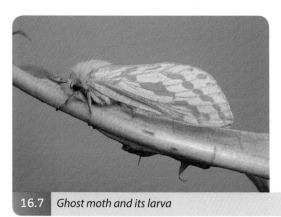

16.7 *Ghost moth and its larva*

Harvesting as an energy crop

Miscanthus is harvested in late winter to late spring (January–April). The crop harvested in spring has a moisture content of approximately 30%. The lower the moisture content, the higher the calorific value of the biomass, which is desirable in an energy crop. If miscanthus is harvested too early, it can have a high moisture content, leaving it unsuitable for some energy crop products. However, if harvesting is left too late, damage can be caused to the new shoots emerging in spring. Miscanthus will start to produce new shoots once temperatures reach 10°C. Therefore, the optimal harvest time is when the crop has sufficiently dried but before temperatures reach 10°C.

Calorific value: the energy content in a fuel.

For energy products, miscanthus is best harvested and stored as a baled product. The crop is cut with a forage harvester and then baled with a baler. This produces a windrow for baling with a higher work rate than a conditioner mower.

The crop can also be cut with a conditioner mower. The miscanthus stems are broken up by conditioning, which aids moisture loss, and it leaves the crop in windrows. Cutting height should be just above the leaf litter layer to minimise wastage of the crop at harvest. Leaf litter is not harvested, as it has a high moisture content and contains soil, which would contaminate the bales or chips.

It is easier to bale the crop if it is left in windrows as it helps dry the material due to better circulation and reduces moisture content.

Miscanthus can also be harvested with a forage harvester with a Kemper header. This cuts and chips the crop in one operation. The chipped product is suitable for combustion in boilers and power stations. The harvester is set to cut chips no bigger than 40 mm, as larger chips are not suitable for combustion in boilers.

Storage

Windrow: a row of cut crop or hay which is left in a swathe by the mower.

Kemper header: a specialised cutting tool attached to forage harvesters to harvest miscanthus and maize.

Bales should be stored inside in a shed or under cover outside, where they can continue to dry. A bale usually weighs between 250 and 600 kg. Bales should be stacked away from overhead power lines, and public roadways, where there may be a fire risk from cigarette ends.

Bales should be stacked on the unstrung side and overlap bale layers should be included at regular intervals. Bystanders should remain at a safe distance when bales are being stacked or loaded on lorries.

Heating risks are reduced when miscanthus is harvested as dry as possible. When the crop is harvested with a moisture content greater than 30%, it still contains enough sugars to allow for microbial activity. Microbial respiration can lead to a temperature rise in stored chips. The increased heat leads to further chemical reactions, which in turn produce more heat and may allow the chips to ignite. The risk of self-ignition is reduced when chip piles are kept below a height of 6 m.

Miscanthus chips with a higher moisture content can sometimes lead to fungal growth and rotting in piles stored for a period of more than a few weeks.

16.8 *Miscanthus being harvested*

16.9 *Miscanthus being stored*

Yield

The crop takes 3 years to produce a mature yield, so the stems are not harvested in the first 2 years but are left in the field until the following season. If application of translocated herbicides is planned for the following season, the stems should be topped to prevent crop uptake of the herbicide. A crop may be harvested in year two producing 4–10 tonnes/ha. From year three onwards a mature crop will produce 10–13 tonnes/ha. Crop yield varies with soil type, climate and planting density.

Crop removal and site restoration

Miscanthus can be removed from a site by allowing the crop to green up after harvest and grow to a height of 1 m. Once foliage is present on the crop, it can be sprayed with a post-emergence herbicide such as glyphosate to kill off the crop. This is followed by rotavation of the soil to eliminate the rhizomes. Continuous mowing can be used as an alternative to the herbicide to kill the miscanthus.

Rhizome harvesting and production

Rhizome harvesting can take place after 4–5 years of growth of the crop. This method of propagation produces rhizomes for planting. After 4 years a crop will produce approximately 150,000 rhizomes per hectare. This will produce enough rhizomes for 10 hectares of newly planted miscanthus, assuming a planting rate of 15,000 rhizomes per hectare. Rhizomes are harvested before new buds appear in March.

Rhizome harvesting is a five-step process:
1. **Biomass harvesting:** the miscanthus crop is harvested and baled or chipped with a conditioner mower and baler or forage harvester. The remaining leaf litter and stubble are then mowed and baled separately.
2. **Undercutting:** the rhizomes are separated from their roots with an undercutter, which operates at a depth of 230 mm.
3. **Rhizome chopping:** a rotavator is used to break up the rhizome mat into pieces, which are suitable for planting. Rotavation is carried out at a depth of 20 cm. The soil and rhizome pieces are then ridged to prepare them for the rhizome harvester.
4. **Rhizome harvesting and sorting:** the rhizomes are lifted from the ground and separated from soil and stones. Very large or very small rhizomes are removed. A potato harvester may be used for this purpose. A de-stoner can be used for rhizome harvesting with an elevator to transfer the rhizomes to a trailer.
5. **Rhizome storage:** if the rhizomes are not being planted immediately, they must be placed in cold storage at 4°C as soon as possible.

Sustainable development of miscanthus production

One of the benefits of growing miscanthus is the reduction of greenhouse gas emissions on a farm. It is described as a carbon neutral fuel, as it absorbs as much carbon during growth as it emits during combustion. Lower amounts of fertiliser are applied to miscanthus, which results in lower greenhouse gas emissions during crop growth.

Herbicides are usually applied only during establishment in the first year. As miscanthus does not suffer heavy damage from pest attacks, pesticide application is also limited. Due to the recycling of nutrients, minimal use of artificial fertilisers is recommended.

It is more economical to produce an energy crop in close proximity to where that crop will be used. This leads to better use of land, and less infringement on wildlife habitats so that fragmentation of habitats is minimised.

Carbon sequestration

Miscanthus can store carbon in its rhizomes and roots, which removes it from the atmosphere. There is an increase in soil carbon when miscanthus is planted into land which was previously used for tillage crops.

Impact on wildlife

Miscanthus production has a number of benefits for wildlife populations and biodiversity.

- There is a greater diversity of species found in miscanthus crops than in cereal crops.
- More earthworms, spiders, birds and mammals are found in miscanthus crops than in cereal crops.
- Up to 10% of land can be left as open ground for management or environmental purposes when planting grant-aided miscanthus. Open ground protects hedgerow habitats. Headlands provide a source of food for mammals such as rabbits and deer.
- Miscanthus provides crop cover for most of the calendar year. There is only a short period of time between harvesting in early spring and growth of the following year's crop. This cover provides wildlife corridors between existing habitats.
- Ground-nesting birds and reed-nesting birds can use miscanthus as a nesting habitat in spring and summer.
- Game birds such as pheasants and partridges may use the crop as cover and protection.
- Numerous mammals have been observed in miscanthus crops, such as hares, mice, foxes, rabbits, voles and shrews. While providing a habitat for these mammals, it also means the food chain for larger carnivores such as barn owls remains intact.
- Leaf litter and a shaded canopy provide a habitat and food source for a wide range of insects, and in turn their predators.
- Numerous species of bird, including skylarks, wrens and goldfinches, use the miscanthus cover for shelter and a source of food.

Health and safety risks and controls in miscanthus production

Like other crops, there are a number of health and safety risks associated with miscanthus production.

- All machinery (tractor, baler, mower, fertiliser spreader, etc.) should be maintained regularly and in proper working order when in use.
- All guards should be on machinery where appropriate.
- When not in use, machinery should be turned off and placed in neutral.
- If there is a blockage in any machine (e.g. mower, baler) do not reach into the machine while it is switched on. Ensure that the machine is turned off before attempting to clear the blockage.
- Ensure that protective clothing, goggles and gloves are worn when handling and spreading fertiliser, pesticides or herbicides.
- Ensure that all chemicals are kept in a locked chemical store and are not accessible by children.
- When stacking or loading baled miscanthus, make sure that bystanders are not near the bales so they do not suffer injury in the event of a falling bale.
- Bales should be staggered when stacked to ensure that they are less likely to fall and cause injury.
- Chipped miscanthus should not be stacked in piles more than 6 m in height to prevent risk of fire.
- Miscanthus should be baled at a low moisture level to prevent build-up of heat in the bale from respiring bacteria. Bales that are stored in a shed are at risk of self-ignition when temperatures rise within the bale.

Summary of advantages and disadvantages of miscanthus as an energy crop

Table 16.3 Advantages and disadvantages of miscanthus	
Advantages	**Disadvantages**
High yield	Wet soil conditions can lead to soil damage during harvesting
Environmentally friendly (carbon neutral)	Low yield in first 2 years means a 3-year delay before there is an economic return for the farmer
No pesticides or fertilisers once it reaches maturity	Crop takes 3 years to reach full production capacity
Annual growing cycle	Some biomass boilers are designed with only one energy crop in mind (e.g. willow) and aren't suitable for miscanthus
Low maintenance and easy to grow	Crop may have to be harvested with a high moisture content due to poor weather conditions, leading to extra drying costs or a poor-quality crop
Increases wildlife biodiversity	Rhizomes produced from rhizome harvesting are susceptible to damage if not planted or stored immediately
Provides game cover	Wet winters in Ireland can lead to crops with a high moisture content
Long lifespan (minimum 15 years)	
Herbicides for cereals can be used for weed control within the crop	
No significant pest or disease issues	
Suitable for carbon sequestration	

Summary

- Miscanthus is a member of the Family Poaceae. Also known as elephant grass, it is a perennial species, originating in Asia.
- It produces a crop every year without the need for replanting. It can grow to over 3 m in a single growing season.
- Miscanthus can spread by means of rhizomes. Once the crop is planted it will produce an annual crop and does not have to be replanted for at least 15 years.
- The main products associated with miscanthus are for combustion. Bales are used in power stations to produce heat and electricity. Chips, pellets and briquettes can be used in boilers and stoves to produce heat. Miscanthus can also be used for animal bedding.
- Miscanthus rhizomes are planted in early spring and the first shoots are produced from the underground rhizomes in March. From late July the lower leaves of the plant undergo senescence.
- In autumn, senescence increases and nutrients are translocated back to the rhizomes. The canes are harvested in winter or early spring, when they are almost bare.
- The optimum pH range for growing miscanthus is between 5.5 and 7.5. It is important that the soil does not get waterlogged, which could cause access issues for heavy machinery and damage soil structure.
- Sunshine, water availability and temperature are the three key factors that affect the yield of miscanthus. Miscanthus has a threshold temperature of 6°C, below which it will not grow.

- Miscanthus has the potential to provide a habitat for wildlife and encourage greater biodiversity. Also, the roots have a deep penetrating ability so impacts on neighbouring archaeological sites and public areas need to be considered.
- In March or April, the site should be rotavated or power harrowed immediately before planting. This aids good root development and improved soil aeration.
- Miscanthus is a sterile crop and does not produce seed. The crop is produced from rhizomes.
- Rhizome division is one of the most common ways of producing plant rhizomes. Two- to three-year-old plants are split while dormant using a rotary cultivator and the rhizome pieces are collected for planting. For best results rhizomes should be planted within 4 hours of harvesting.
- Rhizomes are planted at a depth of 5–10 cm and at a rate of approximately 16,000 rhizomes per hectare. This gives an establishment rate of 10,000–15,000 plants per hectare after the third year.
- Miscanthus can be planted using a specialised miscanthus planter or a potato planter.
- Nutrient off-take is low in miscanthus as most nutrients are translocated to the rhizomes prior to harvest and nutrients in leaf litter are returned to the soil.
- Miscanthus does not have a heavy reliance on artificial fertilisers. Crops show a better response to nitrogen fertilisers on less fertile soils.
- The germination and establishment of weed seedlings is reduced once the full canopy develops in the summer. At this point the main weeds of miscanthus are shade-tolerant weeds such as chickweed and black bindweed.
- The growth and production of miscanthus is not seriously affected by pests. The larvae of two moths, the common rustic moth and the ghost moth, can cause problems to a newly established crop, as the moth larvae feed on the leaves.
- Miscanthus is harvested in late winter to late spring (January–April). The crop is harvested in spring with a moisture content of approximately 30%.
- For energy products, miscanthus is best harvested and stored as a baled product. The crop is cut with a forage harvester and then baled with a baler. This produces a windrow for baling with a higher work rate than a conditioner mower.
- The crop can also be cut with a conditioner mower. The miscanthus stems are broken up by conditioning, which aids moisture loss, and it leaves the crop in windrows.
- Miscanthus can also be harvested with a forage harvester with a Kemper header. This cuts and chips the crop in one operation.
- Bales should be stored inside in a shed or under cover outside. Bales will continue to dry once they are under covered storage.
- Heating risks are reduced when miscanthus is harvested as dry as possible.
- From year three onwards a mature crop will produce 10–13 tonnes/ha.
- Rhizome harvesting can take place after 4–5 years of growth of the crop. After 4 years a crop will produce approximately 150,000 rhizomes per hectare.
- Miscanthus is a carbon neutral fuel as it absorbs as much carbon during growth as it emits during combustion.
- Miscanthus can store carbon in the rhizomes and roots of the crop, which removes it from the atmosphere.
- More earthworms, spiders, birds and mammals are found in miscanthus crops than in cereal crops.

PowerPoint Summary

QUESTIONS

1. Miscanthus is a member of which plant family?

   (a) Apiaceae

   (b) Ranunculaceae

   (c) Poaceae

   (d) Brassicaceae

2. Miscanthus spreads by means of:

   (a) Runners

   (b) Rhizomes

   (c) Stolons

   (d) Tubers.

3. Place the steps of the growth sequence of miscanthus in the correct order.

   (a) The leaves undergo senescence.

   (b) A deep leaf litter forms.

   (c) Shoots develop from the rhizomes.

   (d) The stems dry out.

4. Miscanthus is best suited to soils with a pH range of:

   (a) 5.0–7.0

   (b) 6.5–7.5

   (c) 5.0–8.0

   (d) 5.5–7.5.

5. Why are heavy clay soils not suitable for miscanthus production?

6. Outline the importance of water availability to the growth of miscanthus.

7. Describe how rhizomes are produced for replanting on Irish farms.

8. At what rate, depth and time are rhizomes planted?

9. Explain why little artificial fertiliser is applied to miscanthus and outline how nutrients are recycled in the crop.

10. Identify two common pests of miscanthus and describe the damage they cause to the crop.

11. Describe the process of harvesting miscanthus.

12. Identify three risks associated with the storage of harvested miscanthus and describe how these risks can be minimised.

13. Outline the steps involved in harvesting rhizomes. Why would harvesting rhizomes be beneficial to a farmer?

14. Describe how growing miscanthus can contribute to sustainability on Irish farms.

15. Outline four ways in which miscanthus crops contribute positively to biodiversity.

16. Identify four health and safety risks associated with miscanthus production and outline how those risks can be minimised.

17. Describe four advantages and two disadvantages of growing miscanthus.

18. Outline miscanthus production under the following headings:

    (a) Soil suitability

    (b) Rhizome planting

    (c) Fertiliser requirements in the first year

    (d) Harvesting.

19. Account for the need to plant or store freshly harvested rhizomes within 4 hours.

 Solutions Weblinks

Grassland characteristics and growth

When you have completed this chapter you should be able to:

- Describe the growth cycle of grass
- Discuss the effect of seed selection on the productivity of a crop
- Investigate the botanical composition of an old permanent pasture and a new ley (SPA)
- Carry out an investigation to measure the dry matter (DM) content of a named crop (SPA).

Grassland covers approximately 20% of the earth's land surface. It is extremely important as a habitat, a source of food for animals and in agriculture. In Ireland, over 3.7 million hectares of agricultural land are under grassland. This accounts for 90% of farmland. It provides a readily available source of food for livestock in the form of grazing land and winter fodder.

Table 17.1 Use of grassland in Irish agriculture	
Use of grassland	Hectares ('000)
Pasture	2092.4
Silage	1033.9
Hay	220.3
Rough grazing in use	441.2
Source: CSO	

Grassland ecology

Grassland is semi-natural vegetation that thrives in the temperate climate of Ireland but ultimately is controlled by human activity. If grassland was not grazed by livestock or cut for silage or hay, eventually small shrubs and trees (bramble and blackthorn) would invade the land and become the dominant species.

Since agricultural grassland is used for grazing, grasses are grazed low to the ground; this favours shorter species. These species tend to be leafier. Leafier species are more palatable and nutritious than taller, stemmy species of grass. These taller species of grass, which are of less value agriculturally, can begin to dominate in grassland that is not grazed intensively.

Good grassland management can be the main factor in determining the species of grass present in land used for grazing and conservation as winter fodder.

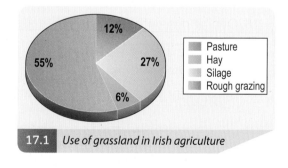

17.1 *Use of grassland in Irish agriculture*

When assessing the value of grassland, it is important to consider the following characteristics:

- **Botanical composition:** the range of grasses, plants and other vegetation present
- **Stocking rate:** the number of animals that can be stocked on a set area of land
- **Production levels:** the amount of herbage produced by the pasture; a high production level will lead to high production levels in livestock (live weight gain).

The three main categories of grassland are: rough mountain or hill grazing, permanent grassland and leys.

Rough mountain or hill grazing

Rough mountain or hill grazing is a category of land under poor-quality grass. It is found on mountains and hillsides that are often peaty in nature. Land is normally acidic and difficult to cultivate. Where cultivation is possible, land can be improved through liming and reseeding.

- **Botanical composition:** highly variable, consisting of poorer grasses such as bent grasses and fescues, heathers and gorse.
- **Stocking rate:** nutritional levels are low in the available grassland, so animals cannot be stocked at a high density.
- **Production level:** low, since grasses are not productive, and livestock will not have a high live weight gain as a result.

Permanent grassland

Permanent grassland is land under grass that is never ploughed. It can be fertilised and limed to maintain and improve quality and productivity.

- **Botanical composition:** variable; it consists of a number of grasses – from the highly productive grasses such as perennial ryegrass to the poorer grasses such as fescues and bent grasses.
- **Stocking rate:** higher stocking rate than rough mountain grazing due to improved grazing conditions.
- **Production level:** higher production levels than mountain grazing, since grassland is of better quality and can be improved through fertilisation and liming.

Leys

A ley is a field or pasture sown by the farmer, which is used for grazing by livestock. Leys are temporary in nature and are reseeded regularly.

- **Botanical composition:** little or no variability; one or two species such as perennial ryegrass and clover dominate, which are sown by the farmer.
- **Stocking rate:** high, since good-quality grassland can support a large number of livestock.
- **Production levels:** high, since the best grasses are sown in leys.

 SPA 17.1 | To investigate the botanical composition of an old permanent pasture or a new ley

SPECIFIED PRACTICAL ACTIVITY

State your hypothesis, prediction, independent variable, dependent variable and controlled variable.

Materials

Access to an old permanent pasture or a new ley, quadrat, pen and paper

Method

1. Throw a pen randomly over your shoulder in the chosen location (pasture/ley).
2. Place the quadrat where the pen lands.
3. Record on your results sheet the plants that are present in the quadrat (see table overleaf for an example of how you might record your results).

4. Repeat ten times in different parts of the pasture/ley.

5. Calculate the percentage frequency by counting how many times a plant is present in a quadrat. For example, if a dandelion is present in six out of ten quadrats then the percentage frequency is calculated at:

$$\frac{6}{10} \times \frac{100}{1} = 60\%$$

6. The experiment may be repeated for the alternative location and the results recorded in a separate table.

7. Compare the results of the old permanent pasture and new ley if both are assessed.

Results

Complete separate tables similar to Table 17.2 below for the old pasture and/or the new ley. The plants found in each area may be different from Table 17.2.

Table 17.2 Sample results table												
Area sampled: _____												
Plant name	**1**	**2**	**3**	**4**	**5**	**6**	**7**	**8**	**9**	**10**	**Total**	**% Frequency**
Perennial ryegrass												
Daisy												
Dandelion												
Dock leaf												
Plantain												
Buttercup												
White clover												
Ragwort												

Validation

1. Do the results of this experiment support the hypothesis? Explain your answer.

2. Is the data quantitative or qualitative in this experiment?

3. Present your data in a graph, comparing the permanent grassland to the temporary ley if both are assessed.

4. Based on your results, is the chosen location the best suited for (a) intensive grazing and (b) biodiversity? Give reasons for your answers.

The growth cycle of grass

Once a grass seed has germinated it goes through three stages of development:

1. Vegetative stage

2. Elongation stage

3. Reproductive stage.

Vegetative stage

During this early stage of growth, the leaves develop on the grass plant. The stem remains compact near the base of the plant. The plant forms tillers and when a critical number of leaves have formed on the plant, the older leaves die off allowing new leaves to grow. The number of leaves on a plant remains constant as older leaves are replaced by new ones.

Elongation stage

During the elongation stage, the stem begins to grow. The stem lengthens between the upper nodes. The plant has finished the elongation stage when the seed head starts to emerge from the leaf sheath at the top of the plant.

Reproductive stage

During this stage, the seed head develops. The stem that grew during the elongation stage is fibrous and strong enough to support the seed head. Wind pollination occurs during this stage of growth. Grass seeds develop as a result of pollination.

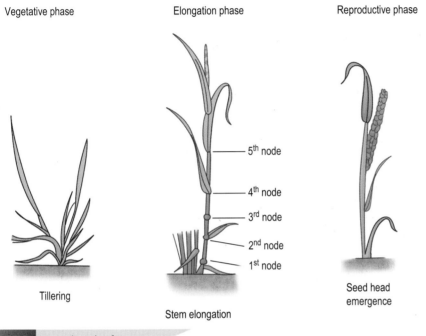

Vegetative phase   Elongation phase   Reproductive phase

5th node
4th node
3rd node
2nd node
1st node

Tillering

Stem elongation

Seed head emergence

17.2   *Growth cycle of grass*

Growth rate of grass

Fig. 17.3 shows the growth rate of a grass plant over the growing season. The plant has a slow growth rate and a low yield in the early vegetative stage. As leaves start to develop on the plant, the area of the plant that can photosynthesise and produce carbohydrate increases. The growth rate increases rapidly in the late vegetative stage and the yield of the plant steadily increases. As the plant enters the reproductive phase, the growth rate slows and the yield levels off. This is due to the development of the seed head, the loss of old leaves on the plant and the conversion of carbohydrates to fibre.

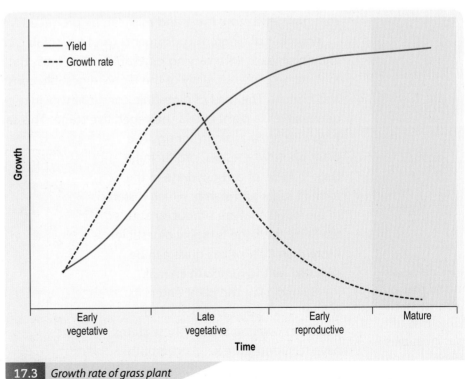

— Yield
---- Growth rate

Growth

Early vegetative   Late vegetative   Early reproductive   Mature

Time

17.3   *Growth rate of grass plant*

Characteristics of grass

The most important characteristics of grass are its palatability, productivity and digestibility. This is because grass is used as an animal feed both for grazing and winter fodder. In Ireland, grass has no other agricultural use. Farmers turn grass into meat and milk through beef and dairy production. Farmers seek grass species that will produce the largest volume of grass that is high in nutrients while also being attractive to their livestock as a foodstuff. Grass species with the highest levels of palatability, productivity and digestibility are the most desirable for grazing and conservation.

Palatability

Palatability is a measure of how pleasant the grass is to taste. Cattle and sheep are selective grazers and will eat only the grasses that are most palatable to them. If there is a variety of grasses in a pasture, livestock will eat the palatable grasses and ignore the unpalatable species. Since the unpalatable species go uneaten, they continue to develop and begin to dominate the pasture. The pasture becomes patchy where certain species have been grazed. Since the unpalatable species replace the palatable ones, the overall productivity and quality of the pasture is lowered. Perennial ryegrass is the most palatable species to grazing animals.

Productivity

Productivity is a measure of the quantity of plant material (herbage) produced by the grass. The higher the productivity, the more grass is available to livestock for consumption. Higher stocking rates are also possible on more productive grasses. Again, perennial ryegrass has one of the highest levels of productivity of all the grass species.

Digestibility

Digestibility represents the proportion of food that can be assimilated and used by the body in comparison to the amount of food consumed. Ideally, digestibility levels should be high, as this means there is little waste. The higher the digestibility of a food, in this case grass, the more meat and milk can be produced from that food. Grass is made up of a number of different constituents (protein, soluble carbohydrates – sugar, cellulose and fibre), each with varying digestibility. The grass that is of most value to the farmer for feeding consists mainly of the highly digestible constituents: soluble carbohydrates and protein. The level of digestible constituents varies over the growing season. After germination, a plant enters the vegetative stage. This same stage occurs when grass

begins to grow again in spring. The plant photosynthesises, producing a large volume of carbohydrate in the form of sugar and starch, which is stored in the leaves that are produced at this time. This herbage is highly digestible. More than 80% of the grass can be digested by the ruminant animal.

By mid-May, the plant enters its reproductive stage and begins to produce flowering stems. These stems have to support the seed head of the grass. Fibre is needed to provide strength in the stem and so it is produced at the expense of protein and

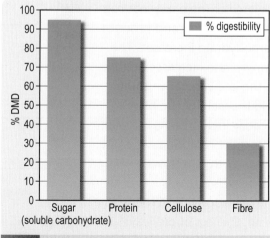

17.4 *Comparison of percentage digestibility of food constituents of grass*

> **Ruminant:** an animal that has a stomach composed of four chambers, specialised for the digestion of plant fibre.

carbohydrate. Since fibre is low in digestibility, this lowers the overall digestibility of the grass plant. The overall digestibility of grass can drop from 80% to 50% within one month.

Digestibility levels vary between grass species. Perennial ryegrass has a higher level of digestibility than any of the other species mentioned in this chapter. When water is removed from the vegetation, the plant material that remains and can be digested is referred to as digestible dry matter. If the dry matter digestibility (DMD) value for grass or silage is low, then the diet of the animal will have to be supplemented with concentrates. In order to maximise output, a dairy farmer will need to feed grass or silage with as high a DMD value as possible.

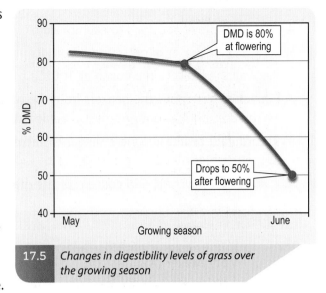

17.5 *Changes in digestibility levels of grass over the growing season*

Dry matter (DM): the matter remaining in a sample of food after the water has been removed.
Dry matter digestibility (DMD): the amount (percentage) of dry matter that can be digested by an animal.
Dry matter intake (DMI): the amount of feed an animal consumes excluding its water content.

Leafy grass will have a high DMD value, since it contains a high level of carbohydrates and protein. Stemmy grass has a low DMD value, since the stems consist of fibres. This is an important factor to consider when saving grass for silage. Cutting grass at the leafy stage is crucial, since the sugars and proteins are contained in the leaves of the plant. As the sugars and proteins are converted to fibre as the stems develop, this leads to a low DMD during conservation.

SPA 17.2 To investigate the dry matter (DM) content of grass

SPECIFIED PRACTICAL ACTIVITY

Note: This experiment can also be used to determine the dry matter content of hay, silage or potatoes.

State your hypothesis, prediction, independent variable, dependent variable and controlled variable.

Materials
Tissue paper, sample of grass, scissors, three beakers, electronic balance, oven, tongs

Method
1. Use a tissue to dry off any excess water on the sample of grass.
2. Use scissors to cut the grass into short lengths of similar size.
3. Weigh each of the empty beakers and record the mass.

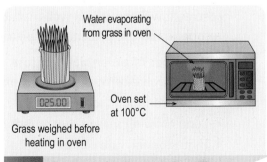

17.6 *Drying grass to determine dry matter*

4. Add a sample of cut grass to each beaker.

5. Weigh each beaker of grass and record its mass.

6. Place all the beakers in an oven at 100°C.

7. Use tongs to remove the beakers from the oven and reweigh each beaker every 10 minutes until a constant mass is achieved.

8. Record your results in a table similar to Table 17.3 and calculate the DM content of the samples.

9. Calculate the average DM content of the grass.

Table 17.3 Results	Sample 1	Sample 2	Sample 3
Mass of empty beaker (A)			
Mass of empty beaker + fresh grass (B)			
Mass of fresh grass = (B) – (A)			
Mass of beaker + grass dried to constant mass (C)			
Dry grass = (C) – (A)			
DM% = $\frac{\text{mass of dry grass}}{\text{mass of fresh grass}} \times \frac{100}{1}$			

Validation

1. Present your data in a suitable table and a graph of your choice.

2. Do the results of this experiment support the hypothesis? Explain your answer.

3. Identify any sources of error.

Seed selection: choosing grass species for leys

A variety of strains of ryegrass and clover is the most common seed mixture sown in leys. The most common grass sown is perennial ryegrass (PRG) and it is usually sown with white clover. It has a higher productivity, palatability and digestibility than other grass species that are suited to growth in Irish soil and climatic conditions.

Perennial ryegrass

Almost all grass seed sold for sowing is perennial ryegrass (approximately 95%).

Perennial ryegrass is suited to well-drained soils with a pH of 6 or greater. The soil should be fertile, and it responds well to nitrogen fertilisation. Since it is a perennial species, it will persist in a well-managed pasture for many years. Its inflorescence is easily recognised by the presence of spikelets on alternate sides of the stem.

Advantages of perennial ryegrass:
- Higher palatability, productivity and digestibility in comparison to other grasses
- High DM production
- Long growing season means reduced costs for winter feed
- High stocking rate can be maintained because of high productivity levels
- Good tillering ability, leading to sward dominance, good ground cover and weed prevention.

Italian ryegrass

The popularity of Italian ryegrass has decreased in Ireland in recent years. It is a biennial plant, which means pastures sown with Italian ryegrass need to be reseeded every 2 years. Some strains of Italian ryegrass may last for a third year. This means that the management of Italian ryegrass pastures is more intensive than that of perennial ryegrass pastures. It requires similar soil conditions to perennial ryegrass and can be recognised by the awns on its spikelets. As it has the ability to produce approximately 20% more herbage than perennial ryegrass, it is most suitable for short-term leys for silage production.

Advantages of Italian ryegrass:
- Longer growing season than that of perennial ryegrass
- Produces 20% more herbage than perennial ryegrass
- High production levels make it particularly suitable for silage production.

Hybrid ryegrasses

Hybrid ryegrasses are produced as a result of a cross between different species of ryegrass, usually perennial ryegrass and Italian ryegrass. The aim is to produce a strain of grass with hybrid vigour. This would combine the persistence of perennial ryegrass and longer growing season with the high production levels of Italian ryegrass.

White clover

Clover is a member of the Fabaceae family. It is a perennial plant with white flowers. It has smooth stems lacking in hairs (described as glabrous). Clover produces stolons and spreads quickly within a sward, since the stolons take root when they are trampled into the soil. This provides good ground cover, preventing weed establishment. Clover is often included in seed mixtures for leys for grazing or conservation as silage. Its inclusion is hugely beneficial in a grass-based enterprise.

Advantages of white clover:
- Good source of protein
- Ability to fix nitrogen: reduces the need for artificial fertiliser, which also reduces costs
- Provides an increased level of productivity, palatability and digestibility of the sward
- Reduces the use of chemicals, particularly in organic farming
- Meets requirements of environmental schemes
- High mineral content
- Provides good ground cover, which controls the spread of weeds.

Red clover

Red clover is not as popular as white clover in grazing systems. It is often used in seed mixtures sown for silage production. It is a perennial plant and can be recognised by its purple flowers. The leaves and stems of red clover are hairy. It grows in similar conditions to white clover.

Advantages of red clover:
- Highly digestible
- Very productive: provides a high yield of silage and can be cut a number of times in a season
- Can fix nitrogen: little need for fertiliser, which reduces costs
- Tap roots improve aeration and soil structure.

17.7 *Red clover*

Seed mixtures and crop productivity

A seed mixture is a combination of a number of different species of grass and clover or a combination of different strains of the same species of grass often mixed with clover. In the past it was commonplace to use a variety of species of grass in a seed mixture. However, this practice has shifted in favour of a seed mixture comprising strains of perennial ryegrass combined with white clover.

The key to good grazing management is to have a constant supply of fresh grass available for grazing livestock. If the seed mixture were uniform, all the grass would head out at the same stage and there would be a point in the grazing season where there was very little grass available to livestock. This can be avoided by using a combination of grasses that have different heading dates. This ensures that the pasture is productive throughout the growing season and there is constant growth of grass with a high nutritional value for livestock.

> The **heading date** of a grass species is the time when the ear emerges on the grass plant. Grass species are categorised as early, intermediate or late heading.

Table 17.4 Heading dates		
Category	**Heading date**	**Use**
Early	Mid-May	Provide grazing in spring (March/April)
Intermediate	Late May	Provide a good silage yield in May–July
Late	Early June	Provide silage (June–late July) and long-term grazing

Seed mixtures for grazing

A seed mixture for grazing may include several strains of perennial ryegrass of early, intermediate and late heading varieties. Early heading perennial ryegrass will give early growth of leafy grass in spring so livestock can be let out to graze earlier. The mid- and late-season varieties will provide grazing pasture throughout the summer and may extend the grazing season into late autumn. Any excess grass produced may be cut for silage.

There are a number of advantages associated with using this type of seed mixture for grazing pasture:
* There is a constant supply of grass over the grazing season, from spring to autumn
* There is always a fresh supply of leafy grass with a high DMD value, since heading dates vary; this ensures that the sward has a good feeding value
* There will not be a dip in production levels at any point in the grazing season, as there would be if only one strain of grass were used
* Since there is a range of heading dates in the sward, the whole sward will not go stemmy at the same time, which would leave unpalatable, poor-quality grass.

Seed mixtures for silage

If land is set aside specifically for silage production, the best-quality silage will be achieved if all of the grass has a similar heading date, since grass growth will be uniform. In order to achieve this, a seed mixture is used with only one strain of grass or a number of strains of the same type of grass with similar heading dates. This means that all of the grass is ready for silage at the same time and can be cut a number of times in one season.

When land is used primarily for grazing, with excess grass being used for conservation as silage, strains with intermediate and late heading dates are advised for use as a silage crop.

Summary

- Leafy grass species are more palatable and nutritious than taller stemmy species.
- Leafy species are more intensely grazed and are found in lowlands. Stemmy species are found on mountains and hillsides.
- The value of grassland is assessed by its botanical composition, stocking rate and productivity.
- The three main categories of grassland are: rough mountain or hill grazing, permanent grassland and leys.
- Rough mountain grass has high botanical composition and low stocking rate and production levels.
- Permanent grassland has a higher stocking rate and production level than mountain grass and there are fewer species present.
- Leys are sown by the farmer. They have high stocking rates and production levels and are dominated by one or two species of grass.
- The grass plant goes through three stages of growth after germination: vegetative, elongation and reproduction.
- Tillers grow during the vegetative stage, the stem develops during elongation, and the seed head emerges during the reproductive stage.
- The growth rate of the grass plant is slow to begin but once it develops tiller growth is rapid. Growth rate slows during the reproductive phase.
- The most important characteristics of grass are its palatability, productivity and digestibility.
- Perennial ryegrass has the highest levels of palatability, productivity and digestibility of the common grass species.
- Early in the growing season, digestibility is high (80%). As the grass produces a seed head, carbohydrates are converted to fibre to support the seed head and digestibility decreases to 50%.
- Dry matter (DM): the matter remaining in a sample of food after the water has been removed.
- Dry matter digestibility (DMD): the amount (percentage) of dry matter that can be digested by an animal.
- Dry matter intake (DMI): the amount of feed an animal consumes, excluding its water content.
- The main species sown in grassland include perennial ryegrass, Italian ryegrass, red clover and white clover.
- A seed mixture is a combination of a number of different species of grass and clover or a combination of different strains of the same species of grass, often mixed with clover.
- Heading dates: the heading date of a grass species is the time when the ear emerges on the grass plant.

PowerPoint Summary

QUESTIONS

1. Which of the following best describes rough mountain and hill grazing land?

    (a) Poorer grasses, low stocking rate, high production levels

    (b) Poorer grasses, high stocking rate, high production levels

    (c) High-quality grasses, high stocking rate, low production levels

    (d) Poorer grasses, low stocking rate, low production levels

2. Which of the following best describes permanent grassland?

    (a) Never ploughed, variable grass species, higher production than hill grazing

    (b) Reseeded annually, only one grass species, high stocking rate

    (c) Never ploughed, usually one grass species, high production levels

    (d) Reseeded annually, lowest stocking rate, lowest production levels

3. Which of the following seeds are most likely to be sown in leys?

    (a) Meadow foxtail only

    (b) Italian ryegrass and clover

    (c) Clover only

    (d) Cocksfoot and clover

4. After germination, what is the correct order of the phases of growth for a plant?

    (a) Elongation, vegetative, reproductive

    (b) Elongation, reproductive, vegetative

    (c) Vegetative, reproductive, elongation

    (d) Vegetative, elongation, reproductive

5. In each phase plant growth is mainly concentrated in one area. Match the phase of growth with the part of the grass plant where most growth occurs during this stage.

Growth phase of plant	Part of grass plant where growth takes place
Vegetative	Seed head
Elongation	Stem
Reproduction	Tillers (leaves)

6. A student carried out an experiment to determine the botanical composition of an old permanent pasture and a ley. In each field she threw a quadrat ten times and recorded the plant species that occurred in each quadrat. If she identified a plant species as present in six out of ten quadrats, she recorded the frequency of that plant as 60%. Her results showing the species found at each site and how frequently they occurred are shown in Table 17.5.

Table 17.5 Results							
Site	Dock	White clover	Perennial ryegrass	Nettle	Cocksfoot	Thistle	Ragwort
Field A		70%	100%				
Field B	60%	60%	100%	40%	50%	40%	30%

    (a) Identify which field was the old permanent pasture and which was the ley.

    (b) Identify one plant species listed in Table 17.5 that would contribute nitrogen to the soil and a source of protein to a grazing animal's diet.

    (c) Identify three plant species in Table 17.5 that would be considered weeds.

    (d) Identify one plant species in Table 17.5 that is described as a noxious weed. State why this plant should be removed from a pasture.

    (e) Outline one way in which the old permanent pasture might be improved.

7. What are the three main characteristics of grass that determine its agricultural importance?

8. What is meant by the following terms?

   (a) Dry matter digestibility   (b) Dry matter intake

9. Why does the DMD value of a grass decline over the summer grazing period?

10. Explain why DMD value is an important characteristic of grass.

11. Read the passage below and answer the questions.

The benefits of quality silage in beef production systems

The potential benefit of improving grass silage DMD depends on the mix of livestock on the farm over the winter period. While 'national average' silage is suitable only for dry suckler cows requiring zero body condition score gain, farm systems requiring higher animal performance stand to benefit from raising silage DMD by at least 6–7 percentage points above this level.

This was demonstrated in a study conducted at Teagasc Grange Animal & Grassland Research and Innovation Centre (Table 17.6) which measured intake and live weight gains for cattle offered silages with a range of DMD values. Results showed that growing cattle fed high-quality silage (75% DMD) gained approximately 0.3 kg more live weight per day compared to those fed on silage at national average DMD (65%). The extra performance was due to a combination of higher daily DM intake (DMI) and greater feed energy value per kg of silage DM.

Table 17.6 Effect of silage quality on silage intake and daily weight gain in growing cattle				
	First-cut silage quality			
DMD%	75	70	65	60
Harvest date	20 May	2 June	15 June	28 June
Silage yield (t DM per ha)	4.8	6.0	7.0	7.7
Dry matter intake (DMI) (kg/day)	9.0	8.3	7.6	7.0
Liveweight gain (kg/day)	0.83	0.66	0.49	0.31
Carcase gain (kg/day)	0.51	0.39	0.27	0.15
Feed efficiency (DMI/kg carcase gain)	17.6	21.1	28.1	46.7

The consequence of feeding the higher quality (75% versus 65% DMD) silage at farm level would include approximately 40 kg extra live weight gain over a 150-day housing period, a 2.0 to 2.5 kg reduction in daily concentrate intake for similar daily gain, and/or a shorter final finishing period. Interestingly, the efficiency of carcase gain per kg of DMI was also significantly improved with higher DMD silage, delivering potential environmental as well as economic advantages. *Extract from 'Grass silage for beef production', Joe Patton; adapted and reproduced courtesy of Teagasc. Adapted by Simon Marsh, Principal Lecturer – Beef Cattle Specialist, Harper Adams University.*

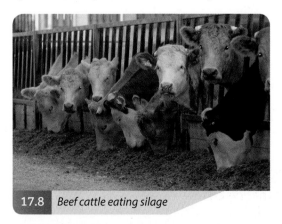

17.8   *Beef cattle eating silage*

(a) What percentage DMD is the national average for silage?

(b) Studies at Teagasc Grange showed an increase in liveweight gain of 0.3 kg/day when silage of what DMD percentage was fed to cattle in comparison to the national average of 65% DMD?

(c) What two reasons were given for the improved liveweight gain in the cattle consuming this silage?

(d) Identify the optimum date for cutting silage from the data above for the following:

   (i) Highest DMD%

   (ii) Highest silage yield.

(e) Give reasons why a farmer might cut grass for silage at 65% DMD rather than 75% DMD.

(f) Table 17.6 outlines the values measured in the study by Teagasc on DMD values for first cut silage during the growing season.

   (i) Plot a graph showing silage yield versus DMD%. Is there a correlation between silage yield and DMD%?

   (ii) Plot a graph of DMD% versus Liveweight gain (kg/day). Is there a correlation between DMD% and liveweight gain?

(g) Account for the digestibility of grass harvested for first-cut silage declining from 20 May to 28 June.

12. Explain why perennial ryegrass is considered superior to all other grasses for sowing.

13. What conditions does perennial ryegrass need in order to grow satisfactorily?

14. Italian ryegrass is 20% more productive than perennial ryegrass, while 95% of all grass seed sold for leys for grazing is perennial ryegrass species. Account for the popularity of perennial ryegrass and suggest reasons that a ley might be sown with Italian ryegrass.

15. Compare the physical characteristics of red and white clover.

16. Why is the presence of clover so important for grazing and grass growth?

17.9 *Cattle grazing on clover-rich pasture*

17. Describe the advantages of using hybrid grass species over Italian ryegrass on its own. Suggest a variety of clover suitable for:

(a) grazing   (b) silage production.

Give reasons for your choices.

18. A farmer has sown a ley with a mixture of early, intermediate and late strains of perennial ryegrass along with clover. Account for the variety of heading out dates of perennial ryegrass sown and state three reasons why clover might be included in a seed mixture for a ley.

19. What type of seed mixture is used for sowing grass for silage? Explain why this seed mixture is used.

Solutions   Weblinks

CHAPTER
18 # Grazing and grassland management

When you have completed this chapter you should be able to:
- Evaluate the impact of different crop management practices on food-producing and other animals
- Identify farm health and safety hazards associated with the management of crops, and discuss the controls and precautions necessary to prevent accidents, injury and ill-health on the farm
- Discuss the various factors involved in crop management, including application of nutrients to match crop requirements.

Uses of grassland

Grassland has two main uses in agriculture: grazing for livestock and conservation of silage and hay for winter fodder. Good management is the key factor in optimising the use of grassland. A farmer must determine how much of the land is to be used for grazing and how much is to be used for conservation. A balance must be achieved to prevent a shortfall in grazing in summer, waste through under-grazing in summer or an inadequate quantity of silage or hay saved for winter fodder.

Farmers must also determine how much grass will be required on an annual basis and how they will achieve this level of production while being cost-effective.

Optimisation of production levels can be achieved by good grazing management and application of the most suitable fertiliser in the correct quantity.

Livestock units

A livestock unit (LU) is a measurement of livestock grazing. One livestock unit (1 LU) is the equivalent of one dairy cow or one suckler cow. It can be used to determine how much grazing and winter fodder is needed on a farm. One livestock unit requires 12 tonnes (1 tonne = 1000 kg) of herbage annually. This value can be used to determine the total quantity of herbage required on the farm for the herd.

- One dairy/suckler cow = 1.0 LU
- Cattle <1 year = 0.4 LU
- Cattle 1–2 years = 0.6 LU
- Sheep = 0.15 LU

Exercise 18.1

Calculate how much herbage would be required annually on a farm containing 20 suckler cows, 15 six-month-old calves, ten 18-month-old cattle and 30 sheep.

Methods of grazing

There are several different methods of grazing. Many of them are based on the concept of a rotational grazing system in which animals are moved around a number of different grazing fields or areas. This allows livestock to graze on fresh grass constantly and allows for regrowth of grazed areas. Grass regrowth takes approximately 3 weeks, so the best rotational grazing systems operate on the basis that a herd will not return to a paddock during this time to allow the grass to regrow and reach the vegetative stage of growth. Grass is at its most digestible and is highly palatable during this vegetative growth stage.

Paddock grazing

Paddock grazing is based on dividing the land into 20–30 paddocks. Ideally each paddock should be of equal size so that it takes the herd 1 day to graze down the paddock. However, due to the layout of a farm, this may not be possible, and some paddocks may be created where cattle spend a shorter or longer time grazing. The herd grazes down one paddock each day and is then moved to the next paddock. They will not return to the previous paddock for at least 3 weeks to give time for the grass to recover. Fertiliser is spread on each grazed paddock after the herd has been moved.

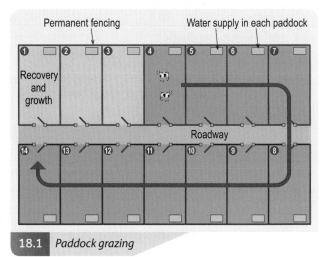

18.1 *Paddock grazing*

Advantages of paddock grazing:
- Fresh, highly digestible leafy grass is available every day for grazing
- No grass is wasted
- Excess grass produced can be saved as silage.

Disadvantages of paddock grazing:
- It is expensive to set up; roadways/access to each paddock need to be created
- Fencing and a water supply is needed for each paddock
- If paddocks are small it can be difficult to cut grass for silage.

Calculating grass cover in paddocks

Good grassland management requires a precise knowledge of how much grass is available for the grazing herd. Paddocks should be grazed to their optimum level, with no wastage. This measurement can be obtained by going on a weekly farm walk ('walking the land') and taking estimates of the grass cover. Farmers use software packages such as Spring Rotation Planner and Feed Wedge, to aid them in managing their grazing block (see Chapter 26 page 381).

Strip grazing

Strip grazing involves dividing a paddock or field into strips using a movable electric fence. Typically, a strip is created that is big enough to provide enough grazing to the herd for 24 hours. The herd is moved forward to a fresh strip of grass each day. A back fence is used to prevent movement of livestock into the pasture that has previously been grazed. Livestock are moved around strips in a rotational manner until they return to the first strip 3–4 weeks later. Each time livestock are moved, the previous strip is fertilised. Strip grazing can be used with a fixed or movable water supply (see Fig. 18.2). Some farmers choose to lay out their fields like the spokes of a wheel, which allows them to have one fixed water supply rather than in strips (see Fig. 18.3).

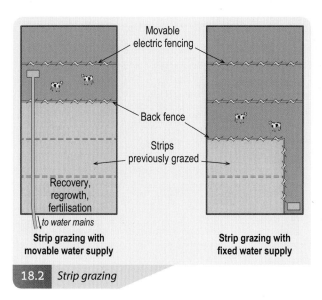

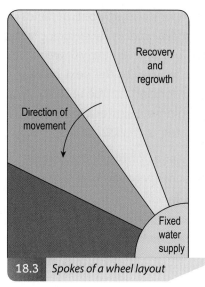

Advantages of strip grazing:

- Fresh, leafy grass is available for grazing each day
- There is no wastage of grass, as each strip is grazed fully
- Grass is not damaged while re-growing, since it is not accessible to livestock.

Disadvantages of strip grazing:

- A lot of labour is required to move livestock, fencing and a movable water supply each day
- The use of a fixed water supply means that part of a field has to be left as access to the water supply. This land cannot be used for grazing and may be damaged by constant use.

Set stocking

Set stocking is the simplest form of grazing management and it is also the least expensive. However, it is the worst form of grazing management and is not associated with intensive farming systems. Livestock have access to all grazing land over one continuous area for the grazing season.

Advantages of set stocking:

- It is a low-cost system with a minimum of fencing and water troughs required
- Poaching is minimised, since livestock are not as densely packed in one area
- Less labour is required.

Disadvantages of set stocking:

- In spring, early heading grasses tend not to be fully utilised; in summer, when grass growth is at its peak, it is not grazed efficiently
- Grass is wasted and much of it turns stemmy, leading to a reduced feeding value for the grass and development of patchy, unpalatable grass with a lower digestibility
- If disease is present in the pasture, livestock are constantly exposed to it.

Block grazing

Block grazing is a popular method of grazing in Ireland, particularly on small farms and for part-time farmers, for whom a reduction in labour is preferable. Block grazing consists of dividing up large fields into smaller blocks. Livestock graze a block for approximately 1 week before moving to the next block. Electric fencing can be used to strip graze blocks. Livestock return to a block after 3 weeks.

Advantages of block grazing:

- It is cheaper than paddock grazing
- Less fencing is needed
- Less labour is required and there is less movement of animals.

Disadvantages of block grazing:

- It is not as efficient as paddock or strip grazing.

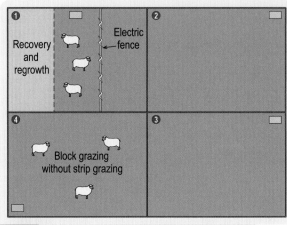

18.5   *Block grazing with and without strip grazing*

Zero grazing

Zero grazing is a system where cattle are housed all year round. Grass or other forage crops are cut with a zero-grazer and brought to the livestock, where they are fed indoors. Cattle do not graze the land. While the system may be labour-intensive, there are a number of advantages to it.

Advantages of zero grazing:

- Land is not poached by animals
- Energy is not wasted by animals through movement and can be used for live weight gain and milk production

18.6   *Cattle housed indoors fed on fresh grass in a zero-grazing system*

- There is less chance of lameness, since livestock are not walking on roads
- Access to fresh grass all the time means that the feed intake of cows increases
- The need for silage decreases due to the intake of fresh grass cut from distant fields, which were previously inaccessible to livestock; all fields are accessible for grazing
- While slurry production increases, this can be spread on the land and can reduce the need for artificial fertilisers, thus reducing costs
- Topping of grass is unnecessary, since all grass is cut at the same time.

> **DEFINITION**
>
> **Topping:** mowing grass to a height of 5–7 cm. It is carried out post-grazing to remove any remaining grass. Topping cuts grass to the correct post-grazing height and encourages tillering. It can also be used to control weeds.

Disadvantages of zero grazing:

- Very labour intensive
- Need adequate shed space for all animals
- Need well-maintained machinery to avoid breakdowns.

Practices complementary to grazing systems

Creep grazing

Creep grazing is used in cattle or sheep systems. It can be used in conjunction with rotational grazing. A creep gate or gap in a fence is created to allow calves or lambs access to another field. This field is disease-free and has fresh grass available for grazing. The size of the gate prevents the older animals from entering the field but allows the young animals to graze and return to their mothers to suckle.

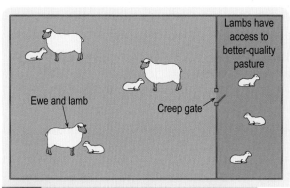

18.7 *Creep grazing, where lambs have access to good-quality pasture but can also return to the ewes*

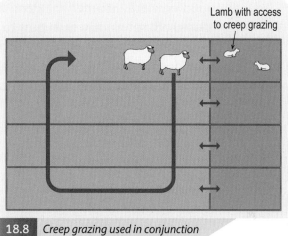

18.8 *Creep grazing used in conjunction with rotational grazing*

Leader-follower system

The leader-follower system is used in conjunction with paddock grazing, where the young animals (calves) are grazed one field ahead of the older animals. Young animals have access to the freshest, leafiest, most digestible grasses, since they are always put on fresh pasture. When the young animals are moved to the next paddock, the older animals are moved into the paddock on which the young animals have been grazing. The older animals graze down the grass that remains. This means that the young animals are always on fresh, clean grass and there is less chance of them picking up disease (since the older animals will have better immune systems). The main difference between leader-follower and creep grazing systems is that the younger animals do not have access to their mothers.

Mixed grazing

Mixed grazing can be used in conjunction with a rotational grazing system. Mixed grazing is the grazing of cattle and sheep together in the same field or paddock.

Advantages of mixed grazing:

- Production levels are increased by 10–15% in both cattle and sheep
- Tillering is increased, since sheep graze closer to the ground; it also reduces the need for topping
- There is less waste of grass due to the close grazing habit of sheep

18.9 *Mixed grazing of cattle and sheep*

- Cows will not eat around their own dung; sheep will eat this grass, ensuring there is no waste and preventing grass from becoming patchy, stemmy and unpalatable
- Cows will eat some grass species that sheep will not consume
- Mixed grazing can reduce the risk of worm infestation in cattle and sheep, since the stocking rate for each is lower when mixed, lowering the risk of infection. Also, some worms are host-specific, so the risk of infestation by endoparasites is reduced.

Extended grazing

Extended grazing is a practice in which the outdoor grazing season is extended between December and March. Grass growth rates begin to decline sharply from August onwards. In order to extend the grazing season beyond November, grazing land is closed off early in July or August to build up grass in late summer and early autumn. The quantity of grass that can be accumulated in this manner is dependent on weather conditions, fertiliser application, date of paddock closure and date of grazing. The yield of grass available to livestock in the extended grazing period also depends on the date of closure and the date of grazing. The earlier the paddock is closed, the higher the yield of grass in the extended grazing period. However, grass yield peaks around 1 November and declines after this time. This is because of senescence. After 1 November, decay rates are greater than growth rates, so yield declines.

Advantages of extended grazing:
- Reduced need for silage, since livestock can graze grass during the winter period
- Reduced costs associated with the smaller quantity of silage produced
- Provides a low-cost, year-round grazing system for farmers
- Reduces the carbon footprint of the farm.

Disadvantages of extended grazing:
- Poor weather conditions (snow, waterlogging) can lead to unsuitable grazing conditions and poached land
- Early closing of the paddock with late grazing means the DMD value of the grass is reduced to that of average-quality silage
- Paddocks are unavailable for rotational grazing for the final few months of the summer grazing season; this may put pressure on the farmer with a high stocking rate
- Extended grazing reduces the content of perennial ryegrass in the sward while increasing the content of grasses of lower feeding value, such as meadow grass and cocksfoot.

Tillering

The more side shoots or tillers that are produced by the (grass) plant, the greater the quantity of herbage produced. Tillering can be encouraged by grazing pasture with sheep or light stock such as calves. Sheep have a close grazing habit and graze grass low to the base of the stem. When the main shoot of the plant is grazed, this encourages the production of side shoots, or tillers. Topping can also encourage tillering.

> **DEFINITION**
>
> **Tillering:** the development of side shoots in a plant.

Impact of grassland management practices on livestock and other animals

While the grazing and grassland management system implemented on a farm is mainly to optimise the amount of grass produced for grazing and conservation of silage and hay, it is also to provide the best-quality grazing for livestock. Several advantages to livestock have been outlined for each grazing system.

These include:

- Less exposure to parasites such as nematodes and liver fluke
- Less exposure to disease, particularly in young livestock
- Increased growth rates in mixed grazing systems
- Access to mothers for calves and lambs in creep grazing systems.

Grassland management systems also have an impact on other animals and insects that live in grassland habitats. The impact the chosen system has can affect animal and insect biodiversity within the grassland system due to the intensity of grazing, or because of a lack of variety of plants in the grassland system.

- A study carried out in the Universities of Aberystwyth and Hull showed that systems which included semi-natural rough grazing support more species of birds and butterflies. A set stocking system, which is a lower intensity system with a greater variety of plant species, may contribute to increased bird and butterfly species. Farmers are also encouraged to plant a variety of wildflowers in meadows, which can also increase biodiversity in this manner.

- In intensively managed grassland, such as a rotational grazing system, the number of arthropod species present may be reduced. This has a knock-on effect on species further up the food chain, such as wasps and bees. Wasps are important in the regulation of pests, and bees are important pollinators. A decline in these species reflects less biodiversity in intensively managed grassland. As 80% of agricultural land in Ireland is under grass, bees and wasps are indicator species of the biodiversity in these grassland habitats.

> **Arthropods:** invertebrate animals, e.g. insects and spiders.

- Earthworms play an important role in maintaining soil structure, which is crucial for the production of grassland pasture for grazing and also for reducing the impact of persistent high stocking rates on soil structure, particularly in dairy systems.

- On dairy farms where an intensive rotational grazing system with a high stocking is implemented, high levels of nitrogen are used on the land. The greater the intensity of stocking, the higher the nitrogen inputs are. This leads to a lower diversity of arthropod populations; however, the density of arthropod populations is greater. Grazing on dairy farms tends to consist of fewer plant species that are grazed intensely, which leads to a lower average sward height. This affects which arthropod species are found in this grassland habitat. In swards with a greater diversity of plant species, and a higher average sward height, there is more diversity in the number of individual arthropod species found in the habitat. An example of this are spiders who depend on taller plant species to survive, and grassland habitats with low stocking rates with taller swards favour their presence in the habitat.

- As a result, the number of organisms found in the grassland habitat on dairy farms is fewer than on farms with low intensity or rough grazing. Species which are indicators of high-intensity grazing and management include aphids, dung beetles and flies. Low-intensity management systems promote the highest diversity and encourage a greater variety of arthropod and bird species in the habitat.

- Grazing systems are not the only practice that affects diversity within grassland habitats. Application of fertilisers, pesticides, ploughing and reseeding also contribute to a reduction in biological diversity, while the inclusion of wildlife corridors, wider field margins and use of hedgerows to create field boundaries all contribute to increased diversity in the habitat.

Fertilisation of grassland

Nitrogen application

On grassland where there is little or no clover, nitrogen should be applied to maintain the quality of the grass. Nitrogen should be applied in accordance with the Nitrates Regulations. Table 18.1 shows the maximum rates that can be applied. A dairy cow (1 LU) produces manure containing a total of 85 kg of nitrogen annually. Under the Nitrates Regulations, the maximum amount of livestock manure applied to farmland in a calendar year must not contain more than 170 kg of nitrogen per hectare. This is equivalent to the manure produced by two dairy cows or a stocking rate of two livestock units per hectare. Most Irish farms do not exceed this stocking rate. Application of nitrogen and phosphorus should not exceed the amount needed by grassland. Quantity and timing of application are determined by whether the land is used for grazing or silage. The application of slurry to the land will lead to a reduction in the quantity of nitrogen fertiliser needed.

Table 18.1 Annual maximum fertilisation rates of available nitrogen on grassland		
Grassland stocking rate kg/ha/year	Grassland stocking rate LU/ha	Maximum N fertiliser kg/N/ha
≤170	≤2.0	206
171–210	2.0–2.47	282
211–250	2.48–2.94	250

If slurry is spread on the land, the rate of nitrogen application can be decreased. Table 18.2 shows nitrogen application levels for first- and second-cut silage with and without the use of slurry.

Table 18.2 Nitrogen application on grass for silage	
Nitrogen application to first-cut silage ground (kg/ha)	
With slurry	Without slurry
85	115

Table 18.3 Annual maximum fertilisation rates of available nitrogen on grassland (cut only, no grazing livestock on holding)	
Maximum nitrogen application rate	kg/ha
First-cut silage	125
Second-cut silage	100
Hay	80

Common nitrogenous fertilisers used on grassland include urea, CAN and 18-6-12. Table 18.4 shows the application rate of nitrogen per hectare for each type of fertiliser.

Table 18.4 Application rate of nitrogen for artificial fertilisers	
Fertiliser name	Application rate of nitrogen (kg/ha) per bag
Urea	56.6
CAN	33.5
18-6-12	22.1

Phosphorus

The application of phosphorus is also subject to regulation under the Nitrates Regulations. Table 18.5 shows the annual maximum fertilisation rates of phosphorus on grassland. Fertilisation rates are dependent on the phosphorus index of the soil.

Table 18.5 Annual maximum fertilisation rates of phosphorus on grassland				
Stocking rate kg/ha/year	Soil phosphorus index			
	1	2	3	4
	Available phosphorus (kg/ha)			
131–170	33	23	13	0
171–210	36	26	16	0
211–250	39	29	19	0

Table 18.6 Annual maximum fertilisation rates of phosphorus on grassland (cut only, no grazing livestock on holding)				
Type of grass	Soil phosphorus index			
	1	2	3	4
	Available phosphorus (kg/ha)			
First cut	40	30	20	0
Second cut	10	10	10	0

Farm safety considerations for grassland management

There are several safety risks to consider in grassland management. Some of the risks involve machinery and the storage and application of chemicals such as fertiliser and pesticides. Many of the risks involve the handling and movement of livestock. Fifty-four per cent of animal-related injuries on Irish farms result from being knocked over or attacked by livestock. Another 40% result from being kicked or crushed by an animal. Therefore, it is important to be careful when working with livestock and to have safeguards in place, so livestock cannot escape from fields or paddocks and cause injury to themselves, to farm personnel or members of the public.

18.10 *Farm safety notice*

Table 18.7 Safety risks associated with grazing and grassland management

Risk	Precaution or control
Livestock	
Injury handling livestock in a field or paddock	• Ensure handlers are experienced, competent and agile. • Work out an escape route or refuge in advance of working with cattle. • Know and understand the basics of cattle behaviour, e.g. cows in heat are unpredictable. • Be careful around cows with newborn calves as they are protective of their offspring. • Do not put a child or inexperienced person at risk with cattle. • Avoid grazing a bull in a field where there is public access or a right of way. If a bull is kept in a field, there should be secure fencing and gates and a notice on the gates alerting people to his presence. • Minimise dangerous behaviour from cattle by breeding stock with good temperament. • Avoid isolating or cornering an animal in a field away from the rest of the herd. • Do not handle livestock with excessive force. Animals will remember past behaviours and react to past experience.
Livestock escaping from field or paddock causing potential hazard or injury	• Check and maintain gate latches and fences. Fences and gates must be able to contain cattle on the farm. • All road boundaries must be stock proof and internal fencing should prevent mixing of stock. • Gates should be strong enough to withstand pressure from livestock.
Moving livestock from one field or paddock to another	• Plan the move in advance, so there is a clear route for the move and gateways are set for herd movement. • Do not beat or shout at cattle unnecessarily. Cattle should be moved with minimal stress and without excessive force. • It should be clear to the herd in which direction they are expected to go. This minimises stress and potential for injury in movement of the herd.
Moving livestock across a public roadway	• Livestock should be moved as a group. Moving one animal can result in the animal trying to re-join the herd. • Personnel on roadways should wear high visibility clothing so they can be easily seen. • Use a stick to assist in directing cattle. A trained dog may also be used to aid movement. • Livestock should be moved in daylight hours to prevent accidents involving livestock, farm personnel or members of the public. • There should be enough people present to move the herd safely. Young children should not be involved in moving livestock. • On dairy farms where accessing the milking parlour involves crossing a public road, the herd should be moved to the parlour as a group and kept together until milking is complete and returned to the paddock as a group, rather than be allowed to wander across the road, increasing the risk of an accident.

Risk	Precaution or control
Fertilisers	
Skin or eye irritation or respiratory problems	• Wear protective clothing, gloves and goggles when handling and applying fertilisers. • Keep fertilisers in a locked storage area so children cannot access them.
Machinery and equipment	
Injury by exposure to moving parts of machinery or by faulty machinery	• Ensure all machinery (tractors, fertiliser spreaders, etc.) is in good working order and that all guards are in place and function correctly.
Electrocution by electric fencing from prolonged contact with fence	• Electric fences usually only deliver a minor shock, but prolonged contact can cause serious injury or death from multiple shocks over minutes or hours.
Entrapment by electric fence	• Avoid entering narrow spaces where electric fences are present. • Do not use barbed wire for electric fencing.
Increased risk of electrocution if neck or head touches fence	• Avoid climbing through or under an electric fence. Go around the fence by another route, or lower the fence (for temporary fencing). • There is an increased risk of electrocution/unconsciousness for people who have a pacemaker or heart abnormality.

18.12 *Moving cattle on a public road*

18.11 *Warning sign for electric fencing*

Summary

- Livestock units: a livestock unit (LU) is a measurement of livestock grazing. One livestock unit (1 LU) is the equivalent of one dairy cow or one suckler cow.

- A rotational grazing system is where animals are moved around a number of different fields, grazing on fresh grass constantly and allowing for regrowth of grazed areas.

- Paddock grazing involves dividing the land into paddocks of equal size. Livestock are moved to a new paddock each day and grass has regrown by the time they return to the first paddock.

- Strip grazing divides a field into strips, using a movable electric fence. A strip is big enough to provide grazing to the herd for 24 hours. The herd is moved forward to a fresh strip of grass each day.

- Set stocking occurs when livestock have access to all grazing land over one continuous area for the grazing season.

- Block grazing involves dividing up large fields into smaller blocks. Livestock will graze a block for approximately 1 week before moving to the next block. This can be further sub-divided for strip grazing.

- Zero grazing is a system where cattle are housed all year round. Grass or other forage crops are cut and brought to the livestock, where they are fed indoors. Cattle do not graze the land.

- Topping is mowing grass to a height of 5–7 cm. Topping cuts grass to the correct post-grazing height and encourages tillering.

- Creep grazing is where a creep gate or gap in a fence is created to allow calves or lambs access to another field. This field is disease-free and has fresh grass available for grazing.

- The leader-follower system is used in conjunction with paddock grazing, where the young animals are grazed one field ahead of the older animals.

- Mixed grazing is the grazing of cattle and sheep together in the same field or paddock.

- Extended grazing is closing off fields in July and August to allow grass to build up so that it is available between December and March for winter grazing.

- Tillering is the development of side shoots in a plant.

- Grassland management systems can reduce exposure to parasites and disease, and increase growth rates in mixed grazing enterprises.

- Greater plant biodiversity can lead to greater animal biodiversity, with bees, butterflies and wasps being indicator species.

- Application of fertilisers such as nitrogen must be according to regulations outlined in the Nitrates Regulations, and the quantity of fertiliser applied to the land is dependent on the stocking rate on the land.

- When moving livestock from paddock to paddock, personnel should be experienced and have a clear route out of the paddock for the livestock.

- Animals should not be unnecessarily stressed or beaten. Fencing should be stock proof and gates should be secure to prevent break-outs.

PowerPoint Summary

QUESTIONS

1. Which of the following factors are involved in good grassland management?

    (a) How much land is used for grazing and conservation

    (b) Calculating levels of production required

    (c) Optimisation of grazing management and fertiliser application

    (d) All of the above.

2. Complete Table 18.8, which calculates the total livestock units on a dairy farm and calculate the total herbage required for the herd annually. One livestock unit will consume 12 tonnes of herbage in 1 year.

Table 18.8 Livestock units and herbage required on a sample dairy farm					
Livestock type	Livestock quantity	LU value	Livestock units	Herbage required (tonnes/year)	Total herbage
Dairy cow	43	1.0			
Cattle <1 year	17	0.4			
Cattle 1–2 years	9	0.6			
Total livestock:		Total livestock units:		Total herbage required:	

3. Identify the total number of livestock units present on a farm which has the following livestock:

    • 90 sheep

    • 38 suckler cows

    • 32 cattle <1 year

    • 27 cattle 1–2 years.

4. Which of the following statements is not true of rotational grazing systems?

    (a) Three-week rotation

    (b) Livestock remain in the same field

    (c) Grass is highly digestible

    (d) Grass is at the vegetative stage of growth

5. Which of the following is not a rotational grazing system?

    (a) Strip grazing

    (b) Paddock grazing

    (c) Set stocking

    (d) Block grazing

6. Identify three advantages of paddock grazing.

7. A movable electric fence, movable water trough and a back fence are all features of which system of grazing?

    (a) Paddock grazing

    (b) Set stocking

    (c) Strip grazing

    (d) Extended grazing

8. Identify two disadvantages of strip grazing.

9. Which of the following is a feature of set stocking?

    (a) Heavily poached land

    (b) Expensive to set up

    (c) High labour costs

    (d) Livestock have access to all grazing land

10. Complete the following paragraph on zero grazing with the words below:

    energy   housed   movement   zero-grazer   poach   indoors

    Grass is cut with a _____. Cattle are fed _____. They are _____ all year round. Livestock do not _____ the land and do not waste _____ through _____.

11. Differentiate between:

    (a) Topping and tillering   (b) Mixed grazing and creep grazing.

12. Categorise each of the following statements under the headings 'Leader-follower system', 'Creep grazing' or 'Mixed grazing'.

    (a) Cattle and sheep graze together in the same paddock.

    (b) A gap in a fence allows calves or lambs to access another field.

    (c) Young animals do not have access to their mothers.

    (d) Young animals graze one field ahead of older animals.

    (e) Young livestock can return to their mothers to suckle, after grazing in a separate paddock.

13. What is the purpose of extended grazing?

14. How can the use of artificial nitrogen fertilisers be reduced on grazing land?

15. Name two artificial fertilisers used in grassland management.

16. How many kg per hectare of phosphorus should be applied to grassland for first-cut silage with a soil phosphorus index of 3?

17. State three advantages to implementing grazing systems on Irish farms.

18. Identify two indicator species associated with rough grazing. Suggest why these species may be present in rough grazing land.

19. Suggest two ways in which farmers might increase biodiversity on their farms.

20. State one reason why each of the following are considered to be important in grassland habitats:

    (a) Earthworm

    (b) Bee   (c) Wasp.

18.13 *Bee on dandelion*

18.14 *Wasp*

21. Describe the effect of implementing a rotational grazing system with intensive stocking and intensive grazing.

22. Suggest three precautions or controls to be taken when handling livestock in a paddock.

23. How can farmers minimise risk to themselves, their livestock and the general public when moving livestock on a public road?

Solutions   Weblinks

CHAPTER 19 Sowing and reseeding grassland

When you have completed this chapter you should be able to:

- Discuss the effect of soil quality, seedbed preparation and sowing on the productivity of a crop
- Compare establishment for grass with that of one other crop (SPA – Higher Level only).

There are a number of different methods of sowing grass. The method of sowing used is determined by a number of factors, including soil type and depth. When choosing methods of sowing, farmers must also take into account how they want to use the land. Often a pasture has been used for grazing or silage for a number of years and needs to be reseeded, and this can be a factor in the sowing method chosen.

Reasons for reseeding grassland

There are many reasons for reseeding grassland. Overall, the aim is to improve the quality of the grass sward.

Weed infestation

After a number of years, weeds can start to take over a pasture, reducing overall productivity. Dock leaves in particular can be prevalent, since their seeds can be spread when slurry is applied. Reseeding can help to remove weeds and improve pasture quality.

19.1 *Grassland infested with weeds*

Infestation: when a habitat or living organism is overrun in such large numbers that the result is damaged or reduced quality.

Low ryegrass content/high content of poor-quality grasses

After a number of years, troublesome weed grasses such as scutch grass and bent grasses can start to dominate a sward. They compete with the good-quality grasses such as perennial ryegrass and they lower productivity, palatability and digestibility. These three factors are used to determine how good a grass is for grazing.

Scutch grass is considered to be a particularly troublesome weed grass for farmers. It spreads by rhizomes and cultivation can cause it to spread by vegetative propagation. It can be difficult to control and requires a systemic herbicide containing glyphosate due to the spread of the rhizomes underground. It is also a weed of cereal crops such as barley and cannot be controlled by rotation.

Glyphosate: a total herbicide used to kill perennial weeds.

Addition of clover

Reseeding a pasture may allow a farmer to increase the clover in the pasture. Clover will increase the protein content of the pasture as well as fixing nitrogen in the soil.

Activity of animals

Livestock may have poached the land, leading to poor-quality pasture. This may be improved by reseeding the land. Establishment of a new sward may improve the root mat system, decreasing the likelihood of poaching. Livestock may also overgraze or undergraze the land: each activity will contribute its own problems to pasture quality. Undergrazing, particularly in a pasture with a variety of grasses, can lead to poorer-quality grasses becoming dominant. This can occur with cattle, since they are selective grazers. As the poorer-quality grasses become dominant, this lowers the overall productivity, palatability and digestibility of the grass. This in turn leads to lowered live weight gain and milk production. Overgrazing a pasture down to the roots can prevent the grass growing back properly and can hinder its ability to tiller. This will also lower the productivity of the grass.

Poor soil fertility

Poaching:
damage caused to wet or waterlogged land where land is cut up by livestock movement on wet soils. It causes surface vegetation to be removed and soil to be washed away. Soil may also be compacted.

Before reseeding takes place, soil tests should be carried out and lime and fertiliser requirements should be determined. Perennial ryegrass has an optimum growth rate at a pH of 6.5, so it may be necessary to lime the land to raise the pH to a suitable level. If phosphorus and potassium are lacking, they should be applied to the land in the form of a compound fertiliser or slurry. Phosphorus is important in the development of plant roots and a soil deficient in phosphorus will lead to poor root development in the grass sward. A soil which has the optimum pH for grass growth, combined with sufficient levels of nutrients can help to maximise the productivity of the grass sward. Other factors which may also play a part in the productivity of the grass sward include soil drainage and method of cultivation, which is outlined below.

Benefits of reseeding:
- Improves grass quality
- Improves silage quality
- Increased meat and milk production
- Higher output allows increased stocking density on land
- Better response to nitrogen fertilisers
- Longer grazing season reduces the need for winter fodder (silage), which reduces overall costs
- Excess grass as a result of increased productivity could be cut for silage and sold.

Effects of seedbed preparation and sowing on grassland productivity

Grassland productivity is affected by several factors: soil quality, seedbed preparation, seed selection and method of sowing. Most of the land sown under grass for agricultural use in Ireland is sown under perennial ryegrass or Italian ryegrass. As described in Chapter 17, perennial ryegrass is mainly used for grazing and Italian ryegrass is used for silage and hay production. Varieties of these grass species may be combined with clover seed when sowing. Perennial ryegrass is more productive than any other grass species in terms of the tonnes of herbage it can produce per hectare, which makes it an obvious choice for reseeding grassland.

The productivity of the grassland is also affected by other factors. When land is selected for reseeding, farmers must take into consideration what type of cultivation is suitable for the land and how long the pasture will be closed off while the grass seed establishes itself in the paddock. Shallow soils are not suitable for all methods of cultivation and farmers may be restricted to direct drilling or slit seeding (see page 283).

As slit seeding does not involve the removal of the old sward the new grass seedlings will have to compete with the older sward. Slit seeding can also be used to stitch-in white clover into an established sward of perennial ryegrass, to improve productivity of the pasture. Direct drilling allows the farmer to maximise productivity on shallow soils by reseeding with a chosen grass species without having to plough the land.

Soil quality and seedbed preparation

A fine, firm and fertile seedbed will provide optimal conditions for maximising grassland productivity. If the seedbed is not levelled and large clods of soil are not broken up by ploughing and harrowing, this allows weeds the opportunity to establish in the seedbed, reducing the overall productivity of the sward. A firm seedbed will also encourage maximum germination rates and will also be at less risk from poaching by livestock.

A firm seedbed can be created by the following steps:
- Take soil samples from the field in a W pattern and check for compaction; if the soil is compacted, sub-soiling might be necessary before reseeding
- Test soil for N, P and K and pH; fertilise and lime where appropriate
- Ensure suitable drainage is in place in wet soils
- In an old pasture spray weeds with a total herbicide and kill off old sward with glyphosate
- Plough and subsoil where necessary; create a fine seedbed by harrowing and rolling the soil.

Methods of sowing and reseeding grassland

There are a variety of methods of sowing or reseeding grassland, each with its own advantages. They include direct sowing, undersowing, direct drilling, slit seeding and slurry seeding. Of these, direct drilling, slurry seeding and slit seeding are examples of minimum cultivation techniques. Minimum cultivation is the practice of sowing a crop (grassland, cereals) or reseeding without ploughing the land. It involves the use of shallow cultivations (harrowing) and/or the use of herbicides to kill off vegetation.

Direct sowing (plough, till and sow)

This is the most common method of sowing grass in Ireland. It is also the most consistent method of establishing a sward. Land is ploughed, which has the advantage of burying the weed seeds. It is harrowed to create a fine seedbed. Seed can be sown using a seed drill or by broadcasting the seed onto the soil surface and covering with a harrow.
- **Fertiliser application:** in autumn-sown leys, nitrogen fertiliser is not applied until the following spring. In spring-sown leys, fertiliser can be applied during seedbed preparation and harrowed into the soil.
- **Time of sowing:** seed has to be sown by September in an autumn-sown ley because frost and winter weather conditions could kill the seedlings. In spring, seed should be sown before May. This will prevent seedlings being killed off due to drought. It will also provide a longer growing season for seed establishment. As this method involves creating a new seedbed, it maximises the productivity of the grass sward in a weed-free pasture.

Undersowing

This method of sowing is most commonly used on farms growing tillage crops. It is particularly suitable for tillage/grassland rotations.

Undersowing means that grass seed is sown with a tillage crop (e.g. barley, wheat). It is not suitable for winter cereals.

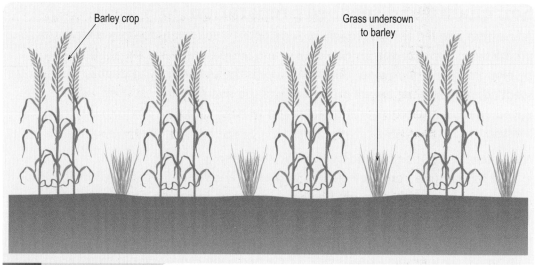

| 19.2 | *Undersowing* |

Grass seed is sown with the spring cereal. The land is prepared for the cereal crop and the cereal seed is then sown. Cereal varieties with short straw should be chosen to reduce the risk of lodging. Lodging will damage the grass. The grass seed is then sown immediately afterwards. Both grow at the same time. When the cereal is harvested in summer, the grass remains and establishes itself in the field. Grass will not be able to maximise production levels while competing with the cereal crop and the field cannot be used for grazing until the cereal crop is harvested. For this reason, grass production will take longer to reach maximum production levels.

Advantages of undersowing:

* Nitrogen leaching can be prevented or reduced, since the grass will take up any excess nitrogen following the cereal harvest
* Soil erosion can be prevented, since the grass is established after the cereal has been harvested
* Grass growing alongside the cereal can provide good ground cover and prevent weed infestation
* Grassland can be used for grazing after the cereal is harvested.

Disadvantages of undersowing:

* Since two crops are growing simultaneously, they are in competition for water, nutrients and space
* Undersowing grass to a cereal will lead to a reduction in yield in the cereal crop, since it competes with the grass
* Herbicide use must be restricted if clover is sown with the grass seed
* Undersowing is not suited to intensive cereal farming, where high crop yields are required.

Direct drilling/direct seeding

A direct drilling machine sows the seed. This machine cuts a slit in the soil and drops a seed into it. The land does not have to be ploughed beforehand. Direct drilling is most successful if the land to be seeded or reseeded is grazed bare or if herbicide is applied beforehand. This is particularly important if the land was infested with weeds.

Glyphosate (a herbicide) should be applied to the land to remove broadleaf weeds such as dock leaves. Seeds have the best chance of germination and establishment if they are drilled into bare land. Slugs can also be a problem with direct drilling. A simple test to check for the presence of slugs in the soil is to take a plastic fertiliser bag and lay it on the soil. Weigh down each corner with a stone and leave it overnight. Check underneath the bag the following day for slugs. If slugs are present, slug pellets should be spread on the soil. A firm seedbed can also reduce the likelihood of slug damage, since most slug species cannot burrow. Production levels are highest on soils which have been treated with herbicides and grazed bare, otherwise production may be reduced in a direct drilling system where new grass seed must compete with weeds/old pasture.

Advantage of direct seeding:
- This method is of most benefit on soils where ploughing is not possible or is difficult. Soils that are easily poached or are shallow are particularly suitable for direct seeding.

Slurry seeding

Slurry seeding is carried out in the same way as direct seeding. After seeding, approximately 10,000 litres of slurry is applied to the land to cover the seed.

Slit seeding/stitching-in

This method of reseeding is very similar to direct seeding. It uses similar machinery to sow the seed. The main difference is that the grassland is not killed off. Seed is always sown into old grassland.

Slit seeding should take place in spring (March or April) when grass growth is not at an optimum level. This will give the new seed a chance to establish itself in the sward without having to compete with the old sward during the rapid growth periods in the summer months. The old sward should be tightly grazed before seeding. Nitrogen fertiliser may be sown with the seed to encourage establishment. If the new seed establishes, the production levels of the field increase as the sward improves.

Advantages of slit seeding:
- No need to plough the land
- Land has not been taken out of use for a prolonged period of time
- Increased production level, quality and yield in grass
- If the seed does not establish itself, the old sward will continue to grow
- Can be used on poached/shallow soils not suited to ploughing.

 **SPA 19.1** (H) | **To compare the establishment of grass with that of one other crop**

SPECIFIED PRACTICAL ACTIVITY   (Higher Level only)

State your hypothesis, prediction, independent variable, dependent variable and controlled variable.

Materials
0.25 m² quadrat, pen and paper

Method
1. Place the quadrat at regular intervals in a W shape in a recently sown pasture.
2. Count the individual grass plants within the quadrat and record in a table.

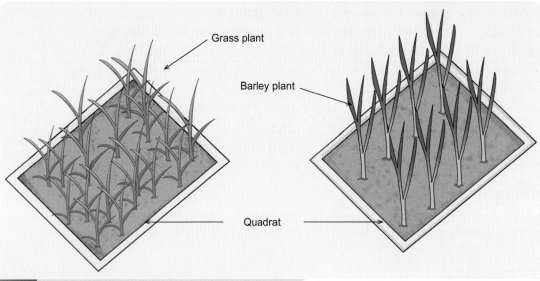

| 19.3 | *Recording established plant numbers in a crop* |

3. Multiply the number of plants recorded by four to calculate the number of plants per metre squared.

4. Repeat for 20 different locations in the pasture.

5. Calculate an average establishment rate per m² for the pasture.

6. Repeat for another crop, e.g. barley.

7. Use the thousand grain weight for the identified grass species and the other crop species to calculate the seeding rate for each crop per m².

8. Use the seeding rate of the grass and crop species to calculate the expected establishment rate.

   Seed rate (kg/ha) = target population × thousand grain weight/expected establishment %

9. Calculate the actual establishment rate as a percentage of the expected establishment.

   Actual establishment / expected establishment × 100/1 = % establishment

10. Plot the results for each crop on a graph and compare the establishment of grass with the chosen crop.

Table 19.1 Results										
Quadrat number	1	2	3	4	5	6	7	8	9	10
Number of established plants per 0.25 m²										
Number of established plants per m²										

Validation

1. Do the results of this experiment support the hypothesis? Explain your answer.

2. Is there quantitative data or qualitative data that supports or falsifies your hypothesis?

3. Identify a safety precaution for this investigation.

4. Identify any sources of error.

Summary

- Grass is reseeded due to weed infestation, low ryegrass content and high content of poor-quality grasses.
- Reseeding improves palatability, productivity and digestibility. It increases clover content in a sward and improves soil fertility.
- Benefits of reseeding grassland include: improved grass quality, improved silage quality, increased meat and milk production, ability to increase stocking density due to higher output, better response to fertilisers, longer grazing season and reduced need for winter fodder. Excess silage can be sold.
- The method of reseeding chosen depends on the type of soil in the pasture. Shallow soils are best suited to slit seeding or direct drilling and pastures can be improved by stitching in white clover. Seeds are sown into the soil without ploughing up the land to maximise productivity.
- A fine seedbed provides optimal conditions for maximum grassland productivity. Soil should be tests for N, P and K and fertilised where necessary. Subsoiling should be carried out on compacted soils.
- Methods of sowing include direct sowing, undersowing, direct drilling, slit seeding and slurry seeding.
- Direct sowing: land is ploughed and harrowed and seed is sown with a seed drill or broadcast on the soil. Nitrogen fertiliser is applied in spring. Autumn-sown leys are sown in September and spring-sown leys are sown before May.
- Undersowing: grass seed is sown with another tillage crop. When the tillage crop is harvested, grass establishes itself in the field. This is suitable only for spring-sown crops. It provides good ground cover and prevents weed infestation, but competition from the two crops reduces the yield of the main crop.
- Minimum cultivation is the sowing of a crop without ploughing the land. For reseeding grassland, it mainly involves shallow cultivations and/or application of herbicides.
- Direct drilling/direct seeding: a slit is made in the ground by a direct drilling machine and the seed is dropped into it. The land is not ploughed but it is grazed bare and herbicides may be used to kill off broadleaf weeds. It is useful on shallow soils that cannot be ploughed.
- Slurry seeding: this is the same process as direct seeding, except that slurry is applied to the land after sowing.
- Slit seeding: this is similar to direct drilling (where grass is sown into a slit in the land) but the grassland is not killed off beforehand. This should be carried out in spring to ensure that the new grass has the optimum chance of establishment. It can be carried out on soils unsuitable for ploughing and helps to improve old grassland.

PowerPoint Summary

QUESTIONS

1. In relation to grassland, what is meant by the term 'weed infestation'?

   (a) Reseeding of grassland due to weeds

   (b) Development of tillers

   (c) Pasture is taken over by weeds

   (d) Removal of weeds by spraying chemicals

2. How can scutch grass be controlled in grassland?

   (a) Rotation

   (b) Contact herbicide

   (c) Systemic herbicide

   (d) Cultivation

3. What is the optimum soil pH for growth of perennial ryegrass?

   (a) 6.5

   (b) 5.5

   (c) 6.0

   (d) 7.0

4. Identify four benefits of reseeding grassland.

5. Place the steps for creating a fine seedbed in the correct order:

   (a) Test soil for compaction and subsoil if necessary

   (b) Plough, harrow and roll soil

   (c) Test soil for N, P and K and fertilise where appropriate

   (d) Spray weeds with total herbicide

   (e) Ensure suitable drainage is in place.

6. In direct sowing state when seeds are sown and explain why this is the optimum time for sowing for:

   (a) Autumn-sown leys

   (b) Spring-sown leys.

7. Identify a suitable sowing method for a mixed farm enterprise where a farmer wants to sow barley but then wants to have the field available immediately after harvest for grazing.

8. State three advantages and three disadvantages of undersowing.

9. What is meant by 'minimum cultivation'?

10. How can a farmer test for the presence of slugs in a grassland pasture?

11. How can a farmer maximise production levels using the direct drilling method of reseeding grassland?

12. State three advantages of slit seeding.

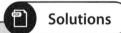 Solutions Weblinks

Conservation of grass

When you have completed this chapter you should be able to:

- Discuss harvesting techniques and storage methods for grass
- Investigate two factors which affect crop preservation
- Identify farm health and safety hazards associated with the management of crops, and discuss the controls and precautions necessary to prevent accidents, injury and ill-health on the farm
- Recognise the need for safe work practices, including the safe handling, harvesting and storage of crops.

Conservation of grass as a winter feed

Grass is the main source of feed for livestock in Ireland. Cattle and sheep get almost all of their nutrition from fresh or conserved grass. During the summer months there is no shortage of fresh grass for grazing animals. During the winter months, where there is no grass growth, it is necessary to feed conserved grass. This is often supplemented with other concentrated animal feeds. As can be seen in Fig. 20.1, excess grass is produced during the summer months, particularly between May and July. This grass can be saved in the form of hay or silage for winter feeding. This provides a relatively cheap source of feed all year round without the need to purchase large quantities of expensive animal feeds. Grass can be conserved as winter feed only if bacterial activity in the grass is inhibited. If bacterial activity were not inhibited, the grass would spoil in a short period of time and would be no use as a winter feed. Silage making and hay making are the two main methods of conserving grass. Each uses a different method of inhibiting bacterial activity.

- **Silage:** fermentation of carbohydrates in the grass produces acids, which lower the pH of the grass and inhibit all microbial activity. Properly fermented and preserved silage can be stored for a few years.
- **Hay:** grass is dehydrated to remove the majority of the water present. In the absence of water, microbial activity is inhibited.

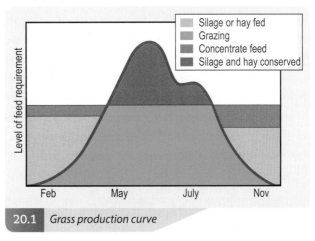

20.1 *Grass production curve*

Silage production

Several factors influence when grass is cut for silage. Silage should be cut when the weather is good, in mid- to late May and again in July to August. Silage making can be delayed by poor summer weather, and second-cut silage can extend into September. Silage is cut from permanent grassland or ryegrass-sown leys. The heading dates of the grasses in these fields can also determine when the silage is cut; an early-heading grass may be cut in May, but it will not be possible to cut a late-heading grass until June. Farmers must consider this when they are sowing grass for silage.

The grass must be cut when digestibility is high, to ensure the highest possible feeding value for the silage. Dry matter digestibility (DMD) is approximately 75% at the heading out stage in perennial ryegrass. For each day that cutting is delayed after this point, the DMD value will fall by 0.5%. This will also affect the quality at ensiling.

Grass cut for silage should also contain a high level of carbohydrates (sugars). Grass is preserved as silage through the process of fermentation. Fermentation is the conversion of carbohydrate to acid by bacteria. The acids produced preserve the grass as silage; therefore, carbohydrates are essential for this process to be carried out properly.

A farmer can provide the optimum conditions for high carbohydrate levels in ensiled grass by following the guidelines below.

- Do not cut grass during or after rainfall, as water dilutes the carbohydrate concentration in grass.
- Cut grass at the vegetative stage, when it is leafy and there is a high carbohydrate concentration.
- Wilt the grass for 1–2 days after mowing. Wilting reduces water content, therefore increasing carbohydrate content.
- Use double chop machinery to cut the grass into smaller pieces. Carbohydrate is more accessible to bacteria for fermentation when the grass is more finely chopped.
- Cut grass in the afternoon when the grass will have been photosynthesising, giving higher carbohydrate content.
- Adding a sugar or molasses solution increases the carbohydrate content in the ensiled grass. This will ensure that fermentation takes place.

Heading out: when half of the grass plants have produced seed heads.

Ensiling: the process of storing grass or another crop in a silo, clamp or pit for preservation as silage.

Biochemistry of silage making: the fermentation process

Fermentation of carbohydrates in grass is carried out by **anaerobic bacteria**. Therefore, the fermentation process cannot begin until all of the oxygen is removed from the cut grass. Grass is rolled when it is brought to the silage pit to remove the air from it. This also prevents the grass from respiring. If oxygen is present, the grass will continue to respire and convert the carbohydrate in the grass to carbon dioxide. This uses up the carbohydrate and lowers the nutritional value of the silage. When the oxygen is removed, the bacteria can begin to respire anaerobically and convert the carbohydrate into acid, which will preserve the silage. The acids produced by fermentation lower the pH to a level that inhibits bacterial activity and preserves the grass as silage for future use.

The concentration of bacteria present in the silage has a huge influence on the type of bacteria that will carry out the fermentation, the type of acid produced and the overall quality of the silage. Two different scenarios are summarised below: for grass with a high carbohydrate concentration and grass with low carbohydrate concentration. Fermentation by *Lactobacillus* produces good-quality lactic acid silage, whereas *Clostridium* produces poor-quality, butyric acid silage.

Table 20.1 Comparison of lactic acid silage and butyric acid silage		
Characteristic	**Lactic acid silage**	**Butyric acid silage**
Carbohydrate concentration	High	Low
Bacteria present	*Lactobacillus*	*Clostridium*
Acid produced	Lactic acid	Butyric acid
Silage quality	Good	Poor
Nutritional value	Good	Poor
Palatability	Palatable to stock	Unpalatable to stock
Storage duration	Several years	A few months

Grassland machinery and fodder production

There are several machines associated with silage production. Their function is outlined below.

Mower conditioner

The mower conditioner is used to cut grass for preservation as silage or hay (as winter fodder). The machine cuts the grass and pushes it through two rollers. This enables the grass to dry faster due to the exposure of a greater surface area.

20.2 *Mower conditioner*

20.3 *High-capacity mower conditioner*

Rotary rake

A rotary rake is used to create rows or swathes of grass ready for baling as silage.

Rotary tedder

A rotary tedder is also known as a hay bob. It is used to shake up swathes of grass to allow for faster drying by exposing the grass to the sun and allowing air to pass through.

20.4 *Twin rotary rake creating a swathe of grass*

20.5 *A rotary tedder is used to speed up the drying of grass for hay production.*

Baler

A baler is used to gather the swathes of grass to create silage or hay bales. Bales may be square (in the case of hay bales) or round. Bales are produced and are then wrapped by the wrapping machine to produce silage bales. Some balers bale and wrap in one operation. Bales can then be easily transported to a shed for storage (in the case of hay bales) or stacked in a suitable place (in the case of silage bales).

20.6 *Creating round bales of hay*

Silage making

Silage can be produced in two ways: in a pit/clamp or in round bales. Both methods are outlined below.

Production of pit silage

Pit silage is more common on large-scale farms. A silage pit normally has three concrete walls and a concrete base. A pit can be expensive to construct and may not be financially viable for the smaller farmer. The pit also needs to have a storage tank for effluent and channels to bring effluent from the pit to the tank. The tank should be leak-proof to prevent pollution. The storage tank and channels should be cleaned out prior to silage production and polythene and tyres should be readily available to cover the pit.

- The field should be closed off to livestock and fertilised 6 weeks before cutting.
- Grass is mowed and left in rows called swathes. It is allowed to wilt.
- It is then picked up by a forage harvester, which cuts the grass and blows it into a trailer.
- The cut grass is brought to the silage pit or clamp and heaped. The pit/clamp should not be located by a waterway (to prevent pollution from effluent) but should be easily accessible for winter feeding.
- A tractor is then used to roll over the layer of grass to remove any air from it. If additives are being used in the silage-making process (see page 292), they can be added to each layer that is rolled. Some additives may have been added during the harvesting process.
- Once the air has been removed by repeated rolling, the pit or clamp is sealed with heavy-duty black polythene sheeting. The polythene keeps the pit airtight to allow for anaerobic respiration to take place. It also prevents water getting into the silage.
- The polythene should be weighed down to keep it in place. One of the most common ways to do this is with old tyres. An alternative is to use a heavy-duty polyethylene mesh cover weighted down with gravel bags. Since it is reusable every year, it removes the need for a large number of tyres.
- The polythene sheet should be inspected after 2–3 weeks and tightened and resealed, since the silage may subside during this time.

20.7 *This grass has been mowed and has been left to wilt.*

20.8 *Forage harvester*

20.9 *Tyres weighed down with a polythene cover, keeping silage airtight.*

Round bale silage

Round bale silage is a very popular method of silage production in Ireland, particularly on small farms.

- Grass for round bales is mown and wilted for 1–2 days, to 30% dry matter (DM).
- Swathes of grass are then collected by the baler and turned into bales.
- They are then wrapped in polythene by the wrapper. Baling and wrapping can be carried out using separate baling and wrapping machines or by one integrated machine that completes both tasks. Most polythene used for wrapping is black, but white, pink or pale green film is also available. The light colour reflects sunlight and helps to keep the bales cool, prolonging their storage life.
- The bales should then be transported to where they are to be stored. Care should be taken in transport to prevent damage or tears to the polythene. Any damage should be rectified immediately.
- Bales should be stored standing on the flat part of the bale. This has a thicker layer of polythene and is less likely to burst. The thicker layer of polythene is also better able to withstand attack from birds.
- To comply with environmental schemes, bales should not be stored closer than 20 m from a watercourse and stacked no more than two bales high.

20.10 *Round bale of silage produced by a baler*

20.11 *Round bales transported by tractor*

Advantages of round bale silage:

- Less dependent on weather conditions
- Quality of baled silage can be as good as pit silage, usually better when well managed
- Lower aerobic spoilage losses compared with pit silage
- Ideal for conservation of surplus grass and grass harvested in autumn
- Lower DM losses during production and storage (<5–10%) than pit silage
- Flexible storage system: bales can be stored in the field or easily transported to any location on the farm
- Less expensive for the small farmer where construction of a silage pit cannot be justified; low transport and storage cost
- If bales are wrapped properly, there is no effluent, which lowers the risk of pollution; effluent storage facilities and disposal is unnecessary
- Excess round bales can be sold.

Disadvantages of round bale silage:

- High unit costs
- Not suitable for very wet silage
- Labour/time at feeding out
- Prone to damage if not properly handled
- Plastic waste disposal cost and compliance with waste regulations.

Additives in silage production

Additives are used in silage making where poor preservation has occurred and carbohydrate concentration in the ensiled grass is low. Additives cannot turn poor grass into good silage; however, they can enhance the quality of the ensiled grass for a relatively small cost. There are a number of different additives available and each has a different mode of action on the ensiled grass.

Acids

Acids are used to aid preservation. They lower the pH of the silage, inhibiting the fermentation process and preventing bacterial activity. They are applied at a rate of 3 litres/tonne grass. Sulfuric acid is one of the most common acids used. Their main disadvantage is that they can reduce the palatability of the grass and they can corrode machinery. They would be more commonly used by silage contractors than individual farmers.

Sugars and molasses

Sugar solutions and molasses are added to ensiled grass to increase carbohydrate concentrations in the pit. This extra sugar is used in the fermentation process. Molasses is one of the more commonly used additives in silage making. It should be applied evenly to each layer of grass in the pit.

Bacterial inoculants

Bacterial inoculant: a bacterial culture that is introduced to a silage pit, increasing bacterial concentrations to speed up fermentation.

The addition of inoculants speeds up the fermentation process and the reduction of pH within the pit. Inoculants can do this more rapidly than acids. They can also aid the preservation of protein.

Enzymes

Enzymes are added to silage in order to break down grass fibres. The breakdown of grass fibres provides additional carbohydrates in the form of sugar for fermentation.

Silage effluent

The fermentation process that takes place in the silage pit releases a liquid known as silage effluent. Effluent is nutrient-rich and contains nitric acid. If effluent seeps into a watercourse it can cause pollution, since it has a high biochemical oxygen demand (BOD) level (see Chapter 8). In order to prevent this happening, silage effluent needs to be collected in a storage tank and stored. It can then be disposed of in a safe manner. Effluent tanks are usually located underground and there is a channel leading from the pit to the tank for efficient effluent collection. Tanks should be leak-proof. Since effluent contains mineral nutrients, it can be diluted and spread on the land as a fertiliser. This reduces disposal costs and recycles nutrients. As with all fertilisers, care should be taken when spreading effluent to prevent run-off and seepage into waterways.

Effluent can be minimised by wilting grass before conservation for silage. This reduces the volume of liquid effluent produced. Silage can be assessed for quality by examining its colour, texture, smell, pH and DM content. Most of these tests can be done at the silage pit. A sample of silage can also be tested in the laboratory if more appropriate.

Factors affecting preservation of grass as silage

As most farmers are reliant on silage as the main source of winter fodder for their livestock, the quality of silage is important. Good-quality silage can provide the majority of nutrients needed by an animal during the winter period. A farmer may have to feed more expensive concentrates to supplement the diet of their livestock if the silage available is poor quality. A high carbohydrate content and the presence of *Lactobacillus* bacteria in anaerobic conditions is necessary for the fermentation of grass to lactic acid silage. The pH of the grass may indicate the production of lactic acid silage. An assessment of the leaf to stem ratio of the grass indicates the carbohydrate levels in the grass. Both of these factors aid in the preservation of grass leading to good-quality silage. Silage can also be assessed for quality on several other factors: smell, texture and colour.

 Activity 20.1 | To assess the factors that affect grass preservation as silage

State your hypothesis, prediction, independent variable, dependent variable and controlled variable.

Materials
Silage sample, microwave, pH meter and probe, beaker, distilled water, weighing dishes

Method
Test 1: Leaf to stem ratio
1. Get a sample of silage and weigh it.
2. Separate the leaves from the stems and divide it into two piles.
3. Weigh two dishes. Place the leaves in one dish and the stems in the other dish.
4. Reweigh each dish. Subtract the mass of the dish from the mass of the dish and leaves. Repeat for the dish containing stems.
5. Record the mass of stems and leaves.
6. Calculate the ratio of leaves to stems.

Table 20.2 Results		
	Leaves	**Stems**
Mass of empty beaker (A)		
Mass of beaker and herbage (B)		
Mass of herbage only (B – A)		

Test 2: pH of silage
1. Squeeze liquid from silage.
2. Place pH probe into the liquid to read pH.

Alternately, if liquid cannot be squeezed from silage, place a small amount of silage (20 g) in a beaker with 20 cm³ of distilled water. Stir the silage and water. Place the pH meter probe in the water and record the pH.

Test 3: Silage quality tests
1. Colour: begin with a visual assessment of the silage. Note its colour.
2. Texture: rub the sample between your fingers. Note the feel of the leaves and stems.
3. Smell: smell the silage and record the smell.
4. DM content: squeeze a sample of silage with one hand. Note if any liquid can be removed from it. Repeat by wringing out a sample of silage with two hands and note if any liquid can be removed from it.

5. DM assessment in lab: place 50 g of silage in a microwave for 30 seconds. Remove from microwave and weigh. Multiply its mass by 2 to calculate the DM.

6. Record your results in a table similar to Table 20.3

Table 20.3 Results				
pH	Colour	Texture	Smell	DM content

8. Compare your results to Table 20.4 and determine the quality of your silage based on your results.

Table 20.4					
Silage type	Colour	Texture	Smell	pH	DM content
Lactic acid	Yellow-green	Soft but firm; fibres do not wear easily	Sharp, acidic, vinegary	<5.0. Ideal range between 3.8 and 4.2	Liquid cannot be removed by hand; DM >25%
Butyric acid	Dark green	Wet and slimy	Putrid or rancid	>5.0 acidic but has not been properly preserved, clostridial bacteria present	Liquid can be wrung out with two hands; DM 20–25%

Hay making

About 18% of conserved grass in Ireland is used for hay making. The popularity of hay has declined over the years, with more farmers choosing to make silage. As hay making is heavily reliant on good weather conditions, silage making has become a safer choice. However, hay has the advantage of being a clean, easily transported winter feed that produces no effluent.

Timing

Grass for hay production should be cut in late May or early June, weather permitting. Ideally it should be cut when DMD is at its highest. This is normally in May, but weather may not allow for this. Do not allow livestock to graze the field for 6 weeks prior to harvest. The pasture should also be fertilised with N, P and K. Teagasc recommend 65–80 kg/ha nitrogen. Calcium ammonium nitrate (CAN), 18-6-12 and 27-2.5-5 are the most common compound fertilisers used in hay making.

Weather

Cut grass for hay only when a prolonged period of dry weather is expected. Warm, sunny, dry weather is needed to remove the moisture from the crop. The moisture levels at storage should be less than 20%.

Machinery

Three machines are essential in the production of hay: a rotary mower, a rotary tedder or 'hay bob' and a baler.

Rotary mower

The rotary mower is the first machine used in the process. The mower cuts the grass and leaves it in rows. It is particularly useful for cutting lodged crops.

Rotary tedder

The tedder or hay bob shakes out the grass, allowing air to pass through it and speed up the drying process. Grass for hay making may be tedded twice before it is baled. Grass should be tedded as soon as possible after cutting. The tedder should be set to minimise damage to the cut grass. The tedder can then be used to gather the grass into rows for baling.

Baler

When the grass has dried out, the baler collects the grass and converts it into bales, which are secured with net wrap or baling twine. Unless there is a prolonged period of dry weather, the quantity of grass cut should be equal to the amount that can be baled in one day, as heavy rainfall can damage the crop. Bales should be moved into storage in a hayshed as soon as possible so that they remain dry.

20.12   *Rotary mower mowing grass*

20.13   *Grass being tedded*

20.14   *Hay baling*

Haylage

Grass can also be preserved as haylage. Haylage is grass that has been cut and left to dry out before baling. The moisture level in the grass is less than is found in silage but higher than is found in hay. The moisture level in haylage is approximately 60%.

Haylage production

Haylage is preserved grass that is used for winter fodder and has been partially dried. Haylage production incorporates aspects of both silage and hay making. Grass for haylage production should be cut in early to mid-June. Moisture levels for haylage production do not have to be reduced to the same levels as those of hay. Grass preserved as haylage requires similar conditions for preservation as grass for silage. An absence of oxygen is required for anaerobic bacteria to ferment the grass. Lactic acid is produced by the bacteria *Lactobacillus* to preserve the grass as haylage.

When producing haylage:

- Close off the field to livestock 6–8 weeks before cutting. Fertilise the pasture with a nitrogen fertiliser such as CAN or 18-6-12.
- Cut the grass with a conditioner mower, since this reduces the moisture content faster, and cut at a height of 8–10 cm above the ground to avoid soil contamination, reducing *Listeria* and *Clostridia* contamination.
- Ted the grass twice a day for 2 days to speed up drying.

- Bale with a baler and wrap with six to eight layers of plastic to prevent damage to the bale.
- High-density bales should be created to ensure an anaerobic environment within the bale.
- Haylage bales should be stored in a similar manner to silage bales, preferably under cover and on a surface free from sharp stones or objects that could damage the bale.

Use of haylage in agriculture

Haylage is a suitable feed for horses. It is a dust-free alternative to hay, which may reduce respiratory problems. It is a good source of fibre in the horse's diet. Since it has a higher moisture content than hay, there is no need to soak it (hay must often be soaked before feeding it to horses with respiratory problems). Haylage bales are denser than hay bales, so less storage space is needed. Haylage bales are wrapped in polythene and can be stored outdoors, while hay bales must be stored under cover. Good-quality haylage should be sweet-smelling and bright in colour. It should also be free from visible mould. Haylage showing mould should be discarded. Rancid-smelling haylage should also be discarded, as it may contain toxins.

20.15 *Grass cut with a conditioner mower*

Health and safety risks when conserving grass

The majority of farming accidents involve machinery. There are a number of risks to consider when making silage or hay as several machines are used in the process. Other risks include crushing by round bales that are not stacked safely or fall when moved. Farmers can take several precautions to minimise the risk of injury during the busy silage- and hay-making season.

Table 20.5 Risks and precautions when making silage or hay	
Risk	**Control/precaution**
Injury by faulty machinery, or from moving part of machine that is exposed	Ensure all machinery is in good working order and that all guards are in place and function correctly.
Injury by getting trapped or crushed by machinery	Ensure that machinery is properly attached to the tractor (e.g. baler, tedder).
Injury from crushing by moving machinery, or injury from inserting limb into moving parts	Ensure machinery is stationery and turned off before clearing a blockage.
Injury to personnel who may be hit by machinery due to lack of light, or because they are wearing dark clothing	Ensure all lights, mirrors and indicators are working correctly, particularly for evening and night-time harvesting. All personnel should wear reflective clothing.
Injury/death by electrocution	Ensure that machinery does not come into contact with overhead power lines when travelling on roadways.
Being hit by machinery causing injury or death	Ensure that children do not enter the cab or have access to fields where silage is being made.
Asphyxiation due to the lack of oxygen	Do not go under the silage cover on a pit once the cover has been put in place.

Risk	Control/precaution
Tractor may topple over if the slope of the pit is too steep	Slope off open silos at an angle of less than 45 degrees.
Increase the risk of a loader/tractor turning over when filling the pit or at feeding out; the walls of the pit may also be overloaded by overfilling	Do not overfill a silage pit. Do not fill above the level of the wall of the silage pit.
Tractor may topple over edge of silage pit	Install guard rails on the top of the pit so the machine operator can see the pit boundary.
Falling bales can cause injury or death from crushing	Ensure bales are stacked safely.
Bales in areas with uneven or poorly drained ground and little room to manoeuvre can lead to incidents with machinery, causing injury	Stack bales on level ground with good drainage in an uncluttered area.
Risk of crushing from falling bales	Do not stack bales more than two rows high when stacking on the flat end of the bale.

Summary

- Grass can be saved in the form of hay or silage for winter feeding.
- Silage: fermentation of carbohydrates in the grass produces acids that lower the pH of the grass and inhibit all microbial activity. Properly fermented and preserved silage can be stored for a few years.
- Hay: grass is dehydrated to remove the majority of the water present. In the absence of water, microbial activity is inhibited.
- Heading out: this is when half of the grass plants have produced seed heads.
- Ensiling: this is the process of storing grass or another crop in a silo, clamp or pit for preservation as silage.
- A farmer can provide the optimum conditions for high carbohydrate levels in ensiled grass by cutting grass when it is leafy, cutting in dry weather, using double chop machinery, leaving the grass to wilt and adding molasses to the ensiled grass.
- Fermentation by *Lactobacillus* produces good-quality, lactic acid silage; fermentation by *Clostridium* produces poor-quality, butyric acid silage.
- Silage produced in a pit needs to be rolled to remove air pockets so that anaerobic bacteria can begin the fermentation process. It must be covered with polythene to keep the pit airtight.
- Round bales are easy to transport, can be sold, are cheaper for the small farmer and produce no effluent.
- Additives can enhance the quality of ensiled grass. Acids, sugar and molasses, bacterial inoculants and enzymes are all common additives.
- Effluent is a nutrient-rich liquid that seeps from silage stored in a pit and can be a pollutant if not stored and disposed of correctly.
- Hay is a clean, easily transported winter feed that produces no effluent. Its production is heavily dependent on prolonged dry, sunny weather.
- A rotary mower, a rotary tedder and a baler are all needed in the production of hay.
- Haylage is grass that is preserved for winter fodder. It has a higher moisture content than hay. Haylage is baled and is a dust-free feed suitable for horses.

 PowerPoint Summary

QUESTIONS

1. Silage is produced through which conservation technique?

    (a) Dehydration   (b) Fermentation   (c) Freezing   (d) Hydration

2. First-cut silage is typically cut in:

    (a) March   (b) May   (c) July   (d) August.

3. At heading out DMD values in grass are typically:

    (a) 95%   (b) 85%   (c) 75%   (d) 65%.

4. Which of the following processes can increase carbohydrate levels in ensiled grass?

    (a) Do not cut during rainfall   (c) Add molasses to the pit

    (b) Wilt for one to two days   (d) All of the above

5. Which type of acid is produced by *Clostridium* bacteria?

    (a) Butyric acid   (c) Carbonic acid

    (b) Lactic acid   (d) Acetic acid

6. Describe two ways in which the activity of bacteria can be controlled.

7. With the aid of a simple graph, describe what happens to the DMD value of the grass after heading out.

8. Explain the terms (a) heading out and (b) ensiling.

9. How does anaerobic respiration help to conserve silage?

10. Identify the bacteria involved in lactic acid fermentation.

11. Describe the steps carried out in the silage-making process.

12. Describe the functions of (a) the conditioner mower, (b) the rotary tedder and (c) the baler.

13. Give four advantages of round bales.

14. Why is molasses used in silage making?

15. Why are bacterial inoculants used as additives in silage making?

16. Why is effluent harmful? How can these dangers be avoided?

17. Describe three ways of assessing the quality of a silage sample.

18. Outline why the leaf to stem ratio is important in silage making.

19. Describe four grassland management practices used to achieve high-quality silage.

20. In relation to hay, what is tedding?

21. Why does grass need to be tedded frequently?

22. In your opinion, are there any advantages to conserving grass as hay rather than silage?

23. Identify the principal steps in haylage production.

24. Differentiate between hay and haylage.

25. Identify three precautions that should be taken at the silage pit when storing grass as silage or at feeding out.

26. Identify the main risks associated with round bale production and state two ways in which these risks can be reduced.

27. During 2018, Ireland experienced a heatwave. Describe how this had an effect on saving grass as winter fodder.

28. Identify reasons that farmers who traditionally make silage might return to making hay when conserving grass as winter fodder.

Solutions   Weblinks

Animals

21	Animal nutrition	300
22	Animal physiology	313
23	Animal reproduction	323
24	Applied animal genetics	335
25	Dairy breeds, nutrition and management of a dairy herd	349
26	Milk composition, milk production and the dairy industry	371
27	Beef breeds and beef production: dairy calf to beef and suckler beef production	394
28	Sheep breeds and production	413
29	Lamb production and husbandry	425
30	Pig breeds, management, nutrition and production	443
31	Animal health and disease	466
32	Environmental impact of agriculture and markets for Irish produce	491

STRAND
4

21 Animal nutrition

When you have completed this chapter you should be able to:

- Describe the nutritive properties of the nutrients in food
- Describe the function of protein, carbohydrates, fats, vitamins and minerals in growth and development
- Discuss the importance of nutrition to meet the protein, energy and performance requirements at different growth/development stages of cattle, sheep and pigs
- Discuss the importance of ration formulation to meet the protein, energy and performance requirements at different growth/development stages of cattle, sheep and pigs.

Nutrients and their function in growth and development

In order to maintain a healthy body, an animal must have a balanced diet composed of carbohydrates, proteins, fats, vitamins, minerals and water. The functions of these nutrients are given in Table 21.1.

Lactating animal: a female animal that is producing milk.

Metabolic processes: collectively a group of chemical reactions, e.g. aerobic respiration, that occur in an animal's body.

Epithelial tissue: a thin layer of cells that forms the lining of the digestive tract, inside of the mouth, the respiratory tract, etc.

Antioxidant: a substance that can remove damaging oxidants from a living organism.

Table 21.1 Nutrients and function	
Nutrient	**Function in animals**
Carbohydrate	• Main source of energy for growth, maintenance and reproduction • Produces heat • Provides fibre (roughage) for the correct functioning of the rumen (in cattle and sheep); stimulates peristalsis
Protein	• Building blocks of an animal's body • Builds muscle • Essential for growth, reproduction and maintenance • Used to produce bones, teeth, blood, skin, hair and wool • Used to produce milk in lactating animals • Used to produce enzymes, hormones, antibodies (immunoglobulins) and pigments (haemoglobin) • Used as a source of energy when an animal's diet contains insufficient amounts of carbohydrate and fats
Fat	• Provides insulation when stored under the skin • Stores excess energy • Carries fat-soluble vitamins A, D, E and K
Vitamins	• Control many metabolic processes • Vitamin A required in cattle for bone development, normal vision and the formation of epithelial tissue; a deficiency in vitamin A is associated with infertility in cattle • Vitamin D required for the formation of healthy bones and teeth; vitamin D deficiency in calves results in rickets • Vitamin E important for normal development and function of muscles; also an antioxidant

	• Vitamin K required for the clotting of blood
	• Vitamin B (group of substances commonly referred to as vitamin B complex) required for many metabolic processes; many of the B vitamins are co-enzymes; folate (folic acid) required for cell division and growth of the embryo during gestation
	• Vitamin C plays a role in building and repairing tissue and also in the prevention of infection
Minerals	**Macro-minerals** required in large amounts:
	• Calcium required to produce teeth and bone, to produce milk in lactating animals, and for the clotting of blood; milk fever (see page 470) is a disease of lactating animals that are deficient in calcium
	• Phosphorus required to produce teeth and bone; also plays an important role in aerobic respiration and energy production
	• Magnesium essential for utilisation of energy in the body; deficiency in magnesium can result in a disease called grass tetany (see page 470)
	Micro-minerals required in trace amounts:
	• Iron required to produce haemoglobin, an essential pigment of red blood cells that carries oxygen around the body
	• Cobalt essential for microorganisms in the rumens of cattle and sheep, to produce some B vitamins
Water	• Essential for growth, digestion, reproduction, transport of nutrients in the body, lactation and elimination of waste products
	• Aids in temperature regulation and involved in many metabolic processes

Protein requirements in animal diets

Cattle, sheep and pigs require many nutrients from their feed in order to maintain good health. An animal's nutrition can depend on its stage in its life cycle. For instance, young animals require more protein in their diet than adult animals do because they are actively growing and putting on lean muscle. Similarly, lactating animals require more protein in their diet than dry animals do. Milk contains 3–4% protein; the source of this protein comes from the diet of the animal or from the animal's own body tissues. An animal in late gestation also has an increased protein demand. Two-thirds of foetal growth occurs in the last 2–3 months of gestation, placing a greater demand on the mother's protein supply.

The type of protein in an animal's diet can also be an important factor. Protein is made up of 20 amino acids. In monogastric animals, ten of these are essential amino acids that must be present in the animal's diet, since they cannot be synthesised by the animal itself. The other ten can be synthesised by the animal's body and are referred to as non-essential amino acids. In the production of feeds for poultry and pigs, high-quality protein must be used to ensure that these amino acids are in the diet. Ruminant animals do not have a dietary requirement for amino acids because microorganisms in their rumen have the ability to synthesise all amino acids (essential and non-essential). The microorganisms in the rumen of cattle and sheep can synthesise microbial protein from non-protein sources of nitrogen such as urea. Rumen microbial protein contributes roughly 50–75% of a cow's total protein supply.

Co-enzyme: a compound that binds with an enzyme to catalyse a reaction.

Dry animal: a cow or other animal that is no longer producing milk.

Monogastric animal: an animal with a single compartment stomach, compared with a ruminant animal which has a four-compartment stomach. Examples of monogastric animals include pigs, horses and humans.

Non-protein source of nitrogen: a term used in animal nutrition that refers to compounds such as urea and ammonia which are not protein but can be converted into protein by the microorganisms that live in the rumen of cattle and sheep.

Young ruminants (calves and lambs) need feeds (e.g. milk) containing good-quality protein until their rumen develops.

> DEFINITION
>
> **Essential amino acids:** amino acids that cannot be manufactured in a monogastric animal's body and must be obtained in the diet, e.g. lysine and methionine.
>
> **Non-essential amino acids:** amino acids that can be manufactured in the body from other amino acids, e.g. alanine and glutamine.

Carbohydrate and fat requirements in animal diets

Sugars and starches are simple carbohydrates that are easily digested by all animals and are a source of energy. Complex carbohydrates such as cellulose are digested only by ruminant animals and provide little energy in the diet of a monogastric animal. Fats are also easily digested and provide large amounts of energy compared with starches and sugars.

Mineral and vitamin requirements in animal diets

Minerals and vitamins are required for a wide variety of functions in the animal's body and are frequently added to animal rations to prevent deficiencies. Table 21.2 lists macrominerals and microminerals.

Table 21.2 Macrominerals and microminerals	
Macrominerals	**Microminerals (trace elements)**
Calcium (Ca)	Iron (Fe)
Phosphorus (P)	Iodine (I)
Potassium (K)	Copper (Cu)
Sodium (Na)	Cobalt (Co)
Sulfur (S)	Fluorine (F)
Chlorine (Cl)	Manganese (Mn)
Magnesium (Mg)	Zinc (Zn)
	Molybdenum (Mo)
	Selenium (Se)

Deficiencies of microminerals such as selenium and copper have been linked with infertility in cattle. These deficiencies can often arise because a mineral is deficient in the soil and, as a result, deficiencies occur in the grass and fodder crops eaten by the cattle. Copper deficiencies in pregnant ewes can result in lambs being born with **swayback**. This is a condition in which the lambs have difficulty standing and walking. A deficiency in cobalt can lead to **pine disease** in sheep and lambs. The symptoms of this disease in lambs include failure to thrive, poor fleece and poor appetite. Pine disease causes poor fertility in ewes. Deficiencies in macrominerals can also lead to disease. Calcium is added to formulated rations to prevent milk fever in lactating cattle and sheep, while magnesium prevents grass tetany. In addition, many farmers tend to supplement the diets of their livestock with minerals.

An animal's diet can be supplemented with minerals using the following methods:
- Dusting mineral supplement onto silage (e.g. Cal Mag)
- Providing the animals with mineral licks
- Dressing the pasture
- Adding to the drinking water
- Oral dose or mineral bullet.

Synthesis: production of compounds or large molecules from simpler materials by chemical reactions in the body.

Microminerals are often called trace elements, since they are required in very small quantities. These minerals can become toxic if consumed in large amounts.

Deficiency: a lack or shortage of a substance in an animal's diet.

Supplementing: adding an extra amount or increasing the amount of a substance.

Formulated: specially prepared.

Mineral bullet: a large pill used to provide a consistent supply of micronutrients to cattle or sheep.

Vitamins are organic compounds and can be divided into fat soluble (A, D, E and K) and water soluble (B and C). Cattle can synthesise Vitamin C. Vitamin supplements are included in many formulated ration feeds. For example, vitamin B is added to rations of young calves and pigs. However, it is not required in adult rations for cattle and sheep as it is produced by the microorganisms in the rumen.

Energy requirements of animals

Metabolisable energy

The total energy contained in any feed is known as the **gross energy**. Gross energy is determined in a laboratory using a bomb calorimeter. The sample of the feed is ignited and burned completely in oxygen. The amount of heat released is used to determine the total energy in the feed. However, not all the energy available in a feed is digestible. Some nutrients such as lignin cannot be broken down by the ruminant or monogastric animal's digestive system. These components pass out of the animal's body as undigested material in the faeces.

Digestible energy is the gross energy minus the amount of energy egested in the faeces.
Metabolisable energy is the digestible energy minus the energy lost in the form of methane gas (formed in the ruminant digestive system) and urine. The loss of energy is far greater for ruminant animals than monogastric animals. Roughly 19% of the digestible energy is lost as urine and methane production by cattle and sheep. The figure is much smaller for pigs, as loss of energy due to methane production is far lower. Metabolisable energy is measured in megajoules per kilogram (MJ/kg) of dry matter. The **net energy** is the amount of energy available for use by the animal after subtracting heat lost during digestion and other metabolic processes in the animal's body. This energy can be used for **maintenance** and **production**.

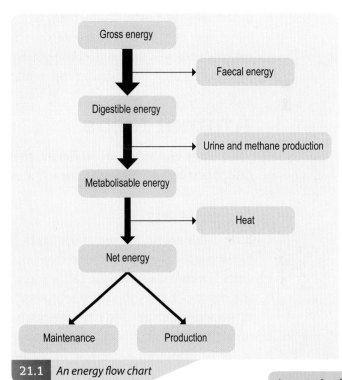

21.1 *An energy flow chart*

A megajoule is equal to one million joules

Maintenance and production diets

As young animals grow, their nutrient requirements change and their diets align with those of adult animals. As mature animals, the diets of dairy cows, sheep and pigs change throughout the course of the year depending on what stage of production they are in.

For part of the year, a production animal can be placed on a plane of low nutrition, commonly called a maintenance diet. At other times, such as during breeding, giving birth and producing milk, the animal must be fed on a high plane of nutrition to meet high energy demands. At these times, the animal is fed a production diet.

DEFINITION

Maintenance diet: the amount of feed that allows an animal to maintain a good health and condition with no loss or gain in weight.
Production diet: the extra amount of feed required to produce 1 kg of LWG, 1 l of milk, 1 kg of wool, or to produce a calf or lamb. Animals on a production diet must be provided with feed that is more than their maintenance requirements.

There are two main categories of animals that would be put on a production diet: pregnant animals and young animals.

Pregnant animals

Pregnant animals need increased energy for:
- The developing offspring (especially in sheep and pigs, which have multiple births)
- Production of colostrum and milk
- Regaining body condition.

> **DEFINITION**
>
> **Colostrum:** the first milk secreted by mammals after giving birth. It is high in nutrients and antibodies and is essential for the survival of the newborn animal.

Growth

Young animals need nutrients for growth and the production of bones, muscles and organs. Milk is a high-quality feed, which is easily digestible by the calf, lamb or piglet. Ninety per cent of the gross energy in milk ends up as metabolisable energy.Once the maintenance requirements of the young animal are met, any additional energy is used to put on muscle and fat, and this leads to live weight gain (LWG).

Animal feeds

Since cattle and sheep are ruminant animals, their feeds can be divided into two categories: bulky feeds and concentrates or formulated rations.

Bulky feeds

Bulky feeds are high in water (grass) or fibre but low in energy. Grass, silage, hay, haylage, root crops and forage crops (kale) are all classified as bulky feeds. Young, leafy grass is a complete food for cattle and sheep and supplies sufficient nutrients to meet the needs of both young and mature animals when eaten in sufficient quantities. Both cattle and sheep need to have adequate levels of fibre in their diet to ensure that their rumen functions correctly. Acidosis can occur when their diet is high in easily digestible starches and sugars and low in fibre (see page 316). Sheep and cattle must be fed silage, hay or straw when concentrates are added to their diet.

Concentrates

Concentrates are feeds that are low in water and fibre and high in energy. Cereals, fats, oil, molasses, beet pulp and feed supplements are all classified as concentrates. Many of the components in concentrate rations are by-products of a food crop that has been processed for human use. Concentrate rations are formulated to give the correct balance of protein, carbohydrates, fibre, minerals and vitamins. Cereals very often make up a substantial part of concentrates. Barley, wheat and maize are commonly used. Cereals have many advantages in a formulated ration:
- They are high in carbohydrates and energy
- Their seed coat contains fibre
- They can be used to supplement poor-quality silage or other fodder crops
- They can ensure that production targets are met.

The following are examples of some formulated rations for dairy cattle, beef cattle, sheep and pigs.

Dairy ration

Components		
Crude protein	18.0%	
Crude fibre	11.0%	Vitamin A
Crude oil	5.0%	Vitamin D
Calcium	1.1%	Vitamin E

List of ingredients
Soya bean hulls, Maize, Wheat, Rapeseed meal, Sunflower, Soya bean meal, Palm kernel expeller, Citrus pulp, Sugar cane molasses, Calcium carbonate, Maize distillers, Magnesium oxide, Selenium, Copper

21.2 *Dairy ration, e.g. Kiernan's Dairy 18%*

21.3 *Soya bean hulls (foreground) and soya bean meal*

21.4 *Dairy ration*

This ration would be fed to dairy cows before calving and in early lactation. Energy and protein are very important in a formulated ration for the production of colostrum and milk. A lactating cow requires more energy and calcium in a formulated feed than a dry cow. Inadequate amounts of energy in a lactating cow's diet can result in lower milk yields, lower milk protein and poor fertility and make the cow more susceptible to disease and metabolic disorders.

The cereals wheat and maize are sources of carbohydrate and, therefore, energy. The inclusion of maize as animal feed is becoming increasingly popular, since prices for maize are lower than other cereals (barley and wheat). Maize distillers is a by-product of distilling (residues of fermented grains) and, like rapeseed meal and soya bean meal, is a source of protein. Soya bean hulls are the seed coat of the soya bean and these are included as a source of fibre. Cane molasses is a source of sugars, which provide energy. Molasses is normally used to bind the meal together into a nut. Palm kernel expeller is the residue of the palm nut once the oil has been removed. Palm kernel expeller is high in fat and energy.

The high fat content of the palm kernel aids in the production of milk fat. Calcium carbonate is added to the ration to prevent milk fever and magnesium oxide to prevent grass tetany. The function of the vitamins has already been described. In soya beans, the meal is the ground-up contents of the seed and is high in protein.

Beef ration for finishing beef for slaughter

This ration is typically fed to a beef animal to ensure it reaches its slaughter weight, commonly known as finishing. The percentage of protein is lower in this ration than in the dairy ration, as finishing beef animals do not require a high percentage of protein, since their frame has reached its mature size. Some components of this feed are the same as the dairy ration. Energy is important in this diet to ensure that the animal reaches its slaughter weight.

Barley, wheat, maize and citrus pulp (a by-product of the citrus fruit industry) are included in this ration as sources of carbohydrate and energy. Soya bean hulls are a source of fibre, which is required for the correct functioning of the rumen. Rapeseed meal is a source of protein. Sugar cane molasses is used to bind the components into a nut and it is also a source of sugars. An acid buff is added to this ration to prevent the animal developing acidosis. A number of trace elements are added to this ration. Zinc is important in enzyme systems and plays a role in the immune system. Iodine is required for the production of the hormone thyroxine by the thyroid gland.

Components		
Crude protein	14%	Vitamin A
Crude fibre	8.1%	Vitamin D
Crude oil	5.0%	
Calcium	0.9%	

List of ingredients
Soya bean hulls, Maize, Wheat, Barley, Wheat feed, Rapeseed meal, Citrus pulp, Sugar cane molasses, Calcium carbonate, Acid buff, Zinc, Iodine, Selenium, Copper

21.5 *Beef ration, e.g. Kiernan's Buffalo Beef Nuts*

21.6 *Citrus pulp*

21.7 *Beef nuts*

21.8 *Maize meal*

Sheep ration

Feeding a concentrate ration to pregnant ewes during the final 6–8 weeks of gestation is common practice, since it helps to prevent twin lamb disease or pregnancy toxaemia (see page 470). This process is called **steaming up** (see page 429). Note the high percentage of protein in this feed. Protein is important for the growth of the lamb in the final weeks of gestation and for good milk production in the ewe.

Many of the ingredients listed above are similar to those in the dairy and beef ration. The proportions of the ingredients in the ration will change to ensure that the correct balance of protein and energy is supplied to the animal. The percentage of calcium is high in this ration, which will help to prevent milk fever.

Components		
Crude protein	19.0%	Vitamin A
Crude fibre	9.0%	Vitamin D
Crude oil	5.0%	
Calcium	1.2%	

List of ingredients
Soya bean hulls, Sugar cane molasses, Soya bean meal, Citrus pulp, Palm kernel expeller, Magnesium oxide, Calcium carbonate, Soya, Palm and rape acid oil, Maize, Wheat, Wheat feed, Rapeseed meal, Maize distillers, Calcium carbonate, Selenium, Cobalt, Zinc, Iodine

21.9 *Sheep ration, e.g. Kiernan's Ewe with Lamb 19%*

21.10 *Concentrate feed for pregnant and lactating ewes*

Pig ration

Unlike cattle and sheep, pigs are monogastric animals. Pig feed has less fibre than cattle or sheep feed, since pigs are unable to digest fibre. Fig. 21.11 is an example of a pig ration. Note the addition of lysine and methionine (both essential amino acids) in this feed. This ration would be fed to pigs in order to fatten and finish them for slaughter. Soya bean is included in this ration for its high energy value and high protein content. Soya bean meal is also high in lysine, whereas cereals (wheat and barley) are deficient in lysine. The soya bean meal is prepared by dehulling the seed to remove the seed coat. This reduces fibre and the seed is toasted to improve the biological value of the protein. Some soya bean hulls are added to ensure that there is some fibre in the ration.

Components			
Crude protein	17.0%	Lysine	1.0%
Crude fibre	4.5%	Vitamin A	
Crude oil	4%	Vitamin D	
Calcium	0.7%	Vitamin E	
Methionine	0.3%		

List of ingredients

Soya bean (dehulled and toasted), Rapeseed meal, Barley, Soya bean hulls, Soya, Palm and rape acid oil, Calcium carbonate, Selenium, Iron, Copper, Lysine (essential amino acid), Maize, Methionine (essential amino acid)

21.11 *Pig ration, e.g. Kiernan's Prime Finisher Pellets*

Rapeseed meal is also a source of protein; however, the amount of rapeseed used in the ration must be limited due to the presence of anti-nutritional factors present in the rapeseed. The soya, palm and rape acid oils are high in fat and provide a good source of energy. Some pig rations will include animal fat as a high source of energy. Iron is also added to this meal to help prevent anaemia (see page 483).

Many of the rations include soya bean meal and rapeseed meal in ground-up form. Grinding up these seeds improves the digestibility of the feeds. Barley is a common example of this: it is processed differently depending on its intended use (ruminant or pig rations). Rolled barley is commonly used in ruminant rations. Rolling breaks the seed coat, allowing the ruminant's digestive system to break down the contents of the seed. If the seeds are not rolled, undigested seeds would be present in the animal's dung. When barley is being fed to pigs, it must be ground down so that it can be easily digested.

Anti-nutritional factors: compounds that interfere with the absorption of nutrients.

Biological value is a measure of how readily the protein in a feed can be incorporated into the cells of an organism.

21.12 *Rolled barley*

Summary

- An animal needs a balanced diet containing carbohydrate, protein, fat, vitamins, minerals and water.
- Carbohydrate provides energy for growth, maintenance and reproduction.
- Protein is required for building muscle and is essential for growth, reproduction and maintenance in animals.
- Protein is required for milk production in lactating animals.
- Fat provides insulation and is a carrier of fat-soluble vitamins.
- Vitamins are required in small amounts in the diets of animals. Many metabolic processes are controlled by vitamins.
- Macrominerals are required in large amounts in an animal's diet. Calcium, phosphorus and magnesium are examples of macrominerals.
- Microminerals are required in trace amounts. Iron and cobalt are examples of microminerals.

- An animal's nutritional requirements will depend on its stage in its life cycle.
- Ruminant animals do not have a dietary requirement for amino acids, as the microorganisms in their rumen have the ability to synthesise all amino acids (essential and non-essential).
- An animal's diet can be supplemented with minerals by dusting mineral supplements onto silage, providing the animals with mineral licks, dressing the pasture, adding them to drinking water or giving the animal an oral dose or mineral bullet.
- The total energy contained in any feed is known as the gross energy.
- Digestible energy is the gross energy minus the amount of energy egested in faeces.
- Metabolisable energy is digestible energy minus the energy lost in the form of methane gas and urine production. The loss of energy due to methane production and urine is far greater in ruminant animals (cattle and sheep) than in monogastric animals (pigs).
- The net energy is the amount of energy available for use by the animal. This energy can then be used for maintenance and production.
- A maintenance diet is the amount of feed that allows an animal to maintain good health and condition with no loss or gain in weight.
- A production diet is the extra amount of feed required to produce 1 kg of live weight gain (LWG), 1 l of milk, 1 kg of wool, or to produce a calf or lamb. Animals on a production diet must be provided with feed that is in excess of their maintenance requirements.
- Bulky feeds are high in water (grass) or fibre but low in energy. Examples include grass, silage and hay.
- Concentrates are feeds that are low in water and fibre and high in energy. Concentrate rations are formulated to give the correct balance of protein, carbohydrates, fibre, minerals and vitamins.

PowerPoint Summary

QUESTIONS

1. One of the functions of protein in the animal's body is to:
   (a) Provide energy
   (b) Be a source of vitamin A
   (c) Provide insulation
   (d) Produce enzymes, hormones and antibodies.

2. Which of the following is a disadvantage of the ruminant digestive system?
   (a) Inability to digest cellulose
   (b) Inability to produce amino acids from non-protein sources of nitrogen
   (c) Inability to produce vitamin K
   (d) Loss of energy due to the production of methane gas

3. A deficiency in vitamin A is associated with:
   (a) Rickets in calves
   (b) Infertility in cattle
   (c) Blood not clotting in sheep
   (d) Milk fever in cattle.

4. Which of the following combinations of vitamins are produced by microorganisms in the rumen of cattle and sheep?

   (a) Vitamin B and vitamin E

   (b) Vitamin K and vitamin E

   (c) Vitamin A and vitamin K

   (d) Vitamin B and vitamin K

5. Which of the following is a disease that is caused by a deficiency of calcium?

   (a) Milk fever

   (b) Grass tetany

   (c) Pine disease

   (d) Swayback

6. Grass tetany is prevented in cattle and sheep by the addition of _____ to formulated rations.

   (a) Calcium

   (b) Manganese

   (c) Cobalt

   (d) Magnesium

7. Fig. 21.13 shows how the gross energy in a diet of an animal is used.

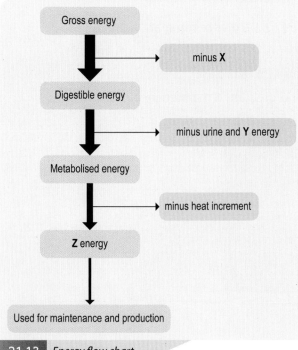

| 21.13 | *Energy flow chart* |

Which row in the grid below correctly identifies the missing terms for X, Y and Z in the diagram above?

	X	Y	Z
(a)	Methane	Carbon dioxide	Net
(b)	Faeces	Methane	Net
(c)	Net	Methane	Total
(d)	Methane	Net	Faeces

8. For each of the following nutrients, give a reason why it is required in the diet of animals.

   (a) Protein

   (b) Carbohydrate

   (c) Fat

   (d) Minerals

   (e) Vitamins

9. Many diseases of plants and animals are caused by a lack of a particular element in the soil or in the animal's diet. In Table 21.3, match each element to the deficiency disease that is caused by a lack of that element. The first one has been completed as an example.

(a) Calcium   (c) Iron   (e) Cobalt

(b) Boron   (d) Copper   (f) Magnesium

Table 21.3	
Deficiency disease	**Element**
Heart rot in sugar beet	Boron
Swayback in sheep	
Anaemia in pigs	
Grass tetany in cattle	
Milk fever in cattle	
Pine disease in sheep	

10. Why are essential amino acids not necessary in the diet of ruminant animals?

11. (a) Why are mineral and vitamin supplements used in the diets of farm animals?

   (b) How are these supplements supplied to farm animals?

12. Explain the difference between a production diet and a maintenance diet.

13. Examine the following concentrate ration which is fed to calves.

Table 21.4 Concentrate ration for calves	
Components	**% of ration**
Protein	16
Oil	3.1
Fibre	8.3
Minerals: calcium, phosphorus	2
Ingredients	
Rolled barley, flaked maize, citrus pulp, rapeseed, soya bean meal, molasses	

   (a) Give a reason for the high protein percentage in this meal.

   (b) Why must high-quality protein be included in this ration?

   (c) Identify one component of this feed that would be a source of protein.

   (d) What is the main nutrient found in rolled barley and flaked maize?

   (e) Why is the barley rolled?

   (f) Why is molasses regularly used as an ingredient in rations?

   (g) Give a reason for the inclusion of calcium in this ration.

14. Table 21.5 shows the nutritional content of two formulated rations.

Table 21.5		
Components	Ration A	Ration B
Energy content (MJ/kg)	10	10
Crude protein (%)	15	18
Fibre (%)	12	3
Fat (%)	0	3

(a) Which of these feeds would be suitable for finishing pigs for slaughter?

(b) Give a reason for your answer.

15. Table 21.6 outlines the constituents of a ration that is fed as a supplement to hay or silage to a pregnant ewe.

Table 21.6	
Constituent	Percentage of ration by weight
Beet pulp	40
Rolled barley	40
Soya bean meal	20
Mineral mixture: Calcium, Magnesium	

(a) (i) Give reasons, in each case, for the inclusion of the four constituents in the diet of a pregnant animal.

(ii) What would the consequence be if the ration were composed of 40% soya bean meal and 20% rolled barley?

(b) Advise the sheep farmer, concerning the feeding of the ration in the table above to pregnant ewes, under the following headings:

(i) When to start feeding the ration

(ii) The consequences for the pregnancy if the above ration is not fed.

16. Explain why there is a greater loss of digestible energy for ruminant animals compared to monogastric animals, e.g. pigs.

17. Explain why a lactating cow has a greater requirement for energy and protein in its feed compared with a dry cow.

18. Explain how the energy and protein requirements differ for a young calf and a beef animal being finished for slaughter.

19. Suckler cows can be fed for **maintenance** for much of the time but they must be fed on a **higher plane of nutrition** for 6–7 months of the year.

(a) Explain the terms in bold.

(b) Give three reasons for the higher plane of nutrition.

20. Fig. 21.14 and Table 21.7 show the feed requirements for pigs at different stages in their production cycle.

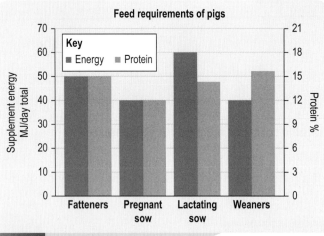

21.14 *Feed requirements for pigs*

Table 21.7 Consumption of pig ration				
	Pig type			
	Fatteners	**Pregnant sow**	**Lactating sow**	**Weaner**
Pig ration consumption kg/day	5	4	5	5

Table 21.8 Information about pig ration			
Pig ration			
Protein (%)	15	Phosphorous (%)	0.5
Lysine (%)	1.2	Fibre (%)	3
Calcium (%)	1.0	Energy (MJ/kg)	10.5

(a) Using the information above, for which of the following pairs of pig types is this ration suitable?

   (i) Lactating sows and weaners   **(iii)** Pregnant sows and weaners

   (ii) Fatteners and pregnant sows   **(iv)** Fatteners and weaners

(b) Identify **one** component of this ration that would be higher in a ration for a ruminant animal.

   (i) Protein   **(iii)** Fibre

   (ii) Lysine   **(iv)** Energy

(c) Explain why lysine is added to this ration but not to a ration for a ruminant animal.

Solutions   Weblinks

22 Animal physiology

When you have completed this chapter you should be able to:
- Compare the ruminant and monogastric digestive systems
- Explain the role of microorganisms in the digestive system.

The intake of food to acquire nutrients is necessary for an animal's survival. The breakdown of food into components that can be used within the body is called digestion. Digestion occurs in two ways: mechanical and chemical. Mechanical digestion is the physical breakdown of food into smaller pieces. Chemical digestion is the chemical breakdown of food by substances known as enzymes. Food is first taken into the body through the mouth, where both mechanical and chemical digestion occur.

The digestive process

Ingestion

The first stage of the digestive process is known as ingestion. Ingestion is the intake of food into the mouth where it is chewed and swallowed. The initial stages of digestion take place in the mouth with the aid of the teeth, tongue and salivary glands.

Mechanical digestion and chemical digestion take place at this stage. Mechanical digestion begins with the teeth.

The teeth

Teeth are used in the first stages of digestion to break up food into smaller pieces by tearing, crushing and grinding it. The tooth is a specialised structure for this task, with a hard outer coating of enamel. There are four types of teeth: incisor, canine, premolar and molar. Each has a different shape and function. The number and type of teeth present in an animal's mouth is related to the diet of the animal.

Herbivores eat plant materials only. They use their premolars and molars for crushing and grinding material such as grass. Sheep, cattle and horses are all herbivores.

Carnivores eat meat. They use their canine teeth for tearing flesh. Omnivores, such as pigs, eat both plant material and meat. They do not have a specialised dentition but use all the types of teeth listed to aid digestion of a variety of foods.

22.1 *Longitudinal section of a tooth*

Incisors: chisel-like teeth used for cutting and biting.

Canines: pointed and sharp teeth used for tearing food.

Premolars: relatively flat teeth used for grinding.

Molars: flat teeth used for crushing food.

Dental formulas of animals

Dental formulas are written to represent the dentition in the upper and lower jaw of the mouth of the animal. The formulas given show the number of incisors, canines, premolars and molars present on one side of the mouth, since the other side of the mouth is identical.

The dentition in Fig. 22.2 shows that the pig has 3 incisors, 1 canine, 4 premolars and 3 molars in the upper jaw and the same in the lower jaw: a total of 22 teeth. As this dental formula represents only one half of the mouth, the same number of teeth are present in the other half, giving the pig a total of 44 teeth.

$$I: \frac{3}{3} \qquad C: \frac{1}{1} \qquad P: \frac{4}{4} \qquad M: \frac{3}{3}$$

22.2 *Dental formula of a pig*

The dentition of a herbivore is quite different from that of a pig. The herbivore has no incisors or canines in the upper jaw. The front upper jaw instead consists of a horny pad, which meets the lower incisors and canines to allow them to crop grass. The gap between the front teeth and the premolars and molars is known as the diastema. It can store ingested material while the animal is chewing.

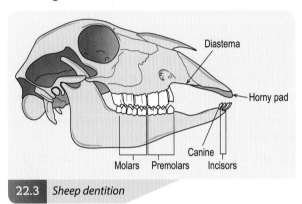

22.3 *Sheep dentition*

$$I: \frac{0}{3} \qquad C: \frac{0}{1} \qquad P: \frac{3}{3} \qquad M: \frac{3}{3}$$

Sometimes the dental formula of sheep is written as:

$$I: \frac{0}{4} \qquad C: \frac{0}{0} \qquad P: \frac{3}{3} \qquad M: \frac{3}{3}$$

22.4 *Dental formula of a herbivore (cow, sheep or goat)*

> **DEFINITION**
>
> **Ruminant:** Cattle and sheep are classified as ruminants as they have four compartments to their stomach (rumen, reticulum, omasum and abomasum). Unlike monogastric animals, ruminants have a digestive system that is specially adapted to ferment plant material. This material, now known as a 'cud', is then regurgitated back up into the mouth, where the food is rechewed (chewing the cud) for a second time before being swallowed again. Chewing the cud is also known as rumination.

Chemical digestion in the mouth

The mouth has three pairs of salivary glands. In the monogastric animal (e.g. pig) the glands secrete an enzyme called amylase. The amylase breaks down starch to maltose. The more the food is chewed by the teeth, the more it can be broken down chemically by amylase.

Saliva also has a secondary function as a lubricant, which wets the food and makes it easier to chew and swallow. This takes place in both the monogastric and ruminant digestive systems. In monogastric animals when food is swallowed it is passed to the oesophagus. It is prevented from entering the trachea by the epiglottis. Food is then moved to the stomach along the oesophagus by peristalsis.

Peristalsis: a rhythmic, wave-like motion of muscular contractions as food entering the oesophagus is moved along to the stomach.

The saliva of cattle contains two enzymes: salivary amylase (which breaks down starch) and salivary lipase (which breaks down fat). The saliva of cattle also contains sodium bicarbonate, a base, which buffers the pH levels in the rumen and reticulum and helps keep the pH between 6.5 and 7.2. This pH is suitable for microorganisms (mainly bacteria) to grow in the rumen. The saliva of cattle also contains an anti-foaming agent, which helps to prevent bloat. Cattle can produce between 40 and 150 litres of saliva a day depending on the type of feed they are eating.

The ruminant digestive system

A ruminant animal (e.g. cattle and sheep) grazes by wrapping its tongue around the grass to grasp it and then pulling the grass to tear it. The lower jaw incisors tear the grass by cutting it against the horny pad in the upper jaw. Cattle will eat forage rapidly without chewing it adequately while they are grazing. When the grass is swallowed it passes down the oesophagus into the rumen.

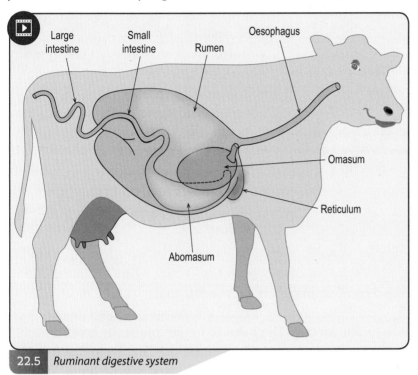

| 22.5 | *Ruminant digestive system* |

The rumen and the role of microorganisms

The rumen is the largest of the four compartments; it occupies 75% of the abdominal cavity and has a capacity of between 150 and 200 litres. The rumen is an anaerobic environment (i.e. there is no oxygen present) and has a pH range of 6.5–7.2. It contains billions of microorganisms such as bacteria, protozoa and fungi. These microorganisms have a symbiotic relationship with the ruminant animal. The bacteria are provided with a suitable living environment and a ready supply of nutrients. In return they produce enzymes to break down cellulose and other complex carbohydrates such as starch by fermentation. The fermentation of these carbohydrates produces volatile fatty acids, which are absorbed directly into the blood through the rumen wall. The volatile fatty acids are a substantial source of energy for the ruminant animal, and some of them (e.g. acetate and butyrate) are precursors of milk fat.

The microorganisms in the rumen also have the ability to synthesise amino acids from non-protein sources of nitrogen in the diet of the ruminant. The bacteria incorporate these amino acids into their own cells, and the amino acids become available when the animal digests the bacteria. The microorganisms in the rumen are also responsible for synthesising B vitamins and vitamin K. A downside to this process is that the microbes themselves utilise some of the energy from the animal's feed.

The process of fermentation produces large volumes of gas – mainly carbon dioxide and methane. The production of these gases also contributes to some energy loss from the animal feed. In order to expel these gases, the cow's rumen contracts, and the cow belches the gases out of the rumen. If these gases are not expelled, they can build up to cause a condition called bloat (see Table 22.1). Another condition that can also affect the rumen is acidosis, which occurs when the pH of the rumen drops below its normal level.

Table 22.1 Digestive disorders of the rumen	
Bloat	**Acidosis**
• Bloat occurs in cattle that have been put on early grass, especially when it contains white clover. This creates a foam in the rumen, which traps gas. • Gases build up in the rumen and the left side of the abdomen becomes distended (swollen). • This can be relieved with an antacid solution or a tube inserted through the mouth to release the gas. • A vet can also create an incision in the abdomen and insert a trocar and cannula. The trocar is removed and the cannula remains, allowing the gas to escape.	• Acidosis occurs when the pH of the rumen falls below 5.5. • It is caused by feeding a diet high in concentrates or low in fibre. This results in the production of high levels of lactic acid, which cannot be absorbed quickly enough. • The rumen stops moving, leading to a loss of appetite. • Increased acidity allows acid-loving bacteria and microbes to flourish in the rumen. • Bacteria and microbes increase the acid levels, which makes the problem worse. • Acid can be absorbed through the rumen wall, which can cause metabolic acidosis.

Metabolic acidosis occurs when the pH of the cattle's blood drops below 7.35. This can result in shock and death of the animal. Metabolic acidosis is also known as systemic acidosis.

The reticulum

The reticulum is the second compartment of the ruminant stomach and is involved in rumination (regurgitation and rechewing of the cud). When cattle regurgitate their food they rechew it with a side-to-side motion. This helps to further physically break down the fibrous material into smaller pieces. In order for the microorganisms to digest the plant material efficiently, cattle regurgitate and rechew their food several times. They can spend anywhere between 3 and 6 hours ruminating per day. The length of time spent ruminating depends on the amount of fibre in their food. Finally, when the plant material becomes small, the rumen contracts and the fluid from the rumen is collected by the reticulum and moved into the omasum.

The reticulum has a honeycomb appearance. Foreign objects, ingested by cattle, often become trapped in this honeycomb structure. Stones and metal objects are examples of items that are generally found in the reticulum. There is a risk that these objects could puncture the reticulum wall, which can lead to the development of hardware disease.

Omasum

The omasum is the third compartment of the ruminant stomach. When food has been broken down enough by the rumen, it is passed to the omasum from the reticulum. The omasum has many folds in it, giving it a large surface area for the absorption of water. The omasum then moves the food into the final compartment of the ruminant stomach, the abomasum.

Abomasum

The abomasum is also known as the 'true stomach'. It acts much like the stomach of a monogastric animal (human or pig) and has a pH of 2. The abomasum produces gastric juices (hydrochloric acid and digestive enzymes) and also receives some digestive enzymes secreted by the pancreas (pancreatic lipase). The cells in the walls of the abomasum produce a mucus that protects the walls of the abomasum from the hydrochloric acid. Due to the large volume of plant material that cattle eat, food tends to flow constantly through the abomasum.

Table 22.2 Enzyme activity in the abomasum		
Enzyme	**Acts on**	**Produces**
Pepsinogen (converted to pepsin)	Protein	Peptides and amino acids
Rennin (chymosin)	Milk protein in calves (caseinogen)	Casein (insoluble milk protein)
Lipase	Fats and lipids	Fatty acids and glycerol

Digestion in the young ruminant

When calves and lambs are born they do not have a fully functional ruminant digestive system. Instead, they are born with an oesophageal groove, which channels milk into the abomasum directly from the mouth, therefore bypassing the rumen, reticulum and omasum. The opening of the oesophageal groove is stimulated by the young animal sucking. As the calves and lambs start to feed, cultures of microorganisms begin to develop in the rumen. As the animals grow and their rumen develops they become less dependent on milk and transition to a diet of grass and concentrates. As a result, the oesophageal groove is no longer required, and it closes. In lambs it usually closes after 8 weeks and in calves after 20 weeks.

The small intestine

The first section of the small intestine is called the duodenum. As with the oesophagus, food is moved through the small intestine by peristalsis.

Bile and pancreatic juices are secreted into the duodenum to aid breakdown of food and absorption of nutrients through the thin intestinal wall. Bile is secreted by the liver and stored in the gall bladder. The role of bile is to emulsify fats and lipids in the duodenum. It also helps to neutralise food that has come from the acidic stomach environment.

Pancreatic juice contains a number of enzymes, including lipase, trypsin and pancreatic amylase, which aid in the digestion of food (Table 22.3).

Table 22.3 Function of pancreatic enzymes in the small intestine		
Enzyme	**Acts on**	**Produces**
Trypsin	Protein	Peptides and amino acids
Amylase	Starch	Maltose
Lipase	Fats and lipids	Fatty acids and glycerol

As the digested food makes its way through the small intestine, it passes through the jejunum and ileum (parts of the small intestine), where approximately 90% of the nutrients released in digestion are absorbed. The lining of the small intestine contains many infoldings called villi. The surface of the villus also has many tiny folds called microvilli. These villi and microvilli increase the surface area for the absorption of nutrients.

The walls of the villi are only one cell thick, which facilitates the diffusion of nutrients into the villi. Each villus has a capillary network and a lacteal (which contains lymph). Amino acids, glucose, vitamins and minerals are absorbed into the blood supply of the capillaries. The capillaries become the hepatic portal vein, which carries nutrient-rich blood to the liver, where the nutrients will either be stored or distributed to other parts of the body. Fatty acids and glycerol are absorbed into the lacteal. They are carried by the lymph and transported to the bloodstream.

> **Oesophageal groove:** a channel, present in calves and lambs, that takes milk from the oesophagus into the abomasum and bypasses the rumen, reticulum and omasum.

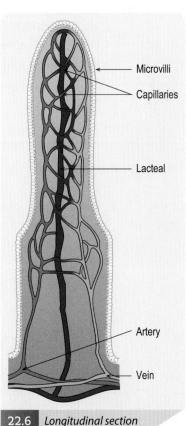

22.6 *Longitudinal section of a villus*

Microvilli
Capillaries
Lacteal
Artery
Vein

Large intestine

The large intestine consists of the caecum and the colon. Its main function is to absorb water and to pass the waste to the rectum for egestion through the anus. Bacteria in the colon manufacture vitamin K, which is absorbed by the body.

The monogastric stomach

Pigs and humans have a monogastric digestive system. This means that they have one stomach; they do not possess a rumen and cannot digest cellulose. Therefore, the diet of a pig is considerably different to that of cattle and sheep. Pigs are fed a concentrate ration, with less fibre and more easily digested nutrients. However, as the pigs digest their feed directly and fermentation is not involved, there is less energy lost by this system.

The type of protein in the diet of a monogastric animal is important. Protein is made up of 20 amino acids. In monogastric animals, ten of these are essential amino acids and they must be present in the animal's diet, since they cannot be synthesised by the animal. In the production of feeds for pigs, high-quality protein must be used to ensure that these amino acids are in the diet.

Table 22.4 Essential amino acids for monogastric animals
Arginine
Histidine
Isoleucine
Leucine
Lysine
Methionine
Phenylalanine
Threonine
Tryptophan
Valine
(Glycine)*
(Glutamic acid)*
Needed by poultry

In the digestive system of a monogastric animal, food is passed from the oesophagus directly to the stomach for digestion. The pig's stomach is equivalent to the abomasum in the ruminant animal. Gastric juices containing hydrochloric acid and pepsinogen are secreted in the stomach. The hydrochloric acid maintains the pH of the stomach at a pH of 2, and also converts pepsinogen to active pepsin. Food can remain in the stomach for several hours as it is chemically broken down. Further digestion and absorption of nutrients in the small intestine and absorption of water in the large intestine is carried out in the same way as in the ruminant animal. Fig. 22.7 shows the digestive system of a pig.

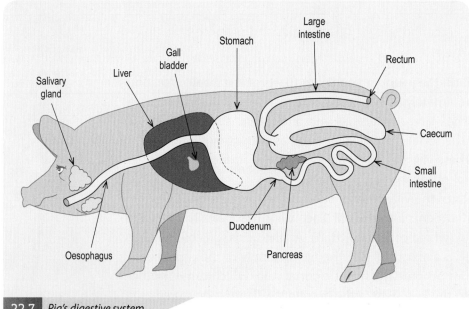

22.7 *Pig's digestive system*

Comparison of the ruminant and monogastric digestive systems

Table 22.5 Summary of the main differences and similarities between the ruminant and monogastric digestive systems		
Feature	Ruminant (cow)	Monogastric (pig)
Diet of animal	• Herbivore – grass, silage, hay, etc.	• Omnivore – both plant and animal material
Dentition	• No incisors or canines in the upper jaw, horny pad on upper jaw and diastema • All adaptations for a plant-based diet	• All types of teeth present
Composition of saliva	• Two enzymes present: amylase and lipase • Sodium carbonate, a base, is also present in the saliva	• Amylase present in the saliva of pigs
Stomach	• Four compartments: rumen, reticulum, omasum and abomasum	• One stomach
Digestion in the stomach	• Rumen and reticulum involved in the fermentation of plant material • Fermentation is carried out by microorganisms • pH of rumen: pH 6.5–7.2 • Rumen and reticulum involved in rumination: regurgitation and rechewing of food • Abomasum (true stomach) produces HCl and enzymes that digest protein and fats • pH of abomasum: pH 2 • Food moves quickly through the abomasum	• No fermentation of food • The stomach does not have the ability to digest plant material • No regurgitation or rechewing of food • Stomach produces HCl and enzymes that digest protein • pH of stomach: pH 2 • Food stays in the stomach for some time
Small intestine	• Bile and pancreatic enzymes are secreted to complete digestion • Nutrients are absorbed into the bloodstream in the jejunum and ileum	• Bile and pancreatic enzymes are secreted to complete digestion • Nutrients are absorbed into the bloodstream in the jejunum and ileum
Large intestine	• Absorption of water	• Absorption of water

Summary

- Mechanical digestion is the physical breakdown of food into smaller pieces.
- Chemical digestion is the chemical breakdown of food by substances known as enzymes.
- Teeth are used to physically break up the food into smaller pieces by tearing, crushing and grinding.

- There are four types of teeth: incisor, canine, premolar and molar.
  - Dental formula of a pig:
    I: $\frac{3}{3}$ C: $\frac{1}{1}$ P: $\frac{4}{4}$ M: $\frac{3}{3}$
  - Dental formula of a herbivore (cow, sheep or goat):
    I: $\frac{0}{3}$ C: $\frac{0}{1}$ P: $\frac{3}{3}$ M: $\frac{3}{3}$
    - Alternative dental formula of a sheep:
      I: $\frac{0}{4}$ C: $\frac{0}{0}$ P: $\frac{3}{3}$ M: $\frac{3}{3}$
- Ruminant animals (cattle and sheep) have four compartments to their stomachs (rumen, reticulum, omasum and abomasum).
- Ruminants have a digestive system specially adapted to ferment plant material.
- The saliva of cattle contains sodium bicarbonate to help maintain the pH of the rumen between 6.5 and 7.2. It also contains enzymes to break down starch and fats.
- The rumen contains microorganisms, which have a symbiotic relationship with the ruminant animal. These microorganisms break down cellulose in plant cell walls.
- The reticulum and the rumen are involved in rumination (regurgitation and rechewing of food).
- The omasum has a large surface area for the absorption of water.
- The abomasum is also known as the 'true stomach'. It produces hydrochloric acid and enzymes that digest protein.
- The monogastric stomach functions like the abomasum in the ruminant animal. It produces hydrochloric acid and is involved in the digestion of protein.
- Monogastric animals do not have the ability to digest cellulose.
- The small intestine in both ruminant and monogastric animals functions in a similar way. The small intestine is responsible for the completion of digestion and the absorption of nutrients in the bloodstream.
- The large intestine is responsible for the absorption of water in both ruminant and monogastric animals.

PowerPoint Summary

QUESTIONS

1. Which types of teeth are commonly found in the upper jaw of a sheep?
   (a) Incisors and canines
   (b) Canines and premolars
   (c) Incisors and premolars
   (d) Premolars and molars

2. The enzyme amylase breaks down starch into:
   (a) Glucose
   (b) Lactose
   (c) Maltose
   (d) Sucrose.

3. The saliva of cattle contains the compound sodium bicarbonate. What is the function of this compound?
   (a) To break down cellulose
   (b) To neutralise the acid in the abomasum
   (c) To maintain the pH of the rumen between 6.5 and 7.2
   (d) To prevent the growth of bacteria in the rumen

4. Identify the third compartment of the ruminant stomach.

   (a) Rumen

   (b) Abomasum

   (c) Reticulum

   (d) Omasum

5. What happens to food that is too big to be broken down by the microorganisms in the rumen?

   (a) It passes out of the ruminant digestive system undigested.

   (b) It passes to the abomasum to be broken down by hydrochloric acid.

   (c) It remains in the omasum and water is added to it.

   (d) It is regurgitated back up to the mouth and is rechewed again.

6. Which part of the ruminant digestive system has the same function as the stomach in the pig's digestive system?

   (a) Omasum

   (b) Rumen

   (c) Reticulum

   (d) Abomasum

7. What is the function of the folds inside the omasum?

   (a) To increase the surface area for the absorption of water

   (b) To increase the surface area for the production of gastric juices

   (c) To increase the surface area for the absorption of nutrients

   (d) To decrease the surface area for the absorption of water

8. The oesophageal groove forms a channel in young calves and lambs from the _____ to the _____.

   (a) Mouth, omasum

   (b) Mouth, abomasum

   (c) Mouth, reticulum

   (d) Mouth, small intestine

9. A cow develops bloat when:

   (a) Foam builds up in the rumen, trapping gas

   (b) Gas cannot be expelled from the rumen

   (c) Cattle are put on early grass that contains a lot of clover

   (d) All of the above.

10. Pigs are monogastric animals and therefore do not have a rumen. As a result, the monogastric animal has difficulty breaking down _____.

    (a) Protein

    (b) Starch

    (c) Fat

    (d) Cellulose

11. Draw a labelled diagram of a longitudinal section through a mammalian tooth.

12. Fig. 22.8 shows a sheep's skull.

    (a) Identify A and B in the diagram.

    (b) State the function of A and the function of B.

    (c) What is the name and the function of C?

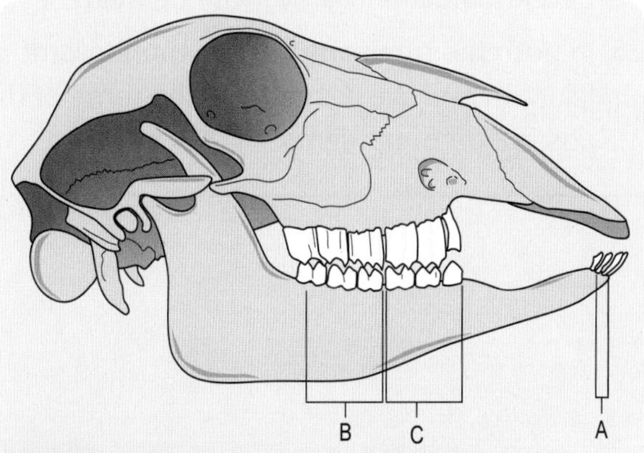

22.8 *A sheep's skull*

13. Give the dental formula of the following animals:

   (a) Sheep   (b) Pig

14. Compare the dentition of a ruminant animal to a monogastric animal, e.g. a pig.

15. Explain the term 'symbiosis'. Describe how the relationship between cattle or sheep and the microorganisms that live in their rumen is an example of a symbiotic relationship.

16. Fig. 22.9 shows the stomach of a ruminant farm animal.

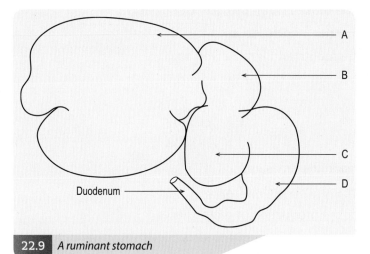

22.9   *A ruminant stomach*

   (a) Name each labelled part of the stomach.

   (b) State the roles of part A and part D.

   (c) Name two farm animals with a ruminant stomach.

   (d) State one advantage of having a ruminant stomach.

17. Describe the process of digestion in the stomach compartments of a ruminant animal.

18. Describe the differences between monogastric animals and ruminant animals in terms of their digestion of starch and cellulose.

19. Compare the dietary protein requirements of both ruminants and monogastric animals.

20. (a) Name the organ that produces bile in the body.

   (b) Where is the bile stored?

   (c) State the function of bile.

21. Name any two substances secreted into the animal's digestive system and in each case name the organ that secretes it.

22. Bloat is a common disorder of the ruminant digestive system. Briefly outline how cattle develop bloat and how it can be treated.

23. In both the ruminant and the monogastric digestive system nutrients are absorbed in the jejunum and the ileum. Describe some of the adaptations of the small intestine for the absorption of nutrients.

 Solutions   Weblinks

CHAPTER

23 Animal reproduction

When you have completed this chapter you should be able to:
- Identify parts of the reproductive system of a bull and a cow
- Describe the role of hormones in the reproductive cycle
- Distinguish between oestrus and oestrous cycle
- Describe methods of fertilisation of two farm animals
- Discuss the importance of genetics in food-producing animals
- Discuss the importance of genetics in the production of animals used for breeding.

The male reproductive system

Fig. 23.1 shows the reproductive system of a bull. The testes are responsible for production of the male gametes, which are called sperm. The testes are suspended in the scrotum, which hangs outside the body cavity. This is to keep it at a lower temperature than the rest of the body. This is necessary to allow the sperm to develop and mature properly.

Sperm produced in the testes matures and is stored in the epididymis. It is also stored in a duct leading out of the epididymis called the vas deferens. As sperm travel along the vas deferens, three fluids are secreted from the seminal vesicle, the prostate gland and Cowper's glands. These give the sperm mobility, and the combination of sperm and fluids is known as semen. These fluids are added to the sperm prior to ejaculation. The sperm is released into the vagina of the female by ejaculation during copulation (mating).

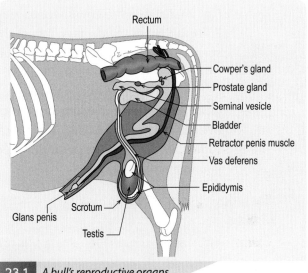

23.1 *A bull's reproductive organs*

Male hormones

Hormones play an important role in reproduction. Follicle stimulating hormone (FSH) promotes sperm production and luteinising hormone (LH) controls the production of another male sex hormone, testosterone. Testosterone is responsible for development of the male sex characteristics and the male sex organs.

Table 23.1 The function of the male hormones	
Hormone	**Function**
Follicle stimulating hormone (FSH)	Sperm production
Luteinising hormone (LH)	Stimulates testosterone production
Testosterone	Plays a role in the development of the testes and prostate gland. Responsible for the male sex characteristics as well as increasing the muscle and bone growth.

The female reproductive system

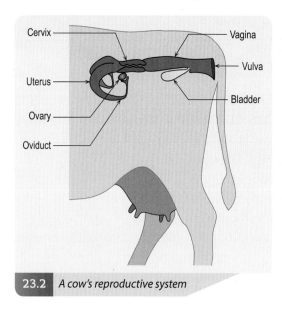

23.2 *A cow's reproductive system*

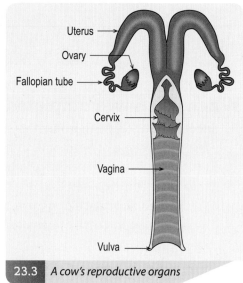

23.3 *A cow's reproductive organs*

Fig. 23.2 shows the cow's reproductive system. The ovaries produce eggs (ova). The Fallopian tubes (oviducts) connect the ovaries to the uterus. Fertilisation of eggs by sperm takes place in the Fallopian tubes. The fertilised egg, known as a zygote, then makes its way to the uterus (womb), where it implants itself in the uterine wall. As the cells divide in the zygote and it starts to develop, it is known as an embryo. The uterine walls are muscular and can stretch to accommodate the developing foetus. The narrow opening at the end of the uterus is called the cervix, which dilates during birth. The vagina, which held the penis during copulation, also serves as the birth canal when the young animal is born.

Dilate: widen, expand or enlarge.

Copulation: sexual intercourse or mating.

> **DEFINITION**
>
> **Oestrous cycle:** a recurring cycle during which a female mammal comes into heat and releases an egg which is available for fertilisation by sperm from the male.

Follicle: a small fluid-filled sac that grows in the ovary and contains an egg.

Ovulation: the release of an egg from the follicle.

Corpus luteum: a structure that forms in the ovary once the follicle has released its egg. The corpus luteum then starts to secrete the hormone progesterone.

Female hormones

As in the male, hormones play a vital role in the reproductive cycle of the female. FSH is produced by the pituitary gland in the brain and promotes the development of a follicle in the ovary. As the follicle grows it produces the hormone oestrogen. Oestrogen stimulates the initial growth and thickening of the endometrium (lining of the uterus). Midway through the **oestrous cycle** the pituitary gland produces LH, which stimulates ovulation and promotes the development of the corpus luteum. The corpus luteum secretes the hormone progesterone.

Progesterone continues the thickening of the endometrium in preparation for the implantation of the embryo. If an egg is fertilised and implants in the uterus then progesterone will continue to be secreted by the corpus luteum and then eventually by the developing embryo. If fertilisation does not occur, the corpus luteum breaks down, removing the source of progesterone and the endometrium is reabsorbed.

Progesterone has a variety of functions during gestation, which include: supporting pregnancy by allowing the uterus to grow, inhibition of lactation prior to birth, inhibition of labour, and the inhibition of an immune response to the embryo. An easy way to remember the function of progesterone is to look at the first part of the word **pro (for) gest (gestation)**.

Oestrogen also promotes the secondary sex characteristics in the female. This includes the development and growth of mammary glands.

Table 23.2 Role of hormones in the oestrous cycle	
Hormone	**Function**
Follicle stimulating hormone (FSH)	To encourage the growth of a follicle in the ovary
Oestrogen	To stimulate the growth of the endometrium in the first half of the oestrous cycle
Luteinising hormone (LH)	To stimulate ovulation and the development of the corpus luteum
Progesterone	To continue the growth of the endometrium, maintain gestation and inhibit labour and lactation prior to birth.

Oestrus and the oestrous cycle

The oestrous cycle in mammals (equivalent to the menstrual cycle in human females) is a recurring cycle that is driven by the hormones already mentioned. When an animal ovulates, it comes into oestrus (otherwise known as 'coming into heat' or 'in heat'). During oestrus an egg is present in the Fallopian tube and the chances of fertilisation are high.

DEFINITION

Duration of oestrus: the length of time during the oestrous cycle in which the female is in heat and an egg is available for fertilisation.
Gestation: the period of development in the uterus from conception to birth.

The length of the oestrous cycle varies from species to species and is outlined in Table 23.3. The duration of oestrus (when a female is in heat) also varies (see Table 23.3). 'Gestation' is the term given to pregnancy in animals. Once an animal conceives she stops oestrous cycling and will not come into oestrus again until after she has given birth.

Table 23.3 Length of oestrous cycle, duration of oestrus and gestation in cattle, sheep and pigs			
Animal	**Length of oestrous cycle**	**Duration of oestrus**	**Length of gestation**
Cow	21 days	18–24 hours	283 days (9.5 months)
Sheep	17 days	36 hours	147 days (5 months)
Pig	21 days	2–3 days	115 days (3 months, 3 weeks, 3 days)

Polyoestrous and seasonally polyoestrous

Animals that have oestrous cycles throughout the year are described as polyoestrous. Cows and pigs are both polyoestrous. Animals that have a number of oestrous cycles, but only during a certain time of the year, are described as seasonally polyoestrous or seasonal breeders. Sheep are seasonal breeders. Seasonal breeding is determined by the length of day (photoperiod).

DEFINITION

Polyoestrous: animals that have several oestrous cycles throughout the year.
Seasonally polyoestrous: animals that have more than one oestrous cycle during a specific time of year. These animals are commonly referred to as seasonal breeders.

Seasonally polyoestrous

Sheep are short-day breeders as they naturally come into oestrus during autumn as daylight decreases. The timing of the onset of oestrus is controlled by the pineal gland, which is located in the centre of the brain, and a hormone called melatonin. As daylight hours decrease, the pineal gland is stimulated to produce melatonin. Melatonin is produced only during the hours of darkness, so as the length of the night increases during autumn, the amount of melatonin increases. This increase in the levels of melatonin in the sheep triggers a chain of other hormonal activities, which ultimately causes ovulation to occur. Goats and deer are also short-day seasonal breeders.

Methods of fertilisation

Dairy production

Artificial insemination

In dairy production the most popular method of inseminating a cow in heat is using artificial insemination (AI). AI is used to improve the genetic merit of the cattle in the dairy herd by selective breeding. Cows of good genetic merit are crossed with superior bulls. AI allows farmers to target particular areas in their herd that they might want to improve. The following are some of the traits that farmers might want to improve within the herd:

- Conformation (see page 330)
- Growth rate
- Feed conversion efficiency (FCE) or feed conversion ratio (FCR) (see page 452)
- Milk yield
- Milk composition (increase percentage fat and protein)
- Fertility.

Prior to AI, an AI company will collect a bull's semen. The semen will be diluted down and packed into a plastic straw. The straw is then frozen and stored in liquid nitrogen at −196°C. When a farmer detects that a cow is in heat (often termed 'standing heat'), the straw will be thawed in warm water. The straw is then placed inside a catheter (also known as an insemination gun). The person carrying out the AI procedure then places their hand inside the rectum of the cow until they feel the cervix of the uterus. The catheter is then guided through the cervix into the uterus and the semen is deposited in the uterus of the cow. If the cow has released an egg, then the egg will be fertilised in the Fallopian tube.

> **Insemination:** the introduction of semen into a female animal by either natural or artificial means.

> **Catheter:** a narrow, flexible tube.

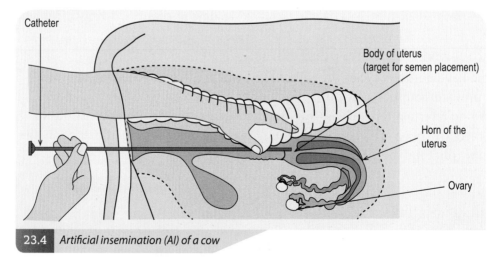

23.4 *Artificial insemination (AI) of a cow*

Table 23.4 Advantages and disadvantages of AI	
Advantages	**Disadvantages**
Allows maximum use of superior bulls	Successful heat detection is crucial
Farmers have a wide choice of bulls that are performance and progeny tested (see page 337)	More labour and management skills required than natural service (e.g. by a bull)
Prevents the spread of sexually transmitted diseases	Lower conception rates compared to using a fertile stock bull
Semen can be sexed to increase chances of heifer calves	Inseminations must be carried out by a trained technician
Cost of an AI straw is little in comparison to the cost of purchasing, feeding and housing a bull	Semen must be stored properly, otherwise it will not be viable
The number of cows serviced by a bull is greater than would be possible by natural means	A stock bull may still be required for mopping up at the end of the breeding season
Wide variety of bulls allows the farmer to target specific genetic traits within the herd	

Sexed semen

In dairy herds, heifer calves are more desirable than bull calves, since heifer calves can be used as replacements or to expand the dairy herd. However, with conventional AI semen or with a stock bull there is only a 50% chance of a heifer calf being born.

Bulls' semen can be collected and separated into two groups: sperm carrying Y chromosomes and sperm carrying X chromosomes.

Table 23.5 Advantages and disadvantages of sexed semen	
Advantages	**Disadvantages**
90% chance of producing a heifer calf	Small chance that a male calf will be produced
High-quality heifer calves can be reared as replacement heifers in the dairy herd	Sexed semen is more expensive than conventional, non-sexed semen
Allows for the expansion of a dairy herd while maintaining biosecurity (see page 486)	Reduced conception rates because sperm can be damaged during the separation process, and sexed semen has fewer sperm per straw than non-sexed semen straws
Reduces the number of male dairy calves being born	
Can reduce the risk of calving difficulties in maiden heifers, since heifer calves are smaller than bull calves	
Sexed semen containing Y chromosomes can be used on genetically superior cows to produce bulls for breeding purposes	

Stock bull

Heifers in particular can be difficult to detect when they are in heat. For this reason some dairy farmers keep a stock bull on their farm for breeding purposes. A bull will detect a cow or heifer in heat or coming into heat.

Heat detection: the means by which a farmer identifies when a cow is in heat. When a cow is in heat, she will stand and allow other cows to mount her. Farmers often rely on heat detection aids to help identify when a cow is in heat. Examples of heat detection aids include tail painting and activity meters (see Chapter 25).

Mopping up: a stock bull detects and services any cows or heifers not in calf.

X and Y chromosomes are the sex chromosomes. Females produce gametes with only X chromosomes; males produce gametes with X and Y chromosomes. A female calf will be XX and a male calf will be XY.

When a cow or heifer is in heat, she will stand and allow the bull to mount her. The bull will ejaculate and deposit semen in the vagina. However, if a cow is coming into heat but not in standing heat, she will move away and not allow the bull to mount her.

Keeping a bull on a farm has several implications:

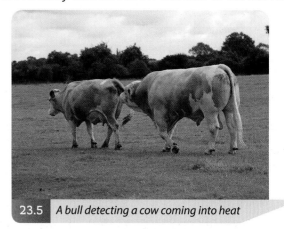

- Bulls are aggressive and can be dangerous
- Bulls are expensive to keep and require additional fencing
- A stock bull must be changed on a regular basis to prevent high levels of inbreeding within the herd
- Bulls can interfere with the breeding programme on a farm, e.g. by serving heifers.

23.5   *A bull detecting a cow coming into heat*

Sheep production

In the majority of cases a ram is used to inseminate ewes in sheep production. Fertilisation takes place naturally in the Fallopian tube as previously described. However, in the production of pedigree sheep (and pedigree cattle) embryo transplantation is used to produce a large number of offspring, which would not be possible by natural means.

Embryo transplantation is a technique that involves collecting a donor animal's embryos and then transferring these into a recipient female, which serves as a surrogate mother. The donor animals are selected on the basis of good breeding history and superior genetic merit. The surrogate mother does not have to be a pedigree animal but must be in excellent health and have good mothering abilities.

- Both donor and recipient ewe are sponged with progesterone-impregnated sponges. This allows synchronisation of the reproductive cycles of both the donor ewes and the recipient ewes. The recipient must be at the correct stage of their reproductive cycle in order to receive an embryo.
- Hormone injections are given to the donor ewes to increase the number of eggs that are released at ovulation. This is known as super ovulation.
- The sponges are removed from both the donor and the recipient ewes after 12 days.
- Ewes should come into heat 36–48 hours after sponges are removed.
- The donor ewes are inseminated using artificial insemination. Using a laparoscope (an optical device), a small incision is made in the abdomen of the donor ewe and semen is inserted into the left and right horns of the uterus.
- Six days later the embryos are flushed from the donor ewes. A small surgical procedure is required. The embryos are collected and graded. The embryos are then transferred to the recipient, inserting two embryos into the horn of the uterus. After removal of the embryos, the donors are given an injection of hormones, which brings them back into heat 4 days later and they are serviced naturally by a ram.

Embryo transplantation in cattle is slightly different from that in sheep, but both have the same basic procedure. It involves the

23.6   *Laparoscopic AI*

Surrogate mother: an animal that takes on the role of mother to another animal's offspring.

Synchronisation: when things occur at the same time.

Super ovulation is the production of more than the normal number of mature eggs at one time.

synchronisation of reproductive cycles, followed by hormone injections to cause super ovulation in the donor cow. Fertilisation of the eggs can take place inside the cow or the eggs can be flushed out and fertilised *in vitro* (in a test tube). The fertilised eggs are then transferred to a recipient cow that will carry and give birth to the calf.

The importance of genetics for food production

Dairy herd

Crossbreeding, or outbreeding, has been an important component in the selective breeding of animals for food production for hundreds of years. It involves the mating of animals from two different breeds. The offspring in many instances inherit favourable genes from both parents, leading to improved health traits. This is referred to as hybrid vigour, or heterosis. Fig. 23.7 shows two purebred animals, Breed A and Breed B. When crossed, they produce the Breed A × B. The performance of all three breeds is represented in the histogram and the line drawn between Breed A and Breed B represents the average of these two breeds. The yellow area on the box shows how the crossbred A × B outperforms the expected averages of Breed A and B.

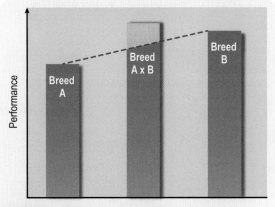
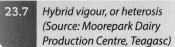

23.7 | *Hybrid vigour, or heterosis (Source: Moorepark Dairy Production Centre, Teagasc)*

23.8 | *Holstein cow*

Successive generations of inbreeding among purebred dairy cows (e.g. Holsteins) has led to decreased fertility rates and decreased productivity over the lifespan of the cow. In addition, the dairy industry has changed, with farmers' milk payments increased by high milk solids content (protein and butterfat) and decreased for high water content of milk.

Purebred Holstein cows are the highest milk producers; however, milk protein and fat content is low in comparison to volume of milk produced. Jersey cows have the highest milk solids in their milk, but low milk yields.

When Holsteins are crossed with Jerseys, the offspring have a reduced milk volume but the yield of milk solids (protein and butterfat) increases. Trials carried out by Moorepark Dairy Production Research Centre show that the Holstein Jersey crossbreed had increased profit per lactation compared with the purebred Holstein-Friesians. Teagasc also noted that the Jersey crossbreed cows had increased production efficiency due to higher grass intake relative to its size and compared to the purebred Holstein-Friesians. In addition, the offspring have increased fertility, health and lifespan in the dairy herd, which reduces the replacement rate.

Milk solids: components of milk (i.e. fat, protein, lactose, minerals and vitamins).

Replacement rate: the number of heifers required to replace culled (or removed) cows from a herd.

Crossbreeding also comes with disadvantages, however: there is a loss of hybrid vigour with subsequent crossing of the hybrids. This results in a reduction in the uniformity of the phenotype in the offspring. Holstein-Jersey cross males have very poor conformation and, as a result, are not suitable for beef production. In addition, crossbreeding requires the maintenance of two purebred herds in order to produce the crossbreeds.

23.9 *Jersey cow*

23.10 *Holstein-Jersey crossbred cow*

Pig production

The two main indoor commercial pig breeds in Ireland are the Large White and the Landrace.

23.11 *Large White*

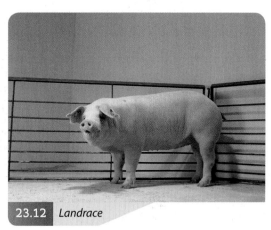

23.12 *Landrace*

These two breeds are crossbred with each other to produce offspring with hybrid vigour. The Large White has a number of desirable characteristics, including high prolificacy, fast growth rate, good meat quality, good feed conversion ratio (FCR; see page 452) and good conformation with good hams.

DEFINITION

Prolific or prolificacy: the breed can produce many offspring.
Conformation: refers to the shape of the animal and the distribution of fat and muscle around its body.

The Landrace has a long muscular body, large hams, lean meat and good conformation.
Breeding sows in a pig production unit ideally would be F1 Landrace-Large White crossbreeds, therefore maximising hybrid vigour. Pig production units practise a criss-cross breeding system which roughly keeps the mix of genes from both breeds around 50% (see Chapter 30). Pig production units also use a Duroc as a terminal sire.

DEFINITION

Terminal sire: a male used in a crossbreeding system to produce offspring with high growth rates and good carcase quality for slaughter.

The Duroc improves the eating quality of the meat due to the high level of marbling in the meat.

Sheep production

Sheep production in Ireland is solely for the production of meat. The ewes used in the production are normally crossbred ewes (offspring of a mountain ewe crossed with a prolific ram). These crossbred ewes are then crossed with a terminal sire. The most commonly used terminal sires used in Ireland are the Suffolk ram and the Texel ram.

23.13 *Suffolk*

The Suffolk has excellent conformation, fast growth rates and good carcase quality. This ram breed is mainly used to produce early lamb or lamb for the Easter market, as Suffolk-cross lambs are early maturing.

The Texel has good conformation and carcase quality and is particularly noted for muscle leanness. It has a slower growth rate when compared with a Suffolk and is usually used as a terminal sire for mid-season lamb (see Chapter 29).

23.14 *Texel*

> **Marbling:** intramuscular fat (fat inside the muscle fibres) or fat that is dispersed within the lean meat. Much of the flavour in meat cuts is derived from the marbling.

> **Carcase:** the body of a slaughtered animal (e.g. pig), which is cut up as meat.

> **Dam:** the female parent of an animal.

> **Replacements:** ewes that have been bred to take the place of a culled ewe in the breeding flock.

> **Suckler herds:** cows that are bred to produce and suckle calves for beef production.

The importance of genetics in breeding

Sheep production

Genetics plays a vital role in the selection of breeding stock. Lowland sheep farmers cross mountain breeds (Blackface Mountain sheep) with prolific rams. Mountain ewes are excellent mothers, but they usually produce a single lamb. Ideally, lowland sheep farmers want every ewe to produce a least two lambs to make sheep production profitable. By crossing the mountain ewes with a Bluefaced Leicester ram or a Belclare ram they produce crossbred daughters that will have good mothering ability from their mountain dam and increased prolificacy from the ram (hybrid vigour).

23.15 *Bluefaced Leicester, a prolific ram breed*

> **Continental beef breeds:** cattle breeds that originate in European countries other than England. They are late maturing breeds of cattle, with high growth rates and large size, and they finish at higher weights without laying down fat. Examples of continental breeds include Charolais, Limousin, Simmental and Belgian Blue.

Beef production – suckler herd

The suckler herd is a type of beef production system in which a suckler dam produces a calf every year and that calf stays with the cow and the feeding of the calf is carried out by the suckler dam. Because the calf is fed milk produced by the suckler dam, the calf has a greater live weight gain compared to some other systems of beef production. The ideal suckler cow has both dairy and continental beef genetics. To produce this type of cow a dairy farmer could cross a purebred dairy cow (Holstein-Friesian) with a continental beef bull (e.g. Limousin or Simmental). The crossbred heifers produced display hybrid vigour and have a number of advantages. Crossbred suckler dams have:

- Higher fertility
- Lower calf mortality
- Longer reproductive life, which lowers replacement rate
- Higher milk yields (trait inherited from the dairy dam), which leads to higher growth rate in the calf, resulting in a heavier calf at weaning
- A shorter calving interval
- A hardier calf.

Even though dairy genes are desirable in a suckler dam, a purebred Holstein-Friesian is unsuitable for suckling a single calf. A purebred Holstein-Friesian would produce too much milk for one calf, which would cause scour in the calf. In addition, the Holstein-Friesian would have poor conformation, which would result in a poor carcase grade on slaughter.

The genetic traits passed on from the continental bull (Limousin or Simmental) in this cross produce higher growth rates, good conformation, higher lean meat content on the carcase and a heavier carcase weight.

Mortality: death or loss of life.

Calving interval: the time that has elapsed between successive calvings.

23.16 *Limousin cattle*

23.17 *Simmental*

Summary

- Follicle stimulating hormone (FSH) promotes sperm production in males. Luteinising hormone (LH) stimulates testosterone production. Testosterone is responsible for the male sex characteristics and increases muscle and bone growth.
- Fertilisation occurs naturally in the Fallopian tube.
- When an egg is fertilised by a sperm it becomes a zygote.
- In females, FSH stimulates the development of a follicle in the ovary.
- The follicle produces the hormone oestrogen, which stimulates the growth of the endometrium.
- LH stimulates ovulation.
- Progesterone has many functions including the continued growth of the endometrium and maintaining pregnancy if fertilisation occurs.
- The oestrous cycle is a recurring cycle during which a female mammal comes into heat, releases an egg which is available for fertilisation by sperm from the male.
- Duration of oestrus is the length of time during the oestrous cycle in which the female is in heat and an egg is available for fertilisation.
- Polyoestrous is when animals have several oestrous cycles throughout the year.

- Seasonally polyoestrous is when an animal has several oestrous cycles during a specific time of year.
- Sheep are short-day breeders as they naturally come into heat during autumn when daylight decreases.
- Artificial insemination (AI) is commonly used in the dairy herd to improve the genetic merit of the herd.
- Sexed semen can be used to increase the chances of a heifer calf being born.
- A stock bull may be kept for mopping up the herd.
- Embryo transplantation is used to produce large numbers of genetically superior animals which would not be possible by natural means.
- Holstein-Friesians are crossed with Jerseys in the dairy herd to produce offspring that display hybrid vigour and have increased productivity.
- In pig production the Large White is crossed with the Landrace to produce offspring with fast growth rates, good food conversion ratio and high prolificacy.
- In sheep production Suffolk and Texel are used as terminal sires to produce lambs for slaughter.
- The suckler cow in beef production can be produced by crossing a purebred dairy breed (Holstein-Friesian) with a continental beef bull. These crossbred cows have higher fertility, higher milk yields and longer reproductive lives.

 PowerPoint Summary

QUESTIONS

1. Which of the following hormones is responsible for the production of sperm in male animals?

   (a) Testosterone

   (b) Luteinising hormone

   (c) Follicle stimulating hormone

   (d) Oestrogen

2. Which of the following hormones stimulates the development of the endometrium?

   (a) Luteinising hormone

   (b) Testosterone

   (c) Follicle stimulating hormone

   (d) Oestrogen

3. Which of the following hormones is responsible for ovulation?

   (a) Follicle stimulating hormone

   (b) Luteinising hormone

   (c) Oestrogen

   (d) Progesterone

4. Which hormone is responsible for maintaining gestation in farm animals?

   (a) Pro-oestrogen

   (b) Progesterone

   (c) Testosterone

   (d) FSH

5. What term is given to the recurring cycle during which a cow will ovulate?

   (a) Oestrus

   (b) Oestrous cycle

   (c) Menstrual cycle

   (d) Gestation

6. What is the length of the oestrous cycle in sheep?

   (a) 17 days

   (b) 18 days

   (c) 19 days

   (d) 20 days

7. The graph in Fig. 23.18 compares the milk production of two different purebred dairy breeds (A and B) and the crossbreed AB.

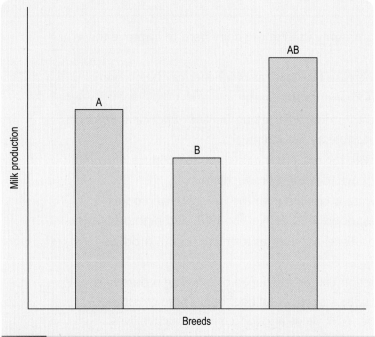

23.18 *Milk production of dairy breeds (A and B) and crossbreed (AB)*

What is the cause of the increased productivity shown in the crossbred animal AB?

(a) Nutrition   (c) Grassland

(b) Hybrid vigour   (d) Dominance

8. (a) Distinguish between the terms 'oestrus' and 'oestrous cycle'.

   (b) Explain the role of hormones in the oestrous cycle of a female animal.

9. (a) Distinguish between the terms 'polyoestrous' and 'seasonally polyoestrous'.

   (b) Name an animal that is seasonally polyoestrous.

   (c) Some animals are short-day breeders. Explain how day length plays a role in the onset of oestrus in these animals.

10. Outline **two** different methods of insemination for a farm animal of your choice.

11. Justify the use of artificial insemination in a dairy herd.

12. Explain the advantages of sexed semen over conventional semen for use on a dairy farm.

13. Describe how genetics plays an important role in the production of breeding stock in an animal production system that you have studied.

14. Describe how crossbreeding can be used to improve the productivity of a food-producing animal that you have studied.

Solutions   Weblinks

CHAPTER 24

Applied animal genetics

When you have completed this chapter you should be able to:
- Describe how genetic improvement and selection are brought about using:
  - Physical traits
  - Performance and progeny testing
  - Genotyping and genomic selection
  - Natural selection
  - Genetic engineering.

Genetic improvement

DNA is the genetic code for living organisms. DNA is present in every cell in an animal's body and it remains the same throughout the animal's life. Within breeds of animals there can be a large amount of genetic variation. Some animals within a breed will carry more favourable genes for a trait, e.g. carcase quality, while others will carry more undesirable genes for that trait. In all animal enterprises, farmers will aim to improve the genetic merit of their animals. To do this, scientists and breeders must identify animals that are of a high genetic merit, whether that is for producing meat or for breeding purposes. Farmers aim to improve the genetic merit of their animals by carefully selecting traits that they require, e.g. growth rate, carcase quality or percentage milk solids, and using sires that impart those traits in their breeding programmes. Genetic improvement takes time as it may take several generations to improve those traits. However, genetic improvement will increase both profitability and productivity of a farming enterprise.

> **Genetic variation:** the difference in DNA among members of a species.

Genetic improvement has several advantages:
- It influences the productivity of the animal over its entire lifetime
- Improvements can be built upon over several generations, thus increasing the overall genetic merit of the herd/flock
- Improvements can be made once genetic variation is included and inbreeding is avoided.

Physical traits

Physical traits or characteristics are features that are visible when you look at an animal. Farmers have selectively bred animals for centuries based on physical traits. Desirable physical traits are often easily identified. For example, Aberdeen Angus cattle are naturally polled (hornless). The gene for the polled condition is dominant over the gene for the presence of horns. When a naturally polled animal is crossed with a horned cattle breed, all the offspring will be polled. This is advantageous as offspring from an Aberdeen Angus do not require dehorning.

24.1 *Aberdeen Angus are naturally polled*

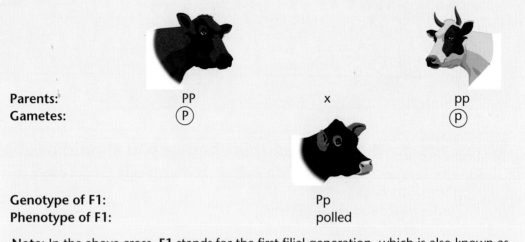

Parents: PP   x   pp

Gametes: (P)   (P)

Genotype of F1:   Pp

Phenotype of F1:   polled

Note: In the above cross, **F1** stands for the first filial generation, which is also known as the first-generation offspring.

24.2 *Inheritance of the polled condition in cattle*

DEFINITION

Selective breeding: the process by which humans breed plants or animals with desirable traits and concentrate those desirable traits in the offspring.
Line breeding: the production of desired characteristics in animals by inbreeding through several generations.

The inheritance of double muscling

The myostatin gene is found in all mammals and its function is to control muscle development. Natural mutations have produced variations of this gene where the gene is either 'switched off' or produces proteins that are less effective at controlling muscle growth and development. Belgian Blues have a mutation of this gene known as NT821, which causes greater muscular growth in the phenotype of the animal, which is commonly referred to as **double muscling**. This trait has been maintained in the Belgian Blue through **line breeding**. Farmers have selected for this physical trait as double muscled breeds produce very lean meat and have a higher meat yield with lower levels of intramuscular fat compared to other beef breeds that are not double muscled. However, there are several well-documented undesirable risks with this breed. They have smaller internal organs, such as heart and lungs. Therefore, the animals have increased risk of respiratory diseases and fatigue easily with exercise. Because of the additional muscle growth and a narrow birth canal, calving difficulties are a common problem with Belgian Blue breeds and other animals that have the double muscled trait. A Caesarean section is commonly carried out to deliver the calf. There is an additional workload and cost as well as welfare issues with this breed.

24.3 *Belgian Blue bull with the additional muscle growth prominent on the rear of the animal*

Some physical traits are undesirable. To prevent these traits from being passed onto the next generation, farmers will cull breeding stock that have these undesirable traits in their phenotype. In sheep enterprises, farmers will cull ewes and rams that have an overshot or undershot jaw. Jaw abnormalities affect the grazing ability of the sheep, which in turn will affect live weight gain and the ability of the ewe or ram to put on

Cull: remove from the herd or flock by slaughter.

condition. In addition, if the ewe were in lamb, the jaw abnormality may make her more susceptible to pregnancy toxaemia or twin lamb disease due to insufficient intake of fodder. In a dairy enterprise udder and teat conformation are extremely important. A strong median suspensory ligament and strong ligament attachment to the pelvic bone and abdomen are essential to support the udder and allow the udder to expand, since a modern dairy cow's udder may weigh up to 50 kg. An

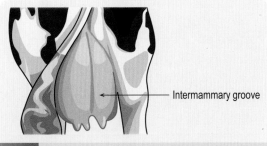

Intermammary groove

| 24.4 | *The intermammary groove marks the position of the median suspensory ligament. In this diagram the median suspensory ligament is prominent, indicating good udder conformation* |

undesirable udder is a pendulous udder, in which the udder does not have adequate support, causing it to swing forward and the rear quarters to hang in a position lower than the front quarter. Cows with pendulous udders are difficult to milk; the lack of internal support for the udder means that the udder hangs lower and interferes with the movement of the animal. In addition, the udder is more prone to injury. Heifers from a cow with a pendulous udder should not be kept as replacements.

Performance and progeny testing

The Irish Cattle Breeding Federation (ICBF) carries out performance testing of bulls. Their aim is to identify genetically superior bulls. During the test period the bulls are all provided with the same type of feed and housing conditions. Their growth potential is assessed by measuring their weight gain, visual muscle and skeletal measurements, ultrasound of fat and muscle and feed intake.

| 24.5 | *ICBF logo* |

In **performance testing** the growth rate and feed conversion ratio (FCR; weight gained in relation to the feed consumed) of a bull is tested and compared to those of other bulls. However, performance testing is not as reliable as **progeny testing**. A bull cannot be assessed for milk production, but the performance of his female offspring can. The ICBF beef bull progeny performance test station is in Tully, Co. Kildare. Each year the test centre purchases around 500 young animals that are the progeny of test bulls. The progeny are provided with the same feed and housing conditions. Results from the testing of these progeny is used to further establish the genetic potential of the particular bulls. Measurements recorded include the progeny's FCR, visual muscle and skeletal measurements, docility and functionality. Once the animals are slaughtered, carcase data are also assessed. The results allow a genetic profile to be developed for all the test bulls in the form of a €uro-Star Index. Bulls with €uro-Star Index values are then used by farmers in breeding programmes. There is a similar system used by the ICBF to identify genetically superior bulls in the dairy sector. Dairy bulls are given an Economic Breeding Index (EBI) (see page 380).

Functionality is a general term used to describe an animal's feet and legs, locomotion and ability to function on a farm. In dairy, functionality takes into account udder suspension, teat size and teat placement.

> DEFINITION
>
> **Performance testing:** the evaluation of a bull's performance by comparing its weight gain and feed conversion ratio with other bulls kept under similar feed and housing conditions.
>
> **Progeny testing:** the evaluation of the performance of a bull's offspring compared to other bull's offspring under similar feed and housing conditions.

Genotyping and genomic selection

Genotyping

Genomics is the study of an animal's DNA. Scientists use genomics to study genes that control important traits such as milk production and carcase weight in animals. To do this, they must have an accurate picture of the animal's genome as every animal's DNA is specific to itself (except for identical twins). **Genotyping** is a technique used by scientists to identify differences in the genetic make-up of an animal's DNA. The animal's DNA is first extracted and isolated from a sample of blood, semen, tissue or hair follicles. The sample that the DNA is extracted from should be uncontaminated and of sufficient quality and quantity. Genotyping the whole of the animal's DNA would be expensive, so scientists have identified positions on the DNA of cattle, known as SNPs (pronounced as 'snips') where variations in the genetic code are related to important traits such as carcase weight, fertility and milk yield.

> DEFINITION
>
> **Genotyping** is the process of identifying differences in the genetic make-up (genotype) of an animal by examining the animal's DNA sequence and comparing it to the sequence of other animals of the same species or to a reference sequence.

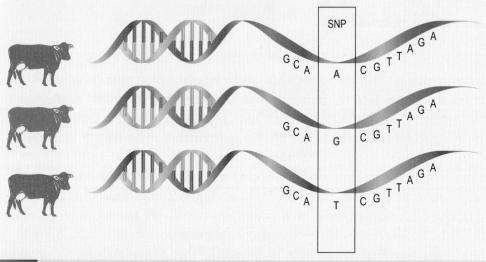

24.6 *SNPs are positions in the genome where one animal has one nucleotide (e.g. an A) and other animals have a different nucleotide (e.g. a G or a T or a C).*

Some of the advantages of genotyping include:
- To check the parentage of an animal
- Traceability of meat
- To identify stolen stock
- Breed transparency: can identify whether an animal is a purebred beef breed or a crossbred beef breed

- Transparency of meat from an animal: can identify whether the meat has come from a purebred beef breed or a crossbred beef animal
- To identify animals that are carriers of lethal genes or congenital defects
- To identify whether an animal contains a variant of the myostatin gene, which will result in the animal being double muscled and flag the possibility of calving difficulties in the future
- To predict the potential genetic merit of an animal from a very young age (a week-old calf)
- To allow for tailor-made management of individual animals. If an animal is known to possess genes for potentially a faster growth rate, then it can be managed differently from an animal that does not have this potential.

By far the most valuable use of genotyping is in the development of tailored breeding programmes for the beef, dairy and sheep enterprises. This will allow farmers to improve the genetic merit of their animals and address issues such as fertility within their herd while avoiding inbreeding.

Genomic selection

Traditional methods of breeding in the past relied on farmers crossing their best sire with their dams in the hope of producing offspring of very good genetic merit. All animals receive half of their DNA from the sire and half of their DNA from the dam. Breeders would then calculate the potential genetic merit of the animal as being the average of its two parents. However, in reality the inheritance of DNA from the sire and dam is a random process, so this can lead to great variation in the genetic merit of the progeny. As a result in the beef and dairy industry, the identification of genetically superior bulls took many years as time was required to build up sufficient information from the progeny testing of the bull's offspring. With the use of genomic selection it is now possible to identify potential genetically superior animals at a very young age by examining the DNA of the young animal and then comparing it with the genotypes of proven animals.

Genomic selection is a breeding technology that was first introduced into Ireland in 2009. The DNA of nearly a thousand AI bulls was genotyped. The objective was to accurately identify how sections of an animal's DNA affected a range of important animal traits, such as growth rate, fertility and milk production. The genotypes of these animals were then compared to their performance records. In 2015 the beef genomic scheme was launched, and a large population of beef cattle were genotyped. Having the genotypes and performance records of a large number of beef animals (both male and female) allowed for greater accuracy of genomic predictions for younger calves. The aim was to identify the optimal DNA profile (genotype) for a range of traits in Irish beef cattle and increase the accuracy of genomic selection in identifying genetically superior replacement heifers for the beef sector.

Genomic selection paves the way for precision breeding of cattle. Cattle have approximately three billion pieces of DNA contained in every cell. Currently tens of thousands of these DNA pieces are examined when an animal's DNA is genotyped. It is possible and probable that in the future all three billion pieces of DNA will be genotyped, and this will lead to more accurate genomic predictions. This will allow for more accurate breeding of animals, which will avoid the mating of animals that carry undesirable recessive genes or deleterious genes, and maximise hybrid vigour.

Natural selection

As described previously, natural selection is the process whereby organisms better adapted to their environment tend to survive and produce more offspring. The basis of natural selection is that variation exists within all populations of organisms, produced by

Lethal genes: genes that can cause the death of an organism.

A congenital defect is also known as a birth defect.

A proven animal is an animal that has been identified as a genetically superior animal based on both performance and progeny testing.

Deleterious gene: a gene that causes harm or damage.

random mutations in the genome. In the case of domesticated animals such as cattle and sheep, some of these variations are more valuable than others. In the past, inbreeding of animals was used as a method of fixing desirable genetic traits such as high milk yields in purebred dairy cattle (e.g. Holsteins) and creating uniformity among the offspring. The disadvantage of inbreeding is that it also concentrates undesirable traits, which are carried by most animals. However, the genes for these traits tend to be recessive and are hidden by the presence of the dominant, normal gene. Closely related animals can have similar genes and inbreeding can increase the inheritance of similar genes, leading to homozygous genotypes (e.g. aa) as shown in Fig. 24.7.

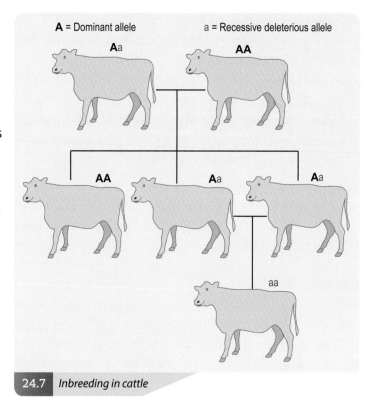

24.7 *Inbreeding in cattle*

These undesirable recessive genes are sometimes called deleterious genes, since they can be harmful or unwanted. This results in an animal that is 'less fit' for survival. Some cases of homozygous recessive genes can be fatal, leading to the failed conception in a cow. The inheritance of two copies of a lethal gene causes the death of the organism. Lethal genes are self-limiting: organisms that inherit two copies of the gene cannot pass them onto their offspring, thereby removing these genes from the population. Therefore, as these animals have inherited variations that do not enable them to adapt better to their environment they are removed by natural selection. Brachyspina is a lethal recessive gene that is carried by a small proportion of Irish Holstein-Friesian animals. If a carrier female were crossed with a bull that was also a carrier of the lethal gene, there would be a 25% chance (1 in 4) that the calf would inherit both recessive genes for Brachyspina. The lethal gene causes embryonic death, stillbirth and other deformities. Lethal genes like this one can be identified by genotyping.

Natural selection is a process that occurs very often in nature. There is one example of natural selection in Irish agriculture that is a cause for concern: the development of antimicrobial resistance. According to the World Health Organization (WHO), antimicrobial resistance occurs when microorganisms such as bacteria, viruses, fungi and parasites change in ways that make the medications used to cure infections they cause ineffective. Microorganisms that are resistant to most medications are commonly referred to as 'superbugs'.

DEFINITION

Antimicrobial resistance: the ability of a microorganism to grow in the presence of a drug, e.g. an antibiotic, that would normally kill it or limit its growth.

Antimicrobial resistance has been caused by the inappropriate use of medicines, which has facilitated its development and spread. The development of antimicrobial resistance is due to variations in the genetic code of microorganisms. As previously stated, some of these genetic variations, which were produced by mutations, has given the microorganisms an improved chance of survival in the presence of the antibiotics and other antimicrobial drugs.

In order to stem the rise in antimicrobial resistance, farmers are working to reduce the incidence of infection and disease by:

- Maintaining good hygiene levels on the farm
- Providing good-quality housing with effective ventilation
- Having a vaccination programme
- Maintaining biosecurity (see page 486 for how farmers do this)
- Administering antibiotics appropriately, and only when needed.

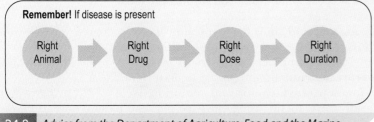

Remember! If disease is present

Right Animal → Right Drug → Right Dose → Right Duration

24.8 *Advice from the Department of Agriculture, Food and the Marine on the appropriate use of antimicrobial medications for the treatment of animals*

Food security: when a population has access to sufficient quantity of affordable and nutritious food.

Antimicrobial resistance is a global threat that has consequences for human health, animal health, food security and the environment. In Ireland there is a National Action Plan on antimicrobial resistance, and one of its main aims is to reduce the overall dependence on the use of antibiotics in agriculture.

Exercise 24.1

Read the following article from the website of the Department of Agriculture, Food and the Marine and answer the questions at the end.

Antibiotics – A farmer's viewpoint

Mike Magan, Dairy Farmer

"I would ask farmers to think carefully before using an antibiotic. Reflect before you inject."

Mike Magan farms 200 dairy cows in Kilashee, Co. Longford in partnership with his son. Mike is Chairman of Animal Health Ireland and is very enthusiastic about working to develop the Irish agricultural industry. He is particularly interested in raising awareness of the issue of antimicrobial resistance (AMR).

Demonstrating this commitment to tackling the issue of AMR head on, Mike is currently trialling a new drying off process on his farm which aims to see if the desired result can be achieved, without antibiotics.

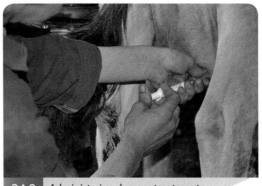

24.9 *Administering dry cow treatment*

So Mike, how does this new process work?
"The drying off of cows is one of those routine processes that has to be done on all dairy farms and the use of both a long acting antibiotic and a sealing agent is the standard procedure for many farmers. I decided to see if this two-pronged approach was really necessary or whether, with careful application, using just a sealing agent would produce the same result.

So two seasons ago we changed the policy on our farm to using the 'antibiotic + seal' procedure only on cows above a certain SCC[1] threshold. That year we had a cut off point of 150,000 SCC at the last milk recording before drying and no reading higher than that during the year. That meant that we had roughly half the cows in each treatment group, i.e. half treated with dry cow tube and seal and half with seal only. The results were that we had no change – no cases of dry cow mastitis and no increase in SCC during the following lactation.

Last year we repeated the policy but changed the threshold figures to 200,000 cells/mL and so had only 20% of the cows in the 'double treatment' category. The results were as before. No dry cow cases and the same profile of SCC throughout the year. The only high SCC cows were the ones that were a problem the year before, and had been on the 'antibiotic + seal' regime anyway.

When the cows calve they get a coloured tape put on their tail, red tape for cows that get the dry cow antibiotic treatment and green tape for cows that got the seal only. I need not tell you how less worrying it is dealing with the milk withdrawal of 'green' cows as compared to 'red' cows!"

It sounds like your experiment has been a success, what would you say was the most important factor in making it so?
"I think it is very important that we take our time and apply the teat seal properly. Carrying out the job as hygienically as possible is what makes the most difference to my mind. In order to best ensure this, we limit the number of cows to dry off on any given day so that we can give the job the care and attention necessary to do it right. We mark the cows clearly as we do them and we separate them to avoid confusion. We use medicated wipes to clean the teat, especially the teat end, using one wipe per teat. I also dip the teat in a 10% iodine solution before they are let out to stand for a while before they lie down.

As well as ensuring the process is carried out as cleanly as possible, our record keeping has also been very important in correctly identifying which of our cows are suitable to receive just the seal without the antibiotic."

You are clearly very committed to doing what you can in terms of protecting against antibiotic resistance, have you personal experience as regards protecting antibiotics for use in human health?
"Yes I do. I lost my son 11 years ago to a brain tumour. He was 12 years old when he was diagnosed, only 16 when he died and he spent a lot of that time in hospital. He had to have a few major operations and he was given antibiotics then to keep down infection. I was always so grateful that those antibiotics worked. It really brought home to me the importance of the latest antibiotic as the last line of defence against a persistent infection. It made me realise the duty we all have to protect antibiotics as an important public health resource. It's a duty I wouldn't have taken too seriously before but having seen at first-hand how vital they are, I decided that if there was any small part I could play, then I would do it."

What message would you like to give farmers about using antibiotics and antimicrobial resistance?
"I would like to send two messages to farmers in relation to their use of antibiotics. Firstly, stop and think. Reflect before you inject. We all want healthy animals but do you really need an antibiotic to achieve that? Talk to your vet and other farmers about what they are doing and their experience and see if a different approach could work for you. I am not saying 'don't ever use antibiotics' and I'm not trying to imply that farmers are not fully responsible in this area but I think it is important that we try and do our best to reserve using antibiotics for animals that really need it.

Secondly, I think it's very important that where a farmer is given a prescription for an antibiotic for an animal that the full course of antibiotic is completed. I believe it is as important to complete the course in the case of a veterinary antibiotic as it is on the human side of things. By not completing the course of treatment you are giving the bugs a fighting chance to develop resistance against that medicine and one day it could be your friend or family member who needs that same antibiotic to work."

[1] Somatic cell count (SCC) is the number of somatic cells found in a millilitre of milk. Somatic cells (or "body" cells) are a mixture of milk-producing cells shed from the udder tissue (about 2%) and cells from the immune system (the other 98%), known as leukocytes (also called white blood cells). Somatic cell counts are useful in identifying intramammary infection in an individual cow or herd.

Department of Agriculture, Food and the Marine

Questions

1. What is the most frequently used procedure for drying off cows and why is this carried out?

2. Write a suitable hypothesis or prediction for the investigation that Mike Magan is carrying out.

3. In your opinion, is Mike Magan conducting a controlled experiment? Give reasons for your answer and reference any variables that you can identify in the article.

4. Were the cows picked for the 'antibiotic and seal' treatment chosen at random? Explain your answer.

5. What quantitative data were recorded during this investigation?

6. Using the internet or some other source of information, find out the meaning of the term 'milk withdrawal period'. Outline reasons why it is a mandatory requirement for farmers to observe withdrawal periods after an animal has been treated with an antibiotic.

7. Research why a creamery will not take milk with antibiotic residues in it.

8. What advantage did the cows that were treated with the seal only have over the animals that were treated with the antibiotic and seal treatment?

9. Identify some of the precautions that Mike took when applying the seal only treatment and explain why he took each of these precautions.

10. Outline the results of Mike's experiment. What modifications did he make to his investigation in the second year? Suggest a reason for these modifications.

11. Why is Mike so passionate about raising awareness about the overuse and misuse of antibiotics in agriculture?

12. One of the last comments Mike makes regarding the use of antibiotics is that if an animal is prescribed antibiotics then it is necessary to ensure that the full course of antibiotics is completed. Why is this necessary?

13. What other sectors of Irish agriculture might use medicated feeds or water as a preventative measure against disease? Why is there concern over this practice and what alternatives are available to farmers as a way of preventing disease?

Genetic engineering
Cloning

DEFINITION

Cloning produces genetically identical individuals.

> A **somatic cell** is any cell of a living organism other than a reproductive cell (egg or sperm).

In horticulture, cuttings, grafting and micropropagation all produce genetically identical plants. Cloning has produced genetically identical animals. In 1996 the first animal to be cloned from an adult mammal was produced: a sheep named Dolly. Dolly was produced when the nucleus from a somatic cell was taken from a donor sheep and then inserted into an egg cell from which the nucleus had been removed. An electric current was applied to cause the egg cell to start dividing. The dividing blastocyst was then implanted into another surrogate sheep.

> A **blastocyst** is an embryo 5–6 days after fertilisation.

24.10 *Dolly the sheep*

The main advantage of cloning is that it makes it possible to produce identical copies of genetically superior animals. The disadvantages of cloning include:

- High failure rate in cloning animals
- Cloning reduces biodiversity
- Cloning results in premature ageing and early death
- Ethical issues surrounding the use of cloning.

Genetic modification

Genetic modification (GM): altering an organism's DNA for the purpose of improvement or to correct a defect in the organism.

Biodiversity: the variety of plant and animal life in the world.

Culture is an artificial substance (medium) containing nutrients and used to maintain the growth of cells.

Genetic modification (GM) can introduce new genes into the genomes of livestock more rapidly than the conventional method of crossbreeding.

GM animals and their products are not widely used. Currently there is only one approved product in the world from a genetically modified animal. ATryn™ is a pharmaceutical drug that is used to prevent blood clotting and is produced in the milk of GM goats. A human gene for the production of a protein molecule that prevents blood clotting is inserted into their genome when the goats are embryos. The European Commission approved the use of this GM product in 2006.

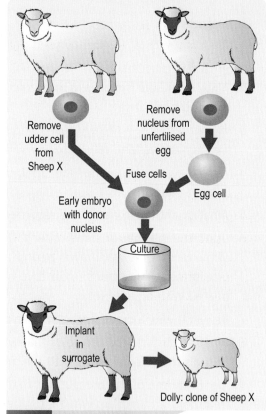

24.11   *Cloning of Dolly*

Labels in figure: Remove udder cell from Sheep X; Remove nucleus from unfertilised egg; Fuse cells; Egg cell; Early embryo with donor nucleus; Culture; Implant in surrogate; Dolly: clone of Sheep X

24.12   *A goat*

Some of the advantages of GM animals include:

- Improved animal production traits, e.g. milk yields, milk composition, carcase quality
- New animal products
- Increased prolificacy
- Improved feed conversion efficiency (FCE)
- Improved growth rate
- Increased disease resistance
- Beneficial impact on human health (e.g. pigs have been genetically modified to contain higher levels of omega 3 fatty acids, the consumption of which may aid in the prevention of coronary heart disease).

However, there are many welfare and ethical issues arising from the genetic modification of animals. There is a risk that the introduced gene might be over expressed, which could have consequences for the health of the GM animal. For example, pigs that have been modified to produce more growth hormone have developed arthritis, altered skeletal growth, gastric ulcers and renal disease.

Genome editing/gene editing

Gene editing enables scientists to add, delete or replace letters in the genome, thereby changing the sequence of the genetic code. CRISPR and TALEN are the two most commonly used gene editing tools. They act like molecular scissors, cutting the DNA at precise locations and allowing scientists to make permanent changes to genes in living cells. The procedure can be carried out just after fertilisation. Scientists in the Roslin Institute in Edinburgh have used gene editing to make pigs resistant to a disease caused by the porcine reproduction and respiratory syndrome virus (PRRSV; see page 484).

This disease causes pig deaths and is very costly. The scientists at the Roslin Institute identified the pig gene that encodes for a receptor on the surface of cells that allows the virus to enter into the cell. The scientists edited the gene sequence, which stopped the production of the sequence. These pigs did not produce the receptor, and as a result the virus could not enter into the cells, thereby making these pigs resistant to the virus.

24.13   *A pig*

Receptor: a protein molecule that chemicals (e.g. hormones) can bind to.

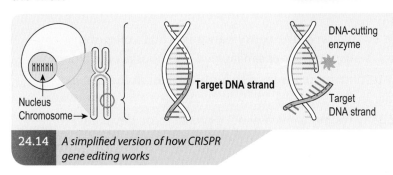

24.14   *A simplified version of how CRISPR gene editing works*

This type of genetic modification involves only small changes to the DNA. Gene editing has proved successful in removing horns in Holstein calves. Dehorning continues to be a welfare concern, due to the stress and pain it can cause an animal. Scientists have identified the genetic sequence that codes for the polled condition in cattle. Scientists edited the gene and the end result was polled Holstein calves that did not require dehorning. It might be suggested that the same result could be achieved by selective breeding. This is true; however, to make this a permanent fixture in the genome of the Holstein breed would require time over several generations, and in the process it could also incorporate other unintended genes into the genetic make-up of the Holstein breed as well as compromise genetic gain in other traits.

Some of the advantages of gene editing include:

- Increased disease resistance
- Ability to dehorn cattle genetically, which results in improved animal welfare
- Ability to castrate male pigs genetically so that the pigs never reach puberty, thus avoiding boar taint in meat
- Prevention of genetic diseases by correcting genetic errors
- Introduction of genetic variability, which is fundamental to genetic gain.

Some of the disadvantages of gene editing include:

- Ethics of editing germline DNA in eggs and sperm, as these changes can be passed on to future offspring
- High cost to implement in a breeding programme.

Germline: inherited material that comes from the eggs or sperm and is passed on to the next generation.

Summary

- Genetic improvement has several advantages:
  - It influences the productivity of the animal over its entire lifetime
  - Improvements can be built upon over several generations
  - Improvements can be made once genetic variation is included and inbreeding is avoided.
- Aberdeen Angus are naturally polled animals that farmers have selected for this physical trait.
- Double muscling is another example of a physical trait that farmers have selected for, as animals with this trait have increased muscle growth.
- The selection for the double muscle trait has some undesirable risks, including calving difficulties.
- Undesirable physical traits in animals include: jaw abnormalities in sheep and pendulous udder in dairy cows. Animals that have these undesirable traits should be culled and should not be used to produce replacement animals.
- Performance testing is the evaluation of the bull's performance by comparing its weight gain and feed conversion ratio with other bulls kept under similar feed and housing conditions.
- Progeny testing is the evaluation of the performance of a bull's offspring compared to other bull's offspring under similar feed and housing conditions.
- Results from progeny testing in bulls is used to further establish the genetic potential of a particular bull.
- Performance and progeny testing allow a genetic profile to be developed for bulls called the €uro-Star Index.
- Genomics is the study of animals' DNA.
- Genotyping is a technique used by scientists to identify differences in the genetic make-up of an animal's DNA.
- Scientists have identified positions on the DNA of cattle, known as SNPs, where variations in the genetic code are related to important traits such as carcase weight, fertility and milk yield.
- Some of the advantages of genotyping include: traceability of meat, identification of animals that are carriers of lethal genes, and the prediction of the potential genetic merit of an animal at a very young age.
- Genomic selection can identify potentially genetically superior animals at a very young age by examining the DNA of the young animal and then comparing it with the genotypes of proven animals.
- Genomic selection will allow for more accurate breeding of animals, which will avoid the mating of animals that carry undesirable recessive genes.
- The inheritance of two copies of a lethal gene is an example of natural selection. The genes make the animal less fit for survival. As a result, the animal does not produce any offspring, thus removing this gene from the population.
- The development of antimicrobial resistance in microorganisms is an example of natural selection. Some microorganisms are resistant to antimicrobial drugs as they have variations in their DNA that allow them to survive in the presence of the drugs.
- Antimicrobial resistance is a global threat that has consequences for human health, animal health, food security and the environment.
- Cloning produces genetically identical individuals.

- Gene editing allows scientists to add, delete or replace a base in the genome, thereby changing the sequence of the genetic code.
- Gene editing has been used to produce pigs that are resistant to PRRSV disease and to dehorn cattle.

📑 **PowerPoint Summary**

QUESTIONS

1. Progeny testing is the:
    (a) Evaluation of the bull's performance compared to other bulls kept under the same conditions
    (b) Evaluation of the bull and his offspring compared to other bulls and offspring kept under the same conditions
    (c) Evaluation of a bull's offspring compared to other bull's offspring kept under the same conditions
    (d) Determination of the genotype of the bull's progeny.

2. Progeny testing involves recording measurements of the progeny's:
    (a) Food conversion ratio
    (b) Docility
    (c) Functionality
    (d) All of the above.

3. Genomics is the study of an animal's:
    (a) RNA
    (b) DNA.

4. Genotyping is a technique that is used to:
    (a) Identify differences in the genetic make-up of an animal's DNA
    (b) Identify similarities in the genetic make-up of an animal's DNA
    (c) Identify similarities in the phenotype of the animal's DNA
    (d) Identify the role the environment plays in the genotype of the animal.

5. Genomic selection allows for the:
    (a) Possibility of identifying potentially superior bulls at a young age
    (b) Tailor-made breeding programmes
    (c) Identification of potentially superior replacement heifers
    (d) All of the above.

6. In a breeding programme a proven animal is one that has been identified:
    (a) Based on performance records only
    (b) Based on progeny records only
    (c) Based on performance and progeny records
    (d) None of the above.

7. A gene that causes death or harm to an animal is called:
    (a) A lethal and desirable gene
    (b) A recessive and desirable gene
    (c) A dominant and desirable gene
    (d) A lethal and deleterious gene.

8. What is the name given to the process in which a characteristic of an animal is modified by inserting a single gene into the genome of the animal?
    (a) Selective breeding
    (b) Inbreeding
    (c) Genomic selection
    (d) Genetic engineering

9. Explain the meaning of the term 'genetic improvement'.

10. State two methods by which farmers can bring about genetic improvement in a production system.

11. Give one example of how farmers have brought about genetic improvement based on physical traits of animals.

12. Outline some of the benefits that genotyping can provide to an animal production system of your choice.

13. Outline how genotyping could benefit each of the following:

    (a) Breeding of replacement stock   (b) Welfare of an animal   (c) The consumer.

14. Explain how scientists can genetically modify an organism by editing a plant's or animal's genes.

15. Describe how genomic selection can be used to improve the productivity of an animal production system.

16. Explain why the development of antibiotic resistance is an example of natural selection.

17. Outline what measures are being put in place to tackle the growing problem of antimicrobial resistance.

18. Discuss the potential benefits of gene editing in animal production.

19. In July 2018, the European Court of Justice ruled that gene edited crops must be labelled as genetically modified organisms (GMOs). However, scientists argue that gene editing is different from the older controversial technique of genetic modification. Older techniques usually involved the introduction of genes from other organisms to produce transgenic organisms. These scientists stress that gene editing only edits DNA within a crop.

    (a) Comment on how the European ruling might affect further research in gene editing.

    (b) Evaluate the argument that the scientists make in favour of gene editing.

    (c) Carry out some independent research into the use of gene editing in animal production systems. Describe the argument that you would put forward in favour of or against the use of gene editing in animal production systems.

20. Distinguish between each of the following pairs of terms:

    (a) Inbreeding and selective breeding

    (b) Genomic selection and genotyping

    (c) Cloning and gene editing

    (d) Natural selection and selective breeding

    (e) Progeny testing and performance testing.

21. Write a brief note on any three of the following:

    (a) Antimicrobial resistance

    (b) Genomics

    (c) Genetically modified organisms

    (d) Genetic improvement by selection of physical traits.

Solutions   Weblinks

Dairy breeds, nutrition and management of a dairy herd

When you have completed this chapter you should be able to:

- Describe the characteristics of common breeds and crosses of dairy cattle
- Describe the management of the life cycle of a dairy cow:
  - From birth to calving down at 2 years in a dairy herd (replacement heifers)
  - As an animal in the dairy herd (production cycle of a dairy cow).
- Describe how breed variety, nutrition, housing and management determine the output and quality of produce from a dairy enterprise
- Discuss the dietary requirements of a dairy calf at different growth/development stages
- Describe the dietary requirements of a dairy cow at different stages in its production cycle
- Identify the potential hazards and risks associated with working with cattle and identify safe work practices and controls
- Identify the role of the Common Agricultural Policy (CAP) and other schemes in establishing standards for animal welfare
- Discuss management practices for:
  - Handling and housing farm animals
  - Optimal animal health and welfare
  - Slurry/farmyard manure
  - Delivering sustainable and environmentally friendly production systems
  - Ensuring quality, safe and traceable food for the consumer.

Dairy breeds and cross breeds

British Friesian

British Friesians were initially bred in the northern provinces of Holland. They became established in England and Scotland during the nineteenth century. The British Friesians are slightly smaller than Holsteins and have a bit more flesh. They are commonly called a dual-purpose breed because the heifers are used to produce milk and the male calves can be fattened for beef. Table 25.1 gives the average milk yield, percentage fat and percentage protein of a British Friesian. British Friesians tend to have a longer calving interval compared with other dairy breeds (average 401 days).

> **Dual-purpose breed:** cattle that can be used to produce both meat and milk.

Table 25.1 Average milk composition and yield of British Friesian		
Milk yield (litres)	% Fat	% Protein
6600	4.1	3.33

25.1 *British Friesian*

Holstein–Friesian

For many years the dairy industry in Ireland was dominated by one dairy breed, the Holstein–Friesian. It is the world's highest-milk-producing cow, producing large milk yields but with a low milk solids content. It is a larger animal than the British Friesian, with black and white markings. It originates from Holland and Germany (Friesland in Holland and Schleswig–Holstein in Germany), where it was bred for high milk production. Unfortunately, breeding for high milk production led directly to a decrease in the fertility and health of this breed. A mature cow can weigh 580 kg. The calving interval of the Holstein–Friesian can be greater than 400 days. The average milk yield for a Holstein–Friesian is around 8000 litres. Table 25.2 shows the average milk yield for a pedigree Holstein–Friesian.

25.2 *Holstein–Friesian*

Table 25.2 Average milk composition and yield of pedigree Holstein–Friesian		
Milk yield (litres)	% Fat	% Protein
8000	3.92	3.18

The purebred Holstein is also a very popular dairy breed in Ireland. Holstein are large cattle with a black and white coat pattern or a red and white coat pattern. They also can produce large volumes of milk, usually in the range of 7300 litres/year up to 8600 litres/year. Holsteins produce milk with an average percentage fat of 3.7% and percentage protein of 3.2%.

Ayrshire

The Ayrshire is a dairy breed that originates from Scotland. It has red and white markings. It is known for its easy calving and longevity, and its milk has a moderate butterfat content and high protein content.

25.3 *Ayrshire*

Table 25.3 Average milk composition and yield of Ayrshire		
Milk yield (litres)	% Fat	% Protein
7000	4.11	3.32

Jersey

The Jersey is a small breed that is light brown in colour and originates from the Channel Island of Jersey. This breed produces milk high in percentage fat and protein and a lower yield compared to the Holstein–Friesian. Since this animal is a much smaller breed of dairy cow (400–450 kg in weight) it has a lower maintenance cost. Other advantages include easy calving, high fertility, resistance to lameness, and longevity.

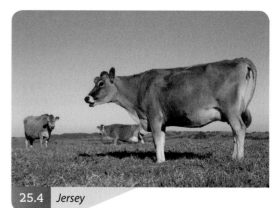
25.4 *Jersey*

Table 25.4 Average milk composition and yield of Jersey		
Milk yield (litres)	% Fat	% Protein
5500	5.41	3.82

Calf: a young animal from birth to 9 months old.

Heifer: a female that hasn't had a calf.

Cow: a female that has had a calf.

Bull: an uncastrated male.

Weanling: a young animal between 9 months and a year.

Yearling: a young animal from 12 months old.

Steer/bullock: a castrated male.

Longevity: long life.

Kerry Cow

The Kerry Cow is a rare breed of dairy cow that is native to Ireland. It is a small animal, weighing 350–450 kg. Its coat is black and it has white horns with black tips. It is an extremely hardy animal and is docile, with easy calving.

Table 25.5 Average milk composition and yield of Kerry Cow		
Milk yield (litres)	% Fat	% Protein
3000–7000	4	3.1

25.5 *Kerry Cow*

Montbéliarde

These cattle originate from the Montbéliarde region of France. Their coat is red and white. Their milk is particularly good for cheese-making, due to its high levels of casein (a type of protein in milk). A mature cow can weigh 600–700 kg. This breed is also known for its good fertility, longevity and low levels of mastitis.

Table 25.6 Average milk composition and yield of Montbéliarde		
Milk yield (litres)	% Fat	% Protein
7846	3.9	3.45

25.6 *Montbéliarde*

Rare breed: a breed of cattle, poultry or other livestock that has a very small breeding population.

Mastitis: an inflammation of one or more quarters of the udder caused by a bacterial infection.

Norwegian Red

The Norwegian Red is a medium-sized dairy breed native to Norway. A mature cow has an average weight of 550–650 kg. It is known for its easy calving, high fertility and health, especially its udder health. Norwegian Reds have a slightly lower milk yield when compared to the Holstein–Friesian.

Table 25.7 Average milk composition and yield of Norwegian Red		
Milk yield (litres)	% Fat	% Protein
7200	3.88	3.35

25.7 *Norwegian Red*

Jersey × Holstein–Friesian

Jersey × Holstein–Friesian cows are smaller, 50–60 kg lighter and tend to be dark brown in colour compared to the purebred Holstein–Friesian (see page 329).

Table 25.8 Average milk composition and yield of Jersey × Holstein–Friesian		
Milk yield (litres)	% Fat	% Protein
5272	4.77	3.88
Source of information: Moorepark Dairy Production Research Centre, Teagasc		

25.8 *Jersey × Holstein–Friesian*

The values for milk yields, percentage fat and percentage protein for each of the breeds described are averages.

Management of the life cycle of a replacement heifer from birth to 2 years

Most dairy calves are born in early spring, because the majority of dairy farmers are seasonal milk producers. As milk is the product in this industry, all calves that are born in a dairy herd are artificially reared.

Calf rearing needs to be well managed, as the mortality rates of calves can be high in the first few weeks of life. Not all calves will be kept on a dairy farm; the majority will be sold on to beef farmers to be reared for slaughter. A proportion of the heifer calves will be kept in a dairy farm as replacements for culled cows from the herd. This section deals with the management of those heifers from birth to when they produce a calf themselves at 2 years of age and join the milking herd.

Once the calf is born a farmer should ensure:

* All the mucus is cleared away from the mouth and the nose of the calf
* The cow licks the calf or the calf is rubbed vigorously with straw to stimulate its circulation
* The calf's navel is dipped in iodine to prevent infection (see page 475)
* The calf receives 2–3 litres of colostrum
* The calf is tagged for identification, traceability and bovine viral diarrhoea (BVD) testing.

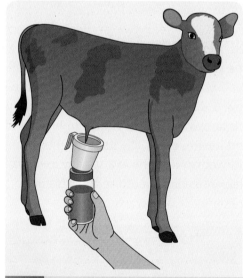

25.9 *A calf's navel being dipped in iodine*

Bovine viral diarrhoea (BVD) is a disease caused by a virus. There is a compulsory testing programme in Ireland to identify calves (both beef and dairy) born with the disease. There is an eradication scheme to eliminate this disease, so calves that test positive for the disease are culled (see page 482).

25.10 *A calf being ear tagged for traceability*

25.11 *A cow licking her calf*

Colostrum

After the birth of a calf, the cow produces colostrum (also known as beastings) for the first 4–5 days. Colostrum is different from normal milk in that it is much creamier and darker in colour and has a higher percentage of protein, fat and other solid non-fats (SNF). Most importantly, it is high in immunoglobulins (antibodies), and this is reflected in the high protein content of colostrum. Table 25.9 compares the composition of colostrum to normal milk.

Table 25.9 Comparison of the average composition of cow's colostrum with normal cow's milk		
Component	Colostrum	Normal milk
Fat (%)	6.7	3–4
Protein (%)	14.9	3.2
Lactose (%)	2.5	4.7

25.12   *A calf being bottle fed*

Feeding colostrum to newborn calves is essential and has a number of benefits.

- The colostrum has a high energy content.
- The calf is entirely dependent on antibodies in the colostrum for protection against disease.
- The colostrum is high in easily digestible nutrients.
- The colostrum has a high fat content, which has a laxative effect and helps to clean out the digestive system of the newborn calf.
- The colostrum warms up the calf.

> **Solid non-fats (SNF):** lactose, protein and minerals make up the solid non-fat component of milk.

At least 2.5–3 litres of colostrum should be fed to a newborn calf within the first 2 hours of its life. Calves are born without any immunity and vital antibodies present in the colostrum are required by the calf to give it resistance to disease. The ability of the calf to absorb these antibodies through the walls of its intestines is greatest within the first few hours of the calf's life. This ability decreases: after 24 hours, the calf is no longer able to absorb these antibodies. Calves that have an inadequate intake of colostrum are at a higher risk of becoming ill and dying. Colostrum is not acceptable by Irish creameries, and a farmer should continue to feed it to the calf until the cow starts to produce her normal milk. If for some reason the cow cannot produce colostrum, a calf can be given colostrum from another cow that has given birth. The calf should be fed colostrum for as long as it is available.

In dairy farms the calf is removed from the cow and is usually grouped with other calves of similar age. The calves are fed milk or milk replacer twice a day. The calves are fed their milk ration at the same times each day. Calves have very sensitive stomachs that are easily upset by irregular feeding times, and this can cause **scour** (see pages 477–478).

Calves are also given access to hay, concentrates and fresh water. Providing hay for the calf is important because this helps to develop the rumen. This is something that is regularly referred to as the 'scratch factor'.

> **Milk replacer** is a dried milk powder that is made up using warm water. It is cheaper to feed milk replacer to calves than whole milk.

Housing

Calves should be housed in well-ventilated, draught-free houses, since poor ventilation can lead to pneumonia in calves. Clean and dry bedding of straw should be used. Calves should have access to clean, fresh water.

Good hygiene should be maintained, especially with feeders and troughs, to prevent scour in the calves.

25.13 *Young calves are bucket fed*

25.14 *Older calves are fed outdoors*

25.15 *Calves out on grass, grazing*

Weaning

Calves are weaned off liquid milk and on to concentrates and grass at 6 weeks old. At this time, the calves should be eating 750 g of concentrates per day. Once out on grass, the feeding of concentrates should be continued until the calf has adjusted to their new diet. Calves are selective grazers and should be provided with high-quality grass. They should graze in the leader-follower system, grazing ahead of older cows. This system of grazing has two advantages: first, the calves have better live weight gain (LWG) and second, it helps to control the number of parasites (worms and flukes) to which they are exposed. By the time the calves are 6 months old they should be 30% of their mature body weight. Calves will continue to graze grass over the summer months and into autumn.

Overwintering

By the time the weanlings are housed for winter they are roughly 9 months old. In order to ensure that weanlings continue to put on good LWG, they should be fed good-quality silage with a dry matter digestibility (DMD) of 75%. If silage quality is poor, it should be supplemented with concentrates. Feeding kale and other catch crops over the winter months has been proven to increase LWG. Weanlings should be dosed for hoose (see page 479) and other worms before housing.

Year 2 replacement heifers

Dairy farmers regularly cull cows from their dairy herd. Dairy cows can be culled for a number of reasons:

- **Age:** as the cow gets older the percentage fat and protein content of her milk decreases
- **Health problems:** lameness, disease (TB, etc.)
- **Problems with milk production:** mastitis, high somatic cell count (SCC) poor milk yield, poor milk quality; many cows last only five or six lactations in a dairy herd
- **Problems with fertility:** decrease in fertility, difficulties with getting the animal back into calf and calving difficulties

CHAPTER 25 DAIRY BREEDS, NUTRITION AND MANAGEMENT OF A DAIRY HERD

- **Grading up the herd:** improving the genetic merit of the herd; replacing older cows with heifers of high genetic merit.

Rearing replacement heifers allows farmers to maintain their herd size and to expand their herd if desired. Teagasc recommends an optimum replacement rate of 17% for a dairy herd each year. If a farmer replaces a higher percentage of their herd, then milk production will drop significantly as younger animals do not produce their maximum milk yield until their fifth lactation. A heifer calving for the first time at 2 years of age will give a peak yield of 70–75% of a mature cow's peak yield. Having a high proportion of animals in their first or second lactation will result in a herd not reaching its full milk potential.

Selecting replacement heifers

Replacement heifers should:

- Be at a **body condition score (BCS)** of 3.25 at mating and reach a target weight of 300 kg (see below)
- Come from a dairy breed: Holstein–Friesian, Jersey, etc.
- Have good teeth and feet and a well-developed udder with four teats of uniform size
- Show good udder conformation
- Come from a mother with high percentage fat and protein in her milk
- Come from a mother that has good fertility, is easy calving and has a good temperament
- Be the offspring of a high economic breeding index (EBI) dairy sire (see page 380)
- Be free of disease.

Body condition score (BCS) is commonly referred to as the **ratio of lean meat to fat.** Scores range from 1 to 5. BCS should be assessed regularly so that a farmer can adjust feeding and management to ensure that the cow is at the correct BCS for each stage of her production cycle (drying off, precalving and start of breeding). Body condition scoring is used to assess an animal's body reserves (fat cover) along the loin (between the hip bone and first rib) and the tail head.

Figs 25.16, 25.17 and 25.18 illustrate the fat cover on dairy cows. Extremes of body condition should be avoided (BCS of 1 and 5). A BCS of **1** indicates an extremely thin animal and a body condition score of **5** indicates they are extremely fat. Management of a cow's body condition score is a critical component of all dairy enterprises.

Table 25.10 Body condition scores for dairy cows	
Stage of production cycle	**Average BSC for herd**
Drying off	3.0
Precalving	3.25
Start of breeding	2.9

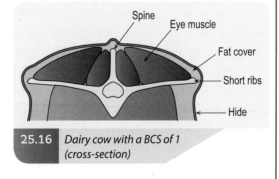
25.16 *Dairy cow with a BCS of 1 (cross-section)*

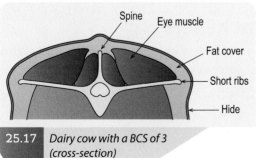
25.17 *Dairy cow with a BCS of 3 (cross-section)*

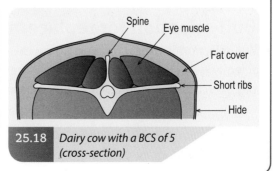
25.18 *Dairy cow with a BCS of 5 (cross-section)*

Farmers are encouraged to rear their own replacement heifers, since this maintains a closed herd and prevents the entrance of disease. This is known as biosecurity (see page 486). If replacement heifers are bought in, there is a greater risk of disease: such animals should be quarantined and vaccinated before they enter the herd. Rearing replacement heifers requires good management, since the aim is to breed a replacement heifer at 15 months so that she will calve down for the first time at 2 years old. It is uneconomical to feed a heifer for an extra year and calving for the first time at 3 years old. It is the recommended practice to calve heifers at 2 years old, as 3-year-old heifers have higher carbon emissions per kg of milk produced.

Target weights for heifers

Target weights are weight goals that a farmer wants an animal to reach at various stages in its growth and development so that the heifer will be able to produce her own calf at 2 years of age. Meeting target weights ensures that a farmer is operating an efficient system of production.

Heifers can be mated once they reach 60% of their mature body weight. Table 25.11 shows a set of target weights for a Holstein–Friesian. Note: bulling target is the weight a heifer needs to reach to ensure that she is oestrous cycling at mating. It is vital that a heifer is at this weight at 15 months in order for her to calve down at 2 years old.

Table 25.11 Target weights for the rearing of Holstein–Friesian replacement heifers			
Age	% Mature live weight	Weight (kg)	Feed
Birth (Feb)		41	Colostrum, milk
6 weeks (April)		63	Milk, hay, concentrates
3 months (May)	15	90	Grass, rotational grazing
6 months (Aug)	30	155	Grass, rotational grazing
9 months (Nov) (Housed)		200	75% DMD silage
12 months (Feb)	50	280	75% DMD silage
15 months (May)	60 (bulling target)	330	Grass, rotational grazing
21 months	80	490	75% DMD silage
24 months	90 (calving target)	550	Silage and concentrates

Target weights for mating and calving vary greatly between breeds and crossbreeds. In order for a heifer to reach the bulling target of 60% mature body weight, the heifer requires an LWG of 0.6–0.7 kg/day. In order to ensure that the heifer reaches this target weight, she needs to be provided with high-quality grass, rotationally grazed during the summer months, and good-quality silage ad lib over winter. Studies at Moorepark Dairy Research Centre found that heifers that overwintered on silage and kale had better LWG than those fed silage alone. The BCS at mating for a first-time heifer should be 3.25 to ensure that the heifer is cycling (coming into oestrus). If heifers are in poor condition at mating, with a BCS less than 3.0, these heifers will calve later and their milk yield will be significantly less. If feed quality is poor, concentrates should be fed to ensure that the heifers meet their target weights.

Bull selection for replacement heifers

Bull selection is critical for a first-time calving heifer. It is important that the dairy farmer selects an easy calving bull for a first-time calving heifer, otherwise the calf may be too big, which can lead to calving difficulties.

Quarantine: a place of isolation in which animals that have arrived from another farm are placed. It prevents any disease that the new animal might be carrying from spreading to the rest of the herd.

Uneconomical: describes something that wastes money.

Ad lib: short for *ad libitum*, which means in farming terms that animals eat as much and as often as they want.

Replacement heifers should be mated to high EBI sires. In the majority of cases, this is done using artificial insemination (AI) unless the farmer has a high EBI stock bull. High EBI sires improve the genetic merit of the herd and their daughters will provide high EBI replacement heifers for the future.

Any cows or heifers not in calf towards the end of the breeding season can be put with the stock bull.

The production cycle of a dairy cow

Factors that determine output and quality of produce from a dairy enterprise

The majority of milk production in Ireland is manufacturing milk (used to produce milk powders and products other than milk for drinking). Farmers producing milk for this sector operate a spring calving system, calving in mid-February (see Fig. 25.19). This is a more cost-effective system, since farmers get maximum utilisation out of their grassland. For this reason, the majority of milk production in Ireland is seasonal, with the bulk being produced over the spring and summer months. The gestation period for a dairy cow is 283 days, or 9.5 months. The length of the oestrous cycle in a cow is 21 days. The average duration of oestrus (when the cow is in standing heat) is 18–24 hours. The calving interval should be maintained at 365 to 370 days to be economical and to ensure that the herd calves down at the same time each year. This is important for seasonal milk producers, since they aim to make full use of the grazing season over the summer months.

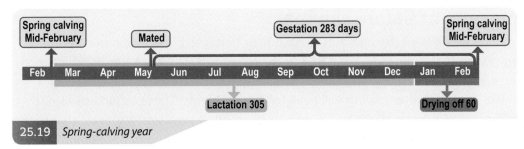

25.19 *Spring-calving year*

Key information on cattle:
Length of oestrous cycle: 21 days
Duration of oestrus (standing heat): 18–24 hours
Gestation period: 283 days (9.5 months)
Lactation period: 305 days
Dried off: 60 days
Calving interval: 365 days ideally

Lactation period: the length of time (days) following birth that a cow produces milk.

Breeds for output and quantity

The breeds of dairy cows used in Ireland has already been discussed at the start of this chapter. The quantity and composition of the milk produced by a dairy cow is determined by its breed. However, you will also have great variation in the quantity and composition of milk within the breed. For this reason, Teagasc and the Irish Cattle Breeding Federation (ICBF) have developed EBI and genotyping of animals to help identify genetically superior animals (see Chapter 24).

Dairy farmers regardless of the enterprise (liquid or manufacturing milk) should breed for:
- Milk solid content of the milk, as farmers are paid on the basis of fat and protein in the milk
- Fertility and survival traits. The focus on fertility traits and survival is to ensure that the farmer can breed their own replacement daughters. To achieve this they should use high EBI bulls in their breeding programme.

The most popular cattle breed used by Irish dairy farmers are Holsteins and Holstein–Friesians. Holstein–Friesian × Jersey crossbreeds are popular with some farmers. However, many farmers are still cautious of using Jersey bulls in their breeding programme as Jersey bull calves have little value for beef production.

Nutritional management of a dairy herd

Dairy farming in Ireland is a grass-based system, and the advantages of this system are explained on page 383. The diet of a dairy cow changes throughout her production cycle based on the availability of grass and the cow's energy requirements. Energy is the most important component in a dairy cow's diet. If the diet is low in energy, this will result in low milk yields and low milk protein. The nutritional requirements of a spring-calving herd are covered under the different stages of the cow's production cycle (calving, early lactation, mid- and late lactation). Dairy farming requires a high level of management. For this reason, dairy farmers are normally full-time farmers. The management of the dairy herd will also change over the course of the production cycle of the dairy herd.

Management before calving

In a spring-calving herd, farmers aim to have their herd calving down in mid-February. Before calving, a cow should have a **BCS** in the range of **3.0–3.25**. A low BCS before calving can decrease the cow's lactation yield. According to research by Teagasc, cows with poor BCS after calving will have fertility problems. These include cows not resuming oestrous cycles after calving, poorer conception rates and a greater chance of death of the embryo. Cows with a BCS greater than 3.5 are at risk of developing milk fever (see page 470), calving difficulties and ketosis.

Ketosis is a disorder in cattle in which an energy deficiency is caused by a high energy output (e.g. milk production) and a low energy intake (e.g. feeding).

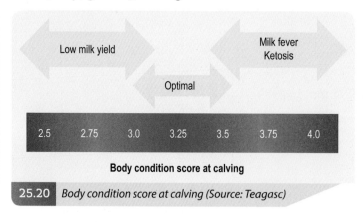

25.20 *Body condition score at calving (Source: Teagasc)*

Calving jack: a device used to assist the birth of a calf.

Records of when the cow was served by the bull or AI dates will help in identifying those cows that are close to calving. Before calving, a farmer should:
- Have used an easy-calving bull on heifers to prevent calving difficulties
- Isolate the cow from the rest of the herd
- Place the cow in a clean, dry calving pen or shed that contains handling facilities
- Have an experienced person on hand, who can inspect the cow regularly and identify problems if they arise
- Ensure that a calving jack, calving ropes and gloves are on hand in case the cow requires assistance.

25.21 A calving jack being used to assist a cow calving. Note that the cow is secured to allow assistance to be given safely.

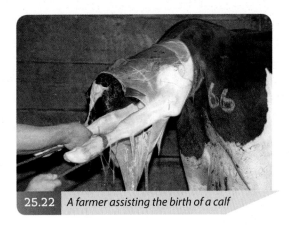

25.22 A farmer assisting the birth of a calf

Management of a cow during early lactation
Feeding and management in early lactation

After calving, a cow will lose weight because her feed intake does not meet her energy output. The cow has used energy to produce the calf, especially in the two months before calving, when the calf was growing rapidly in her uterus. The cow required energy to give birth to the calf and also to produce milk. In order to meet these energy demands, the cow will use up some of her own energy reserves, and the phrase **'milking off her back'** refers to this process.

25.23 Cows eating silage in winter housing

In early lactation, the cow should be kept on a high plane of nutrition. This is achieved by providing the cow with good-quality silage and supplementing her diet with concentrates. This ensures that the cow reaches her lactation peak yield and, therefore, can produce her potential lactation yield. Cows reach their peak milk yield 6–8 weeks after calving. If a cow is not adequately fed, she will not reach her peak yield and will lower her overall total milk yield. Energy is a key component of the dairy cow's diet during this time. The diet of the cow should also be supplemented with minerals to prevent milk fever and grass tetany (see page 470) when she is turned out to grass in the spring. Cows are turned out onto grass as early as possible, and grass should be grazed rotationally using paddocks or strip grazing.

If grass growth is slow, the feeding of concentrates should be maintained. Clean water supply is essential, as lactating dairy cows can drink more than 70 litres of water a day.

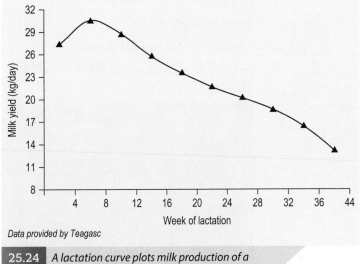

Data provided by Teagasc

25.24 A lactation curve plots milk production of a Holstein–Friesian over the course of her lactation until she is dried off.

Management of cow in mid- and late lactation

Heat detection

The first heat after calving is usually a silent heat, with only a small number of cows in standing heat. Farmers need to record the next normal heat cycle, 21 days later, to ensure that they can plan the starting date for mating. As most dairy farmers use AI, it is vital that they identify a cow in heat in order to have a successful conception from AI. Cows are only fertile (in oestrus) when an egg is released, and the cow is only in oestrus for 18 hours. Farmers often rely on observing cows in the morning and evening to identify cows in heat.

Farmers use the following rule (AM-PM rule) when deciding to artificially inseminate a cow. This rule states that if a cow is observed in heat in the morning (a.m.) she should be artificially inseminated in the evening (p.m.). Likewise, if a cow is first observed in heat in the evening (p.m.) she should be artificially inseminated the following morning (a.m.). There is a risk that the cow may be artificially inseminated too late, since the farmer may not have observed when she first came into heat, so this method of heat detection is not very reliable. When a cow is in oestrus she will stand and allow other cows to mount her. When this happens, a cow may only stand for a few seconds and it may occur at a time when it goes unnoticed. Missing cows that are in heat can lead to longer calving intervals, and this can reduce the profits of a dairy farmer.

To help identify cows in standing heat, many farmers use **heat detection aids**.

Tail painting

Tail painting is a common heat detection aid used by farmers. The top of the cow's tail is painted with a bright colour. When the cow is in heat she is mounted by other cows and they rub off the paint. The colour of the paint can be changed to identify all cows that are cycling before mating.

> **Silent heat:** an unnoticed heat period. There are no behavioural changes in the cow and the heat is not detected by a bull.

> **Heat detection aid:** a device that helps to confirm or identify a cow when she is in heat.

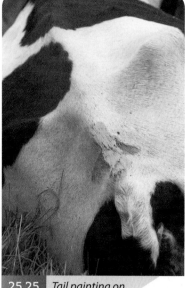

25.25 *Tail painting on a dairy cow*

Kamar device

A kamar device is a pressure-sensitive chamber that contains a dye. It is attached to the top of the tail and when the cow is mounted the chamber bursts and the detector turns red.

25.26 *Kamar device*

25.27 *Cow activity meter*

Activity meter

When cows are in heat they often become very restless. An activity meter measures the activity of a cow and compares it to her activity over the previous few days. The activity meter identifies a cow with increased activity as being in heat. An activity meter can also help determine when AI should be carried out to maximise the chances of success.

Chin ball

A vasectomised bull fitted with a chin ball that contains a dye can be used to mount and mark any cow in heat.

Bull selection for a dairy herd

At the start of breeding, the **BCS** of the herd should be averaging around **2.9**. Dairy farmers use both beef and dairy bulls in their breeding programmes. Their best dairy cows are put back in calf using high EBI dairy sires to breed replacement heifers for the dairy herd. Taking into account that some of the progeny of the dairy bull will be male, the dairy farmer usually doubles their planned replacement rate, unless they are using sexed semen (see page 327). A beef bull will be used on the rest of the dairy herd whose progeny are not destined to be replacements. All the male calves (both dairy and beef cross) and some of the female calves will be sold to beef farmers and reared for beef production. A beef bull will improve the conformation and muscle distribution of its progeny, thus improving the price of the calves when sold.

Feeding the cow in mid- and late lactation

Dairy cows should be rotationally grazing (paddock grazing or strip) perennial ryegrass during the breeding season. Good-quality grass provides adequate energy and protein for the cow at this stage. Concentrate feeding should not be required. During mid-lactation the dairy cow should be back in calf. In late lactation the milk yield is smaller and the cows will need to be milked only once a day. The feed value of autumn grass decreases, and it is recommended by Teagasc that the diets of dairy cows are supplemented with

25.28 Dairy cows grazing

concentrates to help extend the grazing season, maintain lactose levels in milk and increase the BCS of the cow before drying off. The cow will be dried off 60 days before calving, and dry-cow treatment should be administered to treat any mastitis infections,

in combination with a teat sealant. Cows with mastitis have a lower percentage fat, protein and lactose and a higher concentration of somatic cells compared with healthy cows. Drying off cows for 60 days maximises milk yields in the lactation that follows. Studies have shown that lactation yields can be reduced by 25–40% if the drying-off period is less than 40–60 days. Once dried off and housed, the cows should be fed good-quality silage and concentrates to ensure they are at a BCS of 3.25 before calving.

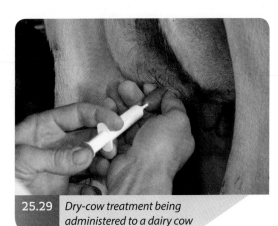

25.29 Dry-cow treatment being administered to a dairy cow

Housing

Dairy parlour

Most dairy parlours in Ireland are herringbone parlours. In a herringbone parlour the cows enter on one side and line up at an angle with their backs to the pit. Since the milker is lower down in the pit, this makes it easier to clean the udder and attach the clusters. The cows are normally given some concentrates to keep them calm and relaxed during the milking process. Usually the cows on one side of the pit are milked first, while the cows on the other side can be checked for mastitis, etc. When the first group of cows are milked, the clusters are swapped over to the other side of the pit. Rinsing the clusters in disinfectant between cows is important in helping to stop the spread of bacteria that cause mastitis. All cows should also be teat dipped after milking to help prevent mastitis (see page 476).

A clean dairy parlour, holding yard and a well-maintained and clean milking machine are important in keeping good hygiene and therefore producing good-quality milk low in total bacterial count (TBC; see page 377). Vigilance in maintaining a healthy, well-fed herd and taking measures to reduce the incidences of mastitis within the herd are important in maintaining a low somatic cell count (SCC; see page 377). Both of these measures will ensure the production of high-quality milk. Milk quality is dealt with in detail in Chapter 26.

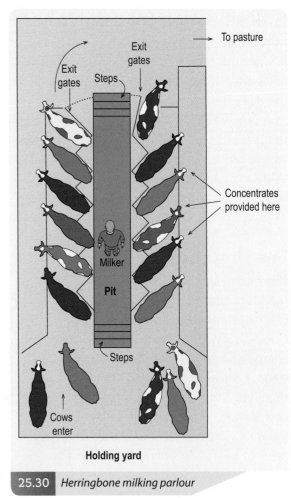

25.30 *Herringbone milking parlour*

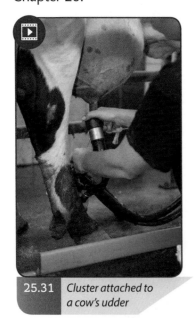

25.31 *Cluster attached to a cow's udder*

25.32 *Receiving vessel*

Winter housing

The most common type of housing for cattle in Ireland is a slatted house. This building can accommodate both the animals and animal waste (slurry). In the slatted house cattle can be grouped according to age (weanlings), body condition and calving date. Slatted houses incorporate a feeding area, a lying area and in some cases a calf creep area (especially useful when housing suckler cows). The main disadvantage of slatted houses is that they are expensive to build and unsuitable for calving. The recommended space for a cow in a slatted house (no cubicles) is 2.5–3 m² per cow.

Another common winter house for cattle is the cubicle house. Cubicles are suitable for heifers and cows but not bulls or steers, as they will urinate in the middle of the cubicle. In the cubicle house there should be one cubicle per cow, with a recommended width of 1.2 m and a length of 2.3–2.6 m. This ensures that the cow has adequate space to stand up and lie down. In addition, cow mats can be used to reduce pressure on the knees of the cows when they stand up and lie down. The cubicles are raised and sloped to provide drainage so that urine and dung fall into a central passage. This passage is then scraped clean of urine and dung each day. The dung passageway can be replaced with slats and slurry storage. Regardless of what type of winter housing is used on a dairy farm, hygiene is important to ensure a low TBC in milk and to reduce the incidences of mastitis.

25.33 *Slatted house*

25.34 *Cow cubicle house*

Farm safety and the safe handling of cattle

Deaths caused by livestock account for 13% of all farm fatalities between 2008 and 2017. Many livestock accidents involving cattle occur when animals are being herded or handled by farmers in the farmyard or farm buildings. Bulls must always be treated with caution and handled vigilantly. Cows and especially heifers can be unpredictable during and/or after calving. Cows have become aggressive after calving and have attacked and killed farmers. To reduce the risk of injury or a fatality, farmers should have proper

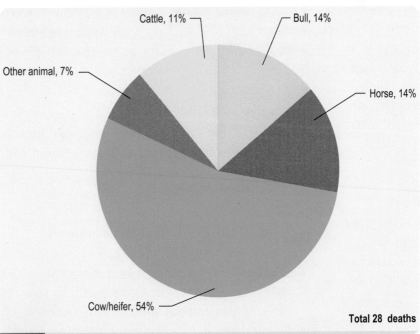

25.35 *Livestock accounted for 13% of all fatalities between 2008 and 2017. Pie chart courtesy of HSA*

Cattle, 11%
Bull, 14%
Other animal, 7%
Horse, 14%
Cow/heifer, 54%
Total 28 deaths

handling facilities on the farm. Farmers should always be vigilant around cattle, especially those that are showing signs of nervousness or excitement.

Livestock is accountable for **14%** of farm fatalities

- Freshly calved cows kill most frequently
- Bulls are most dangerous at end of breeding season
- Protect yourself with good facilities
- Use a vehicle as a sanctuary in fields

Teagasc
AGRICULTURE AND FOOD DEVELOPMENT AUTHORITY

Supporting Farm Safety Week

| 25.36 | A 2018 Teagasc poster as part of its campaign to raise awareness about farm safety |

| 25.37 | Cow in a handling facility. This allows the farmer to handle the cow and calf safely without risk of injury from the cow. |

| 25.38 | Escape gate for a person to get out of a pen quickly |

Table 25.12 Hazards and risks associated with livestock

Risk	Controls and precautions
• Freshly calved cows with newborn calves • Bull attacks • Crushing by animals that are being herded, moved, separated, released or loaded onto trailers • Goring • Kicking • Stressful situations can lead to unpredictable behaviour in animals	• Good handling facilities help to prevent injury from livestock. • Never turn your back on a cow with a newborn calf. • Plan to carry out as many routine procedures as possible when putting cattle through a crush, to reduce the frequency of moving and handling the animals. • Place the race and crush in a location that allows for easy gathering of cattle. • Never enter a crush with animals. • Wear steel-toe-cap boots to help prevent foot injuries. • Always have an escape route when working with bulls. Persons handling a bull should be fit, agile and properly trained. • Use AI rather than keeping a bull. • All bulls should be ringed. • An aggressive bull should be slaughtered. • Two people should handle a bull every time. • Any field in which a bull is kept should be securely fenced. The public should not have access to this field. Use a tractor or some other suitable farm vehicle (as a barrier between you and the animals) when moving a herd containing a bull. • Ensure that you have sufficient help.

Management practices

Handling and housing of farm animals

Many of the precautions necessary for the safe handling of cattle are shown in Table 25.12. Only persons experienced with cattle should be working with the animals. An inexperienced person, an elderly person or a child should never handle or herd cattle. Try to keep the cattle calm when herding or handling them. Difficult and aggressive cattle should be culled. All handling facilities should be regularly checked and maintained. If a stock bull is being kept on the farm, then he should be housed in a purpose-built pen, that is both strong and high to prevent him from escaping. The bull should be able to see other cattle. When installing a milking parlour, it should be designed so that the cows can be milked quickly and safely. A kick rail must be installed to protect the milker from being kicked. A farmer should always wear appropriate personal protective equipment and be vigilant with hygiene to protect themselves against zoonotic diseases (see Chapter 31).

Optimal animal health and welfare

The welfare of all farm animals is discussed in greater detail in Chapter 31.

The Common Agricultural Policy (CAP) has built into it Statutory Management Requirements for the welfare of calves (up to 6 months) and the welfare of all farm animals. All farmers in receipt of CAP payments must adhere to these minimum standards of animal welfare.

Statutory: legally required or expected standards.

Table 25.13 The Statutory Management Requirements for the welfare of calves and all farm animals	
Welfare of calves	**Welfare of farm animals**
• There should be sufficient labour to care for the calves. • Calves must be routinely inspected, twice a day if housed and once a day if they are outside. • Calves must have adequate space. • Ill or injured calves must be treated. • Calves must have suitable bedding. • Housing for calves and all equipment used must be clean and disinfected. • Calves must not be isolated from other calves unless they are sick. • Calves should get sufficient colostrum at birth. • Calves should be fed at least twice a day; once a day feeding is allowed in some systems. Calves must have access to feed, fresh water and straw or hay. • If calves are housed, there should be sufficient natural light or artificial light (equivalent to 8 hours of daylight a day). • Electrical appliances must be kept away from calves.	• There should be no overcrowding in housing, as this restricts the animals' freedom of movement (see page 466). • Yards should be regularly scraped and power washed. • Vermin should be controlled. • If animals are housed regularly, they must be given enough space to avoid unnecessary stress. • Sheds need to have good ventilation. • Sheds must have adequate natural or artificial light. • Animals kept outdoors must have shelter from adverse weather, predators and any other risk to their health. • Animals should be properly fed for their stage of their production cycle. • Animals should have access to feed and fresh water. • Feed and water should always be free from contamination by faeces, urine, etc.

Under no circumstances should a calf ever be muzzled or have its tail docked. Dehorning and debudding of calves older than 14 days should not occur without an anaesthetic. Castration of cattle over 6 months should only be done with a local anaesthetic. Also, calves should not be tethered, as this restricts an animal's freedom of movement and causes discomfort to the animal. **'Freedom from discomfort'** is one of the **five freedoms** discussed in Chapter 31.

Farmers must keep records of all medicinal treatments administered to calves and cattle and also the number of mortalities on the farm. Farmers that are found to be in breach of any of these regulations can have a financial sanction imposed on them.

In addition to the CAP requirements for welfare, there are a number of assurance schemes that also have welfare of animals as part of their requirements. The **Sustainable Dairy Assurance Scheme (SDAS)**, which is an accredited scheme in dairy production, is dealt with below and on page 388. In dairy farming, mastitis and lameness are two ongoing welfare issues. The cell check programme run by Animal Health Ireland provides farmers with guidelines for mastitis control. The use of EBI can bring about improvement, as health traits are one of its sub-indexes, and mastitis, SCC and lameness are all components of this index. Therefore, use of EBI bulls with a high health sub-index will allow farmers to breed replacement heifers with better health traits.

The World Health Organization estimates that 20% of livestock production losses are directly caused by poor animal health. When animals fall sick or ill, it is extremely important that the causative agent (bacterium, virus, protozoan, etc.) is identified quickly, as this will lead to the most effective method of treatment. Vaccination programmes are extremely important in any dairy enterprise. Cattle can be vaccinated for BVD, clostridial diseases, infectious bovine rhinotracheitis (IBR), leptospirosis and salmonellosis. When necessary, cattle should be dosed for worms and fluke. Dairy farmers should maintain biosecurity by rearing their own replacements.

Mortalities: deaths.

Slurry/farmyard manure

Extending the grazing season can reduce the volume of animal manures. However, this is not always possible as weather conditions can result in animals going into winter housing early or delaying them being let out in spring. The storage and management of animal manures has been covered in detail in Chapter 8. Cattle slurry and manure should be spread only on land intended for silage and hay.

Delivering sustainable and environmentally friendly production systems

Protection of the environment is a component of CAP and is commonly referred to as **greening**. The greening payment is a considerable component (30%) of the CAP subsidies, and it rewards farmers for agricultural practices that benefit the climate and the environment. There are also additional schemes, such as the **Green, Low-Carbon Agri-Environmental Scheme (GLAS)**, that encourage farmers to promote biodiversity, protect water quality and combat climate change. **Origin Green** is a Bord Bia initiative and is Ireland's national sustainability programme for the agri-food sector.

In December 2013 the SDAS was launched. Part of the aim of the scheme was to:

- Demonstrate to consumers of dairy products that milk is produced sustainably under an accredited scheme
- Set out best practice in Irish dairy farming.

The SDAS is covered in greater detail in Chapter 26. The environmental impact of agriculture is covered in Chapter 32.

Bord Bia: an Irish state agency with the aim of promoting sales of Irish food and horticulture, both abroad and in Ireland.

Ensuring quality, safe and traceable food for the consumer

The main product of the dairy industry is milk, and this is sold to the consumer as either liquid milk or as butter, cheese, milk powders, etc. The SDAS ensures that food is of high quality and is safe and traceable (see page 388). Milk processors require by law that farmers meet certain standards of milk hygiene. If farmers fail to reach those standards they are penalised. EU law requires all food businesses to have a traceability system in place, and the SDAS checks to ensure they do. This issue is dealt with in detail in Chapter 26.

Summary

- The most popular dairy breed in Ireland is the Holstein–Friesian. This is a large dairy breed that produces high milk yields.

- The British Friesian is a dual-purpose animal: it can be used for dairy and for beef production.

- Holstein–Friesian × Jersey crossbred cattle produce a lower milk yield compared with the Holstein–Friesian but higher milk solids. The crossbred cattle exhibit hybrid vigour.

- All calves on a dairy farm are artificially reared.

- The first milk a cow produces is colostrum. Colostrum has a high percentage of fat and protein. It contains vital antibodies that will give the calf immunity against disease.

- The ability of the calf to absorb these antibodies is greatest in the first few hours of its life.

- Calves should be fed milk or milk replacer twice daily and should also be provided with hay, concentrates and fresh water.

- Calves should be housed in well-ventilated houses with clean, dry bedding of straw. Good hygiene is essential to prevent scour.

- Calves are weaned off milk and onto concentrates and grass at 6 weeks old. Calves should be provided with good-quality grass and should graze in the leader-follower system.

- Calves should be housed for winter at 9 months old and should be fed good-quality silage. Concentrates should be provided if silage quality is poor.

- Replacement heifers should have a body condition score (BCS) of 3.25 at mating and be 300 kg, have good health, be the offspring of a high EBI sire, be free from disease, and come from a mother that has good fertility, easy calving and good milk composition.

- BCS is the ratio of lean meat to fat. BCS should be assessed regularly so that feeding and management can be adjusted so that the cow is at the correct BCS.

- An easy calving bull on a first-time calving heifer reduces the chances of calving difficulties.

- The gestation period of a cow is 283 days, the length of the oestrous cycle is 21 days and the duration of oestrus is 18–24 hours.

- Energy is the most important component in a dairy cow's diet. If her diet is low in energy, this will result in low milk yields and low milk protein.

- After calving a dairy cow will lose weight as her feed intake does not meet her energy output. The cow will make up the deficit in energy by using up some of her energy reserves, which is referred to as 'milking off her back'.

- A dairy cow's diet should be supplemented with concentrates in early lactation to ensure that she reaches her lactation peak. A cow reaches her lactation peak 6–8 weeks after calving.

- Mineral supplements should be provided to prevent milk fever (caused by low calcium) and grass tetany (caused by low magnesium) in early lactation.

- Dairy farmers use heat detection aids such as tail painting and activity meters to identify when a cow is in heat. Most dairy farmers use artificial insemination (AI).

- Dairy farmers use both beef and dairy bulls in their breeding programmes. A beef bull is used to produce offspring for beef production. A dairy bull is used to produce replacement heifers.

- The main housing used on a dairy farm is a dairy parlour and its holding yard and winter housing. A high level of hygiene should be maintained on the farm in order to reduce bacteria and produce high-quality milk.
- Good handling facilities are required to prevent injury from livestock. Carry out as many planned routine procedures as possible when livestock are in the crush, to reduce the frequency of handling the animals.
- Consider using AI as an alternative to keeping a bull. Persons handling a bull should be fit, agile and properly trained.
- The Common Agricultural Policy (CAP) sets out standards of welfare for calves and other farm animals.
- Origin Green Sustainable Dairy Assurance Scheme (SDAS) also sets out standards for both the welfare of animals and the traceability of food.
- Sustainability and environment protection are both components in CAP (Greening) and Origin Green SDAS.

PowerPoint Summary

QUESTIONS

1. Which of the following is the most popular dairy breed in Ireland?

    (a) Jersey   (b) Holstein–Friesian   (c) Ayrshire   (d) Kerry Cow

2. The Jersey is a small dairy breed that originates from the Channel Islands. It is well known for the high _____ in its milk.

    (a) Somatic cell count   (c) Water content

    (b) Mineral content   (d) Fat and protein content

3. The percentage of protein in colostrum (14.9%) is considerably higher than the percentage of protein in normal milk (3.2%). The reason for this is that colostrum is high in:

    (a) Antibodies   (b) Red blood cells   (c) Lactose   (d) Calcium.

4. It is vital that calves get adequate amounts of colostrum in the first 12 hours after birth as these antibodies:

    (a) Warm the calf up   (c) Are high in energy

    (b) Have a laxative effect   (d) Provide immunity against disease.

5. Fig. 25.39 shows the approximate composition of cows' milk.

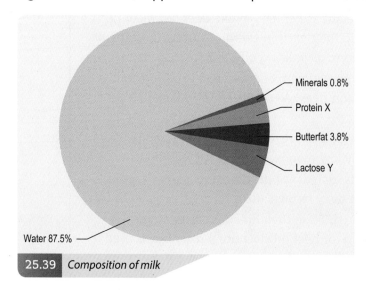

Minerals 0.8%

Protein X

Butterfat 3.8%

Lactose Y

Water 87.5%

25.39 *Composition of milk*

Which of the following is the correct percentage (%) value of protein and lactose in normal milk?

	Protein (%)	Lactose (%)
(a)	5.3	2.1
(b)	0.8	9.5
(c)	3.2	4.7
(d)	4.7	3.2

6. The body condition score (BCS) of a cow before calving should be:
   (a) 2.75
   (b) 2.95
   (c) 3.25
   (d) 3.95.

7. The average gestation period for cattle in days is:
   (a) 255
   (b) 274
   (c) 283
   (d) 300.

8. Why should cattle in late lactation be provided with a mineral supplement along with their feed?
   (a) It makes the feed more palatable.
   (b) It prevents grass tetany and milk fever.
   (c) It increases the digestibility of the animals' feed.
   (d) It increases the energy content of the animals' feed.

9. The most common design of milking parlour in Ireland is a:
   (a) Wishbone parlour
   (b) Salmon bone parlour
   (c) Herringbone parlour
   (d) Rotary parlour.

10. When is a person most likely to be crushed by cattle?
    (a) When the animals are being moved
    (b) When cows are being separated from their young
    (c) When cattle are being released from winter housing
    (d) When cattle are being loaded on to a trailer
    (e) All of the above.

11. When working with bulls a person should always:
    (a) Be properly trained
    (b) Have an escape route planned
    (c) Be fit and agile
    (d) All of the above.

12. The average lactation yield and the fat and protein composition of milk for three dairy breeds are shown in Table 25.14:

Table 25.14			
Breed	Milk yield (kg)	Fat (%)	Protein (%)
A	4350	5.3	4.1
B	6450	4.1	3.5
C	5240	4.8	3.9

   (a) Which breeds are represented by A, B and C?
   (b) Give a reason for your choice in each case.
   (c) State the percentage (%) value of fat and protein in colostrum.

13. How can crossbreeding be used to improve the productivity of a dairy herd?

14. What is colostrum?

15. State **two** differences between colostrum and ordinary milk.

16. Outline the precautions taken by dairy farmers to reduce calf mortality at calving time.

17. Describe the management of dairy calves under the following headings:

    (a) Care at birth

    (b) Housing

    (c) Disease prevention

    (d) Introducing hay into the diet

    (e) Use of milk replacer.

18. Regularly assessing the body condition score (BCS) of a dairy herd is important at different stages of a cow's production cycle.

    (a) Explain the term 'body condition score'.

    (b) What BCS should a dairy cow be at precalving and at the beginning of the breeding season?

    (c) Discuss the implications of not having the cow at the correct BCS precalving.

19. (a) Describe **four** features a dairy farmer would look for when selecting a replacement heifer for a dairy herd.

    (b) Describe the target weights, nutrition and housing of a replacement heifer (Holstein–Friesian) in a spring-calving dairy herd at each of the following stages:

        (i) Newborn calf stage   (ii) Weanling stage   (iii) Yearling stage

        (iv) Mating stage   (v) Precalving.

20. Give **three** reasons for culling cows from a dairy herd.

21. Justify the use of heat detection aids in a dairy enterprise.

22. Discuss how age and condition of breeding heifers in a dairy herd may influence the date of first calving.

23. Describe **two** factors that affect the amount of milk solids in a cow's milk.

24. Discuss **three** factors that affect milk yield in a dairy herd.

25. Explain why it is necessary to dry off cows for 60 days before calving.

26. Describe how the nutritional requirements of a dairy cow can change over the course of her production cycle.

27. The calving records on a dairy farm in 1 year show:

    • 30% purebred Friesian calves

    • 55% continental × Friesian calves

    • 15% Aberdeen Angus × Friesian calves.

    The farmer relies on AI and has no stock bull. He breeds his own replacement stock.

    (a) Why was the Friesian breed used and on which of the cows?

    (b) Why are the continental sires used for most inseminations?

    (c) Why are Aberdeen Angus bulls used?

    (d) What is the replacement rate for culled cows?

28. Describe safety measures that should be taken when handling or moving a bull.

29. Justify the use of AI as a technique for manipulating reproduction in dairy production.

30. Discuss the role of management practices in ensuring safe handling and housing of farm animals.

31. Discuss the role of policies and other accredited schemes in promoting optimal animal health and welfare.

32. Explain how **two** management strategies can be used to improve animal health on a dairy farm.

33. Identify **four** requirements that farmers must provide for the welfare of calves up to 6 months.

 Solutions    Weblinks

Milk composition, milk production and the dairy industry

When you have completed this chapter you should be able to:

- Describe milk composition and how dairy cows produce milk
- Use secondary data to discuss the impact of milk quality on milk price
- Compare the percentage of water and solids in two different milk samples (a.m./p.m.)
- Investigate the quality of a sample of milk over time (SPA)
- Recognise the role and importance of innovation and biotechnological applications in animal science
- Discuss the qualities or features of Irish food based on grass-fed animals
- Appreciate the challenges on sustainable intensification
- Appreciate the impact on farm economics of dairy production
- Appreciate the role of policies related to traceability and animal welfare, and their connection with the food-supply chain
- Appreciate the importance of export markets.

Milk composition and milk production

Milk is a suspension of protein, fat and other solids in water. The composition of cow's milk varies depending on the breed, but the average is given in Table 26.1.

Lactose is the main carbohydrate present in milk. It is a disaccharide sugar made up of glucose and galactose. There are two main proteins in milk: **casein** and **whey**. Casein is the more abundant of the two proteins. Lactose, protein and minerals make up the solid non-fat (SNF) component of milk.

> In a suspension such as milk, the solid particles (protein, lactose, etc.) are dispersed throughout the liquid part (water).

Table 26.1 Average composition of milk.	
Component	**Percentage (%)**
Water	87.8
Butterfat	3–4
Protein	3.2
Lactose	4.7
Minerals (calcium, magnesium, phosphates)	0.8

Milk production by the dairy cow

Milk is produced by specialised cells in the udder called alveoli. The udder is an exocrine gland composed of four quarters that function independently of each other and deliver milk through their own teat.

Fig. 26.1 illustrates the structure and the support tissue of a cow's udder. The right half of the udder is separated from the left half by a membranous wall called the medial (central) suspensory ligament. The udder is further subdivided into the rear and front quarters, which are separated by a thin wall of connective tissue. The udder is composed of connective and fatty tissue between the

> **Exocrine glands** produce and secrete substances through ducts to the outside of the body.

> **Suspensory ligament:** a supporting or holding ligament.

Medial suspensory ligament

Fine membrane between each quarter

Outer wall

Lateral suspensory ligament

Teat

26.1 *A cow's udder*

> **Cistern:** a reservoir or space containing fluid.

> **Alveolus:** the singular form of **alveoli**.

> **Lateral:** sideways or side.

alveoli. The alveoli each has a duct that allows milk to drain out. These ducts meet to produce larger ducts that eventually empty milk into the gland cistern, which can store approximately 500 cm³ of milk. The gland cistern is connected to the teat cistern, which can hold 40 cm³ of milk.

The milk exits the teat through the streak canal. It is through the streak canal that bacteria can enter the udder after milking and cause mastitis. The udder has a rich blood supply. Milk synthesis requires a large amount of nutrients. It is the function of the cells of the alveoli to convert the nutrients in the blood into milk. The average cow will produce 25 litres of milk a day. Blood also carries the hormones prolactin and oxytocin, which control milk synthesis and trigger milk let-down. Prolactin is produced by the pituitary gland and it is responsible for producing and maintaining lactation in mammals. Oxytocin is also produced in the pituitary gland and travels in the blood to the alveoli cells, where it initiates milk let-down.

Milk let-down

The surface of the udder has a number of receptors that are sensitive to touch and temperature. These nerve receptors are stimulated during the preparation of the cow's udder for milking and by a calf attempting to suckle. These actions trigger the sensory nerves to send a message to the brain. The pituitary gland in the brain produces the hormone oxytocin. Oxytocin travels in the blood to the udder where it causes the cells of the alveoli to start secreting milk and this initiates milk let-down. Milking clusters should be attached without delay as oxytocin levels are highest 60–90 seconds after stimulation of the udder and the action of oxytocin only lasts for about 5 minutes. The cow will start milking soon after she has given birth. The average lactation period for a dairy cow is 10 months (**305 days**). After the birth of the calf the cow produces colostrum (also known as beastings) for the first 4–5 days.

Milk quality and milk price

Comparison of liquid milk production and manufacturing milk production

In Ireland the demand for milk is year-round (12 months). However, dairy cows will lactate for only 10 months (305 days) of the year. So how does supply meet demand? The answer is through a mixture of liquid milk production and manufacturing milk production (Table 26.2).

> **Manufacturing milk** is used to produce butter, cheese, milk powders, etc. It is produced between spring and autumn.

Milk price

Dairy farmers are paid for their milk based on the milk's composition (the quantity of protein and butterfat supplied).

Payment is based on an **A + B – C**, plus any bonuses or penalties.

The formula for payment is:

$$(A \times \text{protein \%} + B \times \text{butterfat \%}) - C.$$

> A **co-operative** is an organisation that is owned and run jointly by its members.

A is a set value for protein, **B** is a set value for fat and **C** is the processing charge based on the volume component of the milk and the cost of collection and transport. C is generally a constant. A farmer who produces a moderate volume of milk with a high percentage fat and protein will obtain a higher price for their milk than a farmer who produces a large volume of milk that is low in its percentage fat and protein. Milk is tested for protein and butterfat for payment purposes. Many milk processors are co-operatives and they set a milk price monthly based on global dairy prices for butterfat and protein (see page 386). This milk price will determine the value of **A** and **B** that is used in the formula.

The final price a farmer gets paid for milk will also include any bonuses and penalties. Depending on the processor, farmers can get bonus payments for high protein in milk, supplying early milk (February and March) or for large-capacity storage bulk tanks (this reduces the number of milk collections required). Penalties apply for: having excess water in milk; storing milk at a temperature greater than 4°C; and supplying milk that has high total bacterial count (TBC) and somatic cell count (SCC) (see page 377).

DEFINITION

Total bacterial count (TBC): total number of living bacteria per ml of milk.
Somatic cell count (SCC): mainly the numbers of white blood cells. High numbers of these cells in milk are an indication of mastitis in a herd.

Table 26.2 Comparison of liquid milk production and manufacturing milk production	
Liquid milk production	**Manufacturing milk production**
• Farmers who supply liquid milk for consumption operate both spring- and autumn-calving herds. • This ensures that they have a constant milk supply all year round. • Farmers who supply a dairy with liquid milk are more likely to use a purebred Holstein–Friesian herd. • Farmers who supply the liquid milk market over the winter months usually get paid a flat price, regardless of milk solids, for a portion of their milk. This price is negotiated with the milk processor. The remaining part will be paid using the payment scheme A + B – C. • In addition, there is usually some form of a premium paid to liquid milk farmers to cover the higher feed and production costs incurred by producing milk over the winter months.	• The majority of dairy farmers are seasonal milk producers. These dairy farmers operate a spring-calving herd. • They produce milk between spring and autumn only, when they can take advantage of grass growth. • They select dairy cows that give high milk solids with low milk yields, e.g. a crossbred Jersey may be used. • The milk produced is used to produce commodities such as butter, cheese, yoghurt, infant milk formula and milk powder. • Creameries are looking for the quality of the milk rather than the quantity. Farmers are paid under the payment scheme of A + B – C, with payment related to the amount of protein and fat in their milk, and penalties if milk volume is large. • Under this system, cows are dried off over the winter months.

Milk payment calculation

Example A is of a milk payment calculation. The value of **A** and **B** are determined by the processor. In this example, a farmer has 3.3% protein and 3.6% butterfat in their milk. The percentage protein is multiplied by a factor of 5.466 (**A**) and the percentage fat is multiplied by a factor of 4.218 (**B**). The processing charge is deducted (**C**) and VAT at 5.4% and any bonuses due to the farmer are added to give a final milk payment of 31.27 c/lt.

Value Added Tax (VAT) is a tax on consumer spending.

Example A

Bainne Nua Creamery
Co-operative Society Ltd.

Milk payment

(**A**) Protein   @ 3.3% (3.3 × 5.466) = 18.04 c/lt

(**B**) Butterfat @ 3.6% (3.6 × 4.218) = 15.18 c/lt

(**C**) Volume charge   = –4.0 c/lt

    Bonuses   = 0.45 c/lt

    VAT @ 5.4%   = 1.60 c/lt

    Total milk price   = 31.27 c/lt

In Example B the Brady family farm is producing milk with 3.46% protein and 4.01% butterfat. In addition, they get a storage bonus of 0.45 c/litre for having the refrigerated storage capacity for seven milkings.

Example B

Bainne Nua Creamery
Co-operative Society Ltd.

Milk payment

(A) Protein   @ 3.46 (3.46 × 5.466) = 18.91 c/lt

(B) Butterfat @ 4.01 (4.01 × 4.218) = 16.91 c/lt

(C) Volume charge   = −4.0 c/lt

     Bonuses   = 0.45 c/lt

     VAT @ 5.4%   = 1.74 c/lt

     Total milk price   = 34.01 c/lt

The Brady family has a higher percentage protein and butterfat in their milk compared to the first example. This is increasing their milk price by more than 2c/lt compared to the milk price in example A.

In example C, the Tully family farm is producing milk with 3.78% protein and 3.29% butterfat. The Tully farm has had several cows showing signs of mastitis and this has increased the SCC of the milk to over 255,000 per ml. As a result, the processor is applying a penalty of −0.14 c/lt until the Tully family can reduce their SCC below 250,000 per ml.

Example C

Bainne Nua Creamery
Co-operative Society Ltd.

Milk payment

(A) Protein   @ 3.78 (3.78 × 5.466) = 20.66 c/lt

(B) Butterfat @ 3.29 (3.29 × 4.218) = 13.88 c/lt

(C) Volume charge   = −4.0 c/lt

     Penalties   = −0.14 c/lt

     VAT @ 5.4%   = 1.64 c/lt

     Total milk price   = 32.04 c/lt

In Example C, the lower percentage butterfat and high SCC in the Tully's milk is reducing the total milk price that the farmer is getting.

Improving the percentage butterfat and protein in the milk will lead to a higher milk price. This can be brought about through genetic improvement of the dairy herd using the EBI and good grassland and grassland management. Good grassland results in increased milk yield, fat and protein yields. Lactating cows being fed silage during the winter months show an increase in the percentage butterfat. This is due to increased levels of fibre in their diets. Lowering SCC and TBC will also improve the total milk price.

A high SCC count is an indication of mastitis being present in the herd (see page 377). White blood cells move from the cow's bloodstream into the udder as part of the animal's immune response to the infection (see Fig. 26.2). These cells plus some other body cells make up the SCC of milk. Other factors, such as stress and poor nutrition, can cause a slight increase in the SCC of milk. Mastitis is a costly disease for dairy farmers as it reduces milk yields and increases SCC. The SCC can be lowered by culling cows with chronic mastitis and implementing measures to control mastitis infections in the herd. Cell Check is a national mastitis control programme, co-ordinated and facilitated by Animal Health Ireland. It provides training and guidelines to farmers to aid in mastitis control. Their website is www.animalhealthireland.ie.

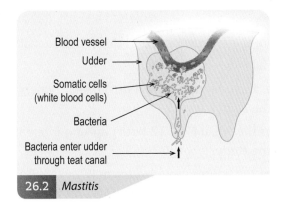

26.2 *Mastitis*

Compare the percentage of water and solids in two different milk samples (a.m./p.m.)

Many factors can affect the composition of milk, including breed, animal feed, the stage of lactation (early, mid- and late lactation), the age of the animal, the presence of disease (e.g. mastitis) and the milking interval. The milking interval is the time between successive milkings. Most farms operate a 14 : 10 hour or a 13 : 11 hour interval.

Exercise 26.1

Scientists at Moorepark Research and Development Division investigated the effect of unequal and equal milking intervals on milk yield and milk composition.

Sixty-six Friesian cows were divided into two groups. Group 1 had a 16 : 8 hour milking interval and Group 2 had a 12 : 12 hour milking interval. Cows on the 16 : 8 hour milking interval were milked at 7 a.m. and 3 p.m. and those on the 12 : 12 hour milking interval were milked at 7 a.m. and 7 p.m. Both groups (1 and 2) grazed side by side on the same land areas in paddocks of similar grass quality and were stocked at the same stocking rate. The cows' milk yields were recorded and the concentrations of fat, protein and lactose were determined.

The results of the investigation are presented in Table 26.3.

Table 26.3 The effects of milking at two different milking intervals in a 24-hour period on milk yield and composition				
	a.m. Milk		p.m. Milk	
Weeks 1–4	16 : 8 hour interval	12 : 12 hour interval	16 : 8 hour interval	12 : 12 hour interval
Milk yield (kg/cow)	16.6	12.8	8.5	12.2
Water (%)	89.45	89.05	87.1	88.77
Fat (%)	2.72	3.17	4.99	3.4
Protein (%)	3.29	3.24	3.34	3.29
Lactose (%)	4.53	4.54	4.56	4.54

Data was adapted. Source of data: Short-term effects of milking interval on milk production, composition and quality. By Bernadette O'Brien, J O'Connor and W.J. Meaney. Teagasc, Agriculture and Development Authority, Moorepark Research and Development Division, Fermoy, Co. Cork.

Questions

1. What were the independent and dependent variables in this study?

2. What variables were controlled?

3. How does the unequal (16 : 8 hour) milking interval affect the milk yield of the cows in the study?

4. How does the equal (12 : 12 hour) milking interval affect the milk yield of the cows in the study?

5. (a) Using the figures provided for milk yield, calculate the total daily milk yield for both the unequal milking interval and the equal milking interval.

   (b) Does an unequal milking interval affect the daily milk yield? Explain your answer.

6. Comment on the effect of the unequal milking interval and the equal milking interval on the % water in the a.m. and p.m. milk.

7. Examine the figures for the percentage fat, protein and lactose.

   (a) Which component is affected the most by having an unequal milking interval?

   (b) Using information in Table 26.3, justify your answer.

8. Using the information in Table 26.3, evaluate whether it is feasible for farmers to use an unequal milking interval as a mechanism to improve profitability in milk production.

Residual milk: milk that remains in the udder after the bulk of the milk has been removed during milking.

The percentage fat content of milk varies between the morning and evening milking if the milking interval is unequal. In studies where milking intervals were unequal, it was found that there was an increase in milk yield but a decrease in percentage fat because of dilution after the longer interval. Another explanation for the higher fat in the 16 : 8 hours milking interval is put forward by researchers at Teagasc, who state that the fat may be higher overall in the daily milk due to more residual milk remaining in the udder after the longer interval (16 hours). The percentage fat changes as the cow is being milked: at the start of milking the milk will contain 1–2% fat; this increases as milking continues – by the end of milking, the percentage fat is at its highest. This is due to the fat globules being trapped in the alveoli at the start of milking. Incomplete milking leads to a lower percentage fat content of the milk. Therefore, residual milk could have a very high fat content and this milk would then be removed at the next milking, leading to an increase in the fat content of the milk at the shorter interval (8 hour). If cows are milked at 12-hour intervals, there is little variation in the percentage fat. However, 12-hour milking intervals may not be practical on dairy farms.

Milk hygiene and milk testing

Depending on the milk processor, milk can be collected from the dairy farmer every second day. Processors use a barcode system so that the milk collected can be traced back to the farm from which it came. In addition, the barcode system allows the milk processor to send a detailed report on the milk back to the farmer. Before the milk is paid for by the processor, it undergoes tests to assess the composition and hygiene quality of the milk. These tests are carried out on every delivery of milk to the milk processor. If the quality of the milk is outside set standards, penalties may be applied, or the milk may have to be discarded. Table 26.4 shows examples of tests carried out by creameries and milk processors.

26.3 *Fossomatic milk analyser from Aurivo milk-testing laboratory in Ballaghadereen, Co. Roscommon. This machine can determine somatic cell count, the presence of excess water and the percentage fat, protein and lactose in milk.*

> **Withdrawal period:** the minimum time that must elapse after the last administration of a drug (e.g. antibiotics) for the treatment of an illness in an animal, before that animal or its products (e.g. milk) can be used for human consumption. Withdrawal periods prevent any residues of the drug being present in the animal or its products.

Table 26.4 Tests to assess the composition and hygiene quality of milk

Tests	Explanation
Milk composition	• The percentage fat, protein and lactose in the milk are determined for payment purposes.
Total bacterial count (TBC)	• **This is an indicator of hygiene on the farm.** • The total number of living bacteria per ml of milk is counted. • High TBC can be caused by farmers failing to wash and dry the udder and teat of the cow, dirty milking machine, unchanged milking machine filters, failure to properly cool milk to below 4°C and mastitis.
Somatic cell count (SCC)	• **This test is an indicator of udder health.** • High SCC counts affect the processing of the milk.
Temperature	• Milk needs to be properly cooled to 2–4°C within 30 minutes of milking. • If the milk is not properly cooled, this will allow bacteria such as *Lactobacillus* to grow. These bacteria convert lactose to lactic acid and cause the milk to sour and curdle.
Antibiotics	• Antibiotic testing is the first test carried out by all milk processors. • **Antibiotics must be absent from milk always,** since antibiotics contribute to bacteria developing antimicrobial resistance (AMR). • Antibiotics affect the bacteria cultures used in the production of yoghurt and cheese. • Antibiotics could be present in milk if a farmer has not observed the entire withdrawal period for cows treated with antibiotics for mastitis. Sometimes there may be residual antibiotics remaining from dry cow treatment administered when the cow was dried off at the end of the previous lactation.
Thermoduric test	• Thermoduric bacteria are an indicator of **hygiene** on the farm. • These bacteria can resist high temperatures and can survive the pasteurisation process. • They cause spoilage of food and shorten the shelf life of these products.
Sediment	• Milk must be free from sediment. • Soil, hair and dung may be on the surface of the udder and teat. It is advisable that farmers clean the udder and teat of the cows and dry them before attaching the clusters. • A milk filter or milk sock will filter and trap any particles that may be present in the milk. This filter is changed at each milking.
Excess water	• Adding water to milk reduces the value of the milk because it dilutes the protein, fat, lactose and other components of the milk. • Milk processors monitor milk for the addition of water by checking the freezing point of milk. The addition of water will change the freezing point of milk.

 **SPA 26.1** To investigate the quality of a sample of milk over time

SPECIFIED PRACTICAL ACTIVITY

State your hypothesis, prediction, independent variable, dependent variable and controlled variable.

What safety precautions should be taken when carrying out this practical activity?

Resazurin is a blue dye that undergoes a colour change caused by the number of bacteria present in a sample of milk. The greater the number of bacteria present in the milk, the more quickly the dye will decolourise.

Before the practical:

A Lovibond milk testing kit and comparator with grading scale could be used to carry out this investigation. Some raw (unpasteurised) milk samples should be pre-aged by incubating them at room temperature before this practical. There is a general rule of thumb that 'Raw milk will double its bacterial number every 20 mins if left at room temperature (approximately 20°C)'. If time allows, raw milk could be left to incubate (pre-age) at room temperature for 1 hour, 2 hours, 4 hours and overnight. Incubating raw milk at temperatures up to 40°C will speed up the souring. Raw milk could be incubated at 40°C for 20 mins, 30 mins and 40 mins.

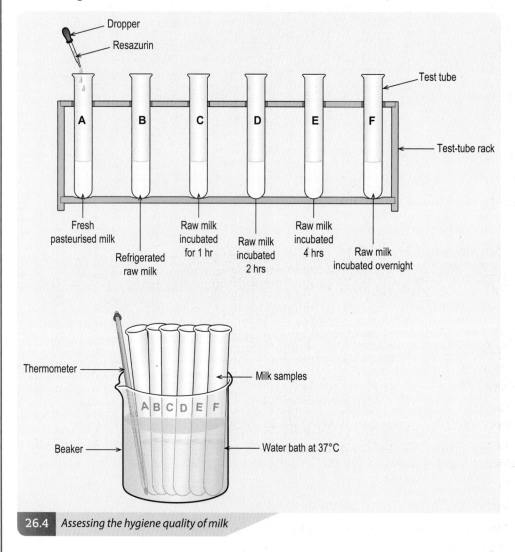

26.4 *Assessing the hygiene quality of milk*

Materials

Six clean and sterile test tubes, a sample of fresh pasteurised milk (control), refrigerated raw milk and four samples of pre-aged raw milk (incubated at 20°C for various lengths of time), resazurin solution (or methylene blue), water bath at 37°C

Method

1. Label six test tubes A, B, C, D, E and F.
2. Add 10 cm³ of fresh pasteurised milk to test tube A.
3. To each of the remaining five test tubes add 10 cm³ of the various raw milk samples as shown in Fig. 26.4.
4. Add 1 cm³ of resazurin solution to each test tube.
5. Place the test tubes in a water bath at 37°C for 15 minutes.
6. Record any colour change that has occurred in a results table. The colour of the milk sample is an indicator of the quality of the milk (see Table 26.5). Good-quality milk will have a low total bacterial count (TBC). It is not possible to quantify the number of bacteria present in the milk samples using this method.

Table 26.5 The meaning of observed colour changes	
Colour of resazurin solution	**Quality of the milk**
Blue (no colour change)	Excellent (low TBC)
Blue to deep mauve	Good
Deep pink	Fair
Light pink	Poor
White	Bad

Validation

1. Do the results of this experiment support your hypothesis? Explain your answer.
2. What type of data is recorded in this experiment?
3. Discuss the effect of incubating raw milk for different lengths of time at 20°C on the hygiene quality of milk.
4. Write a conclusion to this practical activity.
5. Identify any sources of error when carrying out this practical.

Husbandry and management in maintaining high hygiene standards in milking

Measures that a farmer can take to improve the hygiene quality of the milk they produce include:

- Clean and maintain housing, cubicle beds, dairy parlours and holding yards
- Add lime to cow mats in cubicle housing (lime increases pH and helps to reduce bacterial numbers); care should be taken not to add too much lime, since it can be corrosive and cause severe burns to the cow's skin and udders
- Wash the cows' udders and teats and dry them before milking
- Maintain a healthy herd: good breed, low SCC, well fed, good disease control and prevention and good management of herd
- Check for mastitis: use a strip cup and look for any abnormalities in the milk, e.g. watery milk or clots
- Treat mastitis: dry-cow treatment, drying-off period

- Perform teat-dipping after milking
- Control flies in summer using pour-on (this helps to prevent summer mastitis)
- Filter milk through a milk sock and change this before every milking
- Clean and maintain milking equipment; regularly hot wash the milking machine and bulk tank
- Cool milk quickly before it enters the bulk tank
- Store milk at 0–4°C in the bulk tank
- Collect milk regularly
- Be proactive in response to any deterioration in test results.

Innovation and biotechnological applications in animal science

One of Ireland's greatest advantages over dairy industries in other countries is that our system of dairy production is grass based and cattle can graze outside for a large proportion of the year. As a result, there is ongoing research into the genetic improvement of dairy cattle for our grass-based system. EBI and genomic selection are two of the most fundamentally important biotechnological applications in animal science. Genomic selection has been covered in detail in Chapter 24, page 339.

Economic breeding index (EBI)

The economic breeding index (EBI) was developed by Teagasc and the Irish Cattle Breeding Federation (ICBF) to accurately identify genetically superior, profitable animals and to bring about genetic improvement within the average dairy production system.

DEFINITION

> The **economic breeding index (EBI)** is a single-figure profit index given in euros of profit per lactation for the animal's progeny compared to an average dairy cow.

EBI helps farmers to identify sire and dam lines that would be most profitable in their dairy herd. It was first introduced in 2001 and is composed of seven sub-indexes that contain information on a wide range of traits:
- **Production index:** focuses on milk production, fat and protein in the milk
- **Fertility index:** focuses on calving interval and survival
- **Calving index:** focuses on calving difficulty, gestation and calf mortality
- **Maintenance index:** focuses on cull cow weight
- **Management index:** focuses on milking time and milking temperament
- **Beef index:** focuses on carcase weight and conformation
- **Health index:** focuses on lameness, udder (SCC and mastitis) and health.

An animal's EBI is calculated by adding the value of the EBI sub-indexes together.

These seven sub-indexes allow farmers to address issues within their own herd. EBI allows for the selection of cows with high milk solids and good fertility and that require less feed to produce, thus giving a more efficient and productive dairy cow. When a farmer is selecting a sire to cross with their dairy herd, it is important that they use a top-quality bull with a high EBI. These sires can be chosen from the ICBF Active Bull List.

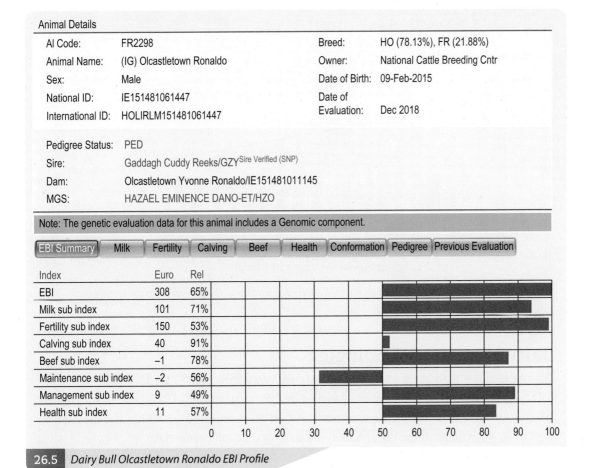

Animal Details

AI Code:	FR2298	Breed:	HO (78.13%), FR (21.88%)
Animal Name:	(IG) Olcastletown Ronaldo	Owner:	National Cattle Breeding Cntr
Sex:	Male	Date of Birth:	09-Feb-2015
National ID:	IE151481061447	Date of Evaluation:	Dec 2018
International ID:	HOLIRLM151481061447		

Pedigree Status:	PED
Sire:	Gaddagh Cuddy Reeks/GZY Sire Verified (SNP)
Dam:	Olcastletown Yvonne Ronaldo/IE151481011145
MGS:	HAZAEL EMINENCE DANO-ET/HZO

Note: The genetic evaluation data for this animal includes a Genomic component.

EBI Summary | Milk | Fertility | Calving | Beef | Health | Conformation | Pedigree | Previous Evaluation

Index	Euro	Rel
EBI	308	65%
Milk sub index	101	71%
Fertility sub index	150	53%
Calving sub index	40	91%
Beef sub index	–1	78%
Maintenance sub index	–2	56%
Management sub index	9	49%
Health sub index	11	57%

26.5 *Dairy Bull Olcastletown Ronaldo EBI Profile*

The EBI of Olcastletown Ronaldo is calculated by adding all the sub-index values together. This bull has a very high index for milk and fertility, and he will pass on half of his genes to his progeny, thereby transferring half of his EBI value (€154). The EBI of any offspring will depend on the cows that the bull is mated to. If this bull was mated to a cow with an EBI of €100, for example, the resultant calf would have an EBI of €204 (€308 + €100 = €408 ÷ 2 = €204). This is called a parent average. This bull has a genomic evaluation, which means a more accurate prediction of his true genetic merit can be generated before he produces any offspring.

Grassland management technologies: Spring Rotation Planner and Feed Wedge

Ireland's grass-based dairy industry allows Irish farmers to produce milk sustainably. Therefore, it is imperative that farmers manage their grazing rotations to minimise costs and maximise profits. Two software packages that allow farmers to do that are **Spring Rotation Planner** and **Feed Wedge**. Spring Rotation Planner divides the total grazing block into weekly portions. It was developed to aid farmers in knowing how much ground they need to graze on a weekly basis, therefore helping them to plan their grazing rotations. Pasture Feed Wedge graphs how much grass is in a particular paddock. It plots the paddocks with the most cover to the paddocks with the least cover of grass. It can help a farmer manage their grassland by identifying paddocks with a surplus of grass (too much grass to graze) so that these paddocks can be used for silage.

Software packages need to be used in conjunction with walking through the paddocks and assessing the grass availability in each paddock. Grass availability is measured either with a plate meter or using a quadrat and shears.

ANIMALS

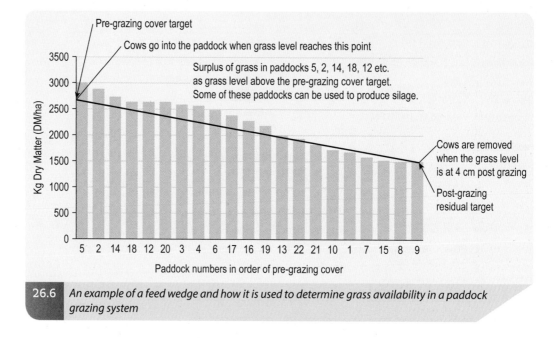

26.6 *An example of a feed wedge and how it is used to determine grass availability in a paddock grazing system*

Dairy parlour technologies

Automation: use of electronic equipment that can carry out a process without the need for manual labour.

The degree of automation in dairy parlours can vary from very little to a great deal. Rotary parlours and milking robots tend to be fully automated. Usually a rotary parlour will require only one person to operate it. A person is required to attach the clusters to the cows, but cluster removal and teat-dipping are usually automatic.

In a rotary parlour the cows walk onto a rotating platform. There is normally a backing gate to keep the cows moving forward onto the rotating platform. The cows are milked as they revolve. Once they are milked, they back off the platform. If a farmer wants a completely automated milking machine, they can choose a 'milking robot'. This type of automated milking machine allows the cows to choose when they want to be milked. It cleans the udder, attaches the clusters, milks the cow, removes the clusters and teat-dips the cow. It can also send a detailed report to the farmer on each cow, including information such as SCC, so that mastitis can be spotted and treated earlier.

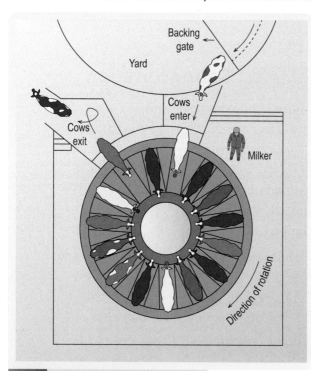

26.7 *Rotary milking parlour*

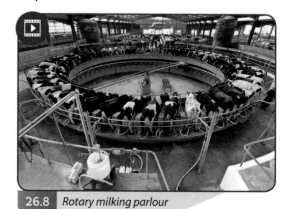

26.8 *Rotary milking parlour*

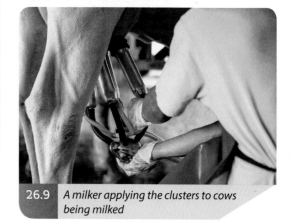

26.9 *A milker applying the clusters to cows being milked*

Qualities and features of Irish food based on grass-fed animals

It is estimated that only 10% of global milk production is based on grass-fed animals. Ireland is in a unique position, as our temperate climate and rainfall facilitates plentiful grass growth, which allows the national dairy herd to graze grass for as long as grass is available. As a result, approximately 68% of an Irish dairy cow's diet is composed of grazed grass (perennial ryegrass pasture). Consumer awareness and interest in purchasing dairy products based on the type of diet (pasture-based diet compared to a mixed ration diet) that the animal is being fed is also growing. Pasture-based feeding

26.10   *Grass-fed dairy cows*

systems are seen to be more natural, healthier and better for an animal's welfare and this is influencing consumers in their choice of dairy products. Ireland has an excellent reputation for producing and selling high-quality food. Ireland is the 12th largest dairy producer in the world.

Teagasc has conducted several research studies to compare the nutrient and processing characteristics of milk derived from cows fed diets based on grazed perennial ryegrass pasture versus total mixed ration (TMR). The findings of the studies were that the grass-fed cows had a greater concentration of fat and protein in their milk. The milk from grass-fed cows was found to have higher levels of unsaturated fatty acids and omega-3 fatty acids. Another study found that milk from cows on mainly pasture-based diets had higher vitamin A and E content compared with milk produced by cows on non-pasture-based diets. Milk produced from grass-fed cows has a more appealing colour, flavour and taste compared to that from animals fed on TMR. This unique colour, flavour and texture is one of the reasons why Irish butter Kerrygold is the second biggest-selling butter brand in the United States and the number one butter brand in Germany. Grass-fed dairy cow's milk is high in beta-carotene. This beta-carotene is what gives Irish butter and cheese their unique colour and flavour. The beta-carotene is responsible for the yellow colour of Irish butter compared with the whiter coloured butter produced in countries where dairy cattle are not pasture fed.

Grass-based milk production is a more sustainable method of milk production. A European Union (EU) survey on livestock contribution to EU greenhouse gas emissions reported that Ireland has the joint lowest (joint with Austria) carbon footprint for milk production in the EU. Milk production in Ireland has a carbon footprint of 1 kg CO_2eq/kg of milk. This is compared to an EU average of 1.4 kg CO_2eq/kg of milk.

> **Total mixed ration (TMR)** is a feed composed of several ingredients blended together. Total mixed ration often consists of some of the following ingredients: maize silage, grass silage, concentrates, molasses and straw. TMR feeding systems are common in the United States and some EU countries.

> **Carbon footprint:** the total CO_2 emissions produced by an individual or product. A product's carbon footprint can be expressed as equivalent carbon dioxide (CO_2eq). This describes the contribution a given greenhouse gas and its concentration will contribute to global warming.

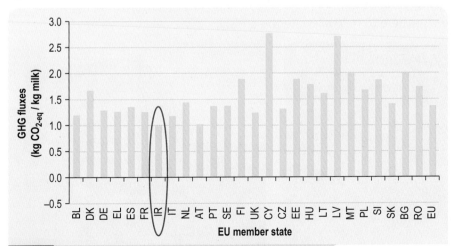

26.11   *Greenhouse gas (GHG) emissions per unit of dairy output. Source: EU Joint Research Centre (JRC)*

Grass-based dairy production systems have the lowest water footprint. Water footprint measures the amount of water used to produce a product. Consumers are becoming more aware of the need for conservation of water supplies and the maintenance of high water quality. A water footprint may become an important deciding factor in a consumer's decision to purchase an Irish dairy product.

26.12 | *Water footprint logo*

The challenges of sustainable intensification

With the continued increase in the global population, worldwide demand for dairy products is on the increase. Ireland is well placed to grow our dairy sector and increase our export of dairy products. The Department of Agriculture, Food and the Marine (DAFM) produced two ambitious plans for the agri-food sector over the last two decades. The first, published in 2010, was called Food Harvest 2020. One of its aims was to increase milk production in Ireland by 50% by 2020, requiring an increase in the national dairy herd by 300,000 to 1.4 million dairy cows. The abolition of milk quotas on 31 March 2015 allowed dairy farmers to expand their herds and sell more milk to their dairy processor. The expansion of the national dairy herd had a knock-on effect for the beef industry, with additional bull calves and heifer calves for the beef sector. Then in 2015 the DAFM updated their Food Harvest 2020 vision and launched Food Wise 2025. This 10-year plan for the agri-food sector aims to make Ireland more competitive in international markets and target the more quality-conscious consumer who looks to buy high-quality food products that are sustainably produced. Both the DAFM Food Harvest and Food Wise strategies aim to intensify food production but to do this sustainably.

This sustainable intensification brings challenges for Irish farmers. The main challenge is the capacity of the farm to produce fodder. If the farm's stocking rate is greater than the farm's ability to produce fodder, expansion of a dairy herd is not possible.

Fodder crises are well documented in the media. There has been a shortfall in fodder for winter feed in 1998, 1999, 2013 and 2018. Weather plays a vital role in the farmer's ability to conserve adequate winter fodder during early summer (first-cut silage) and then later in the summer (second-cut silage). In 2017, a very wet summer prevented farmers conserving as much silage as they would have liked. An extremely cold, wet and long winter meant that turnout of cattle onto the land in 2018 had to be delayed as much of the land nationally was saturated with rainfall. Cold temperatures further compounded the situation, delaying grass growth. What resulted was a fodder crisis across the country, with many farmers running out of fodder to feed their livestock. Fodder was imported from the UK and elsewhere to help alleviate the crisis.

National dairy herd: all dairy cattle throughout Ireland.

Fodder: winter feed for cattle and sheep, e.g. silage and hay.

26.13 | *Fodder crisis 2017–2018*

One of the key causes of the prolonged winter during 2017–2018 was an extreme weather event that caused Ireland and other parts of Europe to experience lower temperatures than normal. Climatologists warn that climate change is making our weather increasingly uncertain. In the summer of 2018, Ireland and the rest of Europe experienced a heatwave. Drought conditions were widespread throughout Ireland, resulting in a large decrease in grass growth. To make up for the shortfall in grass growth, farmers had to feed silage intended for the winter months to the cattle as well as grazing pasture intended for second-cut silage. Teagasc conducted a fodder census in June and early July and reported a fodder deficiency nationally.

Another challenge faced by farmers is limiting or reducing the environmental impact of intensification. Milk production contributes to greenhouse gas (GHG) emissions. Ruminant animals are a source of methane (a GHG) and it is estimated that the expansion of the dairy herd to meet the targets set in Food Harvest 2020 could give rise to a 12% rise in GHG emissions. The Environmental Protection Agency (EPA) states that agriculture is the single largest contributor to Ireland's overall GHG emission, accounting for over 30% of the total. To combat this rise in GHG emission caused by the expansion of the dairy herd, farmers will need to enhance carbon uptake (carbon sequestration) further (see page 106).

Environmental Protection Agency
An Ghníomhaireacht um Chaomhnú Comhshaoil

26.14 *EPA logo*

DEFINITION

Climate change: a change in global or regional climate patterns that is largely caused by increased levels of carbon dioxide and other GHG (nitrous oxide and methane) in the atmosphere. Increased GHG emissions caused by human activities have significantly contributed to climate change.

Intensification of the national dairy herd also faces challenges with increased animal manures from winter housing and increased fertiliser use. According to the EPA, agriculture is one of the main sources of nitrates in groundwater and nutrient enrichment of surface waters (rivers, lakes, etc.). Good water quality is extremely important for public health, the agri-food industry and tourism. Ireland has obligations in relation to water quality and water environments that it must meet under the EU's Water Framework Directive. The Water Framework Directive aims at protecting and enhancing the quality of all waters (rivers, lakes, estuaries, coastal water and groundwaters). The Nitrates Regulations sets out strict measures designed to prevent pollution of surface waters and groundwater from agricultural sources. The Agricultural Sustainability Support and Advisory Programme (ASSAP) has been set up to work closely with farmers to address any potential issues that may be affecting water quality in their area.

Impact of farm economics on dairy production and the importance of export markets

A National Farm Survey has been conducted annually by Teagasc since 1972 as part of the EU Farm Accountancy Data Network. The aim of the survey is to determine the financial situation of Irish farms by measuring the level of costs, gross outputs and incomes across all farming systems (beef, sheep, dairy and tillage). Participants in the farm survey are chosen at random each year in conjunction with the Central Statistics Office. The survey fulfils Ireland's statutory obligation to provide data on farm finances to the European Commission on an annual basis. The results of the 2017 National Farm Survey identified dairy farms as consistently being the most profitable, with the average farm income, after costs and other deductions, of €86,069. The average size of a dairy farm was 56 hectares, with an average dairy herd size of 75 dairy cows.

Dairy farmers' income is composed of their Common Agricultural Policy (CAP) payment and the payment they receive for milk production. The CAP payment is composed of a basic payment scheme and various agri-environmental schemes. Over 90% of farmers applying for their basic payment will automatically qualify for a greening payment (payment for agricultural practices that benefit the climate and the environment) based on their current agricultural practices. The average direct payment for a dairy farmer under CAP was €19,328 and made up 22% of their income. Most of the remainder of their income came from milk production.

Milk production grew nationally in 2017, increasing by 9% compared with milk production in 2016. There was an increase in the average milk price from 27.86 c/l in 2016 to 36.86 c/l in 2017. The biggest challenge for dairy farmers is to weather the volatility of milk prices. Most of the milk produced in Ireland is marketed through Ornua. They sell mostly butter, skim and fat filled powders and cheese. These products are traded on the world market, which is extremely competitive, and the prices that they obtain fluctuate as a result.

26.15 *Milk products*

In 2015 there was a large reduction in milk prices, which coincided with the abolition of milk quotas. The resulting increase in milk production during that year and the following year (2016) allowed farmers to reduce the effect of the fall in milk prices. One of the advantages that allows Irish dairy farmers to compete in such a competitive and volatile market is that Irish farmers have the lowest costs per unit of production of milk compared to any other key dairy region in the EU (source: Teagasc report). The fact that Irish milk is produced on grass-based pasture is one of the contributing factors to this low cost of production.

Cost per unit of production: essentially a breakdown of all the fixed and variable costs that are encountered in the process of producing a single product.

In addition to the volatility of milk prices, we are yet unaware whether a departure of the UK from the EU will have an impact on our dairy industry. The UK is one of our closest trading partners. Over half the cheese produced in Ireland goes to the UK as well as 21% of our milk exports. It is possible that tariffs may be placed on imported Irish goods post-Brexit. We are unsure what our trade relationship will be with the UK, once the UK departs the EU. The Irish government and other agencies are working at diversifying and looking for new markets for Irish agricultural products outside the UK market. The exit of the UK will most likely affect farmers' CAP payments, as the UK contributes to the EU budget and without their contribution, there is likely to be a reduction in CAP payments to farmers. Dairy farmers are not as reliant on their CAP payments as farmers in other farming systems.

The cost of fertilisers, cost of animal feeds (concentrates and fodder), veterinary costs, interest rates on loan repayments, and energy costs are all likely to fluctuate and/or increase and may have a substantial influence on the income of any farmer, not just dairy farmers.

Under the objectives of Food Wise 2025, the Irish dairy industry aims to export 19 out of every 20 litres of milk produced in Ireland by 2025. To achieve this aim will require dairy farmers to continue to work at producing milk sustainably, mitigating any increase in GHG emissions in a market that is extremely competitive, uncertain and with very volatile milk prices.

Policies related to traceability and animal welfare

The Common Agricultural Policy (CAP) is a system of subsidies and support programmes for agriculture operated by the European Union. The CAP combines direct payments to farmers together with price/market supports. It currently accounts for 62% of the EU's budget (source: DAFM).

The objectives of CAP are to:

- Ensure availability of food (food security) at a reasonable price for consumers
- Ensure a fair standard of living for farmers
- Bring stability to markets
- Protect the environment
- Increase agricultural productivity.

CAP consists of two pillars:

- Income support
- Social and environmental development support.

Farmers receiving payments under CAP agree to permit officials or agents from the DAFM to carry out farm inspections.

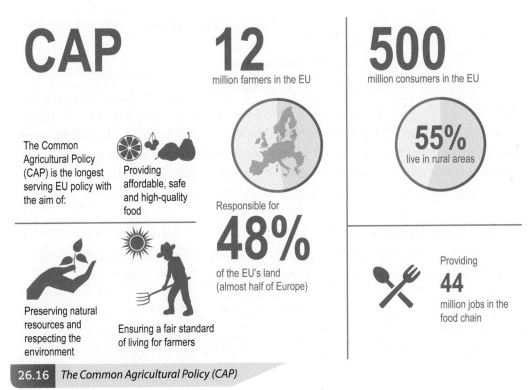

26.16 *The Common Agricultural Policy (CAP)*

Traceability of milk

In Ireland, the main organisations responsible for developing food policies and legislation are the DAFM and the Department of Health (DOH). The Food Safety Authority of Ireland (FSAI) assists in the development of policies and legislation and is also responsible for the enforcement of the legislation.

EU food laws require that all food businesses have in place a **traceability** system, and traceability records must be kept for all foods until it can be reasonably assumed that the food has been consumed. Farmers are required to keep a record of all medicines purchased and administered to animals. In Ireland farmers are legally required **not** to supply milk for human consumption that contains any medicinal residues, including antibiotics. Therefore, milk from dairy cattle being treated with

Legislation: the process of making and enacting laws.

antibiotics must be discarded and kept out of the food chain. To prevent antibiotics and other medicinal residues entering the food chain, farmers must strictly adhere to the withdrawal periods of the animal treatment.

> **DEFINITION**
>
> **Traceability:** the ability to trace and follow a food, feed, food-producing animal or product intended to be incorporated into a food through all the stages of production, processing and distribution.

All milk processors have a testing and traceability system in operation. The raw milk is sampled every time milk is collected from each farmer. One such system involves the collection of a sample of milk in a clean, sterile, uniquely barcoded bottle. The unique barcode allows full traceability of the raw milk back to its source. This sample of milk is immediately tested for the presence of antibiotics as soon as it reaches the processor. If antibiotics are identified in the milk sample, the barcode will identify the supplier of that milk sample. In the event of milk testing positive for antibiotics, that milk will be discarded, and penalties are normally imposed by the milk processor on the farmer that supplied it.

Bord Bia Quality Assurance Scheme

The Bord Bia Quality Assurance scheme was developed by Bord Bia in conjunction with Teagasc, the FSAI, the DAFM, milk producers and processors and other technical experts. Some of the aims of the scheme are to:

- Produce milk sustainably under an accredited scheme
- Provide a uniform mechanism for recording and monitoring
- Set out best practice in Irish dairy farming.

Under the scheme, Bord Bia visits each farm and assesses farm safety and welfare, food safety, traceability and animal welfare. Farmers that meet the relevant criteria will be certified under the scheme. Milk processors in Ireland require their dairy farmers to be certified under the Sustainable Dairy Assurance Scheme (SDAS).

Traceability on the farm

Farmers are required for traceability purposes to keep an accurate record of all movements of animals off and on to their farms. Farmers must comply with each of the following:

- Maintain a herd register for all cattle on their farm
- Ear tag all calves born on the farm within 20 days of birth
- Register all calves born on the Animal Identification & Movement (AIM) system, which is an electronic herd register
- Keep the passports for all registered cattle with the animals each time they move to a new farm and record all movements of an animal throughout its life
- Record all cattle deaths on the AIM system.

This system of traceability reassures consumers that food that enters the food chain can be traced back to its source. It also assures consumers of food safety because if a problem is identified, the traceability system can help prevent a contaminated product reaching the consumer.

Animal welfare

Consumer awareness is growing regarding animal health and welfare, and consumers require assurance that animals are properly treated and managed. Under the SDAS, all cattle must be provided with sufficient feed, fodder, grass and clean water to maintain the health and welfare of the herd. As sustainability is a major component of

Accredited scheme: a scheme that an official body (e.g. the EU) approves or endorses as it recognises that high standards have been met. This means that the scheme has been independently assessed and judged to be as good or better than similar schemes in other countries.

this scheme, dairy cattle must derive the bulk of their feed from grass and grass-based winter fodder (silage or hay).

Other requirements of the SDAS regarding animal welfare include the following:
- Regular inspections of the herd; inspections should be increased around calving time and during adverse weather, etc.
- Appropriate animal handling facilities
- Animals should be treated in a manner that avoids injury and minimises stress
- A euthanisation of an animal should be done under veterinary supervision and carried out humanely
- The herd should be under the routine care of a vet
- All animals should be routinely tested for tuberculosis (TB) and all calves should be tested when tagged for bovine viral diarrhoea (BVD)
- All boundaries and fences must be maintained to minimise contact with neighbouring herds and to prevent injury to animals
- Lactating cows must be milked daily
- All sick animals must be treated promptly and segregated from the rest of the herd if required
- If a notifiable disease is identified on the farm, then the DAFM must be informed.

Farmers participating in this scheme are recommended to participate in the Cell Check programme run by Animal Health Ireland. Some dairy processors also require their dairy farmers to participate in this programme. Animal welfare is dealt with in Chapter 31.

Summary

- Milk is a suspension of protein, fat and other solids in water. The composition of cow's milk varies depending on the breed.
- Milk is produced by specialised cells in the udder called alveoli.
- The udder consists of four quarters and the average cow can produce 25 litres of milk a day.
- Oxytocin is a hormone produced in the pituitary gland that initiates milk let-down.
- The average lactation period for a dairy cow is 305 days.
- The milk dairy industry is composed of liquid milk producers and manufacturing milk producers.
- Liquid milk producers produce milk all year round and operate a spring- and summer-calving system.
- Manufacturing milk producers operate a spring-calving herd and produce milk between summer and autumn, when they can take advantage of grass growth.
- Dairy farmers are paid under the payment scheme A + B − C, with payment based on the amount of protein (A) and fat (B) in their milk minus a processing charge (C).
- The percentage fat in milk varies between the morning and evening milking, if the milking interval is uneven.
- If the milking interval is even, then there is little variation in percentage fat in the milk.
- Milk is tested by the milk processor for a number of things, including: fat and protein (for payment purposes), total bacterial count (TBC), somatic cell count (SCC), antibiotics and excess water.
- TBC is an indicator of the hygiene standards on the farm.
- SCC is an indicator of the health of a cow's udder.

- The quality of a milk sample can be investigated using a blue dye called resazurin.
- Resazurin is incubated with the milk sample at 37°C for 15 minutes. It undergoes a colour change depending on the number of bacteria present. A blue colour indicates excellent quality and a white colour indicates poor quality.
- Economic Breeding Index (EBI) and genomic selection are two of the most fundamentally important biotechnological applications in animal science. The EBI identifies genetically superior, profitable animals and can bring about genetic improvement in a dairy system.
- The use of Spring Rotation Planner and Feed Wedge allows farmers to manage their grazing rotations to minimise costs and maximise profit.
- Grass-based milk production is a more sustainable method of milk production. Ireland has the joint lowest carbon footprint for milk production in the European Union (EU).
- Milk produced from grass-fed animals has a greater concentration of fat and protein. Dairy products produced from grass-fed cattle have a unique colour, flavour and texture.
- The main challenges facing farmers with sustainable intensification are (a) their ability to produce fodder and (b) reducing or limiting the environmental impact of intensification.
- Dairy farming in Ireland is consistently the most profitable farming enterprise.
- Dairy farmers' income is composed of a Common Agricultural Policy (CAP) payment and a payment for the milk that they produce. Milk products are traded on the world market, which is extremely competitive and leads to a lot of volatility in milk prices.
- Traceability is the ability to trace a food, feed, food-producing animal or product intended to be incorporated into a food through all the stages of production, processing and distribution.
- EU law requires that all food businesses have a traceability system in place.
- Milk processors test every milk sample from every dairy farmer for antibiotics and use a traceability system that allows them to trace a sample of milk back to its source if it tests positive for antibiotics.
- Farmers are required to record the movement of animals on and off their farms. Every calf born must be tagged and registered. Registered animals have a passport, which stays with them for life for the purpose of traceability.
- The Sustainable Dairy Assurance Scheme (SDAS) has both traceability and animal health and welfare built into its criteria.

PowerPoint Summary

QUESTIONS

1. The part of the udder that produces milk is called:

   (a) Gland cistern   (b) Streak canal   (c) Alveoli   (d) Teat cistern

2. Which of the following is not a component of the solid non-fat (SNF) fraction of milk?

   (a) Casein   (b) Whey   (c) Lactose   (d) Butterfat

3. Which hormone is responsible for milk let-down in cattle?

   (a) Oxytocin   (b) Prolactin   (c) Adrenaline   (d) Progesterone

4. What is the length of the average lactation period for a dairy cow in days?

   (a) 250   (b) 290   (c) 305   (d) 350

5. Farmers are paid for their milk under the payment scheme A + B − C. What does 'C' stand for?

   (a) Protein value   (c) Processing charge

   (b) Butterfat value   (d) Storage bonus

6. Farmers may have penalties applied to their milk price if they have:

   (a) High TBC   (c) Excess water

   (b) High SCC   (d) All of the above.

7. Why is traceability and welfare a key component of policies and other accredited schemes?

(a)	Consumer confidence in that food that they eat can be traced back to source	To improve the quality of animal products
(b)	To ensure new and improved animal technologies are being used	To minimise stress and unnecessary pain
(c)	To bring about intensification of the production system	To track the movement of animals on to and off a farm
(d)	If a problem arises in a product, it can be traced back to its source	To ensure that all animals are treated and handled in a way that avoids injury and minimises stress

8. Describe an experiment to determine the hygiene quality of milk.

9. A milk processor tests a sample of milk and records (i) a high total bacterial count (TBC), (ii) a high somatic cell count (SCC) and (iii) dirt particles in the milk.

   (a) Give reasons for the results obtained in (i), (ii) and (iii) above.

   (b) Identify ways in which the farmer might reduce the TBC count.

   (c) What actions can a farmer take to reduce the SCC of the milk?

10. How might a dairy farmer improve the composition (fat and protein) of the milk produced by their dairy herd?

11. How can dairy farmers prevent the contamination of milk in their milking parlour?

12. Explain why withdrawal periods must be observed when treating dairy cows for mastitis.

13. Suggest **three** reasons why dairies will not accept milk from cows that have been treated for mastitis.

14. Outline the contrasting management strategies employed in two different dairy farms: one involved in liquid milk production and the other in manufacturing milk production.

15. Read the following information and then answer the questions below.

    A milk processor is paying its farmers using the formula **A + B − C**. The milk processor has set the value of **A** = 5.466 and the value of **B** = 4.218 and a processing charge **C** = −4.5. The VAT rate is 5.4%. Farmers are also given a storage bonus of 0.44 c/lt if they have the storage capacity for seven milkings. Any farmer with an SCC above 250,000 per ml will have a penalty of −0.15 c/lt and a TBC above 51,000 per ml will have a penalty of −0.50 c/lt.

    Example A: The Murphy family farm is producing milk with 4.59% butterfat and 3.65% protein. The Murphy family get a storage bonus of 0.44 c/lt. Their total milk yield for the month of June was 22,650 litres.

    Bainne Nua Creamery
    Co-operative Society Ltd.
    Milk payment June 2018

Protein @ 3.65 (3.65 × 5.466)	= 19.95 c/lt
Butterfat @ 4.59 (4.59 × 4.218)	= 19.36 c/lt
Volume charge	= −4.5 c/lt
Bonuses	= 0.44 c/lt
VAT @ 5.4%	= 1.90 c/lt
Total milk price	= 37.15 c/lt

Example B: The Duffy family farm is producing milk with 3.32% protein and 3.85% butterfat. They also get paid a bonus for storage but in the last 3 months both the SCC count and the TBC in the Duffy's milk has increased. Their total milk yield for the month of June was 22,590 litres.

Bainne Nua Creamery
Co-operative Society Ltd.

Milk payment June 2018

Protein @ 3.32 (3.32 × 5.466)	= 18.15 c/lt
Butterfat @ 3.85 (3.85 × 4.218)	= 16.24 c/lt
Volume charge	= −4.5 c/lt
Bonuses	= 0.44 c/lt
Penalty (SCC)	= −0.15 c/lt
Penalty (TBC)	= −0.50 c/lt
VAT @ 5.4%	= 1.60 c/lt
Total milk price	= 31.28 c/lt

(a) Give reasons why there is such a significant difference in the total milk price paid to the Murphy family compared with that paid to the Duffy family.

(b) Give a reason for the lower percentage of butterfat and protein in the Duffys' milk compared with the Murphys' milk.

(c) Suggest ways in which the Duffys could improve the percentage protein and butterfat in their milk.

(d) What actions would you recommend to the Duffy family in order to reduce the total bacterial count in their milk?

(e) What actions should the Duffy family take to reduce the SCC of their milk?

(f) Why are the Duffys being penalised for the higher TBC and SCC in their milk?

16. Fig. 26.17 is a graph of the effect of an unequal milking interval over 5 days on the milk yield and the milk's composition (percentage fat and protein).

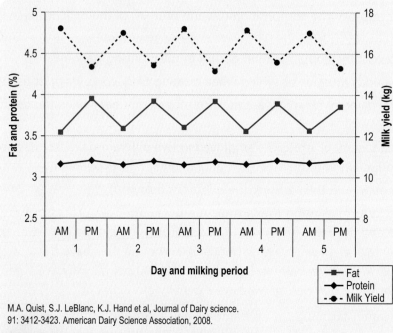

M.A. Quist, S.J. LeBlanc, K.J. Hand et al, Journal of Dairy science.
91: 3412-3423. American Dairy Science Association, 2008.

26.17 *Effect of an unequal milking interval*

(a) What general patterns or trends are shown in the graph above?

(b) Provide an explanation for the patterns or trends you have identified in part (a).

(c) What component (fat or protein) is least affected by unequal milking interval?

17. Distinguish between each of the following pairs:

    (a) TBC and SCC

    (b) Liquid milk producer and manufacturing milk producer

    (c) Withdrawal period and Feed Wedge

    (d) EBI and CAP.

18. How might intensification of the dairy industry affect the profitability and sustainability of Ireland's dairy industry?

19. Discuss the advantages and disadvantages of the intensification of dairy farming.

20. Discuss the effects of the removal of milk quotas on the Irish dairy industry.

21. (a) What benefits has a grass-based dairy industry over other dairy production systems (e.g. total mixed ration system)?

    (b) What advantages does our grass-based dairy system have when it comes to marketing Irish dairy products abroad?

22. What is the Economic Breeding Index (EBI) and why are dairy farmers using high EBI sires on their farms?

23. Outline how advancements in biotechnological applications have brought improvement in animal science.

24. Outline the effect of **one** innovative or technological advancement on milk production in Ireland.

25. Explain why dairy farmers do not receive a set price for their milk.

26. Outline how the economic circumstances beyond the control of a dairy farmer can affect the profitability of a dairy enterprise.

27. Why are calves tagged when they are born?

28. Explain the importance of traceability of milk in the Irish dairy industry.

29. What is meant by the term 'withdrawal period'?

    (a) The time period between administering the dose of an antibiotic or other drug to an animal and when the animal or animal product is fit for human consumption.

    (b) The time period between treating a cow with an antibiotic and when you can milk them.

    (c) The time period between when an animal is treated with an antibiotic and when the infection clears.

    (d) The time period between adding a fertiliser to grass and when the animals can graze the grass.

Solutions   Weblinks

CHAPTER 27
Beef breeds and beef production: dairy calf to beef and suckler beef production

When you have completed this chapter you should be able to:

- Describe the characteristics of common types and breeds of beef cattle
- Compare two different systems of animal production for beef: suckler beef and dairy calf to beef
- Describe the factors that affect output and quality of beef from a suckler herd and a calf to beef herd (breed variety, nutrition, housing and management)
- Discuss the role and importance of genomics and €uro-Star indexes on bringing about improvement in the suckler herd
- Appreciate the impact of beef rearing on farm economics
- Appreciate the importance of export markets
- Discuss the attributes of Irish food based on grass-fed animals
- Discuss management practices for sustainable and environmentally friendly beef production systems.

Beef production in Ireland

Beef production in Ireland is a grass-based system. It is considerably cheaper to produce a beef animal in a grass-based system than in a grain-based system. However, it takes 2 years to have a beef animal ready for slaughter on high production farms, and on other farms it requires 2.5 years. There are many beef production systems in Ireland:

- Calf to beef in 2 years
- Suckler herd
- Bull beef production
- Heifer beef production
- Culled cow finishing
- Several types of store beef cattle to finishing systems.

Beef breeds in Ireland

Beef breeds can be divided into two categories: British beef breeds and continental beef breeds.

British beef breeds

Aberdeen Angus

> **Renowned:** well known for.

> **Finishing weight:** slaughter weight.

The Aberdeen Angus breed originates from Scotland and is renowned for its easy calving. For that reason, it is used as a sire on heifers in both beef and dairy herds. It has a low growth rate and finishing weight compared to other beef breeds. However,

27.1 *Aberdeen Angus*

Aberdeen Angus breed societies have been improving the growth rate of this breed. The Aberdeen Angus has a black coat and skin, is naturally polled, and is of small–medium size. It is an early maturing breed that produces a lean carcase.

Hereford

The Hereford breed originates from Herefordshire in England. It was first introduced into Ireland around the end of the 1700s. This breed is easily recognisable, with its deep-red coat and white face and underside, which gives it the name 'whitehead'.

Some of the characteristics of this breed include: good conformation, strong muscles, strong legs and feet, early maturing and easy calving. They have a growth rate intermediate between the Aberdeen Angus and the continental breeds. Herefords are commonly used as a beef sire on dairy and suckler herds to produce calves for beef production.

27.2   *Hereford bull*

Continental beef breeds
Belgian Blue

This breed originates from southern Belgium. It usually has a whitish-blue coat but can sometimes have a black and white coat. It is a double-muscled beef breed due to a mutation in the myostatin gene. They have a higher growth rate than Charolais.

Belgian Blues have a high kill-out percentage and produce a high percentage of lean meat on the carcase. When a Belgian Blue bull is mated with a normal cow, the calf produced will have some degree of the double muscle. The major disadvantage with this breed is that the double muscle causes calving difficulties. When a purebred Belgian Blue bull is mated with a purebred Belgian Blue cow, the calf is normally delivered by Caesarean.

27.3   *Belgian Blue bull*

DEFINITION

Kill out percentage (%) is the weight of the dressed carcase in relation to the weight of the live animal at slaughter. A dressed carcase will have the head, feet and internal organs removed.

Charolais

Charolais is a very popular beef breed in Ireland. The Charolais is a French breed that was first imported into Ireland in 1964. It is white or cream in colour with a fast growth rate, good conformation and lean carcase. There is a risk of calving difficulties due to the blocky conformation and high birth weight of the calf. For that reason, a Charolais bull should not be used as a sire on a heifer.

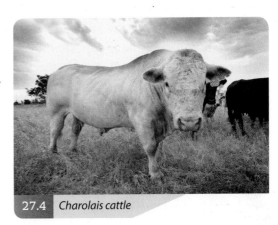
27.4   *Charolais cattle*

Limousin

The Limousin is another popular sire for beef dams in Ireland in 2017 according to the Animal Identification and Movement (AIM) system. The Limousin originates from France. Limousin cattle are recognised by their reddish-brown coat and their long slender bodies. They have a high muscle to bone ratio, good conformation, high fertility and are easy calving. They have a lower growth rate compared to other continental breeds.

27.5 *Limousin cattle*

Simmental

This breed originates from the Simmen Valley in Switzerland. It has a red and white spotted coat, usually with a white face. There are two types of Simmentals: a beef breed that is bred for beef production and a dual-purpose breed that is bred for milk and beef production. The dual-purpose breed is a popular choice for suckler herds because of its beef and milk traits. The growth rate of a Simmental is less than that of a Charolais.

27.6 *Simmental cattle*

Growth, maturity, finishing weight and conformation of beef animals

In the United States, beef animals can be brought from birth to finishing weight for slaughter in roughly 1 year. This type of farming is extremely intensive: animals are fed on a high plane of nutrition. In Ireland there are many different types of beef production systems, and the time it takes to get the animal to its slaughter weight can vary widely depending on the system. In intensive beef production systems, young beef bulls can be ready for slaughter in less than 16 months. Other less intensive systems require 2 years or more to get a calf from birth to finishing weight for slaughter. Intensive beef production systems in Ireland rely on good-quality grass and silage supplemented with concentrates to ensure high live weight gains per day. In less intensive systems, good grassland and more moderate levels of concentrate feeding require 24 months or more to reach slaughter weight. The breed of the beef animal plays a major role in determining the finishing weight of the animal.

Deposition: build-up or accumulation.

Fig. 27.7 shows the deposition of fat and muscle from the birth of the animal until it is 4 years old. A young animal puts on fat very slowly at the start. The rate of muscle deposition decreases as the animal reaches maturity. In contrast, there is an increase in the amount of fat that is deposited from the age of 2 years and onwards. This fat is deposited subcutaneously and in the thoracic cavity. This fat is trimmed from the carcase after the animal is slaughtered. Bone growth has a smaller relative growth rate than either fat or muscle.

Subcutaneous: under the skin.

The weight at which fat deposition increases depends on the breed of the animal. British beef breeds are described as early-maturing beef breeds: they start putting down fat at lower live weights than continental breeds. Continental breeds are later maturing, with high growth rates, larger size and finish at higher live weights without laying down fat. For this reason, continental beef breeds have grown in popularity in

Thoracic cavity: chest cavity in animals.

Ireland. Table 27.1 gives the average finishing weight of British and continental steers. Continental breeds require high levels of feeding to match their high growth rates, while British beef breeds require more moderate levels of feeding.

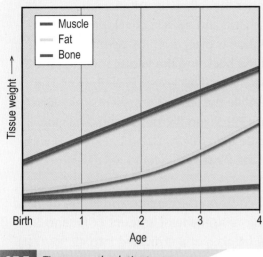

27.7 *Tissue growth relative to age*

Table 27.1 Finishing weights of British (early maturing breeds) and continental (late maturing) beef breeds	
Beef breeds	**Finishing weights (kg)**
British breeds	
Aberdeen Angus	500
Hereford	530
Continental breeds	
Belgian Blue	700
Charolais	700
Simmental	680
Limousin	650

Research work carried out at Grange, Teagasc Animal & Grassland Research and Innovation Centre. Purebred beef breeds were finished at a similar fat cover and slaughtered.

Conformation

Conformation refers to the shape of the animal. It is extremely important in the grading of carcases under the EUROP classification system (see page 398). Conformation traits vary greatly between dairy and beef breeds of cattle. Beef breeds have a block-shaped conformation, with wide shoulders and hindquarters that are well fleshed (see Fig. 27.8).

27.8 *Beef breed conformation*

A purebred dairy animal has a wedge-shaped conformation, with narrow shoulders that are not well fleshed and a neck that is long and thin. The hindquarters of a dairy breed are wide but not well fleshed. Dairy breeds have a wide chest and a large lung capacity, which supports their ability to produce milk. Beef breeds have the best conformation according to the classification scheme, while purebred dairy breeds have the worst. The sex of the animal also affects conformation, with bulls having the best conformation, followed by steers and heifers; cows have the worst conformation.

EU Beef Classification Scheme

The EU Beef Classification Scheme is a common grading scheme for beef throughout Europe. It assesses the slaughtered carcase under the following criteria:

1. **Conformation:** the shape, width of the carcase and muscle development of the carcase is visually assessed. Particular attention is placed on the width and shape of the shoulders, width of the carcase along the back and the width and roundness of the hindquarters. Conformation is divided into five classes: E, U, R, O, P. The letter E represents the best conformation while the letter P represents the worst. The category of P is further subdivided into P+, P and P−, describing declining conformation. A category E animal would be a double-muscled beef animal with excellent carcase quality, while animals in the P category would have very poor conformation (e.g. Holstein–Friesians).

2. **Fat:** visual assessment of the degree of fat cover on the carcase and in the thoracic cavity. There are five fat classes, with 1 indicating the least amount of fat and 5 indicating the greatest amount of fat. The fat class of 4 is divided into 4L (low fat) and 4H (high fat). Consumer demand is for lean meat; therefore, the ideal fat score is 3 and penalties may be applied to carcases with higher fat scores.

3. **Sex:** carcases are also classified by sex and are coded as follows: A is a young bull, B is a stock bull, C is a steer, D is a cow and E is a heifer.

Meat destined for the export market is priced based on this beef classification system.

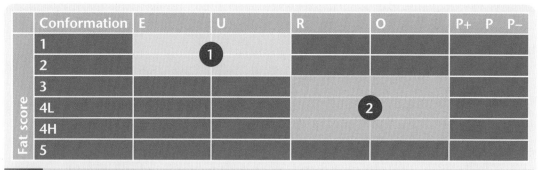

	Conformation	E	U	R	O	P+	P	P−
Fat score	1		①					
	2							
	3							
	4L				②			
	4H							
	5							

27.9 *EU beef grading scheme. 1: Only double-muscled purebred continental animals are classified in this range. 2: Most Irish beef animals score in this range when they are classified after slaughter.*

Comparison of dairy calf to beef and suckler beef as systems of steer beef production

Dairy calf to beef production (24 months)

The calves for this type of beef production are male, with some female calves coming from the dairy herd. Dairy farmers will cross some of their herd with a beef bull to improve the value and conformation of the resulting progeny. However, the most popular sire used in dairy production in 2017 was a Friesian bull (52.1%) followed by Aberdeen Angus (20.6%), Hereford (14.5%) and Limousin (4.7%) (AIM Statistics, 2017). The high use of a dairy bull and early maturing beef breeds will have a knock-on effect on conformation and carcase quality of the resulting progeny. The abolition of the milk quota in 2015 and the subsequent expansion of the dairy herd has led to an increase in the number of dairy calves being born. The AIM Bovine Statistical Report of 2017 reported 1.3 million calves born to Friesian dams, the bulk of which were born in February and March. In addition, the 2017 AIM report also states that 106,889 male dairy calves (dairy sire) between 0 and 6 weeks old were moved from farm to farm in

February and March. Another 10,702 dairy heifers (0–6 weeks old) were also moved from farm to farm during this time. From these numbers alone, it is clear to see that there is a large surplus of dairy calves that will most likely end up in a beef production system. The dairy calf to beef system requires the purchase of calves every year and the rearing of those animals to their finishing weight at 2 years of age. There is a risk of buying in disease, unless the beef farmer is buying the calves directly from the dairy farmer.

Suckler beef production (24 months)

The national suckler herd also supplies a significant number of calves for beef production. The AIM Bovine Statistics Report for 2017 states that over 975,000 calves were born to beef dams. The most popular beef breeds used for suckler production in Ireland are continental breeds: Limousin, Charolais and Simmental. The Aberdeen Angus and Hereford are also very popular due to their easy calving. In contrast to the system of dairy calf to beef, the rearing and feeding of the suckler calf is carried out by the suckler dam. Consequently, a calf in a suckler herd has a greater average daily live weight gain (ADG) compared with the dairy calf to beef system. Approximately 80% of suckler herds in Ireland are spring-calving herds. Under this system, the suckler cow calves in February/March. This allows maximum utilisation of grass and reduces feed cost compared with an autumn-calving system. A productive and efficient suckler herd requires high levels of management.

The suckler dam is a very important component of the suckler system. Ideally the dam should have sufficient milk, good fertility, good ability to calve, good temperament and good beef traits. Crossbred animals display hybrid vigour and can have several advantages as previously described in Chapter 23.

These two systems of beef production (dairy calf to beef system and the suckler beef system) are compared for breed variety, nutrition, housing and management in Table 27.2. These factors will affect the output and the quality of the beef produced by these systems. Both systems require 24 months for steers (castrated males) to reach finishing/ slaughter weight.

DEFINITION

Reproductive efficiency of a suckler herd is defined as the number of calves weaned per 100 cows served. If a farmer has calved 100 cows but just 81 calves have been weaned, the farmer has a reproductive efficiency of 81%.

Reproductive efficiency can be improved by:
1. Selecting replacement heifers with maternal traits
2. Avoiding calving difficulties by using easy calving bulls
3. Ensuring the suckler cow is at the correct BCS at mating (2.5–3.0) and calving down (3.25–3.5)
4. Controlling diseases that affect fertility (BVD and leptospirosis)
5. Management of feeding levels before and after calving – cows that have insufficient feed intake will produce less milk and have poorer milk quality; the growth of the calf relies heavily on its consumption of the dam's milk
6. Low calf mortality
7. Compacted calving and breeding season.

Table 27.2 Comparison of the two systems of beef production

Suckler steer beef production (24 months)	Dairy Friesian calf to beef production (steers)
Breed variety	
Suckler dam	• Majority are purebred dairy steers
• Mainly continental beef breeds: Limousin, Charolais and Simmental. Aberdeen Angus and Herefords are also popular	• Most commonly used dairy sire in the dairy herd is a Friesian bull
• Crossbred dams and purebred dams of both early and late maturing breeds	• Some beef crossed calves, mainly Friesian crossed with early maturing Aberdeen Angus and Herefords
Suckler sire	• Small proportion of Friesian crossed with late maturing continental breeds (Limousin)
• Most popular beef sires (AIM 2017) were Limousin, Charolais, Aberdeen Angus and Simmental	• Dairy breeds have a lower kill out %
• Sires used will influence the conformation, age of the progeny at slaughter and the carcase weight of the progeny	
• Suckler farmers have the ability to improve the genetic merit of their herd's progeny through selective breeding	
• Beef breeds have a higher kill out %	
Suckler steer beef production (24 months)	**Dairy Friesian calf to beef production (steers)**
Nutrition	
• In the suckler system the calf is not removed from the dam	• As the calves in this system of production need to be artificially reared, the feeding and management of these calves is the same as those used to rear dairy calves
• The calf will suckle the dam until it is weaned (7–10 months)	
• Suckler farmers predominately operate a spring-born calving system so that they can maximise the utilisation of grass	• The calves initially should be fed milk replacer, hay (to develop the rumen), concentrates and clean water
• Good grassland management is required to ensure good milk production and fertility in the suckler dam	• Any changes to the diets of the calves should be done gradually so as not to cause digestive upset or scour
• Suckler herds should graze grass rotationally using either a paddock or strip grazing system	• Calves can be put out on grass as soon as there is enough available, and concentrates should be continued to be fed to them until they adjust to their new diet
• Initially when the calf goes out on grass it will depend solely on the milk from its dam; as time goes by, the calf will start to eat grass	• This system of production requires excellent grassland management as calves should be rotationally grazed in a leader-follower system, grazing ahead of older stock
• Calves are selective grazers and should be allowed to creep graze ahead of the herd; creep gates allow calves to have access to better pasture but prevent the cow from doing so	

Suckler steer beef production (24 months)	Dairy Friesian calf to beef production (steers)
Nutrition	**Nutrition**
• Calves are usually weaned in the autumn of their first year • Weanlings should be fed good-quality silage (72% DMD or better) in their first winter with 1–2 kg of concentrates • Yearlings are turned out onto grass in spring and should rotationally graze grass for at least 200 days; the aim is to put on 185 kg over the second season grazing grass • Once housed in winter of their second year, they should be on a diet of high-quality silage (72% or better) and fed 5–6 kg of concentrates a day • To achieve finishing weights in 24 months, suckler farmers should adhere to the target weights as outlined in Table 27.3	• Weanlings need to gain 80 kg over their first winter; they should be housed for their first winter and fed 1–2 kg of concentrates a day as well as good-quality silage (72% DMD) • Yearlings should be turned out on grass in early spring and rotationally graze grass for at least 200 days; they will need to put on 180 kg over their second season on grass • The steers are housed for their second winter and fed good-quality silage (72% DMD or better) and fed 5–6 kg of concentrates to bring them to their finishing (slaughter) weight; during their second winter in housing the steers need a live weight gain of greater than 1.0 kg/day to get to their finishing weight • To achieve finishing weights in 24 months, calf to beef farmers should adhere to target weights as outlined in Table 27.3
Housing	**Housing**
• Suckler beef production systems require a lot of housing: slatted houses for weanlings and yearlings as well as calving sheds; slatted houses can have creep gates fitted to allow calves additional space for resting and creep feeding • A suckler cow and her calf will require 3.5–4 m² of floor space in winter housing • Weanlings require 1.4 m² of floor space per animal in winter housing in their first year • Yearlings require 2–2.3 m² of floor space per animal in winter housing in their second year • Animals should be removed from the land over the winter months to prevent poaching of the land	• Suitable housing and feeding facilities to rear calves (well lit, good ventilation and free of draughts) • Requires housing for weanlings and yearlings • Weanlings are normally housed around November to prevent poaching of the land • Most common type of housing used is slatted housing • Any underweight weanlings should be grouped together and fed extra concentrates • Yearlings require 2–2.3 m² of floor space per animal in winter housing in their second year

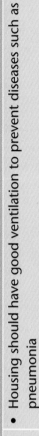

Suckler steer beef production (24 months)	Dairy Friesian calf to beef production (steers)
Housing	**Housing**
• Suckler herds tend to be housed longer as they are not usually turned out onto grass until after calving	• Housing should have good ventilation to prevent diseases such as pneumonia  **27.10** *Cattle in winter housing*
Management	**Management**
• Good parasite control and animal health programme in place	• As this system of production involves the rearing of calves without a dam, there is the potential for losses of calves due to illness, etc.; a farmer should buy in 5% more calves to mitigate these losses
• Suckler beef systems are more suited to drier farms where stocking rates can be kept high	
• There are times in the year where there is a greater workload than others, e.g. calving	• Good parasite control and animal health programme are essential
• Good management of calving and calving interval are required to ensure that the suckler herd is turned out onto grass as soon as grass is available to maximise the grazing season and keep the cost of keeping the suckler cow as low as possible; lower levels of management and having a shorter grazing season makes the cost of keeping the suckler cow greater and reduces profitability	• If grassland is not managed correctly, then this will delay the animals reaching their slaughter weight; more concentrates will be required to get animals to their slaughter weight
	• Purchase the calves from a small number of sources to reduce the risk of buying in disease
• Heat detection is vital as it takes longer for a suckler cow to come back into heat compared with a dairy cow; suckling and the presence of the calf inhibits the onset of oestrus. Farmers should restrict the access of the calf to the cow once the calf is 30 days old, as this will encourage the suckler cow to start oestrous cycling again	• More even workload as there is no breeding stock involved in this production; the farmer doesn't have the cost associated with the keeping of a suckler cow
• Cattle should be finished at the preferred carcase weight of between 280 and 400 kg, as this carcase weight produces steak cut of the preferred size for customers of Irish beef	• Cattle should be finished at the preferred carcase weight of between 280 and 400 kg, as this carcase weight produces steak cut of the preferred size for customers of Irish beef

Suckler steer beef production (24 months)	Dairy Friesian calf to beef production (steers)
Output and quality	

Suckler steer beef production (24 months)

Output

- Key factors that affect output in a suckler herd are reproductive efficiency and calving interval
- Reproductivity efficiency: in a suckler herd the aim is to produce a calf per cow per year
- Calving interval: the calving interval in a suckler herd should be kept at 365; a longer calving interval reduces profitability for a suckler beef farm; if a cow has a calving interval of 395 days, that means she is calving once every 13 months
- Calf growth rate: tends to be higher due to the suckler dam milk supply; in addition beef sires as well as beef dams give higher live weight gains
- Stocking rate: high stocking rates can lead to higher output of beef per hectare
- Long-term investment in stock and capital needed

Quality

- Cattle bred from a suckler herd tend to be more valuable due to their ability to achieve better grades and heavier carcase weights at slaughter compared with dairy beef animals
- Beef from suckler herds generate a higher proportion of high-value cuts that match the requirements of customers across the EU
- Farmers should use the ICBF €uro-Star indexes when breeding replacement heifers and calves for slaughter to improve the maternal and terminal traits of their suckler herd (see page 405)
- Early maturing breeds: farmers aim to have 10% of their beef animals achieve a U grade and 90% achieve an R grade
- Late maturing breeds: farmers aim to have 55% of their beef animals achieve a U grade and 45% achieve an R grade

Feeding and management guidelines are those recommended by Teagasc in their Beef Production System Guidelines.

Dairy Friesian calf to beef production (steers)

Output

- Buy a healthy, good beef crossed calf preferably
- Buy the calf in February to early March, as these calves will be weaned earlier and spend longer grazing grass
- Dairy calves are cheaper than suckler weanlings
- Yearlings need to achieve a 200 day grazing season in their second summer out on grass
- Calf to beef systems are high-cost systems and require high output to cover the costs

Quality

- Beef animals that originate from the dairy herd tend to have poorer conformation and kill-out % compared with beef animals that come from the suckler herd
- Beef animals from the dairy herd are more likely to grade at O or P on slaughter
- Steer beef is in demand by the majority of customers in the UK and Europe; there is a strong demand for beef carcases that have a conformation grade of O or better
- Farmers may struggle to achieve the minimum carcase weight required at slaughter with some dairy crossed heifers

In a farming enterprise, capital is the land, machinery and buildings owned by the farmer.

Comparison of target weights and daily live weight gain in beef production systems

Teagasc produces target weights to aid beef-producing farmers in meeting the required carcase weight for a beef steer for slaughter at 24 months. Target weights and average daily gain (ADG) vary depending on the breed or crossbred animal. Beef cattle rotationally grazing good-quality grass will have an ADG of 0.7 kg/day (purebred dairy steers) to 1.2 kg/day for continental suckler beef steers. When weanling beef steers are housed during the winter months, there is a decrease in their ADG, since they have been moved from a high plane of nutrition (grass) to a low plane of nutrition (silage). This decrease in ADG is commonly referred to as a **store period** (see Fig. 27.11). During this time, the frame of the animal grows but the animal puts on very little muscle. Dairy to beef steers have a target weight of 230 kg at being housed for the winter with the aim of achieving a weight gain of roughly 80 kg over the first winter. Suckler beef steers will be at a higher weight going into winter housing and will aim to put on 80 kg over their first winter.

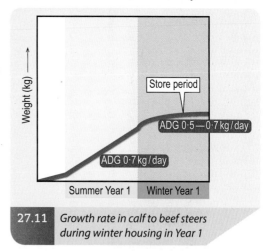

27.11 *Growth rate in calf to beef steers during winter housing in Year 1*

> **DEFINITION**
>
> **Store period:** a period of restricted feeding that occurs during winter housing when there is a change of feed from a high plane of nutrition to a low plane of nutrition. This results in a decrease in live weight gain (LWG) of an animal. Target average daily gain (ADG) over the store period is 0.6 kg/day in beef production.

A farmer needs to feed good-quality silage with a DMD of 72% or greater in order to achieve this live weight gain. To ensure that a target of 80 kg of live weight is achieved over the winter months, steers in both the dairy calf to beef and suckler beef will be fed 1 to 2 kg of concentrates per day. If silage quality is poor (62% DMD) then additional concentrates will need to be fed to the steers to achieve an ADG of 0.6 kg/day. A mineral and vitamin mix or lick should be provided to prevent mineral deficiencies such as grass tetany.

When the steers are turned out onto grass in their second year they are called yearlings. Back on grass, the live weight gain per day will increase and will be higher compared to a yearling kept on a continuous high plane of nutrition. Such growth is called compensatory growth and it occurs when an animal returns to a high plane of nutrition following a period of restricted feeding (see Fig. 27.12).

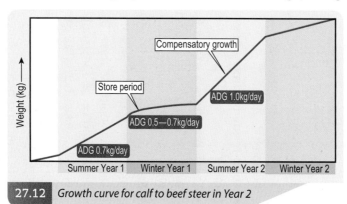

27.12 *Growth curve for calf to beef steer in Year 2*

The compensatory growth effect is used to our advantage in Ireland, since it occurs when grass supply increases naturally during the summer months. The yearlings should again rotationally graze good-quality grass over the summer months. The aim is for the yearlings to put on 180 kg of live weight (calf to beef) and 185 kg live weight (suckler) over a 200-day grazing season. When housing steers for their second winter steers with similar weight and breed should be housed together to allow for better feed management. Steers should be fed high-quality silage (72% DMD or better) with 5.0 to 6.0 kg of concentrates per day to ensure the beef steers reach their finishing weights. Where silage quality is poor, Teagasc recommends that concentrates should be fed ad lib to dairy steers for the last 80–100 days before slaughter. Feeding concentrates ad lib will increase the cost of producing beef.

Table 27.3 Production target weights									
	Suckler beef		Suckler beef		Dairy to calf		Dairy to calf		Dairy to calf
Stage	Early maturing steer		Late maturing steer		Holstein–Friesian steers		Early maturing dairy crosses		Late maturing dairy crosses
	kg LW	ADG (kg/day)	kg LW	ADG (kg/day)	kg LW	ADG (kg/day)	kg LW	ADG (kg/day)	kg LW	ADG (kg/day)
Born	45		50		40		45		50	
Weaned	275	1.10	300	1.20	90	0.70	90	0.8	90	0.8
Winter housing Year 1	290	0.60	320	0.65	220	0.70	240	0.75	240	0.75
Turnout March	350	0.50	390	0.55	320	0.60	330	0.60	330	0.60
Winter housing Year 2			610	0.95	510	0.90	510	1.0	520	1.0
Live weight at slaughter (Feb)	570	0.90	725	1.00	620	1.05	570	1.0	650	1.0
Carcase weight	310–330		400		310–330		295		350	

ADG: average daily live weight gain; kg LW = kg of live weight

Source: Teagasc

Improvement in quality and output of the suckler herd using genomics and ICBF €uro-Star Index (biotechnological application in animal science)

Over the last number of years, breeding in the Irish suckler herd has been dominated by bulls that are used to produce high weight gains and well-muscled calves for slaughter. However, this type of breeding has led to a decrease in the maternal traits (e.g. milk production, fertility and calving ability) in the daughters of these bulls, which are kept as replacement suckler dams.

The **Beef €uro-Star Index** was developed by the Irish Cattle Breeding Federation (ICBF) in conjunction with Teagasc to combat this problem. The €uro-Star Index is designed to aid suckler farms in selecting the most profitable animals for breeding. It is divided into two indexes: a replacement index (used for the selection of bulls to breed replacement heifers) and a terminal index (used to breed beef animals for slaughter). Each bull is ranked in a star system ranging from 0.5 to 5 stars. Stars are allotted within breeds: the left-hand side of the index ranks a bull within his own breed. Stars are also allotted across breeds: the right-hand side ranks a bull against all breeds (see Figs 27.13 and 27.14). A bull that is 0.5 stars is in the bottom 10%. A bull that is 5 stars is in the top 10%. The stars also demonstrate that there is as much variation within each breed as there is across the different cattle breeds.

When suckler farmers want to breed a replacement suckler heifer, they can use the bulls with a high replacement index. Replacement index focuses primarily on maternal traits such as milk production and fertility. If farmers want to breed cattle with high weight gains and well-muscled carcases, they can use bulls with a high terminal index. Terminal index focuses on beef traits such as carcase weight and conformation.

Using high replacement index bulls will not necessarily mean that the calves from these bulls will be poor cattle to slaughter. The replacement index also takes terminal traits into account; therefore, high replacement index bulls offer the right balance between growth and maternal traits.

The ICBF €uro-Star indexes are updated three times a year (April, August and December) after a process called a genetic evaluation. Genetic evaluations involve genotyping. Genotyping increases reliability figures and provides accuracy in gauging the potential performance of the animal. Any data recently recorded on a bull will also be included and all of this will in turn affect the bull's index. Figs 27.13 and 27.14 are examples of very different bulls. The first bull – CF52 (Doonally New) – is a very high terminal index bull. The second bull – JVL (Jovial) – is a very high replacement index bull.

Animal Details

AI Code:	CF52	**Breed:**	CH (100%)
Animal name:	DOONALLY NEW	**Owner:**	NATIONAL CATTLE BREEDING CNTR
National ID:		**Date of Birth:**	18-JAN-1997
International ID:	CHAFRAM007197126709	**Date of**	April 2014

Eurostar Index	Replacement Graphics	Terminal Graphics	Linear Type	Pedigree	Prev Eval (BTAP)

Star Rating (within Charolais breed)	Economic Indexes	€uro value per progeny	Index reliability	Star Rating (across all beef breeds)
★★★★★	Replacement Maternal Cow Traits Maternal Progeny Traits	€8 €236 €228	98% (V high) 98% 98%	★★★★★
★★★★★	Terminal	€152	98% (V high)	★★★★★
★★★★★	Dairy Beef	€	% (N/A)	★★★★★

Poor Replacement Index

Very High Terminal Index (5 stars)

Star Rating (within Charolais breed)	Key profit traits	Index value	Trait reliability	Star Rating (across all beef breeds)
	Expected progeny performance			
	Calving difficulty (% 3 & 4) Breed ave: 7.65%. All breeds ave: 4.99%	9.80%	99% (V high)	
★★★★★	Docility (1–5 scale) Breed ave: 0.04. All breeds ave: 0.00	0.15 scale	99% (V high)	★★★★★
★★★★★	Carcase weight (kg) Breed ave: 31.88 kg. All breeds ave: 22.88 kg	42 kg	99% (V high)	★★★★★
★★★★★	Carcase conformation (1–15 scale) Breed ave: 1.91. All breeds ave: 1.85	2.15 scale	99% (V high)	★★★★★
	Expected daughter breeding performance			
	Daughter calving difficulty (% 3 & 4) Breed ave: 5.05%. All breeds ave: 1.85	2.15 scale	99% (V high)	
★★★★★	Daughter milk (kg) Breed ave: -6.33 kg. All breeds ave: 0.33 kg	-8.38 kg	99% (V high)	★★★★★
★★★★★	Daughter calving interval (days) Breed ave: 0.06 days. All breeds ave: -0.52 days	2.81 days	98% (V high)	★★★★★

Excellent Terminal Traits

27.13 *ICBF €uro-Star Index for Doonally New*

Animal Details

AI Code:	JVL	Breed:	SA (100%)
Animal name:	JOVIAL	Owner:	NATIONAL CATTLE BREEDING CNTR
National ID:		Date of Birth:	29-APR-1994
International ID:	SALFR AMM006327335173	Date of Evaluation:	April 2014

Eurostar Index	Replacement Graphics	Terminal Graphics	Linear Type	Pedigree	Prev Eval (BTAP)

Star Rating (within Salers breed)	Economic Indexes	€uro value per progeny	Index reliability	Star Rating (across all beef breeds)
★★★★★	Replacement Maternal Cow Traits Maternal Progeny Traits	€373 €204 €169	89% (V high) 90% 89%	★★★★★
★★☆☆☆	Terminal	€99	88% (V high)	★★☆☆☆
★★★★★	Dairy Beef	€	% (N/A)	★★★★★

Very High Replacement Index (5 stars)

Star Rating (within Salers breed)	Key profit traits	Index value	Trait reliability	Star Rating (across all beef breeds)
	Expected progeny performance			
	Calving difficulty (% 3 & 4) ℹ Breed ave: 2.35%. All breeds ave: 4.99%	2.90%	94% (V high)	
★★★★☆	Docility (1–5 scale) Breed ave: -0.10. All breeds ave: 0.00	-0.06 scale	91% (V high)	★★☆☆☆
★★★★☆	Carcase weight (kg) Breed ave: 16.75 kg. All breeds ave: 22.88 kg	19 kg	97% (V high)	★★★★☆
★★★★★	Carcase conformation (1–15 scale) Breed ave: 1.19. All breeds ave: 1.85	1.5 scale	97% (V high)	★★☆☆☆
	Expected daughter breeding performance			
	Daughter calving difficulty (% 3 & 4) Breed ave: 5.15%. All breeds ave: 5.29	3.7%	99% (V high)	
★★★★★	Daughter milk (kg) Breed ave: 10.33 kg. All breeds ave: 0.33 kg	18.82 kg	95% (V high)	★★★★★
★★★★★	Daughter calving interval (days) Breed ave: -3.66 days. All breeds ave: -0.52 days	-9.1 days	82% (V high)	★★★★★

Excellent Maternal Traits

27.14 *ICBF €uro-Star Index for Jovial*

Reliabilities

The reliability figures show how well proven a bull is on an index or trait. The more calves that are born from a bull, the higher the reliability figures will become. Bulls such as CF52 have extremely high reliability figures. Thousands of calves have been born and performance-recorded from this bull. He is, therefore, a fully proven bull. Bulls with low reliability indexes do not have many calves born and performance-recorded. The index figures for these bulls are more likely to change as new calves are born.

The impact of beef production on farm economics and the importance of export markets

The profitability of any cattle rearing beef enterprise relies on the cattle achieving a high proportion of their weight gain from grass and grass-based forage. Excellent grassland management is required to ensure that the cattle are always provided with highly digestible leafy grass, and grass conserved as silage must have a high DMD percentage (72% DMD or greater) to maximise weight gains from a grass-based diet.

Variable costs: a cost that varies with the level of output. Variable costs in farming include: concentrates, veterinary fees, animal remedy costs and contractor charges. Animal feed costs make a substantial contribution to variable costs.

By correctly managing grassland this will reduce the need to purchase large quantities of concentrates.

Operating a suckler herd with a spring-calving system is more profitable than an autumn-calving suckler herd. The cost of beef production in Ireland is particularly high compared with other beef producers, both in Europe and the rest of the world, according to a Teagasc report into the competitiveness of Irish beef. Land and labour costs are particularly high in Ireland. The National Farm Survey in 2017 (Teagasc) reported that the average income for cattle-rearing farms was on average €12,529. It reported that 53% of all cattle-rearing farms earned a farm income of less than €10,000.

There are many reasons for such a low farm income. Costs are a contributing factor (e.g. the cost of concentrates, fertiliser, livestock/veterinary costs, machinery hire and operation). Many of the costs mentioned are variable costs but farms also have overhead costs. Cattle prices can also experience volatility as Ireland is vulnerable to low beef prices when EU beef prices fall. This is because we export the majority of our beef to other countries within the EU. A low beef price when animals are finished and fit for slaughter can heavily impact a farmer's income. Low stocking rates and small farm sizes reduce farm output to low levels, and this also directly impacts farm income.

Farm income tends to be higher in the Eastern and Midlands regions compared with the Northern and Western regions of Ireland. Larger farm size, livestock numbers and better soils gave a farm income average of €17,525 to cattle-rearing farmers in the Eastern and Midlands regions. After paying costs and before direct payments under CAP, the cattle-rearing farmer's income is less than or close to zero. Most beef-rearing farmers have an average unpaid family labour unit of 1.1 employed on their farm. Direct payments under CAP are contributing on average 114% of a cattle-rearing farmers' income. Therefore, cattle rearing farmers' income is highly reliant on direct payments under CAP. The possible exit of the UK from the EU may have a knock-on effect on direct payments from the CAP budget. In addition, 50% of our beef exports go to the UK. Additional tariffs may be placed on Irish beef going into the UK post-Brexit.

On the other hand, there is a chance for farmers to improve the price they get for their beef through the Quality Payment Scheme (QPS) for Irish prime beef carcases. This is a bonus payment on top of the sale price to farmers that produce steers that meet certain criteria. For steers to qualify for this quality payment they must be less than 30 months old, have a fat score between 2+ and 4, have a conformation grade of O or better and a carcase weight of 280 to 400 kg. The steers must also come from a certified quality assured farm (according to the Sustainable Beef and Lamb Assurance Scheme). These carcase weights produce moderate size cuts that are at a more affordable price for customers. Heavier steak cuts from carcases (e.g. 460 kg) tend to be sold on the wholesale market at lower prices. A large proportion of steers in Ireland are finished over 30 months of age, so these farmers do not qualify for QPS. Quality assurances now also incorporate a large component on sustainability of beef production, which is being demanded by retail and global consumers.

Overhead costs: ongoing expenses of operating a business. These would include insurance, electricity, renting of land or farm buildings, loan repayments, and telephone or mobile phone bills.

Farm output: commonly referred to as gross output. Gross output determines the profitability of a farm. It refers to the amount and the value of the beef sold from a farm.

Wholesale: the business of selling meal in large quantities at a low price.

Benefits of producing Irish beef on a grass-based system

Ireland is the largest exporter of beef in the EU and the fourth largest in the world. Nearly 90% of Irish beef is exported. According to the EU, Irish beef farms are producing beef sustainably, as beef production in Ireland is predominantly grass based. Ireland has the fifth lowest carbon footprint for beef production in the EU. Dairy beef production tends to have a lower GHG emissions than suckler beef.

The grass-based diet also affects some of the characteristics of the meat produced from it. The carcase fat from a grass-fed beef animal tends to be more yellow in colour compared with that from cattle produced on wheat silage, which is more white in colour. This yellow colour of the fat is caused by the presence of carotenoids that cattle get from their grass-based diet. Grass-fed beef also has a distinct flavour compared with cattle reared on concentrate/straw or a silage/concentrate diet. Consumers are becoming more health conscious, and this is one of the driving forces that is encouraging beef producers to produce lean beef. Lean beef has a higher concentration of omega-3 fatty acids, which have a beneficial effect in protecting against heart disease. Other beneficial fatty acids, such as conjugated linoleic acid (CLA), are also found in beef and dairy products. These fatty acids have been shown to protect against type 2 diabetes and cancers. The concentration of CLA is far higher in beef and dairy products from grass-fed cattle than in cattle that are grain fed. The concentration of CLA in beef can be increased by increasing the number of days cattle spend grazing grass.

Management practices for sustainable and environmentally friendly beef production

The demand from consumers for sustainable meat production is growing. In response, Bord Bia and many other organisations developed the Sustainable Beef and Lamb Assurance Scheme (SBLAS). It is an accredited quality assurance scheme based on sustainability principles. It is operated by Bord Bia and is a voluntary scheme open to all farmers producing cattle and sheep for meat production. The scheme involves minimising the amount of resources used by the enterprise and putting in place measures that enhance its environmental performance. Farmers are assessed over a large number of criteria before a farmer can be a certified beef producer. It makes recommendations to farmers on ways they can reduce their carbon footprint and improve animal welfare, sustainability and their effect on the environment.

Some of the measures that farmers can take to improve the sustainability of their farm include:
- Extending the grazing season; Teagasc data indicated that a 10-day extension of the grazing season can reduce costs and cut the carbon footprint by 1.7%
- Reducing the age of the suckler heifer at first calving from 29 months to 28 months, which can reduce the carbon footprint of the farm by 0.3%
- Participating in agri-environmental schemes such as the Green, Low-Carbon Agri-Environmental Scheme (GLAS)
- Improve water conservation
- Include clover in swards to cut down on nitrogen application.

Other measures that are also included in the schemes include traceability and criteria that promote animal welfare and animal health.

Summary
- Beef production in Ireland is a grass-based system. There are many different types of beef production systems in Ireland.
- Less intensive systems of beef production require 2 years or more to get a calf from birth to finishing weight for slaughter. Good grassland and moderate levels of concentrates are required to achieve the necessary target weights.
- British beef breeds: Aberdeen Angus and Herefords are early maturing beef breeds: they start putting down fat at lower live weights compared with continental breeds.

- Continental beef breeds (Charolais, Limousin and Simmental) are later maturing breeds with high growth rates and larger size, and finish at higher live weights without laying down fat.
- Conformation refers to the shape of the animal and is important in the grading of carcases under the EUROP classification system.
- Beef breeds have better conformation compared with dairy breeds and tend to achieve a better grade upon slaughter.
- The main source of steers for the calf to beef production system is the dairy herd. Dairy bulls and early maturing beef breeds are used extensively in the breeding programme of dairy herds. This has a knock-on effect on the conformation and carcase quality of the resulting progeny.
- The large number of surplus purebred dairy male calves entering beef production is due to the expansion in the dairy herds after the abolition of milk quotas in 2015.
- Dairy calf to beef production involves the purchase of dairy calves annually and there is a high risk of buying in disease in this system.
- Suckler beef herds are mainly composed of continental beef breeds: Limousin, Charolais and Simmental are the most popular beef breeds in Ireland.
- Calves in the suckler beef system have a higher average daily live weight gain (ADG) than calves in the dairy calf to beef system. This is mainly due to the consumption of milk from the suckler dam.
- Suckler herds tend to operate a spring-calving system as this allows maximum utilisation of grass over the grazing season.
- The output and quality of the calves produced by the dairy calf to beef system and the suckler herd are determined by the breeds used, nutritional management, housing and management.
- It is essential that beef farmers ensure that the animals are meeting their target weights to ensure that these animals reach their finishing weight at 24 months.
- When weanlings are housed for the winter, the aim is for a weight gain of 80 kg with an ADG of 0.6 kg/day. This can be achieved by feeding the cattle good-quality silage with a dry matter digestibility (DMD) of 72% or greater and 1 to 2 kg of concentrates a day.
- Yearlings will need to achieve between 180 and 185 kg of live weight over a 200-day grazing season on grass. When housed for their second winter they will be finished on good-quality silage with a DMD of 72% or better and between 5 and 6 kg of concentrates.
- The €uro-Star Index is a biotechnological application that was developed by the Irish Cattle Breeding Federation (ICBF) and Teagasc to identify and select the most profitable animals for breeding in beef production.
- The €uro-Star Index is divided into two indexes: a replacement index and a terminal index. The replacement index is used to select bulls to breed replacement heifers and the terminal index is used to breed beef animals for slaughter.
- Volatility of beef prices, high land and labour costs, low stocking rates, small farm sizes and other costs are factors that contribute to farm incomes for beef-rearing farmers being low. Beef-rearing farmers are very reliant on direct payments from the CAP budget.
- Irish beef production is sustainable as it is a grass-based system. Ireland has the fifth lowest carbon footprint for beef production in the European Union (EU).

- Irish beef produced on a grass-based system has unique colour, flavour and additional health benefits from the composition of its fatty acids.
- The Sustainable Beef and Lamb Assurance Scheme (SBLAS) involves minimising the amount of resources used and putting in place measures to enhance the environmental performance of a farming enterprise.

PowerPoint Summary

QUESTIONS

1. Which of the following is a continental beef breed?
   - (a) Belgian Blue
   - (b) Aberdeen Angus
   - (c) Hereford
   - (d) Friesian

2. Which of the following is an early maturing beef breed?
   - (a) Charolais
   - (b) Limousin
   - (c) Hereford
   - (d) Simmental

3. What is the recommended target live weight gain for weanling steers when they are housed for their first winter?
   - (a) 60 kg
   - (b) 70 kg
   - (c) 80 kg
   - (d) 90 kg

4. What is the recommended average daily live weight gain (ADG) for weanling steers when they are housed for their first winter?
   - (a) 0.55 kg/day
   - (b) 0.60 kg/day
   - (c) 0.70 kg/day
   - (d) 0.80 kg/day

5. The ADG (kg/day) for ten weanling steers during their first winter is shown below.

| 0.82 | 0.75 | 0.55 | 0.58 | 0.64 | 0.58 | 0.70 | 0.68 | 0.59 | 0.55 |

   What is the average growth rate for this group of steers?
   - (a) 0.60 kg/day
   - (b) 0.62 kg/day
   - (c) 0.64 kg/day
   - (d) 0.66 kg/day

6. A beef steer had a grazing season of 220 days. During that time, he put on 190 kg of live weight. What was his average daily live weight gain?
   - (a) 0.80 kg/day
   - (b) 0.82 kg/day
   - (c) 0.84 kg/day
   - (d) 0.86 kg/day

7. What is the recommended ration to be fed to cattle that are on target to finish at 24 months while being housed for their second winter?
   - (a) 65% DMD silage and 5–6 kg of concentrates
   - (b) 68% DMD silage and 2–3 kg of concentrates
   - (c) 72% DMD silage and 1–2 kg of concentrates
   - (d) 72% DMD silage and 5–6 kg of concentrates

8. The table shows the €uro-Star rating for several beef bulls.

Table 27.4				
Bulls	Key profile traits			
	Daughter's milk	Calving interval	Carcase weight	Carcase conformation
Benbulben	★ ★ ★ ★ ★	★ ★ ★ ★ ★	★ ★ ★ ★ ★	★ ★ ★ ☆ ☆
Carrauntoohill	★ ★ ☆ ☆ ☆	★ ☆ ☆ ☆ ☆	★ ★ ★ ★ ☆	★ ★ ★ ☆ ☆
Errigal	★ ★ ☆ ☆ ☆	★ ★ ★ ★ ☆	★ ★ ★ ★ ★	★ ★ ★ ★ ★
Nephin	★ ★ ★ ★ ☆	★ ☆ ☆ ☆ ☆	★ ★ ★ ★ ★	★ ★ ★ ★ ★

Which of the bulls would be most suited to use as a sire on suckler dams to produce replacement heifers?

(a) Benbulben   (b) Carrauntoohill   (c) Errigal   (d) Nephin

9. Give **two** reasons why continental beef breeds are more popular than British beef breeds for suckler beef production.

10. At slaughter the beef carcases are graded for *conformation* and *fatness*. Explain each of the italicised terms.

11. A calf from a suckler herd is at a heavier live weight at weaning compared with a calf in the calf to beef system. Give a reason for this.

12. Explain **two** management practices that suckler farmers must focus on in order to increase output and quality of beef production from a suckler herd.

13. Describe a suitable grazing system for a suckler herd out on grass.

14. When weanlings are put into winter housing they undergo a *store period*. When returned to grass the following spring these animals have increased live weight gains and the animal is described as undergoing *compensatory growth*.

   (a) Explain the meaning of the italicised terms.

   (b) Describe the feeding of a weanling in winter housing in Year 1.

   (c) State the average daily gain for (i) a weanling in winter housing Year 1 and (ii) a yearling out on grass Year 2 for a beef production system of your choice.

   (d) Draw a growth curve for a beef animal showing (i) store period and (ii) compensatory growth.

15. Outline how poor nutrition can impact on the profitability of a beef production system of your choice.

16. Discuss the advantages of suckler steer beef production over dairy steer calf to beef production.

17. Identify methods that a farmer can employ to improve the quality of beef that they are producing in a beef-production system of your choice.

18. Discuss how the €uro-Star Index can improve profitability and breeding within the suckler herd.

19. What are the benefits of a grass-based beef production system?

20. What economic factors affect the farm income of a beef-rearing farmer?

21. Name and describe a programme in which national agencies and farmers work together to produce beef more sustainably.

22. Explain **two** market requirements for beef production in Ireland and how these impact on beef prices for Irish farmers.

Solutions   Weblinks

CHAPTER 28 Sheep breeds and production

When you have completed this chapter you should be able to:

- Describe the characteristics of common types, breeds and crosses of sheep
- Compare two different systems of animal production for sheep: lowland and hill
- Investigate how breed variety determines the output and quality of produce from a chosen enterprise.

Sheep production in Ireland is solely for the production of meat. It is an important export market, with Bord Bia estimating that in 2018 it contributed roughly €315 million to the Irish economy, a 15% increase on 2017 exports. In 2018, one third of all Irish sheep meat was exported to France, with the United Kingdom being the second biggest export market. Other markets for Irish sheep meat are growing in Sweden and Denmark. Many countries, such as Germany, Italy and Libya, import live

sheep. The Irish population consumes less than 30% of the sheep meat produced here. Under EU regulations the Department of Agriculture, Food and the Marine (DAFM) must carry out an annual sheep census. The 2017 census shows that sheep numbers have decreased by 1% in Ireland since 2016. The 2017 sheep census reports a national flock of 3.87 million sheep, which includes 2.65 million breeding ewes. There are roughly 35,000 flocks of sheep, with the average size of a flock at 108 sheep. The counties with the greatest number of sheep are Donegal, Mayo and Galway.

Census: official count or survey of a population.

Live export: transport of living farm animals, usually to another country.

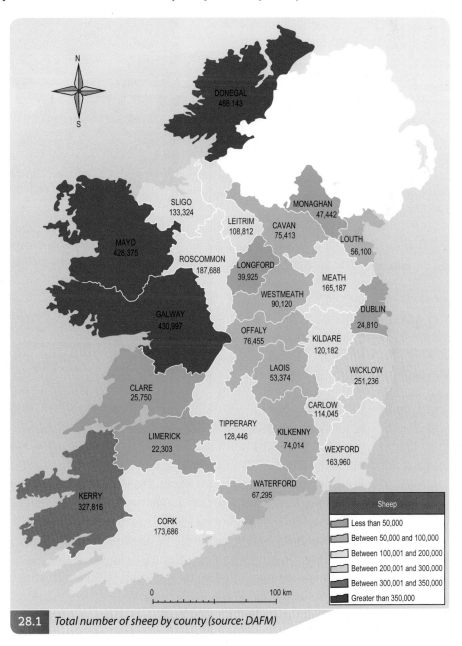

28.1 *Total number of sheep by county (source: DAFM)*

Sheep production in Ireland: factors affecting output and production

Sheep production in Ireland can be divided into two categories: mountain/hill and lowland.

The time of year greatly affects the price of lamb. Easter is traditionally a time when lamb is eaten. As a result, lambs slaughtered for Easter get peak price for the farmer. Mid-season lamb, slaughtered after Easter, gets considerably less than premium price. Live sheep exports also increase around the dates of religious festivals such as Ramadan.

Historically, lowland sheep farming is more intensive and has higher production targets than mountain and hill sheep farming. Better pastures and rotational grazing are used to ensure that lambs are finished off for the Easter and mid-season lamb markets.

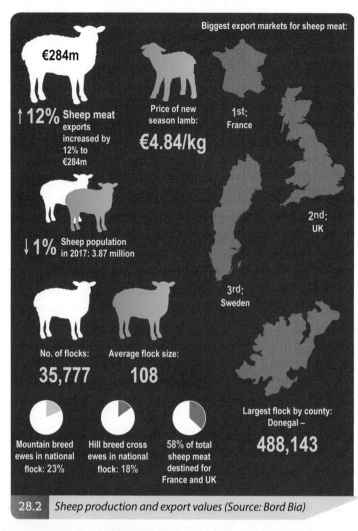

€284m

↑12% Sheep meat exports increased by 12% to €284m

↓1% Sheep population in 2017: 3.87 million

No. of flocks: **35,777**

Average flock size: **108**

Mountain breed ewes in national flock: 23%

Hill breed cross ewes in national flock: 18%

58% of total sheep meat destined for France and UK

Biggest export markets for sheep meat:

Price of new season lamb: **€4.84/kg**

1st: France

2nd: UK

3rd: Sweden

Largest flock by county: Donegal – **488,143**

28.2 *Sheep production and export values (Source: Bord Bia)*

28.3 *Lowland grazing*

28.4 *Mountain grazing*

Commonage: land where two or more farmers have rights to graze.

Botanical composition: variety of plant life.

Variable: not consistent or fixed.

Flora: plants of a particular region or habitat.

Mountainous and upland locations are exposed to harsh weather conditions where sheep graze commonage over large areas. The botanical composition of commonage is highly variable, being composed of heathers and poorer-quality grasses.

Hill and mountain lambs are in demand in some Mediterranean countries due to the smaller and lighter carcases of these lambs. Their meat is slightly darker because of their diet of varied mountain flora and has a distinct flavour, which accounts for the growing popularity of this meat. Mountain ewes are also in demand by lowland farmers as breeding stock. Table 28.1 summarises the main points of these two industries.

Table 28.1 Comparison of mountain/hill and lowland sheep enterprises	
Mountain and hill	**Lowland**
Extensive farming	Intensive farming
Low production targets	High production targets
Rough grazing	Rotational grazing
Ewe and lamb mortality rates can be high	Lambing indoors reduces ewe and lamb mortality
Ewes generally have only one lamb	More ewes give birth to twins and triplets
Sheep breeds suited to exposed conditions	Large muscular sheep used to produce meat
e.g. Blackface Mountain, Wicklow Cheviot	e.g. Suffolk, Texel, Galway, Charollais

There are several factors that contribute to the output on an Irish sheep farm in terms of the number of lambs weaned and also the quality of lambs that are sent for slaughter. Table 28.1 shows that mountain and hill production has higher mortality and lower birth rates than lowland production. This has a direct effect on output from a farm in terms of the number of lambs that can be raised to slaughter. However, the inputs into each system have a major influence on the number and quality of lambs produced.

The inputs that have the greatest effect on output and quality are:

- Breed variety
- Nutrition
- Housing
- Management.

Housing, nutrition and management of sheep will be discussed in more detail in Chapter 29.

Sheep breeds

Mountain and hill breeds

Mountain and hill breeds account for 23% of the national flock, and a further 13% of the national flock consists of hill crossbreeds. The most popular mountain and hill sheep breeds in Ireland are the Blackface Mountain and the Wicklow Cheviot. Both are hardy breeds with long wool and small size, which make them best suited for mountainous areas. Both breeds are also known for their good mothering ability, a trait that is an advantage in a harsh environment. All these traits combined make these breeds particularly suitable for mountain sheep farming; however, they also have small litter sizes. A combination of harsher conditions, poorer quality grasses and a lack of shelter makes survival on mountains and hillsides more difficult. There is also a greater threat from predators. A combination of these factors means that the number of lambs produced from a mountain flock is smaller.

Hardy: robust, tough, able to withstand difficult weather conditions.

Blackface Mountain

Blackface Mountain sheep (also known as Scottish Blackface) and Wicklow Cheviot are the two most popular mountain sheep breeds in Ireland. Mountain ewe breeds are used to produce crossbred ewes for lowland sheep farmers. Blackface Mountain sheep are a small, extremely hardy breed with long wool, black face and horns. Blackface Mountain ewes are known for their good mothering ability and good milk production. This breed of mountain sheep is extremely popular along the west coast of Ireland.

28.5 *Blackface Mountain sheep*

Wicklow Cheviot

Wicklow Cheviot sheep originate from Scotland. These sheep have a white face, are medium-sized and are a hardy mountain breed. The ewes are good mothers. They are a popular breed along the east coast of Ireland.

28.6 *Wicklow Cheviot*

Lowland sheep breeds

Lowland sheep breeds are chosen for two reasons: prolificacy and lambs for slaughter. The breeds that are chosen for lowland production are characterised by fast growth rates, good meat quality, good carcase quality and larger litters. They also have short wool as they do not live in harsh conditions, as winter housing is available. They also graze on better-quality permanent grassland and leys in a rotational grazing system. The most common lowland breeds include Border Leicester, Blue Faced Leicester, Suffolk and Texel.

Prolific breeds

Border Leicester

Border Leicester is a large, long-wool, white, hornless breed easily recognisable by its upright ears. This breed is known for its prolificacy and the breed imparts its prolificacy on its offspring.

28.7 *Border Leicester*

28.8 *Bluefaced Leicester*

Bluefaced Leicester

Bluefaced Leicester is another popular, prolific breed in Ireland and, like the Border Leicester, it originates from England. It is a large breed, with a white head and a slight roman nose. It is also known as the Hexham Leicester. It acquired the name Bluefaced because its skin appears dark blue through its white hair.

These prolific breeds are often used in crossbreeding programmes as **maternal sires**.

> **DEFINITION**
>
> **Maternal sires** are used to produce daughters with excellent genetic traits for reproduction and mothering ability. These offspring are then used as replacement ewes in a sheep flock.

Sire: male parent of an animal.
Common terms in sheep production:
Lamb: a young sheep less than 1 year old.
Hogget: a young sheep between 1 and 2 years old.
Ewe: a fully grown female sheep.
Ram: an intact (not castrated) male sheep.
Wether: a castrated male sheep.

Terminal sires for meat production

A terminal sire is a ram that is used to produce lambs with high growth rates and good carcase quality for slaughter. In Ireland the most popular lowland sheep breeds used as terminal sires are the Texel and the Suffolk.

Suffolk

The Suffolk originates from England and has a distinctive black head and legs. It is a short and solid breed known for its good carcase quality.

The Suffolk has excellent conformation and fast growth rates. Suffolk-cross lambs are early maturing, reaching slaughter weight in less than 14 weeks, making the Suffolk ram an ideal terminal sire for lambs for the Easter market.

28.9   *Suffolk ram*

28.10   *Texel ram*

Texel

The Texel originates from The Netherlands. It has a wide white face, with short ears, and it lacks wool on its head and legs. The breed has good conformation and carcase quality and is particularly noted for muscle leanness. It has slower growth rates than a Suffolk and is used as a terminal sire for mid-season lamb.

Charollais

The Charollais is a French breed and was bred alongside Charolais cattle. It is a medium-sized, heavy sheep with a long loin and muscular hindquarters. It is becoming a popular terminal sire and produces lean, fast-growing lambs.

28.11   *Charollais sheep*

28.12   *Beltex sheep*

What is the difference between lamb and mutton? **Lamb** refers to the meat from a lamb. **Mutton** refers to the meat from an adult sheep.

Beltex

The Beltex is a Belgian breed of sheep that was originally bred from the Texel sheep breed. The name Beltex is derived from a combination of Belgium and Texel. It was first introduced into Ireland in the 1990s. It is a white-faced sheep with medium wool. It is a double-muscled breed, having heavy muscling especially on its hindquarters. Beltex sheep have a high kill-out percentage with good carcase quality.

Irish sheep breeds
Galway sheep and Belclare Improver

The Galway is the only native sheep breed. It is a large, white, polled lowland sheep. It has long wool and is predominantly found in Galway and some surrounding counties.

It has a good growth rate and, when crossed with Suffolk or other continental breeds, it can produce good early lambs. Teagasc undertook research to improve the Galway breed by crossing Galway ewes with the Finnish Landrace, a breed known for its extremely high prolificacy. The ewes were then crossed with a Lleyn ram, a Welsh breed known for high prolificacy, strong mothering instinct and good conformation.

28.13 *Galway sheep*

28.14 *Belclare Improver*

The resulting breed was called the Belclare Improver. Belclare Improvers had improved prolificacy in comparison to the Galway. To improve the conformation of the breed further, the Belclare Improvers were crossed with Texel rams and today's Belclare sheep have originated from these Belclare Improver–Texel crosses. The Belclare ewes normally produce twin lambs, have little lambing difficulty and have good mothering ability.

Breeding strategy in Ireland
Breeding of sheep in mountain and hill farming

In mountain and hill farming, purebred mountain ewes are always crossed with purebred mountain rams. Due to the harsh conditions in these regions and the poor quality of the grass, mountain ewes usually produce a single lamb. These lambs are either kept as replacements or fattened and sold to the Italian market, where there is a demand for smaller carcases. The fertility of the mountain ewes decreases under these harsh conditions after a few years. They are sold as cast or draft ewes to lowland sheep farmers. Mountain ewes are renowned for their good mothering ability and, as a result, are in demand by lowland sheep farmers.

DEFINITION

A **cast** or **draft ewe** is a ewe whose fertility has declined due to the harsh conditions experienced in mountainous areas. It is sold to a lowland farmer, put on an improved plane of nutrition and will continue to produce lambs for many years.

Breeding of sheep in lowland sheep farming

The ultimate goal in lowland sheep farming is to produce lambs for slaughter, and the bulk of sheep meat produced in Ireland comes from these lowland farms. The cast mountain ewes are used in a three-breed crossing system to produce lambs for meat. Other countries, such as Australia and New Zealand, use similar three-breed crossing systems.

Ram selection is a vital part of this breeding programme. A common statement used in sheep farming is that 'a ram is half the flock'. The reason for this is that the ram's genes will spread over a greater proportion of the offspring than a ewe's. In addition, the ram breeds look after the quality of the offspring, while the ewe delivers on quantity (litter size). Purebred rams are used to improve prolificacy, growth rates and carcase quality of the offspring. Rams of superior genetic merit should be used to bring about improvement in the flock. For this reason, many rams have been evaluated and given €uro-Star ratings.

Once the cast mountain ewes are moved to better-quality grass, their fertility improves. The mountain ewe is then crossed with a prolific breed such as the Border Leicester, Bluefaced Leicester or a Belclare ram to produce crossbred offspring that will be used for breeding. In Fig. 28.15, a Blackface Mountain sheep is crossed with a Bluefaced Leicester ram to produce a crossbreed called a Mule. Crossbred ewes show hybrid vigour, having the best characteristics of both parents. They have the hardiness, good mothering ability and good milk production from their mountain dam and good prolificacy from the sire, with an average litter size of 1.71.

Proportion: relative amount or quantity.

Superior: higher quality or better.

€uro-Star ram ratings identify rams with the very best genetics. This rating aids farmers when selecting a breeding ram. A ram with 5 stars is the best ram and a ram with 1 star is the worst.

Dam: female parent of an animal.

Ewe — Blackface Mountain

Ram — Bluefaced Leicester

Crossbred Mule ewes

28.15 *Crossing a Blackface Mountain ewe with a Bluefaced Leicester produces crossbred Mules*

419

> **Prolificacy** in sheep is calculated as the number of lambs reared per ewe mated. If 100 ewes were mated and 160 lambs were produced, the prolificacy of the flock would be 1.6.

Increased prolificacy is extremely important for the output of lamb meat. A female ewe has two teats on her udder – if fed adequately, she can raise two lambs, which increases outputs from the flock. Theoretically, if each ewe had twins instead of a single lamb, this could potentially increase profits for the sheep farmer. This is not always possible, but most farmers will aim for a litter size of 1.7 or 1.8 lambs per ewe. In order to increase litter size, the ram must be carefully selected before it is crossed with the mountain ewe. Table 28.2 shows the litter size produced by crossbred ewes from Blackface Mountain mothers.

Table 28.2 Effect of ram breeds on litter size	
Sire of ewe	**Litter size**
Belclare	1.89
Bluefaced Leicester	1.71
Border Leicester	1.60
Cheviot	1.51
Galway	1.63
Suffolk	1.65
Texel	1.58
Blackface Mountain	1.48

Table 28.2 clearly shows that when the mountain ewe was crossed with a Belclare ram, this increased the litter size that the crossbred ewes produced. The ram with the poorest score for prolificacy was the Blackface Mountain ram. In increasing the prolificacy of a flock, there is an increase in the number of twins, triplets and even quadruplets that the crossbred ewes will produce. It is therefore in the farmer's best interests to choose a lowland ram breed with a greater prolificacy to maximise the number of lambs born and also to produce a lamb with good carcase quality and growth rate. Blackface Mountain rams therefore tend to be used only for mountain sheep production, where the breed is best suited to the harsher conditions. Examine Table 28.3 to see the various types of crossbreeds produced from mountain ewes by lowland ram crosses.

Table 28.3 Progeny of mountain ewes crossed with lowland lambs		
Mountain ewe	**Ram breed**	**Crossbred offspring**
Blackface Mountain	Border Leicester	Greyface
Blackface Mountain	Bluefaced Leicester	Mule
Wicklow Cheviot	Border Leicester	Halfbred
Wicklow Cheviot	Suffolk	Brownface

Crossbred ewes, like the mule, are used as replacement ewes for breeding. These crossbred ewes are crossed with a terminal sire to produce lambs that will be slaughtered for meat. The terminal sires that are used are selected because their traits include good conformation, good carcase quality, fast growth rates and leanness of meat. The lambs produced from this cross are sold as early lamb or mid-season lamb. If a farmer is aiming for early lamb production, such as the Easter market, then the ram used is a Suffolk ram. It has the fastest growth rates; therefore, the lambs reach slaughter weight in time. If a farmer is aiming for mid-season lamb, then a Texel ram is used (see Fig. 28.16).

28.16 *Production of Easter and mid-season lambs*

A Texel ram's offspring do not mature as quickly as a Suffolk ram's offspring, but they have higher carcase quality. Teagasc in Athenry compared the effect of terminal sire breed on their progeny performance and concluded that the three best terminal sire breeds were the Suffolk, Texel and Charollais rams.

Table 28.4 Effect of terminal sire breed on progeny performance			
Sire	**Weaning weight (kg)**	**Extra days to finish**	**Kill-out (g/kg)**
Suffolk	31.8	0	438
Charollais	31.0	5	449
Texel	30.6	9	446
Vendeen	30.0	14	445
Belclare	29.3	15	442
Source: Hanrahan (1994 and 1997, Teagasc, Athenry)			

Replacement ewes

When selecting breeding ewes, a farmer should look at the following:

- Age of the ewe
- Health of the ewe
- Body condition of the ewe: aim for a BCS of 3.5 at mating
- Good conformation
- Mouth of the ewe: no overshot or undershot jaw that could affect the ewe grazing
- Teeth: sheep need good molar teeth for grinding their food
- Sound feet and legs
- Udder: two functioning teats, no lumps in udder, no discharges from udder, good milk supply
- A ewe that will consistently produce twins.

Criteria for selection of ram

- Breed of the ram
- Pedigree and performance tested
- Age of the ram
- Conformation, especially for terminal sire; good muscle distribution
- BCS of 3.5 to 4.0; rams must have a higher BCS than ewes at mating, since they lose a considerable amount of body weight during mating
- Sound feet and legs: lameness will affect the ram's performance during the mating season
- Mouth: no jaw defects, since this could potentially affect many lambs
- Testicle size: there is a direct relationship between testicle size and semen production; a mature ram should have a scrotal circumference of 32 cm; testicles should be firm, the same size and free from lumps.

Summary

- Sheep production in Ireland can be divided into two categories: mountain/hill and lowland. Lowland sheep farming is more intensive, with higher production targets than mountain and hill sheep farming.
- Mountain and upland locations are exposed to harsh weather conditions where sheep graze commonage.
- Hill and mountain lambs are in demand in some Mediterranean countries because of the smaller and lighter carcases of these lambs.
- Mountain ewes are also in demand by lowland farmers, as breeding stock.
- The Blackface Mountain and the Wicklow Cheviot are the two most popular mountain sheep breeds in Ireland. Blackface Mountain sheep are a small and extremely hardy breed with long wool, black face and horns. Wicklow Cheviot are hardy, white-faced and medium-sized.
- The Border Leicester, the Bluefaced Leicester and the Belclare are all prolific breeds that are used to increase litter size. These breeds are also maternal sires used to breed replacement ewes.
- A terminal sire is a ram that is used to produce lambs with high growth rates and good carcase quality for slaughter.
- The Texel and Suffolk are the two most popular terminal sires used in sheep production in Ireland. The Suffolk is predominately used to produce lambs for the Easter market, since Suffolk-crossed lambs will reach slaughter weight in 14 weeks.
- The Galway is the only native Irish breed. Teagasc developed the Belclare breed by crossing the Galway with the Finnish Landrace, Lleyn and Texel breeds.
- A cast or draft ewe is a ewe whose fertility has declined due to the harsh conditions experienced in mountainous areas. Once these ewes are on an improved plane of nutrition, their fertility improves and they will continue to produce lambs.
- Genetic improvement is brought about by the ram in sheep production. 'A ram is half the flock' is stated because the ram's genes will spread over a greater proportion of the offspring than the ewe's genes.
- Prolificacy is calculated as the number of lambs reared per ewe mated.
- Crossbred ewes are crossed with terminal sires (a Texel or Suffolk ram) to produce lambs for slaughter.

- When selecting breeding ewes, a farmer looks at the age, health, body condition score (BCS 3.5), conformation, teeth, feet and udder of the ewe. They will also select a ewe that will produce twins.
- When selecting a ram for breeding, the farmer will look at the breed, pedigree, age, conformation, body condition score (BCS 4), feet and teeth of the ram.

 PowerPoint Summary

QUESTIONS

1. The main product from Irish sheep production is:

   (a) Wool

   (b) Milk

   (c) Meat

   (d) Cheese.

2. Which of the following best describes mountain sheep farming conditions?

28.17 *Mountain sheep*

   (a) High stocking rates with rotational grazing

   (b) Low stocking rates with rotational grazing

   (c) Commonage grazed in harsh conditions

   (d) Sheltered grazing on pastures

3. State why mountain and hill sheep are preferred by:

   (a) Mediterranean countries

   (b) Lowland sheep farmers.

4. Compare mountain and hill sheep farming with lowland sheep farming under the following headings:

   (a) Production targets

   (b) Grazing system

   (c) Mortality rates

   (d) Prolificacy.

5. Describe three characteristics that are important in choosing a mountain or hill sheep breed.

6. Identify two sheep breeds that would be used in mountain sheep production. Give reasons for your answers.

7. Explain how a named mountain breed affects output in the flock.

8. Explain the term 'prolificacy' and identify a breed used to improve prolificacy.

9. In terms of output, why do farmers seek to improve prolificacy in a flock?

10. In lowland sheep production:

   (a) Identify two common breeds

   (b) Describe the characteristics of each named breed

   (c) Explain how the characteristics of the breed affect output and quality in the flock.

11. Explain the term 'terminal sire'. Identify one breed used as a terminal sire.

12. Name the native Irish breed of sheep and explain how Teagasc improved this breed.

13. Explain the term 'cast ewes' or 'draft ewes'. Why does a mountain ewe's fertility decrease after a few years in mountainous areas?

14. What are the advantages of using crossbred ewes as breeding ewes?

15. In the context of output and quality, explain the saying 'a ram is half the flock'.

16. Discuss the effect of terminal sire on weaning weight and finishing time of lambs for slaughter (see Table 28.4 on page 421).

17. Describe the breeding strategy used to produce lambs for the Easter market. Give reasons for your choice of terminal sire in your breeding strategy.

18. Describe the criteria used in the selection of:

   (a) A breeding ewe

   (b) A ram in Easter lamb production.

19. For a lowland breeding system, describe the effect a ram has on the quality of lambs produced. Explain the effect a ewe has on the litter size.

20. Explain the breeding strategy used in a lowland sheep production system of your choice.

21. Outline the strategy involved in mountain sheep production. Identify how the choice of ram and ewe breeds affects output.

Solutions — Weblinks

CHAPTER 29 Lamb production and husbandry

When you have completed this chapter you should be able to:

- Describe the management of the life cycle of a ewe, including dietary requirements at different growth/development stages
- Investigate the factors that determine the output and quality of produce from a lowland sheep enterprise (nutrition, housing, management)
- Appreciate the challenges of sustainable intensification
- Discuss management practices for:
  o Handling and housing farm animals
  o Optimal animal health and welfare
  o Delivering sustainable and environmentally friendly production systems
  o Ensuring quality, safe and traceable food for the consumer
- Appreciate the role of policies related to traceability and animal welfare, and their connection with the food supply chain
- Appreciate the impact on farm economics of lowland sheep production.

The sheep breeding year

The length of the oestrous cycle in sheep is 17 days, meaning a sheep will come into heat every 17 days. The average duration of oestrus or standing heat is 36 hours, with ovulation occurring during the second half of standing heat. Once fertilisation occurs, the gestation period is 147 days, or 5 months.

As mentioned in Chapter 28, in Ireland there are two breeding systems employed to produce lambs for slaughter: early or Easter lamb and mid-season lamb. Both of these systems are outlined in Table 29.1.

Table 29.1 Comparison of early and mid-season lamb production	
Early lamb	**Mid-season lamb**
Lambs born December–January	Lambs born March–April
Higher feed costs: concentrates required	Lower feed costs: better utilisation of grass
Cost of adjusting breeding cycle; breeding out of season	Normal breeding cycle
Lambs finished for Easter market gain a better price	Mid-season lamb: lower price compared to Easter market

Key information on sheep:
Length of oestrous cycle: 17 days.
Duration of oestrus: 36 hours.
Gestation period: 147 days or 5 months.

Flushing

If a farmer is aiming to have lambs finished for the Easter market, when the price for lamb is higher, then planning for this must begin in July (see Fig. 29.1). If a farmer is aiming for mid-season lamb, breeding does not begin until the end of September or the beginning of October (see Fig. 29.2).

> **DEFINITION**
>
> **Flushing:** the process by which ewes are moved from a low plane of nutrition to a high plane of nutrition prior to mating.

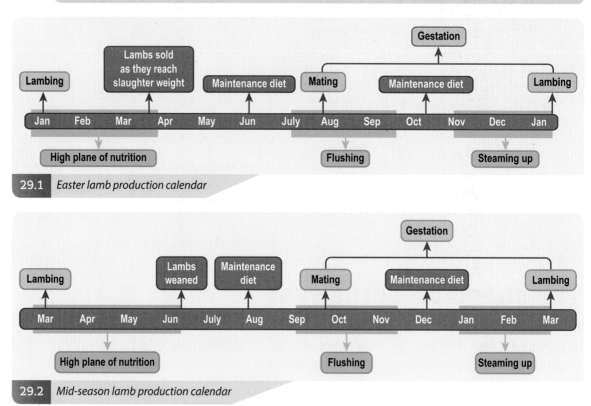

29.1 *Easter lamb production calendar*

29.2 *Mid-season lamb production calendar*

Prior to mating, the breeding ewes are heavily stocked on good pasture. This is known as a maintenance diet. The ewes are then put on an improving plane of nutrition about 3 weeks before mating commences. This can be achieved by decreasing the stocking rate on good pasture. The process of moving ewes from a low plane of nutrition to a high plane of nutrition prior to mating is known as flushing. Research shows that thin ewes with a BCS of 2.0–2.5 respond better to flushing than ewes that are already in good condition (BCS 3.5). Increasing the amount of feed to thin ewes causes them to put on weight and increases their BCS. Some scientists believe that an increase in a thin ewe's weight signals to the ewe's body that she is capable of raising more than one lamb. When mating starts, all ewes should have a BCS of 3.5. If ewes are below this BCS at mating, then they are more likely to produce only one lamb and prolong the lambing season.

Flushing has a number of advantages:

- Increased ovulation rate, leading to more eggs being released
- Increased conception rates
- Better implantation of the embryos to the uterine wall
- Increased litter size, leading to more twins and triplets
- More regular oestrous cycles.

Flushing should continue with the ewes for 4 weeks after mating to ensure that the embryos develop properly. This is because most spontaneous foetal deaths occur during the first 4 weeks of gestation. Lack of energy during this time could result in the embryos being reabsorbed in the uterus.

Synchronised breeding and breeding out of season

Sponging

Allowing ewes to naturally come into oestrus can result in a prolonged lambing season. For this reason, some farmers choose to synchronise the oestrous cycle by sponging the ewes. Sponging involves placing progesterone-impregnated sponges into the vagina of the ewes. The sponges are removed 12 days later. All the ewes come into oestrus 2 days later.

In order to identify those ewes that are in heat, the ram is fitted with a raddle with a coloured crayon. The raddle will leave a mark on each ewe as they are mated by the ram. This allows the farmer to calculate lambing dates. The colour of the marker crayon is changed every 17 days (the length of the oestrous cycle of the ewe) to check for any ewes repeating. If a large number of ewes are repeating, it would be wise to check the fertility of the ram. When synchronising the breeding cycle of the ewes, the ram to ewe ratio should be reduced from 1 : 40 to 1 : 10.

Some sheep farmers will not use a raddle. Instead, they mix grease with a coloured dye and smear the mixture between the front legs and the chest of the ram. This will then mark the back of a ewe when the ram mounts and mates with her.

Groups of rams should be used during the mating season, since this reduces the effect if one ram has poor fertility.

Video
Alternative to using raddle to mark ewes that have been mated

Sponges

Raddle

Ram crayons

The colours used in the raddle should be changed every 17 days. Farmers normally start with lighter-coloured crayons (yellow and green) and then change to the darker colours (red, blue and black) late in the mating season.

29.3 *Sponges, raddle and ram crayons*

Synchronised: occurring at the same time.

Prolonged: continuing over a long period of time.

Impregnate: soak or saturate with a substance.

Raddle: a device or harness that holds a colour-marking device on rams.

Repeating: coming back into heat/oestrus.

Breeding out of season

In order to take full advantage of the higher lamb prices on offer to farmers at Easter, lambs need to be born in December or early January to allow them to be finished in time. This means that the ewe must be mated in July/ August, which is before they would naturally come into oestrus (remember that sheep are short-day breeders). Farmers can induce the onset of oestrus in July/August by inserting progesterone-soaked sponges in the ewes for 12 days and then injecting them with pregnant mare serum gonadotropin (PMSG) once the sponges are removed. The ram is introduced 24 hours after the sponges are removed and all ewes should be in heat 48 hours later. The ram to ewe ratio should be 1 : 10. This process of altering the breeding cycle of sheep is known as 'breeding out of season'.

Induce: bring about, cause or promote.

Onset: start or beginning.

29.4 *Progesterone medication*

Ram effect

Sponging and the injection of PMSG is a very reliable method of breeding out of season; however, some breeds can be encouraged to start ovulating 6 weeks earlier than normal by the sudden introduction of the ram. This is commonly known as the 'ram effect' and is only successful with some breeds of sheep. Rams produce chemical substances called pheromones. The smell of these pheromones initiates the onset of oestrus in the ewes, with ewes ovulating 4 days later. This first oestrus is a 'silent heat', meaning it is not detected by the ram. This will be followed by a normal oestrous cycle 17 days later, when the ewes will be mated by the ram.

The success of the ram effect relies on the ewes and rams being separated (out of sight and smell) for 6 weeks prior to mating, and the rams must be at least 2 km away from the ewes (that includes neighbouring rams and buck goats). The advantage of the ram effect is that it can start the breeding season early and synchronise breeding without sponging and it also helps to compact the lambing period. However, it is not effective if the ewes are already coming into oestrous cycles and it is also not effective with maiden ewes, since they will not start to cycle until they are the correct weight and condition.

29.5   *Ram with flock*

Pheromones: chemical substances that the ram produces in order to attract a female for mating. There are many different types of pheromones and they are widely produced in both animals and insects. They have a variety of roles and are not just involved in reproduction.

Initiate: cause something to begin.

Compact: small, taking up less space.

Improving breeding outputs in hill sheep farming

Intensive breeding systems are usually confined to lowland sheep production. However, with almost a quarter of sheep produced in Ireland originating in hill sheep flocks, with lower litter sizes, increases can be achieved with changes to management systems. Farms that are a part of Teagasc's BETTER Sheep Farm Programme seek to improve breeding outputs in hill sheep flocks. In the programme, farmers:

1. Create a flock breeding plan

2. Seek to improve pre-mating BCS in ewes

3. Increase management of weaned lambs.

In a system that has traditionally required less labour and is categorised as extensive farming, improved management systems can lead to sustainable intensification, particularly in farms in Donegal, Galway and Mayo, where hill sheep farming is most prevalent. Flock numbers can be increased through:

- **Increased pregnancy rates:** improving BCS increased pregnancy rates by up to 10% in Teagasc studies
- **Improved quality of weaned lambs:** crossbred lambs are 3–4 kg heavier at weaning
- **Maximising use of cross breeding:** more saleable crossbred wether and ram lambs; prolific females available for lowland farms.

Mating to lambing

Once mating is completed, the ram should be moved to a separate field. He will have lost some condition during the mating season and will require some extra feeding. Rams, on average, lose 15% of their body weight during the mating season.

Flushing should continue with the ewes for 4 weeks after mating to ensure that the embryos develop properly, since most spontaneous foetal deaths occur during the

29.6   *Sheep out on grazing grass*

first 4 weeks of gestation. At the end of flushing, the ewes can return to a maintenance diet, and their BCS can drop back down to 3.0. During mid-gestation the ewes should be rotationally grazing grass (if available), or if housed they should be fed good-quality silage.

Scanning

Scanning ewes is a vital procedure in determining the correct feed requirement of each ewe in late gestation. Scanning aids separation of ewes carrying singles from ewes carrying twins and triplets, making it easier to feed the ewes the correct amount of feed. It also identifies barren ewes, and these can then be culled from the flock, saving the farmer money on feed. Teagasc recommends scanning sheep 80 days after the ram joined the flock.

> **Video**
> Scanning sheep to check for lambs by IMV imaging

Late gestation and steaming up

In the last 6–8 weeks of gestation, 75% of foetal growth occurs. This rapid growth of the foetus and the uterus restricts the size of the ewe's rumen. Bulky feeds (e.g. silage and hay) will not supply sufficient energy and protein to meet the ewe's requirements. As a result, the ewes are again placed on an increasing plane of nutrition. This feeding practice is referred to as steaming up. Poor nutrition in late gestation, particularly in ewes that are carrying twins or triplets, can cause pregnancy toxaemia. This is also known as twin lamb disease, and it can be fatal to both ewe and lambs.

29.7 *Scanning ewes*

> **Foetus:** unborn young.

> **Restricts:** limits.

In order to prevent twin lamb disease, each ewe should be fed 100 g of concentrates in addition to good-quality hay and silage (high dry matter digestibility) per day and this should be gradually increased to 500 g of concentrates per day for ewes carrying single lambs. Ewes carrying twins should be receiving 750 g of concentrates per day. The concentrates should contain 15–18% crude protein. This level of protein in the feed is required to ensure that the ewe will produce an adequate quantity of colostrum and milk after lambing. Ewes carrying triplets should commence steaming up 10 weeks prior to lambing.

> **DEFINITION**
>
> **Steaming up:** the practice of increasing the amount of concentrates being fed to sheep in late gestation in order to prevent twin lamb disease. This ensures a healthy lamb and promotes good milk production.

Ewes should be vaccinated against clostridial diseases (see page 472) and pasteurella (see page 473). Clostridial vaccinations should be given 4–6 weeks before lambing. Vaccinating the pregnant ewes against these diseases ensures that the ewes will pass on immunity to their lambs through their colostrum. Ewes should be regularly foot bathed to prevent lameness due to footrot. Lameness has been identified as a contributing factor in twin lamb disease. Heavily pregnant ewes are unable to graze properly or compete with other ewes at the forage trough. As a result, they have an inadequate feed intake, and this makes them more susceptible to twin lamb disease. Steaming up also increases the birth weight of the lamb and ensures good milk production in the ewe. It should be noted that feeding the ewes too much concentrates can also be problematic, resulting in big lambs, which can cause lambing difficulties.

> **Susceptible:** more likely, more vulnerable.

Housing

As winter approaches, the ewes should be housed indoors. Winter housing should be clean, draught-free, and have good ventilation with adequate floor space (Table 29.2) and feeding space for the ewes. It can be straw bedded or slats. If pens have slats, faeces and urine are collected in underground tanks.

Table 29.2 The recommended space requirement for housed ewes				
Ewe type	Floor space (m²)		Feeding space (mm)	
	Slats	Straw	Meal	Roughage
Large (90 kg)	1.2	1.4	600	200
Medium (70 kg)	1.1	1.2	500	200
Small (50 kg)	1.0	1.1	400	175
Source: Teagasc				

To maximise output from the flock, sheep should have adequate space for feeding. Twenty-five ewes per pen is recommended for small flocks, and 45–50 ewes per pen for large flocks (see Fig. 29.8). To optimise feeding of ewes, it should be possible to feed all sheep from the feeding passage. All sheep should be able to feed on meals together and it should not be necessary to enter a pen to feed sheep. Larger pens have several advantages, as fewer water troughs and gates are needed, and fewer passageways need to be created between pens. Individual pens should be in the same sheep shed, and there should be one individual pen for every six ewes, each 2.25 m².

The following calculation uses an average floor space of 1.2 m² per ewe and an average trough space of 450 mm per ewe.

Ideal pen depth = floor space per ewe / trough space available per ewe

Example:
Floor space per ewe = 1.2 m²
Feed space per ewe = 450 mm
Pen depth = 1.2/0.45 = 2.7 m

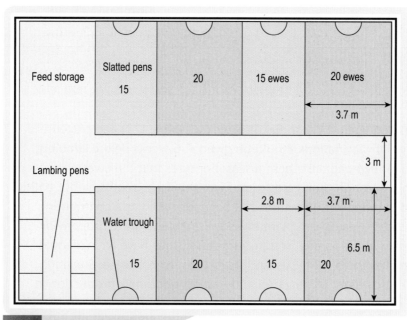

29.8   *Layout of sheep shed*

Lambing

Ewes are normally placed in lambing pens when they are due to lamb. These pens should be clean and disinfected, with plenty of straw. Poor hygiene in the lambing shed can result in the spread of diseases such as scour, watery mouth and navel ill.

Ewes should have a BCS of 3.0–3.5 for those ewes carrying a single lamb and of 3.5–4.0 for ewes carrying twin lambs. Ewes that are too thin at lambing will produce small, weak lambs that increase the mortality rate. Thin ewes will also produce poor-quality colostrum and will have reduced milk production and poor mothering ability.

| 29.9 | *Ewe after lambing* |

| 29.10 | *Lamb suckling a ewe* |

> **Mortality rate:** death rate.

The ewe's behaviour changes once she commences lambing. She will search for a spot to lamb, paw at the ground, get up and lie down frequently. She should be left alone at this time, since the majority of ewes will lamb without difficulty. However, an experienced person should be on hand to give assistance to the ewe if the ewe is experiencing lambing difficulties. Any ewe given assistance should receive an injection of antibiotics to prevent infection. Lambs weigh between 3 and 5 kg when born.

Once the lamb is born, the ewe should be allowed to lick the lamb. This helps to stimulate the circulatory system of the lamb and, more importantly, it helps in the bonding process between the ewe and the lamb. The lamb should get to its feet after a few minutes and start to suckle. The udder of the ewe should be checked to ensure that she is producing colostrum.

It is critical that the lamb gets colostrum, since it contains vital antibodies: the lamb's immune system is not fully developed when born. A lamb should receive at least one litre of colostrum in the first 24 hours. If the ewe has not produced colostrum, then colostrum from a newly calved cow can be used. Artificial colostrum is also available, and this can be made up and fed to the lamb.

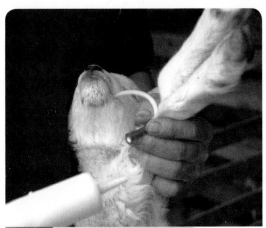

| 29.11 | *Lamb being fed with stomach tube* |

| 29.12 | *Ewe with lambs* |

The navel should be dipped in iodine to prevent navel ill and joint ill. The placenta should be disposed of, since it will attract predators (e.g. foxes and crows). If lambs are born outside, they are at greater risk of suffering from hypothermia or chill. A chilled lamb should be revived by feeding it colostrum through a stomach tube and warming the lamb using an infrared lamp (far enough from the lamb to prevent burning).

Hypothermia occurs when the body loses heat quickly, causing a dangerously low body temperature that interferes with the normal functioning of the body. If the chill is severe, the lamb should be given an injection of glucose. The ewe and her lambs should be placed in a pen of 3.24 m² for a few days to ensure bonding between the ewe and lambs. The lamb should be vaccinated against clostridial diseases in the weeks following its birth.

Fostering

Farmers often foster lambs from multiple births onto ewes with single lambs. There are a number of methods used and one of the most common and most successful procedures involves using the birth fluids of the ewe with the single lamb. This is known as wet fostering. In order to do this, the farmer must be present at the birth. The lamb to be fostered is first washed to remove the scent of its own dam. Its feet are temporarily tied together so that it cannot stand up. When the ewe gives birth to her lamb, the farmer removes it briefly and coats the foster lamb in the birth fluids. The foster lamb is placed in front of the ewe so that she will lick it clean. After 20 minutes, the ties should be removed from the foster lamb's feet and the ewe should be given its own lamb. The ewe with the lambs is observed over the next 24 hours to ensure that both lambs are thriving and that the ewe has not rejected either lamb. It also helps to maximise the number of lambs weaned, improving output.

Other methods of fostering include:

- **Fostering crate:** this prevents the ewe from kicking or hurting the foster lamb while allowing the lamb access to the ewe's udder. After a few days the lamb will have adopted the smell of the ewe and the ewe will accept the foster lamb.

- **Skinning a dead lamb:** if a ewe's natural offspring dies, the dead lamb can be skinned and the skin is attached using string to the foster lamb. The tail of the dead lamb should still be attached to the skin. This is to fool the ewe into accepting the foster lamb. The ewe and her foster lamb should be observed for

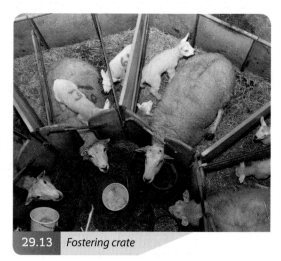

29.13 *Fostering crate*

a number of days to ensure that the ewe does not reject the lamb. Once the ewe has accepted the lamb, the skin can be removed.

- **Fostering products:** fostering products work by interfering with the ewe's sense of smell. The foster spray is sprayed on the ewe's nose and then on the foster lamb. This seems to fool the ewe into thinking the foster lamb is her own. Substituting perfume for a fostering spray works in the same way.

- **A dog:** some farmers will tie a dog outside the lambing pen. This causes the ewe to become protective about the foster lamb, strengthening the bond between the ewe and the lamb.

During the first few days, ram lambs can be castrated, and tail docking is also done. Tail docking is carried out to prevent build-up of faeces and lessen the chances of fly strike. Castration is not necessary if ram lambs are going for slaughter before they are 6 months old, i.e. before reaching puberty. An elastrator (see Fig. 29.19 on page 436) can be used to place a rubber band around the ram lamb's scrotum, where it remains until the scrotum falls off. Ewe lambs reach puberty at 6–8 months old. Lambs should be dosed for worms at about 6 weeks old. Lambs should be provided with hay during their first week to help develop their rumen.

29.14   *Tail docking*

Ewe and lamb mortality

Ewe and lamb mortality is inevitable at lambing time.
Reducing mortality rates will increase lamb output from the farm enterprise.

Ewe and lamb mortality can be reduced by ensuring that there is:

- Adequate supervision at lambing
- Good hygiene in the lambing shed: lambing pens clean, dry and with a plentiful supply of straw
- Ensuring that a strong bond develops between the ewe and her lamb
- Checking the udders of the ewes for colostrum
- Ensuring that the lamb gets adequate quantities of colostrum and milk.

Most sheep farmers aim for a mortality rate of less than 10%.

Factors that contribute to an increase in the mortality rate are as follows:

- Lambs not receiving colostrum (or enough colostrum)
- Lambs and ewes not being vaccinated
- Poor hygiene: dirty and wet lambing pens
- Infectious diseases: scour, watery mouth and navel infections
- Lambing outdoors increases the risk of chilled lambs and abandoned lambs
- Wet and cold conditions increase the risk of lambs developing hypothermia
- Lambs are small and lose heat quickly, especially if their fleeces are wet
- Starvation and mismothering: lambs are often found dead with empty stomachs; this can be due to the ewe abandoning the lamb and not allowing the lamb to suckle
- Lambing outdoors increases the risk of predators (e.g. dogs and foxes)
- Ewes not being steamed up
- Twin lamb disease
- Lambing difficulties, e.g. lambs being born with their hind legs first (breech position) or twin lambs coming together, due to lack of supervision; lambing difficulties can result in birth injuries to lambs that are too big
- Hypocalcaemia (milk fever).

> **Inevitable:** unavoidable, bound to happen.

> **Mismothering:** when a ewe fails to own and care for her lamb.

Post-lambing

The ewes are kept on a high plane of nutrition post-lambing to ensure good milk production. The growth of the lambs during this time solely depends on the ewe's milk. Ewes should have hay or silage (high dry matter digestibility) ad lib and concentrates, particularly for early lambing. Once grass is available in sufficient quantity there is no need to continue feeding concentrates, since good-quality grass is a complete feed. However, if grass is scarce, a farmer should continue to feed concentrates to prevent any reduction in the ewe's milk yield. Ewes should be watched for any sign of grass tetany. Grass tetany (due to a deficiency of magnesium) is one of the biggest killers of lactating ewes. Ewes should be provided with a mineral lick or have Cal Mag dusted onto their meal. Ewes and their lambs should be rotationally grazed on good pasture, rather than set stocked. Lambs being produced for the Easter market should be creep fed concentrates and sold off as they reach slaughter weight (34–40 kg). A Suffolk-cross lamb will reach slaughter weight 12–14 weeks after it is born. Creep gates and creep feeders allow lambs to have access to pasture and concentrates, but not the ewes. Teagasc estimates that lambs creep fed will be 2 kg heavier at weaning and will be ready for slaughter 2 weeks earlier.

29.15 *Lambs creep feeding*

29.16 *Ewe out on grass with her lambs*

Weaning takes place during the months of June and July and the ewes and lambs are separated from each other. The ewes are put onto bare pasture (pasture with very little grass) to dry off (stop lactation) in preparation for flushing, aiming for a BCS of 3.5 for mating. The best lambs (especially those that were a twin) can be selected at weaning.

At this time, the ewes should be checked for chronic health problems:
- Mastitis
- Footrot or chronically lame ewes
- Lambing difficulties (e.g. prolapses)
- Ewes that fail to improve their BCS
- Poor milk production or non-functioning udders (these ewes should be culled)
- Ewes with lots of missing or broken teeth (known as broken mouth): this will affect their ability to graze and make them more prone to twin lamb disease.

Teagasc advises a replacement rate of 23% annually. Rearing your own replacement ewes is always better than bought-in ewes, since there is less risk of diseases. If a farmer is planning to breed their own replacement ewe, a maternal sire like the Belclare, Border Leicester or Bluefaced Leicester should be used.

Breeding ewe lambs

Some farmers will breed their best ewe lambs, since this can increase potential output.

Good management of these ewe lambs is required, since they will require additional feeding compared to mature ewes. Ewe lambs must be fed for growth in addition to producing their own lamb and milk production. A ewe lamb needs to be 45–50 kg at mating, with a BCS of 3.

Since there is an additional workload when breeding ewe lambs, the majority of farmers wait and breed their young ewes as hoggets. A ewe hogget is 18 months old and will weigh roughly 63–65 kg (85–90% of a mature ewe's weight). Charollais rams are a popular choice for mating with ewe lambs and ewe hoggets, since they produce small lambs, which lessens the risk of lambing difficulties.

General management of sheep

These are routine procedures that are carried out on a sheep farm in order to maintain a healthy, productive flock and to maximise output.

Vaccination programme

Vaccinations can be used to prevent a number of diseases in sheep. Sheep are vaccinated against clostridial diseases, pasteurella and orf (see page 470). Vaccinations for footrot and pneumonia are also available.

| 29.17 | *Dosing sheep* |

Dosing

Dosing is used to prevent the build-up of stomach worms, liver fluke and other internal parasites. The dose is usually in liquid or paste form and is administered at the back of the tongue of the animal, either by using a dosing gun for ewes and rams or a syringe (minus the needle) for lambs. Dosing is also commonly referred to as drenching.

Dipping

All sheep are susceptible to fly strike between the months of April and November and sheep scab between September and March. The sheep are dipped in summer to prevent fly strike and in winter to prevent mange mite, which causes sheep scab. For dipping to be effective against sheep scab, the sheep must be in the dip for at least 1 minute with the head immersed twice.

Dipping sheep often provides protection against other parasites (e.g. ticks and lice). The dipping solution must be freshly prepared and dipping should be done on a

| 29.18 | *Sheep dipping* |

dry day to avoid dilution of the dipping solution by rainwater. Due to the hazardous and toxic nature of sheep dips to the operator, risk of contamination of water sources and difficulty with the disposal of the dipping solution, many farmers are choosing not to dip their sheep and instead are using pour-ons or sprays to prevent fly strike and mange mite. These are sprayed along the back and around the tail region of the animal. Mobile sheep showers are also available and are extremely efficient at treating large numbers of sheep.

Dagging and docking

Dagging (also known as crutching) involves the removal of wool around the tail of the sheep. Intestinal worms can cause diarrhoea, causing faeces to soil the wool around the tail. This in turn attracts bluebottle flies. The flies lay their eggs in the soiled wool and when the maggots hatch they feed off the flesh of the animal. This is commonly known as fly strike. Removal of the wool around this area helps to prevent fly strike.

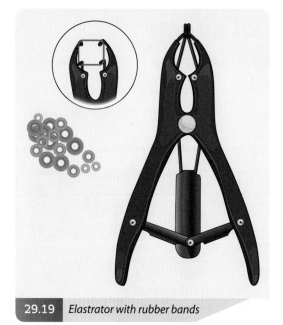

29.19 *Elastrator with rubber bands*

29.20 *Lamb with a docked tail*

Docking is a procedure to remove part of the lamb's tail. Docking the tail prevents the build-up of faeces around the tail and the hindquarters, thus helping to reduce the incidence of fly strike. Docking also aids shearing of the sheep. The most common way to dock a lamb's tail is using a rubber band that is applied using an elastrator. This is a bloodless form of tail-docking. The rubber band cuts off the blood supply to the tail and the tail falls off in 7–10 days. Sheep welfare guidelines state that tail docking, if carried out, must be done in the first week after the lamb is born.

Foot bath, foot trimming and paring

Foot trimming and paring is necessary when the outer surface of the foot grows beyond the soft sole of the foot. This is particularly common in sheep that are housed. If the foot is not trimmed the animal can become lame.

Footrot also causes lameness. Footrot is caused by bacteria that create inflammation and infection of the tissue between the digits of the foot. Regularly walking sheep through foot baths helps to prevent footrot. Foot baths contain a solution of copper sulfate or formalin and the animals are allowed to stand in it to allow the solution to penetrate between the digits. Treatment for footrot includes paring off the infected foot and treatment with an antibiotic. Keeping sheep on clean pasture, which has not been grazed in the previous 2 weeks, helps to eliminate the bacteria.

29.21 *A lame sheep*

29.22 *Sheep being sheared*

Shearing

Sheep are normally sheared in May or June. This prevents the sheep from overheating in warm summer weather and it aids in preventing fly strike. Wool is also a saleable product. Some farmers shear their sheep prior to winter housing, as it gives the sheep more space.

The impact of sheep production on farm economics

There are approximately 12,750 sheep farms in Ireland, with an average size of 51 hectares and an average flock of 138 ewes. Sheep farms in Ireland generate an average income of €16,800 per year.

Sheep farming generates the lowest income per hectare of all the main farming enterprises (dairy, beef, sheep, tillage) in the country, providing €353 per hectare (source: Teagasc). While incomes have risen slightly in recent years, the small increases recorded are largely due to farmer participation in schemes such as the Sheep Welfare Scheme. The majority of farms do not make a profit from production and are heavily reliant on direct payments. The average direct payment is approximately €19,000 per year and contributes 115% of total farm income on the average Irish sheep farm. Sheep farm incomes can be broadly divided into three categories. One third of sheep farmers earn less than €10,000 per year, a third earn between €10,000 and €20,000 and the remainder earn between €20,000 and €50,000. The Sheep Welfare Scheme was the main contributor to the increase in sheep farm incomes in 2017.

Some of the advantages attached to sheep farming include quality assurance schemes such as the Sustainable Beef and Lamb Assurance Scheme (SBLAS). Schemes such as the BETTER Sheep Farm Programme and the Sheep Welfare Scheme improve sheep welfare and encourage breed improvements. These advantages are outlined in Food Wise 2025. Other advantages of Irish sheep farms include our grass-based production system and use of hill and mountain land that would otherwise have limited use.

The export market for sheep meat was valued at €284 million in 2017, with the Irish market being heavily reliant on exports to France and the UK. One third of all sheep meat exports go to France, with a further 19% exported to the UK. As the effect of Brexit is yet unknown, it is important for new markets to be explored. Food Wise 2025 outlines target markets in Asia, Africa and North America, and identifies China as a potential new market as the country has a growing demand for sheep meat products.

Optimising sheep health and welfare

Better management practices can improve sheep health and welfare in a flock, which leads to increased outputs, through better live weight gain, reduction in diseases and lameness, and increased litter sizes. There are a number of schemes farmers can enrol in to enhance welfare standards on their farm, while improving outputs.

Sheep Welfare Scheme

The Sheep Welfare Scheme was introduced to contribute to the continued development of animal and health welfare in the sheep sector and requires farmers to go beyond the relevant mandatory standards to enhance the standards of animal welfare in their flock. Farmers opting into the scheme must complete a sheep census and identify their flock as a hill flock or a lowland flock, depending which has the greater numbers on their farm.

The scheme involves targeted intervention in the areas of:
- Lameness control
- Mineral supplementation for ewes post mating
- Meal feeding lambs post weaning
- Parasite control (faecal egg count)
- Management of pregnant ewes (scanning)
- Flystrike control
- Mineral supplementation to lambs pre weaning.

Farmers must choose one option from Category A and one from Category B, as listed in Table 29.3, for the appropriate flock and implement those processes on their farm.

Table 29.3 Management options in Sheep Welfare Scheme	
Lowland flock	**Hill flock**
Category A	**Category A**
Lameness control	Mineral supplementation for ewes post mating
Mineral supplementation for ewes post mating	Meal feeding lambs post weaning*
Category B	**Category B**
Parasite control (faecal egg count)	Parasite control (faecal egg count)
Scanning	Scanning
Flystrike control	Mineral supplementation for lambs pre weaning*

Cannot be chosen together

Sustainability in sheep farming

Sustainability can be achieved in sheep farming systems while minimising environmental impact. Increasing stocking densities does achieve intensification but at a cost of the use of more fertiliser to improve grass output. Ideally intensification should minimise the impact on the environment in relation to the inputs. This can be achieved by:
- Improved breeds
- Less waste through disease prevention
- Better nutrients available to livestock.

Farmers can also enrol in quality assurance schemes designed to improve sustainability on Irish sheep farms.

Sustainable Beef and Lamb Assurance Scheme

The SBLAS is a quality assurance scheme operated by Bord Bia. The scheme seeks to provide quality assurance that lamb produced under this scheme comes from farms engaged in sustainability initiatives, including good soil management, improving biodiversity, conservation of water and minimising greenhouse gas emissions.

Farmers who are enrolled in the scheme must meet the standards set out in the scheme to be certified by Bord Bia. They must also adhere to regulations set out by the Department of Agriculture, Food and the Marine (DAFM).

Standards required by the SBLAS include:
- Demonstrate competence as a herd owner and have relevant experience and training
- Provide plans for the ongoing health and welfare of livestock on the farm
- Comply with DAFM regulations on identification and traceability (See Table 29.4)

- Comply with regulations on purchase, storage and use of animal remedies
- Provide adequate feed and water to livestock and keep farm feed records
- Comply with regard to livestock and facilities management including: suitable housing facilities, hygiene in lambing facilities, shearing, drafting lambs, castration and tail docking, treatment of disease, nutritional requirements, monitoring of livestock for general health
- Implement biosecurity measures on the farm.

Tagging and traceability

To ensure full traceability of all sheep, a farmer must comply with a number of regulations set out by DAFM. This system of traceability includes farms, marts and meat factories. These are listed in Table 29.4.

Table 29.4 Traceability regulations for sheep farmers	
Regulation	**Practice**
Registration	All flock owners must apply for registration with the DAFM and they will be issued with a flock number.
Identification of sheep	All lambs within a flock must be tagged before they leave the farm or by the time they are 9 months old.
Dispatch/Movement Documentation	Documentation detailing movement must be completed by the sheep owner and accompany sheep moving off a farm, detailing the number of sheep moved, the ID number of each individual sheep tag, and the transfer location (e.g. other farm or slaughterhouse).
Annual sheep census	Sheep farmers must count the sheep on the farm each year and return the details to the DAFM annually as part of the national sheep census.

Summary

- The length of the oestrous cycle is 17 days, the duration of oestrous is 36 hours and the gestation period is 147 days, or 5 months.
- Flushing is the process of moving ewes from a low plane of nutrition to a high plane of nutrition prior to mating.
- Flushing has a number of advantages: it increases the ovulation rate, increases conception rates, promotes better implantation of the embryo to the uterine wall, increases litter size and leads to more regular heat cycles.
- Flushing should continue with the ewes for 4 weeks after mating to ensure that the embryos develop properly.
- Sponging involves placing progesterone-impregnated sponges into the vagina of the ewes to synchronise the breeding cycles of the ewes. The sponges are removed after 12 days and the ewes all come into heat 2 days later. The ram to ewe ratio for synchronised breeding is 1 : 10.
- Rams are raddled (harnessed) with coloured crayons to mark any ewe that they have mated with; in this way, lambing dates can be calculated. The colour of the crayon is changed every 17 days so that ewes that repeat (come back into oestrus) can be identified.

- Breeding out of season involves adjusting the breeding cycle of breeding ewes so that the lambs are born in December and January and can reach slaughter weight in time for the Easter market. In order to breed ewes out of season, the ewes must be sponged in July and injected with pregnant mare serum gonadotropin (PMSG) once the sponges are removed.

- Breeding outputs in hill sheep flocks can be improved by creating a flock breeding plan, improving pre-mating body condition score in ewes and increasing management of weaned lambs.

- Ewes should be returned to a maintenance diet 4 weeks after mating.

- Scanning of ewes is carried out 80 days after the ram joined the flock. Scanning aids in determining the feed requirement of ewes in late gestation. Scanning also identifies barren ewes that can be culled from the flock.

- Steaming up is the practice of increasing the amount of concentrates being fed to sheep in late gestation in order to prevent twin lamb disease, ensure a healthy lamb and promote good milk production. Steaming up should commence in the last 6–8 weeks before lambing.

- The amount of concentrates fed to ewes carrying a single lamb should gradually increase from 100 g to 500 g of concentrates per day. Ewes carrying twins should be receiving 750 g of concentrates per day.

- Ewes should be left alone to lamb unless assistance is required. Once the lamb is born, the ewe should lick the lamb: this helps in the bonding between the ewe and the lamb. Lambs weigh 3–5 kg when born.

- It is critical that the lamb gets colostrum, since it contains vital antibiotics: the lamb's immune system is not fully developed.

- Farmers often foster lambs from multiple births onto ewes with single lambs.

- Ewes should be kept on a high plane of nutrition post-lambing to ensure good milk production. Ewes should have their feed supplement with minerals (especially magnesium and calcium) to prevent grass tetany and milk fever.

- Creep gates and creep feeders are used to provide additional concentrates to lambs and not the ewes. Creep feeding ensures lambs reach slaughter weight in time for the Easter market. Lambs are sold off as they reach their slaughter weight (34–40 kg).

- Lambs are weaned between June and July and the ewes are placed on bare pasture to dry them off and prepare them for flushing. Ewes with mastitis, chronic feet problems, lambing difficulties and poor milk production are culled from the flock.

- When breeding replacement ewes, a maternal sire is used, e.g. Belclare, Bluefaced Leicester or Border Leicester.

- Sheep are dosed to prevent the build-up of worms, liver fluke and other parasites. Sheep are dipped twice a year: once in summer to prevent fly strike and once in winter to prevent sheep scab.

- Tail-docking and dagging are carried out to prevent fly strike. Fly strike is caused by bluebottle and greenbottle flies laying their eggs in the soiled fleece of sheep and lambs.

- Sheep are regularly foot bathed to prevent footrot, which causes lameness. Foot trimming and paring is also regularly carried out to prevent lameness. Sheep are sheared in the summer to prevent them from overheating and to help prevent fly strike.

- The Sheep Welfare Scheme requires farmers to go beyond the relevant mandatory standards to enhance the standards of animal welfare in their flock.
- The Sustainable Beef and Lamb Assurance Scheme (SBLAS) is a quality assurance scheme operated by Bord Bia. The scheme seeks to provide quality assurance that lamb produced under this scheme comes from farms engaged in sustainability initiatives.
- To ensure full traceability of all sheep, a farmer must register their flock, tag sheep, complete dispatch and movement documentation for all sheep and submit an annual sheep census.

PowerPoint Summary

QUESTIONS

1. Give approximate values for each of the following for sheep:
   - (a) Weight of a lamb at birth
   - (b) Finishing weight (slaughter weight) of a lamb
   - (c) Length of gestation
   - (d) Length of oestrous cycle
   - (e) Duration of oestrus.
2. Compare the early lamb production system with the mid-season lamb production system.
3. Define the term 'flushing'. Explain how this is carried out.
4. List three advantages of flushing.
5. Why must flushing be continued for 4 weeks after mating?
6. Explain how a farmer would synchronise breeding in ewes using:
   - (a) Sponging
   - (b) The ram effect.
7. What are the advantages of synchronising the breeding cycles of ewes?
8. Suggest a suitable ram to ewe ratio when synchronising breeding.
9. What is the purpose of each of the following in breeding sheep?
   - (a) Raddling the ram
   - (b) Pregnant mare serum gonadotropin (PMSG)
   - (c) Changing the colour of the ram crayon every 17 days.
10. What is the body condition score (BCS) at mating for:
    - (a) The ewe
    - (b) The ram?
11. Why has the ram a greater BCS at mating than the ewe?
12. Explain why ewes are scanned 80 days after mating.
13. Identify three ways in which breeding output can be increased in hill sheep flocks.
14. Describe how outputs changed on BETTER sheep farms.
15. Describe the feeding and management of the ewe 6 weeks prior to lambing.
16. Define the term 'steaming up'.

17. Explain the importance of each of the following prior to lambing:

    (a) Steaming up

    (b) Addition of Cal Mag to the ewes' feed.

18. Why is lameness seen as a contributing factor to twin lamb disease?

19. Outline why designing a sheep shed with larger pens may be more advantageous than smaller pens.

20. A farmer has a flock of 200 lowland sheep. He wishes to put the flock in his sheep shed for the winter. Each ewe needs space of 1.2 m². The sheep shed contains the following number of pens:

Pen area	Number of pens
6 m × 8 m	2
4 m × 6 m	4
3 m × 4 m	6

    (a) Suggest the most efficient way of grouping the sheep in pens, which will lead to the least labour required when checking pens and placing feed in troughs.

    (b) Does the farmer have any extra space in the shed to expand the flock in the future?

21. Describe the care of a newborn lamb.

22. Describe the management and feeding of lambs and ewes between lambing and weaning.

23. Write a short note on three of the following:

    (a) Dipping

    (b) Dagging

    (c) Foot paring and foot baths

    (d) Vaccination programmes.

24. What is the purpose of the Sheep Welfare Scheme? Describe two practices that a lowland sheep farmer must carry out as part of the scheme.

25. Describe four requirements of the Sustainable Beef and Lamb Assurance Scheme.

26. Outline three requirements of sheep traceability required by the Department of Agriculture, Food and the Marine. Why is traceability of sheep so important?

27. Hill sheep farmers are encouraged to improve output from their flocks under the BETTER Sheep Farm Programme. What difficulties do you think farmers encounter on hill sheep farms, while trying to improve outputs from the flock?

Solutions · Weblinks

CHAPTER 30
Pig breeds, management, nutrition and production

When you have completed this chapter you should be able to:

- Describe the characteristics of common types, breeds and crosses of pigs
- Describe the management of the production cycle of pigs, including nutrition at different development stages:
  - From birth to finishing or selection as a replacement gilt
  - The breeding sow
- Describe the factors that determine the output and quality of produce from a pig production unit:
  - Breed variety
  - Nutrition
  - Housing
  - Management
- Calculate the daily live-weight gain (DLG) and the feed conversion ratio (FCR) of pigs
- Interpret data relating to DLG and FCR (Higher Level only)
- Discuss the role and importance of innovation and biotechnological applications in pig production
- Discuss management practices for:
  - Handling and housing of farm animals
  - Optimal animal health and welfare
  - Slurry/farmyard manure
  - Delivering sustainable and environmentally friendly production systems
  - Ensuring quality, safe and traceable food for the consumer
- Appreciate the impact of pig production on farm economics
- Discuss the importance of export markets for pig producers.

Pig breeds

Indoor pig breeds

The two main indoor commercial pig breeds in Ireland are the Large White and the Landrace. These two breeds are crossbred with each other to produce offspring with hybrid vigour.

Large White

The Large White is an English breed widely used in intensive pig production units. It is a large pig with erect ears. It has a number of desirable characteristics:

- Highly prolific (average litter size is 12–14 piglets)
- Fast growth rate
- Good meat quality

30.1 *Large White*

- Good feed conversion ratio (FCR)
- Good mothers
- Good conformation with good hams.

Landrace

The Landrace is a Danish breed and is also widely used in intensive pig production units. It is a medium-large pig, white, with drooped ears. The characteristics of this breed are:

- Long muscular body
- Small shoulders and large hams
- Lean meat
- Good conformation.

30.2 *Landrace*

Duroc

The Duroc originates from the United States. It is used in both indoor and outdoor pig production units as a terminal sire to produce pigs for slaughter. Durocs are red, with a large muscular frame, and are fast-growing. The Duroc improves the eating quality of the meat due to the high level of marbling.

Crossbred pigs (Landrace × Large White)

30.3 *Duroc*

Since the majority of pig production in Ireland occurs in indoor units, the most popular breed used in this system is a crossbreed between the Large White and the Landrace.

This crossbreed demonstrates **hybrid vigour**, or **heterosis**, since it has the best characteristics of both breeds. To produce crossbred pigs, a breeding strategy known as criss-cross breeding is used. Criss-cross breeding maximises hybrid vigour.

Ideally, all breeding pigs would be a first generation (F1) Landrace–Large White crossbreed. However, maintaining purebred Landrace and Large White pigs to produce these F1 crossbreeds is expensive. Criss-cross breeding reduces the cost of producing quality pigs, while maintaining the best characteristics of both breeds.

In order to start this breeding programme, a number of F1 Landrace × Large White (LR × LW) crossbred gilts need to be purchased. The boars in this criss-cross breeding system are always purebred. The F1 crossbred gilts have hybrid vigour as they have 50% of their genes from both of their purebred parents. The F1 crossbred gilts are crossed with a purebred Large White (LW). The best females (F2) from this cross will be kept as replacement gilts. The remaining females and all of the males will be fattened and finished for slaughter. The replacement gilts from the F2 will be crossed with a purebred Landrace (LR) boar. This step aims to produce offspring in which the inherited genes are roughly 50% from both the Large White and the Landrace. Again, the best gilts will be kept as replacements and the remaining offspring will be fattened for slaughter.

Many pig producers introduce a third breed into their breeding programme. In this example, a Duroc is used as a terminal sire. The Duroc is used in this breeding system to produce progeny with fast growth rate and good carcase yields. All the progeny produced by this cross will be fattened and slaughtered.

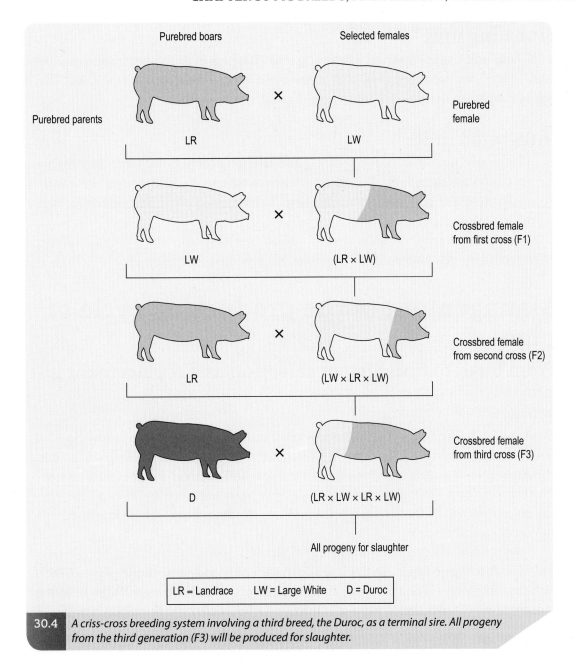

Purebred boars   Selected females

Purebred parents

LR   ×   LW   Purebred female

LW   ×   (LR × LW)   Crossbred female from first cross (F1)

LR   ×   (LW × LR × LW)   Crossbred female from second cross (F2)

D   ×   (LR × LW × LR × LW)   Crossbred female from third cross (F3)

All progeny for slaughter

| LR = Landrace | LW = Large White | D = Duroc |

30.4 *A criss-cross breeding system involving a third breed, the Duroc, as a terminal sire. All progeny from the third generation (F3) will be produced for slaughter.*

Using this system of breeding, the boars must be changed every 2 years to prevent inbreeding. However, more than 95% of pig producers in Ireland are using artificial insemination (AI) instead of natural service using a boar.

Pig production in integrated units

The majority of pigs produced in Ireland are on large commercial farms known as integrated pig production units. These units are comprised of a **breeding unit** and a **finishing unit**.

Breeding unit

A breeding unit involves sows giving birth to piglets in a farrowing house. These piglets remain with the sow until they are weaned at 4–5 weeks old when they have an average weight of 7–9 kg. The piglets are then moved to a weaner house, where they are kept until they reach an average weight of 20 kg. Then they are moved into the second stage weaner house until they reach a weight of 32–38 kg. Boars are kept in these units as 'teaser boars' to bring gilts/sows into heat.

Finishing unit

A finishing unit is also known as a fattening unit. The pigs in this system weigh more than 38 kg. They are raised here until they reach slaughter weight at 100–110 kg. The age of the pigs in these units ranges from 3 months to 6 months.

Integrated unit

In an integrated unit, all breeding, rearing and fattening (or finishing) for slaughter are carried out on the same farm. This reduces the movement of pigs between farms and decreases the risk of disease entering the farm. In integrated pig production units, pigs are raised exclusively indoors.

A very small number of farms concentrate on breeding or finishing only. In addition, a few producers rear pigs outdoors in a free-range or organic enterprise.

Management of the production cycle of pigs

From birth to finishing or selection as a replacement gilt

Birth

Nutrition

> A farrowing crate is a unit that a sow is placed in prior to giving birth. It helps to reduce mortality of piglets by preventing the sow crushing them.

Piglets weigh 1.0–1.5 kg at birth. The sow gives birth to the piglets in a farrowing crate in the **farrowing** house. The first milk that the sow produces is colostrum, so it is important that all piglets are latching onto the sow and suckling. Insufficient intake of colostrum is a cause of piglet mortality. Piglets are born with very low energy reserves and colostrum warms these piglets up as well as providing them with energy and immunity against disease.

Sows produce colostrum for the first 24 hours and then this transitions over 3–4 days into milk. The fat and lactose in the sow's colostrum provide energy to the piglets. The high protein content is due to a high concentration of antibodies present in the milk; the concentration of antibodies is highest in the first 12 hours after the first piglet is born.

Table 30.1 Composition of a sow's colostrum and milk		
Nutrients	**Colostrum (%)**	**Milk (%)**
Fat	5.7	8.2
Protein	13	4.7
Lactose	4	5.1

The fat, protein and lactose percentages are averages for the composition of colostrum in the first 24 hours and are adapted from report by Thiel P.K. et al, 2014.

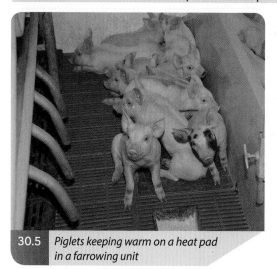

30.5 *Piglets keeping warm on a heat pad in a farrowing unit*

30.6 *Infrared lamp to keep piglets warm. Presence of enrichment material on the ground can aid in preventing tail biting.*

Kiernan Super Creep Ration

Constituents

Crude protein	21%	Lysine	1.8%
Crude oil and fat	10%	Vitamin A	
Crude fibre	2%	Vitamin D	
Crude ash	5.7%	Vitamin E	
Calcium	0.7%		
Phosphorus	0.6%		
Methionine	0.5%		

List of ingredients

Soya bean extruded, maize extruded, extruded wheat, whey powder, whey protein concentrate, oat flour, soya concentrate, soya bean oil, lactose powder, calcium carbonate, monocalcium phosphate, sodium chloride.

30.7	Piglets all suckling a sow in a farrowing crate. Piglets will fight to establish a pecking order for the sow's teat.

30.8	Super creep ration

Farrowing units contain a creep area away from the farrowing crate. Creep feed is introduced to the piglets approximately 1 week after birth. Creep feed contains 21% protein and 1.8% lysine (see Fig. 30.8). Lysine is the most essential amino acid and is required by pigs for producing muscle. It is also important for milk production in sows and gilts.

The sow suckles the piglets for 4–5 weeks; after that the piglets are abruptly removed from the sow (this is known as weaning). The minimum time in which piglets can be weaned is 28 days (4 weeks). Five weeks may be necessary for larger litters.

Management

The greatest risk of piglet mortality is in the first 48 hours. The main causes of death in piglets include starvation and crushing. For these reasons, adequate supervision of farrowing is essential. The sow should be given assistance if she is experiencing difficulties while farrowing. Weak piglets, especially those that weigh less than 1 kg, should be helped to find a teat or be fed colostrum using a syringe. The navels of newborn piglets should be sprayed with iodine to prevent navel infections. Routine tail docking and teeth clipping have been banned on pig welfare grounds since 2008. Teeth clipping can lead to mouth infections. Piglets tend to fight with each other to establish an order within the litter. This can result in facial and tail injuries as well as injuries to the sow's teat. Before carrying out tail docking and teeth clipping, other measures should be taken to prevent tail-biting, taking into account housing environment (ventilation, temperature, draughts), stocking densities and the provision of enrichment materials. Farmers are now required to undertake a risk assessment of the incidences of tail biting in pigs on their farms.

Weaning is the process of changing a young mammal's diet to other food (concentrates and other feeds) while withdrawing the supply of its own mother's milk. In pigs this happens when the piglets are removed from the sow, while in other mammals (sheep and beef) it can be a more gradual process.

30.9	Piglets with enrichment material in the farrowing unit

Piglets that are reared indoors can be susceptible to developing anaemia, which is caused by a lack of iron. To prevent anaemia all piglets are given an injection of iron at 2–3 days old. Ear notching/tagging may also be carried out to identify future replacement gilts for the breeding herd.

Another contributing factor to piglet mortality is the sow crushing the piglets. Crushing is most common in the first 3 days after the piglets have been born and is caused by the sow standing up or rolling over in the farrowing crate. To reduce the risk of crushing, the farrowing unit has a creep area and an infrared lamp or a heat pad. The temperature of the creep area is approximately 30°C. This creep area keeps the piglets warm, since their small bodies can lose heat easily. In addition, the heated area attracts the piglets away from the sow when they are not suckling, thus preventing them from being crushed. The piglets are provided with additional feed (creep feed) in this area. The creep area is separate from the farrowing crate in the farrowing unit. The reason for this is that the temperature of the creep area would be too hot for the sow. If the sow were kept at a temperature higher than 22°C, she would eat less feed, which would decrease her milk production and her energy reserves. A decrease in milk production by the sow would lead to a decrease in the growth rate of the piglets.

Piglets should be vaccinated against *Mycoplasma hyopneumoniae* (see page 484) at 3 weeks of age.

Weaner management and feeding

Litters that have been weaned at the same time are mixed and grouped according to their size and weight. Weaners are normally 7–9 kg on entering the first-stage weaner house.

Weaners are fed a creep ration (21% protein and 1.8% lysine) ad lib for the first 1–2 weeks in the weaner house, then a link ration, which contains 21% protein and 1.45% lysine. The link ration is highly digestible but expensive.

Pig producers should avoid overcrowding in the first-stage weaner house, as this adds stress to the weaners. There should be 0.2 m² per pig and plenty of room at the feeding trough, as these pigs need space and time to adjust to their new diet. It is important that weaned pigs have access to a good supply of water. It is recommended that extra water is provided in the first few days after weaning. Weaners are then moved on to weaner rations, which contain 18–20% protein and about 1.3% lysine (see Fig. 30.10).

> **Environmental enrichment:** objects or materials for the piglets to investigate and manipulate. These materials improve the living conditions of the pigs by encouraging a wider range of normal pig behaviours. Examples of enrichment material include straw, wood, sawdust, grass silage and shredded paper.

Super Weaner Ration

Constituents

Crude protein	19.2%	Lysine	1.3%
Crude oil and fat	6.5%	Vitamin A	
Crude fibre	3.2%	Vitamin D	
Crude ash	5%	Vitamin E	
Calcium	0.7%		
Phosphorus	0.5%		
Methionine	0.4%		

List of ingredients

Wheat, maize, soya bean meal, barley, soya bean oil, cane sugar molasses, soya bean hulls, palm and rape acid oil, calcium carbonate, monocalcium phosphate, sodium chloride.

Instructions for use

This feed may only be fed to growing pigs to a maximum of 12 weeks of age.

30.10 *Super weaner ration*

After 1 month in the first-stage weaner house, the weaners are moved to the second-stage weaner house, where they remain for another month. The weaned pigs are grouped, and this group remains together as much as possible right through to slaughter.

Temperatures in the first-stage weaner house are set at 28°C and decreased by 2°C per week over a 4-week period to 22°C. In the second-stage weaner house temperatures are set at 22–24°C. When the weaners reach 32–38 kg, they are moved to the fattener house.

Fattener management and feeding

Fatteners are fed fattener ration, which contains 14–17% protein and 1.1% lysine, ad lib (see Fig. 30.11). Water is also available. Temperatures are kept at 18°C in the fattening house.

Fatteners remain in the fattening house for approximately 3 months. Pigs are 'finished' when they weigh 100–110 kg. They are approximately 6 months old. Pigs that have been selected as replacement gilts for breeding are housed for a further 4–6 weeks until they reach 130–140 kg. They are then moved to the dry sow house to enter the production cycle.

Prime Finisher Pellets

Constituents

Crude protein	17%	Lysine	1%
Crude oil and fat	4%	Vitamin A	
Crude fibre	4.5%	Vitamin D	
Crude ash	5%	Vitamin E	
Calcium	0.7%		
Phosphorus	0.5%		
Methionine	0.3%		

List of ingredients

Maize, wheat, barley, soya bean meal, wheat flour, rapeseed meal, soya bean hulls, soya, palm and rape acid oil, calcium carbonate, sugar cane molasses, sodium chloride, monocalcium phosphate.

Instructions for use

This feed may only be fed to growing pigs to a maximum of 16 weeks of age.

30.11 Prime finisher pellets

Criteria for the selection of replacement gilts

When selecting replacement gilts for breeding, farmers will look for the following:
- Gilts that come from mothers that are good milkers/mothers
- Correct weight and body condition score (BCS)
- Good conformation
- Good feet and legs: animals with abnormal toes or legs are more prone to lameness
- Gilts that have 12 or more evenly spaced, well-developed teats
- Gilts that have reached puberty and are oestrous cycling
- Gilts that are healthy
- Gilts from sows with a history of low numbers of stillbirths.

The production cycle of a breeding sow

The management and nutrition of a sow

The role of the sow is to produce as many quality piglets as possible in her litters. Potentially, a sow can produce 2.39 litters per year. Herds that participated in Teagasc e-Profit Monitoring (ePM) reported an average litter per sow per year in 2017 of 2.36. A litter can range from 5 to 22 piglets. The average litter size produced by pigs in the Teagasc ePM programme was 13.5 in 2017.

Management of the dry sow

As the name implies, a dry sow is one who is no longer producing milk. Sows and gilts are housed in the dry sow house up until 1 week before they are due to farrow (give birth). Boars are kept in the dry sow house. The boar must be in sight and smell of the sows, since pheromones released by the boar encourage both the gilts and the sows to come into oestrus. The boars are also used to detect which sows and gilts are in oestrus. Physical signs of oestrus in sows and gilts include a swollen, red vulva, erect ears and loud grunting. Sows/gilts in oestrus also display what is called a 'standing reflex', i.e. they stand rigid in the presence of a boar when the farmer applies pressure with his/her hands on the sow's/gilt's back.

30.12 *Sows in a dry sow house*

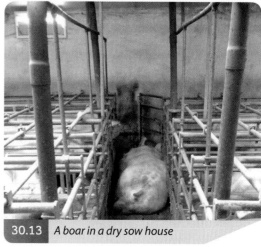

30.13 *A boar in a dry sow house*

Oestrous cycle

The length of the oestrous cycle in pigs is 21 days and the duration of oestrus is 2–3 days. When heat is detected, a sow is double served. This means she is either mated with the boar or artificial insemination (AI) twice within 24 hours. In pig production units, >95% of all servings are now done by AI. Double serving increases the conception rates and the size of the litters. If the sow comes back into heat again after 21 days, she is served twice again. If she repeats (comes back into oestrus again), she will be culled from the herd.

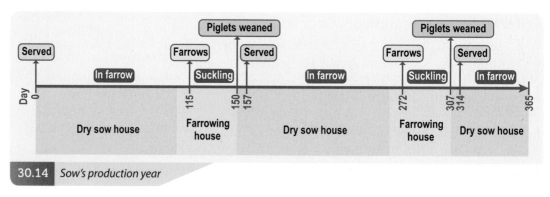

30.14 *Sow's production year*

A gilt should not be served on her first heat, since she will produce a small litter. When she comes into heat the second time, she will be served twice in 12 hours to increase her conception rate and litter size.

Sows and gilts must be loose-housed (kept in groups) from 4 weeks after service until 1 week before farrowing. The gestation period in pigs is 115 days, or 3 months, 3 weeks and 3 days. The pens must have lengths of 2.6 m or greater for groups of six or more sows/gilts. The temperature of the dry sow house is maintained at 20°C. A pig farmer should have vaccination and parasite control programmes in place.

Nutrition

The gilts and sows are fed 2.5 kg of a dry sow ration per day. Sows should not be overfed in the first 3 weeks of gestation, since this will cause them to come back into oestrus. In the final 3–4 weeks of gestation, sows are fed an extra 0.5 kg of ration per day. Dry sow ration typically contains 17.5% crude protein, 4% crude fibre, 0.9–1.0% lysine and vitamins A, D and E. Some research studies have reported that increasing the amount of fibre in a sow's diet in late gestation can increase the fat content of her colostrum.

Management and nutrition of the sow in the farrowing house

One week before the sows and gilts are due to farrow they are moved to the farrowing house. The sows and gilts are washed and disinfected. They are deloused (lice are removed) and dosed for endoparasites (e.g. roundworms). The sows and gilts are also vaccinated against erysipelas, a bacterial disease in pigs (see page 483).

Hygiene is essential in the farrowing house. It is recommended that farmers use an 'all in/all out' movement. Once the previous group of sows and their piglets have left, the farrowing house should be power washed, disinfected and allowed to dry before the next group of pregnant sows moves into the house. The temperature of the farrowing house should be maintained at 20°C until the first piglet is born, when it

30.15 *Sow in a farrowing crate*

should be raised to 22–24°C. The pregnant sow or gilt is then placed inside a farrowing crate. The aim of the farrowing crate is to allow movement of the sow but prevent her from lying on and crushing her piglets. The farrowing crate allows the piglets to suckle with ease. Plastic slats are common in the farrowing pens as they help to prevent foot injuries to the piglets. Sows are fed 1.8 kg of suckling ration daily with an extra 0.5 kg of ration per piglet. Sows should be supervised when farrowing. Most will not require assistance, but if a gilt or a sow is farrowing over a long period of time, or there is long interval between births, then the sow should be inspected, and assistance should be given if required.

The sow produces her maximum milk yield at 3 weeks and after that it starts to decline. Once the piglets are weaned from the sow at 4–5 weeks, the sow is returned to the service house. Sows are often thin after rearing a litter and are fed ad lib to bring them back up to their normal weight and body condition score between weaning and service. A sow that has weaned a litter will come back into heat 5–7 days later. The sow is checked for signs of oestrus each day. She will be served by AI when she comes back into oestrus and she will start her next gestation period. A sow will produce litters in this manner for 4–5 years until she is culled. Roughly 50% of a pig herd is culled on an annual basis. Three to four days after the sow is served she is moved back to the dry sow house.

Factors that determine the output and quality of a pig production unit

Nutrition

Pigs are monogastric animals and therefore require a good source of protein in their diet and less fibre than a ruminant animal's diet. Pig rations are specially formulated for every stage of the production diet (creep feed, link ration, weaner ration, fattener ration, dry sow ration and lactating sow ration). These feeds contain protein, fibre, fats, minerals, vitamins and an essential amino acid (lysine) at the appropriate concentration for pigs.

The feeds also provide energy. The efficiency at which a pig will convert feed into live weight gain (LWG) is calculated as a feed conversion ratio (FCR) or what is more commonly known in pig production as feed conversion efficiency (FCE). Animals with a **low FCR** are efficient converters of feed to LWG. For example, if an animal has an FCR value of 2 : 1, this means that the animal would have to consume 2 kg of feed to put on 1 kg of LWG. FCR is extremely important in pig production, and there are recommended FCR values for each stage of the production cycle from birth to slaughter. Improvements in FCR will allow pig farmers to increase pig output while maintaining or reducing production costs.

The **service house** is a distinct house from the dry sow house. Sows are moved to the service house after weaning. Ideally the sow should be within sight of, sound of, smell of, and have fenceline contact with the boar. This helps bring the sow back in oestrus.

Feed conversion ratio (FCR) is also known as **feed conversion efficiency (FCE)**. FCR is a measure of an animal's efficiency at converting a mass of feed into live weight gain. It is expressed as a ratio of the feed consumed to the live weight gained.

Table 30.2 Target FCR values in pig production units	
Stage of production	**FCR value**
Weaners	1.75 : 1
Fatteners	2.65 : 1

Breed variety

In commercial pig production, the breeds commonly used are selected based on output (e.g. prolificacy or litter size) and quality of pig meat. The Large White is a prolific breed with an average litter size of 12–14 piglets. Many pig production units in Ireland will have litter sizes greater than this. Farmers in the ePM programme in 2017 had an average litter size of 13.5, with litter sizes of 14 or more on the increase. This increase in litter size can be attributed to genetics and the selection for prolificacy when breeding. It is likely that this trend will continue with the use of genomics and the identification of genes associated with prolificacy. Increased litter size does present several challenges (see the section on Management below).

The Large White is used to confer a good FCR value onto their offspring. A fast-growing breed will have a better FCR. The offspring of a breed with a good FCR will reach slaughter weight sooner and will cost less to feed in comparison to a pig with a poorer FCR kept under the same conditions. This in turn will increase the output of pig meat from a pig enterprise.

Pig meat quality is influenced by genetics. Crossbred pigs (LW × LR) are the most commonly used pigs for pig production. The reason for this is that the crossbred pig has hybrid vigour. Genes from both the Large White and the Landrace pig contribute to the quality of the pig meat produced by a pig enterprise. The crossbred pigs get good meat quality, good conformation and good hams from the Large White and a long muscular body, large hams and lean meat from the Landrace. Terminal sires such as Duroc are often used to produce progeny with good eating quality and fast growth rates.

Management

Healthy, disease-free animals will have a low FCR and will reduce the incidence of pig mortality. Pigs are regularly vaccinated against common diseases and dosed for parasites. Maintaining strict biosecurity and operating an 'all in/all out' policy will help to reduce the risk of disease. Diseases and parasites can increase FCR value, which decreases profitability and reduces output. Nutrients are diverted away from LWG and used by the immune system to fight disease. In addition, diseases normally reduce feed intake. A farmer who maintains a pig production unit with an efficient feeding regime and proper disease control will have a healthy herd with a low FCR.

Some diseases directly affect litter size. Bacterial diseases such as erysipelas (see page 483) and viral diseases such as PRRS (see page 484) and parvovirus (also known as SMEDI; see page 483) increase the number of mummified and stillborn pigs as they can cross the placenta, infecting the litter and causing embryonic or foetal death. Having high standards of hygiene, biosecurity and a vaccination programme in place will help to reduce losses caused by disease and increase pig output.

Increases in litter sizes over the last number of years has led to an increase in the number of little piglets that are less than 1 kg. Reducing the mortality of newborn pigs is critical where sows are having large litters. Many pig producers will move some piglets from large litters onto sows with smaller litters. This process is commonly known as cross-fostering. Some producers will also use nurse sows by placing surplus piglets from a large litter onto a sow whose own piglets have been weaned. Cross-fostering and the use of a nurse sow should be carried out when the newborn piglets are between 12 and 24 hours old, once they have had adequate intake of their own mother's colostrum. Some farms use 'rescue decks' where cross-fostering is not an option (all sows with large litters) or nurse sows are not available. In this process the pigs are weaned onto artificial milk replacer in a separate dedicated rearing pen.

Housing

In pig production the housing is extremely important, since each house is a different stage in the production of pigs for meat. In addition, each house is temperature controlled to prevent pigs using energy from feed to keep warm. The houses in a pig production unit are maintained at appropriate temperatures for good FCR values: dry sow house at 20°C, weaner house at 24–28°C and fattener house at 18–20°C.

Table 30.3 Housing temperatures for pig production	
Housing	**Temperature**
Creep area (within the farrowing unit)	30°C
Dry sow house	20°C
Farrowing house	20–22°C
Weaner house	24–28°C
Fattener house	18–20°C

All housing should be dry, draught free and well lit. Houses should be well ventilated to minimise airborne diseases and prevent the build-up of toxic gases, factors that could increase pig mortality and reduce pig output. Pig housing should not be overcrowded as overcrowding results in stress and stressed animals are more likely to succumb to ill-health and disease. There should be adequate room for all pigs to lie down together, for pigs to feed and to have access to fresh water, which will prevent bullying occurring.

Calculation of daily live weight gain and the feed conversion ratio for pigs

Calculating the FCR of pigs involves the collection of data on the weight the pigs are gaining on a daily basis and the amount of feed the animals are consuming. In pig production units it would be highly unlikely that the piglets or young pigs would be weighed this frequently as it would cause undue stress to the animals and would be counterproductive. Instead, when farmers have to carry out a number of routine procedures, they will record the weights of the young pigs then. As the time between consecutive weight measurement can vary, farmers tend to use average daily live weight gain (ADG) compared to daily live weight gain (DLG).

DEFINITION

Average daily live weight gain (ADG) or **daily live weight gain (DLG)** is a performance measure that many animal producers monitor. ADG or DLG is the rate of weight gain per day over a specified period of time.

Exercise 30.1

How to calculate DLG and FCR

The following is an example calculation of the DLG of a group of fattener pigs over a period of 4 weeks (28 days). In the example the young pigs are weighed on a weekly basis and after 28 days their DLG is calculated.

Pig number	TN 579 Weight (kg)	DT 658 Weight (kg)	CN 988 Weight (kg)	LT 357 Weight (kg)
01/02/'19	35.2	34.8	34.9	35.3
08/02/'19	41.5	41.9	42.2	41.6
15/02/'19	47.7	48.2	48.8	48.1
22/02/'19	54.0	54.6	55.8	54.2
01/03/'19	60.2	61.0	63.7	61.2
08/03/'19				
15/03/'19				

Pig number TN 579 DLG is calculated as follows:

Initial live weight: 35.2 kg

Live weight after 28 days: 60.2 kg

Weight gain = 60.2 – 35.2 = 25 kg

$$DLG = \frac{total\ weight\ gain}{number\ of\ days}$$

$$= \frac{25}{28} = 0.893\ kg\ DLG$$

Questions

1. Calculate the DLG for pigs DT 658, CN 988 and LT 357.

2. If the pigs continue to put on live weight at the same DLG, predict the live weights of all four pigs on the 15/03/'19.

3. If the finishing weights for all four pigs is 110 kg, calculate how many days it will require to get the pigs to their slaughter weight if they maintain the same daily live weight gains.

   To calculate the feed conversion ratio (FCR) for pig number TN 579, we need data on the amount of feed the pig is consuming. It takes 84 days for pig TN 579 to reach a slaughter weight of 110 kg. During that time the pig consumes 200 kg of weaner and finisher ration.

   (a) How much feed is consumed by pig TN 579 per day?
   $$Feed\ per\ day = \frac{feed\ in\ kg}{number\ of\ days} = \frac{200}{84} = 2.38\ kg\ /\ day$$

   (b) What is the FCR of pig TN 579?
   $$FCR = \frac{feed\ per\ day\ (kg)}{DLG\ (kg)} = \frac{2.38}{0.893} = 2.66$$

4. If it takes 84 days and 200 kg of feed to get pigs DT 658, CN 988 and LT 357 to their slaughter weight, using the DLG in question 1, calculate the FCR values for each pig.

5. Which of the pigs is the most efficient at converting feed into DLG?

6. If all the pigs are fed the same amount of ration, with the same proportion of nutrients and kept at the same temperature, what factor may be responsible for the variation in FCR values between the pigs?

Exercise 30.2 (H) (Higher Level only)

Interpret secondary data relating to DLG and FCR

A research centre is carrying out an investigation into DLG and FCR of feeds on finishers in a pig production unit. There are 120 pigs in the trial, divided into three groups. Each group is composed of 40 pigs, of similar weight at the start of the trial. The pigs are kept in the same house, given access to water and all have been vaccinated and treated for both external and internal parasites. The pig groups are given different rations ab lib at the same time each day and the amount of feed that the pigs consume is calculated at the end of each day and recorded. The pigs are regularly weighed to calculate their DLG. The results are recorded in the table below.

	Group 1	Group 2	Group 3
Temperature of the house (°C)	18	18	18
Ration crude protein (%)	17	15	13
Ration crude oil and fat (%)	4	4	4
Ration crude fibre (%)	4.5	4.5	4.5
Feed consumed (kg)	2.3	2.5	2.7
DLG (kg)	0.9	0.85	0.8
FCR			

Questions

1. What is the independent variable in this trial?

2. What is the dependent variable in this trial?

3. What additional factors, not mentioned at the start, were also controlled in the trial?

4. What is the trend or pattern between the independent variable and the feed consumed by the pigs in the trial?

5. What is the trend or pattern between the independent variable and the DLG of the pigs in the trial?

6. Calculate the FCR values for each of the groups 1, 2 and 3.

7. Which group is the most efficient at converting feed into live weight gain?

8. Explain the relationship between the independent variable and the FCR values of the pigs in this trial.

9. How could the accuracy of this trial be improved?

10. Summarise the results of this trial and make a recommendation on which of the rations would be the most efficient to use to finish pigs.

11. A second pig trial was carried out by the research centre. For the second trial, 300 pigs were used. The pigs were separated into three equal groups into three different houses. The results of the trial are presented below.

	Group 1	Group 2	Group 3
Temperature of the house (°C)	20	18	16
Ration crude protein (%)	17	17	17
Ration crude oil and fat (%)	4	4	4
Ration crude fibre (%)	4.5	4.5	4.5
Feed consumed (kg)	2.1	2.3	2.9
DLG (kg)	1.0.	0.85	0.8
FCR			

(a) What is the independent variable in this trial?

(b) What is the dependent variable?

(c) Identify factors that will need to be controlled in this trial.

(d) Calculate the FCR values for each of the groups above.

(e) Which group of pigs had the most efficient FCR?

(f) Present the results of this trial using either a graph or bar chart of the independent variable versus FCR value.

(g) Explain how the independent variable affects the FCR values of each of the groups. Discuss reasons for the trend that is seen in the results.

(h) Summarise the results of this trial and make a recommendation on the appropriate temperature at which to keep finishers to ensure an efficient FCR.

Effect of age on FCR

FCR values increase with age and weight. In other words, the efficiency at which an animal converts feed into LWG decreases as the animal gets older or heavier. Young animals (piglets) have low FCR values, since they will convert most of the feed they consume into bone and muscle growth. As the animal gets older, and as it reaches slaughter weight, its FCR value increases. The reason for this is that fat deposition has started, and this requires more energy than the production of lean muscle, therefore decreasing feed conversion efficiency. The higher the quality of the feed, the more efficiently the animal will convert it to body tissue. If a pig is not getting enough protein from the ration provided it will consume more food, thereby increasing its FCR.

Innovation and biotechnological applications in pig production

There are several breeding companies that operate in Ireland, from which farmers can source pigs and semen. Some of the breeding companies use estimated breeding values (EBV), which are calculated on both individual and family performance information. Farmers can then use these EBV to bring about genetic improvement in their own herd.

Some companies have moved to genotyping and genomic selection to identify the best breeding pigs in a herd. Their research claims that the genetic gain they achieve by using genomic selection is 30% greater than non-DNA-tested pigs. Pig breeders have been using genetic technology since the 1990s to remove deleterious genes, such as halothane gene (HAL), from pig breeds. This gene causes porcine stress syndrome in pigs, which can cause sudden death, often after the pigs have been transported. The presence of the gene in pigs has a negative effect on meat quality of the slaughtered pig.

Gene editing technology, which has been described in Chapter 24, could in the future play an important role in disease control. African swine fever is highly contagious and is a notifiable disease both here in Ireland and in the EU. The disease is not present in Ireland currently, but it is in wild boar populations in many Eastern European countries. Researchers identified a gene in warthogs that made the warthogs resistant to African swine fever; they were then able to use a gene editing tool to flip one letter of the genetic code in a similar gene in pigs to make the gene slightly like that of a warthog. Scientists hope that this change in the DNA will make these pigs resistant to African swine fever.

There are many innovative technological applications in pig production. Feed and ventilation systems are mostly computerised. Sows can be electronically ear tagged, so that when a sow goes to a feeder, the computer reads her tag and feeds the sow her allocated amount of feed. This system identifies to the farmer the sows that have eaten and more importantly the sows that haven't eaten so a farmer can check if the sow is sick. The computer can also identify sows that need to be vaccinated, pregnancy scanned or moved to the farrowing house by drafting these sows to a separate holding pen. This system can also identify sows that are coming into oestrus as it will identify sows that are hanging around the boar pen and the system will then notify the farmer. The use of antibiotics in European pig production systems is banned due to antimicrobial resistance (AMR), unless a veterinary surgeon has prescribed antibiotics to treat a disease. Pig farmers are moving away from the use of medicated feeds to water medication instead, which allows the farmer to target individual pens of pigs rather than all the pigs throughout the feed system. Automated systems (e.g. the Dosatron system) can deliver medicated water to these targeted pigs.

Management practices

Handling and housing of pigs

Pig housing has been dealt with in some detail early in this chapter. As well as the main housing, farrowing house, dry sow house, etc., a pig unit must have isolation units/ housing with comfortable bedding for sick, injured or bullied pigs. Each isolation unit should have water and be power washed, disinfected and allowed to dry after the pigs have returned to the herd. Pigs should move in one direction in the pig production unit. Pigs should not return to a previous stage (e.g. stage-two weaners do not return to the first-stage house). One-way movement reduces the risk of infection and can disrupt the spread of a disease. Pig producers should operate an 'all in/all out' procedure so that houses can be thoroughly cleaned and disinfected before a new batch of pigs move into the house.

Bord Bia operates a quality assurance scheme for the production of pig meat. It is an accredited scheme that sets out best practice for pig production at farm level. Certified pig farmers must provide a safe, secure, hygienic and comfortable environment for pigs, and housing must be maintained to avoid injury and distress. Each house should have

a ventilation system that controls temperature and keeps toxic gases such as carbon dioxide, ammonia and hydrogen sulfide at low levels. Housing should also be vermin-proof.

Pigs should never be handled roughly, as it can cause injury and lead to stress. Stress and rough handling of pigs prior to slaughter affects the quality of the pork, causing changes to the colour and texture of the meat.

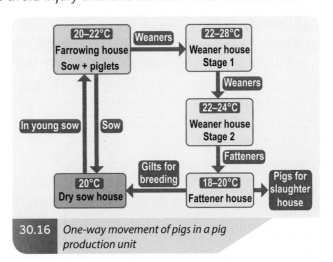

30.16 One-way movement of pigs in a pig production unit

Optimal animal health and welfare

Animal health and welfare go hand in hand. If a farmer can provide good pig welfare, this can lead to healthier pigs. Low pig welfare leads to an increase in unnatural pig behaviours such as tail biting.

Currently there is a big focus on reducing the usage of antibiotics in pig production units due to the increase of AMR. Zinc oxide is commonly fed for 14 days post-weaning to prevent diarrhoea in weaners. The use of zinc oxide in feeds is due to be banned in 2021.

Having a vaccination programme (see Table 30.4), high standards of hygiene and strict biosecurity protocols in place are the most important barriers in preventing the entrance of disease onto a farm. Breeding all replacement stock is key in preventing the buying in of disease. Many pig farmers will allow only essential personnel to have access to the pigs on their farm and require those personnel to have a 72-hour period away from other pig farms (known as 'clean time') before they enter their farm. They must also shower in and out, wear full protective clothing and footwear and disinfect their footwear.

Table 30.4 A sample vaccination programme for a pig farm	
Vaccination	**Given to**
Erysipelas	Gilts and sows
Parvovirus	Gilts and sows
E. coli and Clostridium	Gilts and sows
Mycoplasma hyopneumoniae	Piglets
PRRS	Piglets and gilts

Under the EU legislation scheme all pigs over 2 weeks of age must have access to sufficient quantities of fresh water. Pigs must be supplied with the correct nutrition for their stage of production. Dry sows, pregnant sows and gilts must have sufficient levels of fibre in their diet to maintain a suitable body condition score and to meet their nutritional requirements.

Environmental enrichment

In 2016, the European Commission recommended that enrichment materials should be provided to pigs as one of several steps that should be taken in order to reduce the incidence of tail biting. Tail biting is a sign of stress in pigs caused by inadequate environmental conditions and management practices. Pigs have a natural rooting instinct that they use to explore their environment. If pigs are unable to do this, then they get bored, frustrated and stressed. The European Commission states that pigs should be provided with enrichment materials that are edible, chewable, investigative and manipulable. Some suggested materials include straw, hemp rope, branches with leaves, wood chip, hay, grass silage, shredded paper and other edible materials. Pigs that have their tails bitten need to be treated with antibiotics to prevent infections developing, so by reducing the incidence of tail biting in a unit the use of antibiotics will also be reduced. Tail biting can lead to spinal abscesses in a pig, which is then rejected at the slaughterhouse as a condemned carcase, unfit for human consumption. Pig farmers are not paid any money for condemned pigs.

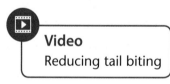

Video
Reducing tail biting

30.17 *Pigs in an environment with enrichment materials*

30.18 *A sow in her nest with piglets, also known as free farrowing, as the sow is not placed in a farrowing crate*

Sows exhibit nesting behaviour about a day before they farrow. It is recommended that sows be provided with nesting material such as straw, as this reduces behaviours such as chewing on the bars of the farrowing crate. Allowing the sow to carry out this natural behaviour is thought to encourage her to be more protective of her newborn piglets. Research carried out in Denmark found that providing enrichment material to sows reduced the number of piglets crushed compared with sows that were not provided with any enrichment materials. Provision of nesting material also reduces the length of time for farrowing to be completed, thereby reducing the incidence of stillborn piglets. Prolonged farrowing leads to increases in the number of stillborn piglets due to a reduced supply of oxygen to the piglets prior to birth.

Lameness

Lameness of sows and gilts is a significant welfare issue and a common reason for the culling of sows on a farm. Lameness can also affect growing pigs and boars. It is a painful condition for pigs, as they have difficulty standing and walking. Lame sows will not stand to be served when in oestrus and boars will not serve if they are lame. Lame pigs will not stand long for feeding, which results in a decrease in intake of feed, and this can cause reduced growth rate of growing pigs and a reduction in milk production of lactating sows. Lame sows are also more likely to crush piglets compared with normal sows as lame sows are less able to stay in the normal lying-down position that enables piglets to suckle. The most common causes of lameness in a pig production unit include poor floor quality, poor hygiene, infections (e.g. erysipelas) and claw overgrowth. All lame pigs should be removed to a hospital pen and treated. A vaccination is available to prevent erysipelas. Overgrowth of the hoof horn should be trimmed and infections should be treated with antibiotics. Any pig with broken bones should be euthanised.

Noise

Loud noises cause stress to pigs. They can be particularly stressful for farrowing sows, which can result in a sow harming her own piglets. The farrowing room should be kept as quiet as possible.

Animal health and welfare are key components of Bord Bia's quality assurance scheme. The following is a summary of some of the criteria that farmers must have in place to be certified.

- Pig farms must be under the routine care of a veterinary surgeon.
- Farmers must have a documented hygiene plan.
- Daily checks must be carried out on all animals to ensure they are adequately fed, and maintained in good health and vigour. Animals close to farrowing, young pigs and sick pigs should be checked more often.
- Pig driving boards and paddles must be used to move pigs; sticks or any device that causes pain are prohibited.
- All pigs must have permanent access to sufficient quantities of manipulable material such as straw and hay to enable them to undertake natural investigation and manipulative activities.
- Piglets are not to be weaned before 21 days except in rare circumstances such as the death of a sow.
- Teeth clipping and tail docking are not permitted unless recommended by a veterinary surgeon on welfare grounds after all management procedures have been checked (e.g. stocking densities, housing environment, proper feed and water, provision of enrichment materials).
- Pigs should not be exposed to constant noise, sudden noise or very loud noises.

Slurry and farmyard manures

Pig manure in Ireland tends to be mainly in the form of slurry. The solid content of the slurry averages between 4 and 12% depending on the amount of water the pigs consume and additional water from washing of houses, etc. All pig production farms must have adequate facilities to collect and store all manures and effluents including dirty water and yard run-off. Under the Nitrates Regulations, pig farms must have 6 months of slurry storage. Pig farms with more than 750 breeding sows or 2000 finisher pigs must get an Industrial Emissions Activities (IEA) licence from the Environmental Protection Agency (EPA) to produce pigs.

Pig slurry is a valuable fertiliser. The exact composition of the slurry (nitrogen (N), phosphorus (P) and potassium (K) content) will vary between farms. All of the P and K in pig slurry is available for crop uptake. Many pig farmers have arrangements with tillage or other farmers who will take the slurry and spread it on their crops. All farmers who supply organic manure/fertiliser produced on their farms to other farms are required to submit a record of this to the DAFM.

Delivering sustainable and environmentally friendly production systems

Like all other animal production systems, pig production is changing to make it more environmentally sustainable. Pig production has the lowest carbon footprint of all the main agricultural enterprises. It is a highly specialised intensive farming operation. According to the DAFM, pig meat production increased by 76% between 1990 and 2015, but pig production has also increased in efficiency. Increase in efficiency has been brought about by improvements in genetics, feed, management, health, welfare and housing. According to the EPA, there has been a reduction in the amount of phosphorus excreted by pigs over the last 25 years (from 26 kg to 17 kg per sow), and this has been achieved through better formulation of pig rations and the addition of enzymes to improve the digestibility of phosphorus. Phosphorus contributes to eutrophication of rivers and other water bodies (see page 127). Bord Bia's quality assurance scheme has sustainability built into its criteria, as part of its Origin Green initiative.

As energy is required to heat the houses, each house should be well insulated to keep down energy costs. Pig producers that are building new houses or updating existing buildings should consider investing in more energy-efficient ways of heating their houses (for example, using air-to-water heat pumps). New LED lighting is the most energy-efficient means of lighting the houses. Installation of solar photovoltaic (PV) panels on south-facing roofs of the houses can convert light energy into electrical energy, therefore reducing electrical cost. Some of these systems are expensive to install, but there are grants available and this can reduce the time it takes to pay back such an investment.

Many farms in the Netherlands, Denmark and Germany use biogas as a source of heat and electricity. In Ireland, Ashleigh Farm in Ballinameela, Co. Waterford, which has 13,000 pigs, uses an anaerobic digestion system to produce biogas from pig manure, thus creating a sustainable waste management system. The anaerobic digestion unit generates methane gas, which can then be converted into electricity. The anaerobic digestion unit also produces a nutrient-rich fertiliser. The nutrients are more readily available in this fertiliser than in raw slurry, therefore making it easier to be utilised in the soil.

30.19 *The anaerobic digestion unit on Ashleigh Farm*

Targets set for pig production under Food Wise 2025 will require increased production from pig farmers. Pig production is a very efficient animal production system. Over the last few years the productivity of sows has increased without the need to increase the number of breeding sows (which has remained unchanged at 150,000). The number of piglets produced by each sow has increased and, combined with low levels of mortality of piglets, has led to increased numbers of pigs produced per sow. An increase in the sale weight of fattener pigs in recent years has also helped to increase pig meat production. Teagasc and other research centres are continuing to conduct research in a number of areas including the production of more pig meat from less feed, reducing the use of antibiotics in farming, pig health and welfare, nutrition, pig management and genetics.

Ensuring quality, safe and traceable food for the consumer

Under the Bord Bia quality assurance scheme, all pig meat must be traceable back to the source farm. The National Pig Identification and Tracing System (NPITS) was set up in 2002 to record all pig movements. All pigs moved off a farm must be ear tagged or slap marked. Breeding stock (sows and boars) are issued with an individual number. In addition to tagging and slap marking, all pigs under the Bord Bia scheme must be DNA traceable back to a DNA-tested boar. All breeding boars kept on a farm must therefore be DNA tested.

The impact of pig production on farm economics and the importance of export markets

There are roughly 300 commercial pig farms in Ireland, with approximately 150,000 breeding sows, and an average herd size of 500 sows. Under targets for Food Wise 2025, the aim is to increase sow productivity to 27 pigs per sow per year (currently around 26) and to improve weaner and fattener FCR. Increasing the productivity of the sow will require an increase in litter size while maintaining very low levels of piglet mortality. Improvements in FCR at every stage of production will reduce production costs. Formulation of rations, management of feeding and genetics have the greatest impact on FCR.

Pig meat is the most consumed meat in Ireland. Ireland is approximately 118% self-sufficient in pig meat, and for this reason we export 50–60% of our pig meat with roughly half of our export going to the UK market. Approximately 95%+ of pig producers in Ireland are certified under the Bord Bia quality assurance scheme. For a certified farm in this scheme, all breeding boars must be DNA tested. This is very important, as pig meat produced and reared in Ireland can be identified by DNA analysis. This is an important issue regarding transparency for consumers, who choose to buy and consume pig meat produced here in Ireland. Although Ireland is a net exporter of pig meat, Ireland also imports pig meat. DNA analysis is another link in the traceability of Irish pig meat.

In pig production, feed is the biggest cost, accounting for 70% of total production costs. Profitability is severely affected by volatility of pig and feed prices. The cost of pig feed can fluctuate on a year-by-year basis, especially when homegrown cereals do not meet home demand. When this happens, cereals along with other components not grown in Ireland (e.g. soya beans) have to be imported. This pushes up the cost of pig feed. The wet weather in spring 2018, which resulted in a fodder shortage, followed by the heatwave conditions that Ireland and the rest of Europe experienced in the summer

Slap mark: a unique identification number that is tattooed directly onto the pig's skin. The tattoo should be placed on each front shoulder area and should last for the lifetime of the pig. Slap marking needs to be done with accuracy and efficiency to minimise stress to the pig.

of 2018, pushed feed costs up due to reduced crop yields and increased concentrate feed demand from the dairy, beef and sheep sectors.

For pig farmers to be profitable they need to sell their pigs for a price that will cover their feed costs and other additional costs and give them enough of a margin left over. Supply and demand for pig meat, both in Europe and large export markets such as China, affect the price a farmer is paid for their pigs. There are no support subsidies for pig producers in Europe, so Irish pig farmers get paid based on world market prices. Ireland is a small producer of pig meat on the world market, so the price of pig meat here tends to follow what happens abroad. The threat of disease is another factor that affects pig meat price. The presence of disease could cause an export ban, and if it is a notifiable disease, then whole herds could be culled to prevent the spread of the disease. African swine fever has spread through China and there has been confirmed outbreaks of the disease in wild boar in Belgium and in domesticated pigs in Eastern Europe. If there were an outbreak of the disease in Ireland it would have devastating consequences for pig producers all over the country.

Summary

- The Large White is highly prolific, has a fast growth rate, good feed conversion ratio (FCR), good conformation and good mothers.
- The Landrace has a long muscular body, small shoulders and large hams, and produces lean meat and has good conformation.
- Duroc is used as a terminal sire as it has fast growth rates and the eating quality of the meat is good.
- Landrace–Large White crossbreeds are used in commercial pig production as they demonstrate hybrid vigour.
- Piglets weigh 1.0–1.5 kg at birth; it is important that they have sufficient intake of colostrum, as piglet mortality is highest in the first 48 hours.
- The piglets should be provided with some environmental enrichment in the farrowing unit to try to reduce the incidence of tail biting among the piglets.
- Piglets are given an iron injection at 2–3 days old to prevent anaemia.
- The creep area in a farrowing unit is approximately 30°C and its function is to attract the piglets away from the sow, therefore reducing the chance of the sow crushing them. Piglets are provided with creep feed in this area.
- Piglets are weaned at 28 days old when they are between 7 and 9 kg.
- Weaners are fed ab lib weaner ration that contains 18–20% protein.
- Lysine is an essential amino acid added to all pig rations.
- The temperature in the weaner house is kept at between 24°C and 28°C.
- Weaners are moved to the fattener house when they reach 32–38 kg.
- Fatteners are fed a ration ab lib, with 14–17% protein. The temperature in the fattener house is kept at 18–20°C.
- Pigs are finished at 100–110 kg; replacement gilts are selected and enter the dry sow house when they reach a weight of 130–140 kg and are oestrous cycling.
- Sows can produce roughly 2.36 litters per year, with an average litter size of 13.5.
- Boars are kept in the dry sow house to encourage the sows and the gilts to come on heat. The temperature of the dry sow house is 20°C.
- The length of the oestrous cycle in pigs is 21 days; the duration of oestrus is 2–3 days; the gestation period is 115 days.
- Sows are moved to the farrowing house 1 week prior to farrowing; they are washed, dosed, vaccinated and placed in a farrowing crate.

- Farmers operate an 'all in/all out' procedure and houses are power washed, disinfected and allowed to dry before the next group of animals move in. This aids in the prevention of disease.
- Daily live weight gain (DLG) is a performance measure that many animal producers monitor. It is the rate of weight gain per day over a specified period of time. It is calculated as: DLG (kg/day) = total weight gain / number of days.
- FCR is a measure of an animal's efficiency at converting a mass of feed into live weight gain (LWG). It is expressed as a ratio of the feed consumed to the live weight gained: FCR = feed per day (kg) / DLG (kg).
- Genotyping and genomics are being used to identify the best breeding pigs in a herd. Gene editing may play an important role in disease control in the future.
- Stress and rough handling of pigs prior to slaughter affects the quality of the pork, causing changes to occur to the colour and the texture of the meat.
- All pigs should be provided with environmental enrichment materials to encourage their natural rooting instinct and to help prevent unnatural pig behaviours such as tail biting.
- Pig production is a highly specialised and efficient operation. Improvements in efficiencies have been brought about by improvements in genetics, feed, management, health, welfare and housing.
- All pig meat must be traceable back to the source farm. All pigs moving from a farm must be ear tagged or slap marked and recorded on the National Pig Identification and Tracing System (NIPTS). All boars in the Bord Bia quality assurance scheme must be DNA tested.
- Pig meat is the most consumed meat in Ireland. Fifty to sixty per cent of our pig meat is exported, with roughly half of our export going to the UK.
- Feed costs are 70% of the total cost of pig production. Feed costs can be volatile depending on the cost of importing some components of the ration (e.g. soya bean and cereals) into Ireland.
- Pig farmers are not subsidised, so the price pig farmers get paid for their produce depends on the world market.

 PowerPoint Summary

QUESTIONS

1. Bacteria entering the navel of a newborn piglet may cause:
   - (a) Lameness
   - (b) Navel ill
   - (c) Scour
   - (d) PRRS.

2. What is the length of the oestrous cycle in pigs?
   - (a) 28 days
   - (b) 25 days
   - (c) 21 days
   - (d) 17 days

3. What is the length of gestation in pigs?
   - (a) 95 days
   - (b) 115 days
   - (c) 125 days
   - (d) 130 days

4. What is the temperature of the creep area in the farrowing unit?
   - (a) 20°C
   - (b) 24°C
   - (c) 28°C
   - (d) 30°C

5. An iron injection is given to piglets when they are 2–3 days old to prevent:

    (a) Tail biting   (c) Navel ill

    (b) Scour   (d) Anaemia.

6. What is the temperature of the dry sow house?

    (a) 18°C   (c) 25°C

    (b) 20°C   (d) 30°C

7. Which of the following methods is used for the purpose of traceability in pig production units?

    (a) DNA testing of sows   (c) Micro-chipping

    (b) Ear notching   (d) Slap marking

8. Which of the following are notifiable diseases of pigs?

    (a) African swine fever and anaemia

    (b) PRRS and bovine TB

    (c) Erysipelas and SMEDI

    (d) African swine fever and foot and mouth disease

9. What is the purpose of environmental enrichment material in pig production units?

    (a) It provides all the necessary feed the pigs need.

    (b) It eliminates disease and odours in the pig unit.

    (c) It provides material for the pigs to investigate and manipulate, encouraging normal piglet behaviour.

    (d) It improves the FCR of the pigs.

10. Name **two** breeds of pigs used in commercial pig production in Ireland. Describe **one** feature of each breed.

11. Name **three** types of housing used in a pig production unit and give a function of each.

12. Explain the term 'terminal sire'. Identify **one** pig breed that is commonly used as a terminal sire in pig production.

13. The critical period within which there is the greatest risk of mortality of piglets due to crushing is:

    (a) In the first 3 days   (c) 14 days old

    (b) Days 6 to 10   (d) 28 days old.

14. Describe the nutrition and management of a newborn piglet.

15. Describe **two** features of pigs' colostrum and explain how these benefit newborn piglets.

16. Describe the management of pigs in:

    (a) The weaner house   (b) The fattener house.

17. List **four** criteria a farmer would look for when selecting a replacement gilt.

18. Describe the management practices involved in preparing the sow at the end of gestation for transfer from the dry sow house to the farrowing house.

19. Explain the meaning of the term 'all in/all out' and discuss the importance of this procedure in a pig production unit.

20. Describe the management and feeding of a sow on return to the service house after weaning from her litter.

21. Distinguish between each of the following terms:

    (a) FCR and DLG   (c) Farrowing house and dry sow house

    (b) Duroc and Landrace   (d) Nurse sow and gilt.

22. Write a brief note on each of the following:

    (a) Factors that affect litter size in sows

    (b) Factors that decrease the mortality rate of piglets within the first 48 hours after farrowing.

23. Discuss any **three** factors that will affect the FCR of fatteners in a pig production unit.

24. The graph in Fig. 30.20 shows the weight of two pigs over a 24-week period.

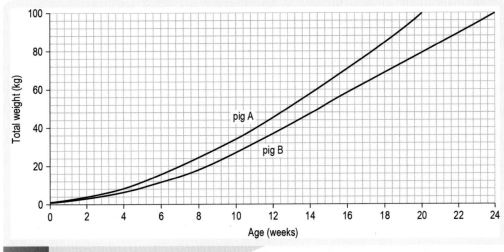

30.20 *Question 24*

(a) Calculate the daily live weight gain (DLG) for both Pig A and Pig B.

(b) Suggest **two** reasons why there is a difference in the time taken for Pig B to reach its finishing weight compared to Pig A. **H** (Higher Level only).

(c) If the average daily feed intake for Pig A is 1.585 kg, calculate the FCR for Pig A.

(d) If the average daily feed intake for Pig B is 1.727 kg, calculate the FCR for Pig B.

(e) Give a reason why FCR decreases with the age of a pig.

25. Good biosecurity is essential in helping to prevent the spread of disease in pig production units. State and explain **three** ways pig farmers ensure good biosecurity in a pig production unit.

26. Describe ways in which stress or harm to pigs is minimised when performing routine pig husbandry practices.

27. Pig farmers need to make a profit to be a viable business. Identify **two** costs and explain how these affect the profitability of a pig production unit.

28. Name **two** examples of innovative or biotechnological applications used in pig production. Describe how these two examples benefit pig farmers.

29. Bord Bia supports farmers by offering various accredited schemes. Name **one** scheme that Irish pig farmers participate in. Discuss the requirements that pig farmers must meet for animal welfare and traceability as part of this scheme.

30. Outline how financial circumstances beyond the control of the farmer can affect the profitability of a pig production unit.

31. Give a scientific explanation for each of the following:

(a) Keeping a boar in the dry sow house

(b) Maintaining the creep area in a farrowing unit at 30°C

(c) Minimising noise in the farrowing house

(d) Providing environmental enrichment material to piglets

(e) Using criss-cross breeding in pig production

(f) Using a nurse sow in a farrowing unit.

 Solutions Weblinks

Animal health and disease

When you have completed this chapter you should be able to:

- Discuss factors that should be taken into account when considering the welfare of farm animals
- Identify diseases of cattle, sheep and pigs
- Discuss the transmission of diseases between farm animals
- Identify controls and measures to prevent entry of disease onto a farm
- Explain the term 'zoonose' and identify examples of zoonotic diseases
- Recognise the potential hazards to humans of animal disease.

Welfare of animals

The health and welfare of agricultural animals are intertwined and ultimately are the responsibility of the farmer. In 1965, the Brambell Report was published. It studied the welfare of animals kept under an intensive livestock husbandry system in the UK. From this report came the **five freedoms**. These describe the conditions required to ensure the good physical health and mental state of farm animals.

Five freedoms

1. **Freedom from hunger, thirst and malnutrition:** animals should have access to fresh water and food to maintain good health and vigour.
2. **Freedom from discomfort:** animals should be provided with shelter and a comfortable resting area.
3. **Freedom from pain, injury and disease:** animals should receive disease prevention and prompt diagnosis and treatment when a disease does occur.
4. **Freedom to express normal patterns of behaviour:** animals should have sufficient space, proper facilities and the company of their own kind.
5. **Freedom from fear and distress:** animals should have good conditions and treatment to avoid causing mental stress.

Animal health and welfare criteria are built into the Common Agricultural Policy (CAP) and all Bord Bia quality assurance schemes, as previously described. Under CAP requirements, any farmer found to be in breach of the health and welfare regulations can have a financial sanction imposed on them. Cruelty to animals, including farm animals, is an offence in Ireland and any individual convicted of such an offence is punishable by law.

Freedom from hunger, thirst and malnutrition

- The diets of all animals should always be adequate to maintain full health of the animal.
- Animals should have access to fresh palatable feed. Any feed that is spoiled or stale should be removed.
- Feed troughs should be constructed in a way to avoid contamination of feed with urine or faeces.
- When feeding cattle and sheep, any sudden changes in type and quantity of feed should be avoided. Changes to feed should take place gradually, allowing the animal time to adapt to the change.

- Ruminant animals need sufficient amounts of roughage in their diets for the correct functioning of the ruminant stomach.
- There should be sufficient space for all animals at a feeding trough to avoid competition and aggression when animals are being fed all together.
- Animals should always have access to fresh clean water.
- Water toughs should be situated and constructed in an area to minimise the risk of water freezing in cold weather.
- There also needs to be an adequate supply of water troughs to ensure all animals have access to water.
- Care should be taken to ensure small animals such as lambs cannot climb into and drown in a water trough.

Freedom from discomfort

Cattle are usually housed during the winter months to provide them with shelter for inclement weather and also to prevent damage to grassland (poaching). Some animals, such as pigs, can spend their entire life indoors. Regardless of the length of time an animal is housed, the housing needs to be cleaned regularly and the animal should be provided with clean and dry lying areas. The flooring in the housing needs to be even to avoid injury to the animal's feet and it should also be non-slip. Animals should be provided with enough room for movement, lying down, grooming and other normal animal-to-animal interactions.

Housing should be adequately ventilated (to help prevent diseases such as pneumonia) and it should have enough natural or artificial light. Animals should not be kept in permanent darkness.

If cattle are calving indoors, then there should be separate calving pens with handling facilities. Sheep and pigs should also be provided with separate pens to give birth in. Shelter should be provided for young stock, e.g. calves, from the wind and rain when they are let outside for the first time.

Freedom from pain, injury and disease

A farmer must be able to recognise when animals are not well. Signs of ill-health include loss of appetite, listlessness, lack of rumination in ruminant animals, discharge from the eyes, nose or excessive dribbling, persistent cough, lameness, scouring, rapid loss of weight or condition, and excessive scratching. Sometimes there can be a change in the behaviour of the animal.

Animals should be given appropriate veterinarian treatment when required. Animals that are sick or injured should be housed in a separate area or facility away from the rest of the herd or flock. Terminally ill animals should be euthanised to avoid unnecessary suffering to the animal. A vaccination programme should be in place to prevent clostridial diseases, Pasteurella and orf in sheep. Cattle should be vaccinated against blackleg.

Animals should also be dosed against lice and other external parasites that can cause irritation, excessive scratching and discomfort to the animal. They should also be dosed against internal parasites such as stomach and intestinal worms as well as liverfluke. 'Pour-on' rather than a dosing gun should be used where possible, as this reduces handling stress on the animal. Any farmer using a dosing gun should be competent in the use of the gun and administration of the dose. When dosing, the equipment should be appropriate to the size of the animal, it should be properly calibrated and care should be taken not to injure the animal's throat when

Listlessness: when an animal lacks energy, has no interest in anything and is lethargic.

Rumination: chewing the cud.

Scouring: diarrhoea in animals.

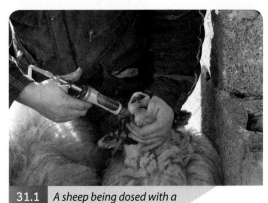

31.1   *A sheep being dosed with a dosing gun*

administering the dose. Good grassland management (e.g. a leader-follower system for grazing young calves) can decrease exposure to stomach worms.

Lameness can be a common problem in sheep and cattle. Lameness is a welfare problem in dairy. Correct hoof trimming and paring is necessary when the hoof grows beyond the soft sole of the foot. This is particularly common in sheep that are housed. Footrot causes lameness in sheep. Sheep should be regularly walked through a foot bath to prevent footrot. Keeping sheep on clean pasture that has not been grazed in two weeks can also help to eliminate the bacteria that cause footrot.

31.2 *Lame sheep*

Animals should be inspected at least once a day. Young animals or animals in late gestation should be checked more frequently.

Freedom to express normal patterns of behaviour

When housing cattle, animals of similar age and size should be grouped together, which allows for social groups to develop. A hierarchy exists in a cattle herd, with one animal being dominant. Cattle should also have enough room to exhibit their normal behaviour when feeding. Cattle graze standing up and then lie down to ruminate.

Chickens need space to forage and ground scratch. Another common behaviour of chickens is dust bathing, and they often do this several times a day.

Sheep are very sociable animals, with a strong flocking instinct. They band together in large groups for protection. If a sheep becomes separated from the flock it will become stressed and agitated.

31.3 *Free-range chickens*

31.4 *Battery hens*

Freedom from fear and distress

If cattle or sheep need to be handled, proper handling facilities should be used to restrain animals with minimum risk of injury or stress. Movement of cattle and sheep should be done without use of excessive force. Cattle are easily stressed by loud noises and yelling, and they have very poor depth perception. When moving cattle it is important that they can see where they are going and that there are no obstacles in their way.

Debudding or dehorning of calves should be carried out by a competent person before the calf is 2 weeks old. If the animal is older than 2 weeks, then a local anaesthetic should be administered before dehorning.

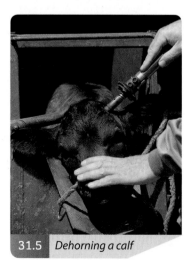
31.5 *Dehorning a calf*

Castration of male cattle should be carried out when the calf is between 8 and 12 weeks old. Having proper handling facilities to carry out debudding and castration is vital to minimise stress.

A sheep's tail should be docked only if there is a real threat of fly strike, and adult sheep should be shorn in summer to prevent heat stress caused by hot weather.

| 31.6 | *Tail of a lamb being docked using a rubber band that is being applied using an elastrator* |

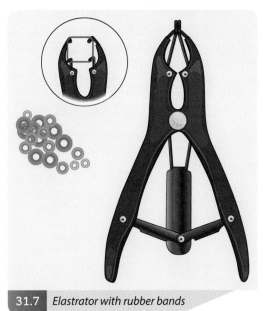

| 31.7 | *Elastrator with rubber bands* |

Weaning a suckler calf from its mother can be stressful on both the calf and the mother. It is recommended that this be done gradually. First, it is important that the calves are being creep fed concentrates. Then the cows are gradually removed (a quarter at a time) to an area away from the calves. Having the calves already weaned onto concentrates can help prevent any drop in live weight gain caused by the weaning process.

The Farm Animal Welfare Advisory Council

The Farm Animal Welfare Advisory Council (FAWAC) was set up in 2002 within the DAFM to promote animal welfare. It is a forum of different interest groups with a variety of perspectives on animal welfare, who meet to discuss the challenges facing farm animal welfare.

The group's main functions are to:
- Conduct formal meetings with government officials
- Publish reports and opinions advising the Minister of Agriculture, Food and the Marine on specific topics
- Provide a forum for different interest groups to meet, exchange divergent views and reach consensus on the broad mandate of challenges facing farm animal welfare
- Build relationships between different representative groups; all members have a common purpose and share the view that animal welfare is an issue of very high importance.

The FAWAC has published several codes of practice for the welfare of pigs, beef animals, broiler chickens, etc.

Diseases of cattle, sheep and pigs

Diseases of sheep

Disease transmission is the means by which contagious, pathogenic microorganisms are spread from one farm animal to another.

Table 31.1 Diseases of sheep and lambs

Disease	Cause and transmission	Symptoms	Treatment	Prevention
Twin lamb disease	**Cause:** • Underfeeding ewes carrying multiple lambs • Breakdown of fat reserves in the ewe's body, leading to liver failure	• Separates from flock • Staggers, tremors • Collapse and death	• Fatal disease unless caught early • Administer energy solution (glucose)	• Steaming up with concentrates in the late gestation. Growing foetus limits the intake of hay and silage, since it restricts the size of the rumen
Orf	**Cause:** • Viral (highly contagious) • **Zoonose** **Transmission:** • The orf virus can survive many years in a dry environment, e.g. inside a sheep shed • Minor cuts of the skin of the sheep or lamb is enough for an infection to become established	• Small spots on udder, ewe's teats, lips, gums, nose of young lambs and genitals of rams • Secondary bacterial infection of lesions can occur • Lambs of ewes with orf are at risk of starvation as ewes will not allow lambs to suckle if lesions are present on the teat • Poor growth in lambs • Very painful	• No treatment for virus • Secondary bacterial infections of the lesions can be treated with antibiotics • May need to bottle feed lambs if ewe is refusing to allow the lamb to suckle • Ewes may develop secondary mastitis: treat with antibiotics	• Vaccinate ewes before lambing • Vaccinate lambs at a few weeks old • Thoroughly clean and disinfect buildings • Biosecurity
Milk fever (hypocalcaemia) **Can affect all lactating animals**	**Cause:** • Low levels of calcium in late pregnancy or early lactation	• Similar to twin lamb disease • Listlessness, unable to stand • Unconsciousness and death	• Injection of calcium borogluconate	• Dust ewes' feed with Cal Mag concentrates with • Feed ewes concentrates with added calcium or mineral lick
Grass tetany **Affects cattle as well**	**Cause:** • Occurs when ewes and lambs are turned out onto lush grass low in magnesium	• Twitching, muscle spasm • Coma and death	• Injection of soluble magnesium	• Dust ewes' feed with Cal Mag concentrates with • Feed ewes concentrates with added magnesium or mineral lick

Prevalent: widespread or common in an area.

Endoparasite: a parasite that lives inside the body of the host.

Disease	Cause and transmission	Symptoms	Treatment	Prevention
Watery mouth (affects lambs)	**Cause:** • *E. coli* bacteria: a result of poor hygiene in lambing shed or lambing in dirty and wet conditions • Bacteria is prevalent in the environment • *E. coli* bacteria are ingested and build up in large numbers in the small intestine of the lamb • Insufficient intake of colostrum is a contributing factor	• Lambs are lethargic • Lambs are unwilling to suckle • Profuse salivation • Wet lower jaw	• Antibiotics • Feed lambs electrolyte solution	• Clean and disinfect lambing pens between lambing ewes • Use dry, clean straw in lambing pens • Ensure lamb gets adequate amounts of colostrum • Collect and dispose of placentas
Nematodirus	**Cause:** • Roundworms • Endoparasite **Transmission:** • The adult roundworm lays their eggs in the lamb's gut; the eggs pass out onto grass and overwinter as eggs; the eggs hatch in spring after a cold spell • Large numbers can hatch together; young lambs are most at risk, since they lack resistance	• Many lambs showing signs of scour • Lambs stop eating, become dehydrated and die	• Dose lambs for worms at regular intervals	• Put lambs on clean pasture that has not been grazed by lambs in the previous year

Protozoan: a single-celled microscopic animal.

Oocyst: a cyst containing a zygote formed by a parasitic protozoan.

Endemic: a disease or condition that is regularly found.

Disease	Cause and transmission	Symptoms	Treatment	Prevention
Coccidosis **Can also affect calves**	**Cause:** • Protozoan, parasite found in faeces • Endoparasite • Affects young lambs 4–8 weeks old • Parasite invades the lining of the intestines **Transmission:** • Oocysts can overwinter on pasture • Lambs can become infected by grazing pasture that was grazed by lambs the previous year • Endemic in all sheep flocks	• Lamb fails to thrive • Bloody scour • Dehydration • In worst cases, death	• Lambs have initial immunity while suckling (ewe immune) • Oral dose the lambs	• Clean grazing: pasture that was not grazed by sheep the previous year • Low stocking density • Moving creep and feeding troughs regularly as wet and mucky conditions around troughs can help the spread of the parasite • Clean bedding/straw in lambing sheds • A medicated creep feed gives protection
Clostridial diseases	**Cause:** • Variety of bacteria that cause pulpy kidney, blackleg, lamb dysentery, tetanus, bloody scours and braxy (infection of the abomasum) **Transmission:** • Clostridial bacteria are always present in the environment	• Varied, most lead to sudden death	• Treatment is difficult	• Vaccine available • Vaccinate using a '10 in 1' vaccine • Vaccinate lambs • Give ewes an annual booster shot

Disease	Cause and transmission	Symptoms	Treatment	Prevention
Pasteurella	• Most common cause of sudden death in sheep **Cause:** • Bacterial **Transmission:** • Sheep are carriers of the bacteria in their throat and tonsils • Outbreak can be brought about by stress to the animal caused by transport, weaning, castration, etc.	• Causes septicaemia (blood poisoning) in lambs • Pneumonia in older sheep • Mastitis in lactating ewes	• Can be treated with antibiotics if caught in the early stages	• Vaccinate adult sheep and lambs annually
Fly strike	**Cause:** • Maggots • Ectoparasite **Transmission:** • Bluebottle and greenbottle flies lay their eggs in fleeces soiled with faeces • Eggs hatch into maggots and the maggots eat into the sheep's flesh	• Maggots irritate sheep; tail wags constantly followed by dark staining on the wool • Sheep with fly strike will lie on its own, away from the flock • Weakness • Scour	• Spray with insecticide • Treat flesh eaten by maggots with antiseptic cream to prevent bacterial infection	• Dip sheep in summer • Dose sheep for worms to prevent diarrhoea • Use insecticide sprays

Ectoparasite: a parasite that lives on the surface of the host.

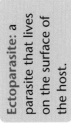

Disease	Cause and transmission	Symptoms	Treatment	Prevention
Sheep scab Notifiable disease	**Cause:** • Mange mite • Ectoparasite **Transmission:** • Picked up by sheep that rub up against fences, posts and trees that infected sheep have rubbed up against • It can also be spread by the clothing and equipment of the farmer or sheep handler • Sheep-to-sheep contact at marts, in lorries, contact with infected stray sheep or in winter housing	• Sheep irritated by mites rub against fences and gates, causing wool loss • Sheep nibble and bite at their fleece • Rubbing and head tossing becomes excessive • Sheep's skin becomes very sensitive to touch • Yellow scabs visible on skin • Sheep lose condition and can start fitting • **Serious welfare concern**	• **Notify district veterinary office immediately** • Dip sheep • Maintain tight biosecurity	• Winter dip sheep • Seek veterinary assistance (administer injections) 31.8 *Sheep being dipped to prevent sheep scab* 31.9 *Mange mite*

Notifiable disease: a disease that must immediately be reported to the Department of Agriculture, Food and the Marine. Diseases that are notifiable are normally infectious and highly contagious.

Disease	Cause and transmission	Symptoms	Treatment	Prevention
Navel ill/joint ill	**Cause:**	**Navel ill:**	• Treat with antibiotics and painkillers	• Fully bathe the navel in iodine
Disease of both calves and lambs	• Bacterial	• Navel is swollen and painful	• Vet is required to remove abscesses if they develop	• Strict hygiene in lambing and calving sheds
	Transmission:	• Thick pus may ooze out		• Clean and dry bedding in sheds
	• Bacteria that enter the navel shortly after birth, either from a contaminated environment (dirty lambing/calving sheds) or a dirty knife used to cut the umbilical cord	**Joint ill:**		• Ensure newborn animal has an adequate intake of colostrum
		• High temperature		• Do not let young animal out on contaminated fields until the navel has dried up
		• Swollen, stiff and painful joints		
	• Initial infection starts in the navel and then spreads to the joints	• **Welfare implications as animal can be in severe pain**		• Navels of bulls take longer to dry than those of heifers, putting bulls at a greater risk of infection
	• Usually affects calves and lambs that are less than 1 week old	• Death in severe cases		

Common diseases of lactating cows

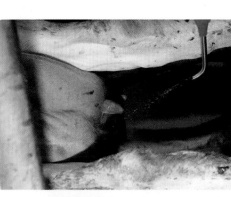

31.11 *The bacterium Staphylococcus aureus can cause mastitis in lactating cows*

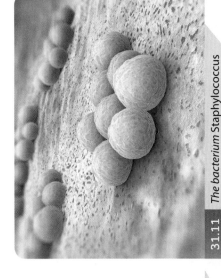

31.12 *The teats of the udder are disinfected after milking to prevent mastitis*

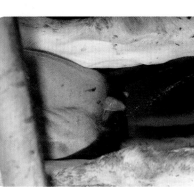

31.10 *A cow with mastitis being treated with antibiotics*

Subclinical: a disease that is not severe enough to present signs or symptoms.

Inflammation: when part of the body becomes reddened, swollen, hot and often painful.

Clinical: where the cow displays definite and obvious symptoms of the disease.

Table 31.2 Diseases of lactating cows

Disease	Cause and transmission	Symptoms	Treatment	Prevention
Subclinical mastitis	**Cause:** • Bacterial (most commonly *Staphylococcus aureus*, *Streptococcus uberis* and *E. coli*) **Transmission:** • Bacteria are constantly present in the environment • Bacteria are spread through dirty housing, through the operator's hand when milking, cloths used to wipe the udder prior to milking, milking clusters and teat injuries	• No obvious change in milk • Possibly some inflammation of the udder • Only clear indication is a high somatic cell count	• Treat affected cows with long-lasting dry-cow treatment to regenerate tissue and prevent new infection • Treatment during drying off ensures no milk loss during lactation period	• Dry-cow treatment during drying off • Ensure milking machine works correctly; faulty machines damage teats • Change milk liners regularly: cracks in milk liners can harbour bacteria • Use teat disinfectant after milking: dirt on udder and teat increases chances of infection • Strip teat regularly to check for mastitis • Ensure clean and dry bedding in winter housing and calving shed • Cull chronically infected cows
Clinical mastitis **Can also affect sheep and pigs**	• Same **cause and transmission** as subclinical mastitis	• Inflammation of the udder, affecting one or more of the quarters • Visible changes in the milk, presence of clots • Milk may be watery	• Treat with antibiotics • Milk from the cow is withheld from the bulk tank	• Same prevention measures as per subclinical mastitis

Disease	Cause and transmission	Symptoms	Treatment	Prevention
Summer mastitis Seen in dry cows and heifers between June and September	**Cause:** • Bacterial (*Actinomyces pyogenes*) **Transmission:** • Spread by flies	• Infected quarter becomes swollen and hard • Foul smelling discharge from infected udder • High temperature • Severely affected cows may abort their calf • Infected quarters are generally lost	• Early detection is vital; look for flies constantly around a single teat • Irrigation of the infected quarter • Administer antibiotics and anti-inflammatories	• Treat sores and wounds on teat of the animal • Control flies with pour-on or spot-on • Use long-lasting dry cow treatment • Apply Stockholm tar as a physical barrier on the teat

Diseases of calves

Table 31.3 Diseases of calves

Disease	Cause and transmission	Symptoms	Treatment	Prevention
Nutritional scour	**Cause:** • Calf is fed too much milk • Irregular feed times • Milk ball develops in the calf's stomach • Can develop into infectious scour	• Diarrhoea • Dehydration, weak calf • Not life-threatening unless it develops into infectious scour	• Frequent small feeds of water with glucose and electrolytes in addition to milk • Feed weak calves with a stomach tube	• Good feeding routine • Make gradual changes to the calves' diet • Avoid overcrowding • Ensure calves have sufficient clean, dry bedding • Sheds should be dry and warm to reduce stress caused by cold weather • Strict hygiene

Disease	Cause and transmission	Symptoms	Treatment	Prevention
Infectious scour **Can also affect lambs and piglets** 31.13 *E. coli bacteria can cause scour in cattle, sheep and pigs*	**Cause:** • Variety of pathogens • Bacteria: Salmonella and *E. coli* • Viruses: rotavirus • Protozoa (*Cryptosporidium*) endoparasite **Transmission:** • Exposure to infected faeces • Calves become infected from calf pen, contaminated buckets and clothing of the farmer • Cows can be carriers of the virus that causes scour	• High temperature • Calves reluctant to feed • Bright yellow or white faeces • Foul-smelling diarrhoea • Dehydration • Listlessness • Hypothermia • Shock followed by death	• Frequent small feeds of electrolyte solution and milk to prevent dehydration • Consult vet • Identify causative agent (bacterium, virus or protozoan) • Treat with antibiotics, if bacterial • If calf's temperature falls below 37°C, place it under an infrared lamp • Isolate infected animal	• Clean and disinfect calf houses, buckets and bedding • Maintain strict hygiene • Don't mix older calves with newborn calves, the younger calves will be more susceptible • Ensure calf gets adequate colostrum at birth • Cows can be vaccinated against rotavirus, which can increase the number of antibodies, against the virus, in the colostrum • See also points for prevention of nutritional scour
Viral pneumonia	**Cause:** • Initial infection caused by a virus, secondary infection caused by bacteria due to weakened immune system **Transmission:** • Caused by a number of factors: insufficient intake of colostrum, poor nutrition, poor ventilation in sheds, overcrowding, poor hygiene and mixing older animals with younger calves, exposure to extreme cold weather	• Rise in temperature • Discharge from nose and eyes, rapid breathing and coughing • Calf lies down a lot • Weight loss, loss of appetite • Death in severe cases	• Isolate calf • Vet required • Treat bacterial infection with antibiotics	• Well-ventilated, dry, warm, draught-free housing essential • Good hygiene • Prevent scour • Avoid overcrowding • Ensure calf receives adequate intake of colostrum • Ensure proper nutrition for growing calf • Vaccinate calves • Prevent BVD in the herd by testing and culling infected calves

Disease	Cause and transmission	Symptoms	Treatment	Prevention
Ringworm 31.14 *Ringworm infection on the face and neck of a young calf*	**Cause:** • Fungal • Zoonose **Transmission:** • Direct contact with infected cattle • Cattle are infected from contaminated walls of sheds, feeding barriers, etc. • Can be a problem with cattle that are housed	• Circular patches of hair loss develop into grey, crusty scabs on the animal's head, neck and flank	• Apply a topical medicine to infected skin • Animals recover in a few weeks	• Clean and disinfect housing (spores can survive on walls of buildings) • Vaccine available • Some farmers hang large pieces of holly from the ceilings of their winter housing, which can help to prevent ringworm
Hoose (lungworm)	**Cause:** • Nematodes (roundworms) • Endoparasite **Transmission:** • Parasite is widespread • More prevalent in wet areas • Cattle ingest the larvae from the grass • The larvae can survive a long period of time on pasture	• Young calves are susceptible to hoose • Causes coughing and failure to thrive • Increases the risk to lung infections, leading to viral and bacterial pneumonia	• Dose cattle	• Good grassland management, rotational grazing • Low level exposure to lungworm over time builds up a natural immunity • Graze calves in leader-follower system ahead of older animals • Vaccinate young calves
Stomach worms	**Cause:** • Nematodes (roundworms) • *Ostertagia* • *Cooperia* **Transmission:** • The calves ingest the larvae when grazing grass	• Young calves susceptible to stomach worms • Causes scouring • Failure to thrive	• Dose cattle	• Good grassland management • Graze animals in leader-follower system ahead of older stock

Diseases of cattle

Table 31.4 Diseases of cattle

Disease	Cause and transmission	Symptoms	Treatment	Prevention
Fasciolosis (liver fluke) **Infects both cattle and sheep** 31.15 *Liver fluke*	**Cause:** • Liverfluke • Flatworm, endoparasite **Transmission:** • Animals ingest the cercaria (larval stage of the liverfluke) when they are grazing grass	• Failure to thrive • Reduction in milk production in dairy cattle • Lower FCR in beef animals • Causes liver damage • Diagnosed by faecal examination for fluke eggs • Cows with chronic infections will have chronic diarrhoea	• Dose animals	• Dose animals regularly • Drain land and fence off wet areas • Keep vulnerable stock such as calves away from wet areas • Treat dairy cows for fluke when drying them off
Blackleg	**Cause:** • Bacterial (*Clostridium chauvoei*) **Transmission:** • Bacterial spores lie dormant in the soil for many years • The spores are ingested when cattle are grazing grass • Under low oxygen conditions in an animal's muscle, the endospore germinates and starts to multiply	• Highly fatal disease • Animals usually die within 12–48 hours of the bacteria becoming active in their body • Lameness • Loss of appetite • High fever • Rapid breathing	• Usually fatal • Kills very quickly, making treatment difficult	• All animals should be vaccinated against the disease

Failure to thrive: animal is not putting on sufficient weight gain or has inappropriate weight loss.

Disease	Cause and transmission	Symptoms	Treatment	Prevention
Bovine tuberculosis (TB) **Notifiable disease** **31.16** *Testing cattle for bovine tuberculosis with the tuberlin test*	**Cause:** • Bacterial (*Mycobacterium bovis*) • **Zoonose** **Transmission:** • The bacteria spread within the herd from cow to cow by inhalation, especially in winter housing • It is also spread through water supply, urine and faeces • It is spread from cow to calf through colostrum and milk	• The bacteria replicate slowly so it can take years for the disease to develop • Swollen lymph nodes in the animal's neck • Failure to thrive • Weakness and lethargy • Large loss of body weight (emaciation) • Soft chronic cough	• No treatment • Cattle are tested annually under a national eradication programme • Animals that show a reaction to the testing are called reactors and are culled • Restrictions are then put in place so that animals cannot be moved on or off the affected farms • Restrictions are lifted only when a herd has two clear tests 60 days apart	• Biosecurity • Strong fencing to prevent mixing of herd with neighbouring stock • Breeding own replacement stock • Isolating and quarantining bought-in stock • Ensure cattle have access to fresh water • Raise feeding and drinking troughs to 84 cm in height so that wildlife cannot have access to it • Keep feed storage areas and cattle sheds closed so that wildlife cannot gain entry
Johne's disease (pronounced yoh-nays) **Can also affect other ruminants, e.g. sheep**	**Cause:** • Bacterial (*Mycobacterium paratuberculosis*) **Transmission:** • The disease is usually introduced onto the farm through the purchase of an infected animal • Calves become infected with the disease by ingesting the bacteria in contaminated milk and feed • Adult animals shed the bacteria in their dung and milk • A calf can be born with the disease if the dam is in advance stages of the disease	• Bacteria infect the digestive tract of cattle and sheep • The disease develops slowly • Progressive wasting of the animal, despite eating well • Watery diarrhoea • Low milk yields • Death of the animal	• No known treatment	• Strict hygiene standards, particularly in relation to calving • Do not pool milk and colostrum from many cows to feed to replacement calves, which can spread the disease • Calves should not come into contact with dung from infected animals • Cull infected animals • Keep a closed herd • Biosecurity • Rear own replacement heifers

Disease	Cause and transmission	Symptoms	Treatment	Prevention
Bovine viral diarrhoea (BVD) **Notifiable disease**	**Cause:** • Viral **Transmission:** • Virus is spread through saliva, semen, urine, milk, nasal secretions and faeces • Calves can be born with the virus if the dam is exposed to BVD during the first 4 months of gestation; these calves are described as persistently infected (PI) • PI's shed huge quantities of the infection over the course of their lives	• Diarrhoea • Respiratory infections • Infertility • Abortion • Weak and ill-thriving calves • Virus is an immunosuppressive agent	• No treatment for infected animals • All newly born calves are tested • Ear tissue sample is sent away to be tested • PI animals should be culled as soon as they are identified • Eradication programme for BVD	• All bought in animals should have tested negative for BVD • Ensure cattle have no contact with neighbouring cattle • Don't buy in calf heifers • Biosecurity • Vaccinate breeding cows

31.17 *Modified tags for BVD testing*

31.18 *BVD viral particles seen as small round red particles in cell organelles through an electron microscope*

Eradication programme: a programme run by the DAFM in conjunction with the district veterinary laboratories for the compulsory testing of the national herd with the aim of completely removing a disease.

Immuno-suppressive agent: reduces the activity of the immune system. It makes the animal's immune system less effective at dealing with pathogens.

Common diseases of pigs

Table 31.5 Diseases of pigs and piglets

Disease	Cause and transmission	Symptoms	Treatment	Prevention
Erysipelas	**Cause:** • Bacterial **Transmission:** • Pigs can be carriers of the bacteria in the herd • Spread in faeces, saliva, nasal secretions and urine	• Fever • Abortion of piglets • Mummified piglets • Stillborn piglets • Raised red lumps on skin of the sow	• Antibiotics	• Clean water supplies • Clean housing: bedding, dung, feed and water can harbour the bacteria • Vaccinate sows • Piglets up to 8–12 weeks old are protected by the antibodies in the sow's colostrum
Anaemia in piglets	**Cause:** • Lack of iron	• Pale skin • Rapid breathing • Weakness • Scour	• Iron injection	• Iron injection is given to piglets at 2–3 days old
Porcine parvovirus (SMEDI)	**Cause:** • Gut-borne viruses specific to pigs **Transmission:** • Spread by the ingestion of contaminated food and water with infected faecal material	• Stillborn piglets • Mummified embryos • Embryonic death • Infertility (all caused by the virus entering the uterus across the placenta)	• No treatment	• Piglets are normally protected by the antibodies in the sow's colostrum • Good hygiene
Internal parasites	**Cause:** • Roundworm; tapeworm **Transmission:** • Pigs ingest the eggs	• Coughing • Vomiting • Diarrhoea • Loss of condition	• Dosing	• Dosing every 6 months

Carrier: an organism infected with a pathogenic microorganism that does not display any signs or symptoms of the disease.

483

Disease	Cause and transmission	Symptoms	Treatment	Prevention
Mycoplasma hyopneumoniae (Porcine enzootic pneumonia)	**Cause:** • Bacteria **Transmission:** • Windborne infection • Aerosols produced by the pigs when coughing • Carrier pigs: bought-in pigs from infected herds	• Disease is endemic in most herds • Typically affects pigs aged 8–20 weeks old • Persistent dry cough • Can cause breathing difficulties • Decrease in growth rate • Poor FCR • Causes lesions in the lungs • Secondary infections by PRRS can lead to more severe respiratory infections, which can result in huge economic losses	• Antibiotics • Reduce pig numbers • Maintain a closed herd	• Avoid overcrowding • Good ventilation • Strict biosecurity • Operate an 'all in/all out' policy • Vaccinate piglets at 3 weeks of age • Rear own replacement gilts • Avoid mixing pigs of different ages
Porcine reproductive and respiratory syndrome (PRRS)	**Cause:** • Viral (first identified in 1991) **Transmission:** • Virus is spread by nasal secretions, saliva, faeces and urine • Pigs can carry the disease for some time	• Virus kills macrophages (white blood cells) • Lowers the ability of the pig to fight disease • Loss of appetite during farrowing period • Respiratory problems • Early farrowing, causing an increase in stillbirths and weak newborn piglets	• No treatment • Antibiotics are given to treat secondary infections by bacteria	• Biosecurity • Only buy replacement gilts and boars from PRRS-free herds. Use AI that is guaranteed free from PRRS • Vaccinate pigs

Aerosols: minute particles that are suspended in the air.

Non-infectious diseases

A non-infectious disease is a disease that is not caused by a pathogen (microorganism). Milk fever and grass tetany are examples of diseases that are caused by environmental factors (e.g. the deficiency of a mineral in the diet of an animal). Milk fever is due to low calcium levels in a mammal's blood after giving birth and commencing lactation. Grass tetany is caused by low levels of magnesium in lush spring grass.

Notifiable diseases

A notifiable disease is a disease that must be immediately reported to the DAFM. These diseases are notifiable because they are normally infectious and highly contagious. Notifiable diseases can cause significant economic hardship, through loss of productivity and the death of affected animals. By notifying the DAFM, it allows the authorities to monitor the disease and co-ordinate a response to the disease. Notification to the DAFM is not required in the case of tuberculosis as there is an eradication programme in place, or for Johne's disease and BVD, where there is a dedicated surveillance or control programme in place.

Notifiable diseases are:

- Diseases of national importance
- Spread quickly (are highly contagious)
- Cause significant economic loss
- Decrease productivity
- Result in both affected and unaffected animals being destroyed to prevent the spread of the disease
- Pose a threat to human health (some notifiable diseases are zoonoses)
- Cannot easily be treated or controlled.

Prion: a misfolded protein.

Table 31.6 Notifiable diseases in Ireland			
Notifiable disease	**Animal affected**	**Infectious agent**	**Description**
African swine fever	Pigs and wild boar	Virus	Fatal disease
Avian influenza	Poultry	Virus	Zoonose
BSE (bovine spongiform encephalopathy)	Cattle	Prion	Zoonose spread when contaminated meat and bone meal are eaten
Bluetongue	Ruminants	Virus	Spread by midges; vaccination available
Brucellosis	Cattle	Bacteria	Zoonose causes undulant fever in humans
Contagious bovine pleuropneumonia	Cattle	Bacteria	Affects the lungs
Foot and mouth disease	Cattle, sheep, pigs	Virus	Highly infectious; causes significant economic loss; blisters occur in the mouth and on the feet of infected animals
Newcastle disease	Poultry	Virus	Highly contagious
Rabies	Mammals	Virus	Zoonose; spread through saliva
Scrapie	Sheep and goats	Prion	Same symptoms as BSE
Bovine tuberculosis	Cattle	Bacteria	Zoonose; herd testing and eradication programme in place
BVD	Cattle	Virus	Newborn calves tested; eradication of calves that test positive (PIs)

Bluetongue (sheep), brucellosis (cattle), foot and mouth disease, bovine tuberculosis, BVD (cattle) and sheep scab are all examples of diseases that are notifiable. A full list of notifiable diseases can be found on the website of the DAFM.

When a notifiable disease is identified on a farm, the movement of animals and animal products is restricted to prevent the spread of the disease. The animals are then slaughtered humanely and their carcases are disposed of by incineration or burial. For many years Ireland has had eradication programmes for bovine tuberculosis and brucellosis, with regular testing of the national herd. These eradication programmes have had considerable success, with Ireland being declared brucellosis-free in 2009.

The Animal Health Surveillance website contains many articles on common diseases, their symptoms, diagnosis, treatment and control. It is a valuable resource for all farmers, giving accurate information on all animal diseases.

Biosecurity

Prevention is always better than cure. This is especially true with notifiable diseases, since treatment of the disease itself is usually impossible. The following is a list of measures a farmer should take to prevent entry of disease onto their farm.

- Maintain a closed herd; breed all replacement stock where possible and only buy in stock from herds certified disease-free.
- Quarantine all bought-in stock. A farmer should have a separate building away from their own stock animals for bought-in animals.
- Use good fencing to prevent contact of stock with animals from a neighbouring farm.
- Limit access to the farm for people and vehicles. Both can carry disease onto a farm through clothing, footwear, tyres, etc.
- Ensure that vermin and wildlife do not have access to animal feed and bedding.
- When using AI, ensure that semen and embryos have disease-free status.
- Do not house cattle and sheep together: cattle can become infected with malignant catarrhal fever during lambing time.
- Ensure all newborn animals receive colostrum from their mothers.

Zoonotic diseases

A zoonotic disease is a disease caused by an infectious agent that can spread between animals and humans. Zoonotic diseases are also called zoonoses. Some zoonotic diseases can cause serious illness and even death.

Zoonoses can be passed on to humans through several routes:
- **Direct contact:** saliva, blood, urine, faeces and other bodily fluids
- **Indirect contact:** contaminated water and feed, bedding and other contaminated materials
- **Vector:** an organism, usually a parasite that is carrying a disease; e.g. ticks (ectoparasite of sheep) carry the bacterium that causes Lyme disease
- **Foodborne:** drinking unpasteurised milk.

In order to avoid the risk of contracting a zoonose, farmers should:
- Maintain healthy animals
- Clean and cover all wounds, cuts and scratches
- Get immunised against tetanus
- Use protective clothing (gloves, aprons, overalls, etc.)
- **Wash hands regularly.** (See Exercise 2.1 in Chapter 2, pages 23–25).

An **infectious** disease is caused by a bacterium, virus or protozoan.

Lyme disease: a bacterial infection carried by ticks. Ticks are a common ectoparasite of sheep and feed on the sheep's blood. When a tick bites a human, it produces a rash that looks like a bull's eye on a dart board. A person that develops this rash should seek medical advice.

Summary

- Farmers are responsible for the welfare of farm animals.
- The five freedoms are:
  - Freedom from hunger, thirst and malnutrition
  - Freedom from discomfort
  - Freedom from pain, injury and disease
  - Freedom to express normal patterns of behaviour
  - Freedom from fear and distress.
- Twin lamb disease is a disease that is caused by the under-feeding of ewes carrying multiple lambs. It can be prevented by steaming up.
- Orf is a zoonose and can be passed from sheep to humans. Sheep can be vaccinated against orf.
- Milk fever is a disease of lactating animals that have a deficiency in calcium.
- Grass tetany is a disease of ruminating animals caused by a deficiency of magnesium.
- Watery mouth is a disease that affects lambs and is caused by poor hygiene.
- Nematodirus and coccidosis are both endoparasites that are ingested by lambs when grazing pasture.
- Sheep scab is a notifiable disease. It is caused by mange mites that feed on the flesh of sheep.
- Navel ill and joint ill are diseases that affect newly born animals. Navel ill is caused by an infection of the navel. It can be prevented by bathing the navel in iodine.
- Mastitis is a bacterial infection of the udder of a dairy cow. There are several symptoms determined by the severity of the disease. In subclinical mastitis there is an increase in the somatic cell count. In clinical mastitis the udder is swollen and there are visible changes in the milk. All forms of mastitis are treated using antibiotics.
- Infectious scour is caused by several microorganisms (bacteria, viruses and protozoans). Treatment depends on the type of infectious agent. Maintaining strict hygiene can prevent the spread of the disease.
- Ringworm is caused by a fungus and is a zoonose.
- Liverfluke, hoose and stomach worms are all endoparasites. They all cause an animal to fail to thrive. They are treated by dosing the animal and prevented by employing a good grassland management system.
- Bovine tuberculosis is a notifiable disease and a zoonose. It is a bacterial infection that is transmitted by direct contact with the infected animal or indirectly by coming into contact with contaminated water, urine and faeces. Calves can become infected by drinking milk from an infected cow.
- Anaemia in piglets is caused by a deficiency in iron. It is treated and prevented by administering an iron injection.
- A notifiable disease is a disease that must be immediately reported to the district veterinary office or the DAFM. These diseases are normally infectious and highly contagious. Tuberculosis and sheep scab are examples of notifiable diseases.
- Biosecurity is the name given to measures that a farmer should take to prevent entry of disease onto their farm.
- Zoonotic diseases are diseases that can be passed from animals to humans. Zoonotic diseases are also called zoonoses. Ringworm and tuberculosis are examples of zoonotic diseases.

PowerPoint Summary

QUESTIONS

1. What is the purpose of the five freedoms?

    (a) To ensure animals get enough food

    (b) To ensure animals are provided with water

    (c) To ensure animals get the right conditions to maintain them in good physical and mental health and to prevent cruelty to them

    (d) To ensure that animals can reproduce

2. Which of the following is a sign of ill-health in a calf?

    (a) Clear eyes and nose

    (b) Bright and playful

    (c) Calf wants to drink milk

    (d) Rattling noise when the calf is breathing

3. A farmer needs to dehorn (debud) several calves. Which statement correctly describes the correct procedure for minimising stress to the animal?

    (a) Pour on and handling facilities

    (b) Carried out before the calves are 2 weeks old and using handling facilities

    (c) Carried out before the animal is 8 weeks old without anaesthetic

    (d) Using an elastrator, handling facilities are not necessary

4. A farmer wants to move cattle into a shed. Which of the following will stress the cattle and make it difficult to move them?

    (a) Having the passageway cleared of obstacles

    (b) Having lights on in the shed

    (c) Speaking to the animals calmly

    (d) Yelling and shouting at the animals

5. What is the correct name given to an organism that carries a disease?

    (a) A pathogen

    (b) A microorganism

    (c) A zoonose

    (d) A vector

6. What is a zoonose?

    (a) A disease that can be transferred from animals to birds

    (b) A disease that cannot be transferred from animals to humans

    (c) A disease that can be transferred between ruminant animals

    (d) A disease that can be transferred from animals to humans

7. A farmer has several ewes expecting twins and triplets in January. He is feeding these ewes extra concentrates and a mineral supplement containing calcium. What two diseases is the famer trying to prevent?

    (a) Milk fever and twin lamb disease

    (b) Orf and grass tetany

    (c) Grass tetany and milk fever

    (d) Grass tetany and twin lamb disease

8. A number of lambs have the following symptoms: scabby lesions around their nose and inside and outside their mouths, and their feet are also affected. Which of the following diseases have the lambs got?

(a) Milk fever

(b) Watery mouth

(c) Nematodirus

(d) Orf

31.19   *Question 8*

9. The only way to prevent clostridial diseases from affecting a flock of sheep is:

(a) Vaccination of all animals

(b) Good grassland management

(c) Adequate amounts of concentrates

(d) Strict hygiene levels in all housing.

10. Sheep scab and Newcastle disease are examples of diseases that are:

(a) Zoonoses

(b) Notifiable diseases

(c) Caused by ectoparasites

(d) Caused by endoparasites.

11. The only sign that a cow has subclinical mastitis is that there is:

(a) Clots in her milk

(b) High somatic cell count

(c) A lot of inflammation of her udder and it is sore to touch

(d) Blood in her milk.

12. A calf has been diagnosed with bacterial scour. What factors may have contributed to the calf developing scour?

(a) Overcrowding

(b) Insufficient intake of colostrum

(c) A build-up of dung in the pens containing the calves

(d) All of the above

13. Identify the disease that the calf in Fig. 31.20 has.

(a) Orf

(b) Ringworm

(c) Hoose

(d) Mastitis

14. Which of the following pathogens is responsible for causing a disease called blackleg in cattle?

(a) Bacterium

(b) Virus

(c) Fungus

(d) Lungworm

31.20   *Question 13*

15. Which of the following diseases is a notifiable disease and a zoonose?

    (a) Ringworm

    (b) Sheep scab

    (c) BVD

    (d) Bovine tuberculosis

16. Which of the following is not a symptom of bovine tuberculosis?

    (a) The onset of the disease is rapid

    (b) Swollen lymph nodes

    (c) Emaciation

    (d) Soft chronic cough

17. A national eradication programme exists for which of the following diseases?

    (a) Tuberculosis and anaemia

    (b) Tuberculosis and BVD

    (c) BVD and sheep scab

    (d) BVD and milk fever

18. Which of the following diseases is caused by a pathogen?

    (a) Anaemia

    (b) Milk fever

    (c) Grass tetany

    (d) Tuberculosis

19. SMEDI and PRRS in pigs are both caused by a:

    (a) Bacterium

    (b) Fungus

    (c) Virus

    (d) Roundworm.

20. Cattle, sheep and pigs are all affected by internal parasites such as roundworms. The most common source of infection is by:

    (a) Inhalation of eggs or larvae

    (b) Ingestion of eggs or larvae

    (c) Egestion of eggs or larvae

    (d) Digestion of eggs of larvae.

21. Explain why lameness in cattle and sheep are a welfare issue.

22. What signs should a farmer look out for that would indicate to them that a calf was unwell?

23. A farmer needs to dose his cattle against liverfluke and lungworm. Briefly outline some key points that the farmer should take into account when considering the welfare of these animals.

24. Outline some key requirements for cattle and sheep when housing them for the winter months. Identify which of the five freedoms each of these requirements facilitates.

25. Intestinal worms are a common problem in all animal production systems.

    (a) Identify ways in which a farmer can control the problem in a production system of your choice.

    (b) Describe how good grassland management can help reduce the problem in a grass-based system.

26. (a) Name two examples of production diseases that occur in farm animals.

    (b) In the case of one of the diseases you have mentioned, state the cause, how the disease is transmitted, the main symptoms and a method of prevention or cure.

27. Name three notifiable diseases of farm animals in Ireland.

28. Name two bacterial diseases of pigs. Give one symptom of each disease.

29. 'Maintaining strict hygiene, ensuring newborn animals have sufficient intake of colostrum and avoiding overcrowding are key features in preventing disease on a farm.' Choosing an animal production system of your choice and using examples, discuss the validity of this statement.

30. A number of calves have developed infectious scour on a farm. Suggest an appropriate plan to treat infected animals and prevent the spread of the disease to healthy calves.

31. Identify three practices a pig farmer should carry out to prevent disease in a pig unit.

32. Briefly outline the importance of biosecurity in all animal production systems.

 Solutions   Weblinks

CHAPTER 32 — Environmental impact of agriculture and markets for Irish produce

When you have completed this chapter you should be able to:

- Discuss the environmental implications of animal production
- Recognise the importance of markets for Irish produce including value-added, niche market and artisan produce
- Read and evaluate scientific information from a variety of sources
- Describe a farm that you have studied in terms of:
  - Farmyard layout (sketch) in which you identify and discuss potential hazards on the farm and how they are prevented
  - Best layout practice, including economic, health and safety, social and environmental sustainability aspects (SPA).

Environmental implications of animal production

Greenhouse gas emissions

By far the greatest environmental impact of agriculture is the emission of greenhouse gases (GHG). In Ireland, agriculture accounts for 32% of our overall GHG emissions (see Fig. 32.1). This figure is relatively high compared with the contribution of agriculture in other EU countries (average 10%), and this is mainly due to our lack of heavy industry. The three main GHG produced by farming are:

- Carbon dioxide (CO_2)
- Methane (CH_4)
- Nitrous oxide (N_2O).

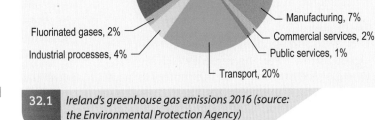

32.1 Ireland's greenhouse gas emissions 2016 (source: the Environmental Protection Agency)

> The **global warming potential of a gas** is a measure of how much energy the gas will absorb over a given period relative to carbon dioxide. It allows the comparison of the impact of different gases on global warming.

Table 32.1 Greenhouse gases produced by agriculture and their source	
Gas	**Source**
Carbon dioxide	Combustion of fossil fuels for energy and transport
Methane	Product of fermentation in the ruminant stomach (cattle and sheep)
Nitrous oxide	Artificial fertilisers and manures

Each of these GHG contributes to global warming to different extents. The global warming potential of nitrous oxide and methane are 298 and 25 times that of carbon dioxide, respectively.

Exercise 32.1

Read this Teagasc article and answer the questions that follow.

Reducing Greenhouse Gas Emissions from Agriculture

23 May 2017
Gary Lanigan – Teagasc, Soils, Environment & Land-Use Programme, Johnstown Castle, Wexford.

The Problem

The facts are simple, the solutions are more complicated. The undeniable fact is that Earth is warming up, with the average global temperatures having increased by 0.85°C between 1880 and 2012. The Intergovernmental Panel on Climate Change (IPCC), a UN body of hundreds of expert scientists who assess the science of climate change, has stated that man-made greenhouse gases (GHG) are the primary cause of this warming.

The main man-made gas is Carbon dioxide (CO_2) which accounts for 76% of global emissions. However, agricultural emissions are dominated by methane (from ruminants and manures) and nitrous oxide (N_2O from fertiliser and animal deposition) and contribute to 16% and 6% respectively towards man-made warming. While there is much less methane and N_2O in the atmosphere, as outlined in IPCC reports, these gases have different capacities to trap heat. As a result, they are assessed using Global Warming Potential which compares the ability of 1 kg of each gas to trap heat over a 100-year time horizon. Using this measure, methane has 25 times the warming potential of CO_2, and N_2O 298 times higher than CO_2. These gases also remain in the atmosphere for different lengths of time. CO_2 does not break down easily and it remains in the atmosphere for several centuries. N_2O has a lifetime of 121 years. In contrast, the atmospheric lifetime of methane is much shorter at 12.4 years.

The Challenge

In order to address climate change, 197 countries signed up to the Paris Agreement which seeks to limit global temperature rise this century to below 2°C above pre-industrial levels. The EU has also set emissions reduction targets, with Ireland allocated a 20% reduction in emissions to 2020 and 30% to 2030. Recently the Department of Communications, Climate Action and Environment (DCCAE) published the National Mitigation Plan Consultation which aims to set out Ireland's roadmap to reducing emissions. Teagasc has submitted a response to this consultation outlining both the challenges and options available for emissions reduction in the agriculture and land-use sector.

Why are these Climate targets a challenge to Irish agriculture? Well, firstly agriculture accounts for one-third of national GHG emissions. Secondly, agricultural production, particularly in the dairy sector, is increasing post quota removal and Foodwise 2025 has set ambitious targets for primary production, exports and jobs.

The Footprint

Projections suggest that increases in global population and changing patterns of wealth will increase demand for dairy and meat by more than 50–80% by 2050. As a result, there are significant concerns that increasing food production will lead to increased global GHG emissions. As a result, there is currently a strong focus to reduce the carbon footprint across commodities. Comparisons of the carbon footprint of international livestock production by FAO and the EU Joint Research Council have demonstrated that the carbon footprint of dairy and beef production was the lowest in temperate grass-based systems, with the footprint of Irish produce amongst the lowest in Europe. Recent Teagasc data showed that the carbon footprint of Irish produce has been reduced by c. 15% since 1990. Similarly, the 'Nitrogen-footprint' of Irish produce has been reduced by c. 25%.

The Solutions

Teagasc's strategy for reducing agricultural emissions is a) to stabilise GHG emissions, particularly methane, by enhanced efficiency measures, b) to further reduce emissions, particularly nitrous oxide, c) to offset GHG emissions with carbon sequestration from afforestation and agricultural land management and d) displace fossil fuel emissions with wood fuel and biogas.

> **Commodity:** a raw material or an agricultural product that can be bought or sold.

Over the last number of years, Teagasc's Greenhouse Gas research group has been working to develop solutions. Much of the answer lies in farm efficiency: so if we can produce food with fewer inputs, then this reduces emissions to the atmosphere and costs to the farmer. This will be achieved through adoption of measures such as dairy Economic Breeding Index (i.e. improve the genetics of our dairy cows), beef genomics (to improve the genetics of our beef herd), improved animal health, and extending the grazing season. These efficiencies will reduce the C footprint of dairy and beef and stabilise methane emissions via increased product per head. Improved nutrient management planning in combination with optimal use of slurry and legumes will help increase nitrogen efficiency and reduce nitrous oxide emissions. Other strategies can reduce greenhouse gas emissions even

> **Afforestation:** the process of planting large numbers of trees on land that was not previously forested.

further. Examples include the development of novel, low-emission fertilizers, reducing crude protein in bovine and pig diets, fatty acid supplementation to reduce methane, drainage of poorly drained mineral soils and adding amendments to manures during storage. In addition, enhancing carbon sequestration and/or reducing soil C losses are key strategies to reducing sectoral emissions. This will principally be achieved through increased afforestation, reducing losses on organic soils and enhancing pasture sequestration.

As both the 2020 and 2030 GHG reduction targets are multi-year targets, the total GHG reduction will be highly dependent on rates of uptake. This means that the role of knowledge transfer (KT) and education will be more important than ever. Research by itself will not lead to emissions reductions without strong linkage to advisory and education and the involvement of farmers. Initiatives, such as the Teagasc eProfit Monitor, Pasture Profit Index, NMP online, the Teagasc/Bord Bia Farm Carbon Navigator, the Teagasc/Farmers Journal BETTER farms beef programme, the Teagasc BETTER farm sheep and tillage programmes, and the many other Teagasc-joint industry programmes, will all play vital roles in getting the message out to farmers.

In summary, CO_2, methane and nitrous oxide all contribute to climate change. There is potential to reduce the more long-lived nitrous oxide and CO_2, whilst stabilising methane in the short term. Ultimately, achieving timely and substantial levels of mitigation will require the whole sector including farmers, industry, research, advisory/education and policymakers working in concert. Effective large-scale mitigation will only occur if best practice can be communicated on the ground. This will involve a closer linkage between research/analysis to the development of relevant policies and effective translation on the ground via knowledge transfer.

Amendments: addition of something.

Mineral soils: soils that are derived from rocks and contain very little organic matter or humus.

Mitigation: the process or action of reducing the severity or lessening the effects of something, e.g. climate change.

Knowledge transfer: the process of communicating knowledge or information from one organisation to another.

Questions

1. What is the main factor responsible for an increase in the average global temperatures over the last century?

2. Identify the main GHG produced by the agricultural sector.

3. Identify a source for the gas named in question 2.

4. How is the global warming potential of each of these gases assessed?

5. What is the main aim of the Paris Agreement?

6. Under the Paris Agreement, what EU emission reduction targets have been set for Ireland?

7. What are the main challenges faced by the agricultural sector in achieving these emission reduction targets?

8. Describe the strategies Teagasc aims to employ in reducing GHG emissions from the agricultural sector.

9. Identify ways in which farmers can enhance their herd efficiencies.

10. In the second last paragraph, what does the author identify as being vital to achieve a reduction in GHG emission from the agricultural sector?

11. In the article the author mentions several initiatives: Teagasc eProfit Monitor, Pasture Profit Index, NMP online, the Teagasc/Bord Bia Farm Carbon Navigator, the Teagasc/Farmers Journal BETTER farms beef programme, the Teagasc BETTER farm sheep and tillage programmes.

    Select one of the above initiatives. Using the internet or other sources, write a report:

    (a) Summarising the initiative/programme

    (b) What farm enterprise the programme is aimed at

    (c) How the initiative/programme will benefit our environment.

Water quality

The potential risks to water quality in Ireland from agriculture are the addition of nitrates and phosphates (eutrophication), sediment and pathogens. The effect of the addition of nitrates and phosphates has been dealt with in Chapter 8. Farmers must ensure that they have adequate storage for all washings from dairy parlours, collecting yards and pits and that these washings are collected and prevented from entering any watercourse.

Slurry and farmyard manures can have a significant loss of nitrogen during storage and spreading. Most of the nitrogen loss is by the volatilisation of ammonia and nitrous oxide. Nitrous oxide is a potent GHG. Ammonia emissions have a negative impact on air quality as well as a damaging effect on soil ecosystems. Method of slurry spreading as well as timing and weather conditions can have a large effect on nitrogen loss from the slurry. A slurry tanker fitted with a splash-plate has the potential for large nitrogen loss. Using a tanker with a trailing shoe or band spreader can reduce nitrogen loss, as it places the slurry below the grass and closer to the soil in comparison to broadcasting the slurry with a splash-plate, which leaves the slurry on top of the grass. Nitrogen loss from slurry is also greatest when slurry is spread during warm, dry and sunny weather. Nitrogen losses can be reduced by spreading slurry during spring rather than summer.

> **Volatilisation:** vaporised easily.

Biodiversity

> **DEFINITION**
>
> **Biodiversity:** the variety of plants and animals that are living in a particular habitat.

Changes in agricultural practices over the last century have led to a loss of diversity of wildlife in Ireland. The National Parks and Wildlife Service published a report under Ireland's Habitat Directive in 2013, and they identified the following as principal pressures on biodiversity as a result of agricultural activities:

- Land drainage
- Pollution
- Climate change
- Unsuitable grazing regimes.

32.2 *The marsh fritillary butterfly was once widespread across Ireland but its population has declined and its conservation status is listed as vulnerable*

Land drainage

Land drainage and reclamation has led to a decrease in peatlands and wetlands. These are a unique habitat to many plants, mammals and insects. With the targets set out in Food Harvest 2020 and Food Wise 2025, Birdwatch Ireland warned that the intensification of production would require the expansion of farm areas further into habitats. Lowland wet grassland habitats are vital breeding grounds for waders. One such wader, the curlew, once a common bird in Ireland, has seen its breeding

> **Reclamation:** the process of changing land that is unsuitable for farming into land that can be used.

32.3 *The curlew population has dramatically declined since the 1980s*

population decline by 96%. It is red listed in Ireland and is an endangered species. The curlew nests in damp, rushy pastures. Changes in agricultural practices have decreased the curlew's natural breeding habitat and have also caused fragmentation of its habitat.

Pollution

Pollution of aquatic habitats due to nutrient run-off from fertilisers, animal manures, milk and silage effluent has already been dealt with in Chapter 8, page 127.

Climate change

Agriculture in Ireland contributes to over 30% of GHG emissions as previously described. These GHG emissions are contributing to global warming and climate change. The climate in Ireland is predicted to lead to warmer and drier summers, milder and wetter winters and an increase in extreme weather events. The Environmental Protection Agency (EPA) carries out analysis of meteorological records and identified that temperatures in Ireland rose by 0.7°C between 1890 and 2008 and by 0.4°C between 1980 and 2008. The knock-on effect of this increase in temperature is changes in the growing season, which directly affects farmers and agriculture. In addition, the increase in temperature is changing the life cycles of plants, insects, birds and mammals. It is also causing changes in the distribution of both plant and animal species, with the warmer temperatures increasing the number of animals suited to those warmer temperatures. There is the additional threat that warmer temperatures will bring new pests and diseases to this country (e.g. blue tongue virus).

32.4   *Flooding in the west of Ireland*

Unsuitable grazing regimes

Agriculture has drastically changed from one of subsistence farming to intensive farming in many parts of Ireland. Consequently, the way farmers utilise and manage their grassland has changed.

Subsistence farming: where a farmer grows crops to feed themselves and their families.

The change from natural grassland (wide variety of grass species and wildflowers) to more productive grass species, perennial ryegrass, has led to a decrease in pollinators (bees, butterflies and hoverflies). The Federation of Irish Beekeepers has reported that 30% of Ireland's 101 bee species is on the verge of extinction.

The change from traditional hay making to silage making has had consequences for farmland birds, and these birds have experienced the largest decline in numbers and distribution. In Ireland, hay meadows are traditional nesting ground of the corncrake. Corncrakes build their nests on the ground and are reliant on tall, open grassland throughout their breeding season (May to September). Silage making occurs earlier than hay making; as a result, grass cover is removed and nesting sites are exposed or destroyed. The use of faster tractors and large machinery has contributed to the decline of this bird species.

32.5   *The corncrake is an endangered species due to a severe decline in the breeding population*

Measures employed by the farming community to lessen its environmental impact

There are many ways to reduce the environmental impact of farming. For example, increasing the grazing season reduces the volume of slurry that needs to be stored and spread. Incorporating clover in grassland swards reduces the emission of nitrous oxide by reducing the need for artificial fertiliser. Conservation and management of hedgerows on farmland provides important habitats for birds, insects and other animal species. Legislation prohibits the cutting of hedgerows during bird nesting season (March to August). When planting new hedgerows, the use of native tree species such as blackthorn, crab apple, hazel, holly and elder are recommended, as these are adapted to the Irish climate. Afforestation and increasing the amount of grassland on a farm increases carbon sequestration. Increasing the economic breeding index (EBI) of a dairy herd can reduce the carbon footprint of the farm, as high EBI dairy cows are more efficient.

Other measures include:
- Using genomics in beef production
- Using low emission slurry spreading equipment and timing the application of animal manures to reduce nutrient loss
- Carrying out soil testing to establish the correct amount and type of fertiliser required and timing the application of the fertiliser to reduce nutrient loss
- Applying lime
- Regulating nitrates
- Participating in agri-environmental schemes such as GLAS
- Installing bird and bat boxes around the farm
- Allocating 10% of farmland to habitats for native flora and fauna.

Custodian: a person or persons who are responsible for taking care of or protecting something.

Irish farms tend to have been in families for many generations, and there is a strong tradition in Ireland of handing a farm down to the next generation. Irish farmers are very aware that they are the custodians of the land and they play a primary role in protecting it for future generations. Legislation at both European and national level further reinforces the protection of the environment and of its biodiversity through the Habitats Directive, Water Framework Directive, Nitrates Regulations, the Birds Directive, etc. The protection of the environment against pollution, conservation of wild birds, conservation of natural habitats of wild flora and fauna are all key components of the Common Agricultural Policy (CAP), and farmers in receipt of subsidies must comply with the statutory management requirements of CAP.

In 2012 the EU launched its European Innovation Partnership for Agricultural Productivity and Sustainability (EIP AGRI). Its aim was to develop a new way of helping the agricultural and forestry sectors to become more sustainable. The Department of Agriculture, Food and the Marine (DAFM) selected 23 projects in Ireland to participate in EIP AGRI. One of these projects is the Biodiversity Regeneration in a Dairying Environment (BRIDE) in the Bride Valley in East Cork. It is an agri-environmental scheme that rewards participating farmers for increasing and maintaining biodiversity on their farms. It has 62 farmers committed to the project, in which the farmers allocate 10% of their land as a biodiversity managed area (BMA). A BMA can include hedgerows, bogs, drains, field margins, etc. A biodiversity management plan is then drawn up by an ecologist, who will walk through and make note of the habitats on each of the participating farms. The project will advise the farmers on how to improve the habitats in their BMA. Every September, the ecologist assesses the BMA and scores them on the quality of the habitats: the higher the quality of the habitats, the higher the payment the farmer receives. This project is different from other agri-environmental schemes as it involves an ecologist liaising with the farmer and providing the farmer with information on best practice for maintaining and improving biodiversity on the farm. Participation in the scheme can also aid in reducing the carbon footprint of the farm: for example, allowing hedgerows to grow and fully mature not only provides habitats for birds, insects and other small animals, it also increases carbon sequestration on the farm. The project doesn't differentiate between enterprises as it is the land of the Bride catchment area that determines the biodiversity.

Exercise 32.2

Read this article from the Farm Ireland section of the Independent.ie and answer the questions that follow.

New project to reward farmers with biodiversity habitat plans

Margaret Donnelly
April 24 2018 9:00 AM

A new project in the Bride Valley in east Cork will reward participating farmers for wildlife on their farms.

The 'Biodiversity Regeneration In a Dairying Environment' (BRIDE) project will provide participating farmers with farm habitat plans that identify the most appropriate and effective wildlife management options for individual farms. Farmers will be paid for their conservation actions.

[. . .]

An innovative element of the project is its higher payments for higher wildlife gains (a results-based approach). Thus, the more flowers in a hedgerow or field margin, the higher the payment. The greater reward for a higher quality product is very familiar to farmers, and the BRIDE project applies this principle to the management of wildlife habitats.

This also means that farmers will be paid for the ongoing management of selected existing wildlife habitats, which is an important feature of the project.

Donal Sheehan, the BRIDE Project Manager, who lives in Castlelyons, places great emphasis on the fact that "the BRIDE Project has been designed by local farmers for local farmers and this is one of the most important distinguishing features of the project."

[. . .]

The Project will run for five years and is designed to increase and maintain biodiversity on intensively managed farms in the area through simple, innovative measures.

The effects on wildlife will be monitored through the project, which aims to create suitable habitats for local important populations of wildlife include skylarks,

32.6 Field margins that are allowed to flower and form a dense vegetation provide a habitat for flowering plants, as well as cover and food for farmland wildlife such as birds and bumblebees.

32.7 Hedgerows are an important source of food and habitat for wildlife in the Irish countryside. Their management has a large impact on wildlife; here, the flowering hedge is a wonderful resource for bees and butterflies, and the berries will be a major food item for birds later in the season. The taller emerging trees are perfect for breeding birds.

yellowhammers, bumblebees and frogs and newts. The BRIDE Project differs from traditional agri-environment schemes through its use of a results-based payment system i.e. more farmland habitats will result in higher financial payments.

An ecologist will work with participating farmers to develop a farm plan and advise on how to maximise the wildlife on their farm, and will focus on important habitats such as hedgerows, bogs, woodland, ponds, derelict buildings,

etc. Wild birds and other animals don't respect farm boundaries, and the BRIDE Project is also designed to work at a landscape scale.

It will involve several clusters of neighbouring farms to collectively enhance biodiversity on a much larger scale than would be possible on an individual farm basis. Farmers will improve the environment for the wider community and local participation will help forge a strong identity that values local wildlife and the 'farming with nature' concept.

Questions

1. What is the BRIDE project?

2. How is this project different from other agri-environmental schemes?

3. What is the expected duration that the project will run for?

4. What are the aims of the BRIDE project?

5. What supports are on offer to aid farmers participating in the BRIDE project?

6. How will this project benefit conservation of wildlife compared with farmers working individually?

7. Find out if there are similar projects promoting conservation and biodiversity in your locality. What steps are local farmers taking to promote and protect biodiversity on their farms?

8. Should all agri-environmental schemes be on a 'results-based payment'? Discuss and justify your answer.

Rare Irish breeds

Endangered: in danger of becoming extinct.

Herd book: a record of the pedigrees of a breed.

Conservation grazing: the use of grazing livestock to maintain and increase biodiversity of natural or semi-natural grassland by controlling more aggressive plant species and preventing the development of scrub (vegetation dominated by shrubs).

The intensification of agriculture has not only led to a reduction in the biodiversity of many of the wild flora and fauna, it has also led to a reduction in many local Irish native breeds, which have been replaced by more economically profitable breeds. The Kerry Cow, Irish Moiled cattle, Dexter cattle and Galway sheep are native Irish breeds that are designated as **endangered**, and the DAFM has management schemes for these breeds. Recently the DAFM recognised another native Irish cattle breed, the Droimeann, and a herd book for this breed was formally established in April 2018. These native breeds, many dating

32.8 *Droimeann cattle in Fernhill Park, Co. Dublin*

back hundreds of years, are well adapted to the Irish landscape and climate. They can thrive on poorer pasture and they are hardier, smaller and lighter breeds than their continental counterparts – and therefore suited to grazing land that would not be suited to heavier animals. The Kerry Cow is a dairy breed, while Dexters, Droimeann and Irish Moiled cattle can be used for suckler beef production. Dexter cattle have been used for **conservation grazing** in the uplands of Kerry, and Droimeann cattle are being used to help manage biodiversity in Fernhill park in County Dublin. The development of niche markets and artisan produce from some of these rare breeds, along with the dedication and determination of the breed societies, has ensured the survival of these rare native Irish animal breeds.

32.9   *Dexter cattle*

32.10   *Irish Moiled cattle*

Markets for Irish produce

Value-added

The importance of export markets has already been discussed in previous chapters on dairy, beef, sheep and pigs. Ireland also exports live animals, both to the EU and to other non-EU countries. There is the possibility that in the future live export may be banned to non-EU countries that fail to meet animal welfare standards. Therefore, this can only increase the importance of the export market for our value-added products. Value-added can be used to increase the level of income to the producer or the processor of the product. For example, dairy processors buy raw milk from dairy farmers; this milk is then pasteurised, homogenised and packaged and sold at a higher price than the price at which it was bought. This increases the economic return from the initial raw material as well as creating jobs in the food industry here in Ireland. Value-added food involves some degree of processing of the raw material into the final product. Dairy value-added products include cheeses, butter, flavoured milks, yoghurts and milk powders. The most important value-added product in the dairy industry is infant milk formula. Three of the world's biggest infant nutrition companies, Abbott, Wyeth and Danone, have infant milk manufacturing facilities in Ireland and buy their milk from the Irish market. The production of infant milk formula requires good-quality milk, strict hygiene standards and diet formulations. Ireland roughly supplies 20% of the world's infant formula. China is Ireland's second largest market for dairy products, and it is our largest importer of infant milk powders. This is a sector that is likely to see further growth in the future, and there is ongoing research and investment in this area.

32.11   *Cheese, butter, flavoured milk (as shown above), yoghurt and milk powder are all examples of value-added products.*

Pasteurisation: heating the milk to 72°C for at least 15 seconds and then cooling the milk quickly to 3°C. This process kills any pathogens in the milk, making it safe to drink and extending the shelf life of the product.

Homogenisation: reduction of the size of the fat globules in milk so that they can be dispersed uniformly through the milk.

Economic return: profits made based on an investment.

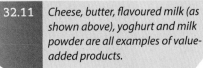

DEFINITION

Value-added is the process of changing or transforming a product from its original state to a more valuable state.

Niche markets

> **DEFINITION**
>
> **Niche market:** a specialised market with products aimed at satisfying the specific needs of consumers.

As well as export markets, there are many home-grown markets that are just as important for Irish produce. A niche market is a specialised market that meets the needs, quality and price range of a customer. Organic produce is considered a niche market; however, this area is growing continuously. Currently Ireland is importing roughly 70% of its organic fruit and vegetables in order to meet consumer demand. Organic food tends be more costly than food produced by conventional means. However, customers are willing to pay a higher price for organically produced food as they see it as a more natural means of food production with greater regard for health, the environment and animal welfare. One such supplier of organic food is Drumanilra Organic Farm, Knockvicar, Co. Roscommon. They produce and sell their own organic meat and vegetables in their café and farm shop.

Case Study

Drumanilra Farm Kitchen and Organic Farm

The Drumanilra Farm Kitchen and Organic Farm is owned and run by Liam and Justina Gavin. The farm is situated on the shore of Lough Key and the Farm Kitchen shop and café are located in the town of Boyle. All the pork, lamb and Dexter beef used in the Farm Kitchen shop and café is certified organic and is fully traceable back to their own

family farm. They also grow many of the salads and vegetables that they use in their farm kitchen. They have a farm-to-fork philosophy about the food they use, preferring to source all additional produce locally, as they believe that this food is healthier and tastier than food imported from overseas. Selecting locally produced food also supports the local economy and local community.

The Gavins manage their farm so that they produce food in a sustainable manner with a low carbon footprint. The cattle and sheep on their farm are all predominantly grass fed, with some certified organic grain ration provided in the lead up to calving and lambing. The breeds of animals that they keep on the farm include Dexter cattle, Tamworth pigs, Jacob and Shetland Sheep. Dexter cattle are a native Irish breed that produce excellent beef yields. The Dexter meat is well marbled and has excellent flavour. The meat from the Dexter cattle is used in the café to produce their Dexter burgers and steak sandwiches. The location of the Gavin's family farm means that the land

32.12 *Dexter cattle on Drumanilra Farm*

32.13 *Dexter burger*

can be wet and boggy. The Dexters are naturally adapted to the Irish landscape and by using low stocking densities as well as the Dexters' small size there is little damage to the ground.

As Drumanilra is an organic farm, no synthetic fertilisers or pesticides are used. Antibiotics are used only to treat sick animals and then only under veterinarian supervision. The withdrawal period for organic meat is three times longer than in other non-organic production systems. Drumanilra keeps outdoor, free-range pigs, including Tamworth, Berkshire and Large White crosses. Both the Tamworth and Berkshire breeds are rare, heritage breeds and have excellent taste and flavour. The pigs live outdoors and are free to forage in the fields. They live on a diet of grass, vegetables and certified organic and GM-free pig ration. Drumanilra Farm Kitchen and shop has won awards for its food, including a Georgina Campbell Natural Food Award in 2019. This is just one example of many farm-to-fork enterprises that are growing in Ireland.

There has been an increase in functional foods in recent years. Functional foods are foods that have a potential positive health benefit above supplying basic nutrition. These are often unique products that target a very specific consumer. An example of this is Lullaby Milk, which is produced by the Burns family in North Cork.

Case Study

Lullaby Milk

Lullaby Milk contains higher levels of melatonin compared with normal milk. Melatonin is a natural hormone that is produced by mammals and helps regulate sleep–wake cycles. Cows also produce this hormone during hours of darkness. Julian and Gerald Burns are third-generation dairy farmers in Kanturk, Co. Cork. Gerald's father initially started to research night milk when he came across it while travelling in Europe. Gerald started producing Lullaby Milk in 2005, having researched the benefits of melatonin in aiding sleep.

32.14   *Lullaby milk*

32.15   *The Burns family and their pedigree Holstein herd*

32.16   *The Burns family with some young calves*

The Burns family have a pedigree Holstein herd of 120 cows that have a grass-based diet. They operate a spring and autumn calving system as Lullaby Milk is produced all year round. The Burns family milk their dairy herd twice a day. The morning milk is kept in a separate milk tank to the evening milk. The morning milking occurs before dawn (at 2 a.m. during the summer months and at 4 a.m. in the winter months) when the cow's milk is naturally higher in melatonin. Therefore, Lullaby Milk naturally contains higher levels of melatonin compared with milk from cows that are milked during daylight hours.

Research studies have been conducted on the effectiveness of consuming melatonin-rich night-time milk on sleep quality, and these studies have shown that melatonin-rich milk can significantly enhance sleep efficiency compared with normal milk. Lullaby Milk is currently on sale in a number of supermarket outlets. The primary market for Lullaby Milk is children and pregnant women that are experiencing difficulties with their sleep patterns. However, this milk is suitable for anyone, from 12 months of age right up to and including the elderly. The Burns have a large customer base, including people that are going through illness or therapy and people suffering from jet lag or stress, and feedback from their customers is that Lullaby Milk helps them to sleep. Some doctors have also advised parents of children with sleeping difficulties to try Lullaby Milk instead of using prescription melatonin. The Burns family relaunched and rebranded their Lullaby Milk in 2015. They have won two golden Blas na hÉireann awards in 2015 for their Lullaby Milk and a best in the Dairy Category in the Quality Food and Drinks Awards in 2017.

Exercise 32.3

Read the case studies on the Gavin family and Burns family related to their agri-food enterprises. Answer the questions below using and referencing a variety of sources of information. Consider the reliability and validity of any data you use.

Questions

1. Give the advantages and disadvantages of purchasing organic produce.

2. Outline some of the environmental benefits of purchasing organic food.

3. What scientific evidence is there to support the theory that organic food production is better for the environment compared with conventional farming techniques?

4. Lullaby Milk is higher in melatonin compared with normal milk. What is the function of melatonin in the body?

5. How does the Burns farm obtain milk high in melatonin from their dairy herd?

6. Explain why cows milked at night have higher levels of melatonin in their milk compared with cows milked during the day.

7. What scientific evidence or findings support the theory that melatonin-rich milk can improve sleep quality?

Artisan food

Artisan: describes a food or drink that is made in a traditional manner using high-quality ingredients.

The Food Safety Authority of Ireland (FSAI) issued guidelines describing the criteria that a product must meet to be labelled **artisan**. In order to be labelled as artisan, a product must:

- Be made in a limited quantity by skilled craftspeople
- Follow a traditional method, which is not fully mechanised
- Be made in a micro-enterprise at a single location
- Use characteristic ingredients (e.g. the milk in cheese or yoghurts) that are grown or produced locally.

The artisan food sector is extremely important to the economy of rural Ireland. The growth in this sector has been helped by the large number of farmers' markets and country markets around Ireland. Artisan food is also contributing to food tourism, in which a person looks to enhance their travel experience by sampling the local food and drink. One such example is Blasket Island Lamb, which is available in limited quantities between July and October.

Case Study

Blasket Island Lamb

Donncha Ó Céileachair raises his lambs naturally on the Blasket Islands off the Dingle Peninsula. He has a flock of crossbred Dorset Horn ewes. He introduced the Dorset Horn several years ago to improve the carcase conformation of his lambs, and the Dorset Horn is a relatively hardy sheep. Donncha Ó Céileachair's philosophy on managing his sheep flock is 'to keep everything as natural as possible, minimal interference but plenty of supervision'. He handles his flock twice a year and monitors them closely for fly strike over the summer months.

32.17 *Donncha Ó Céileachair and Jerry Kennedy and their Blasket Island lamb (Photo by: Don MacMonagle – macmonagle.com)*

Sheep have grazed the land of the Blasket Islands for centuries, and their presence on the Islands is essential to the ecosystem. The grazing habits of the sheep prevent the vegetation on the islands going wild and assist in ensuring that there are suitable habitats for nesting birds. In turn, the birds and sheep provide natural nitrogen for the soil, and no artificial fertilisers are used on the Islands. The ewes and the rams stay on the Islands all year round, with the ewes lambing in spring (March to April). The ewes and lambs are free to roam the Islands. The lambs initially depend solely on their mother's milk for nutrition but gradually wean themselves onto a diet of heather, herbs and grasses. It is this diet that contributes to the unique flavour of the meat. The meat is tender, burgundy in colour, with marbled fat and a saltiness from its island environment.

The natural production methods used to produce Blasket Island lamb is the opposite to normal intensive lamb production. This means that there is a very limited supply of the lamb and due to the unique environment that the lambs are reared on, there is no opportunity to expand the enterprise. Donncha supplies his best-quality lambs to Jerry Kennedy's butchers in Dingle. The supply of the lambs is completely weather dependent, as the lambs must be transported from the Islands to the mainland to be slaughtered. Jerry Kennedy is a craft butcher, and he deals with the slaughter and the final processing of the meat. Because there is a close relationship between the farmer and the butcher, there is full traceability of the meat from farm to fork, making the Blasket Island lamb a much sought-after meat by locals of the Dingle Peninsula and restaurants in Cork.

Other very popular artisan food products in Ireland are farmhouse cheeses. Artisan cheeses are produced by skilled cheesemakers using traditional methods with as little mechanisation as possible. There are roughly 50 or more farmhouse cheese producers in Ireland, making cheese from their own herds of cows, sheep and goats. Some of these cheeses are made using raw milk (unpasteurised milk), while others are made with pasteurised milk. There is a large variety of farmhouse cheeses available, as cheesemakers use various recipes, and age and mature their cheeses differently to develop flavours and textures. Producing a farmhouse cheese from a farmer's own herd is an example of a value-added product.

Case Study

Killeen Farmhouse cheese and Killeen goat's cheese

32.18 *Killeen goat's cheese*

32.19 *Killeen farm goats zero grazing*

Marion Roeleveld, originally from the Netherlands, has been making goat's cheese in Ballyshrule, just outside Portumna, since 2004. In 2004 the milk quota restrictions made it difficult to set up a dairy enterprise with cattle; however, there was no quota restrictions for producing goat's milk. It was difficult to make an income from selling goat's milk, as the demand for milk was very unpredictable. As Marion had grown up on a dairy farm and had previously worked on a cheese farm in the Netherlands, she decided to make a Gouda-style cheese with goat's milk. Marion and her business partner Haske have a herd of 200 goats, which were originally Swiss breeds, Saanen and Toggenburg, along with some British Alpine. These breeds of goat are productive dairy breeds. The goats have a lactation period similar to that of dairy cows and usually produce milk for roughly 300 days a year.

The goats are milked twice a day in a milking parlour and are kept indoors all year round on straw bedding and are zero grazed. They are fed a grass-based diet of fresh grass cut daily and grass haylage during the winter months in addition to some meal. Although Killeen farm is not an organic farm, they do not use any artificial fertilisers on their grassland and instead have a lot of clover incorporated into their grassland sward. Killeen Farm operates two kidding systems in the year. The first lot of goats kid around February/March and the second lot of goats kid around April. About a quarter of the goats are not put in kid at all for a few years in a row; instead they stay milking continuously. This allows Killeen Farm to produce milk all year round. The gestation period for a goat is roughly 150 days and the goats are dried off 2 months before they kid. Once the goats give birth they produce colostrum. Killeen Farm waits 3 days before they use the milk from a newly kidded goat to produce cheese. The kids are artificially reared on milk replacer.

Gouda: a style of Dutch cheese that is usually mild and creamy. Traditionally Gouda would have been made with cow's milk.

Kidding: a female goat giving birth to a baby goat, commonly called a kid. A female goat is called a nanny goat and a male goat is referred to as a billy goat.

The process for producing the cheese from the goat's milk requires a lot of skill to ensure that the cheese produced has the quality, texture and flavour that the cheesemaker is looking for. The milk used to produce the Gouda-style cheese is first pasteurised. A starter culture of lactic acid bacteria is added to the milk when the milk is at a temperature of 29°C. The lactic acid bacteria break down the lactose in the goat's milk to produce lactic acid. It is the lactic acid that preserves the cheese. Then Marion adds traditional rennet which makes the milk coagulate. After 30 minutes the gel is cut into curds. Marion spends roughly 2 hours working the curd so that the curd expels more whey. This causes the curd to become drier. The curd is then moulded and pressed for 3 hours. That evening the cheese is placed in a brine solution for 2 days, after which the cheese is allowed to mature for a minimum of 6 weeks. During the maturing process the cheese is stored at 15°C, to allow the starter culture and enzymes to continue working, thereby developing taste and texture.

Marion emphasises the importance of hygiene on the farm and in the milking parlour, as poor hygiene affects the quality of the cheese produced. In addition, poor feed quality also affects the taste and the flavour of the cheese. Goat's cheese is a popular cheese, as goat's milk is easier to digest than cow's milk. Goat's milk has smaller fat globules compared with cow's milk. The characteristic golden colour of cow's milk cheese is caused by the presence of beta carotene; this is not seen in goat's cheese. Goats convert beta carotene into vitamin A, which is colourless, hence goat's milk is always white no matter what diet the goats are on. Marion sells her cheese mainly to delicatessens, farmers' markets, hotels and restaurants. Marion can just about supply enough of her farmhouse cheese to meet demand. Her Gouda-style goat's cheese is creamy, smooth and sweet with no distinct goat flavour. For Marion to supply supermarket chains with her artisan cheese would require a large expansion of both her herd of goats and her cheese-making facility. This would lead to greater mechanisation, which could reduce the quality of the cheese she is producing, and the cheese would not stay true to its nature.

Rennet: an enzyme produced in the stomachs of young calves to digest milk. Traditional rennet is obtained from the stomachs of slaughtered milk-fed calves.

Curd: a soft substance formed when milk coagulates (clots or thickens).

Whey: the watery part of milk that remains after the formation of the curds.

Brine solution: a saturated salt solution.

Exercise 32.4

Read the previous case studies on artisan produce in Ireland. Answer the following questions using and referencing a variety of research sources. Consider the reliability and the validity of any data presented.

1. Define conservation grazing.

2. Discuss or describe the scientific evidence that exists to support the benefits of conservation grazing.

3. Has there been any research conducted in Ireland on the use of conservation grazing? Give a summary of the information you have found.

4. Discuss the factors that influence a person to purchase an artisan cheese rather than a mass-produced cheese.

5. Many people eat goat's milk cheese because it is easier to digest compared with cow's milk cheese. Discuss the scientific evidence that shows or proves that goat's milk is easier to digest compared with cow's milk.

 **SPA 32.1** To plan the layout of a farm

SPECIFIED PRACTICAL ACTIVITY

The following are some guidelines to consider when completing this SPA. The farm layout should include:

- The farmhouse and buildings
- The farm (land surrounding the farmhouse and buildings).

You must be able to identify and discuss **potential hazards** on the farm and how they can be prevented.

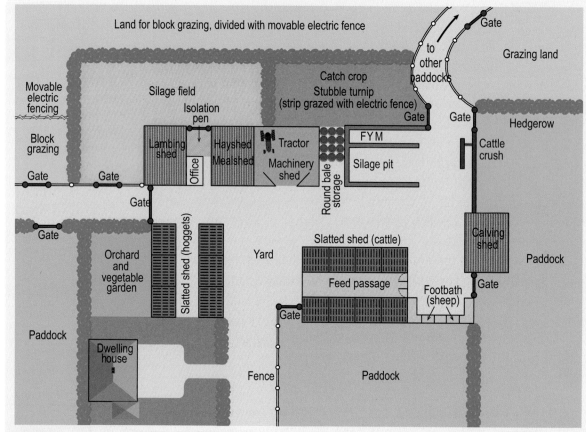

32.20 *Example of a farm plan*

Discussion points on farm layout

Some of the following points are recommendations made by Teagasc and the Health and Safety Authority Ireland.

1. **Planning for economy of labour:** this will be dictated by the type of farm enterprise.

   (a) **Dairy parlour:** dairy farmers producing milk over the summer months will situate their dairy parlour so that cows have easy access to and from the farm's grazing platform. Farmers who milk all year round may situate the milking parlour close to winter housing.

   > **Grazing platform:** the grazing land that is adjacent to the milking parlour.

   (b) **Calf sheds:** these should be located where the calves have access to paddocks in good weather but can return to the shed if the weather gets cold.

   (c) **Milk collection lorry:** there must be enough space to allow easy and safe access for a milk collection lorry. For health and safety reasons, access should be sufficiently wide to avoid having the lorry reverse into the yard.

(d) **Animal and machinery access routes:** keep animal access routes and machinery routes separate. This reduces the workload of opening and closing gates and eliminates machinery wheels driving over soiled routes.

(e) **Storage of silage and feed:** if animals are being fed with a diet feeder, locate feed storage areas close together, e.g. silage pit/concentrate storage etc. This is to facilitate the fast loading, mixing and dispensing of feed.

2. Health and safety

There should be:

(a) Good visibility at the farm entrance so that there is no obstruction for vehicles entering or leaving the farmyard

(b) Adequate farmyard lighting for working after dark

(c) A separate play area for children that is fenced off and is in sight of the house

(d) Secure fencing around slurry pits and water sources

(e) A separate storage area for chemicals and animal remedies, with all chemicals kept in locked storage

(f) Sliding doors on sheds and dairy parlours; swinging doors are dangerous in high winds

(g) A designated area for the parking of any tractors and other machinery

(h) Waterproof electrical sockets for outdoor use

(i) Good handling facilities for animals on the farm

(j) Stock-proof fencing

(k) Safety signs

(l) A storage area for ladders and equipment when not in use.

3. Social and environmental sustainability aspects

(a) **Soiled water:** use one tank to collect all soiled water, e.g. washings from collecting yard, houses and dairy washings. This tank should be separate from the slurry tank otherwise it would fill up the slurry tank too quickly and would be classified as slurry for storage and for spreading.

(b) **Slurry tank:** sufficient space to store slurry for 16–22 weeks.

(c) **Aspect:** most of our wind and rain comes from a southwesterly direction. Shed entrances should not be open to the southwest. Silage pit faces should be on a sheltered side of a shed.

(d) **Habitats:** incorporating new or rejuvenating old hedgerows into the farm will not only provide habitats for wildlife but it will also help with carbon sequestration and reducing the carbon footprint of the farm. Hedgerows also contribute to the aesthetics of the farm. Creating field margins to allow wildflowers to grow will provide a habitat for insects and butterflies. Fence off wet or water-logged grassland and allow it to develop into a wet grassland meadow, which will provide habitats for birds such as curlews and lapwings.

> **Aesthetics:** contributes to the enjoyment or the beauty of the farm.

(e) **Buffer zones:** buffer zones are strips of land maintained in permanent vegetation adjacent to rivers and streams that help maintain water quality and prevent run-off from fertilisers and pesticides reaching and polluting the river or steam. Fence off waterways to prevent cattle and other farm animals having access to rivers and streams.

Suggested features for inclusion on your sketch

- Aspect (direction of North)
- Topography
- Roads and gates
- Water supply

Farm buildings

- Animal houses (general or purpose-built)
- Sheep or cattle handling facilities (crush, foot bath, dipping, etc.)
- Crop storage (winter feed, concentrates, etc.)
- Silage storage (pit or bale)
- Grain storage (silos)

Grassland and tillage fields

- Grazing fields and systems of grazing
- Silage/hay fields
- Crop fields

Summary

- Agriculture accounts for 32% of our overall greenhouse gas emissions. The three main greenhouse gases produced by farming are: carbon dioxide, methane and nitrous oxide.
- Carbon dioxide is produced by the combustion of fossil fuels, methane is produced by ruminating animals and the main source of nitrous oxide is artificial fertilisers and animal manures.
- Eutrophication (from the addition of nitrates and phosphates), sedimentation and the addition of pathogens are the main risks to water quality from agriculture.
- Changes in agricultural practices over the last century have led to a loss of biodiversity.
- Biodiversity is the variety of plants and animals living in a habitat.
- Land drainage, pollution, climate change and unsuitable grazing systems are the agricultural activities that cause a decrease in biodiversity.
- Land drainage has led to a reduction in peatlands and wetlands, important breeding grounds for birds such as the curlew.
- Climate change is likely to cause changes in the life cycles of plants, insects, birds and mammals.
- Climate change is likely to bring new pests and diseases to this country, e.g. blue tongue virus.
- The use of more productive grass species (perennial ryegrass) has led to a reduction in pollinators such as bees, butterflies and hoverflies.
- Increasing the grazing season, incorporating clover into grass swards, conservation of hedgerows, increasing herd EBI or use of genomic selection in beef production, soil testing, afforestation and participating in agri-environmental schemes are just some of the measures farmers can take to reduce their environmental impact.
- The intensification of agriculture has led to a reduction in many native Irish breeds of cattle and sheep.

- Native Irish breeds such as Dexter, Irish Moiled cattle and the Galway are adapted to the Irish landscape and climate and can thrive on poorer pasture and are hardier, smaller and lighter breeds.
- Many native Irish breeds are used for conservation grazing, where livestock are used to maintain and increase biodiversity of natural and semi-natural grassland.
- Value-added is the process of changing or transforming a product from its original state to a more valuable state.
- Cheeses, butter, flavoured milks, yoghurts, milk powders and infant milk are examples of value-added products produced by the dairy industry.
- Niche market: a product that is aimed at satisfying the specific needs of consumers.
- Organic produce is considered a niche market and consumers are willing to pay a higher price, as they see it as a more natural means of food production.
- Artisan is food or drink that is made in a traditional manner using high-quality ingredients.
- The artisan food sector is extremely important to the economy of rural Ireland. Artisan food also attracts food tourism.

PowerPoint Summary

QUESTIONS

1. Which of the following greenhouse gases has the greatest potential to contribute to global warming?
   (a) Oxygen
   (b) Carbon dioxide
   (c) Methane
   (d) Nitrous oxide
2. What is the main agricultural source of the greenhouse gas nitrous oxide?
   (a) Slurry and farmyard manure
   (b) Combustion of fossil fuels
   (c) Fermentation of grass in the rumen of cattle and sheep
   (d) Silage additives
3. Which of the following can help reduce the use of artificial fertilisers on a dairy farm?
   (a) Extending the grazing season
   (b) Increasing a dairy herd's EBI
   (c) Addition of clover or other legumes into grassland swards
   (d) Afforestation
4. Land drainage and monoculture has led to a decrease in:
   (a) The volume of slurry that needs to spread on land
   (b) Biodiversity
   (c) Winter temperatures
   (d) Air quality.
5. Which of the following is an example of value-added?
   (a) Selling cheese made on the farm
   (b) Selling weanlings at the mart
   (c) Selling chicken eggs at the farm gate
   (d) Selling pigs to the factory (slaughterhouse)

6. An agri-environmental scheme in which a farmer is assessed and paid based on his or her maintenance and improvement in wildlife habitats on their farm is called a:

    (a) Greening scheme

    (b) GLAS scheme

    (c) Results-based scheme

    (d) The Common Agricultural Policy.

7. Due to genetic variations, cow's milk can contain two different types of milk proteins, called A1 and A2. Some research suggests that a small number of people have difficulty digesting the A1 protein. A milk company in Australia and New Zealand sells A2 milk, which is cow's milk that lacks the A1 protein. This company claims that A2 has health benefits and is easier to digest compared with normal milk containing the A1 protein. This milk is marketed at people who have trouble digesting normal milk. This is an example of:

    (a) An artisan product

    (b) A value-added product

    (c) A niche market

    (d) An export market.

8. Discuss the contribution of farming activities to the amounts of greenhouse gas emission produced by Irish agriculture.

9. Identify measures farmers are taking to reduce the environmental impact of farming.

10. Explain using an example how value-added can increase the profitability of an agricultural product.

11. Discuss markets available to farmers for them to sell their farm produce.

12. Name **one** artisan product that you have studied. Describe the requirements that this farm product must meet in order to be labelled an **artisan** product.

13. (a) Explain the term 'niche market'.

    (b) Name **one** niche market you have studied.

    (c) Give a brief description of the product produced for this market.

    (d) Identify the consumer needs that this market is meeting.

 Solutions Weblinks

1. A trial was conducted to investigate the effect of temperature on the growth of weaner pigs. The parameters of the trial are listed below.

   - Four insulated sheds each housing 200 fattener pigs.
   - Each shed was maintained at a different temperature.
   - The pigs were all at a similar weight at the start of the trial (50 kg).
   - Each pig was provided with 0.55 m² of space.
   - All pigs were fed the same diet with the same amount of crude protein (17%) as recommended for their stage of development and growth. The pigs were fed at the same time each day.
   - After 30 days 50 pigs in each shed were randomly selected and weighed.

   The results of the trial were as follows:

Temperature of the house (°C)	Average weight of the pigs (kg)
10	62.5
14	68.2
18	77.4
22	74.3

   (a) Construct a graph that represents the results of this trial.

   (b) Calculate the DLG for each group of pigs based on the average weights given above.

   (c) Identify the independent and dependent variables in this trial.

   (d) Identify **four** features of this trial that were controlled in order to make the trial fair.

   (e) Based on this trial, what recommendation should be made to pig producers of the appropriate temperature in which to house fattener pigs to ensure optimal weight gain? Justify your choice.

   (f) Discuss ways to reduce stress and improve animal welfare in a pig production unit.

2. (a) Describe **two** market requirements for finished beef animals in a production system of your choice.

   (b) Explain **two** grassland management practices that can be used to improve the quality of beef.

   (c) Distinguish between the effects of continuous tillage and permanent grassland on soil organic matter.

   (d) List **three** ways of improving soil organic matter.

   (e) Describe an experiment to determine the percentage organic matter in a soil sample and convert that to organic carbon.

   (f) Explain the term 'carbon sequestration'. Outline the importance of carbon sequestration in reducing greenhouse gas emissions in agriculture.

3. (a) List **three** reasons why good soil structure is necessary.

   (b) Describe **two** management practices that promote soil structural development.

   (c) Explain **four** factors a farmer should take into account when deciding how much fertiliser should be applied to a crop.

   (d) Identify a safety hazard and the precautions necessary for the safe handling of a fertiliser.

(e) Describe the main characteristics a farmer would consider when selecting a grass variety for grazing.

(f) Discuss the benefits and characteristics of Irish food produced by grass-fed animals.

(g) Identify **two** sources of water pollution on a farm. Explain how farm management and legislation help to maintain the quality of water sources.

4. (a) Name a plant or animal disease.

(b) Outline the effect of this plant or animal disease on the productivity of an agricultural enterprise of your choice.

(c) Describe how this plant or animal disease is prevented or controlled.

(d) How does biosecurity help protect a farming enterprise?

(e) Outline the beneficial roles of microorganisms in soils.

(f) Identify **two** soil management techniques that can increase populations of microorganisms in soil.

(g) Describe a field investigation to estimate the number of earthworms in a pasture.

5. (a) Distinguish between the monogastric and ruminant animals' digestive systems.

(b) Explain why pigs produce less methane gas than ruminant animals.

(c) Explain how the nutritional requirements of a dairy cow should be managed at different stages of her production cycle.

(d) Using an example from the dairy industry, explain the potential benefits of producing a value-added product.

6. (a) Outline **two** welfare issues relating to an animal production system of your choice.

(b) Explain how policies play an important role in the production of safe and traceable food in Ireland.

(c) Discuss the various markets available to farmers for selling their plant or animal produce.

(d) Identify management practices that farmers can employ to reduce the environmental impact of farming and improve the sustainability of a farming enterprise.

(e) Describe how crossbreeding can be used to improve the productivity of an animal or crop production system of your choice.

(f) A dairy farmer has a purebred Holstein herd of 150 cows. He is selling milk to a local creamery. The milk has moderate levels of protein and butterfat. The creamery has applied a number of penalties (High SCC and High TBC) to the last delivery of milk to the creamery. This has led to a reduction in the milk price the farmer has received. Outline management practices that a farmer could use to improve the quality of the milk in order to achieve a better milk price.

(g) Describe a biotechnological application in animal science and how this has led to an improvement in the productivity of a dairy enterprise.

7. (a) What is the length of the oestrous cycle and the length of gestation in sheep?

(b) Describe the key steps involved in 'breeding out of season' to produce lambs for the Easter market.

(c) Outline the management practices required to reduce ewe and lamb mortality at lambing time.

(d) Distinguish between flushing and steaming up.

(e) Explain how the role of the EU and national legislation improve animal welfare in sheep or pig production units.

(f) Describe the changes in the diet of a dairy calf, from birth to weaning.

8. **(a)** Identify **two** factors that can affect the fertility of a farm animal.

   (b) Explain how breed variety, nutrition and management can be used to improve the output of lambs from a lowland sheep production enterprise.

   (c) Explain the term **body condition score** (BCS). State the optimum BCS of a dairy cow at:

       (i) Calving

       (ii) Mating.

   (d) Explain the consequences of an animal not being at the correct BCS at calving and mating.

9. **(a)** Describe a suitable grazing system that might be used in a dairy enterprise to achieve optimum output for milk production.

   (b) Describe how the dry matter digestibility (DMD) of a grass plant alters during its various stages of growth.

   (c) Describe **four** measures that can be used to maintain a high grass DMD for longer during the grazing season.

   (d) Explain how the ruminant stomach is suited to the digestion of grass.

   (e) Suggest **one** reason why a farmer would include clover in a grassland sward.

   (f) Discuss the potential benefits of genetically modified crops.

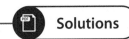 Solutions

Glossary

A

Accredited scheme: a scheme that an official body (e.g. the EU) approves or endorses as it recognises that high standards have been met. This means that the scheme has been independently assessed and judged to be as good or better than similar schemes in other countries.

Active transport: the movement of a substance from an area of low concentration to an area of high concentration against a concentration gradient. Active transport requires energy.

Ad lib: short for ad libitum, which means in farming terms that animals eat as much and as often as they want.

Aerobic respiration: the controlled release of energy from glucose in the presence of oxygen.

Aerosols: minute particles that are suspended in the air.

Aesthetics: contributes to the enjoyment or the beauty of the farm.

Afforestation: the process of planting large numbers of trees on land that was not previously forested.

Agrochemical: a chemical used in agriculture, e.g. pesticide, herbicide or fertiliser.

Allele: an alternative form of a gene, e.g. a gene for petal colour in flowers may have alleles for red or white.

Amendments: addition of something.

Analysis: an identification of trends and patterns in data; examining or scrutinising results.

Antimicrobial resistance: the ability of a microorganism to grow in the presence of a drug, e.g. an antibiotic, that would normally kill it or limit its growth.

Anti-nutritional factors: compounds that interfere with the absorption of nutrients.

Antioxidant: a substance that can remove damaging oxidants from a living organism.

Artisan: describes a food or drink that is made in a traditional manner using high-quality ingredients.

Available water capacity: the amount of water between the field capacity and permanent wilting point that is available for absorption by plant roots. Available water capacity = field capacity – permanent wilting point.

Average daily live weight gain (ADG) or daily live weight gain (DLG): a performance measure that many animal producers monitor; ADG or DLG is the rate of weight gain per day over a specified period of time.

B

Bacon: meat from the pig that has been cured (preserved using salt).

Barrow: a castrated male pig.

Bias: prejudice or a preconceived opinion about something.

Biochemical oxygen demand (BOD): the amount of dissolved oxygen needed to break down organic material in a water sample.

Biodiversity: the variety of plants and animals that are living in a particular habitat.

Blastocyst: an embryo 5–6 days after fertilisation.

Blind and double-blind experiments: a blind experiment is an experiment in which information is withheld from the participant. A double-blind experiment is when information is withheld from both the participant and the experimenter. Blind and double-blind experiments eliminate or prevent bias.

Boar: an uncastrated male pig.

Bord Bia: an Irish state agency with the aim of promoting sales of Irish food and horticulture, both abroad and in Ireland.

Bovine viral diarrhoea (BVD): a disease caused by a virus. There is a compulsory testing programme in Ireland to identify calves (both beef and dairy) born with the disease. There is an eradication scheme to eliminate this disease, so calves that test positive for the disease are culled.

Brine solution: a saturated salt solution.

Bull: an uncastrated male.

C

Calf: the offspring of a cow from birth to 9 months old.

Calving interval: the time that has elapsed between successive calvings.

Calving jack: a device used to assist the birth of a calf.

Canines: pointed and sharp teeth used for tearing food.

Capital: in a farming enterprise, is the land, machinery and buildings owned by the farmer.

Carbon footprint: the total CO_2 emissions produced by an individual or product. A product's carbon footprint can be expressed as equivalent carbon dioxide (CO_2eq). This describes the contribution a given greenhouse gas and its concentration will contribute to global warming.

Carbon sequestration: the removal of carbon dioxide from the atmosphere by plant photosynthesis and storing as plant biomass or organic soil matter.

Carcase: the body of a slaughtered animal (e.g. pig), which is cut up as meat.

Carrier: an organism infected with a pathogenic microorganism that does not display any signs or symptoms of the disease.

Cast ewe (draft ewe): a ewe whose fertility has declined due to the harsh conditions experienced in mountainous areas. It is sold to a lowland farmer, put on an improved plane of nutrition and will continue to produce lambs for many years.

Catch crops: fast-growing crops grown between two main crops when land would otherwise lie idle.

Catheter: a narrow, flexible tube.

Cation exchange: the ability of soil particles (clay and humus) to attract, retain and release cations.

Cation exchange capacity (CEC): the quantity of cations that a soil adsorbs. It can also be described as the capacity of a soil to exchange cations between the soil surfaces and the soil solution (water).

Causation: indicates that a change in one variable is the direct result of a change in another variable (i.e. that there is a cause-and-effect relationship).

Cementation: the binding together of soil particles, e.g. when silt and sand particles are cemented together in aggregates during flocculation by clay particles.

Census: official count or survey of a population.

Cisgenic: describes an organism that has been modified with a gene from an organism of the same species or a closely related species.

Climate change: a change in global or regional climate patterns that is largely caused by increased levels of carbon dioxide and other greenhouse gases (nitrous oxide and methane) in the atmosphere. Increased greenhouse gas emissions caused by human activities have significantly contributed to climate change.

Clinical: where an animal displays definite and obvious symptoms of a disease.

Cloning: a process for producing genetically identical individuals.

Co-enzyme: a compound that binds with an enzyme to catalyse a reaction.

Colostrum: the first milk secreted by mammals after giving birth. It is high in nutrients and antibodies and is essential for the survival of the newborn animal.

Commodity: a raw material or an agricultural product that can be bought or sold.

Compound fertiliser: any fertiliser that contains two or more elements. Compound fertilisers are often produced by the combination of two or more straight fertilisers.

Confirmation bias: the tendency to search for, interpret or favour information that confirms our existing beliefs or ideas.

Conformation: refers to the shape of the animal and the distribution of fat and muscle around its body.

Congenital defect: a birth defect.

Conservation grazing: the use of grazing livestock to maintain and increase biodiversity of natural or semi-natural grassland by controlling more aggressive plant species and preventing the development of scrub (vegetation dominated by shrubs).

Continental beef breeds: cattle breeds that originate in European countries other than England. They are late maturing breeds of cattle, with high growth rates and large size, and they finish at higher weights without laying down fat. Examples of continental breeds include Charolais, Limousin, Simmental and Belgian Blue.

Control: The control is commonly the normal or usual state; the only difference between the control and the experimental group is the independent variable. The results of the control can be compared to the results of the experimental group.

Co-operative: an organisation that is owned and run jointly by its members.

Corpus luteum: a structure that forms in the ovary once the follicle has released its egg. The corpus luteum then starts to secrete the hormone progesterone.

Correlation coefficient: a statistical measure (expressed as a value between –1 and +1) that describes the size and direction of a relationship between two or more variables. The correlation coefficient is denoted by the letter *r*.

Cotyledon: part of the embryo within the seed of a plant. When the seed germinates, or begins to grow, the cotyledon may become the first leaves of the seedling. The cotyledon is often called the seed leaf and can provide energy to the germinating seed until the true leaves have formed and can photosynthesise.

Cow: a female that has had one calf.

CRISPR (clustered regularly interspaced short palindromic repeats): a gene editing technology that allows scientists to change an organism's DNA. Using this technology, genetic material can be altered at particular location in the DNA (see page 153).

Crossbreeding: the mating or crossing of animals or plants from two different breeds, varieties or species.

Cross-compliance: a set of legal requirements a farmer must adhere to under the Common Agricultural Policy (CAP).

Cull: remove from the herd or flock by slaughter.

Culture: an artificial substance (medium) containing nutrients and used to maintain the growth of cells.

Curd: a soft substance formed when milk coagulates (clots or thickens).

Custodian: a person or persons who are responsible for taking care of or protecting something.

D

Dam: the female parent of an animal.

Degree day: a unit of measurement of heat calculated by subtracting the plant's threshold temperature from the average daily temperature. It is used by plant growers to calculate heat available for crop growth.

Deleterious gene: a gene that causes harm or damage.

Diffusion: the movement of a substance from an area of high concentration to an area of low concentration, along a concentration gradient. It is a passive process and so does not require energy.

Disease transmission: the means by which contagious, pathogenic microorganisms are spread from one farm animal to another.

Dominant: describes an allele expressed in the phenotype when present in the genotype; normally represented by a capital letter, e.g. T.

Drift: the unintentional movement of a pesticide from an area of application to any unintended site. Drift can cause the accidental exposure of the pesticide to people, animals and plants.

Dry matter (DM): the matter remaining in a sample of food after the water has been removed.

Dry matter digestibility (DMD): the amount (percentage) of dry matter that can be digested by an animal.

Dry matter intake (DMI): the amount of feed an animal consumes excluding its water content.

Dual-purpose breed: cattle that can be used to produce both meat and milk.

Duration of oestrus: the length of time during the oestrous cycle in which the female is in heat and an egg is available for fertilisation.

E

Economic breeding index (EBI): a single-figure profit index given in euros of profit per lactation for the animal's progeny compared to an average dairy cow.

Economic return: profits made based on an investment.

Ectoparasite: a parasite that lives on the surface of the host.

Eluviation: the transport of soil particles or minerals from the upper layers of a soil to the lower layers by precipitation of water.

Endangered: in danger of becoming extinct.

Endemic: a disease or condition that is regularly found.

Endoparasite: a parasite that lives inside the body of the host.

Environmental enrichment: objects or materials for the piglets to investigate and manipulate. These materials improve the living conditions of the pigs by encouraging a wider range of normal pig behaviours. Examples of enrichment material include straw, wood, sawdust, grass silage and shredded paper.

Environmental Protection Agency: an independent public body that is responsible for protecting and improving the environment for the people of Ireland.

Epithelial tissue: a thin layer of cells that forms the lining of the digestive tract, inside of the mouth, the respiratory tract, etc.

Eradication programme: a programme run by the DAFM in conjunction with the district veterinary laboratories for the compulsory testing of the national herd with the aim of completely removing a disease.

Essential amino acids: amino acids that cannot be manufactured in a monogastric animal's body and must be obtained in the diet, e.g. lysine and methionine.

Eutrophication: the artificial enrichment of a habitat or environment with nutrients.

Exocrine glands: glands that produce and secrete substances through ducts to the outside of the body.

Extrapolating: the extension of a graph/data to estimate something by assuming that an existing trend will continue.

F

Failure to thrive: when an animal is not putting on sufficient weight gain or has inappropriate weight loss.

Farm output: commonly referred to as gross output. Gross output determines the profitability of a farm. It refers to the amount and the value of the produce sold from a farm.

Farrowing crate: a unit that a sow is placed in prior to giving birth. It helps to reduce mortality of piglets by preventing the sow crushing them.

Feed conversion ratio (FCR) or feed conversion efficiency (FCE): a measure of an animal's efficiency at converting a mass of feed into live weight gain. It is expressed as a ratio of the feed consumed to the live weight gained.

Fertiliser: an inorganic, manufactured material that may contain one or more of the essential elements required for crop growth.

Field capacity: the amount of water in a soil after the gravitational water has drained away.

Flushing: the process by which ewes are moved from a low plane of nutrition to a high plane of nutrition prior to mating.

Fodder: winter feed for cattle and sheep, e.g. silage and hay.

Follicle: a small fluid-filled sac that grows in the ovary and contains an egg.

Food security: when a population has access to sufficient quantity of affordable and nutritious food.

Frequency distribution table: a table that summarises values and their frequency (how often that value occurs).

Functionality: a general term used to describe an animal's feet and legs, locomotion and ability to function on a farm. In dairy, functionality takes into account udder suspension, teat size and teat placement.

Fungicide: a chemical that kills or inhibits the growth of fungi.

G

Gametes: sex cells, e.g. egg and sperm.

Genetic modification (GM): altering an organism's DNA for the purpose of improvement or to correct a defect in the organism.

Genome: an organism's complete set of DNA, including all of its genes. Each genome contains all of the information needed to build and maintain that organism. It is a complete list of nucleotides (A, T, C, G) that make up the individual or species.

Genome editing (also known as gene editing): the use of any technology that allows a change to an organism's DNA. Genetic material can be added, removed or altered at specific locations in the genome.

Genotype: the genes present in the organism, whether they are expressed or not, e.g. Tt.

Genotyping: the process of identifying differences in the genetic makeup (genotype) of an animal by examining the animal's DNA sequence and comparing it to the sequence of other animals of the same species or to a reference sequence.

Germline: inherited material that comes from the eggs or sperm and is passed on to the next generation.

Gestation: the period of development in the uterus from conception to birth.

Gilt: a female pig that has not had a litter of piglets.

Global warming potential of gas: a measure of how much energy the gas will absorb over a given period relative to carbon dioxide. It allows the comparison of the impact of different gases on global warming.

Gouda: a style of Dutch cheese that is usually mild and creamy. Traditionally Gouda would have been made with cow's milk.

Grazing platform: the grazing land that is adjacent to the milking parlour.

Greenpeace: an international nongovernmental environmental organisation that campaigns on worldwide issues such as climate change, deforestation, overfishing and genetic engineering.

Gross margin per hectare: the amount of money available to pay for costs, e.g. hired labour, insurance, veterinary costs, loans, repairs and maintenance, and electricity. When these costs are deducted from the gross margin what remains is the net margin (farm family income).

H

Heat detection: the means by which a farmer identifies when a cow is in heat. When a cow is in heat, she will stand and allow other cows to mount her. Farmers often rely on heat detection aids to help identify when a cow is in heat. Examples of heat detection aids include tail painting and activity meters (see Chapter 25).

Heat detection aid: a device that helps to confirm or identify a cow when she is in heat.

Heifer: a female that hasn't had a calf.

Herbicide: a chemical that kills plants or inhibits their growth.

Herd book: a record of the pedigrees of a breed.

Heterosis (hybrid vigour): the increased productivity displayed by offspring from genetically different parents.

Heterozygous: when the alleles present in the genotype are not the same, e.g. Pp.

Homogenisation: reduction of the size of the fat globules in milk so that they can be dispersed uniformly through the milk.

Homozygous: when the alleles present in the genotype are the same, e.g. PP or pp.

Humification: the process by which soil organic matter is converted to humus.

Hydrolysis: chemical breakdown of a substance when it reacts with water.

Hygroscopic water (adsorbed water): water that forms a thin film around a soil particle and is held on the surface of the particle by force of attraction. It cannot be removed from the soil and is unavailable to plants.

Hypothesis: a proposed explanation for an observation. A hypothesis must be both testable and falsifiable.

I

Illuviation: the accumulation or deposition of soil particles or minerals from one soil horizon to another by percolating water or leaching.

Immunosuppressive agent: reduces the activity of the immune system. It makes the animal's immune system less effective at dealing with pathogens.

Inbreeding: the mating of closely related organisms, which increase the chances of offspring being affected by undesirable recessive traits.

Incisors: chisel-like teeth used for cutting and biting.

Incomplete dominance: when two alleles are equally dominant. When both occur together in the genotype, the resulting phenotype is a blend of the two.

Indirect control of pests and diseases: the implementation of agricultural practices that discourage the establishment of pests and diseases.

Inflammation: when part of the body becomes reddened, swollen, hot and often painful.

Insemination: the introduction of semen into a female animal by either natural or artificial means.

Interpretation: the process of explaining the meaning of your data and drawing conclusions or findings.

K

Ketosis: a disorder in cattle in which an energy deficiency is caused by a high energy output (e.g. milk production) and a low energy intake (e.g. feeding).

Kidding: a female goat giving birth to a baby goat, commonly called a kid. A female goat is called a nanny goat and a male goat is referred to as a billy goat.

Kill out percentage (%): the weight of the dressed carcase in relation to the weight of the live animal at slaughter. A dressed carcase will have the head, feet and internal organs removed.

Knowledge transfer: the process of communicating knowledge or information from one organisation to another.

L

Lactation period: the length of time (days) following birth that a cow produces milk.

Leaching: the process in which soluble matter, such as minerals, dissolves in water filtering through soil and is carried downwards. The leached minerals may accumulate at a lower horizon.

Legislation: the process of making and enacting laws.

Lethal genes: genes that can cause the death of an organism.

Line breeding: the production of desired characteristics in animals by inbreeding through several generations.

Listlessness: when an animal lacks energy, has no interest in anything and is lethargic.

Live export: transport of living farm animals, usually to another country.

Loam soil: soil that contains equal amounts of sand, silt and clay.

Lodging: the tendency of cereal crops to bend over so that they lie almost flat on the ground. This makes it difficult to harvest the crop and reduces the yield.

M

Maintenance diet: the amount of feed that allows an animal to maintain a good health and condition with no loss or gain in weight.

Manufacturing milk: milk used to produce butter, cheese, milk powders, etc. It is produced between spring and autumn.

Manure: an organic material that consists of the wastes of plants and animals.

Marbling: intramuscular fat (fat inside the muscle fibres) or fat that is dispersed within the lean meat. Much of the flavour in meat cuts is derived from the marbling.

Mastitis: an inflammation of one or more quarters of the udder caused by a bacterial infection.

Maternal sire: a male used to produce daughters with excellent genetic traits for reproduction and mothering ability. These offspring are then used as replacement animals in a flock or herd.

Mean: the sum of all the values in a set of data divided by the total number of values.

Metabolic acidosis: when the pH of the cattle's blood drops below 7.35. This can result in shock and death of the animal. Metabolic acidosis is also known as systemic acidosis.

Metabolic processes: collectively a group of chemical reactions (e.g. aerobic respiration) that occur in an animal's body.

Microbiome: a community of microorganisms (e.g. bacteria and fungi) that inhabit a particular environment.

Microminerals: minerals often called trace elements, since they are required in very small quantities. These minerals can become toxic if consumed in large amounts.

Milk replacer: a dried milk powder that is made up using warm water. It is cheaper to feed milk replacer than whole milk.

Milk solids: components of milk, i.e. fat, protein, lactose, minerals and vitamins.

Mineral bullet: a large pill used to provide a consistent supply of micronutrients to cattle or sheep.

Minerotrophic: describes a fen or peatland supplied with dissolved minerals from groundwater or surface water.

Minimum tillage (conservation tillage): a method of cultivation in which ploughing is not carried out at any stage during the seedbed preparation.

Mitigation: the process or action of reducing the severity or lessening the effects of something, e.g. climate change.

Molars: flat teeth used for crushing food.

Monogastric animal: an animal with a single compartment stomach, compared with a ruminant animal which has a four compartment stomach. Examples of monogastric animals include pigs, horses and humans.

Mopping up: when a stock bull detects and services any cows or heifers not in calf.

Mortality: death or loss of life.

Mutalistic relationship: a close relationship or interaction between two different organisms in which both organisms benefit, e.g. *Rhizobium* and clover.

N

Niche market: a specialised market with products aimed at satisfying the specific needs of consumers.

Nitrification: conversion of ammonia or ammonium compounds into nitrite or nitrate.

Non-essential amino acids: amino acids that can be manufactured in the body from other amino acids, e.g. alanine and glutamine.

Notifiable disease: a disease that must immediately be reported to the Department of Agriculture, Food and the Marine. Diseases that are notifiable are normally infectious and highly contagious.

Nucleotide: a structural component or building block of DNA or RNA.

O

Objective: describes a way of looking at something that is not influenced by personal feelings or opinions.

Oesophageal groove: a channel, present in calves and lambs, that takes milk from the oesophagus into the abomasum and bypasses the rumen, reticulum and omasum.

Oestrous cycle: a recurring cycle during which a female mammal comes into heat and releases an egg which is available for fertilisation by sperm from the male.

Ombrotrophic: describes a bog or its vegetation which depends on atmospheric moisture for its nutrients.

Oocyst: a cyst containing a zygote formed by a parasitic protozoan.

Open pollination: pollination that takes place between two plants of the same species, or by self-pollination. It also means pollination that takes place naturally by wind, insect, or water, i.e. without interference.

Osmosis: the movement of water from an area of high concentration to an area of low concentration across a semi-permeable membrane. Osmosis does not require energy.

Overhead costs: ongoing expenses of operating a business. These would include insurance, electricity, renting of land or farm buildings, loan repayments, and telephone or mobile phone bills.

Ovulation: the release of an egg from the follicle.

P

Pasteurisation: heating the milk to 72°C for at least 15 seconds and then cooling the milk quickly to 3°C. This process kills any pathogens in the milk, making it safe to drink and extending the shelf life of the product.

Pathogen: a disease-causing organism such as a bacterium, virus or fungus.

Performance testing: the evaluation of a bull's performance by comparing its weight gain and feed conversion ratio with other bulls kept under similar feed and housing conditions.

Peristalsis: a rhythmic, wavelike motion of muscular contractions as food entering the oesophagus is moved along to the stomach.

Permanent wilting point: the point at which no more capillary water can be removed from a soil (by plant roots). Plants will die from drought if the soil in which they are growing reaches its permanent wilting point.

Pesticide: a chemical used to kill pests (particularly insects and rodents).

Pesticide run-off: caused by rain washing the pesticide off plants and carrying it into drains, streams and rivers or washing the pesticide through the soil and into the groundwater. Pesticide run-off contributes to water pollution.

pH: a measure of the concentration of the hydrogen ions in a solution. It can also be expressed as the negative log of the hydrogen ion concentration: $pH = -log_{10}[H+]$.

Phenotype: the outward appearance of the organism.

Pheromones: chemical substances that male animals produce in order to attract a female for mating. There are many different types of pheromones and they are widely produced in both animals and insects. They have a variety of roles and are not just involved in reproduction.

Photoperiod: the length of time each day that a living organism (plant or animal) receives exposure to light.

Phyllochron: the time that elapses between the emergence of two successive leaves. It is influenced by the sowing date and the seed variety sown.

Piglet: a baby pig.

Placebo: a substance that resembles a drug but contains inactive ingredients such as sugar or starch.

Poaching: damage caused to wet or waterlogged land where land is cut up by livestock movement on wet soils. It causes surface vegetation to be removed and soil to be washed away. Soil may also be compacted.

Podzolisation: occurs in acidic pH conditions where minerals such as iron and aluminium are leached from the A horizon, leaving it bleached in colour. They accumulate in the B horizon, forming an iron-pan that is impermeable to water.

Polyoestrous: animals that have several oestrous cycles throughout the year.

Pork: any meat that comes from the pig.

Prediction: the outcome you would expect to observe if the hypothesis is correct. A prediction is often written as an 'If … then …' statement.

Premolars: relatively flat teeth used for grinding.

Prevalent: widespread or common in an area.

Prion: a misfolded protein.

Production diet: the extra amount of feed required to produce 1 kg of LWG, 1 l of milk, 1 kg of wool, or to produce a calf or lamb. Animals on a production diet must be provided with feed that is more than their maintenance requirements.

Progeny testing: the comparison of an animal or plant's offspring with another animal or plant's offspring kept under the same conditions. The plants grown from the seeds of one plant can be compared with the plants grown from the seeds of another plant of that species when grown in trials under the same conditions.

Prolificacy: when a breed can produce many offspring. Proflicacy in sheep is calculated as the number of lambs reared per ewe mated. If 100 ewes were mated and 160 lambs were produced, the prolificacy of the flock would be 1.6.

Protozoan: a single-celled microscopic animal.

Proven animal: an animal that has been identified as a genetically superior animal based on both performance and progeny testing.

Q

Qualitative data: data that we observe with our senses, e.g. colour changes, smells, tastes.

Quantitative data: data that involve measurement and will always be numerical values.

Quarantine: a place of isolation in which animals that have arrived from another farm are placed. It prevents any disease that the new animal might be carrying from spreading to the rest of the herd.

R

Raddle: a device or harness that holds a colour-marking device on rams.

Randomised controlled experiment: an experiment in which the subjects are randomly divided into two groups: an experimental group and a control group. The experimental group receives the treatment under investigation while the control group receives no treatment or the standard treatment. Using a randomised control experiment reduces bias.

Rare breed: a breed of cattle, poultry or other livestock that has a very small breeding population.

Receptor: a protein molecule that chemicals (e.g. hormones) can bind to.

Recessive: describes an allele that is expressed only when an individual has no dominant allele present; usually represented with a lower-case letter, e.g. t.

Reclamation: the process of changing land that is unsuitable for farming into land that can be used.

Rennet: an enzyme produced in the stomachs of young calves to digest milk. Traditional rennet is obtained from the stomachs of slaughtered milk-fed calves.

Replacements: ewes or heifers that have been bred to take the place of a culled animal in the breeding flock or herd.

Replacement rate: the number of ewes or heifers required to replace culled (or removed) animals from a flock or herd.

Reproductive efficiency: the number of offspring weaned per 100 animals served. For example, if a farmer has calved 100 cows but just 81 calves have been weaned, the farmer has a reproductive efficiency of 81%.

Residual milk: milk that remains in the udder after the bulk of the milk has been removed during milking.

Rhizome: an underground stem that can send out both shoots and roots. If a rhizome is broken into pieces, each piece can produce a new plant.

Rhizoplane: the external surface of the roots and adhering soil particles.

Rhizosphere: the zone of soil surrounding a plant root where the biology and chemistry of the soil are influenced by the plant root. It is the most biologically active part of the soil with microorganisms benefitting from the chemical compounds released by the plant roots.

Ruminant: describes an animal that has a stomach composed of four chambers, specialised for the digestion of plant fibre.

Rumination: chewing the cud.

S

Safety data sheet (SDS): a sheet that provides information on chemicals describing hazards, handling, storage and disposal of the chemical, as well as emergency measures in case of an accident.

Scouring: diarrhoea in animals.

Seasonally polyoestrous: describes animals that have more than one oestrous cycle during a specific time of year. These animals are commonly referred to as seasonal breeders.

Selective breeding: the process by which humans breed plants or animals with desirable traits and concentrate those desirable traits in the offspring.

Senescence: the process in which a plant starts to die back.

Separation: when soil aggregates are broken up within the soil. Large cracks may develop in the soil, which damages its overall structure.

Service house: housing to which sows are moved after weaning. Ideally the sow should be within sight of, sound of, smell of, and have fenceline contact with, the boar. This helps bring the sow back in oestrus.

Silent heat: an unnoticed heat period. There are no behavioural changes in the cow and the heat is not detected by a bull.

Slap mark: a unique identification number that is tattooed directly onto the pig's skin. The tattoo should be placed on each front shoulder area and should last for the lifetime of the pig. Slap marking needs to be done with accuracy and efficiency to minimise stress to the pig.

Soil biomass: the total mass of living organisms in the soil.

Soil texture: a measure of the proportion of different-sized mineral particles (sand, silt, clay) that are found in a sample of soil.

Solid non-fats (SNF): lactose, protein and minerals make up the solid non-fat component of milk.

Somatic cell count (SCC): mainly the numbers of white blood cells. High numbers of these cells in milk are an indication of mastitis in a herd.

Sow: a female pig that has had a litter of piglets.

Statistical uncertainty: random fluctuations in measurements (also known as random errors). Random errors can occur in either direction, above and below the true value.

Steaming up: the practice of increasing the amount of concentrates being fed to sheep in late gestation in order to prevent twin lamb disease. This ensures a healthy lamb and promotes good milk production.

Steer/bullock: castrated male cattle.

Stolon: a horizontal stem that grows above the ground from the base of a plant and produces a new plant from its tip.

Store period: a period of restricted feeding that occurs during winter housing when there is a change of feed from a high plane of nutrition to a low plane of nutrition. This results in a decrease in live weight gain (LWG) of an animal. Target average daily gain (ADG) over the store period is 0.6 kg/day in beef production.

Straight (simple) fertiliser: fertiliser that contains only one of the essential elements.

Subclinical: describes a disease that is not severe enough to present signs or symptoms.

Subgenic engineering: the alteration of the genetic makeup of a plant by the removal of a gene or addition of DNA without inserting genes from other species.

Subjective: a way of looking at something that is based on personal feelings, tastes or opinions.

Subsistence farming: where a farmer grows crops to feed themselves and their families.

Suckler herds: cows that are bred to produce and suckle calves for beef production.

Super ovulation: the production of more than the normal number of mature eggs at one time.

Surrogate mother: an animal that takes on the role of mother to another animal's offspring.

Suspensory ligament: a supporting or holding ligament in a cow's udder.

Symbiotic relationship: a close relationship between two different organisms in which at least one of the organisms benefits, e.g. parasitism (see also mutualistic relationship).

Synchronisation: when things occur at the same time.

Synthesis: production of compounds or large molecules from simpler materials by chemical reactions in the body.

Systematic uncertainty: consistent, repeatable error usually caused by measuring instruments that are incorrectly calibrated, a defect in the measuring equipment or the measuring equipment being used incorrectly. Systematic errors are always of the same value in the same direction, e.g. +0.05 g.

T

Terminal sire: a male used in a crossbreeding system to produce offspring with high growth rates and good carcase quality for slaughter.

Theory: an explanation for some aspect of the natural world that is based on facts that have stood up to repeated testing by the scientific method over a period of time.

Tillering: the development of side shoots in a plant.

Topping: mowing grass to a height of 5–7 cm. It is carried out post-grazing to remove any remaining grass. Topping cuts grass to the correct postgrazing height and encourages tillering. It can also be used to control weeds.

Total bacterial count (TBC): total number of living bacteria per ml of milk.

Total mixed ration (TMR): a feed composed of several ingredients blended together. Total mixed ration often consists of some of the following ingredients: maize silage, grass silage, concentrates, molasses and straw. TMR feeding systems are common in the United States and some EU countries.

Traceability: the ability to trace and follow a food, feed, food-producing animal or product intended to be incorporated into a food through all the stages of production, processing and distribution.

Transgenic species: any organism that has had part of the DNA of another species (animal, plant, microorganism, etc.) inserted into its own DNA by genetic engineering.

Transpiration: the loss of water by evaporation from the leaves.

Transpiration stream: the uninterrupted passage of water in the xylem tissue from the roots up to the leaves in plants.

V

Validity: how well a scientific test measures what it set out to measure. Can the results of the study be trusted or believed?

Value-added: the process of changing or transforming a product from its original state to a more valuable state.

Variable: any factor or condition that can be changed in an experiment.

Variable cost: a cost that varies with the level of output. Variable costs in farming include concentrates, veterinary fees, animal remedy costs and contractor charges. Animal feed costs make a substantial contribution to variable costs.

Volatilisation: the evaporation or sublimation of a substance into a gas.

W

Weaning: the process of changing a young mammal's diet to other food (concentrates and other feeds) while withdrawing the supply of its own mother's milk. In pigs this happens when the piglets are removed from the sow, while in other mammals (sheep and beef) it can be a more gradual process.

Weanling: a young animal between 9 months and a year.

Whey: the watery part of milk that remains after the formation of the curds.

Wholesale: the business of selling meal in large quantities at a low price.

Withdrawal period: the minimum time that must elapse after the last administration of a drug (e.g. antibiotics) for the treatment of an illness in an animal, before that animal or its products (e.g. milk) can be used for human consumption. Withdrawal periods prevent any residues of the drug being present in the animal or its products.

X

X and Y chromosomes: the sex chromosomes. Females produce gametes with only X chromosomes; males produce gametes with X and Y chromosomes. A female calf will be XX and a male calf will be XY.

Y

Yearling: a young animal from 12 months old.

Z

Zoonose or zoonotic disease: a disease that can be passed from animals to humans.

Index

A

accidental discoveries 26

accuracy 16, 21

acidosis 316

acids 47, 292

actinomycetes 101

active transport 139–140

activity meter 360–361

adsorption 73, 82

aerobic respiration 136, 137, 300

agrochemicals 45–47

alleles 29, 148, 149, 150, 158

alluvial soils 67

amino acids 301, 302

amylase 5–7, 314

animal feeds 304–307

animal nutrition 300–312
    carbohydrate and fat requirements 302
    maintenance and production diets 303–304
    mineral and vitamin requirements 302–303
    nutrients and function 300–301
    protein requirements 301–302

animal production, environmental implications 491–498

animal welfare 387, 388–389, 466–469

animal(s)
    energy requirements 303–304
    handling and housing 365
    impact on soil 126–127

antimicrobial resistance 340–341

aphids 157, 195, 197, 213, 221, 226

Apiaceae 175

arthropods 271

artificial insemination (AI)
    cows 326–327
    pigs 445, 450
    sheep 328

artisan food 502–505

Asteraceae 169–170

B

bacteria 101, 107, 108, 198–199, 292

barley 206–218
    cultivation 209–215
    diseases, pests and weed control 212–214
    growth cycle 207–208
    machinery used in barley production 215–216
    production and harvesting safety considerations 214–215
    uses 206
    varieties and seed selection 209

basalt 59

bases 47

beef cattle
    breeds 394–396
    conformation 397
    growth, maturity, finishing weight 396–397

Beef €uro-Star Index 405–406

beef production 394–397
    daily live weight gain 404–405
    dairy calf to 398–403
    EU Beef Classification Scheme 398
    grass-based system 408–409
    impact on farm economics 407–408
    quality and output 405–407
    suckler 399, 400–403
    sustainable 409
    target weights 404–405

beef ration 305–306

biochemical oxygen demand 127

biodiversity 105, 157, 344, 494–497

biological control 194–195

biotechnology 150–157

blackleg
    in cattle 467, 480
    in potatoes 225

blastocyst 343

blind experiments 26

bloating 316

body condition score 355

bogs 62

Bord Bia Quality Assurance Scheme (dairy) 388

Bordeaux mixture 198

bovine viral diarrhoea (BVD) 352, 482

bract 165

Brassicaceae 170–171

brown earth soils 68

brown podzolic soils 68

brown rot 225–226

buffer zone 129

bulls 405–407
    genomic selection 339
    performance and progeny testing 337–338
    reliability index 407
    safe handling of 363, 364
    selection for dairy herd 361
    stock 327–328

C

calcium 116

calcium ammonium nitrate (CAN) 107, 119–120, 121, 294

calves
    diseases 477–479
    housing 354
    weaning 354
    welfare 365

carbohydrates 300, 302

carbon cycle 104–106

carbon sequestration 88, 102, 106, 129, 247

carbonation 62

carpel 165

Casparian strip 140

catch crops 106, 171, 187, 231–239
    advantages and disadvantages 231–232
    kale 232–237

cation exchange capacity of soils 94–95

cattle see also beef cattle; dairy cattle
    diseases 480–482
    farm safety and safe handling 363–364
    rare Irish breeds 498–499

causation 12–13

cereals 180

cheese, Killeen Farmhouse 504–505

chin ball 361

chlorophyll 135

chloroplasts 135

chromosomes 158

clay 59

climate change 129, 385, 495

cloning 343–344

clover 108, 169, 259, 279

club root 232, 235, 236

cohesion–tension model 139
colostrum 304, 353
Common Agricultural Policy (CAP)
    365, 386, 387, 496
common scab 225
conformation 330, 398
conservation 128–129
control group 13
controlled experiments 4, 5–7
correlation coefficient 11, 12–13
cotyledon 165
CRISPR 34–35, 153–155
crop production and management
    184–205
    control of pests, weeds and
        diseases 194–198
    factors affecting 186–187
    GM crops 156–158
    impact on animals 187
    safe work practices 202–203
    soil and crop productivity
        188–191
    sustainable development
        practices 199–201
crop(s)
    rotation 191–192
    seed certification 184
crossbreeding
    animals 329–330
    plants 177–178
cultivars 177
cytosol 137

D
daily live weight gain 453
dairy cattle
    breeds 349–352, 357–358
    bull selection for 361
    diseases 475–477
    heat detection 360
    housing 362–363
    management 358–361
    production cycle 357–363
    replacement heifer from birth to
        2 years 352–357
    selective breeding 329–330
    tail painting 360
    winter housing 363
dairy parlour 362, 382
dairy ration 305
data 7–12
decibels 52
dental formulas 313–314
diamondback moth 236
dicotyledon (dicot) 139

digestive process 313
    chemical, in the mouth 314
digestive system
    monogastric 318, 319
    in ruminant animals 315–318,
        319
diseases
    bacterial 198–199
    control of 194–198
    lactating cows 475–477
    non-infectious 485
    notifiable 485–486
    prevention 486
    quarantine 199, 225–226
    zoonotic 23, 486
double muscling 336–337
double-blind experiments 26
Drumanilra Farm Kitchen and
    Organic Farm 500–501
dry matter 147, 257

E
earthworms 109–111
economic breeding index (EBI)
    337, 380–381, 496
embryo transplantation 328
energy crops 240–251
environmental enrichment 448,
    458–459
environmental impact 496–497
Environmental Protection Agency
    24, 385, 460, 495
enzymes 292
erosion 87–88
essential elements 114–117, 119
EU Beef Classification Scheme 398
European Innovation Partnership
    for Agricultural Productivity and
    Sustainability (EIP AGRI) 496
eutrophication 127
evaluating evidence 21–32
experimenting 4–13
    analysis and interpretation of
        data 10–12
    collection, organisation and
        presentation of data 8–10
    designing the experiment 4–8
    drawing conclusions 26–27

F
F1 hybrid seed production 178
Fabaceae 169
farm accidents 39, 40
Farm Animal Welfare Advisory
    Council (FAWAC) 469
fat 300, 302

feed conversion ratio 451, 452,
    453–456
feldspar 58, 59
fertilisation 326–329
    dairy production 326–328
    sheep production 328–329
fertilisers 118–122, 235, 243–244
    application 122, 211–212,
        223–224
    handling, use and storage 122
    spreading restrictions 128
flea beetles 235–236
flocculation 79, 92–93
flushing 426
fodder 384
fungi 101, 102
fungicides 196–197
Fusarium head blight 155, 213

G
gametes 29
genetic engineering 151–153,
    343–345
genetic improvement 144, 335
genetic modification 151, 344
genetic variation 335
genetically modified (GM) crops
    156–158
genetic(s)
    applied animal 335–348
    applied plant 144–164
    beef production 331–332
    crosses 29, 159
    dairy herd 329–330
    pig production 330–331
    sheep production 331
genome editing 153–155, 345
genotypes 29
genotyping and genomic selection
    148–150, 338–339
germination 87, 175
gley soils 67
glyphosate 167, 200–201, 244,
    279, 283
granite 59, 63
grass
    characteristics 256–257
    conservation 287–298
    diploid and tetraploid 180
    dry matter content 257–258
    growth cycle 254–255
    growth rate 255
    inflorescence 166
    seed mixtures and crop
        productivity 260

seed selection 258–259

seed varieties 179

structure 166–167

grassland 252–264

  ecology 252–253

  farm safety considerations 273–275

  fertilisation 272–273

  impact on livestock and other animals 271–272

  management 381

  permanent 253

  productivity 280–281

  reseeding 279–280

  rough mountain or hill grazing 253

  sowing and reseeding 281–283

  uses 265

grazing methods 265–270

  block 267–268

  creep 269

  extended 270

  leader-follower system 269

  mixed 269–270

  paddock 266

  set stocking 267

  strip 266–267

  zero 268

Green, Low-Carbon Agri-Environmental Scheme (GLAS) 172, 366

greenhouses gases 129, 247, 383, 491

guttation 138

H

hay 287

hay making 294–295

haylage 295–296

heifers, replacement 352–357

herbicides 196

heterosis (hybrid vigour) 178

hormones

  female 324–325

  male 323

humidity 139

humification 100

humus 63, 100, 102

hydration 61

hydrolysis 61

hypothesis 3–4

I

inbreeding

  dairy cattle 329

  plant 177

incomplete dominance 160

infiltration 86

inflorescence 166, 167

ingestion 313

inheritance of traits 158–161

intensive farming 495

ion exchange 73

K

kale 232–237

  benefits 237

  cultivation and feeding 233–235

  diseases 236

  feeding livestock 236

  fertilisers 235

  growth cycle 232

  health and safety production risks 237

  pests 235–236

  weed control 235

Kamar device 360

kill out percentage 395

L

lamb, Blasket Island 503–504

lamb production and husbandry see also sheep 425–442

  breeding ewe lambs 434

  ewe and lamb mortality 433

  fostering of lambs 432–433

  lambing 431–432

land drainage 494–495

leaf rust (brown rust) 213

leaf structure 135–136

leatherjackets 213

lethal genes 339, 340

leys 253, 258–259

lichen 62

lime (calcium carbonate) 47

limestone 63, 98

line breeding 336

lithosols 67

livestock units 265

loam soil 73

lodging 116

luvisols 68

M

machinery

  barley production 215–216

  grassland and fodder production 289

  hay production 294–295

  safety hazards 50–51

  silage production 289

macronutrients 115, 116

macroorganisms 109–111

magma 58

magnesium 116

manures 118–119, 122–125

  farmyard manure 106, 123, 125, 366

  organic 212

  slurry 123–125, 366

  straw/stubble 125

marble 60

margin of error 14

mastitis 351, 476, 477

maternal sires 416

mean 11

Mendel, Gregor 22

metabolisable energy 303

mica 58, 63

microbiome 100

micronutrients 115, 116–117

milk 371–393

  composition 371

  from grass-fed animals 383–384

  hygiene and milk testing 376–380

  let-down 372

  Lullaby Milk 501–502

  payment calculation 373–375

  price 372–373

  production 371–372, 373

  quality 378–379

  sustainable production 384–385

  water and solids 375–376

mineral matter 72–73

minerals 301, 302–303

miscanthus 240–251

  advantages and disadvantages 249

  crop removal and site restoration 247

  factors for growth 241–242

  growth cycle 240–241

  harvesting 245–246

  health and safety risks 248

  impact on wildlife 248

  pests and diseases 245

  planting and establishment 242–244

  rhizome harvesting and production 247

  site selection 242

  storage 246

sustainable production 247–248

weed control 244

yield 246

molecular markers 155

monogastric animals 301

mutualistic relationship 101

N

National Farm Survey 385–386

natural selection 144–145, 339–341

nematodes 81

net blotch 213

niche markets 500

Nitrates Regulations 128

nitrogen 115, 272, 301

nitrogen cycle 106–109

nitrogen fixation 107

nucleotides 148

nutrient absorption 139–140

nutrient off-take 243

nutrient recycling 104–108

O

observations 3

oesophageal groove 317

oestrous cycle 324, 325

organelles 137

organic carbon 102–103

organic farming 201–202

organic matter 88, 102–104, 105, 129

organic parent material 62

osmosis 138

oxidation and reduction 61

P

parent material 58, 62, 63

pathogens 23

peat soils 66

peer reviews 22

performance testing 146–147, 337–338

peristalsis 314

pest control 194–198

petals 165

pH of soil 96–97

phenotype 29, 150

phloem 135

phosphorus 115, 273

photoperiod 188

photosynthesis 135–136

physical traits

animals 335

crops 147–148

pig production

breeding sow 449–451

impact on farm economics and export markets 461–462

innovation and biotechnological applications 456–457

integrated units 445–446

output and quality 451–453

production cycle 446–449

sustainable 460–461

pig ration 307

pig(s) 330–331

average daily live weight gain 453

breeds 443–445, 452

daily live weight gain 453–456

digestive system 318, 319

diseases 483–484

environmental enrichment 458–459

fattener management and feeding 449

feed conversion ratio 453–456

handling 457

housing 453, 457

lameness 459

and loud noises 459

management 452–453, 457–461

manure 460

National Pig Identification and Tracing System (NPITS) 461

nutrition 446–447, 450, 451

oestrous cycle 450

optimal health and welfare 457–459

slurry 460

placebo 26

plant(s)

annual 175–176

applied genetics 144–164

biennial 176

breeding 177–178

classification 165–183

life cycles 175–177

perennial 177

physiology 134–143

selective breeding 177

varieties 177

water transport in 137–138

Poaceae 165–168

poaching 125, 126–127, 280

podzols 67–68

pollination 146

pollution 127, 495

Polygonaceae 171–172

polyoestrous 325

potassium 116

potato blight 224

potato(es) 219–230

categories 220

cultivation 222–224

diseases 224–226

genomics research 227

growth cycle 219–220

harvest and storage 226–227

health and safety production precautions 228

micropropagation 155–156

pests 226

seed production 221

seed selection 220–221

sustainable production 227

powdery mildew 213

precipitation 63, 87, 125

precision 16

predictions 3–4, 27–32

progeny testing 145–146, 337, 338

protein 156, 300, 301–302

Punnett square 159

Q

Quality Payment Scheme (QPS) for Irish prime beef carcases 408

quartz 58, 63

R

randomised controlled experiment 13

Ranunculaceae 172–173

rare breeds 351, 498–499

reliability 22, 26

rendzinas 66

reproduction 323–334

female reproductive system 324–326

male reproductive system 323

reproductive efficiency 399

reproductive technologies 179–180

respiration 137

Rhizobium bacteria 108, 140, 169

rhizomes 167

rhizosphere 101–102

Rhynchosporium 212

ring rot 226

risk assessment 39, 153

rock

biological decomposition 62

igneous 58–59

metamorphic 59–60
sedimentary 59
weathering 60–62
root pressure 138
Rosaceae 174
Rubiaceae 174
rumen 315–316
ruminant 256, 314
abomasum 316–317
digestive system 315–318, 319
large intestine 318
omasum 316
reticulum 316
small intestine 317

S
safe work practices 52–53, 202–203
safety data sheet (SDS) 47
safety hazards 40–53
agricultural machinery and equipment 50–51
agrochemicals 45–47
and ill-health in farmers 48–49
preventing accidents and injury 40–45
scientific evidence 25–26
scientific method 2–3, 25
scutch grass 167, 279
seasonally polyoestrous 325, 326
sedimentation 75, 88
seed 175
certification 184–185
germination 188–191
varieties 179
selective breeding 149, 150, 177, 336
sepals 165
sexed semen 327
sheep 413–424
breeding 418, 419–421, 427, 428
breeding year 425
breeds 415–418
diseases 470–475
fertilisation 328–329
flushing 426, 428–429
general management 435–437
health and welfare 437–438
housing 430
late gestation and steaming up 429
post-lambing ewes 433–434
ram effect 427–428
replacement ewes 421

scanning ewes 429
sponging 427
sheep production 331, 413
factors affecting 414–415
impact on farm economics 437
selection of ram 422
sustainability 438–439
sheep ration 306
Sheep Welfare Scheme 437–438
silage 260, 287–288, 290–294
machinery used in silage production 289
production 290–291
single nucleotide polymorphism (SNP) 148–149
slate 60
slugs 226
soil
air 80–81
biological properties 100–113
chemical properties 92–98
classification 64
colour 87
compaction 81–82, 126–127
composition 72
and crop productivity 188
drainage 125–126
fertility 280
formation 63–64
functions 58
health and fertility 114–117
management 114–132
microbiome 100–101
nutrients 97–98, 117
physical properties 73–78
porosity 80–85
profiles 64
structure 79–80
temperature 87
testing 117–118
texture 73–78
water in 82–86
soil index system 118
Solanaceae 173
somatic cell 343
sowing
direct (plough, till and sow) 281
direct drilling/direct seeding 282–283
slit seeding/stitching in 283
slurry seeding 283
undersowing 282
winter versus spring 187–188
spikelets 166

sprouting (chitting) 223
stamen 165
standard deviations 14
stolons 172
store period 404
sugars and molasses 292
sulfur 116
Sustainable Beef and Lamb Assurance Scheme (SBLAS) 409, 438–439
Sustainable Dairy Assurance Scheme (SDAS) 366
symbiotic relationships 101
symbolic representations 29–30

T
teeth 313–314
terminal sires 330, 417
theory 4
tillering 270
tissue culture 155
traceability
animals 388
food 366
milk 387–388
sheep 439
transgenic species 151
transpiration 138–139
transpiration stream 137

U
uncertainty, statistical and systematic 14–16
urea 120–121
Urticaceae 173

V
validity of experiments 22, 27
value-added products 499
variables 4–5
vascular tissue 134–135
vitamins 300–301, 302–303

W
water 301
quality 494
in soil 82–86
water footprint 384
water pollution 128
water table 67
wireworms 213, 226

X
xylem 134

For permission to reproduce photographs and copyright material, the author and publisher gratefully acknowledge the following:

Photographs
Alamy: Page 3: Nigel Cattlin; Page 22: History and Art Collection; Page 38: MShieldsPhotos; Page 40: Mark Richardson, Bonekimages; Page 117: Nigel Cattlin; Page 132: Arterra Picture Library, Martin Shields; Page 136: Martin Shields; Page 138: Derek Croucher; Page 150: Nigel Cattlin; Page 152: Charlie Newham; Page 167: FLPA; Page 168: imageBROKER, Carmen Hauser, imageBROKER; Page 178: Johnny Greig; Page 182: Arco Images GmbH, FloralImages, Nature Photographers Ltd; Page 183: Photo Central, inga spence; Page 195: Denis Crawford, Nic Hamilton; Page 196: Nigel Cattlin; Page 199: Nigel Cattlin; Page 201: Joerg Boethling, Nigel Cattlin; Page 222: Nigel Cattlin, clynt Garnham Agriculture, Tim Scrivener; Page 235: Nigel Cattlin; Page 236: Nigel Cattlin, Photogenix; Page 243: michael smith; Page 245: Hakan Soderholm, Nigel Cattlin; Page 264: Tim Scrivener, Jennifer MacKenzie; Page 269: Wayne HUTCHINSON; Page 273: Andy Gibson; Page 278: Liam O'Hara, Richard Becker; Page 279: Nigel Cattlin; Page 290: Reinhard Tiburzy; Page 330: Nigel Cattlin, Grant Heilman Photography; Page 331: Marilyn Shenton, FLPA; Page 332: hans engbers, Dieter Hawlan; Page 335: WILDLIFE GmbH; Page 336: Jeremy Pardoe; Page 343: Colin McPherson; Page 349: Jane Williams; Page 351: PhotoAlto sas; Page 352: Doug Houghton40; Page 354: Wayne HUTCHINSON, age footstock; Page 359: Les Gibbon, David Platt; Page 360: FLPA; Page 362: FLPA; Page 363: Mrs. Bakker; Wayne HUTCHINSON; Page 382: Terry Mathews; Page 384: Andy Gibson; Page 394: peter mcdonald; Page 395: Nigel Cattlin, Jeremy Pardoe, Design Pics Inc; Page 414: Gareth McCormack; Page 416: keith morris; Wayne HUTCHINSON; Page 417: Marilyn Shenton, FLPA, Wayne HUTCHINSON; Page 419: Wayne HUTCHINSON; Page 421: Marilyn Shenton, FLPA; Page 423: Ros Drinkwater; Page 428: Kathy deWitt; Page 429: Wayne HUTCHINSON; Page 431: catherine lucas, Robert Garrigus; Page 432: Wayne HUTCHINSON; Page 433: FLPA; Page 435: FLPA, Nigel Cattlin; Page 436: FLPA; Page 443: Nigel Cattlin; Page 444: Grant Heilman Photography, Nigel Cattlin; Page 446: FLPA; Page 450: FLPA; Page 467: FLPA; Page 468: Wayne HUTCHINSON; Page 469: FLPA; Page 474: Nigel Cattlin, Science Photo Library; Page 475: Wayne HUTCHINSON; Page 479: Wayne HUTCHINSON; Page 481: RGB Ventures; Page 483: Zoonar GmbH; Page 498: Nigel Cattlin; Page 495: Design Pics Inc.

Alfie Shaw Photography: Page 499

Ashleigh Farms: Page 460

Aurivo/Connacht Gold: Page 499

The BRIDE Project: Page 497

Don MacMonagle – macmonagle.com: Page 503

Drumanilra Farm: Page 500

Dún Laoghaire-Rathdown County Council: Page 498

Environmental Protection Agency: Page 385

ESB Networks: Page 56

Getty Images: Page 22: Hulton Archive/ Stringer

Irish Cattle Breeding Federation (ICBF): Pages 337

iStock: Page 350: JoeGough; Page 361: Lakeview_Images; Page 428: pahham; Page 446: RachelDewis.

Kiernan Milling: Pages 305, 306

Killeen Farmhouse Cheese: Page 504

Kverneland Group Ireland Ltd.: Pages 215, 216, 289, 291, 295, 296

Lullaby Milk: Page 501

Matthew Gammon, Yew Tree Studio: Pages 499, 500

Mayo Mule and Greyface Group: Pages 419, 421

MSD Animal Health: Pages 427, 488

Nicola Reddy Photography: Page 384

Oisín Joyce: Pages 415, 419

Science Photo Library: Page 134: Power and Syred; Page 135: DR KEITH WHEELER, DR JEREMY BURGESS; Page 137: CNRI; Page 140: Steve Gschmeissner; Page 168: BRUNO PETRIGLIA; Page 185: JOHN HOWARD; Page 482: MOREDUN ANIMAL HEALTH LTD.

Shutterstock: Page 4: By justwanderto, Olexandr Panchenko; Page 8: goodluz, Elliot Photography; Page 13: Mitar Vidakovic, Yurlick, kristnu, Ewa Studio; Page 14: sima, Claudia Harms-Warlies; Page 21: Monkey Business Images; Page 27: Matej Kastelic; Page 31: LEDOMSTOCK; Page 33: Jarretera; Page 34: Anna Om; Page 52: Keith Gentry, tirc83, Martin Ludlam; Page 55: Standard Studio; Page 56: Chii Chobits, Zoart Studio, Ruud Morijn Photographer; Page 59: Zelenskaya, Attila JANDI, Sakdinon Kadchiangsaen, vvoe, Aleksandr Pobedimskiy; Page 60: www.sandatlas.org, bogdan ionescu, Tyler Boyes; Page 62: Kadamedo; Page 109: sivivolk; Page 120: iamporpla; Page 122: oticki; Page 123: Hans Verburg, BELINDA SULLIVAN; Page 127: Trixcis; Page 140: Worachat